RETHINKING THE NEW YORK CONVENTION

European Studies in Law and Economics Series

1. *Group Litigation in European Competition Law. A Law and Economics Perspective,* Sonja E. Keske
2. *Behavioural Economics in Consumer Policy,* Hanneke Luth
3. *Ex-Post Liability Rules in Modern Patent Law,* Rosa Castro Bernieri
4. *Competition and Innovation in the EU Regulation of Pharmaceuticals: The Case of Parallel Trade,* Claudia Desogus
5. *The Law and Economics of Organ Procurement,* Fırat Bilgel
6. *Law and Economics in the RIA World. Improving the use of economic analysis in public policy and legislation,* Andrea Renda
7. *Regulatory Competition in European Corporate and Capital Market Law,* Lars Hornuf
8. *Economic Criteria for Criminalization: Optimizing Enforcement in Case of Environmental Violations,* Katarina Svatikova
9. *Definition of the Relevant Market. (Lack of) Harmony between Industrial Economics and Competition Law,* Hila Nevo
10. *Patents as Protection of Traditional Medical Knowledge? A Law and Economics Analysis*, Petra Ebermann

RETHINKING THE NEW YORK CONVENTION

A Law and Economics Approach

SHEN Wei

intersentia
Cambridge – Antwerp – Portland

Intersentia Publishing Ltd.
Trinity House | Cambridge Business Park | Cowley Road
Cambridge | CB4 0WZ | United Kingdom
Tel.: +44 1223 393 753 | Email: mail@intersentia.co.uk

Distribution for the UK:
NBN International
Airport Business Centre, 10 Thornbury Road
Plymouth, PL6 7 PP
United Kingdom
Tel.: +44 1752 202 301 | Fax: +44 1752 202 331
Email: orders@nbninternational.com

Distribution for the USA and Canada:
International Specialized Book Services
920 NE 58th Ave. Suite 300
Portland, OR 97213
USA
Tel.: +1 800 944 6190 (toll free)
Email: info@isbs.com

Distribution for Austria:
Neuer Wissenschaftlicher Verlag
Argentinierstraße 42/6
1040 Wien
Austria
Tel.: +43 1 535 61 03 24
Email: office@nwv.at

Distribution for other countries:
Intersentia Publishing nv
Groenstraat 31
2640 Mortsel
Belgium
Tel.: +32 3 680 15 50
Email: mail@intersentia.be

Rethinking the New York Convention. A Law and Economics Approach
Shen Wei

ISBN 978-1-78068-112-2
D/2013/7849/6
NUR 820

British Library Cataloguing in Publication Data. A catalogue record for this book is available from the British Library.

To my parents

FOREWORD

There has been a very large literature devoted to the law of arbitration, a considerable portion of which focuses upon the New York Convention. Much of this writing is practical in nature, directly contributing through exposition and commentary to the law and practice of international commercial arbitration.

Dr Shen argues in this book that contemporary scholarship can reasonably aspire to go beyond that, invoking appropriate strands of legal and socio-political theory. He is surely right, in that the present surge of pluralist scholarship offers us fresh opportunities to re-examine the legal regimes of international commerce in a broader light. The New York Convention is an important – and arguably a largely successful – feature of the contemporary global governance regime, so fifty-five years after the birth of the Convention, it is appropriate to re-examine the evolving operation of this instrument, self-consciously invoking a range of theoretical resources, including but going beyond jurisprudence, in doing so.

Any new attempt to analyse the New York Convention is a formidable challenge given the vast array of topics and issues touching international commercial arbitration in general and the New York Convention in particular – not to mention the diversity of judicial opinions in more than 145 Convention States.

Dr Shen meets this challenge by reducing the issues surrounding the application of the New York Convention into four key topics: the evolution of the treaty; the competition among various jurisdictions in the context of enforcing an annulled award; *lex mercatoria* and governing law in arbitration; and the doctrine of public policy. Dr Shen approaches this challenge in an extremely innovative way. From a perspective broadly informed by economics, he draws specifically upon both Darwinian evolutionary theory and game theory. This is a brave initiative, clearly marking off his analysis from existing research in the field.

Dr Shen is to be warmly congratulated on making a fresh and important contribution to this field; his book deserves every success and will surely become an essential work of reference.

Simon Roberts
Professor of Law
London School of Economics
August 2012

ACKNOWLEDGMENTS

I am particularly grateful to Professor Simon Roberts for his guidance, support and encouragement, which made my PhD thesis, and now this book, an updated version, possible. I am indebted to Professor Michael Palmers and Professor Anthony Bradley who commented on an earlier draft of the manuscript. Special thanks also go to Trevor Goh and Yvonne Xu who read through the whole manuscript with great care and patience, and Dr Iris H.Y. Chiu for her insightful comments on Chapter 4. Certainly, responsibility for any error, defect or omission rests with me.

My interest in international commercial arbitration dates back to twenty years ago when I took a commercial arbitration course with Professor Chen Zhidong, who has become my mentor in many respects since then. I truly thank Professor Chen for his endless support, guidance and encouragement.

This book is a product of collective efforts. I want to thank two anonymous referees' endorsement for the publication of this book in this series. My gratitude further extends to Rebecca Pound for her patient proofreading and editorial input, and to Ann-Christin Maak for publication support. They have done their job with great efforts and tolerance for my failings; without them, this book would be a mission impossible.

As always, my greatest debt and most heartfelt thanks are owed to my parents even though our cultural tradition may restrain me from expressing that in a refined manner. As a merely tiny token of appreciation, this book is dedicated to them.

CONTENTS

Chapter 3.
Enforcement of Annulled Awards, Delocalisation and Game Theory 81

Chapter 4.
***Lex Mercatoria* and the New York Convention**.......................... 159

LIST OF TABLES AND DIAGRAMS

CHAPTER 1

RETHINKING THE NEW YORK CONVENTION: FROM A JURISPUDENCE-ORIENTED PERSPECTIVE

There are numerous critical but unsettled issues in today's international commercial arbitration, ranging from the enforcement of arbitral awards to the spectacular rise of both mandatory arbitration and arbitration without contractual relationships under investment treaties. It is then not a surprise to see so many published articles and books in this field addressing a large number of legal and practical issues. The purpose of this book, nevertheless, is not to supplement the vast array of existing writings on international commercial arbitration, which may have easily convinced us that there is no such need to repeat this effort. Nor is this book intended to offer a day-to-day tool or a comprehensive manual to help professionals or experts who are faced with a specific issue relating to the application of the New York Convention and domestic arbitration laws. Therefore, this book is not an endless-seeming work merely concerned with the detail of arbitration in the light of the New York Convention or reflecting some thoughts on those topics frequently written by scholars and practitioners. The most frustrating experience which can be encountered in studying arbitration law is that so much emphasis is placed on the practical topics that the subject is of little jurisprudential significance. In other words, very little discussion has been undertaken on arbitration, or more specifically the New York Convention, at a jurisprudential level.

Jurisprudence and a jurisprudential analysis, while esoteric, have a role in legal research. Like philosophy, jurisprudence can also be practical, and can approach practical issues pragmatically. At first glance an attempt to approach something as mundane as institutional rules for arbitration from a jurisprudential perspective might seem somewhat presumptuous. However, beneath the surface of the rule-making and practice, there is a clear purpose which is future-oriented. Scholars have decried the extent to which arbitrations have increasingly become carbon copies (in their systemic design) of traditional dispute resolution through judicial systems, rather than remaining true alternatives.[1] For these reasons, while this book offers a reasonably concise explanation of several crucial academic issues involved in international commercial arbitration, more emphasis has been placed on the illustration of how a particular issue can be explored via some new jurisprudential tools. Rather than putting another spin on received doctrine, the research is an attempt to explore whether what has been studied can be more convincingly presented with the help of new strands of theory and, moreover, treated in a way which is sufficiently forward-looking to meet the demands of future developments. This book does not provide a machete to hack at the undergrowth along the way. What it does is to demonstrate the pathway of logics and the jurisprudential questions one ought to consider in search of common principles in the next few decades.

This is a study of how the New York Convention might be reformed or evolved on a jurisprudential basis. It is not a functional study, and cases of the application of the New York Convention are not extensively referred to as often as in other writings. There are several reasons for this. First, it would be premature to decide how the New York Convention's framed legal discourse will function in a new framework or how the New York Convention's currently-designed legal discourse for the future functions in the existing framework. Second, functionalism is too narrow an approach to the jurisprudential study of law because it ignores or underestimates the power of legal discourse.[2] Third, the practical difficulty with the New York Convention is that the courts of more than 140 jurisdictions are unlikely to use the same, or even a similar, approach regardless of a uniform conclusion when they apply the New York Convention in real cases. The cases cited in this research therefore are key decisions which illustrate the ways in which other decisions in different jurisdictions or, more importantly, the jurisprudential development path of the New York Convention, might go.

The study of legal discourse is important because language, cultural values and political ideologies not only affect how law is formed and evolved but also suggest how law will be interpreted and applied. Legal discourse is also important due to its political function, as it expresses ideas which constitute part of the ruling legal ideology and shape social behaviours. Legal discourse is the heart of law's methodological autonomy[3] which contributes to the fact that the

---

1 Thomas I.A. Allen, 'Institutional Rules: Straitjacket or Scaffold?', in Martin Odams De Zylva and Reziya Harrison (eds.), *International Commercial Arbitration – Developing Rules for the New Millennium*, Bristol: Jordans (2000) p. 54.

2 For a critique of this tension with legal realism and functionalism in comparative law, see George Fletcher, 'The Universal and the Particular in Legal Discourse', (1987) 2 *BYU Law Review* 335.

3 "Law is autonomous at the methodological level when the ways in which specialised institutions [for adjudication] justify their acts differ from the kinds of justification used in other disciplines or practices. This means that legal reasoning has a method or style to differentiate it from scientific explanation and from moral, political, and economic

legal order is "separate from any other identifiable set of non-legal beliefs or norms, be they economic, political, or religious".[4] Take one classical example. The importance of legal discourse is illustrated by Alan Watson's thesis that there are two primary features of Roman private law discourse which explain its historical domination of modern civil law systems.[5] First, relying on Max Weber's characterisation of Roman private law as a formally rational system of applying law to factual problems,[6] Watson argues that Roman private law has an inherent authoritativeness with an emphasis on rules, not obscured by local interests, and set out independently of practical problems in real cases.[7] Second, Roman private law became divided into discrete "blocks" of substantive legal institutions, such as categories of contracts, property rights and delicts, and was thus apt to be received in such blocks rather than as individual rules or as a whole theoretical system.[8] This "block" effect allowed some institutions to be received without others, though they related to one another, and individual rules could then be adapted to the host legal system.

Similarly, the New York Convention to a certain extent is also a host legal system, a discourse with some crucial norms such as cost-effectiveness, efficiency, party autonomy, justice and the split of powers (involving judicial review and sovereignty). Social, historical, economic and even cultural factors also affect the formation and application of norms and rules in this discourse. The search for a developing direction of international commercial arbitration lies at the heart of this book. Do we have a direction? Why? What is the purpose of the direction? How are we to navigate? Whence should the direction of navigation be best derived? Is it to be universal or particular to distinct contexts? These questions frame the structure of this book.

In determining the methodology to be used in this study, it is of great importance to ensure that the issues discussed here are studied in a pragmatically jurisprudential way. With this in mind, the major objective that shaped the methodology of study is to find the path along which the New York Convention may further evolve. The methodology also, ideally, can help to justify the space for some core norms such as public policy and *lex mercatoria* to survive or even revive and spread.

discourse." See Roberto M. Unger, *Law in Modern Society: Towards a Criticism of Social Theory*, New York: Free Press (1976) p. 53.

4 Roberto M. Unger, above n. 3, 52.

5 See generally Alan Watson, *The Making of the Civil Law*, Cambridge, MA: Harvard University Press (1981).

6 See Max Weber, '"Economy of Law" or "Sociology of Law"', in Guenther Roth and Claus Wittich (eds.), *Max Weber, Economy and Society: An Outline of Interpretive Sociology*, Vol. 2, Berkeley: University of California Press (1978).

7 Alan Watson, above n. 5, 32.

8 Alan Watson, above n. 5, 14–22.

In recent years, with the realisation that law is no longer a closed system of rules[9] but an instrument of social policy, the importance of other disciplines to the study of law has been noticed and some innovative responses have appeared in the legal scholarship. This novelty in part is a consequence of the increasing influence of academic disciplines and intellectual traditions previously unconnected with the study of law. For the time being, the burden of these new methods of legal study has discouraged scholars from pursuing them. Some scholars have chosen to avoid moving in these directions altogether, whilst others have chosen to specialise in one of the new forms and to neglect the others. Yet these interdisciplinary methodologies have rarely been adopted in studying international commercial arbitration. However, it is not the plan to base this book systematically on the disciplines of law, sociology, economics, literature,[10] psychology and social policy,[11] even though, from time to time, some of these approaches will be adopted. Among others, two major analytic approaches, that is, Darwinian legal theory and game theory, are adopted in this book where appropriate. The use of these theoretical resources is briefly discussed below.

No research on arbitration would be complete without some discussion of the historical context. Legal history can provide us with a good understanding of arbitration so that crucial reasons for its development can be scrutinised. A historical analysis can help explore the differences between different times and show the gradual development of critical theories. A historical analysis can also provide a full picture of the critical concepts and issues, *e.g.*, arbitrability and de-localisation (*lex loci arbitri*). Arguing that the New York Convention needs new qualifications itself needs a strong theoretical basis. Chapter Two provides a

---

9 This line of thinking has developed alongside the recent resurgence of neo-systems theory such as Luhmann theory etc. See further discussion in Chapter 2 in this book.

10 The Law and Literature movement instructs legal scholars in techniques of literary analysis for the purpose of interpreting laws and in the reciprocal use of legal analysis for the purpose of interpreting literary texts. According to the Law and Literature movement, law should be understood as an essentially literary activity. Judicial opinions should be read and evaluated not primarily as political acts or as attempts to maximise society's wealth through efficient rules, but rather as artistic performances. The "contract reading" theory can characterise the role an arbitrator plays in construing an arbitration agreement and a judge plays in reviewing an arbitral award. A "contract reading" approach proposes a new calculus, that is, the contract (literature) analysis of party's intention manifested in the arbitration agreement for determining the scope of review of awards. See generally Richard A. Posner, *Law and Literature*, Cambridge, MA: Harvard University Press (2000); James Boyd White, *The Legal Imagination. Studies in the Nature of Legal Thought and Expression*, Boston: Little, Brown and Co. (1973); James Boyd White, 'Law as Language: Reading Law and Reading Literature', (1982) 60 *Texas Law Review* 415, 429–430.

11 The social analysis of law is dedicated to the study of law in a social context. The emphasis is placed on both empirical research and the social development of the theoretical framework and legislative activities. See generally, Lawrence M. Friedman, 'The Law and Society Movement', (1986) 38 *Stanford Law Review* 763–780; Roger Cotterrell, *The Sociology of Law – An Introduction*, London: Butterworths (2nd edn. 1992).

full discussion of Darwinian legal theory and the New York Convention. The idea of Darwinian legal theory is that patterns of legal evolution are closely analogous to those which occur in the natural world as a result of the interaction between genes, organisms and environments. In this sense, Darwinian legal theory can be used to explain that the New York Convention has been out of step with the developing changes to the "environment". Thus, a change of the "meme", an equivalent term for gene in the legal sense, is necessary.[12] The theory can be a tool for examining the future development of the New York Convention in a changing legal environment. Some driving forces such as globalisation and high technology, which will result in new changes to legal terms, will also be discussed.

One very influential analytical tool in current legal study has been the Law and Economics Movement.[13] According to legal economists, law ought to consist of rules that maximise a society's material wealth and aid the efficient operation of markets designed to generate wealth. Economic analysis has been extended to a wide range of human behaviours and interactions that had been traditionally considered outside the boundaries of this discipline. The theory-building potential of economic methods, however, has met with resistance from legal professionals, for the analytical models used by economists to generate predictions and propose reforms are often regarded as simplified and sometimes counterfactual assumptions about the empirical world. As a relatively new methodology, economic analysis can provide a new, pragmatic and empirical view, and respond in particularly technical ways to legal issues in the regulatory environment. Although it could be argued that reduced expenses or cost-savings are not the essence of arbitration and the arbitration agreement determines the process, an economic approach to arbitration is useful to illustrate some critical issues in international commercial arbitration such as the relationship between arbitration institutions and courts and the cooperation among signatory states to the New York Convention.

---

12 See generally Kate Distin, *The Selfish Meme – A Critical Reassessment*, Cambridge: Cambridge University Press (2005).

13 There are several schools in the law and economics movement. The approach taken here may largely side with the Chicago school theory in the analysis. Apart from that, there are "Austrian School" and "neo-classical" economic theory school. The Austrian school is an economic theory based on the idea that what economics needs to deal with is the actions of individual, subjective goals in the face of shortages of the goods, services and time needed to reach these goals. Important factors for economists of this school are the influence of time on human action, and the fact that, in acting, people need to deal with the uncertainty regarding the effect of their actions due to their lack of precise knowledge regarding the present, past and future. This is to be contrasted with the more dominant "neo-classical" economic theory which is based on the idea of a mainly mathematical model of "perfect" competition and seeks to describe the behaviour of a market in terms of equations. See generally, http://en.wikipedia.org/wiki/Neoclassical_economics and http://en.wikipedia.org/wiki/Austrian_School (last accessed on 4 February 2013).

Among others, game theory has been utilised by legal scholars to study legal phenomena such as jurisdictional competition and legal harmonisation in a number of legal areas such as corporation law, securities regulations, labour standards and environment protection rules. The basic idea is that states act in their self-interest like private parties in the game, which requires a "federalism" system in place to harmonise self-interest-oriented national rules. Game theory has often been used to study the substantive law. Procedural rules in arbitration and litigation have rarely been tested. It will be interesting to see if game theory can be used in arbitration to study the possibility of harmonising national rules in the trend of de-localisation and, in a wider sense, globalisation.

It has been argued that it is difficult to use Darwinian legal theory and game theory simultaneously because of their incomparable and incompatible natures. Darwinian legal theory is in essence a historical approach which studies the vertical development of biological or human behaviours in a chronological way, whereas game theory focuses on the horizontal plane with a view to harmony. There seems a potential conflict in using different approaches in one research project. This requires some preliminary discussion of the nature of the rules in the New York Convention.

The rules in one law or treaty differ in nature, that is, in their values, structures, norms and processes. They vary in the extent to which their values, structures, norms and processes are contained in a hierarchy or legal discourse. They may differ in respect of those characteristics which are often associated with the application of the law, including the reliance on case law, the use of precedent and the binding force of norms. They may also differ in their role or function in realising or serving the purpose of legal discourse. Different characteristics of various rules in one convention result in different ways in which they allocate risk or solve the problem, and the different roles they play in this legal discourse or hierarchy. Besides, rules are interrelated, for example, in relation to institutional arrangements such as jurisdiction, copying or borrowing of norms, and the interactions with outsiders.

The rules in the New York Convention, by their very nature, may be classified provisionally into two rough categories. Some rules are market-based, being generated by economic actors as part of the economic process, or polity-based, in that they form part of the established political structure. Other rules are more convention-based, deriving from their very beginning from historical development. This classification distinguishes between different types of rules according to their origins and modes of function. The basic allocation of tasks set out in the New York Convention is realised by utilising the functions of these two types of rules.

A variety of norms is contained in the New York Convention such as procedural autonomy, applicable law (the use of *lex mercatoria* or similar constructs), the remedies available to arbitral tribunals, and the recognition and enforcement of awards. The rules relating to the procedural autonomy and applicable law, *inter alia*, *lex mercatoria*, are convention-based rules and can be studied by using Darwinian legal theory. These rules attempt to maintain the basic features of arbitration. Other rules such as the grounds for refusing to recognise and enforce arbitral awards are more polity-based rules, which recognise the differentials between signatory states but also attempt to harmonise local practices to a certain extent. Since the polity-based rules inevitably involve human players (*i.e.*, the agency), game theory is appropriate as a methodological tool. The classification scheme distinguishing convention-based and polity-based rules in the New York Convention is convincing in the sense that Darwinian legal theory and game theory can be adopted simultaneously in one research project because they can be used to solve different legal problems.

In view of all the developments that have occurred since 1958, the application of the New York Convention in arbitral tribunals, the courts of the forum of the arbitration and courts of third-party States may no longer be sound and is in need of a revision or new qualification. This is the core purpose of this book.

CHAPTER 2

THE NEW YORK CONVENTION AND DARWINIAN LEGAL THEORY

The aim in bringing Darwinian evolutionary theory into a legal context is to unite legal and biological evolution and then account for processes of cultural transmission and legal change with a conception of "genetic metaphor". The Darwinian evolutionary theory provides a mechanism for understanding legal evolution. The patterns of cultural and legal evolution are closely analogous to those which occur in the natural world as a result of the interaction between the gene, organism and environment.[1] This chapter explores the significance of discovery and development of legal evolutionary theory which is associated with the notion of Darwinian evolutionary theory and its specific application in the field of international commercial arbitration.

2.1. DARWINIAN EVOLUTIONARY THEORY

Charles Darwin first proclaimed the biological evolutionary theory[2] in *The Origin of Species* in 1859,[3] the objective of which was to show how speciation occurs spontaneously through natural selection in the natural world. Due to the scarcity of resources, species struggle for life in a competitive environment. "Owing to this struggle for life, any variation, however slight and from whatever cause proceeding, if it be in any degree profitable to an individual of any species, in its infinitely complex relations to other organic beings and to external nature, will tend to the preservation of that individual. The offspring, also, will thus have

1 In this chapter, "culture" is broadly defined to include human practices such as law. See Henry Plotkin, 'Culture and Psychological Mechanisms', in Robert Aunger (ed.) *Darwinising Culture. The Status of Memetics as a Science,* Oxford: Oxford University Press (2000).

2 As surprising as it sounds, Darwin never uses the term "evolution" in *The Origin of Species.* Rather, he speaks of "descent with modification". For Darwin, the process of modification is, in principle, continuous. The difference between these terms is not merely semantic. Darwin realised that evolution is a teleological term. To say that something evolved is to say that it has evolved toward something. Darwin eschews such teleological thinking.

3 Charles Darwin, *On the Origin of Species by Means of Natural Selection or the Preservation of Favoured Races in the Struggle of Life,* London: John Murray (1859).

a better chance of surviving".[4] It is the organisms that inherit traits or characteristics from their parents. Traits which are advantageous in aiding the survival and reproduction of speciation accumulate across successive generations and have more chances to be passed on to the next generation. A selective pressure is therefore applied invisibly.

The core of Darwinian evolution is natural selection. As Darwin pointed out:

> "natural selection is daily and hourly scrutinising, throughout the world, every variation, even the slightest; rejecting that which is bad, preserving and adding up all that is good; silently and insensibly working, whenever and wherever opportunity offers, at the improvement of each organic being in relation to its organic, and inorganic, conditions of life".[5]

This suggests that natural selection is a two-step process consisting of, first, mutations and rearrangements of the germ-line that are random with respect to the future of organism and species; and second, the sorting and selecting by the environment of the most adaptive organisms produced by the mutations.

For Darwin, change is a universal characteristic of the organic world and results from "natural selection", a blind and automatic process by which species adapt to environmental changes by weeding out variations that jeopardise their survival. In Darwin's view, nature is intrinsically mechanistic and responds to external forces of chance and necessity. The environment, in the Darwinian sense, consists of two major factors: the physical features of the natural world, *e.g.*, weather, and the activities of other organisms. The changes in the landscape or the migration or the separation of the members of a single species can lead over time to the emergence of new species as each group adapts to new conditions. This process will result in greater diversity due to the possibility of combining two separate lines of descent. The emergence of distinctive forms of species are all "fitted" in or "adapted" to the environment by possessing features which co-evolved with those of the surroundings.

Darwinian evolution theory has a three-fold distinction among genotype ("code"), phenotype ("organism"), and environment. The first element, vitally, explains the nature of the links between the other two. The environment's past, in the form of information and code, is embedded in the organism. In this sense, the organism and environment are "fitted" to each other. The pressures from the environment gradually lead to the changes in the composition of the code which then in turn influences the structure of the organism. Nevertheless, this does not happen to all individual organisms but only to those which carry the code and make it feasible for it to be reproduced. The process is dependent upon the

4 Charles Darwin, 'On the Origin of Species by Means of Natural Selection', in Duncan Porter and Peter Graham (eds.), *The Portable Darwin*, Harmondsworth: Penguin Books (1993) p. 147.

5 Ibid. 162.

different survival rates of individual organisms. The "data" contained in the code is transmitted through the incremental processes of inter-generational development and selective retention. The change in the structure of the code is non-teleological or blind.

The contribution of modern genetics to the evolutionary theory has been to identify the precise way in which inheritance and variation occur. Inheritance takes place through the copying of the genetic code from the parent to offspring. The genetic code, the "genotype",[6] is a "replicator" or self-replicating entity and contains the genetic material which is "encoded" in the sense of embodying previous adaptations or successful "survival strategies". Genetic material is a form of stored and coded information,[7] and has a peculiar chemical composition (DNA) which makes this cross-generational copying possible. The DNA "code" transmits information to proteins so as to enable them to "build" the organism which then becomes the carrier or vehicle for the replication of the genetic material through reproduction. Along with this process, the effect of natural selection is expressed through shifts in the genetic composition of particular species. This has been summarised as "the process of … extracting useful information from the environment and encoding it in the genes".[8] Meanwhile, it is through random mutations in the genetic composition of individual organisms and their recombination through reproduction that variation in inherited traits takes place.[9]

The variations in the characteristics of different organisms do not represent the impact of immediate environmental pressure. Rather, they are the consequence of the inherited, cumulative effects of environmental change over successive generations or the result of random mutations in the genetic code. According to Darwinian theory, variation precedes selection. From the perspective of mutation, variations are "errors" in the copying process. However, it is the "errors" that help those individual organisms to survive and reproduce because variations make them more able to adapt to a challenging environment. To copy the "errors" or variations in the code is a process of genetic change. This observation seems different from the Lamarckian accounts of evolutionary change.[10] According to the Lamarckian theory, individual organisms respond

---

6 The term "genome" is used to refer to a complex of genes.

7 See Kim Sterelny and Paul Griffiths, *Sex and Death: An Introduction to the Philosophy of Biology,* Chicago: Chicago University Press (1999), and Matt Ridley, *Genome: The Autobiography of a Species in 23 Chapters*, London: Harper Perennial (2000).

8 Matt Ridley, above n. 7, 247.

9 Mutations have both light and dark sides. They are essential to natural selection because they provide genetic variability which results in new phenotypes for the environment to sort out, the bountiful speciation presently observed, and the minor variations that embellish the basic design of lineages.

10 An outline of Lamarck's theory is available at http://www.ucmp.berkeley.edu/history/lamarck.html. Lamarckianism or Lamarckism is now often used in a rather derogatory sense to refer to the theory that acquired traits can be inherited. As a matter of fact,

with varying degrees of "mutation" to the changing conditions of environment. In order to ensure that the more efficient characteristics endure, more successful individuals "acquire" traits that can be passed on to their offspring.[11]

In brief, Darwinian evolutionary theory has three basic building blocks, which are the code, organism and environment. The functional and adaptive nature of codes persists through time. This theory is not specific to biology, and can be applied in a social science context where it is feasible to substitute "social system" for "organism", and the "institutional" or "cultural" environment for nature.[12] In addition, the "evolutionary algorithm" of natural selection can also be expressed at a general or specific level applicable to the social sphere. The algorithm predicts that where four conditions are observed: (i) self-replicating entities, (ii) a mechanism of variation, (iii) a mechanism for inheritance, or the inter-generational transmission of entities, and (iv) differential survival rates brought about through environmental pressures, a process of cumulative evolution, leading to the emergence of complex and diverse forms, will occur.

2.2. LEGAL EVOLUTIONARY THEORY[13]

The process of development or growth is not only one of the most important processes in the biological world but also occurs universally among modern,

---

Lamarck's theory is more complicated. The theory is that organisms are not passively altered by their environment. Instead, a change in the environment causes changes in the needs of organisms living in that environment, which in turn causes changes in their behaviour. Altered behaviour leads to a greater or lesser use of a given structure or organ; use would cause the structure to increase in size over several generations, whereas disuse would cause it to shrink or even disappear. The rule that use or disuse causes structures to enlarge or shrink is called the "first law" by Lamarck in his book *Philosophie Zoologique*. Lamarck's "second law" stated that all such changes were heritable. The result of these laws was the continuous, gradual change of all organisms, as they became adaptable to their environments; the physiological needs of organisms, created by their interactions with the environment, drive Lamarckian evolution. Lamarckian inheritance, at least in the sense Lamarck intended, is in conflict with the findings of genetics and has now been largely abandoned. Lamarck's theory was accepted by some scholars. For instance, Herbert Spencer was convinced by Lamarck's arguments for evolution and began to see the possibility of constructing a synthesis that would unite all aspects of natural and human evolution under the same laws.

11 See Geoffrey Hodgson, 'Is Social Evolution Lamarckian or Darwinian?', in John Laurent and John Nightingale (eds.), *Darwinism and Evolutionary Economics*, Cheltenham: Edward Elgar (2001).

12 Gunter Teubner, *Law as an Autopoietic System*, Oxford: Blackwell (1993).

13 The last few decades of the 20th century saw a climate of uncertainty surrounding the social science. Scholars tried to rebuild the theoretical framework for legal history. Among others, Marie Theres Fögen adopted a radical approach and similar terms to describe the change and development of social world. For instance, she used autopoiesis to replace the hierarchy and domination, the key terms in politics and history. As a result, a "system of communication" constitutes a social world without human actors. This extreme theory, although is criticised by other scholars, effectively means that legal history can be reformulated by adopting new

higher, multicellular and complex animals. The theory of evolution is more than a scientific theory or paradigm.[14] It has become the philosophical foundation of the naturalistic view of the universe that has replaced the Judeo-Christian worldview which once dominated Western culture.[15] Darwinian theory then offers at least a new perspective on the social development of life of human beings. Social Darwinism attempts to utilise the evolutionary theory of Darwin to describe society or prescribe its best constitution, and culturally transmitted behavioural information exhibits and supports a Darwinian evolutionary dynamic.[16] By analogy to its biological counterpart, social Darwinism argues that the struggle for survival among humans may be expected to yield social progress, just as the struggle among biological communities produces evolutionary adaptive results.[17] Social behaviours and legal systems and institutions came into existence as evolutionary responses to "species-threatening" changes in mankind's environment.

In order to apply Darwinian theory to the legal sphere, a key aspect of social evolution or development, it is critical to identify the specific dynamics of the upstream replicative process. This requires a medium corresponding to the "gene" in the biological evolutionary process so that the three basic blocks in the Darwinian theory can be built up in the legal context. The term "meme" is created as an analogue to the gene in the social sphere.[18] One theme focusing on the evolution of the cultural elements is sometimes called "memetics".[19] However, the diffusion of the term "meme" owes much to the philosophical

---

elements and philosophical ideas. See Simon Roberts, 'Against a Systemic Legal History' (on file with the author).

14 *e.g.*, Edward O. Wilson popularised evolutionary psychology or socio-biology and interpreted all human behaviours in light of the evolutionary process, such as the origins and ends of every human behaviour and institution. See Marc D Guerra, 'The Delusion of Darwinian Natural Law', (2001) 11(4) *Religion & Liberty* 8–11. Marx and Engels were much interested in Darwin's work, and used his theory to underpin their notion of the historical evolution of class struggle.

15 It is widely agreed that international law was the product of dominant European nations that were Christian, capitalist and imperialist. See Louis Henkin, *How Nations Behave: Law and Foreign Policy*, New York: Columbia University Press (2nd edn. 1979) p. 121.

16 See Robert Aunger, above n. 1; Susan Blackmore, *The Meme Machine*, Oxford: Oxford University Press (1999); Ward H. Goodenough, 'Outline of a Framework for a Theory of Cultural Evolution' (1999) 33 *Cross-Cultural Research* 84; Mark R. Flinn, 'Culture and the Evolution of Social Learning', (1997) 18 *Evolution and Human Behaviour* 23–67; William H. Durham, 'Advances in Evolutionary Culture Theory', (1990) 19 *Annual Review of Anthropology* 197.

17 Herbert Spencer, an English sociologist and philosopher, was the pioneer of this approach even though he was not a convinced Darwinist. In the field of social science, social Darwinism is also called "social Spencerism", which proclaimed a progressive view of human society.

18 The notion is originated by the evolutionary biologist Richard Dawkins in his works *The Selfish Gene*, Oxford: Oxford University Press (1976; 2nd edn. 1989) and *The Blind Watchmaker*, London: Norton & Company, Inc. (1986).

19 See Susan Blackmore, above n. 16.

work, *Darwin's Dangerous Idea* by Daniel Dennett.[20] Antecedents of memetics have been found in the theory of cultural inheritance.[21]

As a matter of fact, a "meme" is used to mean a replicating entity and a unit of social, cultural or legal information, a concept that is shared in a population of individuals through social transmission. A meme is made of information, which can be carried in any physical medium. A meme is also subject to similar Darwinian principles of heredity, variation and selection as applicable to a gene. Thus, cultural norms or legal concepts develop in a cumulative evolution process, through which incremental changes occur over time in a manner which reflects surrounding environmental pressures. The basic evolutionary "algorithm" can be applied to the emergence of complicated social or legal institutions. An individual meme, as a unit or entity equivalent to the gene, must be able to copy itself with accuracy. Errors in the self-copying process are recognised as random mutations which occur in the memetic code along with the transmission through inheritance. Similarly, changes in memetic material must not occur as a consequence of the volition of individual agents, even though it is difficult to envisage that this process may be blind or spontaneous.[22] Memes can also be identified as memory items stored in the human brain, such as fashions, tunes, catchphrases and so on.[23] In terms of this wide coverage, memes are more complex verbal formulas mainly transmitted through imitation.[24] This definition also prefers a behavioural account of memetics to a purely neural one.[25] The problematic aspect of this memory-like definition is that cultural evolution would possess few features of biological evolution. For instance, the change would be probably rapid rather than being slow and incremental. The copying process through imitation would be inaccurate and threaten the integration of the "memetic code". Individual volition would replace collective volition in playing a major part in the transmission process. Last but not least, cultural change would lack the dominant feature of genealogical character in the biological evolution, namely the impossibility of recombining different lines of descent once they have separated.[26] However, this

---

20 See Daniel C. Dennett, *Darwin's Dangerous Idea: Evolution and the Meanings of Life*, New York: Simon & Schuster (1995).

21 See Luca Cavalli-Sforza and Marcus Feldman, *Cultural Evolution and Transmission: A Quantitative Approach*, Princeton: Princeton University Press (1981); Robert Boyd and Peter J. Richerson, *Culture and the Evolutionary Process*, Chicago: University of Chicago Press (1985).

22 See Daniel C. Dennett, above n. 20, 352–30.

23 See Richard Dawkins, above n. 18, 194.

24 See Susan Blakemore, above n. 16, and Jack Balkin, *Cultural Software: A Theory of Ideology*, New Haven: Yale University Press (1998), Chs. 3 and 4.

25 See Dan Gatherer, 'Why the thought contagion metaphor is retarding the process of memetics', (1998) 3 *Journal of Memetics – Evolutionary Mechanisms of Information Transmission* (available at http://www.cpm.mmu.ac.uk/jom-emit.1998/vol12/gatherer_d.html).

26 See Robert Aunger, 'Introduction', in Robert Aunger, above n. 1.

discouraging speculation does not stand well in the current emergent discipline of memetics.[27]

As rightly described, the genome is "an information-processing computer that extracts useful information from the world by natural selection and embodies that information in its design … the human genome [is] four billion years' worth of accumulated learning".[28] One account of cultural evolution argues that human imitative processes can be classified into three categories – non-linguistic transmission (uncoded), stories (partially coded), and formulas (fully coded).[29] The replication is of a formula of context and action: a recipe, recommendation, or rule. The authority for these formulas for action can be varied: observational, parental, religious or legal. Legal concepts or terms, the linguistic formulas which supply the basis for systematising legal materials, can be regarded as embodying in shorthand form information about the social (legal) world which is filtered through the processes of legal argument, debate, consultation, litigation, arbitration and exposition. Like the genetic code, legal concepts develop slowly, compared to the more rapid rate of change in the substance of legal rules. In addition, the change of a legal concept is apparent in retrospect, reflecting the non-teleological and path-dependent aspect of the genetic change. Like the genome, a legal concept or term also has the ability to copy itself (*i.e.*, largely its critical feature) faithfully so that the necessary condition for inheritance of information contained in the genetic code can be satisfied. Therefore, the memetic information in the legal concept can be vertically transmitted. This process is similar to the relative continuity of the genetic code. Legal evolution is only possible if there are sufficiently powerful information-processing devices capable of storing information and reliably transmitting it to or replicating it in other information-processing devices.[30]

In the legal context, a legal doctrine can be thought of as a particular mechanism of cultural transmission which works through coding information into a conceptual form, thereby assisting its inter-temporal dissemination. This mechanism is a "Darwinian" type of process, in the sense of operating through a cycle of inheritance, variation and selection, which results in temporal sequences and patterns of morphological changes. Legal discourse possesses basic elements of autonomy and self-reference which provide it with the capacity for self-replication, while it is linked to wider social and biological processes through

27 This problematic aspect stands in contrast to associations which have long been made between the Darwinian evolution and processes akin to lineal descent within legal doctrine.

28 See Matt Ridley, above n. 7, 220.

29 Non-linguistic, uncoded transmission depends upon the direct observation. In its simplest form, an action by person A in a particular context is observed by person B. The action and the context for it are stored in the brain of B, waiting for the context to reoccur for B. Once the language enters the human repertoire, it can be used to tell a story. The third mode, the "fully coded" transmission through linguistic formulas, uses language to transmit abstracted behavioural information.

30 See Jack Balkin, above n. 24, 55.

Ancient Law to identify the characteristic movement of "progressive societies" from their archaic condition to the modern one.[54]

Maine was not alone in placing the growth of law and legal systems in an evolutionary context. As a matter of fact, he was followed by a group of sociologists in Europe and America. Lewis H. Morgan, an American anthropologist, published *Ancient Society* in 1877 and put forward a theory of the three stages in the cultural and social evolution of mankind, *i.e.*, from Savagery through Barbarism to Civilization.[55] Like Maine's *Ancient Law*, Morgan's *Ancient Society* greatly influenced European social theorists such as Karl Marx and Friedrich Engels.[56] In England, Leonard T. Hobhouse produced far more complex evolutionary schemes of social growth as well as legal development.[57] Although these early works substantially contributed to the legal evolutionary theory as a subject or "science", an apparent weakness or defect was that all the key questions discussed therein were formulated in an ethnocentric way and premised on the assumption that western legal categories were sophisticated enough to offer an analytical framework for understanding legal institutions and concepts in "primitive" societies.

The first several pages of Holmes's *The Common Law* in 1881 also reflected an evolutionary legal thinking. Holmes's major concern was the disjuncture between form and substance in the common law and the different speeds at which the two appeared to evolve. Holmes argued that legal forms or concepts tend to persist long after the justification for them has been lost, a process which he thought required "ingenious minds" to discover new rationales for their existence. Once a new ground of policy was found, "the rule adapts itself to the new reasons which have been found for it, and enters upon a new career. The old form receives a new content, and in time even the form modifies itself to fit the

54 They are from sentiment to contract as the basis of social cohesion; from family to territory as the basis of the polity; from collective family property to private individual property; from tort to crime; from status to contract; from kinship to the individual as the basis of rights.

55 Lewis H. Morgan, *Ancient Society*, London: MacMillan & Company (1877).

56 Friedrich Engels published his historical materialist treatise *The Original of the Family, Private Property, and the State* in 1884 and the first part of the book was an extensive discussion of *Ancient Society*. Emile Durkheim published his book *The Division of Labour in Society* in 1893, in which Durkheim associated successive forms of social organisation with different types of legal system and purported to test his well-known hypothesis concerning the relationship of "mechanical" and "organic" solidarity. During the period from 1860 to 1945, there was social Darwinism movement in both Europe and the United States. The social Darwinism theory was closely related to the theories of Darwin, Jean-Baptiste Lamarck and Herbert Spencer and was widely used in a number of crucial ideological debates and social movements such as socialism, imperialism, liberalism, Fabianism, democracy and anti-democracy. For a detailed account, see Mike Hawkins, *Social Darwinism in European and American Thought 1860–1945: Nature as Model and Nature as Threat*, Cambridge: Cambridge University Press (1997).

57 Leonard T. Hobhouse, *Morals in Evolution: A Study in Comparative Ethics*, London: Chapman & Hall (6th edn. 1906).

meaning which it has received".[58] Although Holmes was writing at a time when the nature of genetic processes of transmission was not fully understood, the process he described in *The Common Law* is not dissimilar to those aspects of the modern neo-Darwinian synthesis in its account of "blind" legal evolution occurring in an incremental, cumulative fashion as the result of selective inheritance. Nevertheless, Holmes's work, like much of the early evolutionary thoughts about human society, shared in the flaws of social Darwinism which helped lead to such approaches being eclipsed.[59]

In the last several decades of the twentieth century, this line of thinking has resurfaced based on memetics,[60] along with the popularity of the "law and economics" movement.[61] Some have continued at the level of metaphor,[62] and others have drawn on the complexity theory as well as evolution.[63] Most recently, evolutionary terms such as the notions of autopoiesis[64] and path dependence[65] have merged as a new version.

Law is a fruitful field for testing Darwinian evolutionary theory and the notion of memetics. This, however, is not a simple transplantation of theories from biological to social sciences. More precisely, there is a possibility of developing a genuinely cross-disciplinary exchange and synthesis of ideas.[66] As a matter of fact, legal evolutionary theory also provides terminology for the biological evolution theory. For instance, the opportunistic adaptation of

58 Oliver Wendell Holmes Jr., above n. 47, 8.

59 See Albert W. Alschuler, *Law Without Values: The Life, Work, and Legacy of Justice Holmes*, Chicago: Chicago University Press (2000). See generally Oliver R. Goodenough, 'Biology, Behaviour and the Criminal Law: Seeking a Responsible Approach to an Inevitable Interchange', (1997) 22 *Vermont Law Review* 263.

60 See Michael Fried, above n. 48, 291; Jeffrey E. Stake, 'Are We Buyers or Hosts? A Memetic Approach to the First Amendment', (2001) 52 *Alabama Law Review* 1213; Sam Vermont, 'Politics and Literature: New Perspective: Memes and the Evolution of Intellectual Dishonesty in Law', (1998) 22 *Legal Studies Forum* 655.

61 Among others, major contributions include Richard A. Posner, *Economic Analysis of Law*, New York: Wolters Kluwer (8th edn. 2011); Paul Rubin, 'Why is the Common Law Efficient?', (1977) 5 *Journal of Legal Studies* 51; George Priest, 'The Common Law Process and the Selection of Efficient Rules', (1977) 5 *Journal of Legal Studies* 65.

62 See William H. Rodgers, Jr., 'Where Environmental Law and Biology Meet: Of Pandas, Thumbs, Statutory Sleepers and Effective Law', (1993) 65 *University Of Colorado Law Review* 25.

63 See J.B. Ruhl, 'Complexity Theory as a Paradigm for the Dynamical Law-and-Society System: A Wake-up Call for Legal Reductionism and the Modern Administrative State', (1996) 45 *Duke Law Journal* 849; J.B. Ruhl, 'The Fitness of Law: Using Complexity Theory to Describe the Evolution of Law and Society and its Practical Meaning for Democracy', (1996) 49 *Vanderbilt Law Review* 1407; Thomas E. Geu, 'Chaos, Complexity, and Coevolution: The Web of Law, Management Theory, and Law Related Services at the Millennium', (1998) 65 *Tennessee Law Review* 925.

64 Gunther Teubner, above n. 12.

65 Mark Roe, above n. 42, 641.

66 The widely adopted notions of bounded rationality and conventions, which were derived from the organisation theory and the economics of law, are often used by biologists to explain the persistence of behavioural traits and regularities.

existing legal forms to new ends which Holmes highlighted has parallels in the concept of "bricolage" which has entered into the biological literature from social anthropology.[67]

The ontological dimension concerns the status of legal norms, concepts, and processes as the objects of study and the nature of legal reality. A purely internal legal perspective does not offer a viable account of how norms operate in the social or economic realm.[68]

The law's self-descriptive nature does not provide a secure foundation for a socio-legal understanding of how law and society inter-relate.[69] The evolutionary approach sees social structures in general and legal systems in particular as "emergent" orders with distinctive evolutionary dynamics of self-reproduction and replication.[70] It is the emergence that creates "a relationship between two features or aspects such that one arises out of the other and yet, while perhaps being capable of reacting back on it, remains causally and taxonomically irreducible to it".[71] The evolutionary theory offers a means of studying law as emerging from the interactions of individual agents.[72] Moreover, the pattern and path of legal change and development may be subject to evolutionary mechanisms which share elements in common with those governing biological evolution.

By way of example, legislation encodes information about solutions to coordination problems. The legislative process collects information through the processes of parliamentary debate, interest-group lobbying, and public investigation. Like litigation, it contains elements of spontaneous order and is subject to the selective process by which certain rules are taken up and persisted with while others are discarded. In addition, legal rules derived from the

---

67 "Bricolage" implies that innovation in design, instead of involving the construction of a new model from scratch, tends to make use of structures or devices which lie immediately to hand. When a design feature is adapted from one use to another in this way, it remains embodied in the relevant structure long after its original function has disappeared. It is also possible that a design feature which is an essentially accidental by-product of an earlier adaptation finds a new use in a changed environment. See Claude Levi-Strauss, *The Savage Mind*, Chicago: Chicago University Press (1966). Also Daniel C. Dennett, above n. 20, 225–226.

68 Attempts to describe law run the risk of imposing an inappropriate conceptual framework which denies the distinctive social reality of legal phenomena.

69 Law's self-description is of interest in its own right, from both an internal, doctrinal and an external, sociological point of view.

70 The evolutionary approach may push the theory to an extreme form of reductionism in which legal forms are seen as driven by a sub-individual unit, a "selfish meme", and in which biological laws dictate the nature of social institutions.

71 See Tony Lawson, *Economics and Reality*, London: Routledge (1997) p. 63; see also Geoffrey Hodgson, above n. 11.

72 Memetic structures such as information, code, convention and culture cannot exist without human agency. The legal order represents more than the sum total of these interactions. Once the legal order is established, it frames the conditions for the exercise of human agency, just as much as it is framed by them.

legislation change over time without necessarily being formally repealed, thanks to judicial interpretations of statutes and codes. The widely-held misconception of the role of legislation among adherents of spontaneous order owes much to the belief that statutory rules are the product of conscious or planned intervention, while those of the common law derive from the "blind" interplay of litigation and adjudication. In both cases, the conscious human agency acts with the elements of evolution. Legislation, in many respects, provides a form of information retrieval which is more broadly-based and open to a plurality of influence than the judge-made law merely available through litigation.[73]

The evolutionary approach also sheds some light on the methodological implications. The approach is a functionalist one, a link between the function and form. The basic rule is that existing forms contain significant elements of adaptation to past environments. Like genetic information, the memetic information encoded in memes provides information about the structure-building which was adaptive in environments encountered by our ancestors. This may lead us not to easily adopt the optimality approach to observed institutions on the basis of their persistence. In the social institution context, the "fitness" or "survival of the fittest" only refers to the institution that has become "fitted" to the environment over time. In this sense, there may not be the best available institution.[74] It is not wise to conclude that the existing form of social institution or legal rules is a near-complete norm and is fully functional in the current environment.[75] A genealogical methodology requires a close inspection of the historical record, with the aim of reconstructing the line of descent of institutional forms from an examination of the circumstances of their origins. The reconstruction shows that the development of forms is dependent upon contingencies and chance configurations of events.[76]

---

73 A good example is the world-wide discussion of the use of land-mines and the proposed international treaty banning such weapons. The movement that launched this new rule of international law was surely innovative, and must have involved deliberate foresight, but the process by which such potential innovation was transformed into international practice was one of extended social selection, involving information companies, social organisations, and coalition-building, conference bargaining and negotiation, and has been and will be followed by voting in national assemblies and, ultimately, in national selection (an election campaign is the paradigmatic social-political selection process). The fact that such memes originate in individual or collective experience does not preclude the operation of social selection processes that ultimately add to, or subtract from, the world stock of memes. See George Modelski, 'An Evolutionary Theory of Culture?' (1999) 3 *Journal of Memetics – Evolutionary Models of Information Transmission* (available at http://jom-emit.cfpm.org/1999/vol3/modelski_g.html, last accessed 10 September 2012).

74 As there is not a best available institution, once the effect of interaction between the institution and environment has been amplified, other paths may be closed off.

75 The existing forms have been inherited as a result of past adaptations. These forms may possess the functionality to survive, but have acquired unnecessary features by way of adaptations to current conditions.

76 As a matter of fact, the study of cultural evolution is more likely to be more empirically orientated than their biological counterparts because "a fossil record of cultural change exists

Normative issues are related to this reconstruction issue. Selection can only work through the feedback mechanism between the code and the system or environment. Horizontal and vertical transmissions exist in the social context or process. As the long tradition of comparative law illustrates, the legal models are often diffused by direct copying of concepts and the content of rules.[77] This, however, does not undermine the basic observations that the vertical transmission of coded information through the legal system and the inheritance of the adapted knowledge contained in the legal norms are subject to Darwinian theory. In addition, the capacity of the code to assimilate new information is limited by the need to ensure a high consistency in the copying process. The relative stability and continuity of legal concepts suggest that legal evolution is out of sync with the process of social and economic change.

Memetic theory has been widely adopted in legal research. For instance, Russell Williams reasons that the application of memetics and business offers potential explanations as to "why some theories take off and come to dominate in our culture for periods of time, perhaps even when there is a lack of empirical evidence to support them".[78] Joshua Frank applies memetics to financial markets by asking the question of "do markets evolve toward efficiency?" Based on the memetic theory, he reasoned that "if there are many possible competing financial memes and only a small percentage of those memes are economically sound, chances are that the most psychologically appealing memes are not the most economically sound".[79] It has also been constructively diagnosed and claimed[80] that prevalent anti-takeover defence mechanisms that occur frequently in the commercial world such as "poison pills", "lock-up" strategies, "pac man" defences, "supermajority" amendments, "scorched earth" strategies, and "shark repellent" defences, are the results of the groupings of memes (or meme-plexus)[81] that aid survival.[82]

The evolutionary theory has also been adopted to rationalise the policy-making process. The use of evolutionary theory to "mememise" policy-making is based upon the understanding that the environment is exogenously determined

---

for our species that puts the biological fossil record to shame". See David Sloan Wilson, 'The Challenge of Understanding Complexity, Commentary on Laland *et al*: "Niche Construction"', (2000) 23 *Behavioral and Brain Sciences* 165.

77 See Gunther Teubner, 'Legal Irritants: Good Faith in British Law, or How Unifying Law ends up in New Divergences', (1998) 61 *Modern Law Review* 11.

78 See Russell Williams, 'The Business of Memes: Memetic Possibilities for Marketing and Management', (2000) 38(4) *Management Decisions* 272–279. See also Betsy D. Gelb, 'Creating "Memes" Whilst Creating Advertising', (1997) 37(6) *Journal of Advertising Research* 57–9.

79 Joshua Frank, 'Applying Memetics to Financial Markets: Do Markets Evolve Towards Efficiency?', (1999) 3(2) *Journal of Memetics – Evolutionary Models of Information* 87–99.

80 Ed Vos and Ben Kelleher, 'Mergers and Takeovers: A Memetic Approach', (2001) 5(2) *Journal of Memetics – Evolutionary Models of Information Transmission* 1.

81 See Susan Blackmore, above n. 16.

82 This theory makes sense because the grouping of memes can decrease the chance of outside memetic attacks thus enhancing its replicative ability.

and that existing forms must have adapted themselves efficiently to it. The rationale of this view is that the relationship between the environment, system and code is not linear but cyclical.[83] In other words, the environment is constituted by the presence of the systems within it, and co-evolves with them. In the case of memetic or cultural evolution, this implies that there is a complex relationship between conscious attempts to shape or construct the environment, the selective pressures, and unpredicted and unintended outcomes. It also means to get away from a deterministic "meme's eye view" of the world, in favour of a focus on the complex, multi-causal relations between the system and the environment. In evolutionary biology, such an idea is associated with the concept of niche construction, which "occurs when an organism modifies the functional relationship between itself and its environment by actively changing one or more of the factors in its environment, either by physically perturbing these factors at its current address, or by relocating to a different address, thereby exposing itself to different factors".[84] In the legal debate, the development of techniques which seek consciously to shape the environmental framework, with the aim of inducing desired "second-order effects" on the part of social and economic actors. This so-called "reflexive law" has increasingly come to the fore in the context of economic regulation over the past decade.[85] A technique which involves the legal rule "thinking about" the conditions for its own application marks an advance on more traditional "command and control" mechanisms. It would seem that in the social sphere, as in the biological one, "evolvability", or the capacity of systems to co-evolve in line with their environment, is itself an emergent property. With the advent of reflexive law, the possibility arises that learning about evolution itself will become a property of the legal code.

2.4. THE NEW YORK CONVENTION AND DARWINIAN EVOLUTIONARY THEORY

To fit Darwinian theory into the New York Convention seems to be novel to most scholars and practitioners. The fundamental questions here are (i) whether the New York Convention itself has any inherent meme which may need Darwinian theory to interpret; and (ii) whether Darwinian theory truly provides a new perspective to study the New York Convention or, in a broad sense,

---

83 See Richard Lewontin, 'Gene, Organism and Environment', in D.S. Bendall (ed.) *Evolution from Molecules to Men*, Cambridge: Cambridge University Press (1983).

84 See Kevin Laland, John Odling-Smee and Marcus Feldman, 'Authors' Response: Niche Construction Earns its Keep', (2000) 23 *Behavioral and Brain Sciences* 166.

85 See Ralf Rogowski and Ton Wilthagen (eds.) *Reflexive Labour Law*, Deventer: Kluwer (1994); Julia Black, *Rules and Regulators*, Oxford: Oxford University Press (1998); Simon Deakin and Alan Hughes, 'Economic Efficiency and the Procedualisation of Company Law', (1999) 3 *Company, Financial and Insolvency Law Review* 169.

international commercial arbitration more convincingly. This section explores the answers to such questions.

The answer to the first question involves a philosophical consideration of the separation of litigation and arbitration, and historical discussion of the New York Convention or, in a wider sense, international commercial arbitration. The historical review of the development of international commercial arbitration may illustrate the core meme of arbitration. A recurring question in jurisprudence – and, indeed, much of philosophy concerns the separation of litigation and arbitration. This distinction in all likelihood reflects different processing pathways in human history. The distinction may also reflect different transmission pathways at the cultural level. Our picture of arbitration may be formed through direct observation and through stories, while litigation may be explicitly more formulaic, language-based rules. One of the strengths of the common law system may be a cross-fertilisation between these two normative streams.

2.4.1. THE ORIGIN OF ARBITRATION AND CORE MEMETIC CODE

Many social sciences involve historical patterns and therefore are revealed and explained in narratives. Law including arbitration is also a historical narrative. Arbitration arises not only in history[86] but also in mythology.[87] Arbitration is not a unique feature of the modern age even though only in the modern age has it been officially recognised and codified.[88]

---

86 It is said that arbitration was established in some of the most refined systems of law ever almost three thousands years ago, which shows that arbitration has accompanied mankind throughout its history.

87 In classical literature, in the Greek myth of the golden apple, a golden apple was found by the three goddess Aphrodite, Hera and Athena. The apple was labelled "to the most beautiful". Each goddess claimed the precious prize (out of vanity and not because they were interested in the intrinsic value of the golden object). The dispute as to whom the golden apple should be awarded could not be decided by Zeus whose wife is Hera. In order to maintain independence and neutrality, the dispute was referred to Paris, a young shepherd believed to have great appreciation of beauty. Paris made a choice in favour of Aphrodite.

88 The Jay Treaty of 1794, promoted by the United States to resolve boundary and compensation issues with the United Kingdom for the purpose of adjudicating claims of British creditors who were unsatisfied with their treatment at the hands of US courts and vice versa, gave birth to the modern method of public arbitration. The landmark commissions that the treaty established to deal with the north eastern boundary of the United States with Canada, and compensation for American citizens during the pre-Napoleonic wars, are an important precedent for dispute settlement without resorting to war. It is said that public arbitration existed in North Italy in the 12th and 13th centuries. Cited in Derek Roebuck, 'Sources for the History of Arbitration: A Bibliographical Introduction', (1998) 14(3) *Arbitration International* 270.

It is usually thought that the origins of contemporary private arbitration lie in mediaeval Western Europe.[89] In its origins, the concept of arbitration as a method of resolving disputes was a simple one:

> "The practice of arbitration ... comes ... naturally to primitive bodies of law; and after courts have been established by the state and a recourse to them has become the natural method of settling disputes, the practice continues because the parties to a dispute want to settle it with less formality and expense than is involved in a recourse to the courts".[90]

According to the Oxford English Dictionary, at the time of the first Arbitration Act, the word "arbitration" had recently come to have the meaning it still has in the Dictionary:

> "the settlement of a dispute or question at issue by one to whom the conflicting parties agree to refer their claims in order to obtain an equitable decision".

The first citation under this meaning (from 1634) confirms this concept of an informal proceeding "to mediate in a friendly manner in a way of arbitration".[91] The German word for "arbitrator" is "Schiedsrichter", which is the same word as a referee, umpire or judge in a sporting contest. The standard wording for many international arbitration clauses still uses the word "settle" rather than "determine". What all these definitions had in common, then, was a quick and less expensive, but nonetheless final, disposal of disputes pursuant to a voluntary submission. These objectives contained in the definitions have failed over time to provide the desired means of dispute resolution, at least in the sense that we are still trying today to solve the same problems of delay and cost.

Two thousand years ago, Confucius was advocating ADR over litigation. A good public judicial service could become the victim of its own success by increasing the burden on the state. This thought reflects the greater Chinese concern for order in the community than for individual rights[92] and was no doubt at the forefront of the mind of the 18th century Chinese Emperor Kang Xi when he issued the following decree:

> "The Emperor, considering the immense population of the empire, the great division of territorial property and the notoriously litigious character of the Chinese, is of the

89 Michael Mustill, 'Is It a Bird...' in *Liber Amicorum Claude Reymond*, Paris: Editions du Juris-Classeur (2004) p. 209. The history of public arbitration can be traced back to ancient Greece. Sheila L. Ager, *Interstate Arbitrations in the Greek World 337–90 BC*, cited by Derek Roebuck, above n. 88, 243.

90 William Searle Holdsworth, *A History of English Law*, Vol. XIV, London: Methuen (1964) p. 187.

91 The word "arbitration" first came into the language with Chaucer in about 1386 with the now obsolete meaning: "a deciding according to one's will or pleasure; uncontrolled or absolute decision". This meaning persists in the word "arbitrary".

92 Derek Roebuck, above n. 88, 256.

> opinion that lawsuits would tend to increase to a frightful extent if people were not afraid of the tribunals and if they felt confident of always finding in them ready and perfect justice ... I desire, therefore, that those who have recourse to the courts should be treated without any pity and in such a manner that they shall be disgusted with law and tremble to appear before a magistrate. In this manner ... the good citizens who may have difficulties among themselves will settle them like brothers by referring them to the arbitration of some old man".[93]

Arbitration was common in medieval England and was important in municipal life.[94] Arbitration was used as a means of dealing with the most important and intractable disputes of the time.[95] During the period between 16th and 18th centuries, arbitration appeared at every level of society and in a wide range of matters.[96] Some research has shown that international arbitral jurisprudence was vast in the nineteenth century. For instance, during the period between 1814 and 1898, there were no less than 158 different international tribunals.[97] More salutary still is to consider that arbitration has been conceived as means of replacing litigation as an expeditious and fair means of dispute resolution for an equally long time. Mr Manson's City of London Chamber of Arbitration was to be:

> "... expeditious where the law is slow, cheap where the law is costly, simple where the law is technical, a peacemaker instead of a stirrer up of strife ... there is really no reason why they should not be attained under a summary system of rough-and-ready arbitration..."[98]

The key here is that a dispute among people belonging to a well-defined community was referred to an independent person in possession of special expertise on the subject matter. It was rightly observed that "arbitration ... was not primarily to ensure the rule of law but rather to maintain harmony between persons who were destined to live together".[99] On the one hand, the modern arbitral process has become more complex, legalistic and institutionalised. This line of development shows the trait of evolution. Most of the characteristics present in the early age still exist in today's arbitration. Impartiality, independence and the great skills of the arbitrator in a particular industry are now accompanied by speed, confidentiality, flexibility and the easier recognition and enforcement of arbitral awards. More particularly, the parties to the dispute grant power to arbitrators or an arbitral panel instead of a court.

93 National Geographic Magazine, June 1927.
94 Derek Roebuck, above n. 88, 259.
95 Rawcliffe's writings, ibid. 260.
96 Writings of Burdick and Comish as well as Guy, ibid. 261.
97 W. Evans Darby, *International Tribunals: A Collection of Various Schemes Which Have Been Propounded, and of Instances Since 1815*, London: Peace Society (1899) pp. 285–304.
98 The City of London Chamber of Arbitration (1893) 9 LQR 86.
99 René David, *Arbitration in International Trade*, Deventer: Kluwer Law and Taxation (1985) p. 29.

As we have seen from reviewing the origin of arbitration, although the content of legal rules in different places may shift considerably from one period to another, there is a surprisingly high degree of conceptual continuity. This simple survey from the dictionary to Confucius' teaching, and from the City of London to Far East China, demonstrates some core memetic codes in arbitration in a historical context. The conceptual substance of a legal term maintains a continuing presence while the form of the rules themselves has in many cases been completely transformed. This seems consistent with Darwinian legal theory.

Power is a cultivator through which thought contagion breeds, evidenced by the various ideas that can be spread in a society by those that hold power, reinforcing the notion of memetic transfer. "Memes are ideas that propagate themselves around the world by jumping from brain to brain, memes are stored in human brains and passed on by imitation, individuals learn from society by imitation instruction. Ultimately, human life is permeated through with memes and their consequences".[100] Historically speaking, arbitration can be used as an example of thought contagion (memetic transference), with large groups sharing beliefs in alternative dispute resolution. In the past, arbitration that promoted dispute resolution was successful because it caused more people to adopt the faith from their own experience. This example draws resemblance from the memetic advantages of arbitration activity, with faiths very much likened to business ideas and practices, both of which are spread by one person copying another, creating large fellowship and beliefs.

As discussed, the way that we see and understand the world is guided by thought contagion (or the replication of memes). Certain characteristics enable thoughts or ideas to enhance their replicative ability. As Dawkins pointed out, the criterion for a successful replicator, in the sense that they create multiple duplicates, consists of three elements: fidelity, fecundity and longevity.[101] When examining arbitration on this three-factor success scale, the theme remains that the greater market strength places arbitrators in a position where they are further able to supply the market with their ideas. Logically, arbitration allows this to happen because arbitrators have the enhanced power and distribution channels to make a vast number of exact copies (fidelity and fecundity), with the pooled research, design and marketing capabilities to defend against competitors and ensure continued expression (longevity).

Clarifying the relationship between thought contagion and power, arbitration can be regarded as a type of activity in which the judicial power is transferred, where the arbitrators hold the power and in turn memetic transference ensures that the story is replicated. In biological terms, Mokyr states that "the environment into which seeds are sown is of course the main determinant of

---

100 See Susan Blackmore, above n. 16, 6.

101 See Richard Dawkins, *The Selfish Gene*, above n. 18.

whether they will sprout".[102] Whether or not comparisons between evolution and cultural or legal progress are valuable has been the focus of a substantial and spirited debate in the literature. As Mokyr said, the parallels are inevitably incomplete and do not provide the researcher with sharp analytical conclusions.[103] Arbitration with power has a stronger ability to dictate the flow of information and resources ultimately shaping the services, systems and ideas that arbitration maintains.

The power of history to shape the direction of evolution is also captured by the theory of "path dependence" which derives from new institutional economics. This stresses the sense in which structural features of an "exapted" technology or practice may be "locked in" by the high costs of switching to what appears to be a more efficient or effective alternative.[104] The widespread and unavoidable practice of providing after-the-event rationalisation to doctrinal innovations often obscures the historical process by which they were formed. A "genealogical" analysis, by revealing this process, can shed some light not only on the inherited constraints, but also on the capabilities, of legal concepts. An analysis of the origins of the concept of arbitration indicates what is possible from this kind of methodology.

2.4.2. THE HOSTILITY TOWARDS ARBITRATION BY COURTS IN COMMON LAW JURISDICTIONS

By way of an example, the legal continuity and inheritance can be found in the hostile attitudes of the courts towards arbitration in most common law jurisdictions.[105] The perspective from which we can understand these narratives is what we can call the intentional stance: the strategy of analysing the flux of events into agents and their rational actions and reactions.

Arbitration has been recognised as a viable dispute resolution mechanism in the mercantile community since the 17th century.[106] The Civil Procedure Act 1833 modernised the procedures for enforcing awards and authorised arbitrators

---

[102] See Joel Mokyr, *The Lever of Riches: Technological Creativity and Economic Progress*, Oxford: Oxford University Press (1990) p. 299.

[103] Ibid. 275.

[104] See Paul David, 'Clio and Economics of QWERTY', (1985) 75 *American Economic Review* 332; Brian Arthur, 'Competing Technologies, Increasing Returns, and Lock-in by Historical Events', (1989) 99 *Economic Journal* 116; Douglass C. North, *Institutions, Institutional Change, and Economic Performance* Cambridge: Cambridge University Press (1990); Mark Roe, above n. 42.

[105] The study revealed that the civil law countries were also hostile to arbitration as being "too primitive" a form of justice. In France, for instance, arbitration was described as an "apparently rudimentary method of settling disputes". See Philippe Fouchard, *L'Arbitrage Commercial International*, Paris: Dalloz (1965) pp. 1–31.

[106] See Statute 9 & 10 William III c 15, discussed in Michael J. Mustill and Steward C. Boyd, *Law and Practice of Commercial Arbitration in England*, London: Butterworths (2nd edn. 1989)

to take sworn statements from the parties, at a time when they were not admissible in the common law courts. The Common Law Procedure Act 1854 improved the procedure whereby a submission was made a rule of court. However, courts, as the agent through their actions and reactions, did not give full recognition to this consensual form of dispute resolution based on party autonomy until very recently in England.[107] Such agents – courts, in our case – do things for reasons, and their actions can be predicted up to a point by cataloguing their reasons, beliefs and desires, and calculating what would be the most rational course of action. For instance, the relatively recent growing importance and increased recognition of arbitration can contribute to more realistic considerations such as efficiency and cost effectiveness which the courts are seeking currently.

Until well into the 20th century, US courts were hostile towards arbitration.[108] Like English courts, American judges refused to grant specific enforcement of arbitration agreements, and permitted their revocation at any time. This grudging approach to arbitration agreements reflected a variety of factors, including the concern about private agreements "ousting" the courts from their jurisdiction, scepticism about the adequacy and fairness of the arbitral process, and suspicions that arbitration agreements were often the product of unequal bargaining power. The parties to disputes in the US courts concerning an international arbitration are often confronted with a procedural and substantive masse of applicable laws that is some distance away from the often-repeated promise that international arbitration provides a simple, efficient and predictable dispute-resolution mechanism.[109]

Historically, Canada has adopted a more hostile stance towards arbitration than England. For instance, most provincial courts exercised broad latitude in

---

p. 432. Also see Robert B. Ferguson, 'The Adjudication of Commercial Disputes and the Legal System in Modern England', (1980) 7(2) *British Journal of Law and Society* 141.

107 See the leading decision in *Scott v. Avery* (1856) 5 HL Cas 811, which upheld a clause making it a condition precedent to any litigation that arbitral proceedings be first instituted to resolve any dispute, and no right of action should arise until after an award had been made. Recent scholarship shows that there was also a continuous working relationship between judges and arbitrators in the medieval period. Derek Roebuck, above n. 88, 260.

108 By the 20th century, the willingness of the US to allow an impartial third party outside of its jurisdiction to settle its international disputes had begun to wane. The United States never joined the League of Nations that arose out of World War I; it did join the United Nations that grew out of World War II, but at least twice the US Congress restricted conditions that would allow US participation in cases before the UN's International Court of Justice.

109 The young and weak United States during the 19th century was generally willing to mediate international disputes rather than go to war over them. For example, the United States and Britain nearly went to war over the case of the British-built Confederate battleship Alabama. They avoided war through the agreement to an arbitrated claims settlement in which Britain paid $50 million in gold to the United States. The blot on that shining record of the 19th century came when the United States confirmed the Monroe Doctrine, which drew an American boundary around the Americas, and the US Senate claimed the right to oppose arbitration to settle international disputes.

refusing to stay court proceedings or enforce arbitral awards even in the presence of *ex ante* agreements to arbitrate. UK courts generally refuse to compel proceedings or enforce awards only in egregious cases such as arbitrator's misconduct or unconscionability. Canadian courts have refused to compel arbitration in far less egregious circumstances. Before Canada enacted arbitration legislation based on the UNCITRAL Model Law in 1986, Canadian arbitration law had largely adopted 19th century English doctrines and rendered the arbitration process unattractive to disputants even though it in principle allows arbitration in almost all contexts.[110]

A brief comparison between English and Australian laws illustrates a historical link between common law jurisdictions. The commercial arbitration legislation of Australian States has been modelled on the successive Arbitration Acts of the UK. In 1979, following the demands by the commercial community, the UK Commercial Court Committee recommended a far-reaching reform, which was implemented by the Arbitration Act 1979 (UK). The 1979 UK Act replaced all pre-existing remedies against arbitral awards with two means of recourse, namely, an appeal to the High Court against an award and an application to the High Court with respect to questions arising in the course of arbitral proceedings. This reform was intended to drastically curb the number of arbitrations which end up in a court, a factor which the business community once feared would make London arbitration less attractive. The provisions of this Act were copied into the Australian statutes such as ss 38 and 39 of the Commercial Arbitration Act 1984 until that Act was amended in 1990. The Commercial Arbitration Act 1984 retains the remedy of setting-aside which is limited to the grounds of misconduct of the arbitral tribunal, misconduct of the arbitral proceedings or the improper procurement of the arbitration agreement or the award.[111] The court's power to remit matters also survives in a very restricted form in s 43. Indeed, even a prima facie mistake of fact or law does not constitute sufficient grounds for judicial intervention. The 1979 UK Act was later superseded by the Arbitration Act 1996.[112] Australia has also been undergoing a complete transition by leaving behind its ties to the 19th century common law tradition on arbitration.[113]

The traditional model used by historians and anthropologists to explain the cultural evolution uses the intentional stance as its explanatory framework. These theorists regard culture as composed of goods and possessions of people.

---

110 John J. Kerr, Jr., 'Arbitrability of Securities Law Claims in Common Law Nations', (1996) 12(2) *Arb. Int'l* 176–77.

111 s 22 of the Arbitration Act 1950 (UK).

112 The 1996 Act consolidates all the previous Acts and was meant to simplify the law of arbitration in the UK and to further limit the powers of courts to intervene in arbitral proceedings or outcomes. Gabriel Moens and Peter Gillies, *International Trade and Business: Law, Policy and Ethics*, Australia: Cavendish Publishing Pty Limited (1998) p. 747.

113 John J. Kerr, Jr., above n. 110, 178.

Accordingly, people preserve their traditions of justice and trade cultural items as they trade other goods. It is clear from this perspective in our context that there will be a competitive market where agents both "buy" and "sell" legal wares. If a method of dealing with arbitration sweeps through the common law jurisdictions, it may be because courts perceive advantages to such novelties. This perspective is typical of Richard Dawkins's meme's-eye point of view which recognises the possibility that cultural or legal entities may evolve according to selective regimes. Due to the common law tradition, it seems reasonable to conclude that the "hostile" memetic code was inherited (or more precisely, spread) from one jurisdiction to the other, providing that the basic legal tradition is compatible in these jurisdictions.

The hostile attitudes of the courts towards arbitration exist in most developing countries for various reasons. In Latin America, for example, the long-standing policy such as the Calvo doctrine would render an arbitration clause not enforceable, which was a natural reaction to the "gunboat diplomacy" that was prevalent in the Western Hemisphere for many decades.[114] The anti-arbitration policy in Latin America was enhanced by a variety of obstacles such as a broad range of grounds for attacking the validity of an arbitral award, non-acceptance of the competence-competence doctrine, and the imposition of rigid formalities on the arbitral process including the prohibition of non-nationals from serving as arbitrators.[115] In the Middle East,[116] due to the lack of clear arbitration rules in the Koran, some countries do not have detailed and codified arbitration laws.[117] Although the hostility towards arbitration in these countries may be caused by different ideological reasons, the hostile memetic code does exist. There has been a perception that international commercial arbitration was developed by, and was biased in favour of, Western commercial interests, and is loaded with traps for the unwary. The underlying rationale behind this hostility is a distrust of the impartiality of Western judicial systems, and the fear that arbitration would be prejudiced against national interests. At the international level, the widespread hostile atmosphere has been described in a brief but vivid statement, that is, "denial of justice was a dominant theme in early international arbitrations".[118] There certainly is an exception to this general perception. For

---

114 Robert Layton, 'Changing Attitudes Toward Dispute Resolution in Latin America', (1993) 10(2) *Journal of International Arbitration* 125.

115 Houston Putnam Lowry, 'The United States Joins the Inter-American Arbitration Convention', (1990) 7(3) *J. Int'l Arb.* 83–5.

116 This geographic description usually includes Bahrain, Egypt, Iraq, Jordan, Kuwait, Lebanon, Oman, Qatar, Saudi Arabia, Syria, and the United Arab Emirates. Some of these countries can be categorised as Arab countries. Abdul Hamid El-Ahdab, 'Enforcement of Arbitral Awards in the Arab Countries', (1995) 11(2) *Arb. Int'l* 230.

117 Samir Saleh, *Commercial Arbitration in the Arab Middle East*, Oxford: Hart Publishing (2006) p. 20.

118 Jan Paulsson, *Denial of Justice in International Law*, Cambridge: Cambridge University Press (2005) p. 131.

instance, some Arab legislation on international arbitration is more advanced than the New York Convention in that they have made enforcement of foreign arbitral awards even easier. This is the case in Lebanon and Algeria, whose international arbitration acts were strongly influenced by French law in this field.[119] These phenomena illustrate that the memetic code can not only be inherited vertically (from one generation to the other) but also spread horizontally (in the same generation but in various species) in the legal sphere. From the perspective of mutation, the exceptional examples set by Lebanon and Algeria can be regarded as an "error" in the copying process. Such variation is the consequence of random mutations in the genetic code. In general, this hostility has waned somewhat over the past decade, with many states acceding to the New York Convention and enacting "pro-arbitration" legislation.

What is to account for the conceptual continuity of this kind? It appears that the mechanism of inheritance is the legal system's self-imposed rule of internal conceptual order, which requires new legal norms to refer back to the pre-existing conceptual forms. The conceptual content of the norm endows it with legitimacy in the context of the "self-referential" operation of the legal order. There are many illustrations of this principle of legal consistency, the most obvious being the rules of precedent which confine the scope of legitimate judicial interpretations, and which are monitored, modified and enforced by the appellate courts. It is precisely such principles that mean similar cases should be decided alike, and that ensure faithful copying most of the time, while also allowing certain scope for variations to emerge in response to novel factual situations.

2.4.3. THE LONG JOURNEY TO THE NEW YORK CONVENTION

Yet no state can stand back and be willing to allow a system of private justice, which largely depends on the goodwill of the participants, to regulate commercial activities. The sovereignty reason would at some stage force the national state to step in and regulate arbitration.

The first English Statute was the Arbitration Act of 1698, although in *Vyniors* (8. Co. 80a, 81b) the Court ordered the defendant to pay the agreed penalty for refusing to submit to arbitration as he had agreed to do. In France, an Edict of Francis II promulgated in August 1560 made arbitration compulsory for all merchants in disputes arising from their commercial activities. During the French Revolution, arbitration came back into favour as "the most reasonable device for the termination of disputes arising between citizens".[120] The right to

119 Abdul Hamid El-Ahdab, above n. 116, 175.

120 René David, above n. 99, 89–90.

arbitration was guaranteed by the French Constitution of 1792.[121] The French Code of Civil Procedure in 1806 turned arbitration into the first stage of a procedure which would lead to the judgment of a court.[122]

International commercial arbitration does not stay within national boundaries. The national law of one state alone could not deal with all problems arising from cross-border arbitration. What the international community needed was an international treaty or convention that would link national laws together and provide a uniform solution on arbitration. The development of international conventions is "the most effective method of creating an international system of law governing international commercial arbitration".[123] In the long journey of arbitration through the history of mankind, the New York Convention stands as a landmark between the ancient and modern world. Thanks to the New York Convention, arbitration has overcome the uncertainty of the past.[124] The New York Convention obliges Member States to recognise and enforce both international commercial arbitration agreements and awards, subject to limited exceptions. Prior to the New York Convention, intergovernmental efforts to unify arbitration law began under the League of Nations, which produced two Geneva treaties after World War I.[125] They removed a number of obstacles then facing international arbitration,[126] and provided conditions governing the enforcement of arbitral awards. These two treaties remain of some relevance, as they led the international community to undertake a formal appraisal of common values in arbitration later on.

The Geneva Protocol of 1923

The Geneva Protocol of 1923 on Arbitration Clauses in Commercial Matters was the first modern and genuinely international treaty, which was drawn up by the ICC under the auspices of the League of Nations, and entered into force on 28 July 1924. Thirty-three countries ratified or acceded to the Protocol.[127] Although the Protocol is brief, with merely four articles covering the validity and

---

121 Derek Roebuck, above n. 88, 267.

122 In 1791, the judges were abolished and replaced by "public arbitrators".

123 Alan Redfern and Martin Hunter, *Law and Practice of International Commercial Arbitration*, London: Sweet & Maxwell (3rd edn. 1999) p. 64.

124 See Domenico Di Pietro and Martin Platte, *Enforcement of International Arbitration Awards, The New York Convention of 1958*, London: Cameron May (2001) p. 13.

125 In modern times, the first was the Montevideo Convention, the Treaty concerning the Union of South American States in respect of Procedural Law, signed at Montevideo on 11 January 1889. It was made and provided for the recognition and enforcement of arbitration agreements between certain Latin American States. See *Register of Texts of Conventions and other Instruments concerning International Trade Law, Vol. II, United Nations (1973)*, p. 5.

126 See Giorgio Balladore Pallieri, 'L'arbitrage privé dans les rapports internationaux', in *Collected Courses of the Hague Academy of International Law*, Vol. 51, Part I (1935) p. 291.

127 It also applied to those former dependent territories to which it had been extended.

effect of arbitration clauses, it had a decisive impact on the future of arbitration throughout the world.[128] In France, the signing of the Protocol prompted the legislature to make arbitration clauses valid in commercial transactions.[129]

The Protocol's main objective was to ensure the international enforcement of arbitration agreements. It laid a foundation for the worldwide development of international arbitration, which is dependent on the effectiveness of arbitration agreements in international contracts. The Protocol's subsidiary objective was to ensure that arbitral awards made pursuant to such arbitration agreements would be enforced in the territory of the states in which they were made. The Protocol's approach to differentiating between the enforceability of arbitration agreements and awards[130] was inherited by the New York Convention.

The Geneva Protocol is certainly limited in its range and effect even though some terms can be found in the New York Convention. For instance, it was meant to apply to submission agreements and arbitration clauses concluded "between parties subject respectively to the jurisdiction of different contracting states", whether by their nationality, domicile, registered office or principal place of business, and hence to proceedings and awards resulting from such agreements.[131] It also left the parties free to determine the arbitral procedure[132] and obliged states and national courts to ensure that arbitration agreements[133] and the resulting awards[134] could be enforced.

From a technical viewpoint, of all these states, only Albania, Brazil, the Democratic Republic of Congo, the Gambia, Guyana, Iraq, Jamaica, Malta, Myanmar (formerly Burma), Pakistan and Zambia have yet to accede to the New York Convention. In their relations with each other and with other countries bound by both the Protocol and the New York Convention, they remain bound by the terms of the Protocol.[135] This effectively means that the Protocol, as a disappearing "species" in the legal evolutionary process, may still function in the form of a new generation of "species" even though it has been out of the scene.

---

128 Philippe Fouchard, Emmanuel Gaillard and Berthold Goldman, *International Commercial Arbitration,* The Hague: Kluwer Law International (1999) p. 121.

129 Article 631 (last paragraph) of the Commercial Code (Law of 31 December 1925).

130 The former were to be recognised and enforced internationally, the latter however only in the state where the award was made.

131 On ratifying or acceding to the Protocol, many countries implemented the "commercial reservation" provided for in Article 1, para. 2, whereby "each contracting state reserves the right to limit the obligation mentioned above to contracts which are considered as commercial under its national law".

132 See Article 2.

133 See Article 4.

134 See Article 3.

135 See the New York Convention Art VII(2). Philippe Fouchard, Emmanuel Gaillard and Berthold Goldman, above n. 128, 120. It is said that "two forerunners are no longer relevant, except in relations between countries which are not bound by the New York Convention".

The Geneva Convention of 1927

The Geneva Protocol of 1923 was soon superseded by the Geneva Convention of 1927 on the Execution of Foreign Arbitral Awards that came into force on 25 July 1929.[136] The scope of the 1927 Geneva Convention is based on that of the 1923 Protocol, with certain unsatisfactory restrictions.[137] This seems consistent with the idea presented here that the development of a new generation meme is based on the old generation. On the other hand, the aim of the Geneva Convention of 1927 was to widen the scope of the 1923 Protocol and to provide for international enforceability of the Protocol awards within the territory of contracting states (and not merely within the territory of the state in which the award was made). In this sense, the 1927 Geneva Convention moves one step further. Moreover, the states which have adhered to the 1927 Geneva Convention are mostly those states which adhered to the Geneva Protocol with some notable omissions such as Brazil, Norway and Poland.[138] From this perspective, the core memetic code of extending the enforceability of arbitration awards is inherited from the 1923 Protocol by the 1927 Convention.

The 1927 Convention contains uniform conditions for the recognition and enforcement of "foreign" arbitral awards, and excludes any review of the merits of the award. Some of the terms in the 1927 Convention are presented in the form of substantive rules which constitute universal conditions governing the international validity of awards. These include the parties' right to a fair hearing and the respect of the limits of the arbitrator's brief. Unfortunately, these conditions are expressed in obscure and restrictive terms.[139] Some problems still remain unsolved in the 1927 Convention. It has the disadvantage of limiting the scope of the 1927 Convention to awards made in a contracting state and, in particular, to awards between the parties both of which are contracting states. The conditions of location and nationality hardly represent a realistic approach to international commercial arbitration. A party seeking enforcement has to

---

136 It has been ratified or acceded to by 27 countries, and also applied to countries to which, as former dependent territories, the Convention had been extended. For a text of the Convention as well as a table of member States, see http://www.asser.nl/ica/eur.htm.

137 The Protocol only applies to awards made "in the territories of any high contracting party … between persons who are subject to the jurisdiction of one of the high contracting parties".

138 Alan Redfern and Martin Hunter, above n. 123, 67 n. 55. Similarly, of all these states, only the Democratic Republic of Congo, Guyana, Jamaica, Malta, Myanmar (formerly Burma), Pakistan and Zambia have yet to accede to the New York Convention. In their relations with each other and with other countries bound by both the 1927 Protocol and the New York Convention, they remain bound by the terms of the 1927 Protocol (the New York Convention Art VII(2)). Philippe Fouchard, Emmanuel Gaillard and Berthold Goldman, above n. 128, 120.

139 See Articles 1 to 4. Assessing the validity of the various stages of arbitration involves the reference to a number of national legal systems, and the courts in the host country can only grant enforcement if it has been established that the award is "final" in its country of origin. In practice, this amounts to requiring two enforcement orders.

prove the conditions necessary for enforcement. Another problem of the 1927 Convention is the so-called "double exequatur" requirement. The successful party in arbitration, prior to commencing enforcement of an award in the courts of the place of enforcement, needs to show that the award had become final in the country of origin by seeking a declaration in the courts of the country where the arbitration took place to the effect that the award was enforceable in that country. The Convention also imposes the requirement that the award shall not be contrary to "the principles of the law of the country in which it is sought to be relied upon", which has also posed problems. This requirement suggests that an award might be open to attack not only on the grounds of public policy but also on the grounds that it offended the legal principles of the forum state. These problems are part of the target issues in the 1958 New York Convention. The double exequatur problem was later dealt with by the draftsmen of the New York Convention in Article V, and the "principles of the law of the country in which it is sought to be relied upon" was not carried through to the New York Convention. Overall, the Geneva Protocol of 1923 and Geneva Convention of 1927 were unsuccessful and failed to attract much support outside Europe due to their limitation in aim and objective.[140] However, theoretically, they should have had a well-deserved place in the history of international commercial arbitration as they represented an early generation of effort on the road towards harmonisation of commercial arbitration.

The New York Convention of 1958

The ICC proposed a "Draft Convention" governing international commercial arbitration in 1953.[141] The proposal was taken up by the United Nations Economic and Social Council but its panel of experts produced a second draft which was more conservative than the ICC text.[142] An international conference was then held in New York beginning on 20 May 1958 under the UN banner. The text adopted on 10 June 1958 was considerably more liberal than that put forward by the panel of experts and came closer to the ideas, if not to the wording, of the ICC text.[143]

---

140 René David, 'The International Unification of Private Law', in *International Encyclopaedia of Comparative Law: The Legal System of the World, Their Comparison and Unification*, Vol. II, Ch. 5, Tübingen: JCB Mohr (Paul Siebeck); The Hague, Boston and London: Martinus Nijhoff Publishers (1972) pp. 130–133.

141 ICC, Enforcement of International Arbitral Awards: Report and Preliminary Draft Convention (ICC Publication No. 174, 1953), reprinted in (1988) 9(1) *ICC Bulletin* 32 .

142 Reprinted in M. Domke (ed.), *International Trade Arbitration* (1958) p. 288.

143 On the legislative history of the Convention, see United Nations Economic and Social Council Docs. E/Conf. 26/2 to E/Conf.26/7 and E/Conf.26/SR.1 to E/Conf.26/SR.24, reprinted in International Commercial Arbitration – New York Convention – Part III – Preparatory Works (G. Gaja ed., 1978).

The New York Convention is eulogised as "perhaps ... the most effective instance of international legislation in the entire history of commercial law",[144] "the most successful multilateral instrument" and "the centrepiece in the mosaic of treaties and laws" in the field of international commercial arbitration.[145] It can be regarded as the major driving force or the cornerstone of developing arbitration as a means of resolving international commercial disputes in the modern world. It thus was labelled "the single most important pillar on which the edifice of international arbitration rests".[146]

The New York Convention has been ratified by more than 147 states, including all major trading nations.[147] A resounding success came gradually because it was not until the 1970s and 1980s that a number of key countries ratified the Convention: the US in 1970, the UK in 1975, Canada in 1986, China in 1987; and in the late 1980s and 1990s, more developing countries ratified the Convention: Algeria and Argentina in 1989, Saudi Arabia in 1994, Venezuela and Vietnam in 1995, Lebanon in 1998, Brazil in 2002, Pakistan in 2005 and United Arab Emirates in 2006. Among others, the accession of Argentina, Brazil, Saudi Arabia, Venezuela and Vietnam are particularly significant, as those signatory countries have traditionally, for various political or legal reasons, been hostile towards international arbitration.[148] The number of Member States is so great that it is now easier to point out the few "conspicuous absences": there are no longer any in the world. In this sense, the Convention in substance has become the universal instrument that its proponents intended it to be.

The New York Convention is a considerable improvement compared to the Geneva Protocol of 1923 and the Geneva Convention of 1927. One feature of the New York Convention is its recognition of the parties' freedom in the constitution of the arbitral tribunal and the determination of arbitral procedure. These two aspects need only be "in accordance with the agreement of the parties, or, failing such agreement, ... the law of the country where the arbitration took place".[149] This reflects the primacy of party autonomy in the Convention and the purely subsidiary role of national law which, unless the parties have stipulated

144 Michael J. Mustill, 'Arbitration: History and Background', (1989) 6 *J. Int'l Arb.* 43; Stephen M. Schwebel, 'A Celebration of the United Nations' New York Convention', (1996) 12(1) *Arb. Int'l* 823. There were some statistics supporting this claim: 98% of awards in international arbitrations were honoured or successfully enforced, and enforcement by national courts was refused in less than 5% of cases. Albert Jan van den Berg, 'The New York Convention: Its Intended Effects, Its Interpretation, Salient Problem Areas', (1996) *ASA Special Series* No. 9, 25.

145 Pieter Sanders, Foreword to *The ICCA's Guide to the Interpretation of the 1958 New York Convention: A Handbook for Judges*, International Council for Commercial Arbitration (2011), p. v.

146 J. Gillis Wetter, 'The Present Status of the International Court of Arbitration of the ICC: An Appraisal', (1990) 1 *American Review of International Arbitration* 91.

147 http://www.uncitral.org/uncitral/en/uncitral_texts/arbitration/NYConvention_status.html (last accessed on 14 September 2012).

148 Abdul Hamid El-Ahdab, above n. 116, 169.

149 See Article V(1)(d) of the New York Convention.

otherwise, will be that of the seat of arbitration.[150] As a result, the influence of the seat of arbitration and, more generally, that of national laws on the arbitral procedure, is substantially reduced. As the New York Convention also confirms the existence and legitimacy of institutional arbitration,[151] in the absence of a specific agreement between the parties as to the procedure, the rules of arbitral institutions are considered to be the principal source of rules governing arbitral proceedings.

The scope of the New York Convention is not limited by reference to the nationality of the parties to the arbitration agreement or the award. This is significant progress compared to the 1927 Convention, which only applies where the parties were subject to the jurisdiction of one of the contracting parties. This change indeed detaches arbitration from the national regime and paved the way for globalisation or de-localisation, which is more popular nowadays. The change itself seems a variation of the memetic code inherited from the old generation, that is, the Geneva Protocol of 1923 and the Geneva Convention of 1927. The application of the New York Convention is not restricted to international arbitration as well. The text contains no "internationality" requirement. Article I of the Convention provides that, in principle, a "foreign" award is an award made in a country other than that in which its recognition and enforcement are sought. This effectively means that whether the dispute involves the interests of international business is not a relevant issue. One or more foreign components of arbitration are also of little relevance. In order for the Convention to apply in a contracting state, all that is necessary, in principle,[152] is for an award in question to be made in another country. The award may have been made in a purely domestic dispute following an arbitration in which all elements were connected to that country. The arbitration would then be national, but the award becomes foreign when enforcement is sought outside the country where it was made. The concept of a "foreign" award, as indicated by the title of the Convention – the Convention on the Recognition and Enforcement of Foreign Arbitral Awards – still suggests a national connection. The criterion adopted by the New York Convention is in the middle ground between "national" and "international", which is the same as the development route of international treaties in international arbitration, from the 1923 Protocol with a rather "national" standard, to the 1958 New York Convention with a quasi-international standard. This route may suggest that the next action, if taken, may go one step further by completely erasing the "national" trace and adopting a truly "international" criterion.

---

150 See Pieter Sanders, 'The New York Convention', in Pieter Sanders (ed.), *Union International Des Avocats, Arbitrage International Commercial – International Commercial Arbitration,* Vol II (1960) p. 293.

151 See Article I(2).

152 That is, except where the reciprocity reservation has been made.

Although the title of the Convention does not suggest it, the New York Convention gives a much wider effect to the validity of arbitration agreements than the Geneva Protocol of 1923 and the Geneva Convention of 1927 did, thereby improving efficiency and efficacy of the regulatory regime as a whole. In order to enforce arbitration agreements, the New York Convention adopts the technique in the Geneva Protocol of 1923. For instance, the Convention requires the courts of contracting states to disallow a dispute that is subject to an arbitration agreement to be litigated before its courts, if an objection to such arbitration is raised by any party to the arbitration agreement. The New York Convention, instead, provides for a more effective and simple method of obtaining recognition and enforcement of foreign arbitral awards and makes significant progress in three areas as compared to the 1923 and 1927 Protocols. First, the burden of proof is reversed. Once the award and arbitration agreement have been submitted by the party applying for recognition and enforcement of the award,[153] the party opposing enforcement must prove why the award should not be enforced against it.[154] Second, there are fewer grounds on which an application resisting enforcement will be admissible, and such grounds are defined in more restrictive terms, which preclude the judicial power to review the award on its merits. For example, it is no longer necessary that the award should be "final" in its country of origin but the award must simply be "binding". Although that term may create difficulties of interpretation in some countries, the setting-aside procedure no longer prevents enforcement abroad. Third, under the New York Convention, the requirement for a "double exequatur" is precluded. An arbitral award is entitled to enforcement without the need for any order of any court in the country of origin.[155] The procedure governing recognition and enforcement[156] is still determined by each contracting state, although the contracting states agree not to impose on the recognition and enforcement of foreign awards more onerous conditions than those imposed on the enforcement of domestic awards.

Despite its apparent simplicity, the criteria governing the application of the New York Convention have raised a number of difficulties. Some are the results of courts in the host jurisdiction, whose lack of a uniform approach to the interpretation of the Convention, and taking into account other factors connecting arbitration with that jurisdiction, has led them to exclude the

153 See Article IV.

154 See Article V.

155 Under the Geneva Convention of 1927, a party seeking enforcement had to prove the conditions necessary for the enforcement. This was known as the problem of "double exequatur". In order to show that the award had become final in its country of origin, the successful party was often obliged to seek a declaration in the courts of the country where arbitration took place to the effect that the award was enforceable in that country, before it could go ahead and enforce the award in the courts of the place of enforcement.

156 See Articles III and IV.

Convention and to exercise their discretionary power to set aside an award which they consider to be "national". Published case law contains very few examples of this kind of confusion: one example is the much criticised decision of the Indian Supreme Court, which in 1992 held that the substance of the dispute before it was governed by Indian law and, on that basis, allowed an ICC award made in London to be set aside in India.[157]

Another difficulty stems from how to define the country where the award is made. For example, prior to the 1996 UK Arbitration Act, the mere fact that an award was signed by a sole arbitrator in Paris, whereas the arbitration had been held in London, led the English courts to exercise their power to review the award under the New York Convention.[158] The 1996 Arbitration Act ensures that such a decision cannot recur.[159] This is an obvious practical difficulty because there has not been a uniform approach to interpreting the New York Convention by the courts in various contracting states. In practice, the detachment of an arbitration award from the national regime has caused problems in application of the rules set out in the New York Convention.[160] Thus, in France, the Rouen Court of Appeals had no hesitation in applying the New York Convention to an award made in Switzerland, in the context of an application for enforcement, as both Switzerland and France had ratified the Convention. It was irrelevant that Yugoslavia, which was a party to arbitration, had only ratified the Convention on the condition that it would not apply to awards made prior to such ratification, because "the parties' nationality does not affect the application of the Convention".[161] Likewise, in another French case, the Paris Court of Appeal and the *Cour de cassation* applied the New York Convention to the enforcement in France of an arbitral award made in Vienna, rightly disregarding the fact that the award was in favour of a Turkish company and that, at that time, Turkey was not bound by the Convention.[162]

The chronological study of the development of the New York Convention matches our discovery of the core memetic code and evolutionary theory. We may also look back to earlier times in order to trace the origin of the core provisions of the New York Convention. The first English Arbitration Act of 1698

---

157 *National Thermal Power Corp. v. The Singer Corp.*, 7 May 1992; XIII *Yearbook of Commercial Arbitration* (hereinafter: *Yearbook*) (1993) 403. Also V.S. Deshpande, '"Foreign Award" in the 1958 New York Convention', (1992) 9 *J. Int'l Arb.* 51.

158 *Hiscox v. Outhwaite (No. 1)* [1992] 1 AC 562; [1991] 3 All ER 641; [1991] 3 WLR 297; [1992] 2 Lloyd's Rep. 435; XVII *Yearbook* (1992).

159 See Section 3. The English legislature adopts a definition of arbitration based on legal rather than purely geographical criteria in the provision.

160 More detailed discussion will be made in Chapter 3 of this book.

161 CA Rouen, 13 November 1984, *SEEE v. Republique de Yougoslavia*, XI *Yearbook* (1986) 491; (1985) 24 ILM 345, 349.

162 *Norsolor v. Pabalk Ticaret Sirketi*, XI *Yearbook* (1986) 484, 2 *J. Int'l Arb.* 67 (June 1985) with comments by D. Thompson; XI *Yearbook* (1986) 484; (1985) 24 ILM 360; XXI *Yearbook* (1996) 617.

contained just two provisions, which foreshadowed the mainstays of the New York Convention: a stay of court proceedings in favour of a valid arbitration clause, and a right to enforcement in the absence of misconduct or fraud.

> "Now for promoting trade and rendering the awards ... the more effectual in all cases for the final determination of controversies referred to them by merchants and traders or others concerning matters of account or trade or other matters ... it shall and may be lawful for all merchants and traders and others desiring to end any controversies suit to the award or umpirage of any person or persons should be made a rule of any of His Majesties courts of record".[163]

The example of these two key provisions indicates the "qualified efficiency" or sub-optimal nature of opportunistic adaptations and exaptations.[164] There is a potential cost in making do with what lies at hand. It may also show the potential for what in biology are called "frozen accidents".[165] These are structural features which are difficult to explain by reference to existing environmental conditions, but which can be regarded as adaptations to previous environmental conditions. The functional approach of Darwinian theory implies that the persistence of certain traits at the expense of others is a product of adaptation to environmental change. In principle, "any functioning structure carries implicit information about the environment in which its function works".[166]

What is striking is the continuity of concept throughout this period as a point of reference when a series of mutations occurred in the relationship between the courts and arbitration organisations. Through shifts in the conceptual form, the notion of the finality of arbitral awards emerged by way of a response to the rise of the independence of arbitration and the tolerance of arbitration by the state courts. Mutations in legal forms were therefore the result of a complex interplay of social, economic and political forces. Long periods of relative stasis alternated with intervals of rapid innovation, often triggered by legislative intervention in a pattern reminiscent of "punctuated equilibrium".[167]

---

163 See Robert Hunter: 'Anticipating Trends in Dispute Resolution', in Martin Odams De Zylva and Reziya Harrison (eds.), *International Commercial Arbitration: Developing Rules for the New Millennium* Bristol: Jordans (2000) p. 10.

164 The evolutionary biologist Stephen Jay Gould coined the term "exaptation" to convey the feature in the biological evolution that a design feature which is an essentially accidental by-product of an earlier adaptation finds a new use in a changed environment. See generally Stephen Jay Gould, *The Individual in Darwin's World*, above n. 37.

165 Francis Crick, 'The Origin of the Genetic Code', (1968) 38 *Journal of Molecular Biology* 367; Daniel C. Dennett, above n. 20, Chs 7–8.

166 Daniel C. Dennett, above n. 20, Chs 7–8.

167 On punctuated equilibrium, see Niles Eldredge and Stephen Jay Gould, 'Punctuated Equilibria: an Alternative to Phyletic Gradualism', in Niles Eldredge, *Time Frames: The Rethinking of Darwinian Evolution and the Theory of Punctuated Equilibria*, New York: Heinemann (1985) (originally published in 1972); Niles Eldredge, *Reinventing Darwin: The Great Evolutionary Debate*, London: Phoenix Giant (1995); Stephen Jay Gould, *The Structure of Evolutionary Theory* above n. 37, Ch. 9. The evidence for punctuated equilibrium in the

Uneven rates of development and discontinuities brought about by exogenous shocks, rather than continuous, linear adjustment to an external environment, characterised the path of legal change. Certainly, the New York Convention itself is also beginning to show its age.

2.4.4. MUTATION AND THE NEW YORK CONVENTION

A simple historical survey of the 1923 Geneva Protocol, the 1927 Geneva Protocol, and the 1958 New York Convention demonstrates that a core memetic code was inherited from one generation to the other. Nevertheless, the memetic code has varied with time as well. A question may then naturally arise. Why did the New York Convention appear in the 1950s? Why didn't it appear in 1920s? The birth of the New York Convention may be a consequence of the environmental changes in the 1950s, when there were some factors which were mature enough to bring new changes to the international law regime of commercial arbitration.

In the economy of the world as a whole, there are convincing social and economic reasons in favour of an increased role for private dispute resolution in the 1950s. Dispute resolution was increasingly seen as a part of a continual process of conflict management from the inception of the business community. After World War II, business perspectives and strategies have become transnational to an unprecedented degree in response to the development of international markets and the infrastructures that serve them. Multinational corporations have emerged as a principal steward of wealth and a potent force in the financial markets, and remain the cardinal vehicle for global development. Recognising that reality, even most developing countries welcome such enterprises. Obstacles to free trade have been under attack for years. The main supranational vehicle for these initiatives has been the GATT. At the same time, the globalisation of trade was supposed to promote a harmonisation of commercial law and practice, since a globalised commercial community is entitled to expect that obligations should be construed similarly in different jurisdictions and legal cultures. Following the subsequent growth of international trade, the weakness of the 1927 Geneva Protocol, which neither the United States nor the Soviet Union had ratified, became very apparent. It needed to be improved if arbitration was to become an efficient means of resolving international disputes. These environmental changes also gave birth to a number

social or cultural evolution can be taken to mean that social evolution and biological evolution are subject to distinct evolutionary processes; alternatively, its presence in the social sphere may be used to cast light on biological processes, on the assumption that they share some common elements with social evolution, but to do so would be beyond the scope of this chapter.

of regional conventions on international commercial arbitration, which impose comparable obligations on the Member States with respect to particular categories of disputes or with respect to particular bilateral or regional relationships. Although no conventions since 1958 have had the same impact on international commercial arbitration, a brief examination of later conventions is a worthwhile exercise because of the direction of development they indicate and the approach they take.

European Convention on International Commercial Arbitration of 1961[168]

The European Convention was signed in Geneva in 1961 under the aegis of the Trade Development Committee of the UN Economic Commission for Europe as a supplement to the New York Convention.[169] It does not confine itself to the membership of European States.[170] In other words, it applies to international arbitrations to settle trade disputes between parties from different states, whether European or not. However, it is designed mainly for disputes arising out of contracts between European parties, in particular East-West disputes. Unlike the New York Convention, the European Convention only applies when the parties to arbitration reside in contracting states. Several key features of the European Convention include the limitation of grounds on which awards can be set aside;[171] and an express recognition of the capacity of the state or other public body to enter into an arbitration agreement even though the Convention allows the contracting state to reserve this recognition. However, the Convention failed to realise its objectives since the approach taken in the Convention is not practical; and it does not deal with the recognition and enforcement of awards but leaves this to the New York Convention.[172]

---

168 The European Convention has been ratified by only 26 states and lacks the significance of the New York Convention.

169 The European Convention does not deal with recognition and enforcement of awards, which is left to other treaties, such as the New York Convention, to handle.

170 For a text of the Convention as well as a table of Member States see http://www.asser.nl/ica/eur-a.htm.

171 Article IX.1 provides that the setting aside of an award in a contracting State will only constitute a ground for the refusal of recognition or enforcement of that award in another contracting State if the award has been set aside for reasons specified in the Convention. These reasons correspond closely to the first four grounds for refusal of recognition and enforcement of awards under the New York Convention.

172 There is one improvement made in the European Convention, which may avoid local annulment: see Chapter 3 of this book. An award vacated in a contracting State can still be recognised and enforced in another contracting State if the reason for setting aside the award is not recognised by the Convention as a valid ground for setting aside the award.

Brussels Convention on Jurisdiction and the Enforcement of Judgments in Civil and Commercial Matters of 1968

As its title suggested, the Convention excludes the enforcement of awards, since the definition of judgment for recognition and enforcement purposes embraces decisions that are made by the courts of a contracting state.[173] Nevertheless, by merger of the award into a court judgment, an arbitral award can indirectly fall within the scope of the Convention.[174] In the contracting states, the award creditor may find an interest in relying upon the judgment absorbing the award rather than on the award itself because the enforcement scheme under the Convention achieves more uniformity than does the New York Convention, as the 1968 Convention's aim is to increase the mobility of judgments in the European Union.[175] Unlike the New York Convention which does not regulate but leaves the procedure for enforcing awards in the sphere of competence of national law, the Convention sets out a two-tier enforcement procedure[176] which is uniform to all contracting states, and national law only governs the procedure for making the application.[177] It has been stated that the enforcement of the claim granted in the award would be made considerably easier if the claim were incorporated in the judgment which is enforced under the more effective Convention regime.[178]

Moscow Convention of 1972

The Moscow Convention was signed in 1972 as part of the process of implementing the "socialist economic integration" of those East European States that formed the Council of Mutual Economic Assistance.[179] The Convention provides that arbitral awards are to be enforced voluntarily by the parties, failing which they are to be enforced like court judgements of the country where the enforcement is sought. The grounds on which enforcement can be denied closely resemble those set out in the New York Convention, namely, the lack of

173 Article 25 of the Convention.

174 Schlosser Report, on the Convention of 9 October 1978 on the Association of the Kingdom of Denmark and the United Kingdom of Great Britain and Northern Ireland to the Convention on Jurisdiction and the Enforcement of Judgments in the Civil and Commercial Matters and to the Protocol on its Interpretation by the Court of Justice, OJ No. C59, 5.3.79.

175 Dominique T. Hascher, 'Recognition and Enforcement of Arbitration Awards and the Brussels Convention', (1996) 12(3) *Arb. Int'l* 234, 248.

176 Brussels Convention, Articles 34 and 36.

177 Brussels Convention, Article 33.

178 Peter Schlosser, 'The 1968 Brussels Convention and Arbitration', (1991) 7(3) *Arb. Int'l* 234.

179 Some former Member States have either ceased to exist or have withdrawn their membership for obvious reasons after the collapse of the Soviet Union in 1991.

jurisdiction, lack of due process and that the award has been set aside at the place where it was made.[180]

Inter-American Convention on International Commercial Arbitration (Panama Convention of 1975)

Latin American countries were "rather secluded in their world outlook" and "trust[ed] global organisations less than they trust themselves".[181] As a consequence, these countries were once reluctant to ratify the New York Convention because of their long-established distrust of American and European business interests, and treated the New York Convention as a result of Western influence. Therefore, the Member States of the Organisation of American States strongly preferred to have their own treaty regime. The Panama Convention was signed at the conclusion of the Inter-American Conference on Private International Law in 1975 by twelve South American States.[182] The Convention represented an important change of attitude away from wariness and even hostility towards arbitration. Arguably, this Convention is key to opening up Latin America, now a vital market for arbitration.

It is said that the Panama Convention "was carefully drawn up so as to be fully compatible with the New York Convention",[183] and that "the New York Convention and the Inter-American Convention are intended to achieve the same results, and their key provisions adopt the same standards..."[184] It is apparent that the Panama Convention was strongly influenced by the New York Convention, although there are some technical differences. For instance, the Panama Convention used the term "execution" to mean "enforcement". Nevertheless, the discrepancy between the New York Convention and Panama Convention is also obvious in that the latter does not contain provisions regarding its field of application,[185] the referral by a court to arbitration,[186] and

---

180 The Moscow Convention now only applies to Bulgaria, Cuba, Mongolia, Romania and Russia. The Convention is now rarely used. Nigel Blackaby and Constantine Partasides, *Redfern and Hunter on International Arbitration*, Oxford: Oxford University Press (5th edn. 2009) p. 664.

181 J. Lliteras, 'The Panama Convention Strengthens Arbitration in the Americas', in *Inter-American Arbitration*, IACAC (2nd edn. 1975) p. 2.

182 For a text of the Convention as well as a table of Member States, see http://www.asser.nl/ica/iaci.htm.

183 Charles Robert Norberg, 'General Introduction to Inter-American Commercial Arbitration', in *International Handbook on Commercial Arbitration* (Suppl. 7, 1987) p. 3.

184 The House Report by the Judiciary Committee accompanying the bill implementing the Panama Convention in the United States, H.R. Rep. 101–501, 101st Cong., 2nd Sess. 5 (1990), reprinted in 1990 *US Code Cong. & Adm. News* 675, 678.

185 The New York Convention adopts reciprocity and commercial reservations to define the scope of application. The Panama Convention does not provide for any express definition of its field of application.

186 One basic action of the New York Convention is the referral by the court to arbitration. Article II(3) imposes the obligation on the courts in the contracting State to stay their

the conditions to be fulfilled by the party seeking enforcement of the award.[187] In addition, if the parties fail to agree upon the arbitral procedure, the Inter-American Commercial Arbitration Commission Rules of Procedure will apply.[188] In cases of concurrent applicability, no major conflict between both Conventions would seem to arise, except with respect to the applicability of the IACAC Rules. Such conflicts may be resolved by the rule of conflicts of treaties of maximum efficacy. In sum, the Panama Convention can be considered to constitute a bridgehead to international arbitration in general and the New York Convention in particular.

Riyadh Arab Agreement on Judicial Cooperation of 1977[189]

The Riyadh Convention on Arab Judicial Cooperation is a regional multilateral convention among a variety of Arab States concerning enforcement of arbitral awards and court judgments. The Convention affirms the executory character of arbitral awards made in a contracting state, without taking into account the nationality of the successful party. The Convention is a step backwards for those Arab States which ratified the New York Convention since it requires the enforcing party to obtain leave for enforcement from the judicial authority of the country in which the award was made in order to grant leave for enforcement in another Arab State. This implies that the Convention requires two leaves for enforcement whereas the New York Convention only requires that of the enforcement country. The enforcing court can only accept or refuse enforcement but is not allowed to examine the substance of the dispute when the judgment or award is referred to it for enforcement. Like the New York Convention,[190] the Convention imposes some restrictions on the refusal of enforcement such as the arbitrability, validity of arbitration clause, lack of jurisdiction, due process, breach of public order, Moslem Shari'a good moral or Constitution.[191] To those

proceedings and to refer the parties to arbitration. This mandatory requirement is absent in Panama Convention.

187 Article IV of the New York Convention imposes a minimum condition to be fulfilled by the party seeking enforcement. The Panama Convention does not contain any provisions similar to Article IV.

188 These are now the UNCITRAL Arbitration Rules.

189 This Convention was ratified by Iraq, Yemen, Mauritania, Jordan, Syria, Somalia, Tunisia and Libya, and was approved by the Council of Arab Ministers of Justice on 6 April 1983. The Convention came into force on 30 October 1985. Now Morocco, Lebanon, Kuwait, Qatar, Palestine, Oman, Sudan, Saudi Arab, Djibouti, Algeria, Bahrain and the United Arab Emirates are also members to the Convention.

190 It has been argued that the New York Convention, like numerous treaties, was designed to promote more efficient and effective transactional relations without reflecting universal moral norms. David Sloss, 'Treaty Enforcement in Domestic Courts: A Comparative Analysis' in David Sloss (ed), *The Role of Domestic Courts in Treaty Enforcement: A Comparative Study*, Cambridge: Cambridge University Press (2009) p. 9.

191 Article 30 of the Convention.

Arab States which did not sign the New York Convention,[192] the Convention is a step forward because it provides a multiple regime for cross-border enforcement of arbitral awards in this region. In this sense, the Convention is a supplement to the New York Convention.

Amman Arab Convention on Commercial Arbitration of 1987[193]

This Convention was signed in 1987 and is open to all the Arab States.[194] It is modelled on the 1965 ICSID Washington Convention and created the Arab Centre of Commercial Arbitration with its seat in Rabat. The Convention provides that the High Court of each country has jurisdiction to grant enforcement of arbitral awards. Arbitral awards made by the Rabat Centre are executory; the High Court must grant leave to enforce and the award can be rejected if it is contrary to public order, which has not been specifically defined. The Convention further provides that an award made by the Rabat Centre can only be set aside by the Centre and is not subject to appeal before the judicial authorities of the country where enforcement is sought. The Convention is of limited interest in international business, which, given the importance of the Arabic States, is unfortunate. This demonstrates a real trend towards the purposive construction of contracts less bound to esoteric national rules of interpretation, no longer just defining legal relationships but also containing the machinery to ensure a continuing mutuality of interest and effective communication.

These regional arbitration conventions are largely modelled on the New York Convention for the similar purpose of promoting the convergence of national arbitration laws of Member States in the region. In particular, like the New York Convention, they provide a clear platform for Member States to recognise and enforce foreign arbitral awards. The environmental factors connecting to the emergence of these regional conventions are similar to those for the New York Convention. The economic and political convergence and regional legal harmonisation perhaps play a much more important role in the promulgation of these regional conventions due to the fact that regional convergence developed much earlier and faster than global harmonisation. Functionally, these regional conventions may fairly be seen as a supplement to the New York Convention if the critical norms established in the New York Convention were not spread to these regions.

Some regional arrangements may come to interact with the New York Convention by "piggybacking" on the randomisation procedure to possess the

192 These countries are Iraq, Oman, Qatar, Libya, the United Arab Emirates, Yemen and Sudan.

193 This Convention was ratified by Iraq, Jordan, Libya, Tunisia, Yemen, Lebanon and Sudan.

194 For a text of the Convention, as well as a table of Member States, see http://www.asser.nl/ica/eur-a.htm.

casual impact of the New York Convention.[195] The New York Convention was referred to in the North American Free Trade Agreement in the context of observance of agreements to arbitrate and enforcement of arbitral awards.[196] Other regional arrangements such as the 1979 Inter-American Convention on Extra-territorial Validity of Foreign Judgments and Arbitral Awards, while piggybacking on the New York Convention, may also help improve the mechanism of the New York Convention with the objective of strengthening the global regime for enforcing arbitral awards.[197]

The Model Law

In spite of various international and regional treaties, international commercial arbitration still suffers from a lack of uniformity in the state laws applicable to other aspects in arbitration, which, however, are not the main subject of the New York Convention and other treaties. The United Nations Commission on International Trade Law (UNCITRAL) has attempted to provide a solution to the widely shared concerns relating to the actual quality and diversity of national arbitration laws. The Model Law began with a proposal to reform the New York Convention. This led to a report[198] from UNCITRAL to the effect that the harmonisation of state arbitration laws and clarification of some uncertainties surrounding them could be achieved more effectively by reference to a model. The technique adopted by UNCITRAL to deal with the discrepancy among state arbitration laws was to encourage states to adopt, borrow or imitate the rules of the Model Law in their own laws of arbitration. As an inducement to inception, states were not obliged to do so. Rather, the states may depart from it to the extent they consider necessary to accommodate important elements of their own law or policy which would otherwise be in conflict with it. The final text of the Model Law was adopted by resolution of UNCITRAL in June 1985 (and as amended in 2006), and a recommendation of the General Assembly of the

195 Consideration of fairness and transparency are a fertile ground for piggyback analyses because they often drive legal processes toward randomized queuing procedures. Some related research includes Bruce Sacerdote, 'Peer Effects with Random Assignment: Results for Dartmouth Roommates', (2001) 116 *Quarterly Journal of Economics* 681; David S. Abams and Albert H. Yoon, 'The Luck of the Draw: Using Random Case Assignment to Investigate Attorney Ability', (2007) 74 *University of Chicago Law Review* 1145; Daniel E. Ho and Kosuke Imai, 'Randomization Inference with Natural Experiments: An Analysis of Ballot Effects in the 2003 California Recall Election', (2006) 101 *Journal of the American Statistical Association* 888.

196 NAFTA, Art. 2022.2, 3.

197 Francisco Orrego Vicuna, *International Dispute Settlement in an Evolving Global Society: Constitutionalization, Accessibility, Privatization*, Cambridge: Cambridge University Press (2004) p. 111.

198 "Study on the Application and Interpretation of the Convention on the Recognition and Enforcement of Foreign Arbitral Awards", UN Doc. A/CN 9/168.

United Nations commending the Model Law to Member States was adopted in December 1985.

The soft law approach has enabled the Model Law to achieve great success by being adopted in over seventy countries and federal states[199] as "it is a text that any state proposing to adopt a modern law of arbitration is bound to take into consideration".[200] Many states have modernised their arbitration laws in recent years by modelling national laws on the Model Law. The Model Law, as one of the twin pillars of modern international commercial arbitration,[201] certainly represents a new generation of international rules on commercial arbitration.

2.5. ENVIRONMENTAL CHANGES AND THE NEW YORK CONVENTION

The foregoing discussion of the interaction between Darwinian evolutionary theory and the New York Convention may provide a platform to answer the second question, that is, whether Darwinian evolutionary theory may give us a new perspective to look at the New York Convention in the 21st century. What are the new environmental changes in the 21st century? A quick answer is globalisation and new technology. We will review their respective impact on international commercial arbitration.

2.5.1. GLOBALISATION AND ITS IMPACT ON ARBITRATION LAW

The discussion of the emergence of a global regulatory framework for international business transactions is not new.[202] The governance of global

---

199 Pieter Sanders, above n. 145, v.

200 Alan Redfern and Martin Hunter, *Law and Practice of International Commercial Arbitration*, London: Sweet & Maxwell (3rd edn. 1999) p. 70.

201 Neil Kaplan, 'Introduction' to the *ICCA's Guide to the Interpretation of the 1958 New York Convention: A Handbook for Judges*, International Council for Commercial Arbitration (2011) p. x.

202 See *e.g.*, John Braithwaite and Peter Drahos, *Global Business Regulation*, Cambridge: Cambridge University Press (2000); Loukas Mistelis, 'Regulatory Aspects: Globalisation, Harmonisation, Legal Transplants and Law Reform', (2000) 34(3) *The International Lawyer* 1055–69; Klaus Peter Berger, 'The New Law Merchant and the Global Market Place: A 21st Century View of Transnational Commercial Law', (2000) *International Arbitration Law Review* 91–102; Alex Y. Seita, 'Globalisation and the Convergence of Values', (1997) 30 *Cornell International Law Journal* 429–91; Yves Dezalay and Bryant Garth, *Dealing in Virtue – International Commercial Arbitration and the Construction of a Transnational Legal Order*, Chicago: University of Chicago Press (1996), and Richard P. Appelbaum, William L.F. Felstiner and Volkmar Gessner (eds), *Rules and Networks, the Legal Culture of Global Business Transactions*, Oxford: Hart Publishing (2001). The issue of the globalisation

economic activities and networks requires a concept of globalisation, which refers to an aggregate of multifaceted economic, political, social and cultural processes. While globalisation in the aftermath of 11 September is no longer fashionable,[203] the main premise, that as far as international commercial relations are concerned one could observe the incremental organic creation of an autonomous system and increasing homogeneity in political and legal ideas, which operate on the basis of the rule of law, is increasingly appealing. The world appears to be marching towards a new version of the rule of law with some 21st century characteristics, which does have an impact on legal practice, in particular on international commercial arbitration. According to Maine, contractual obligations are characteristic of modern societies.[204] If this is the case, contract-based arbitration shall become dominant in modern societies and the new century needs and seems able to nurture such developments.

It is now common to begin every discussion of globalisation with a definition, even though the term is used in multiple, often contradictory ways. In line with settled expectations, globalisation is defined as the processes of convergence in the economic, political, cultural and legal realms around the world as evidenced in rules, institutions, norms and practices. The emphasis on the processes of globalisation captures both the active and resultant dimensions by bridging cause and effect,[205] while also drawing attention to the dynamic, multifaceted and proactive nature of globalisation. In terms of commercial arbitration, the role of globalisation is to facilitate the convergence of substantive and procedural rules.

Law is widely defined as "a body of rules for human conduct within a community",[206] or "a coercive order".[207] Law in a global world shall affect social conduct of human beings through a common interest, economical, social or cultural. This is particularly true in a decentralised international community, where enforcement of law is accomplished through the application of the

of law pertaining to international business is approached from the perspective of legal theory, empirical sociology, economics, relational anthropology and formal law and legal reasoning.

203 The World Trade Organisation Doha Ministerial Declaration (November 2001) makes no reference to globalisation, which seems to have been put on hold for the time being. Instead, harmonisation at a regional level is encouraged. See http://www.wto.org/english/thewto_e/minist_e/min01_e/min01_e.htm.

204 "We may say that the movement of the progressive societies has hitherto been a movement from status to contract". See Henry Maine, *Ancient Law,* above n. 46 (1861, 1894) p. 170.

205 Globalisation is both a cause of convergence and a measure of the degree to which convergence has occurred.

206 Oppenheim, *Oppenheim's International Law*, Oxford: Oxford University Press (9th edn. 2008) p. 10, para. 5.

207 Hans Kelsen, *Principles of International Law*, New York: Rinehart (1952) p. 5. Max Weber, *Economy and Society*, Berkeley: University of California Press (1978) pp. 311–14.

principle of cooperation and self-compliance.[208] Besides, a global world also contains an autonomous community of merchants, which is governed by a separate set of rules or moral postulates, *inter alia*, the general assent or tolerance of the community. Legal systems in both communities are a community-minded kind of law.[209]

We may have to set the scene by locating the impact of globalisation on international commercial arbitration within the general context of globalisation in the economic, political and legal realms. Globalisation can be measured in many ways. Indeed, whether one finds convergence or divergence depends on the particular indicators that one chooses. Market, democracy, human rights and rule of law are broad standards, and each is capable of causing variations in theory and practice. Assessing the impact of globalisation requires these broad standards to be refined and supplemented by other measures. The effect of globalisation is most noticeable in the economic realm, where the world economy has become increasingly integrated in global and regional spheres. By contrast, political and cultural convergence has been much slower.[210] Legal convergence falls in the middle.

Culture is one of "the elementary forms of social unanimity"[211] or the "traditional authority".[212] The globalisation of business and finance has increased the range and depth of inter- and intra-national cultural conflicts, major causes of which are cultural misunderstandings and an increased resistance to new forms of cultural imperialism. Globalisation has implied the emergence of a new global culture and helped transform some, if not many, cultural elements. Nevertheless, the globalisation of culture is much more difficult to capture because it is hard to tell the impact of globalisation on more fundamental modes of values that are more constitutive of a community, people or nation. On the other hand, culture is so pervasive that it shapes the way the forces of globalisation operate and their ability to affect change in the aspect of economic, political and legal reforms. In this case, culture is a key factor shaping the legal map. Today, when cultural difference is offered as a legitimation for and

208 Friedmann has called this "the international law of cooperation". See Philip C. Jessup, *Transnational Law*, New Haven: Yale University Press (1956) pp. 15–16.

209 Among the nations, there is also a development of the international law of human rights and international environmental law which are a particularly community-minded kind of law.

210 For instance, China has resisted the trend towards Western-like democracy and challenged the universality of human rights by stressing the right for economic development. This comment was made by Chinese Premier Wen Jianbao in an interview on 21 November 2003 with the Washington Post Executive Editor Leonard Downie Jr., Assistance Managing Editor for Foreign News Philip Bennett, and Washington Post Correspondents John Pomfret, Philip P. Pan and Peter S. Goldman prior to his state visit to the United States of America in December 2003.

211 Emile Durkheim, *The Elementary Forms of the Religious Life*, New York: Simon & Schuster Ltd. (1997).

212 Max Weber, *Economy and Society*, above n. 207, 226–40.

explanation of legal difference, the cultural context often comes up as an aspect of a consciously mobilised collective identity in the midst of a political struggle, and it arises in relation to constitutions, collective inequalities, and other aspects of law. While legal convergence has become a response to the forces of globalisation today, such as WTO rules and the demands of foreign investors, the main driving force behind it may be a reaction to the highly diversified business and/or regulatory environments, which call for a more law-based order; a global governance for the convenience of doing business; an economic efficiency world-wide with the support of local governments; and an increasing demand from the reality that the rights recognised in one jurisdiction can be enforced in the other as well.

Globalisation has shaped developments in all legal areas, not only commercial law and international law but also some theoretical subjects such as jurisprudence and law and economics, although the degree of impact differs from one to the other. In the area of international commercial arbitration, some widely accepted notions such as party autonomy, independence of arbitration and finality of arbitral awards have found their viability in most major economic powers. The discrepancy between jurisdictions has been diminished to a certain extent. In the economy of the world as a whole, there are convincing social and economic arguments in favour of an increased role for private dispute resolution. The globalisation of trade will promote a higher level of harmonisation of commercial law and practice since a globalised commercial community is entitled to expect that obligations should be construed similarly in different jurisdictions and legal cultures. This may form a trend towards a purposive construction or operation of arbitration less bound to esoteric national rules. Dispute resolution will come to be seen increasingly as part of a continual process of conflicting management from the inception of a project to its completion and the resolution of residual claims.

The future of arbitration lies not in mimicking assisted settlement processes but rather in harnessing itself to assist the process of voluntary dispute resolution. Its function should therefore be two-fold. First, it is to act as an ultimate determinant of the rule of law, for which purpose the determination must result from acceptably rigorous factual investigations. Second, it is to act flexibly and according to the parties' needs, and to promote the materials for a successful settlement. Based on the foregoing discussion of the current "environmental" factors in the world-wide commercial sphere, such as global electronic commerce, standard-development organisations and "informational regulation", we can then explore what changes in the New York Convention may be brought about by environmental changes.

2.5.1.1. *Lex Mercatoria*

A sense of legality and modernity in the trend of globalisation requires us, with a neo-system theory, to understand law by embracing "legal pluralism". Legal pluralism, as Teubner put it, is defined "no longer as a set of conflicting social norms in a given social field but as a multiplicity of diverse communicative processes that observe social action under the binary code of legal/illegal".[213] Early formulations of legal pluralism reveal a movement in the environment of a system as metaphors of "turbulence" or "noise", implying a restricted view of the interchange and penetration taking place across boundaries but bringing about an internally shaped response from the system.[214] Global legal pluralism involves a variety of institutions, norms, and dispute resolution processes located, and produced, at different structured sites around the world.[215] In this sense, "pluralism" can be referred to as "societies which incorporate a diversity of institutionally distinct collectivities",[216] or "an exclusive, systematic and unified hierarchical ordering of normative propositions".[217] There are different approaches to eliminating the effect of cultural and legal differences that may hinder the globalisation of international business. In particular, unification or harmonisation of law or, more appropriately, the organic global convergence of law is distinguished from less formal mechanisms (soft law or less rigid law)[218] which also aim at increasing predictability; *lex mercatoria* and international arbitration.

The perception proclaimed by exponents of the neo-systems theory in the social sciences is helpful in understanding the universality of law. Luhmann asserted that "all collective human life is directly or indirectly shaped by law. Law is, like knowledge, an essential and all pervasive fact of the human condition".[219] Fögen took this one step further by saying that "law is everywhere"

---

213 See Gunter Teubner, above n. 43, 1451.

214 Niklas Luhmann, *A Sociological Theory of Law*, London: Routledge (1985) (the English translation of *Rechtssoziologie*, Opladen: Westdeutchser Verlag, 1972).

215 Snyder defines the "site" as states, regional and international organisations, and a diversity of other institutional, normative, and processual sites, such as commercial arbitration, trade associations and so on. The totality of these sites can be described as a network to represent a new global form of legal pluralism. See Francis Snyder, 'Governing Economic Globalisation: Global Legal Pluralism and European Union Law', (1999) 5(4) *European Law Journal* 334–374. According to Pospisil's theory, law could be generated from the multiple sites. Every social sub-group such as families, clans, and communities had its own internal "law". See Leopold Pospisil, *Anthropology of Law: A Comparative Theory*, New York: Harper & Row (1971). Pospisil said: "We have to ask whether a given society has only one consistent legal system … or whether there are several such systems".

216 See generally Stanley J. Tambiah, *Leveling Crowds*, Berkeley: University of California Press (1996).

217 John Griffiths, 'What is Legal Pluralism?', (1986) 24 *Journal of Legal Pluralism and Unofficial Law* 1–55.

218 René David, above n. 99, 29.

219 See Niklas Luhmann, above n. 214, 1.

and "there has been and there still is law without jurisprudence, even law without laws and without legal doctrine and without lawyers".[220] These views effectively suggest that human societies may not necessarily involve only binary coding marking right/wrong, lawful/unlawful, state/non-state.[221] Exponents of neo-systems theory have seen that the category of normative discourse is not peculiar to the state law only.[222]

The evolution of differentiated legal orders and an ideology of pluralism have been closely associated, in a global and multi-cultural context, with human beings' activities of establishing the non-state legal structure. In formulating law in a globalised world, the real "modernity" exists in a broad evolutionary trajectory, that is, a global legal order's containing an autonomous natured, self-determined, internally shaped, functionally differentiated, and non-state legal structure. A multi-dimensional approach relating human action or practice to the global structure or environment[223] inevitably leads to a multi-layered legal system, in which, apart from the States, the inter-state system, extra-state system, regional legal system and sub-systems for smaller groupings, an autonomous *lex mercatoria* all play a unique role through a system of informal, unofficial, negotiated settlements. Weber characterised the non-state (or extra-state) system as "[the] non-violent means of coercion which may have … even greater effectiveness than the violent ones".[224]

It is obvious that arbitration of the post-classical mercantile world was conducted within, and drew its strength from, communities consisting either of participants in an individual trade or of persons enrolled in bodies established under the auspices and control of geographical trading centres.[225] On the other hand, the geographical separation of the global commercial community needs widely recognised governing norms. Thus, the real authority of *lex mercatoria* resides in the fact that some communities gave birth to the implicit expectations and peer-group pressures which both shaped and enforced the resolution of disputes by an impartial and separate prestigious personage; and, more recently, the international society's recognition of it as a system that *ipso facto* binds nations and the global commercial community as members (or players) of the whole international society, regardless of their individual wills and roles. It also has to be pointed out that external formal legal sanctions would have been largely redundant in such communities even if a legal framework had been

220 See Simon Roberts, 'Against a Systemic Legal History', at 2 (unpublished paper on file with the author).

221 Max Weber adopted a binary coding state/extra state law in Max Weber, above n. 207, 311–14.

222 See, *e.g.*, Gunter Teubner, above n. 43, 1451.

223 See Richard Nice (tr.), Pierre Bourdieu, *Outline of a Theory of Practice*, Cambridge: Cambridge University Press (1977), and Anthony Giddens, *The Constitution of Society*, Berkeley: University of California Press (1986).

224 See Max Weber, above n. 207, 311–14.

225 See Michael Mustill, above n. 89.

available to bring them into play. More importantly, within a particular trade or market, a trader's concern for his reputation – or the risk of sanctions being imposed by a trade association such as the Grain and Feed Trade Association – would probably be sufficient to ensure compliance. In a global world, cultural, religious or other non-legal coercive measures are available and may be even better than the coercive apparatus of the political and legal community.

International law has been classified as a branch of ethics rather than of law.[226] If this classification can be agreed upon, *lex mercatoria* can be defined as a branch of values, which is more than international morality. *Lex mercatoria* contains two layers of values. One is an economic test, judging the "feasibility" of an act; and the other a moral test, judging the "rightness" of an act. Every business entity habitually commits acts of selfishness which are often gravely injurious to other business players, and yet are not contrary to national or international law. Nevertheless, we do not on that account necessarily judge them to have been "right". *Lex mercatoria* exists in the form of the customary law system, upon which it has been erected over several centuries and mainly consolidated within the last several generations. Unlike international law, it is a superstructure of "traditional" law rather than treaty-made law. This view is consistent with a wider sense of law that includes a set of ideas, materials, and institutions that were being used as a resource by people pursuing their own interests.

The paradox of international society is that its "spiritual" community is vulnerable even though the material side is much more than primitive, and thus needs a corresponding refined system of law for the regulation of the clashes to which the material interdependence of various business entities from different states is constantly giving rise. The most serious shortcoming of the current system is the rudimentary character of the institutions which exist for the making and application of the uniform commercial law at the global level. There is no legislature to keep the law abreast of new needs in the international society; no authoritative law-making machinery; no executive or judicial power to enforce the rules of *lex mercatoria*;[227] no compulsory character of international business rules; no wide range of application of a limited number of dispute resolution mechanisms.

The phenomenon of "globalisation" reflects not only an increase in the extent to which business is done internationally but also the emergence of entirely new

[226] See Humprey Waldock, *General Courses on Public of International Law,* 106 Hague Recueil 54 (1962-II) (6th edn. 1963) pp. 41–42, 68–76.

[227] The majority of rules of *lex mercatoria* are generally unaffected by the weakness of its system of enforcement because of voluntary compliance, which prevents the problem of enforcement from arising altogether. The rules of *lex mercatoria* may not recognise sanctions, such as the adoption of reprisals and other counter-measures. In this sense, *lex mercatoria* obviously is another kind of law.

markets and new ways of doing business.[228] Inherent in this process is the emergence of new demands for a system of international dispute resolution that is responsive to previously unknown issues and expectations. Globalisation may require an autonomous arbitration system that is more compatible with the rules of many of the major international arbitration institutions.[229] This autonomous system requires *lex mercatoria*, which has a significant role to play in trade facilitation and commercial dispute settlement. A possible advantage of such a system may be that it is culturally neutral. When it expresses a legal culture this may not be universally acceptable and practically feasible. However, one can argue that to the extent that lawyers and law firms are ultimate users of this autonomous system, those who participate in major business dispute resolution share the same culture, irrespective of their place of work. Effectively one could speak of a *lex arbitralis materialis* which consists of transnational substantive rules,[230] general principles of law and practice as generally expressed in the work of leading arbitration institutions and international firms. Autonomous rules, largely the new *lex mercatoria* and self-regulations such as the rules of arbitration institutions, are becoming more and more important. This trend may challenge the scope of the New York Convention, which usually only recognises and enforces an arbitral award in a national framework rather than an autonomous regime.

2.5.1.2. Sovereignty and De-nationalisation

Law is said to exist in a society, and there can be no society without a system of law to regulate the relations of its members with one another.[231] The only essential conditions for the existence of law are the existence of a political community, and recognition by its members of settled rules binding upon them

228 The quest for predictability and certainty as well as an economically based "time-space" compression invariably lead to a set of rules of amorphous and irregular character. Conflicts amongst existing constituencies are not necessarily detrimental.

229 See *e.g.*, AAA International Rules Art 28; ICC Art 17; LCIA Art 22.3; Stockholm Art 24. Also see the traditional UNCITRAL Rules Art 33.

230 See *e.g.*, Klaus Peter Berger, *The Creeping Codification of Lex Mercatoria*, The Hague and Boston: Kluwer Law and Taxation Publishers (1999); Thomas Carbonneau (ed.), *Lex Mercatoria and Arbitration: A Discussion of the New Law Merchant*, Dobbs Ferry NY: Kluwer and Juris Publishing (revised edn. 1998); Roy Goode, 'Usage and Its Reception in Transnational Commercial Law', (1997) 46 *International and Comparative Law Quarterly* 1–36; Martin Hunter, 'Publication of Arbitration Awards and Lex Mercatoria', (1988) 54 *Arbitration: The Journal of the Chartered Institute of Arbitrators* 55; Ole Lando, 'The *Lex Mercatoria* in International Commercial Arbitration', (1985) 34 *International and Comparative Law Quarterly* 747; Andreas F Lowenfeld, '*Lex Mercatoria*: an Arbitrator's View', (1990) 6 *Arb. Int'l* 133; Lord Mustill, 'The New *Lex Mercatoria* – the First Twenty-Five Years', (1988) 2 *Arb. Int'l* 86.

231 See Humprey Waldock, above n. 226, 41–42, 68–76.

in that capacity.[232] The construction of national governments is not a process that can be divorced from transnational matters. If and when slogans like the "law of globalisation", "law in a global world" or "global legalism" are talked about,[233] it is assumed that a "society of a global world" exists, and that the entire world constitutes a single community or society. In the trend of globalisation, there has been an immense growth of the factors that makes states mutually dependent on one another. What we are witnessing today is a powerful micro-globalism, in which states or other sub-groups in the world assert their distinctiveness and compete for recognition and control over some part of the polity. The interdependence of states would lead to a strengthening of the feelings of community. In general terms, this interdependence is not sufficient to maintain material bonds without a common social consciousness. The necessary force behind a corresponding legal system is some sentiment of shared responsibility for the conduct of a common interest. Globalisation and its surrounding institutions require a unique process of norm-setting, the standardisation of practices, the rationalisation of claims that are attached as part of the discourse, and the interaction of multiple power structures.

Darwinian perspectives of law at the transnational and national levels have become more de-centralised. De-centralised institutional arrangements seem to be the crux of the matter. From a political standpoint, globalisation has witnessed the rise of new political actors such as multinational firms, non-governmental organisations and social movements. The emergence of multi-players has tended to weaken, fragment, and sometimes even restructure the state. In the last quarter century, the increasing globalisation of trade and finance has resulted in a wholesale transformation of traditional markets, a State's political or sovereign function,[234] and the relationship between governance and territory. Particularly significant is an awareness of the many sites of regulation and sources of ideas and standards that are in play. This

232 See Frederick Pollock, *First Book of Jurisprudence for Students of the Common Law*, London: MacMillan and Co. Ltd. (1896) p. 28.

233 One aspect of "globalism" can be global legalism, the international rule of law, which many believe ethically necessary and in each nation's best interests especially given globalisation and recent financial crisis. However, some have viewed this globalism or "global legalism" as "a dangerously naive tendency" or "idealistic belief" that cannot be effective in the absence of legitimate institutions of governance. This "realistic" view of international law, globalism and global legalism warns us that neither globalism nor global legalism is a panacea. All nations only make commitments to international law or an international governance regime if such a legalist movement serves their short or long term interests. For a realistic account of global legalism, see generally Eric A. Posner, *The Perils of Global Legalism*, Chicago and London: Chicago University Press (2009).

234 Along with this trend is the fact that the conceptions and practices of the West are spreading globally together with its economic power. The legal aspects of Westernisation are sometimes conceived of in a positive light as steps toward greater justice, economic or technical modernisation and political democratisation. Others, however, may see it as pernicious domination.

requires an investigation of "the connections between policy, power, subjectivity and changing form of government".[235] Business has become increasingly international in nature and scope. In virtually every major field of commerce, transnational contracts have proliferated, together with parties from far-flung regions and widely divergent cultural and legal backgrounds. Therefore, "alternative spaces and spheres of power may indeed be emerging, notwithstanding the overwhelming weight of Western legal norms".[236] Globalisation has blurred the boundaries between the domestic and external spheres of nation-states, fostered the articulation of systems of multi-level governance and interlocked politics and policy networks. The discourse on this topic gets mixed with arguments about current transformations of the state through the empowerment of sub-national collective entities. Through "globalism", the state acknowledges diverse social fields within the society and represents itself ideologically and organisationally in relation to them, and acknowledges that the law may depend on the collaboration of non-state social fields for its implementation. Within the state, the internal diversity of the state administration, the multiple directions in which its official subparts struggle and compete for legal authority are all consistent with de-centralisation. Externally, the state is interdigitated with non-government, semi-autonomous social fields which generate their own (non-legal) obligatory norms to which they can induce or coerce compliance.

Another trend, which is recorded, is that legislators are often forced to change their laws and attitudes in order to attract foreign investment. The use of legal rules is inevitable and often, despite its pitfalls, the only alternative. Traditional private and commercial laws and rules have been in the process of reform under the pressure of global transactions. The international order plays an important role in driving the changes of state laws. On the other hand, in the 1970s a curious test of informal institutions appeared when informality was officially embraced by the American judicial system. The US courts added alternative dispute resolution (ADR) to options open to litigants. ADR was publicised as a response to the needs of the poor and of those who had minor claims that would otherwise have gone unheeded. Alternatives to the courts were sought in many countries.[237]

---

235 See Cris Shore and Susan Wright (eds.), *Anthropology of Policy,* London and New York: Routledge (1997) p. xiii.

236 See Eve Darian-Smith, 'Structural Inequalities in the Global Legal System', (2000) 34(3) *Law and Society Review* 826.

237 See Mauro Cappelletti and Bryant Garth (eds.), *Access to Justice: A World Survey* (2 Vols.), London, Boston and Milan: Siftoff & Noordoft (1978–9); Mauro Cappelletti and Denis Tallon (eds.), *Fundamental Guarantees of the Parties in Civil Litigation,* Dobbs Ferry NY: Oceana Publications (1973). Less felicitously, some judges remarked that they wanted to get garbage cases out of courts. See Laura Nader, 'From Legal Processing to Mind Processing', (1992) 30(4) *Family and Conciliation Courts Review* 468–73.

The emerging globalisation departs from the traditional global liberal values of generality, clarity and prospectiveness. The new global environment of business transactions needs a low portfolio of sovereignty and law in a de-nationalised world. Some of the roles of states have been delegated or diffused to post-national constellations of statehood.[238] The twentieth century experienced an important change, that is, the dilution, dissipation and, in some extreme cases, disappearance of state power. This shift in the locus of authority reflects a widespread popular realisation but a critical controversy that the collective public responsibility of the state cannot fully substitute on a broad basis for individual responsibility privately exercised. So far a four-tiered global system, consisting of private adjudication under agreed rules, supported by national laws and soft law necessary to ensure its integrity, and an international exercise of state power to the extent required to guarantee enforcement of the results, has been set up. The dilution of the state power strengthens a system whereby the parties of different nationalities agree to mandatory and binding arbitration of disputes between them pursuant to a particular set of arbitration rules before an arbitration panel. The growth in private adjudication is matched stride for stride. Indeed it is made possible by the concomitant convergence of relevant national laws and the elaboration of facilitative international agreements, resulting in the internationalisation of adjudicated commercial dispute resolution. Statutes in major industrial jurisdictions have been modernised so as to minimise state or judicial intervention in the arbitral process, while offering judicial review to the extent merely necessary to ensure the integrity of the process by which the arbitral tribunal arrived at its award. For example, the procedural aspect of the French legal reform relating to enforcement and means of recourse was seen as a way to harmonise domestic and international arbitration. There are many rules of law with national and international origins which are shaped by techniques, habits and customs of national or regional characters. The social regulation of economic activities and how private governance and decentralised law can emerge are evident in a variety of settings. Businesspeople increasingly prefer and embrace more flexible "general principles" of contract law. These soft law principles operate within the limits set by public law. Major countries, to a certain extent, have concocted for themselves a jurisprudential corpus that either is divorced from its own original system of law or combines certain rules from international conventions.

This trend is parallel to the global legislation of international commercial arbitration. The relative reduction in the role of states today necessarily requires the unification of state laws in most aspects, which has spawned an explosion in

[238] The correlation between de-nationalisation and globalisation in light of the new architecture of statehood and the role of non-state actors is always a hot issue in theory and practice. As far as international commercial arbitration is concerned, de-nationalisation may give arbitration more flexibility and autonomy than before.

the development of international commercial arbitration. The international community has adopted a series of conventions and treaties ensuring mutual and uniform enforcement of agreements to arbitrate, and also of the resulting awards, of which the New York Convention of 1958 is the most prominent. In this regard, tremendous achievements have been made by international organisations, for example, the International Center for Settlement of Investment Disputes, International Chamber of Commerce, International Institute for the Unification of Private Law, along with others, in promoting international commercial arbitration at a global level. All these legislative and practical efforts result in important legal consequences. For example, the distinctions between the civil law and common law traditions are gradually fading. Nevertheless, it has to be pointed out that "de-nationalised" or "de-localised" arbitration, as a controversial concept,[239] is indeed explicitly rejected by some countries such as Singapore,[240] which indicates the pragmatic difficulty in implementing this concept in the whole international community.

2.5.1.3. Harmonisation of Arbitration Law

A global economy ideally requires a global system for defining rights and obligations and providing for their determination. Despite this, differences in the legal systems of countries, even within the Europe Union or among common law jurisdictions, are still substantial. The most obvious differences are on both substantive and procedural levels.[241] For instance, there is an Anglo-Saxon belief in the innate superiority of an "adversarial" judicial process and a corresponding mistrust of a possible superficiality, or at least lack of pragmatism, of an "inquisitorial" process.[242] These procedural differences reflect underlying

239 Albert Jan van den Berg, 'The New York Convention of 1958: An Overview', in Emmanuel Gaillard and Domenico di Pietro (eds.), *The Enforcement of Arbitration Agreements and International Arbitral Awards, The New York Convention in Practice*, London: Cameron May (2009) p. 42.

240 At the second Parliamentary Reading of the International Arbitration (Amendment) Bill, the Minister of State for Law commented that Singapore did not recognise the concept of a "delocalised" arbitration unconnected with any system of municipal law. Singapore Parliamentary Debates, Official Report (5 October 2001), vol. 73 at col. 2215, the Review of Arbitration Laws Committee, Law Reform and Revision Division, Attorney-General's Chambers, Review of Arbitration Laws (LRRD No. 3/2001), 4 October 2001, para. 2.1.1.

241 Northcote Parkinson's satire of the English parliamentary system could equally have been of our legal system: "the British instinct is to form two opposing teams, with referee and linesmen, and let them debate until they exhaust themselves … [The individual Member's] training from birth has been to play for his side, and this saves him from any undue mental effort … But the British system depends entirely on its seating plan. If the benches did not face each other, no one could tell truth from falsehood, wisdom from folly…" C. Northcote Parkinson, *Parkinson's Law or The Pursuit of Process*, Penguin (1965/1985).

242 "The changes [in the civil justice system] … would assimilate the role of the judge in this country to that of his brethren in continental Europe. But there is no reason to fear that judges would not continue … to bring to their task an invaluable practical experience of the

cultural differences in approaches to the application of the substantive law.[243] It must be recognised that it is an over-simplification to see the differences in terms of "common law" and "civil law" systems. Beyond the superficial similarity of a system based on precedent or on a codified law, there are innumerable differences between the legal systems of the countries which fall within one or other broad description.

One effect of the globalisation of business is to force the pace of change towards harmonisation. Just as globalisation need not be the only reason for convergence, neither need globalisation mean one-size-fits-all. Convergence is a matter of degree. Arbitration law is one area in which there is tremendous variety among legal systems around the world. Simply put, there is not a single correct way to deal with common arbitration problems. Thus, while all states rely on generally applicable laws to limit abuses of discretion and provide predictability and certainty, they may differ on how much judicial and legislative discretion is desirable. For example, the East Asian developing states tend to favour a larger, more flexible role for the executive in managing the economy than western liberal states, in part because the rapidly changing economic environment requires a certain level of flexibility. In light of the diversity among arbitration laws, the lack of a single blueprint for success, and the presence of a distinctive set of institutional, cultural, economic and political constraints, the development of a world-wide unified arbitration law regime inevitably will be determined primarily by its own contingent, context-specific conditions.

There is an increasing degree of cooperation between national legislatures to harmonise both substantive and procedural law. There are many examples particularly within the European Union. The national arbitral laws of many European countries have been reformed in the last decade of the 20th century: England, Germany, Sweden and Belgium enacted new, or amended existing, arbitration laws. Jurisdiction, recognition and enforcement of judgments, and governing law have all been addressed by Europe-wide Conventions. Various directives are driving forward the process of harmonising substantive law in the realm of contractual relationships. On a macro level, the Treaty of Amsterdam

law; professional distinction; integrity; independence; and a sense of fairness which is the great distinguishing feature of the common law." Sir Thomas Bingham, 'The Price of Justice', (1994) 60 *Journal of the Chartered Institute of Arbitrators* 247 (proposing reforms to the civil justice system).

243 "The historical fact that common lawyers have been reared on a diet of case law has had a profound effect on our judicial method. Common lawyers tend to proceed by analogy, moving gradually from case to case ... We tend to reason upwards from the facts of the cases before us, whereas our continental colleagues tend to reason downwards from abstract principles embodied in a code ... It is this fundamental distinction between the English and the continental European cultures which ... lies at the heart of the misunderstanding about the possible creation of a federal Europe. Continental Europeans love to proclaim some great principle, and then knock it into shape afterwards. Instead, the boring British want to find out first whether and, if so, how these ideas are going to work in practice". Lord Goff, 'The Future of the Common Law', (1997) 46 *ICLQ* 745.

(signed in July 1997) contains amendments to the European treaties of potentially far-reaching significance in the area of procedural and substantive law.[244] The whole process may justify the belief in the ultimate possibility of a harmonisation of European national laws, a Darwinian exercise of the survival of the fittest.[245]

In relation to arbitration, in the area of substantive law, there is an increasing willingness among English judges to undertake comparative legal exegesis. The most notable example has been Lord Hoffmann's judgment in *Kleinwort Benson*,[246] which was based in part on a comparative analysis of the law of unjust enrichment in other countries as an aid to deciding whether the public policy required the maintenance of the rule against the recovery of money paid under a mistake of law. Judicial techniques of construction of statutes and contracts start to lose some of their previous unique harshness, and foreign concepts (such as "gross negligence") begin to enter the law.[247] Another profound change is in the area of procedural law. The English judicial process has recently been reformed by the adoption of the Civil Procedure Rules 1998.[248] The reforms introduced a shift in the balance of procedural determination from the parties' advocates to the judge.[249] The importance of this shift should not be underestimated in terms of European harmonisation because this will be much easier for English procedure to gradually take on elements of continental procedure. In this sense, the reform should be regarded as a first but greatest step taken in the transition to an "inquisitorial" system. Besides, the dilution of specialist advocates will gradually demystify and simplify the procedure.

---

244 Article 65 of the resulting draft amended Consolidated Version of the European Treaty defines the measures which the Council must adopt progressively over five years in the field of judicial cooperation in civil matters for the purpose of progressively establishing an area of freedom, security and justice. The scope of these measures is very wide and may include improving and simplifying the recognition and enforcement of decisions in civil and commercial cases, including decisions in extrajudicial cases; promoting the compatibility of the rules applicable in the Member States concerning the conflict of laws and of jurisdiction; and eliminating obstacles to the good functioning of civil proceedings, if necessary by promoting the compatibility of the rules on civil procedure applicable in the Member States. Following the Tampere conference in October 1999, the European Council has invited the Council and the Commission to prepare new procedural legislation in cross-border cases and has requested the Council to report on the need to approximate Member States' legislation in the area of substantive law by 2001.

245 Lord Goff, above n. 243, 745.

246 *Kleinwort Benson Limited v. Lincolnshire County and Ors* [1998] 4 All ER 513.

247 *Per* Mance LJ in *Red Sea Containers v. Papachristidis & Ors, The 'Hellespont Ardent'* [1997] 2 Lloyd's Rep 547, 586.

248 The reform is known as the 'Woolf Reforms' as of 26 April 1999. See *The Civil Procedure Rules 1998*, London: Sweet & Maxwell (1999).

249 "One of the most radical features of the Rules is that the *reactive judge* (for centuries past at the heart of the English common law concept of the independent judiciary) will go. Instead, we shall have a proactive judge, whose task will be to take charge of the action at an early stage and manage its conduct in a way we have never seen before in this jurisdiction." R.L. Turner, *Foreword, The Civil Procedure Rules 1998*, London: Sweet & Maxwell (1999).

The globalisation of international trade, finance and investment has seen a progressive change in the global legal field. The WTO, the WIPO and other inter-governmental organisations respond to the needs of international commerce, and harmonise the cross-border trading and business environment by distilling operative common principles. With the comfort of a huge bureaucracy and the need to serve corporate entities, the inter-governmental bodies can implement and enforce these rules. It is reasonable to expect such a trend to continue, along with the increased number of contracts among private parties before arbitral tribunals and courts. In the global marketplace, the private dispute resolution system has proved popular and workable over time. Parties are afforded the flexibility to choose a set of rules that best suits their commercial needs in a given context. Arbitration institutions are more specialised and service-oriented and their rules are moving ever closer. The New York Convention and the Model Law[250] are adopted by more countries and arbitration institutions. There has been an increasing trend towards the time of the "flu of modernisation" of arbitration.[251] Since the economic globalisation aims at minimising state interference in cross-border transactions,[252] the liberalisation of the private justice system through modernised international commercial arbitration is considered to be vital and constructive in this respect.[253] International commercial arbitration is believed to contribute to

250 See the text at http://www.uncitral.org/en-index.htm. As discussed above, the objective of the Model Law is to globally harmonise the law and practice in international commercial arbitration. As of November 2003, legislation based on the Model Law has been enacted in Australia, Azerbajian, Bahrain, Bangladesh, Belarus, Bermuda, Bulgaria, Canada, Croatia, Cyprus, Egypt, Germany, Greece, Guatemala, Hong Kong, Hungary, India, Iran, Ireland, Japan, Jordan, Kenya, Lithuania, Macau, Madagascar, Malta, Mexico, New Zealand, Nigeria, Oman, Paraguay, Peru, Korea, Russia, Singapore, Sri Lanka, Tunisia, Ukraine, the UK, the states of California, Connecticut, Illinois, Oregon and Texas of the United States, Zambia and Zimbabwe.

251 The "flu of modernisation" of arbitration is obviously driven by the global economy. For instance, in tune with the global phenomenon of modernisation of international commercial arbitration, Bangladesh has recently enacted a new arbitration law, known as the Arbitration Act 2001. The Act is principally based on the Model Law and consolidates the law relating to both domestic and international commercial arbitration. The new legislative step was urgently taken in the face of increasing foreign investment in Bangladesh in various sectors, especially in natural gas and power and its ever-growing export trade with the rest of the world. This modernisation gives Bangladesh a facelift as an attractive place for dispute resolution in the field of international trade, commerce and investment. Since the new Act embodies the modern practices of arbitration, it is considered to help build confidence in prospective foreign investors in Bangladesh. In today's highly competitive world, since Bangladesh is keen to maintain its current momentum of economic growth and to improve its image as a rapidly developing economy, it expects to see the new Act as a boon in that respect.

252 See Gunther Teubner (ed.), *Global Law Without a State,* Dartmouth: Aldershot (1997); Jarrod Wiener, *Globalisation and the Harmonisation of Law,* London and New York: Pinter (1999); Michael Likosky (ed.), *Transnational Legal Process: Globalisation and Power of Disparities,* London: Butterworths/LexisNexis (2002).

253 See Katharine Lynch, *The Forces of Economic Globalisation – Challenges to the Regime of International Commercial Arbitration,* The Hague: Kluwer Law International (2003).

market integration by safeguarding and improving the efficiency and fairness of international private transactions.[254]

2.5.2. NEW YORK CONVENTION AND NEW TECHNOLOGY

Science has had considerable impact on law. For example, it has added at least several new territorial areas – outer space and the deep seabed – for which international law theories and rules need to be developed. Law reflects societal and technological concerns. The impact of new technology has extended to various legal spheres.[255] As rightly observed, "in this age of science we must build legal foundations that are sound in science as well as in law".[256] Legal doctrine and process have to be adapted to the use of new technology. Also, new technology has been widely used in legal proceedings. One example of using modern means of communication in the legal process is using video conferences, which took place in the United States[257] and Germany[258] as well as the International War Crimes Tribunal for the former Yugoslavia.[259] In this sense, new technology has brought us into a new legal era. Along with globalisation, new technology such as the Internet has a deep impact on society and drives the rapid development and diversity of international commercial arbitration. There has been a range of developments suggesting that new technology may not only facilitate international commercial arbitration but also bring new challenges to the New York Convention.

2.5.2.1. New Technology, Commerce and Law

The Internet is listed as one of the ten forces that "flattened" the world.[260] The non-traditional area of e-commerce has not grown merely by replicating offline patterns of commerce but has experienced extraordinarily rapid growth. By the end of 2000, the number of items offered for sale online increased to more than 5,000,000 and the number of transactions per week had increased to over

254 See Alessandra Casella, 'On Market Integration and the Development of Institutions: The Case of International Commercial Arbitration', (1996) 40 *European Economic Review* 155.

255 New technology obviously brings a lot of new legal issues relating to, for instance, the Internet, freedom of speech and privacy, nanotechnology and intellectual property law, network effects and antitrust law, sustainability, and trade and environment,.

256 Associate Justice of the Supreme Court Stephen G. Breyer at http://www7.nationalacademies.org/stl.

257 See Eugene Volokh, 'Technology and the Future of Law', (1995) 47 *Stanford Law Review* 1400.

258 'Some Lawyers in Germany Agitate for the Cyber Trial', *International Herald Tribune*, 26 October 1995, at A10.

259 See *Dusan Tadic*, Case No. IT-94-I-T.

260 For a general picture as to how the Internet changed the world, see Thomas L. Friedman, *The World is Flat – The Globalised World in the Twenty-First Century*, Harmondsworth: Penguin Books (2006).

2,000,000.[261] U.S. e-commerce sales grew from $72 billion in 2002 to $256 billion in 2011.[262] Disputes often occur in such new environments where the established practices, understandings and behaviours have not been solidified. The emergence of online dispute resolution is likely to occur much more quickly than we might expect.

Like fax transmission, email communication increases efficiency and flexibility but also affects the commercial and legal environment. In addition to being more easily authenticated than faxed documents, email communication can serve widely dispersed parties throughout the world in a more efficient way. The increasingly routine use of email was adopted in the Microsoft antitrust case. Before US District Court Judge Thomas Penfield Jackson issued his ruling that Microsoft had violated the antitrust laws, he appointed Federal Court of Appeals judge Richard Posner to try to mediate a settlement. In late March 2000, it was reported that Judge Posner "peppered both sides with faxes, emails and phone calls about proposals and counterproposals. The parties have not dealt face to face, but instead have been working through Posner, who has been acting in the role of an electronic shuttle diplomat".[263] Email, therefore, becomes the document manager for place-independent dispute resolution. The use of email in any dispute settlement process may be a valuable means of communication. When email is the only use of the network and only occasionally used, we would not even suggest that our figurative "fourth party" is present. The "fourth party" begins to appear as network-based tools and resources acquire a larger role, one in which the network is used for something more than the telephone or some other means for exchanging communication.

2.5.2.2. New Technology and E-based Arbitration

Changes in communications technology have often been heralded as "revolutionary". Transactions such as facsimiled contracts, credit-card transactions made via static or mobile telephony, on-line television sales, and e-financial transactions such as automated clearing house and electronic funds transfer share the same problem as internet-based transactions have: the lack of certainty as regards the place where the contract is concluded. The parties in Internet-based transactions will more often be located in different jurisdictions. Therefore, Internet-based transactions can more likely be subordinated to one national domestic legal system. It is also unclear at which point the contract becomes binding upon the parties. National laws and their legal doctrines have already been adapted to the use of new technology in a commercial world. For

---

261 Ethan Katsh and Janet Rifkin, *Online Dispute Resolution: Resolving Conflicts in Cyberspace*, San Francisco, Jossey-Bass: A Wiley Co. (2001) pp. 4–5.

262 http://www.statista.com/topics/871/online-shopping/.

263 See J.V. Grimaldi, 'Microsoft, Justice Remain Far Apart; Sources Say Pact Unlikely by Tuesday', *Washington Post*, 25 March 2000, E1.

instance, doctrines such as the declaration theory, expedition theory, mail-box rule (or reception theory), information theory, and Entores rule[264] are adopted in contract laws to determine the moment of formation of contract via telefax, electronic data interchange (EDI), or, more recently, email. Many countries have restructured consumer banking and payment systems, as well as private international law, for financial transactions via ATM machines.

As a response to the rise of e-commerce, various supranational organs are devoting significant time to the resolution of the problems. By way of example, the European Union has proposed a regime for digital signatures[265] and distance contracts,[266] and the United Nations Trade Commission has proposed a law on electronic commerce.[267] In the UK, the DTI is seeking to introduce measures[268] to give legal recognition to the UNCITRAL Model Law and electronic signatures, which, however, specifically excludes tax, convergence and content issues,[269] and consumer protection. New technologies are already widely utilised in international commercial arbitration. For instance, applications for arbitration and arbitral awards may be often delivered by fax or email. The Internet no doubt has substantially changed the traditional features of commercial arbitration. A number of recent projects which seek to encompass dispute resolution in the virtual marketplace are worthy of note: The Virtual Magistrate, the On-line Ombuds Office,[270] and the Internet Good Faith Code E-arbitration™ scheme.[271]

2.5.2.3. *Impact of New Technologies on the New York Convention*

New technologies have already brought many special difficulties into the legal sphere, including in international commercial arbitration[272] and the New York

264 *Entores Ltd. v. Miles Far East Corp.* [1955] 2 QB 327 CA. Also see Benjamin Wright, *The Law of Electronic Commerce: EDI, Fax and E-mail,* (Supplement) New York: Little, Brown & Company (1996), para. 15:14.

265 Proposal for a Directive on a Common Framework for Electronic Signatures, Directive 98/0191 of 13 May 1998.

266 Directive on the Protection of Consumers in Respect of Distance Contracts, June 1997, 97/7/EC OJ R 144/19.

267 UNCITRAL Model Law on Electronic Law 1996.

268 Report of 19 October 1998 in which OFTEL is proposed as the regulator for the virtual marketplace.

269 Such as materials of a pornographic and/or obscene nature.

270 http://www.ombuds.org.

271 http://www.e-goodfaith.com.

272 E-commerce or e-based disputes usually require special legislation or regulatory regime. For instance, in relation to the telecoms industry, the EU has a Directive 2002/21 on a common regulatory framework for electronic communications and services (Framework Directive); Directive 2002/20 on the authorisation of electronic communications networks and services (Authorisation Directive); Directive 2002/19 on access to, and interconnection of, electronic communications networks and associated facilities (Access Directive); Directive 2002/22 on universal service and users' rights relating to electronic communications networks and services (Universal Service Directive).

Convention. Questions are being raised about how e-based arbitration operates and how different the arbitration agreement, arbitration process, and arbitration award will be in such an arbitration. Arbitration conducted through the Internet would seem to challenge the New York Convention regime in various respects.

The New York Convention requires an "agreement in writing".[273] This writing requirement is reflected in three perspectives. An arbitral clause shall be signed and included by the parties in a contract or an arbitration agreement. Alternatively, an arbitral clause in a contract or arbitration agreement shall be contained in an exchange of letters or telegrams.[274] In addition, an award is enforceable only if it is presented as a duly authenticated original award or a duly certified copy, together with an agreement to arbitrate furnished in the same form.[275] The reason for imposing the writing requirement is mainly to ensure the existence of an arbitral clause or agreement which will eventually exclude the jurisdiction of national courts and allow a private method of dispute resolution. Nevertheless, the "writing" requirement creates difficulties for arbitration clauses in contracts evidenced by certain brokers' notes, bills of lading, sales confirmations, charterparty recaps and other instruments granting rights to non-signing parties. Similar difficulties may arise in contracts which include standard written terms with an arbitration clause only by reference.[276] In addition to the practical difficulties, the writing requirement has also given rise to judicial difficulty and multiplicity. Italy is a particular illustration because of its unduly formalistic approach to the "writing" requirement requiring the formal signature of an arbitration provision as a separate agreement.[277] The English view seems to support the idea that "the definition is not exhaustive and [is] wide enough to cover contracts made by reference to the conditions of sale of the London Commodity Markets, provided the contract or an arbitration agreement is signed by the parties".[278] A US court parsed Article II(2) to separate "an arbitral clause in a contract" from an arbitration agreement "signed by the parties or contained in an exchange of letters".[279] This approach was also adopted by other countries.[280]

---

273 Article II(2) of the New York Convention.

274 The requirement of writing is also contained in Article 7(2) of UNCITRAL Model Law on International Commercial Arbitration, which is described as "contained in a document signed by the parties or in an exchange" of communications.

275 Article IV(1) of the New York Convention.

276 Neil Kaplan, 'Is the Need for Writing as Expressed in the New York Convention and the Model Law out of Step with Commercial Practice?', (1996) 12(1) *Arb. Int'l* 27.

277 Michael Kerr, 'Concord and Conflict in International Arbitration', (1997) 13(2) *Arb. Int'l* 135, 139.

278 Explanatory Note in the Fifth Report of the Private International Law Committee (Cmnd. 1515) 26.

279 *Sphere Drake Ins. v. Marine Towing*, 16 F.3d 666 (5th Cir.), cert. denied, 155 US Sup. Ct. 195 (1994), reprinted in XX *Yearbook* (1995) 937.

280 *Compagnie de Navigation v. Mediterranean Shipping Co.*, Swiss Sup. Ct. January 1995, reprinted in XX *Yearbook* (1995) 690.

At the first glance, the wide use of email and other modern methods of communications has made this "writing" requirement distinctly old-fashioned. Is an agreement formed by the exchange of emails an "agreement in writing"? Some commentators have expressed doubts on this, but more recent work has suggested that email should not be treated differently from more tangible forms since the essential features of an exchange of telegrams may be reproduced via email even though critical technical differences between telegrams and emails do exist.[281] Obviously, there is not a uniform approach to interpreting the "writing" requirement. Because of various interpretations of the "writing" requirement, it is questionable whether all courts of the enforcement regime would accept the printout of an email message as an "agreement in writing" by virtue of Article II(2) of the New York Convention. The exchange of emails to form an arbitration agreement may deserve some special considerations in practice. The interpretation of the writing requirement in the New York Convention needs to take into account the legislative history of the New York Convention, the purpose of enacting such a requirement, the state of technology at the time of drafting the provision, and the general trend in defining the "writing" requirement in recent international conventions.

It is obvious that the drafters of the New York Convention wished to exclude the oral or tacit acceptance of a written proposal to arbitrate.[282] There is evidence that the drafters of the New York Convention may have intended the term "agreement in writing" to have a uniform interpretation and rejected possibilities including unsigned documents where the assent of one of the parties had to be implied from its failure to object.[283] However, in view of *travaux préparatoires*, the drafters did not want to impose this on all parties to the Convention, as new principles of contract formation had not been widely accepted.[284]

It seems reasonable to interpret Article II(2) in a facilitative manner that it supports and recognises international contracts concluded by the exchange of correspondence. The flexibility of means of communication will facilitate and enhance greater opportunities for international trade.[285] The most advanced communication technology at the time of drafting and passing the New York Convention was the telegram, which was obviously considered and adopted by the delegates of signatory countries. However, the New York Convention did not give an exhaustive list of communication technologies, which effectively means that future developments in ways to transmit written words may be acceptable under the New York Convention. There has been a revolution in communications since 1958 when the New York Convention was drawn up. Telegrams, a frequent

281 Richard Hill, 'On-line Arbitration: Issues and Solutions', (1999) 15(2) *Arb. Int'l* 200.

282 Albert Jan van den Berg, *The New York Arbitration Convention of 1958: Towards a Uniform Judicial Interpretation*, The Hague: Kluwer Law and Taxation Publishers (1981) p. 196.

283 See generally Neil Kaplan, above n. 276, 172–73.

284 *Fothergill v. Monarch Air Lines Ltd* [1981] AC 251.

285 See Neil Kaplan, above n. 276, 27–43.

method of communicating a message in writing at that time, were largely replaced by telex, and later by fax and now by email. Courts have applied Article II(2) to telexes in several cases and some authorities hold the view that it should be extended to facsimiles as well.[286] Technically speaking, an email seems to be much more secure than a telegram, which cannot show the identity of its sender. By contrast, an email easily displays a sender's email address and the delivery time. There is no technical reason to speculate that the New York Convention would not recognise an arbitration clause or agreement made by a more reliable communication technology than a telegram.

From a legislative perspective, national laws and international treaties usually attempt to accommodate new technologies in commercial activities. The Netherlands Arbitration Act 1986 requires that the arbitration agreement be proven by an instrument in writing expressly or impliedly accepted by the parties.[287] The 1988 UNIDROIT Convention on International Factoring adopted a broad definition of notice which includes but is not limited to "telegrams, telex, and any other communication capable of being reproduced in tangible form".[288] Swiss law requires "an agreement to be made in writing by telegram, telex, telecopier or by any other means of communication which permits it to be evidenced by a text".[289] Unlike the approach of defining the writing requirement only by reference to the mode of imposition of the medium, the UK Arbitration Act 1996 seems to extend the "writing" requirement to cover "anything being written or in writing … being recorded by any means".[290] This seems to suggest that arbitration clauses may be in all forms of enforceable written contracts. The US Uniform Commercial Code provides that "written or writing" includes "printing, typewriting, or any other presentational reduction to tangible form".[291] The common law in the US is also moving in the same direction by accepting that an email is a "writing" for contractual matters.[292] The national legislation appears to be moving towards the relaxation of the formal writing requirement.[293] In these modern laws, there has in effect been a triumph of substance over form. As long as there is some written evidence of an agreement

---

286 UNCITRAL Model Law on Electronic Commerce.

287 The Netherlands Arbitration Act 1986, Article 1021.

288 Article 1(4)(b) of the UNIDROIT Convention on International Factoring.

289 Swiss PIL Act 1987, Article 178(1).

290 Section 5(6) of UK Arbitration Act 1996.

291 UCC Section 1-201(46).

292 Richard Hill and Ian Walden, 'The Draft UNCITRAL Model Law for Electronic Commerce: Issues and Solutions', (1996) 13(3) *The Computer Lawyer* 18.

293 Toby Landau, 'The requirement of a written form for an arbitration agreement. When "written" is "oral"', 16th ICCA Congress, 12–15 May 2002, London. It should be pointed out that there remain states such as Argentina and Uruguay in which special requirements of form are imposed in respect of agreements to arbitrate. In these two countries, for example, a clause to submit future disputes to arbitration is not operative until a submission agreement (or "compromise") has been executed. National laws still need to be examined to ensure that there is no special requirement imposed on the form of arbitration agreement. See Nigel

to arbitrate, the form in which that agreement is recorded is immaterial.[294] Due to its flexibility, it is urged that local statutes be adopted to expand the definition of arbitration agreements in "writing" for the purpose of harmonising the "writing" requirement.[295]

The practical trend appears to be that drafters of national laws are more willing to make allowances for the use of new technologies,[296] or to define the "writing" requirement as widely as possible.[297] More recent case law has also adopted this view, either holding that "the words in Article II(2) [of the New York Convention][298] are merely illustrative and inclusive of what an arbitration agreement is, and is not an illustrative list of what constitutes an arbitration agreement"[299] or echoing a liberal approach to interpret the definition of "arbitration agreement" in the New York Convention as a looser and wider term.[300] The standard judicial view on this appears to suggest that an agreement under Article II(2) is not limited to a document signed by the parties. Rather, the requirement is more about a record to evidence the agreement of the parties to arbitrate.[301] Closely intertwined with this widespread trend is the reluctance the courts have shown in construing Article II(2) as the minimum international requirement,[302] according to which courts were not entitled to require less than provided for the written form under the New York Convention. Thus, Article II(2) has been increasingly understood as not precluding the application of less stringent standards of form by contracting States. This latter view is also supported by the reading of Article VII(1).[303]

Blackaby, David Lindsey and Alessandro Spinillo, *International Arbitration in Latin America*, The Hague: Kluwer Law International (2002) p. 12, pp. 31–32 and p. 73.

294 *Oonc Lines Ltd v. Sino-American Trade Advancement Co. Ltd.*, (1994) *Arbitration and Dispute Resolution Law Journal* 291; *Aster-Reiniger Joint Venture v. Argos Engineering Co. Ltd.*, (1995) *Arbitration and Dispute Resolution Law Journal* 41.

295 Neil Kaplan, above n. 276.

296 Richard Hill and Ian Walden, above n. 292, 18.

297 For example, the UK Arbitration Act 1996 defines "writing" as including an agreement made orally, provided that there is reference to a written form which itself contains an agreement to arbitrate.

298 Article II(2) of the New York Convention defines an arbitration agreement as follows: "The term 'agreement in writing' shall include an arbitral clause in a contract or an arbitration agreement, signed by the parties or contained in an exchange of letters or telegrams".

299 *Proctor v. Schellenberg* [2003] 2 WWR 621.

300 *Aloe Vera of America, Inc. v. Asianic Food (S) Pte Ltd* [2006] 3 SLR(R) 174 at [16].

301 *Denmark Skibstekniske Konsulenter A/S I Likvidation v. Ultrapolis 2000 Investments Ltd* [2010] 3 SLR 661 at [24].

302 The opposite way of interpreting this writing requirement is to treat Article VII(2) as a maximum standard that precludes contracting states from requiring additional or more demanding formal requirements under national law.

303 Article VII(1) of the New York Convention contains a "more favourable right" provision, which will be discussed in Chapter 5 of this book. Article VII(1) reads: "[T]he provisions of the present Convention shall not … deprive any interested party of any right he may have to avail himself of an arbitral award in the manner and to the extent allowed by the law or the treaties of the country where such award is sought to be relied upon".

This liberal and purposive approach to interpreting the "written" requirement has also been codified into UNCITRAL's interpretative instrument, which recommended that: "[A]rticle II, paragraph 2 [of the New York Convention] be applied recognising that the circumstances described therein are not exhaustive".[304] More modern international legal instruments such as the UNCITRAL Model Law on Electronic Commerce,[305] the UNCITRAL Model Law on Electronic Signatures[306] and the United Nations Convention on the Use of Electronic Communications in International Contracts[307] are reflective of or in line with this interpretative approach. A more flexible way of applying the "writing" requirement in the New York Convention is consistent with widespread business usage as well as the pro-enforcement thrust of the New York Convention.

However, the legislative flexibility towards email and other modern means of communications technology does not guarantee that courts in these jurisdictions will recognise and enforce arbitration agreements that are not in a written document signed by the parties or otherwise contained in an exchange of letters or telegrams,[308] even though it has been argued that courts are usually able to find a way to modernise the judicial interpretation and there is no need to cure the problem at the legislative level.[309] The practical difficulty often arises when an arbitral agreement that is regarded as valid by an arbitral tribunal or a court in one country (the place of arbitration) may not be treated as valid by the court in the enforcement country.[310] This uncertainty justifies a "legislative" solution that the New York Convention be amended to overcome the judicial multiplicity.[311] For the time being, the Model Law maintains the requirement for

304 'Recommendation Regarding the Interpretation of Article II, Paragraph 2, and Article VII, Paragraph 1, of the Convention on the Recognition and Enforcement of Foreign Arbitral Awards, done in New York, 10 June 1958, Adopted by the United Nations Commission on International Trade Law on 7 July 2006 at its thirty-ninth session', in *Convention on the Recognition and Enforcement of Foreign Arbitral Awards (New York 1958)*, UN Sales No. M.08.V.5, p. 18, para. 1.

305 *UNCITRAL Model Law on Electronic Commerce with Guide to Enactment 1996 with additional article 5 bis as adopted in 1998*, UN Sales No. E.99.V.4.

306 *UNCITRAL Model Law on Electronic Signatures with Guide to Enactment 2001,* UN Sales No. E.02.V.8.

307 *United Nations Convention on the Use of Electronic Communications in International Contracts*, UN Sales No. E.07.V.2.

308 See the decision of the Second Circuit Court of Appeals in *Kahn Lucas Lancaster Inc. v. Lark International Ltd* 186 F.3d 210 (1999); the US District Court of the Southern District of California's decision in *Chloe Z Fishing Co. Inc. v. Odyssey Re (London) Ltd* 109 F. Supp. 2d 1048 (2000) and the US District Court of the Western District of Washington's decision in *Bothell and Bothell v. Hitachi Zosen Corp.* 97 F. Supp. 2d 1048 (2000).

309 Gerold Herrmann, 'Does the World Need Additional Uniform Legislation on Arbitration?', (1999) 15(3) *Arb. Int'l* 215.

310 *Decision of the Halogaland Court of Appeal (Norway),* 16 August 1999, XXVII *Yearbook* (2002) 519.

311 Neil Kaplan, above n. 276, 44–45.

an arbitration agreement to be "in writing" but sets out a more modern definition of this term. It recognises agreements made by any means of telecommunication "which provides a record of the agreement", and an exchange of statements of claim and defence in which "the existence of an agreement is alleged by one party and not denied by another".[312] Therefore, for the purposes of the Model Law, the requirement for writing may be satisfied by any means of telecommunication that provides "a record of the agreement".

The "writing" requirement is always accompanied by the requirement for signatures. The function of a signature is the key point in understanding the "writing" requirement. A signature no doubt helps identify the parties in the transaction and specify the date of documents in the final form. The New York Convention expressly requires the signature of both parties where arbitration is conducted on the basis of an arbitral agreement or clause.[313] This requirement for signatures has given rise to problems in some states[314] because several courts' decisions have strictly requested the signature in the arbitration agreement or clause.[315] The arbitration clause or agreement may be problematic if it is concluded by the exchange of email messages or electronic data interchange. In reality, notarisation, or authentication and authoritative dating of documents can now be easily implemented by using digital signatures and "digital notary" services available online. Digital signatures can be employed if desired, and agreements should also be allowed by clicking on a "submit", "transmit" or "accept" button on a web site. Modern cryptography can also provide very secure methods of authentication. These new technologies may satisfy the signature requirement where there is exchange by other means of communications. In the modern laws of arbitration the traditional signature requirement will disappear.

According to the doctrine of party autonomy, the parties to arbitration are entitled to the use of electronic means for the conduct of arbitral proceedings, which, however, brings legal difficulties as to the "place of arbitration". Most legal systems attach great importance to the place of arbitration, since it is the connecting point to the governing law of arbitration. The arbitration laws of most countries recognise that some hearings, testimony of witnesses, meetings of arbitrators, or even actual signature or publication of award must occur in the "place of arbitration". The importance of the "place of arbitration" is also

---

312 Model Law, Article 7(2).

313 New York Convention, Article II(2).

314 Michael Marks Cohen, '"Agreements in Writing": Notes in the Margin of the Sixth Goff Lecture', (1997) 13(3) *Arb. Int'l* 273.

315 William Laurence Craig, William W. Park and Jan Paulsson, *International Chamber of Commerce Arbitration*, Dobbs Ferry, NY: Oceana Publications and ICC Publishing (1990) p. 76; Alan Redfern and Martin Hunter, *Law and Practice of International Commercial Arbitration*, London: Sweet & Maxwell (1991) p. 135; Albert Jan van den Berg, 'The New York Convention: Summary of Court Decisions' in Marc Blessing (ed.), *ASA Special Series No. 9*, Basel: Swiss Arbitration Association (1996).

reflected in determining the law governing the arbitral procedure.[316] The parties to arbitration often fail to specify the governing law of arbitration. In some cases, the governing law of arbitration chosen by the parties to arbitration may not necessarily cover all aspects of the arbitral procedure. The lack of clear rules on the arbitral procedure will require the law of the arbitral seat to govern such issues as the validity of the arbitration agreement and the composition of the arbitral panel. The law of the arbitral seat is also critical in the setting-aside and enforcement of arbitral awards because only a foreign arbitral award can be enforced under the New York Convention.

In this sense, the place of arbitration or arbitration seat will become extremely important if the governing law of arbitration is not specified. In an arbitration case in which each party in the hearing is located in different countries, and arbitrators conduct their deliberations from three different continents and an award is a multimedia report collectively stored in cyberspace, it seems impossible to administer the network from any particular country and any judicial intervention on the network will lead to extraterritorial jurisdiction. The use of email to conduct the proceedings may pose a problem as to where the arbitration takes place because of the lack of an identifiable physical seat of arbitration,[317] which may essentially result in an unseated, stateless or free-floating award.[318] The argument has been made that the physical place of hearings or other proceedings is of little relevance as the seat of arbitration is often the seat chosen by the parties or arbitrators in accordance with applicable arbitration law and rules.[319] The courts seem to support this view by placing little significance on the seat of arbitration in setting aside an arbitral award.[320] This line of argument is consistent with the long-held judicial viewpoint that arbitration can take place anywhere and the seat of arbitration would be the seat specified by the parties in the arbitration agreement or determined in accordance with the applicable arbitration rules regardless of the location of hearings or exchange of writings.[321] More controversially, the use of emails in conducting

---

316 The academic circle has different views on to what extent the parties to arbitration may derogate from the law of the arbitral seat as the governing law of arbitral procedure. Filip De Ly, *International Business Law and Lex Mercatoria*, North Holland, Amsterdam and London: Elsevier Science (1992) pp. 103–05.

317 Alan Redfern and Martin Hunter, *Law and Practice of International Commercial Arbitration*, London: Sweet & Maxwell (1991) p. 95 and n. 89; Jasna Arsic, 'International Commercial Arbitration on the Internet', (1997) 14(4) *J. Int'l Arb.* 219.

318 Gerold Herrmann, above n. 309, 232.

319 Richard Hill, 'The Internet, Electronic Commerce, and Dispute Resolution: Comments', (1997) 14(4) *J. Int'l Arb.* 103.

320 *Bundesgericht, I. Zivilabteilung, T AG v. H Company* (24 March 1997) in [1997] ABA Bulletin 2, 329–30.

321 Philippe Fouchard, Emmanuel Gaillard and Berthold Goldman, *Traite de l'Arbitrage Commercial International,* Paris: Litec (1996) p. 785; No. 1410 and Departmental Advisory Committee on Arbitration Law, '1996 Report on the Arbitration Bill', (1997) 13(3) *Arb. Int'l* 281.

arbitral proceedings may also result in the exercise of extraterritorial jurisdiction over international commercial arbitration, which is contrary to the principles of the New York Convention to encourage the contractual freedom and party autonomy outside of the national judicial system. The use of networks and other modern telecommunication technologies will necessarily lead to the dissolution of national legal boundaries, which may inevitably result in more *forum shopping.*[322] Due to the uncertainty of online arbitration, the suggestion was made to amend the New York Convention and national arbitration laws.[323]

The fact that deliberations take place exclusively online or through a combination of communications media would interfere with the designation of a "seat of arbitration". Designating a formal place of arbitration can be achieved through one traditional solution, that is, *lex loci arbitri.* The place of arbitrator or arbitral panel will be regarded as the place of arbitration. Regardless of the floating or movable nature of the arbitrator or arbitral panel,[324] e-arbitration may increase the difficulty in applying the principle of *lex loci arbitri.* In e-arbitration, the place of arbitration can be determined by the rule of "*lex loci server*", the geographical location of the computer server through which arbitration takes place.[325] Nevertheless, the rule of *lex loci arbitri* or *lex loci server* may not guarantee the certainty of jurisdiction. In *Hiscox v. Outhwaite*, the House of Lords accepted the fact that the arbitral award was signed in Paris constituted the basis for finding that the whole arbitral procedure took place in Paris even though the hearing was held in London.[326]

Along with the popularity of e-commerce, it is foreseeable that the parties in international business will prefer their disputes to be arbitrated through the same medium as which they do their business. Due to the obvious advantages of e-arbitration, arbitral awards made on the Internet will eventually become more common. The purpose of law is not only to regulate the current situation but also to provide feasible solutions to future developments. The traditional "writing"

---

322 Advanced telecommunication facilities allow a meeting of people for the "live" exchange of arguments and testimony. For instance, chat rooms, virtual spaces created by computer software, allow each party working at network-connected computer to type messages that are broadcast to all other parties in the chat room. All parties can read whatever is typed by each party and can make contributions to the conversation by typing his own transcript. "Video conferencing" software further permits multiple parties to hear audio signals and see photos or full motion video.

323 Frank A. Cona, 'Internet Arbitration of International Commercial Disputes', available at http://www.ipwarehouse.com/IP_Library/general_articles/arb_art.htm (1996) and 'Application of Online Systems in Alternative Dispute Resolution', (1997) 45 *Buffalo Law Review* 975.

324 There are several factors which can be used to determine the location of arbitrator, such as the place at the commencement of arbitration procedure, place of domicile or residence of arbitrator, the place of chairman of arbitral panel, the place of arbitral organ, etc.

325 Technically speaking, it may not be desirable to use the choice of "server" as the connecting factor because multiple servers can be used in the process of arbitration and can be anywhere on the globe.

326 [1991] 3 WLR 297; XVII *Yearbook* (1992) 599–609.

requirement and the long established territorially based principles such as *lex loci arbitri* will be no longer suitable for the critical changes brought about by email and/or the Internet.[327] It may be necessary to adapt territorially based arbitration rules into a virtually based environment. A feasible solution may be to re-invent traditional arbitration rules to a virtual type of rules (*e.g.*, rule of virtual place) under the auspices of UNCITRAL, UNIDROIT or other international institutions. The recognition of such rules will lead to a wider or even uniform adoption of these rules, and better facilitation of international trade and business in cyberspace. Without new-generation rules applicable to cyberspace, a new wave of *forum shopping* (or cyber-shopping) will naturally emerge.

2.6. NEW DIRECTION OF THE NEW YORK CONVENTION

When the New York Convention was signed in 1958, shortly after the end of World War II, it represented a major step in the direction of international cooperation. The New York Convention, with a focus on a pro-arbitration bias, has facilitated and safeguarded the enforcement of arbitration agreements and arbitral awards, thereby promoting international trade and commerce. Needless to say, it provides a legal measure, with a certain level of security and reliability, for parties entering into cross-border transactions, and more importantly, for the international community as a whole to achieve harmonisation and rule of law in the fields of commerce and arbitration.

Fifty-five years later, some adjustments to new developments, legal, technological, political and economic, seem to be more than necessary. Immense commitment needs to be made so that sensible solutions to difficult problems will be found. There have arisen two roadmaps offering different routes to deal with the problems and challenges facing the New York Convention. On the one hand, the Hypothetical Draft Convention on the International Enforcement of Arbitral Agreements and Awards was prepared with the aim of replacing the New York Convention.[328] The rationale for this initiative is the existence of a great deal of shortcomings, omissions and inconsistencies when the New York Convention was interpreted and applied by the arbitrating parties, practitioners,

---

327 Matthew Burstein, 'Conflicts on the Net: Choice of Law in Transnational Cyberspace', (1996) 29(1) *Vanderbilt Journal of Transnational Law* 75.

328 Albert Jan van den Berg, 'Hypothetical Draft Convention on the International Enforcement of Arbitration Agreements and Awards – Explanatory Note', in Albert Jan van den Berg (ed.), *50 Years of The New York Convention*, Peace Palace, The Hague: The Permanent Court of Arbitration (2009) pp. 649–678. Also see 11th IBA International Arbitration Day, The New York Convention: 50 Years, 1 February 2008, available at http://www.uncitral.org/pdf/uncitral/NYarbday-programme.pdf.

arbitrators and courts all over the world. The urgency and necessity of these problems call for an overhaul of the entire regime. On the other hand, contrary to the idea of upgrading, reshuffling or modernising the New York Convention is a more "conservative" proposal – that not making any changes to the New York Convention, and keeping the status quo, is more urgent than any reform itself.[329] This proposed approach is premised on the reasoning that embarking on a revision to the New York Convention would result in more losses than gains.[330] The counter arguments to the revision initiative are owing to (i) the difficulty of obtaining unanimous consent from 147 States for the passing of a new convention; and (ii) the lack of serious flaws in the New York Convention that justify such a massive undertaking.[331] While both proposals have some merits, the critical question is how to solve internal and external difficulties or challenges or remedy the problems the New York Convention has encountered in the past fifty-five years. In the second decade of the 21st century, it is fair and reasonable to expect the emergence of one proposal with strong jurisprudential support.

329 Emmanuel Gaillard, 'The Urgency of Not Revising the New York Convention', in Albert Jan van den Berg (ed.), *50 Years of The New York Convention*, Peace Palace, The Hague: The Permanent Court of Arbitration (2009) pp. 689–696.

330 Ibid. 690.

331 Ibid. 691–92.

CHAPTER 3

ENFORCEMENT OF ANNULLED AWARDS, DELOCALISATION AND GAME THEORY

This chapter explores the issue as to whether it is desirable to enforce an award under the New York Convention even though the award has been set aside in the state where it is rendered. This issue is an important one in the context of the New York Convention, other similar conventions,[1] and national arbitration laws[2] modelled on the New York Convention. A thorough analysis of this issue requires an in depth review of Articles V and VII of the New York Convention.

Part 1 of this chapter involves a detailed analysis of the two most well-known cases on this topic. The cases of *Hilmarton* and *Chromalloy* provide an overview of the legal issues involved in this debate, from perspectives of both the state of origin and the state of enforcement. Part 2 discusses the technical and doctrinal sides of the New York Convention, *inter alia*, Articles V and VII. An innovative analysis of legal and policy issues on this topic is contained in Part 3 by reference to game theory, which has been widely adopted in other legal areas within strategic settings. For this purpose, a theoretical introduction of game theory is first provided. Game theory is used to illustrate in Part 4 the doctrinal issue of the degree of independence of arbitral proceedings from the law of the arbitral *situs*. Part 5 touches upon the issue of "delocalisation" which has been partially addressed in Chapter 2. Before the conclusion of this chapter, Part 6 reviews the goals of the New York Convention. A summary follows at the end of the chapter in Part 7.

---

1 For instance, the Inter-American Convention on International Commercial Arbitration (Panama, 30 January 1975), UNCITRAL Model Law on International Commercial Arbitration, as well as some bilateral treaties such as the Convention concerning the Reciprocal Recognition and Enforcement of Judicial Decisions, Arbitral Awards and Authentic Acts in Civil and Commercial Matters (between Belgium and Austria).

2 UK Arbitration Act 1996.

3.1. FROM *HILMARTON* TO *CHROMALLOY*: CASE LAW STUDY

In relation to enforcement of foreign awards which have been set aside in the country of origin on the basis of the New York Convention, Belgium took an early step.[3] In respect of an award rendered in Algiers which an Algerian court had declared to lack force and effect, the Court of First Instance in Brussels held that the New York Convention did not apply to the lack of retroactive effect but granted enforcement, as in its view the decision by the Algerian court was not a decision relating to the setting aside of the award.[4]

In a decision of 26 May 1994, affirmed on 26 July 1995 by the Court of Appeal of Zurich, the Court of First Instance of Affoltern am Albis, Switzerland, refused to grant recognition and enforcement to an award issued in Ankara after an action to set aside the award had been rejected by the Turkish Supreme Court on 14 July 1992. The Court of First Instance noted that the arbitral clause in the underlying contract violated Swiss public policy and rejected the application to enforce the award pursuant to Article V(2)(b) of the New York Convention. The Court reasoned that, under Swiss law, the principle of independence and impartiality of the arbitrator pertains to the fundamental requirements of legal protection and public policy. The Court opined that the fact that (i) the underlying contract contained a clause referring all disputes to Dr E. as a sole arbitrator when Dr E. himself was the drafter of the contract and had been the claimant's lawyer for many years, and (ii) the contract provided that the sole arbitrator could not be removed under any circumstances otherwise there would be a penalty of 1 million Swiss Francs, violated *bonos mores*.[5]

3.1.1. *HILMARTON* SAGA IN FRANCE

The *Hilmarton* case is unprecedented in the sense that various court judgments led to two contradictory arbitral awards between the same parties being recognised in France.[6]

The *Hilmarton* case began with an ICC arbitration in Geneva by Hilmarton Ltd., a UK company, against Omnium de Traitement et de Valorisation ("OTV"), a French company. Hilmarton initiated the arbitration proceedings in order to

---

3 See *Sonatrach v. Ford, Bacon & Davis, Tribunal de Première Instance,* Brussels, 6 December 1988, reported in XV *Yearbook* (1990) 370; *Cour d'Appel,* Brussels, 9 January 1990, cited in William W Park, 'Illusion and Reality in International Forum Selection', (1995) 30 *Texas International Law Journal* 135, 180, n. 274.

4 *Sonatrach v. Ford, Bacon & Davis, Tribunal de Première Instance*, Brussels, 6 December 1988, reported in XV *Yearbook* (1990) 370–377.

5 XXIII *Yearbook* (1998) 754.

6 The two decisions of the Court of Appeal of Versailles of 29 June 1995, (1995) *Rev. Arb.* 639.

recover a fee allegedly owed by OTV under a consultancy agreement between the parties for Hilmarton's services to assist OTV in obtaining a contract in Algeria. In the arbitral proceedings under ICC Rules in Geneva, the sole arbitrator issued an award which denied Hilmarton's claim for payment against OTV on the grounds that the contract was contrary to *bonos mores* and hence unenforceable. OTV then tried to bring the award to France for its exequatur. Prior to the French court's ruling on OTV's application, the award was annulled on 17 November 1989 by the Canton of Geneva's Court of Justice (*Cour de Justice du Canton de Genève*), an appellate court, for "arbitrariness".[7] The annulment was later confirmed on 17 April 1990 by the Swiss Federal Tribunal (*Tribunal fédéral Suisse*), the Swiss supreme court.[8]

Notwithstanding these annulment procedures, the Paris Tribunal of First Instance (*Tribunal de grande instance de Paris)* on 27 February 1990 granted OTV's application for exequatur of the award. The Court of Appeal in Paris (*Cour d'appel de Paris*) upheld the enforcement by rejecting Hilmarton's appeal of the exequatur. This decision was confirmed on 23 March 1994 by the Court of Cassation (*Cour de Cassation*), which held that, as the annulment of an international arbitral award in its country of origin, unlike under Article V of the New York Convention, is not grounds for refusing its enforcement in France under French law,[9] OTV was entitled to avail itself of the more favourable internal law in France and hence obtain the enforcement of the award pursuant to Article VII of the New York Convention.[10] France eventually enforced a Swiss award previously vacated by a Swiss court.[11] In summary, the French court's approach was that a vacated award is nonetheless enforceable in France provided it satisfies French standards of enforcing arbitral awards.[12]

After the annulment of the ICC award by the Swiss Federal Tribunal, the dispute was resubmitted by Hilmarton to a new arbitration panel against OTV in Geneva for the same claim. A new award was rendered on 10 April 1992 but in favour of Hilmarton this time.[13] Contrary to the finding of the first arbitrator, a different arbitrator decided that the contract in question was enforceable and

---

7 Judgment of 17 November 1989, (1993) *Rev. Arb.* 214.

8 Judgment of 17 April 1990, (1993) *Rev. Arb.* 315.

9 Article 1502 of the New Code of Civil Procedure.

10 Article VII of the New York Convention states that: "[t]he provisions of the present Convention shall not … deprive any interested party of any right he may have to avail himself of an arbitral award in the manner and to the extent allowed by the law … of the country where such award is sought to be relied upon".

11 *Société Hilmarton v Société OTV.*

12 See *Hilmarton Ltd. v. Omnium de traitement et de valorization (OTV), Cour de cassation*, 23 March 1994, in XX *Yearbook* (1998) 663 (enforcing an award in France that was vacated in Switzerland).

13 See Hamid G. Gharavi, 'A Nightmare Called Hilmarton', (1997) 12(9) *Mealey's International Arbitration Report* 22; Hamid G. Gharavi, 'Enforcing Set Aside Awards: France's Controversial Steps Beyond the New York Convention', (1996) 6 *Journal of Transnational Law and Politics* 93.

Hilmarton was entitled to its fee from OTV. Hilmarton then went with the new award to France to request its exequatur, which was granted by a court of first instance in Nanterre, notwithstanding the existing order of exequatur in respect of the first award. OTV then filed an appeal in respect of the new order of exequatur before the Versailles Court of Appeal and argued that the second order of exequatur was inconsistent with the first one, which had already acquired *res judicata* effect. Moreover, the recognition of two contradictory decisions would be contrary to French international public policy. The Versailles Court of Appeal rejected the appeal.[14] The second order of exequatur was left intact. The French approach to the recognition and enforcement of foreign arbitral awards precluded consideration of the revised status of the first award, and left Hilmarton with no possibility of recovery in France on the second, arguably "correct" award.

3.1.2. *CHROMALLOY* CASE: A DILEMMA

The US District Court for the District of Columbia in *In the Matter of the Arbitration of Certain Controversies between Chromalloy Aeroservices and the Arab Republic of Egypt* allowed the enforcement of a foreign arbitral award set aside in its country of origin.[15] The decision is often described as "a major victory for supporters of binding international arbitration".[16]

The dispute arose out of a contract between Egypt and Chromalloy Aeroservices Inc., a US company, as to the supply, maintenance and repair of a fleet of Sea King Commando helicopters owned by the Egyptian Air Force. The total contract price was US$ 32 million, with a commencement date of 3 December 1988 and a three-year term. On 2 December 1991, the Egyptian Air Force informed Chromalloy that it regarded the contract as terminated because the three-year term had expired. Chromalloy, however, responded to the Egyptian Air Force that it did "not accept the notice of cancellation" (attributing the delay of performance to obstruction by the Air Force) and commenced arbitration proceedings.[17] The contract contained an arbitration clause according to which the dispute was to be submitted for arbitration pursuant to "Egyptian laws" and with "Cairo [as] the seat of court of arbitration". Furthermore, the parties agreed that the decision was to be final and binding and could not be made subject to any appeal or other recourse. Chromalloy initiated the arbitration proceedings against Egypt for damages caused by the alleged

14 See two decisions of the Court of Appeal of Versailles of 29 June 1995, (1995) *Rev. Arb.* 639.

15 *Chromalloy Aeroservices v. Arab Republic of Egypt*, 939 F. Supp. 907 (D.D.C. 1996).

16 See Gary H. Sampliner, 'Enforcement of Foreign Arbitral Awards after Annulment in their Country of Origin', (1996) 11 *Mealey's Int'l Arb. Rep.* 22.

17 *Chromalloy Aero-Services v. Arab Republic of Egypt*, (1996) 11(8) *Mealey's Int'l Arb. Rep.* C-1; XXII *Yearbook* (1997) 1001–12.

improper termination of the contract. The arbitral tribunal on 24 August 1994 rendered an award in favour of Chromalloy,[18] and a majority of the arbitral tribunal found Egypt to be liable for the breach of contract to Chromalloy for approximately US$ 16 million plus interest. Although the Egyptian party participated without objection in the arbitration proceeding, it subsequently applied to the Court of Appeal of Cairo to set aside the award under Article 53(1) of the Egyptian Law of Arbitration 1994 which was largely modelled on the UNCITRAL Model Law.[19]

According to Article 53(1) of the Egyptian Law of Arbitration 1994, Egypt argued that the arbitral tribunal had mistakenly "applied the rules of the Egyptian Civil Code to the exclusion of the administrative law" of Egypt,[20] although the contract in question was allegedly an administrative contract. The Court of Appeal in Cairo agreed with that contention and later set aside the award in December 1995 on the grounds that the arbitral tribunal "failed to apply the law agreed upon by the parties to govern the subject matter in dispute". The court opined that the tribunal should have applied Egyptian administrative law, which was agreed upon by the parties when entering into an arbitration clause. The parties' agreement that the award was not subject to appeal did not preclude the action to vacate the award in Egypt because under Egyptian law the grounds for vacating awards are mandatory rules.[21] Regardless of the annulment of the award by the Court of Appeal in Cairo, Chromalloy sought to enforce the award against assets of Egypt in France and the United States. The US District Court for the District of Columbia decided to enforce the arbitral award. So did the French court.[22]

The District Court reasoned that:

> "Under the New York Convention, 'recognition and enforcement of the award may be refused' if Egypt furnishes to this Court 'proof that … the award has been set aside

---

18 The arbitration in Cairo was conducted by a prestigious international arbitral tribunal under the chairmanship of Dr Robert Briner, a former President of the Iran-US Claims Tribunal.

19 Egypt added as a possible ground for the annulment of an international award made in Egypt, that is, the arbitrator's failure to apply the law that the parties had agreed to the dispute. See Article 53(1)(d).

20 The arbitration panel held that it did not need to decide whether the contract was governed by Egyptian civil or administrative law. *Chromalloy Aero-Services v. Arab Republic of Egypt*, (1996) 11(8) *Mealey's Int'l Arb. Rep.* C-17.

21 Law No. 27 Concerning Arbitration in Civil and Commercial Matters (Egypt), Article 54(1), in Egypt, International Council for Commercial Arbitration, *International Handbook on Commercial Arbitration*, Annex 1–1, 1–14 ("The admissibility of the action for annulment shall not be prevented by the applicant's renouncement of the right to request the annulment of the award prior to the making of the arbitral award").

22 The Paris Court of Appeal allowed the enforcement in France of the arbitral award in *Chromalloy* notwithstanding its annulment in Egypt (judgment of 14 January 1997, (1997) 12 *Mealey's Int'l Arb. Rep.* B-3).

> ... by a competent authority of the country in which, or under the law of which, that award was made.'"[23]

Of particular importance to the discussion here, the District Court continued that:

> "... the award was made in Egypt, under the laws of Egypt, and has been nullified by the court designated by Egypt to review arbitral awards. Thus, the [District] Court *may*, at its discretion, decline to enforce the award. While Article V provides a discretionary standard, Article VII of the Convention requires that, 'the provisions of the present Convention shall not ... deprive any interested party of any right he may have to avail himself of an arbitral award in the manner and to the extent allowed by the law ... of the country where such award is sought to be relied upon'. 9 U.S.C. §201. In other words, under the New York Convention, Chromalloy maintains all rights to the enforcement of this arbitral award that it would have in the absence of the New York Convention. Accordingly, the Court finds that, if the New York Convention did not exist, the US Federal Arbitration Act would provide Chromalloy with a legitimate claim to enforcement of this arbitral award. See 9 U.S.C.§§1–14."[24]

The Court noted that "the parties agreed to apply Egyptian Law to the arbitration, but, more important, they agreed that the arbitration ends with the decision of the arbitral panel".[25] This seems to suggest that the Court considered the arbitral award final and binding and therefore valid under US law.[26]

As to Egypt's request to grant *res judicata* effect, the Court's analysis of the relevant US law is confined to an examination of the grounds for vacating an award in the US under Section 10 of the Federal Arbitration Act, although, on the face of it, Section 10 has nothing to do with the enforcement of foreign arbitral awards. Section 10 merely sets out the grounds upon which an award made in the United States may be vacated, which are not the same as the grounds for refusing enforcement.[27] The Court therefore concluded "that the award is valid as a matter of US law". The Court further concluded that it "need not grant *res judicata* effect to the decision of the Egyptian Court of Appeal at Cairo".[28] As a result, the Court granted Chromalloy's petition to recognise and enforce the arbitral award.

---

23 New York Convention, Articles A(1) and V(1)(e).

24 XXII *Yearbook* (1997) 1001.

25 939 F. Supp. at 912.

26 See the decision in 939 F. Supp. 907, in Arthur T. von Mehren, Tibor Varady and John J. Barcelo, *International Commercial Arbitration: A Transnational Perspective*, St. Paul: West Group (1999) p. 784.

27 It is doubtful that a US court would have had any authority to vacate the arbitrators' award as the award was made in Egypt under Egyptian law. See *International Standard Electric Corporation v. Bridas Sociedad Anonima Petrolera*, Industrial Commercial, 745 F. Supp. 172 (SDNY 1990).

28 939 F. Supp. at 914.

The right to appeal is one aspect of *Chromalloy* that calls for analysis. In refusing to recognise the judgment of the Egyptian Court, the US District Court held that the parties were precluded from applying to the Egyptian courts for the award's annulment and that, in making such an application, Egypt repudiated "its solemn promise to abide by the results of the arbitration". The District Court observed that the parties had provided in the arbitration clause that the award could not "be made subject to any appeal or other recourse". The Court then brought the public policy issue into consideration. In the District Court's view, "the US public policy in favour of final and binding arbitration of commercial disputes is unmistakable, and supported by treaty, by statute, and by case law. The Federal Arbitration Act and the implementation of the Convention in the same year by amendment to the Federal Arbitration Act, demonstrate that there is an emphatic federal policy in favour of arbitral dispute resolution, particularly in the field of international commerce. A decision by this Court to recognise the decision of the Egyptian court would violate this clear US public policy".[29]

In *Chromalloy*, the District Court enforced the award even though it had been vacated in Egypt. However, other courts in the United States have not followed its lead. In two subsequent cases,[30] notwithstanding *Chromalloy*, the United States Court of Appeals for the Second Circuit and the United States District Court for the Southern District of New York refused to enforce vacated awards and distinguished *Chromalloy* on the grounds that in neither case did the parties violate any promise not to appeal the arbitration award.[31] Therefore, enforcement of a vacated award, or the *Chromalloy* approach, is not the entirety of the US approach. Rather, more precisely, the *Chromalloy* ruling was conditional upon (i) the arbitration clause explicitly providing that any award "cannot be made subject to any appeal or other recourse"; and (ii) by having the award vacated, Egypt failed to abide by the arbitral award. The other two cases, however, did not contain such elements.[32] In this sense, the *Chromalloy* approach, indeed, treats vacated awards as unenforceable in the US, unless the award satisfies American standards for enforcing arbitral awards *and* the parties agreed in their contract that the arbitral award would not be subject to

---

29 939 F. Supp. at 913.

30 *Baker Marine (Nig.) Ltd. v. Chevron (Nig.) Ltd.*, 191 F. 3d 194 (2nd Cir. 1999); *Spier v. Calzaturificio Tecnica, S.p.A.*, 71 F. Supp. 2d 279, *on reargument*, 77 F. Supp. 2d 405 (SDNY 1999).

31 In *Baker Marine*, the court of appeals also distinguished *Chromalloy* on the grounds that "Baker Marine is not a United States citizen, and it did not initially seek confirmation of the award in the United States". These distinctions seem unimportant. The court emphasised that the agreement language in *Chromalloy*, prohibiting appeal of the arbitral award, was not present in *Baker Marine*. Also, the parties' agreement did not mention US arbitration law, which shall play no role in the resolution of the dispute. Without better reasons than those given by *Baker Marine*, the Court was unwilling to apply US law under Article VII. 191 F. 3d at 197 n. 3.

32 *Baker Marine*, 191 F.3d at 197 n. 3; *Spier*, 71 F. Supp. 2d at 287, and 191 F. 3d at 197 n. 3.

appeal.[33] In substance, the *Chromalloy* approach recognises party autonomy to solve their disputes through the contractual arrangement. Accordingly, the parties can choose either to contract for judicial supervision of the arbitral award at the arbitral *situs* or to opt for a rule of enforceability in the enforcement *situs*.

Even in the US, the *Chromalloy* ruling's precedential value is limited. The court in the case of *Baker Marine* did not enforce an annulled foreign arbitral award because "[that] would seriously undermine finality and regularly produce conflicting judgment".[34] By the same token, the court in the *Spier* case held that the party seeking enforcement could not "introduce domestic US law, statutory or decisional, into the case at bar through the vehicle of Article VII of the Convention".[35] The court in the *Termorio* case refused to follow *Chromalloy* and called it "questionable on the merits and distinguishable on the fact".[36]

3.1.3. WHY ARE *HILMARTON* AND *CHROMALLOY* SPECIAL?

There is no uniform practice of enforcing an annulled award in major jurisdictions. The "traditional approach" is that an award vacated by the court of in a country with primary jurisdiction is not enforceable in another jurisdiction.[37] Germany adopts this approach whereby the courts usually refuse

---

33 See *In re Chromalloy Aeroservices*, 939 F. Supp. 907 (D.D.C. 1996); *Baker Marine (Nig.) Ltd. v. Chevron (Nig.) Ltd.*, 191 F.3d 194 (2nd Cir. 1999); *Spier v. Calzaturificio Tecnica, S.p.A.*, 71 F. Supp. 2d 279, *on reargument*, 77 F. Supp. 2d 405 (SDNY 1999).

34 *Baker Marine (NIG) Ltd. v. Chevron (NIG) Ltd.* 191 F.3d 194 (decided in 1999), XXIVa *Yearbook* (1999) 909 (US Court of Appeal for the 2nd Circuit US), at 197.

35 *Spier v. Calzaturificio Tecnica, S.p.A.* 71 F. Supp. 2d 279 (decided in 1999) XVIII *Yearbook* (2000) 159 (US District Court for the Southern District of New York, US), at 288.

36 *Termorio S.A., E.S.P v. Electrificadora Del Atlantico S.A., E.S.P.*, 421 F. Supp. 2d 87 (decided in 2006), XXXI *Yearbook* (2006), 1457 (US District Court for the District of Columbia, US), affirmed 487 F.3d 928 (decided in 2007) (US Court of Appeals for the District of Columbia Circuit, US).

37 It must be clarified in the beginning that an award annulled by a court in a country with secondary jurisdiction can still be enforced without too much trouble. In these countries, the parties to arbitration can contest whether that State should enforce the arbitral awards but not vacate them. The New York Convention is clear in the sense that "the country in which, or under the [arbitration] law of which, [an] award was made". This was clearly demonstrated in the case of *Karaha Bodas Co LLC v. Perusahaan Pertambangan Minyak Dan Gas Bumi Negara* 364 F. 3d 287 (5th Cir. 2004). Karaha Bodas Co obtained an arbitral award made in Geneva, Switzerland against Perusahaan. KBC applied to enforce the award in numerous jurisdictions. After failing in its appeal before the Swiss court, Pertamina obtained an order from an Indonesian court annulling the award and sought to rely on the decision to resist enforcement in the US and Hong Kong. The challenges to enforcement in the US and Hong Kong failed. *Karaha Bodas Co LLC v. Perusahaan Pertambangan Minyak Dan Gas Bumi Negara* [2003] HKCU 1. The US Fifth Circuit Court rejected the defence by saying that only a court in a country with primary jurisdiction over an arbitral award may annul that award. In Canadian

the recognition and enforcement of awards in a manner that is responsive to the review process by national courts of the *situs*.[38] An annulled award is highly unlikely to be enforced in Singapore.[39] Against this backdrop, cases like *Hilmarton* and *Chromalloy* were said to be unusual decisions where enforcement was permitted notwithstanding the fact that the awards had been set aside in the jurisdictions where they were made.[40]

There are some rare exceptions. Enforcement may be granted under English law where the award has in fact been annulled in the country in which it was made.[41] Compared to others, France is well-known in that it has declared an award enforceable notwithstanding the fact that the award had been set aside in the country of origin. Under French law, arbitral awards shall be recognised if their existence is proven by the party relying on the award and the award satisfies French standards of enforcing arbitral awards.[42] The existence of an arbitral

---

case of *Powerex Corp. v. Alcan Inc.*, Justice Brown explicitly identified the appropriate court for the setting aside proceeding as one of the threshold tests the parties must satisfy while applying to seek an adjournment. *Powerex Corp. v. Alcan Inc.* [2004] BCSC 876 at [24] to [26].

38 See Erica Smith, 'Vacated Arbitral Awards: Recognition and Enforcement Outside the Country of Origin', (2002) 20 *Boston University International Law Journal* 355. Also see *Zivilprozebetaordnung* (German Code of Civil Procedure), Section 1061 of which states that "if the award is set aside abroad after having been declared enforceable, the application for setting aside the declaration of enforceability may be made". An unofficial translation by the German Institute of Arbitration (DIS) and the German Federal Ministry of Justice is available at http://www.dis-arb.de.

39 Chan Leng Sun, *Singapore Law on Arbitral Awards,* Singapore: Academy Publishing (2011) para. 7.99.

40 Simon Greenberg, Christopher Kee and J. Romesh Weeramantry, *International Commercial Arbitration: An Asia-Pacific Perspective*, Cambridge: Cambridge University Press (2011) p. 70.

41 Article 103(2) of the UK Arbitration Act 1996; J.C.T. Chuah, *Law of International Trade*, London: Sweet & Maxwell (1998) p. 413; Lawrence Collins *et al., Dicey and Morris on The Conflicts of Laws*, London: Sweet & Maxwell (13th edn. 2000) p. 640; Roy Goode, 'The Role of the *Lex Loci Arbitri* in International Commercial Arbitration', (2001) 17 *J. Int'l Arb.* 19.

42 Article 1498 of the French Code of Civil Procedure. See also *Hilmarton Ltd. v. Omnium de traitement et de valorization (OTV) (Cour de cassation,* 23 March 1994), in XX *Yearbook* (1995) 663 (enforcing an award in France that was vacated in Switzerland); *Arab Republic of Egypt v. Chromalloy Aeroservices Inc.* (*Cour d'Appel* Paris, 14 January 1997), in XXII *Yearbook* (1997) 691; *Pabalk Ticaret Sirketi v. Norsolar S.A.* (*Cour de cassation,* 9 November 1984), in (1985) 24 ILM 360 (enforcing in France an award vacated in part in Austria); *SEEE v. Yugoslavia* (*Cour d'Appel* Rouen, 13 November 1984), in (1985) 24 ILM 345 (enforcing in France an award vacated in Switzerland); *Ministère Tunisien de l'Equipment v. Société Bec Frères* (*Cour d'Appel,* 24 February 1994) (enforcing in France an award vacated in Tunisia), cited in David W. Rivkin, 'The Enforcement of Awards Nullified in the Country of Origin: The American Experience', in Albert Jan van den Berg (ed.), *Improving the Efficiency of Arbitration Agreement and Awards: 40 Years of Application of The New York Convention,* The Hague: Kluwer Law International (1999) p. 534; see also *Sonatrach v. Ford, Bacon & Davis Inc.* (*Tribunal de Première Instance,* Brussels, 6 December 1988), in XV *Yearbook* (1990) 370 (enforcing in Belgium an award vacated in Algiers). See Emmanuel Gaillard, 'Enforcement of Awards Set Aside in the Country of Origin: The French Experience', in Albert Jan van den Berg (ed.), *Improving The Efficiency of Arbitration Agreement and Awards: 40 Years of Application of the New York Convention,* The Hague: Kluwer Law International (1999) p. 505; Bruno Leurent, 'Reflections on the International Effectiveness of Arbitration Awards', (1996)

award is established by the production of its original text together with the arbitration agreement, or by copies of the said documents accompanied by proof of their authenticity.[43] In *Putrabali*, the *Cour de cassation* held that "an international award, which does not belong to any state legal system, is an international decision of justice and its validity must be examined according to the applicable rules of the country where its recognition and enforcement are sought".[44] Following this line of logic, French courts enforced an award set aside in England.[45] As a general rule, sophisticated commercial parties have the certainty that enforcement in France is a possibility under French law (rather than the New York Convention) regardless of annulment elsewhere.[46]

3.2. ARTICLES V AND VII OF THE NEW YORK CONVENTION

The US District Court which decided to enforce the *Chromalloy* award, notwithstanding its annulment by the Egyptian courts, based its decision upon Articles V and VII of the New York Convention acting in tandem. One critical issue here is how to interpret Articles V and VII of the New York Convention, which requires various approaches.

Article V(1)(e) of the New York Convention reads:

> 1. Recognition and enforcement of the award may be refused … only if the party against which the award is invoked furnishes to the competent authority where the recognition and enforcement are sought, proof that:
>
> …

12 *Arb. Int'l* 269, 270; Albert Jan van den Berg, 'New York Convention of 1958 Consolidated Commentary Cases Reported in Vol. XVII (1992)', XIX *Yearbook* (1995) 475 and 592 ("If an award is set aside in the country of origin, a party still can try its luck in France").

43 Article 1499 of the French Code of Civil Procedure.

44 The case was quite similar to *Hilmarton* and *Chromalloy*. There were two awards in this case. The first award was annulled by the High Court of London and the second one was issued with the opposite outcome. Both awards were sought to be enforced in France by the claimant and respondent. The *Cour de cassation* enforced the first annulled award and refused to accept the losing party's argument that the enforcement of this award would be contrary to international public policy. The Court then refused to enforce the second one on the basis that *res judicata* was attached to the decision enforcing the first award which was incompatible with the second one.

45 *Société PT Putrabali Adyamulia v. Société Rene Holding et Société Mnogutia Est Epices* (2007) *Rev. Arb.* 507.

46 See Philippe Fouchard, 'L'Arbitrage International en France après le Decret du 12 mai 1981', (1982) 109 *J.D.I.* 374, 419. That level of certainty should be acceptable for planning business contracts decisions. See Friedrich A. Hayek, *The Road to Serfdom*, London: Routledge Press (1944) Ch. VI; Joseph Raz, 'The Rule of Law and its Virtue', (1977) 93 *Law Quarterly Review* 195, 198, 204 and 210.

(e) The award has not yet become binding on the parties, or has been set aside or suspended by a competent authority of the country in which, or under the law of which, that award was made ...

At first glance, Article V(1)(e) of the New York Convention does not seem to be compatible with the whole regime of the New York Convention. Subsections (a) to (d) lay down grounds for refusal of enforcement which are intrinsic to the awards or proceedings and authorise the court in the enforcement forum to examine afresh the regularity or legality of the awards. They work in tandem and form a semi-integrated legal regime. Subsection (e), however, refers to an extrinsic factor, annulment by a court in the jurisdiction in which or under the law of which the award is rendered. The finality of an award is the major concern of this subsection, which indirectly or potentially opens the door for judicial review over the content of the award or the arbitral proceedings. The court may guard against lack of due process, fraud, corruption or other improper conduct on the part of the arbitral tribunal. However, the New York Convention has not made it clear how far this judicial control should go and whether it should be limited to the first grounds in subsections (a) to (d). On the other hand, if one takes the view that the New York Convention authorises a judge to exercise his discretion to grant enforcement of an award when one (or more) of the grounds listed in Article V(1)(a) to (d) is present, then it must be appreciated that the Convention also authorises a judge to exercise his discretion to grant enforcement of an award that has been set aside on the grounds of Article V(1)(e).[47] The text of the Convention may not justify treating point (e) any differently from points (a) to (d). If Article V, as a whole, is read as leaving a discretion to the court for granting enforcement to foreign awards notwithstanding the presence of one (or more) of the grounds listed therein, enforcement of annulled awards would also be permissible and warranted by the virtue of Article V.

Technically speaking, Article V(1)(e) is a *lex specialis* on *res judicata*. Its logic is premised on some specifics. First, the courts of the country of rendition and/or of the country of the law under which arbitration is conducted and the courts of the country of enforcement are internationally competent. These two countries must adopt similar substantive and/or procedural standards in the field of international commercial arbitration. The similarity or compatible levels of the court systems, even though in different jurisdictions, may facilitate the recognition and enforcement of arbitral awards of each other. Second, the annulment proceedings have a collateral effect under Article V(1)(e),[48] which has to be reflected in another jurisdiction where an award is sought to be enforced, so that the refusal of enforcement of an annulled award can be legitimised.

---

47 Albert Jan van den Berg holds a different view. See Albert Jan van den Berg, 'Enforcement of Annulled Awards?', (1998) 9(2) *The ICC International Court of Arbitration Bulletin* 18.

48 This is consistent with the scope defined in Article I of the New York Convention.

Third, the realisation of the collateral effect depends on the exertion of the discretionary power by the enforcing court according to its own standards. The collateral effect would not be materialised in an enforcement forum if the court in the enforcement forum uses its "may"-created discretion under Article V(1)(e), or Article VII where Article V(1) fails to apply in part or in its entirety,[49] to grant enforcement.

A collateral effect needs a margin of residual discretion to be given to an enforcing court. It has been argued that Article V leaves discretion to the judge in the country where enforcement of an arbitral award is sought even when one (or more) of the grounds listed in Article V(1) is present.[50] The debate that has been and is still intense among commentators focuses on whether the word "may" really means the enforcing judge has a discretionary power to grant enforcement despite the presence of one or several grounds listed in Article V(1), or whether it actually means "shall" and leaves the enforcing judge no discretionary power at all. The argument arises because Article V is not formulated in the same way in all of the equally authentic versions of the New York Convention. Among the five languages, the Russian, Chinese and Spanish versions provide inconclusive first-hand evidence for or against the English version.[51] There is an obvious linguistic discrepancy between the English and French versions of the New York Convention.[52] The English version provides in Article V(1) that "recognition and enforcement of the award may be refused" so that the competent courts of the state in which enforcement is sought are not obliged to refuse enforcement if the provision of subsection (e) or any other item of Article V is fulfilled, but leaves the discretion with the enforcing court. The French text reads as "*La reconnaissance et l'execution de la sentence ne seront refusée ... que si ...*" which could be understood to exclude any discretion.[53] One

49 Adam Samuel, *Jurisdictional Problems in International Commercial Arbitration*, Zurich: Schulthess (1989) pp. 307–308.

50 Albert Jan van den Berg, *The New York Arbitration Convention of 1958: Towards a Uniform Judicial Interpretation*, The Hague: Kluwer Law and Taxation Publishers (1981) p. 265, and Jan Paulsson, 'Enforcing Arbitral Awards Notwithstanding a Local Standard Annulment', (1998) 9(1) *The ICC International Court of Arbitration Bulletin* 14–17.

51 The Russian and Spanish versions, like the English version, use the expressions "may be refused". The Chinese version on this point is relatively neutral and the term can be interpreted as either "may be" or "can be".

52 Another well-known linguistic discrepancy in the New York Convention is Article II(2). The English version reads that "the term 'agreement in writing' shall include certain forms of agreement" whilst the French text apparently limits the valid forms of agreement in writing to those enumerated in Article II(2) by providing that "*On entend par 'convention écrite'* [those forms]". The Spanish and Chinese versions are closer to the French version. The Russian version sides with the English version.

53 In the French version, Article V provides that "enforcement will not be refused ... unless...", from which it might be inferred that enforcement will be refused if one of the stated grounds applies. On other occasions, the English and French versions seem to be close. For instance, the English text of Article V(2) reads that "recognition and enforcement of an arbitral award may also be refused;" while the French text of Article V(2) reads: "*La reconnaissance et l'execution d'une sentence arbitrale pourront aussi être refusés si ...*", which literally means

argument is that the word "may" indeed enables but does not mandate the enforcing court to use its own discretion in enforcing or refusing to enforce an annulled award, if one of those grounds is found to be in existence in a case. Although the English and French versions differ from each other, to some extent they are compatible. As the English text stands, a margin of discretion is accommodated, which is reflected in its indicative mood and negative formulation.[54] It was argued that in four of five authentic versions of the New York Convention, a textual interpretation leads to the conclusion that the discretion is given and can be exercised under Article V.[55] The counter argument, however, is that the English text "may be refused only if…" is the same as "may not be refused unless", which exactly resembles the French version. Therefore, even the English text leaves no room for discretion as it addresses exclusively the situation where none of the grounds exists whereby the judge must or shall enforce an arbitral award.[56]

The New York Convention did not explicitly state that the discretion conferred upon the courts to enforce awards notwithstanding the presence of one (or more) of the grounds listed in Article V(1) does not apply to the grounds in Article V(1)(e). The reading of the New York Convention itself cannot demonstrate the drafters' intention as to the enforceability of the annulled awards. It may be reasonable to assume that there was no such intention in the first place.[57] A very early draft of the New York Convention produced by the ICC used the word "shall"[58] which was later replaced by the word "may" in the version prepared by the UN Economic and Social Council.[59] The Federal Republic of Germany then recommended that "shall" be re-introduced in the draft Article IV.[60] A joint French-German-Dutch working group further

that "recognition and enforcement of an arbitral award may also be refused if …" The suggestion that the French text of the Convention is mandatory rather than permissive is demolished by some commentators. See Jan Paulsson, 'May or Must under the New York Convention: An Exercise in Syntax and Linguistics', (1998) 14 *Arb. Int'l* 227.

54 The French term did not provide "*auxquels cas elles seront refusés*" at the end of Article V(1). This way of interpretation is also supported by Article 27 of the Brussels Convention on Jurisdiction and Enforcement of Judgment in Civil and Commercial Matters, the English version of which similarly reads "shall not be recognised if" while the French text adopted "*ne sont pas reconnues si*".

55 Jan Paulsson, above n. 50.

56 Gerold Herrmann, 'Does the World Need Additional Uniform Legislation on Arbitration?', (1999) 15(3) *Arb. Int'l* 235.

57 In the drafting process no one actually discussed and even less thought of this question, as it was obvious that refusal of enforcement would follow if any of the V(1) grounds for refusal was proved.

58 See ICC, *Enforcement of International Arbitral Awards* (Brochure No. 174, 1953). Also see UN Doc. E/C.2/373 (1955): Preliminary Draft Convention (1953), Article IV, reproduced in (1998) 9 *ICC International Court of Arbitration Bulletin* 35.

59 See Draft Convention, UN Doc. E/2704 and Corr. 1 (1955, original: English) at 7, Article IV. The primary motivation behind the New York Convention was to do away with the requirement of finality. See Albert Jan van den Berg, above n. 50, pp. 333–334.

60 See UN Doc. E/Conf.26/L.34 (28 May 1958).

re-phrased Article IV to its current wording.[61] This brief historical overview may help confirm the intention of the parties in incorporating the word "may" in the draft so that a compromise can be made among various parties. In this case, there is no room to dismiss it *pro non scripta*. The *travaux préparatoires* of the Convention are of limited help in that they only indicate that the inclusion of the word "may" was not accidental. Even though various understandings (or misunderstandings) arise from five different language versions, a linguistic analysis may lead to a conclusion that a margin of discretion is allowed under the New York Convention because four out of five versions adopt the word "may" in the context and the French version did not clearly and directly contradict this interpretation.[62] This proposition seems consistent with the rule of interpretation of customary law contained in Article 33(4) of the Vienna Convention on the Law of Treaties.[63] The rule requires that the interpretation of the meaning "which best reconciles the texts" should prevail, if an application of Articles 31 and 32 does not resolve the difference as in the present situation.

The word "may" in Article V(1) is permissive in inviting the judge in the country of enforcement to form his own view and to make a decision on the elements that have or should have been reviewed and decided upon by the court of rendition that decided on the action to set aside the award. It also preserves the discretion of the court to defer enforcement in certain circumstances in addition to those contemplated in Article V and where such deferral would warrant the quality of foreign judgments or domestic awards.[64] The principle of "maximal efficiency"[65] and the generally accepted standpoint that the New York Convention favours enforcement of foreign arbitral awards also support this "discretionary" interpretation.

A large number of cases increasingly support the view that the discretion is granted to the court to a certain extent.[66] The High Court in Hong Kong has had opportunities to apply the "residual" discretion in several cases.[67] Recent case

61 See UN Doc. E/Conf.26/L.40 (2 June 1958, original: French).

62 There is no other discrepancy between the English and French texts where the Convention provides for some discretion. Article VI reads "may" or "*peut*".

63 The Vienna Convention on the Law of Treaties is the foundational legal source in interpreting any international law issues in relation to the treaties.

64 See *Far Eastern Shipping Co. v. AKP Sovcomflot* [1995] 1 Lloyd's Rep 520, XXI *Yearbook* (1996) 699; *Hewlett-Packard Inc v. Berg*, 61 F.3d 101 (1st Cir. 1995), vacating 867 F. Supp. 1126 (D Mass. 1994). See Richard Allan Horning, 'Deferral of Enforcement of New York Convention Awards for Prudential Reasons', [1997] 1 *Int. A.L.R.* 3.

65 The principle of "maximum efficiency" is consistent with the pro-enforcement bias and applies to the scenario in which two or more treaties could be applicable. In this case, the courts should apply the treaty under which the award is enforceable. Article VII of the New York Convention.

66 See *China Agrobusiness Development Corporation v. Balli Trading* [1998] 2 Lloyd's Rep 76, 79.

67 See *Hong Kong High Court, Qinhuangdao v. Million Basic Company*, XIX *Yearbook* (1994) 675, 676. For a general discussion of "residual discretion", see Albert Jan van den Berg, 'Residual Discretion and Validity of the Arbitration Agreement in the Enforcement of Arbitral Awards under the New York Convention of 1958', in Teo Keang Sood et al (eds.),

law seems to offer clearer views. The UK Supreme Court, for instance, has recognised the existence of discretion but attached a condition to the exercise of such discretion, *i.e.*, where the award is made by an arbitration panel without jurisdiction.[68] Canadian courts have applied a "balance of convenience and irreparable harm" test in deciding whether or not the court should adjourn the enforcement proceedings by looking into a number of factors, "including the estimated time to complete the case in the originating jurisdiction; whether the party opposing enforcement is merely delaying the inevitable; whether a court in the originating jurisdiction has already refused to set aside the award; the availability of security and the possibility of resisting enforcement to undertake diligent prosecution of the action in the originating jurisdiction".[69]

Case law in this field is still uncertain and sometimes controversial.[70] Mance LJ expressed his doubt over an open discretion to allow enforcement despite proof of one of the grounds of non-enforcement.[71] The same doubt was also expressed by Lord Phillips CJ elsewhere.[72] Even if judges are sympathetic to the idea of attaching a discretionary force to "may", they prefer to be restrictive in exercising such discretion in reality. In addition, Lord Mance was inclined to consider other circumstances, "which might on some recognisable legal principle affect the *prima facie* right to have enforcement or recognition refused", such as estoppel.[73] Lord Collins added one example where the foreign law that renders the arbitration agreement invalid outrages the English court's "sense of justice or decency".[74]

The uncertainty and controversy in case law is derived from the lack of guidance in the New York Convention as to when and how such discretion should be used. In other words, the problem still rests on the uncertain scope of such discretion.[75] The enforcement forum may encounter difficulty in

---

Current Legal Issues in International Commercial Litigation, Singapore: National University of Singapore Press (1997) p. 327, pp. 330–336.

68 *Dallah Real Estate and Tourism Holding Company v. The Ministry of Religious Affairs, Government of Pakistan* [2010] UKSC 46.

69 *Powerex Corp v. Alcan Inc* [2004] BCSC 876 at [24] to [26].

70 *Dallah Real Estate and Tourism Holding Company v. The Ministry of Religious Affairs, Government of Pakistan* [2010] UKSC 46, *per* Lord Mance at [67] to [68], and *per* Lord Collins at [126] to [128]; for the Court of Appeal's comments, see *Dallah Real Estate and Tourism Holding Company v. The Ministry of Religious Affairs, Government of Pakistan* [2009] EWCA Civ 755, at [75] and [89]. Also see *Société Hilmarton v. Société Omnium de Traitment et de Valorisation* (*Cour de Cassation*, France, 23 March 1994), (1994) *Rev. Arb.*, 327; *In the Matter of the Arbitration of Certain Controversies Between Chromalloy Aeroservices and the Arab Republic of Egypt* 939 F. Supp. 907 (DDC 1996).

71 *Dardana Ltd v. Yukos Oil Company* [2002] EWCA Civ 543, [2002] 2 Lloyd's Rep 326.

72 *Kanoria v. Guinness* [2006] EWCA Civ 222, [2006] 1 Lloyd's Rep 701; *Dardana Ltd. v. Yukos Oil Company* [2002] EWCA Civ 543, [2002] Lloyd's Rep 326.

73 *Dardana Ltd v. Yukos Oil Company* [2002] EWCA Civ 543, [2002] 2 Lloyd's Rep 326 at [68].

74 Ibid. at [128].

75 *Dallah Real Estate and Tourism Holding Company v. The Ministry of Religious Affairs, Government of Pakistan* [2010] UKSC 46, *per* Lord Mance at [67] to [68], and *per* Lord Collins

circumscribing its obligations and prescribing limits for its exercise.[76] As rightly pointed out,[77] this uncertainty may require a court to confront a number of "vexatious questions" in deciding how to exercise its discretion. The diversity of judicial practices owing to different legal and judicial cultures may further cause a higher degree of uncertainty and unpredictability, which the New York Convention tried to eliminate eventually by standardising or harmonising the grounds for refusal of recognition and enforcement.[78] This can be the counter argument against the idea of granting discretion to the courts in the enforcement jurisdiction. As a matter of fact, this line of argument was adopted by German courts.[79]

Article VII gives some guidance in this regard. The material part of this Article reads:

> The provisions of the present Convention shall not ... deprive any interested party of any right he may have to avail himself of an arbitral award in the manner and to the extent allowed by the law or the treaties of the country where such award is sought to be relied upon.

This is the "most favourable right" provision in the New York Convention, which has a wider *ratione personae* scope of application than Article V(1) in that it applies to "any interested party" rather than merely the award creditor.[80] Article VII grants the beneficiary of the award an option to elect the more favourable course of action for the purpose of enforcing an arbitral award. Consequently, the award creditor or any interested party is able to rely upon a more favourable domestic law (of the forum) or international treaty (applicable in the territory where recognition and enforcement are sought), instead of relying upon the New

---

at [126] to [128]; *Dallah Real Estate and Tourism Holding Company v. The Ministry of Religious Affairs, Government of Pakistan* [2009] EWCA Civ 755 at [75] and [89].

76 An equivalent example is the European Convention on Human Rights (Convention for the Protection of Human Rights and Fundamental Freedoms (Rome, 4 November 1959) (1955) 213 UNTS 221), which contains such general guidelines in the second paragraph of Articles 7–11. Such paragraph has been held by the European Commission and Court of Human Rights to provide a "margin of appreciation", reviewed by the European institutions, in favour of the domestic implementing authorities.

77 See Jan Paulsson, 'Rediscovering the New York Convention: Further Reflections on *Chromalloy*', (1997) 12(4) *Mealey's Int'l Arb. Rep.* 20.

78 Ulrich Hass, 'Convention on Recognition and Enforcement of Foreign Arbitral Awards, New York 1958', in Frank-Bernd Weigand (ed.), *Practitioner's Handbook on International Arbitration*, Munich: C.H. Beck (2002) p. 401.

79 *OLG Düsseldorf* (decided by Dusseldorf Court of Appeal, 21 July 2004), XXXII *Yearbook* (2007) 315, 318–321.

80 A closer reading of Articles I and III may indicate that the scope may not be that broad. See Albert Jan van den Berg, above n. 50, 82–83, who is of view that "any party" in practice is only the party seeking enforcement. The drafting of Article VII appears to be a product of a copy-and-paste exercise from Article 5 of the 1927 Geneva Convention. See Convention on the Execution of Foreign Arbitral Awards (Geneva, 26 September 1927) (1929) 92 LNTS 301.

York Convention, for enforcement.[81] Article VII has been cited by some courts, such as the German Supreme Court, in enforcing some arbitral awards.[82] In *Hilmarton*, French courts enforced the annulled award on the basis of the more arbitration-friendly French law (instead of the New York Convention) due to the "more favourable right" provision, Article VII(1) of the New York Convention, which allows French courts to opt out of the New York Convention in order to honour and enforce the award.

It appears logical to assume that if the word "may" in Article V were to mean "shall", leaving no discretion to the court in the country of enforcement, Article VII could not have been included in the New York Convention as it stands. That is to say, if a court were compelled to refuse enforcement of an award in the presence of one of the grounds listed in Article V, these grounds listed in Article V would be of such importance that awards so affected by any grounds must never be enforced in any jurisdiction. Therefore, the New York Convention would not have authorised any interested party to take advantage of Article VII to bypass the requirements of Article V. Rather, a provision may have been included in Article VII to the effect that it could not be used to circumvent the requirements of Article V, since these requirements were strictly mandatory.[83] The UNCITRAL Working Group's early attempt to remove uncertainty in the form of court discretion by introducing the word "shall" into Article 36(1) in the Model Law 2006 may easily defeat this analysis[84] even though it eventually reverted to "may be refused" in the final wording for the sake of consistency with the New York Convention.[85]

The New York Convention would be better understood as a discretionary authority allowing the court to enforce an award even if one of the grounds in Article V appears, since, under Article VII, the enforcement forum may enforce an annulled award if its law does not include the grounds of Article V(1)(e) as a basis for refusing enforcement.[86] This line of thinking is consistent with the judicial opinions in some countries such as the US District Court for the District of Columbia in *Chromalloy* and the Hong Kong High Court's *Paklito*

81 The "more favourable right" principle derogates from the classical rules of international law on conflicting treaties (*lex posterior* and *lex specialis*). Pursuant to the "more favourable right" principle, the more favourable treaty prevails.

82 *Jacob Boss v. Sohne KG*, judgment of 14 April 1988, *Bundesgerichtshof*, Ger., 1988 RIW 642.

83 It may be more incoherent if the New York Convention had set mandatory rules requiring that enforcement of awards must be refused in the presence of certain grounds (listed in Article V), and then further accepted enforcement of awards (according to Article VII and the law or the treaty of the country where enforcement is sought) despite the presence of the same grounds.

84 *UNCITRAL Model Law on International Commercial Arbitration, 1985 with amendments as adopted in 2006*, UN Sales No. E.08.V.4.

85 Peter Binder, *International Commercial Arbitration and Conciliation in UNCITRAL Model Law Jurisdictions*, London: Sweet & Maxwell (3rd edn. 2009) pp. 423–424.

86 See French and Belgian law, as well as *Nouveau Code de Procedure Civile*, Article 1502 (France), *Code Judiciaire*, Article 1723 (Belgium).

decision.[87] At this juncture, the Convention does not provide for a partial application of its provisions. If an award falls into the category of an "arbitral award" as defined in the Convention, then all provisions of the Convention apply to that award regardless of the fact that a ruling has been granted that is detrimental to the legality of the award. It is legitimate for a contracting state to grant enforcement to all Convention awards provided that they do not violate the public policy rule in Article VII of the Convention. Annulled awards, like any other awards, shall benefit from the "most favourable rule" provision in Article VII. This rule refers the enforcement court to the more favourable provisions in its domestic law or the treaty its state belongs to, and further makes those domestic provisions prevail over the New York Convention.[88] Therefore, survival of an annulled award in one domestic legal system is legally sensible.[89]

3.3. LEGAL NATURE OF AN ANNULLED AWARD

One critical issue here is what exactly the nature of an annulled award is. There are two approaches. First, it can be examined by defining the existence of an annulled award. A more liberal interpretation of Article V does not solve this problem, which was raised at the outset, namely, the award's continued existence after it has been annulled. Does an annulment by the courts of the state of rendition leave behind a truncated award? It has been argued that an arbitral award that has been set aside is no longer in existence.[90] The second approach is an analysis of the text of the New York Convention, which may furnish us with a more concrete answer.

A fundamental difference between a judgment and an arbitral award is that, while the former results from the legal order of a country where it is rendered, the latter is a private act, chosen by private parties, and is a product of the procedure decided by the agreement reached by the parties to arbitration in solving their dispute through arbitration. Hence, whereas the root of a judgment is in the legal system of a specific country, the root of arbitration more or less lies

---

87 See XIX *Yearbook* (1994) 664.

88 Article V(2)(b) directly grants courts the power to refuse enforcement of an award if it would be contrary to the public policy of the enforcement forum.

89 This pro-enforcement argument may not prevail over a pro-arbitration argument derived from the New York Convention itself. The primary purpose of the New York Convention is to promote arbitration as an effective means of resolving international commercial disputes, while the secondary (but direct) purpose is to reach a degree of uniformity among contracting states on the subject of refusing recognition and enforcement of arbitral awards. The over-emphasis on the "more favourable right" provision may be formalistic and counter-productive, and would compromise the harmony the New York Convention is supposed to achieve because the "more favourable right" provision may potentially exclude the New York Convention as the applicable rule.

90 Albert Jan van den Berg, above n. 47, 15–16.

in the agreement of participating parties to arbitration. Logically, the court in a given case has exclusive jurisdiction to confirm judgments rendered by lower courts of the same state, thereby making a judgment final and binding. In this sense, it is rather doubtful whether the courts of any state have jurisdiction to grant international effect to a decision setting aside an award rendered in international arbitration merely because that award is rendered in its territory.

In the framework of international commercial arbitration, an award is foremost a national award drawing its legal existence from a national judicial monopoly.[91] This is apparent if arbitration is viewed from the standpoint of its effectiveness. It has been rightly observed that "arbitration cannot exist outside of a legal context. An agreement to arbitrate, the rules governing the arbitral process, and the arbitral award itself can be given effect only by reference to some body of law prescribing such effect".[92] In *Chromalloy*, the award formerly drew its legal existence from a concession by the Egyptian judicial monopoly. Being deprived of such existence under Egyptian law, the award may freely float through time and space until one jurisdiction shows respect and mercy and grants enforcement. Then, an award may have not existed from the beginning if it is annulled in its home jurisdiction. Some commentators, however, have disagreed with this view. Instead, it has been opined that, "as long as the courts of country X have properly established their jurisdiction in a given case, they may conclude – and have indeed done so for generations, as any glimpse of a textbook on conflicts of law will confirm – that a contract or a marriage or an adoption is valid and produces effects in country X, even if the relevant act had its origin in country Y and has been annulled there. The same is true for arbitral awards".[93] Parallels drawn between contracts, marriages or adoptions and arbitral awards, or more specifically, arbitral agreements, are actually less convincing. Legal relationships such as contracts, marriages or adoptions are mainly based on reciprocal promises or subject to state regulations, whilst arbitration derives its effectiveness mainly from consent of the parties and concessions of the national judicial monopoly. Therefore, the nature of a vacated award must be considered and determined in a unique context, a home jurisdiction where an independent arbitration regime and a national judicial system co-exist. Due to its independence and the judicial scrutiny available in the national court system,[94] the jurisdictional role of the arbitration panel which renders an arbitral award needs to be respected and recognised. This seems to suggest that an annulled award is a truncated award ceasing to exist because the court ultimately vacates it.

---

91 See Eric Schwartz, 'A Comment on *Chromalloy* and *Hilmarton*, à l'americaine', (1997) 14(2) *J. Int'l Arb.* 128.

92 See Hans Smit, 'A-National Arbitration', (1989) 63 *Tulane Law Review* 631.

93 Jan Paulsson, above n. 50.

94 See William Laurence Craig, 'Uses and Abuses of Appeal from Awards', (1988) 4(3) *Arb. Int'l* 174, 180.

A simple review of the New York Convention, however, may lead to an opposite conclusion. The term "award" as defined by Article I(2) of the New York Convention not only includes awards made by arbitrators, but also refers to awards made by permanent bodies to which the parties have submitted. Neither Article I nor any other Articles in the New York Convention exclude annulled awards from the category of awards for the purpose of the Convention and to which the Convention applies. Rather, the Convention applies to all awards as defined in Article I. The only article in the Convention dealing with annulled awards is Article V(1) under which an annulled "award" is regarded as not being different from other awards which may have a defect contemplated in Article V(1). For this provision to make any sense, it must be read as applying to annulled awards, which are regarded as an "award" within the ambit of the New York Convention, otherwise the second part of Article V(1)(e) could not have been part of Article V.

The foregoing discussion seems to have left a critical issue unresolved, that is, whether an annulled award actually amounts to a continuing award recognisable in other contracting states to the New York Convention. The *Chromalloy* Court failed to address the issue of an award's continuing legal existence.[95] Some commentators have argued that the New York Convention itself may breathe new life into the body of an annulled award.[96] The rationale behind this argument is that Article V of the New York Convention allows but does not require a rejection of foreign arbitral awards that fall under any of its five subparagraphs, due to the language that "recognition and enforcement may be refused … only if" one of the subparagraphs applies.[97] Enforcement notwithstanding annulment elsewhere is a matter left to the State members to the Convention. The same discretionary power is passed on to the judge(s) of a state that incorporates the rules of the New York Convention into its own law.[98] *Chromalloy* appears to also adopt this view. From this, it appears that the annulment does not bring an award to a definite end in the New York Convention regime. Instead, an annulled award may still be "alive" or revived at a later stage, and is effective in other jurisdictions except its home jurisdiction. To a certain extent, the New York Convention saves a "dying" award and creates a new legal foundation for it. In any event, the New York Convention merely deals with an existing and effective award but does not create a brand new award. It is only the home jurisdiction that has the legitimate and natural power to grant a *raison d'être* in the field of monopolised judicial powers.

The process through which the Court arrived at its decision in *Chromalloy* was relatively straightforward. First, the Court observed that it was not obliged

95 See Eric Schwartz, above n. 91, 131.

96 See Pierre Lastenouse, 'Why Setting Aside an Arbitral Award is not Enough to Remove it from the International Scene', (1999) 16(2) *J. Int'l Arb.* 31.

97 See Article V of the New York Convention.

98 See Jan Paulsson, above n. 50, 20, and Gary H. Sampliner, above n. 16, 22.

under Article V of the New York Convention to refuse enforcement of an award that had been set aside. Rather, Article V permitted, but did not require, the Court to do so. The Court then noted that, under Article VII of the Convention, it was required to enforce the award if Chromalloy had a legitimate claim for enforcement under the US Federal Arbitration Act. The Court drew this conclusion from a detailed comparison of the grounds for vacating an award under the FAA and the reasons for the award's annulment by the Egyptian Court. Finally it considered whether the Egyptian Court's annulment decision, which it assumed to be proper under Egyptian law, should be recognised as a valid foreign judgment in the United States. Nevertheless, the Court decided that it should not recognise the judgment because US public policy favours enforcement of the award made in Egypt and the Court would violate "its solemn promise to abide by the results of the arbitration" if it recognised the Egyptian judgment to vacate the arbitral award. The Court then proceeded to conclude that the award was "valid as a matter of US law" and should be enforced in the United States. All that the District Court established was that the award would not have been set aside under US law if it had been made in the US. The line of reasoning indicated that the Court did not touch upon the residual issue, *i.e.*, the nature or existence of an annulled arbitral award. Instead, it focused on the legal effect of an annulled award in rendering and enforcing jurisdiction. This analytical approach is obviously innovative in light of its extraterritorial nature. The *Chromalloy* case shows the possibility of enforcing an annulled award, which may be revived and become re-existent if some other jurisdictions never regard it dead or invalid in its home jurisdiction according to domestic laws. The annulled award is thus furnished with legal effect deriving from the monopoly embodied in the US Constitution's Article III. Ultimately, the award became a US title and, arguably, is outside of the scope of the New York Convention.

The conclusions drawn from different analytical angles seem to contradict each other. The nature of arbitration and arbitral awards may emphasise the fact that an award is always effective in a specific jurisdiction and has some legal effect locally. Accordingly, an award may no longer be effective once it is set aside. On the other hand, it makes more sense if the nature of arbitral awards can be recognised in the international framework under the New York Convention, which effectively brings an award, even though vacated, into a multiple-jurisdiction regime, with the aim of promoting party autonomy in cross-border commercial transactions. An award annulled in its home jurisdiction may still be effective in another jurisdiction which follows the route set by the New York Convention. Nevertheless, the New York Convention only refers to or governs effective awards. An ineffective award may not fall within the New York Convention regime at all. Moreover, the Convention is, at least on a technical level, silent on the continuing existence of an award. Even though international commercial arbitration is now firmly based on the New York

Convention, which, as a matter of fact, has changed the whole landscape of arbitration, the effect of an arbitral award may still be restricted within a domestic boundary. Therefore, an annulled award may have not been in existence from the beginning.

3.4. GAME THEORY AND ITS APPLICATION

3.4.1. PRISONER'S DILEMMA AND STRATEGIC BEHAVIOUR

Game theory is a set of tools describing and predicting strategic behaviour.[99] Strategic settings are various scenarios in which two or more decision-makers are involved and one party takes account of its counterpart's behaviour in order to make its own decision. Accordingly, one decision may be linked to another decision, and vice versa. Oligopolistic industries are normally natural settings for strategic interactions. For instance, in the aviation industry, whether Virgin Airlines will cut fares may depend on how British Airways will take action, and vice versa.

A simple example of game theory is the widely discussed Prisoner's Dilemma[100] in which there are two players (*i.e.*, prisoners) and several sets of choices or strategies (usually two contrasting options, *i.e.*, either to be silent or to confess). The outcomes of the game would be in four different strategy pairs as demonstrated in the simplified diagram below.

Diagram: Prisoner's Dilemma

		Prisoner 2	
		Silent	Confess
Prisoner 1	Silent	–2, –2	–10, 0
	Confess	0, –10	–6, –6

In this scenario, two prisoners both have committed a serious crime. However, the prosecutor cannot convict either of them of this crime without extracting at least one confession. The prosecutor is likely to convict them both of a lesser offence without the confession of either. The prosecutor tells each prisoner that

99 See generally Richard A. Posner, *Economic Analysis of Law*, New York: Aspen Publishers, Inc. (5th edn. 1998) pp. 21–24.

100 The Prisoner's Dilemma was originally framed by Merrill Flood and Melvin Dresher in 1950. Albert W. Tucker formalised the game with prison sentence payoffs and gave it the name of "Prisoner's Dilemma". See generally William Poundstone, *Prisoner's Dilemma*, New York: Doubleday (1992).

both of them will be convicted for the lesser offence and each will go to prison for two years if neither confesses. This outcome is represented in the upper left cell. However, if one of them confesses but the other does not, the prisoner who confesses will go free but the other will be tried for the serious crime and given the maximum penalty of ten years in prison. This applies to both prisoners and is represented in the lower left and upper right cells. Alternatively, if both confess, the prosecutor will prosecute both for the serious crime, but not ask for the maximum penalty and both prisoners will go to prison for six years. This is the lower right cell.[101]

Obviously, each prisoner wants to spend as little time as possible in prison. It is also clear that each is indifferent as to how much time the other will spend in prison.[102] Without any communication in advance, each prisoner must make a decision as to his confession strategy without knowing what his counterpart will do. In such a game, it is known to both prisoners that each is better off confessing regardless of what the other does. Likely, each prisoner may presume that he may better off confessing if the other prisoner were to decide to keep silent. This strategy would avoid his two-year period in prison. The other possibility is that one is also better off confessing if the other prisoner confesses. As unpleasant as serving a six-year sentence may be, serving a ten-year sentence is even worse. Whatever the other person does, one would be better off confessing. It is very likely that both prisoners will follow this line of thinking. Likely, the chance to see both prisoners confess is very high.

The outcome of the Prisoner's Dilemma seems counterintuitive because the prisoners would have been better off if both had remained silent. The underlying rationale of the game is that the players are both selfish. Even if each prisoner erroneously believed that the other was altruistic and would confess, the same outcome will arise, given the assumption that the prisoners care only for themselves. If a prisoner believes the other would remain silent, confessing is one way of avoiding prison altogether, so the best outcome will be the same. The result is not at all odd once it is recognised that the prisoners lack a means of committing themselves to remaining silent. As long as the two prisoners cannot reach any agreement and as long as their only concern is their own interest (*i.e.*, time spent in prison), their individual interests will lead them to confess even though they are jointly better off remaining silent.

The fundamentals of the Prisoner's Dilemma originate from the incongruence between private benefit and collective good. Individually rational decision-making may possibly result in a collective disaster. It is generally accepted that individuals attempt to maximise utility or profits subject to

101 For details, see http://plato.stanford.edu/entries/prisoner-dilemma/ and http://en.wikipedia.org/wiki/Prisoner's_dilemma.

102 A simplified case ignores any factors such as altruism.

constraints.[103] The fundamental strategic interdependence that game theory tries to address is that rational actors need to be concerned about the actions of others in a game-theoretic setting. It is also seen as one of the main theoretical rationales for government intrusion into private decision-making. In a legal context, the Prisoner's Dilemma is adopted as a theoretical basis for legislation and judicial cooperation. A sizable amount of legal literature has grown out of applying the discipline of the microeconomist's marginal analysis to legal issues in a range of regulatory domains, such as securities regulations, corporate governance, banking supervision, labour standards and insolvency and bankruptcy regimes. Many legal settings can be represented as normal form games and can be solved by identifying dominant interests and strategies. One of the topics more relevant in the context of the New York Convention is the inter-jurisdictional regulatory competition, which could trigger a welfare-reducing "race to the bottom".

3.4.2. RACE TO THE BOTTOM IN REGULATORY CONTEXTS – SOME EXAMPLES INVOLVING STATES

The "race to the bottom" label has been applied in a wide variety of regulatory contexts such as races to the bottom caused by interstate competition over corporate[104] and banking charters,[105] securities regulations,[106] labour standards,[107] antitrust rules[108] and, in a broader sense, over programs of

103 As Harold D. Lasswell and Myres S. McDougal pointed out, "game theory provides a mathematical technique for determining the ratio of the various strategies open to a player that maximizes his value position and minimizes his losses". Harold D. Lasswell and Myres S. McDougal, *Jurisprudence for a Free Society: Studies in Law, Science, and Policy*, New Haven: New Haven Press/Martinus Nijhoff Publishers (1992) Ch. 4.

104 See Elisa Westfield, 'Globalisation, Governance, and Multinational Enterprise Responsibility: Corporate Code of Conduct in the 21st Century', (2002) 42 *Virginia Journal of International Law* 1075.

105 The major cause for this race is that, in a federal system, the Federal Deposit Insurance Corporation (FDIC) charges banks a deposit insurance premium that is independent of the bank's risk of default. See Henry N. Butler and Jonathan R. Macey, 'The Myth of Competition in the Dual Banking System', (1988) 73 *Cornell Law Review* 680, 714.

106 See Norman S. Poser, 'The Stock Exchanges of the United States and Europe: Automation, Globalisation, and Consolidation', (2001) 22 *University of Pennsylvania Journal of International Economic Law* 497; John C. Coffee, Jr., 'Racing Towards The Top? The Impact of Cross-Listings and Stock Market Competition on International Corporate Governance', (2002) 102 *Colum. L. Rev.* 1757.

107 See John Hancock, 'Finding A Solution: How To Have Free Trade While Upholding International Labour Standards', (2002) 11 *MSU-DCL Journal of International Law* 23.

108 See Karl M. Meessen, 'An International Antitrust Challenge: Competition of Competition Laws', (1989) 10 *Northwestern Journal of International Law and Business* 17; Anu Piilola, 'Assessing Theories of Global Governance: A Case Study of International Antitrust Regulation', (2003) 30 *Stanford Journal of International Law* 207.

economic redistribution.[109] In addition to commercial laws, game theory has also been utilised in the research of public law areas such as environment protection, which is of more relevance to our topic given the involvement of state governments in regulating commercial arbitration.

Under public laws, the fundamental issue is how to regulate self-interest among states and to allocate responsibilities between various states to deal with related social and policy issues such as protection of ecology (*i.e.*, numerous classes of terrain, wildlife and plant life) and natural resources, control of air quality and waste, soil and energy preservation, water regulation, attraction of tourism, promotion of leisure business, agriculture, population, industrial, transportation, culture and sustainable development policies.[110] The analysis here indeed has a more general application whenever states impose costs on the physical assets or even intangible lawful rights of individuals and firms in order to promote the welfare of their citizens.

The underlying theory of the effects of interstate competition over economic redistributions, principally welfare programs, relies heavily on the mobility of individuals and firms across jurisdictions. The idea is that wealthy individuals or firms, who would bear the burden of paying the cost of economic redistribution, are likely to move to jurisdictions with lower taxes and business costs, and consequently lower welfare payments. By contrast, welfare beneficiaries would move to jurisdictions that impose higher taxes in order to finance generous welfare programs. Such mobility of human capital is phrased as "voting with the feet".[111] Ultimately, the jurisdiction with higher tax rates would lose all its wealthy residents or firms, its tax base would shrink or even be destroyed, and there would be no funds for welfare recipients.[112] Migration patterns in the United States have revealed that the states with the lowest tax, spending and regulatory burdens are the winners in the contest for the human capital.[113]

---

109 See Richard L. Revesz, 'Rehabilitating Interstate Competition: Rethinking the "Race-to-the-Bottom" Rationale for Federal Environmental Regulation', (1992) 67 *NYU Law Review* 1210; Richard L. Revesz, 'Federalism and Interstate Environmental Externalities', (1996) 144 *University of Pennsylvania Law Review* 2341; Richard L. Revesz, 'The Race to the Bottom and Federal Environmental Regulation: A Response to Critics', (1997) 82 *Minnesota Law Review* 535; Richard L. Revesz, 'Federalism and Environmental Regulation: Lessons for the European Union and the International Community', (1997) 83 *Virginia Law Review* 1331.

110 See Casey J. Caldwell, 'The Black Diamond of Harmonisation: The Alpine Convention as a Model for Balance Competing Objectives in the European Union', (2003) 21 *B.U. Int'l L.J.* 137.

111 Arthur Laffer and Stephen Moore, 'The (Tax) War between the States', *The Wall Street Journal*, 11 December 2007 at 19.

112 See Paul E. Peterson, *The Price of Federalism*, Washington, DC: Brookings Institution (1995) pp. 108–28; Jacques LeBeouf, 'The Economics of Federalism and the Proper Scope of the Federal Commerce Power', (1994) 31 *San Diego Law Review* 555, 579; Sheryll D. Cashin, 'Federalism, Welfare Reform and the Minority Poor: Accounting for the Tyranny of State Majorities', (1999) 99 *Colum. L. Rev.* 552, 598–99.

113 Arthur Laffer and Stephen Moore, above n. 111.

This phenomenon constitutes a picture of the "race to the bottom" game.[114] In reality, consumers are free to choose according to the quality and price of what is offered by suppliers of a product or service. This simple proposition is also applied to the supply of legal systems or laws amongst the competing states. Empirical research in the United States has indicated that the states with the highest taxes and spending and the most intrusive regulations may attract fewer people and create less job growth than the more economically and legally free states.[115] This was the same in France and Germany in the last two decades of the twentieth century.[116] In globalisation, free movement in goods and services matches free movement in legal rules. A state seeking to attract investors to set up businesses there, and thereby obtaining chartering fees and service business, as well as increasing social welfare and benefits to local labourers and residents, will offer a regulatory regime most attractive to investors, shareholders or managers, who will naturally prefer to make risk choices that are unconstrained by a rigid regulatory regime. Accordingly, states may have incentives to set sub-optimally lax regulatory regimes.

In the area of environmental protection, states usually use air or water quality standards or waste control standards as a tool to control pollution. Occasionally a state could meet ambient standards but export a great deal of pollution to downwind states (through tall stacks or location near the interstate borders). As a matter of fact, a state might meet its ambient standards precisely because it exports a large proportion of its pollution. The problem of interstate externalities arises because of a combination of inadequate information, public process bias and traditional economic externalities. In most instances of economic externality, costs and benefits are not directly priced by the market system and therefore not necessarily considered by a market actor.[117] In this scenario, the benefits of the polluting activity are enjoyed by one actor but the costs are externalised on other actors or societies as a whole.[118] For instance, Country A unilaterally takes protective measures to protect the environment in order for its citizens to enjoy clean water and air. Country B sends pollution to State A and obtains the labour and fiscal benefits of the economic activity that

---

114 See Steven G. Calabresi, 'The Era of Big Government Is Over', (1998) 50 *Stanford Law Review* 1015, 1019; Anne L. Alstott, 'Federalism and U.S. Social Welfare Policy: Fundamental Change and New Uncertainties', (1996) 2 *Columbia Journal of European Law* 441, 452; Thomas S. Ulen, 'Economic and Public Choice Forces in Federalism', (1998) 6 *George Mason Law Review* 921, 935–36; Jerry L. Mashaw and Dylan S. Calsyn, 'Block Grants, Entitlements, and Federalism: A Conceptual Map of Contested Terrain', (1996) 14 *Yale Law and Policy Review* 297, 321.

115 Arthur Laffer and Stephen Moore, above n. 111.

116 Ibid.

117 See Henry N. Butler and Jonathan R. Macey, 'Externalities and the Matching Principle: The Case for Reallocating Environmental Regulatory Authority', (1996) 14 *Yale L. & Pol'y Rev.* 29.

118 See Daniel C. Esty, 'Environmental Protection in the Information Age', (2004) 79 *NYU L. Rev.* 115, 154.

generates the pollution but does not suffer the full costs of the activity. Country A, with regulation, indeed pays for a public good enjoyed by the non-regulating states. Country A tries to get Country B to make similar efforts on the basis that B's citizens should not free ride off Country A's efforts.[119] This scenario gives rise to the proposition that, in an effort to induce geographically mobile firms to locate or relocate within their jurisdictions, states may lower environmental standards so as to bring in other benefits such as additional jobs and higher tax revenues.[120] Such a "race to the bottom" scenario calls for federal governance and adjudication, a regulatory mechanism with the aim of internalising externalised costs,[121] balancing competing interests, and dividing the responsibility for environmental regulation among states.

Compacts or treaties can serve an indicative and binding function, which can change Country B's law and governance behaviour so as to effectively redistribute the costs of providing clean water and air or innovative technologies. By increasing the efficiency and distributive justice and lowering transactions costs,[122] co-ordinated standards such as those for air quality and emissions can be used as the primary policy tools to facilitate cross-jurisdictional trade and investment. It then follows that co-ordinated standards are essential to address public policy problems that span political boundaries and to control interstate externalities. This has been a particularly important motivation for passing international treaties (*i.e.*, environmental protection conventions), whose main purpose is to address problems that exist between multiple jurisdictions and that cannot be adequately ameliorated without centralised policies binding on more than one political jurisdiction. Although international compacts, treaties or conventions involve transaction costs due to the fact that the uniform ratification and approval process by the national legislative bodies is a political obstacle course, they are nevertheless useful in overcoming the self-interests of the national states.

More recently, advocates of centralised regulation have devoted considerable attention to the public choice rationale for federal intervention, which notes that the US- or EU-like cooperative horizontal regulation is a must because state political processes lead to the systematic imperfect public governance problems such as local protectionism at the state level. For example, pro-environmental

---

119 See Adriana Lieders, 'A New Chapter in Brazil's Oil Industry: Opening the Market While Protecting the Environment', (2001) 13 *Georgetown International Environmental Law Review* 781, 797.

120 See R. van den Bergh, M. Faure and J. Lefevere, 'The Subsidiarity Principle in European Environmental Law: An Economic Analysis', in E. Eide and R. van den Bergh (eds.), *Law and Economics of the Environment*, Oslo: Juridisk Forlag (1996) p. 121; Ludwig Kramer, *E.C. Treaty and Environmental Law*, London: Sweet & Maxwell (2nd edn. 1995) p. 62.

121 See Henry N. Butler and Jonathan R. Macey, above n. 117, 29.

122 See Ronald H. Coase, 'The Problems of Social Cost', (1960) 3 *J. L. & Econ.* 1; Guido Calabresi and A. Douglas Melamed, 'Property Rules, Liability Rules, and Inalienability: One View of the Cathedral', (1972) 85 *Harv. L. Rev.* 1089.

interests can be under-represented or anti-environmental interests over-represented at the state level. Therefore, the centralised regulation promotes the harmonisation of environmental rules and standards and further encourages the establishment of a common market or even a uniform legal regime.[123] The centralised regulation model has some force in the era of globalisation. The harmonisation of environmental standards creates the effect of removing a competitive advantage from such states with lower and non-harmonisable standards[124] and of protecting states from the outside pressure to impose sub-optimally lax environmental standards as a means of attracting jobs and tax revenues.[125] Regional agreements to protect environment and natural resources can help facilitate cooperation and produce positive results without having to expect states to renege on commitments. Nevertheless, the European Union's efforts to control interstate externalities by adopting various standards such as emission standards are criticised. This is largely because primary tools of environmental policy such as standards do not effectively combat the problem of interstate externalities, as these standards do not regulate the number of sources within a state or the location of the sources.[126] Very often, regional and international integration may lead regions, nations, sub-national authorities or even private organisations to compete with one another by enacting or implementing less stringent environmental regulations. Likely, environmental standards may not necessarily function well in reality because the costs of compliance with stricter regulatory standards have not been sufficient to force relatively affluent nations or sub-national authorities to choose between competitiveness and environmental protection. In addition, centralised protective regulations may produce public benefits. Therefore, in some respects, economic openness, capital mobility and liberal trade policy have actually encouraged states to take advantage of other states' environmental protection measures and policies by avoiding adoption and implementation of higher

---

123 A real example is the Convention on the Preservation of the Alps (1991), which was passed by the European Community to recognise the dual threat posed by increasing transport-related pollution and unsustainable levels of tourism to the ecology of the Alpine region. The Convention imposes a series of general obligations on the signatory states to "maintain a comprehensive policy of protection and preservation of the Alps, taking into account in an equitable way the interests of all Alpine States and their Alpine regions, as well as those of the European Economic Community in using resources wisely and exploiting them in a sustainable way".

124 In a perfect competition scenario, the state environmental regulations would be optimal. However, in an imperfect competition model, these regulations could either be overly stringent or overly lax.

125 See R. van den Bergh, M. Faure, and J. Lefevere, above n. 120, 121; Ludwig Kramer, above n. 120, 62.

126 For instance, federal ambient air quality standards are not well-targeted to address the problem of interstate externalities since they are over-inclusive in the sense that they require a state to restrict pollution that has only in-state consequences.

standards than they would have in the absence of increased economic interdependency.

Other critical questions are how to deal with the problem of interstate externalities, and what is the appropriate level of effective public (*i.e.*, environmental) governance. The problem is not simply that competitive pressures will force some jurisdictions to lower their standards due to their fear of being competitively disadvantaged. In the international community, the effectiveness of the centralised regulation and economic integration are different, due to the extreme differences in wealth and economic development in the international community. The presence of inter-jurisdictional externalities has pushed for and justified centralised intervention or even sanctions worldwide, for example, the increased level of centralisation in the environmental protection policy-making within a federal-type framework such as the United States or a common market like the European Union. Coordinated standards or sanctions may be appropriate and necessary if the costs of pollution abatement are perceived as seriously burdening domestic producers *vis-à-vis* their competitors in other political jurisdictions. As a result, there is a need for a viable centralised enforcement mechanism at the "federal" level in the international community.

Take another example. The WTO's dispute resolution mechanism can be understood as an iterated prisoner's dilemma.[127] Any two states will be better off if they can agree to open borders to each other. Domestic interest groups, however, put pressure on the states to restrain trade so as to protect domestic industries from competition and domestic workers from being marginalised. Consequently, each state may adopt some restrictive policies or measures to encourage export but restrict import. Without a treaty, based on their calculation of costs and benefits of protectionism in a single iteration, both sides are likely to end up in the sub-optimal, high protection-low trade equilibrium in which both choose protectionist policies. The WTO's institutional design is to address this prisoners' dilemma and to help maximise each "prisoner's" interests in a more coordinative way.

In commercial arbitration, the parties, either respondent or claimant, as in other strategic games, may compete for a better position. The claimant may search for an enforcement-friendly jurisdiction where he can get the award enforced without any difficulty. The respondent deciding on the same will take into account the anticipated behaviour of the claimant. For example, the court will not easily resort to domestic public policy or reject enforcement simply because of an annulled award. The respondent, by contrast, would prefer to see the enforcement proceeding end up in a "harsh" jurisdiction where the court will exert "substantive" or merit review. This would be addressed in the early stage when the parties negotiate an arbitration agreement or contact. As in the

[127] Ernst-Ulrich Petersmann, 'Constitutionalism and International Organisations', (1997) 17 *NW U. J. Int'l L. & Bus.* 398, 453.

typical prisoners' dilemma, each party, fearing that the other party will not cooperate, ends up in a worse situation than the one that would be reached had the parties coordinated their actions.

In the context of enforcing a foreign arbitral award, without a central enforcer (or a centralised institution), compliance with a pro-arbitration principle in enforcement by any given court depends in part on each state's belief that other states will comply with the same principle. This in turn will likely be affected by the enforcing court's (less likely the tribunal's) reputation for quality and for generating compliance in earlier cases.

3.5. GAME THEORY, ENFORCEMENT OF ANNULLED AWARDS AND THE NEW YORK CONVENTION

Economic analysis of law has strong explanatory and predictive power. Game theory helps generate counterintuitive insights into legal problems. Law, as is often recognised, should be criticised and evaluated by reference to the principle of utility.[128] There has been a tendency to treat law-making authority as a matter of political legitimacy, appealing to a version of social contract theory as an explanation of the authority of the legislature to enact laws. In a contractual context, game theory may help solve collective action problems between the parties.[129] Can issues relating to the New York Convention such as enforcement of annulled awards involving both courts in the countries of rendition and enforcement, be solved in the game theory context as well?

The environmental, corporate, banking, and redistribution "races to the bottom" scenarios, respectively, have the following distinct elements: (i) divergence of interests among competitors over decisions regarding location; (ii) coherent defects in the interstate competitive process; (iii) interstate externalities such as the relationship between principals and their agents; and (iv) mobility of

128 Legal writers such as Blackstone and Rawls represented the law as enforcing natural rights. The systematic classifications they employed, and the principles they extracted, were based upon a theory of natural rights. See William Blackstone, *Commentaries on the Laws of England*, Oxford: Clarendon Press (1765-69), Vol. I, Intro., s. 2. Unlike Blackstone and Bentham (whose maxim is "the greatest happiness of the greatest number"), I adopt the term "utility" in a sense of economic analysis, which parallels the utilitarian approach. For instance, where Bentham spoke of the greatest happiness of the greatest number, the economic analyst speaks of the "efficient" solution.

129 Game theory proceeds on the assumption that the outcome of each strategy can be estimated in advance on the postulate that the other party acts rationally in choosing the strategies open to him. However, the common conception of "games" includes many situations, not all of which are relevant to game theory. In some games, it is not necessary to take the strategy of the other players into consideration because the results are beyond the control of the participants.

wealth and wealthy players in the market, either individuals or firms. These elements also appear in the context of arbitration.

In international commercial arbitration, jurisdictional (legislative or judicial) competition exists among various jurisdictions and arbitral sites due to divergence of interests. Such competition is both jurisdiction-oriented and market-oriented. In England, it is said, the court decisions which concern choice of forum clauses all involved a competition between jurisdiction of English courts and jurisdiction of foreign courts.[130]

First, there is a market which is expanding with more involvement of arbitration institutions, judges, businessmen and lawyers in more arbitration cases. "International arbitration has become a serious industry ... for the proliferating institutions that seek to maintain, increase, or establish a caseload of important arbitrations".[131] The expansion of the arbitration industry indicates a demand for arbitration that sets the price and need for services, information, arbitration infrastructure and judicial assistance. This demand triggers supply.

Second, "if international commercial arbitration is regarded ... as a service industry ... in the field of economic activities, it becomes natural in each truly free market economy to treat it as being subject to the same standards and exigencies as those which govern the business community ... notably in terms of competence and cost-effectiveness".[132] The user-unfriendly arbitration law and regime inevitably influence the choice of the business community as regards arbitration services. In the 1960s and 1970s, members of the international commercial community viewed international arbitration held in England with much disdain because it was not only considered slow and expensive, but also as making a nonsense of the notions of finality and certainty in arbitration proceedings and awards.[133] As a consequence, very few foreign businesses or enterprises chose England as a venue for the settlement of their disputes by arbitration. This resulted in a considerable loss of income in the form of invisible earnings for the various professions concerned in England.[134] The Arbitration

---

130 Andrew Rogers, 'Forum Non Conveniens in Arbitration', (1988) 4(3) *Arb. Int'l* 251.

131 Jan Paulsson, 'Introduction (to the first issue of *Arbitration International*, quarterly journal published by The Chartered Institute of Arbitrators)', (1985) 1(1) *Arb. Int'l* 2–3.

132 J. Gillis Wetter, 'The Conduct of the Arbitration', (1985) 2(2) *J. Int'l Arb.* 7.

133 The English assumption was that parties agreeing to arbitrate in England themselves "want" judicial review. E.J. Cohn, 'The Rules of Arbitration of the International Chamber of Commerce', (1965) 14(1) *ICLQ* 132, 152; Mark Littman, 'England Reconsiders "The Stated Case"', (1979) 13 *International Lawyer* 253, 256; Michael Kerr, 'International Arbitration v. Litigation', (1980) *J. Bus. L.* 164; Michael Kerr, 'The Arbitration Act 1979', (1980) 43 *Mod. L. Rev.* 45, 47; Lord Hacking, 'The "Stated Case" Abolished: The United Kingdom Arbitration Act of 1979', (1980) 14 *Int'l Lawyer* 95, 98; William W. Park and Jan Paulsson, 'The Binding Force of International Arbitration Awards', (1983) 23 *Va. J. Int'l L.* 253, 272–73; Kodwo J. Bentil, 'Judicial Intervention and International Commercial Arbitration', (1986) 130 *Solicitors' Journal* 191.

134 Anthony Thornton, 'Appeals in Construction Arbitrations', (1984) 1 *Construction Law Journal* 103.

Act 1979 was then drafted in an attempt to draw back some of the arbitration-related business to London. In 1996, England took another significant step by formulating its *lex arbitri* to be in line with the UNCITRAL Model Law approach (or the modern "hands off" approach to the award).[135] Latin American countries have been hostile towards arbitration for a long time. In these countries, foreign awards will be ordinarily tested against the same standards as are applied to foreign court judgments. For example, enforcement of foreign awards needs to satisfy the reciprocity requirement. These unnecessary requirements served as a deterrent to foreign investors otherwise inclined to enter into international commercial agreements with Latin American opposite contracting parties. The deterrent to foreign investment is one of the prices these countries paid for such a hostile policy.[136] Swiss[137] and Belgian[138] law represent a more liberal position by allowing parties, through express agreement, to opt out of any judicial review process if neither party is Swiss or Belgian. These rules favour finality of the award and give effect to the autonomy of the parties thereby attracting international arbitration business.

Third, with the changes in national legislation to keep pace with the developments in international arbitration, states have begun a quest for more visibility and expansion of their services in the field of international commercial arbitration to satisfy the market demand. Some states have tirelessly pushed and prodded to shape the infrastructure and to increase the popularity of arbitration in their jurisdiction. For instance, New York hosts several experienced arbitration institutions: the American Arbitration Association's Headquarters and the New York Regional Office, the IACAC's US National Office, the US Council for International Business for the ICC Court of Arbitration, the Society of Maritime Arbitrators, Inc. for maritime arbitration, and specialised arbitration under the rules of the stock and commodity exchanges. In addition to "hard" facilities, the US and New York law have made an effort to package New York as a well-equipped and hospitable forum. For example, the US courts will apply a restrictive notion of sovereign immunity[139] and the conclusion of an arbitration agreement by a foreign state is considered to be a waiver of sovereign immunity.[140] Another example is that the New York State Legislature amended

---

135 Joseph Lookofsky and Ketilbjorn Hertz, *Transnational Litigation and Commercial Arbitration – An Analysis of American, European, and International Law*, Copenhagen: JurisNet LLC (3rd edn. 2011) p. 908.

136 Robert Layton, 'Changing Attitudes Toward Dispute Resolution in Latin America', (1993) 10(2) *J. Int'l Arb.* 126–7.

137 The Swiss Federal Statute on Private International Law, Art. 192.

138 The Belgian Judicial Code, Art. 1717(2).

139 Section 1602 of the Foreign Sovereign Immunities Act 1976 reads: "under international law, states are not immune from the jurisdiction of foreign courts insofar as their commercial activities are concerned".

140 Gabriel M. Wilner, *Domke on Commercial Arbitration*, St. Paul: West Group (revised edn. 1995) §18:02.

the New York arbitration statute in 1985 by adding a new paragraph entitled "provisional remedies", the goal of which was to make pre-award attachments available in New York arbitrations and to allow the Supreme Court to grant such remedies if arbitration may otherwise be rendered "ineffectual".[141] In the international business arena, New York or London, as centres for international business, are often chosen by the parties to appear in the choice-of-law and choice-of-forum provisions in cross-border transactional contracts.[142] Developing or emerging countries have also followed this trend. Romania, for example, acceded to the New York Convention, the European Convention on International Commercial Arbitration 1961, the ICSID Convention 1965 and other bilateral treaties, in order to achieve a climate of confidence that would be appealing to foreign investors and commercial partners.[143] However, emerging or transitional jurisdictions may not share the same high degree of reliability and sophistication in complex transnational transactions as advanced economies have displayed.[144] This may explain the preferred choice of New York or London as the arbitration venue.

Fourth, the competition among international arbitration *situs* may well be considered a good and healthy sign, as it is likely to lead to improvements in arbitration procedure and to modernisation and harmonisation of arbitration statutes. Opening arbitration law, centred on party autonomy, to the arbitrating parties and recognising the private parties' free choice of law among competing jurisdictions and arbitration *situs* would altogether foster a salutary level of regulatory competition, which may likely produce more efficient rules.[145] Ultimately the competition among various arbitration *situs* or jurisdictions may benefit market players by providing greater choice for the "arbitration cake" with varied options in both legal and geographical terms. For instance, because of the fact that England became a less attractive centre for the settlement of transnational commercial disputes by arbitration in the 1960s and 1970s, the British legislature passed the Arbitration Act of 1979 which was a legislative response to the dissatisfaction of the business community with the practice of "too much interference by the [English] courts with the finality of the arbitral awards".[146] The Arbitration Act of 1979 granted the parties to an international arbitration agreement the right to oust the jurisdiction of the English superior

141 Joseph M. McLaughlin, *Supplementary Practice Commentaries, N. Y. Civ. Prac. Law and Rules §7502:4,* Cum. Ann. Pocket Part, New York: McKinney (1990).

142 Geoffrey P. Miller, 'Choice of Law as a Precommitment Device', in F.H. Buckley (ed.), *The Fall and Rise of Freedom of Contract*, Durham and London: Duke University Press (1999) p. 366.

143 Grigore Florescu, 'The Evolution of Commercial Arbitration in Romania', (1993) 10(1) *J. Int'l Arb.* 95, 103.

144 Geoffrey P. Miller, above n. 142.

145 This is the jurisdictional competition theory which can be generally applicable to other cross-border legal scenarios. Andrew T. Guzman, 'Choice of Law: New Foundations', (2002) 90 *Georgetown Law Journal* 883, 914.

146 [1987] 2 All ER 751.

courts in determining any question of law arising from arbitration proceedings or from an arbitral award. In addition, the Arbitration Act of 1979 showed Parliament's intention to promote greater finality in arbitral awards[147] by discouraging or removing judicial intervention or supervision in England so as to make England a more attractive arbitration *situs* to the international commercial community. From the international business or commercial standpoint, the Arbitration Act of 1979 was a welcome legislative reform which restored confidence in the arbitration regime in England.[148]

The generalisation of the "race to the bottom" arguments indicates that states are able to promote the interests of their citizens by imposing costs on physical assets or intangible rights, through tax and other regulatory programs and/or economic means. Similarly, it is natural to assume that if the New York Convention is a response to a common pool problem (*i.e.*, a pool of international arbitration awards), then the content of the procedure "supplied" by different judicial systems, *i.e.*, national laws and court precedents, will immediately affect the efficiency of the process. This assumption relies upon a third limitation of the common pool model: it neglects the role played by renegotiation, given a unified procedure.[149] In most cases national courts retain some supervisory authority over arbitral awards. A court in the arbitral *situs* has the authority to vacate an award under standards set out in its national arbitration laws. Meanwhile, when the prevailing party seeks to enforce the award in another jurisdiction, the court where the enforcement is sought is also entitled to exert its judicial authority to decline enforcement under the standards set out in its national arbitration law, which may be constrained by international conventions. Due to differences between the grounds for vacating awards and the grounds for non-enforcement of awards, an award may be vacated by a court in the arbitral *situs*, yet nonetheless be enforceable under the national arbitration law of the enforcement *situs*. In such a case, the conflict inevitably arises between two states' judicial interests, or even commercial interests. Without a uniform enforcement standard, there may be no grounds – other than that the award was vacated in the *situs* – for declining to enforce a vacated arbitral award. The existence of a centralised or superior power among contracting states affecting a collective action or transformation of some sort is probably far more important, in terms of efficiency, than the content of the procedure which will thereby be invoked. If the content of the procedure is inefficient, then the award creditors may well be better off by arranging a solution amongst the states' and private parties' "right" distress without initiating formal proceedings.

---

147 [1987] 2 All ER 743.

148 Lord Hacking, 'Where We Are Now: Trends and Developments since the Arbitration Act 1979', (1985) 2 *J. Int'l Arb.* 7, 14.

149 The existence of the legal procedure "in the shadows" means that the prisoner's dilemma problem is no longer one of the obstacles to renegotiation.

Some public choice considerations[150] offer an insightful angle to interpret, in the specific context of a global "federal" system,[151] why a more flexible approach to the legal nature of annulled awards may make more sense. Jurisdictional competition in the field of international commercial arbitration is an important effect of permitting free choice of law in arbitration. In essence, this is a natural result of the bargaining freedom not only allowed but also encouraged in contract-based arbitration given an array of autonomy-oriented arbitration rules. Jurisdictional competition also gives rise to or remoulds regulatory patterns in almost all countries that host arbitration venues or activities.

Like in many other consensual settings,[152] free choice of law and legal regime in arbitration improves arbitration laws and rules. Rule-makers (the scope of which is wider than the conventional concept of lawmakers in the arbitration arena, since arbitration commissions or centres also "legislate" arbitration rules)[153] may impose costs (or spillovers) on the competing rule-makers in other arbitration venues. Competition between rule-making bodies may help constrain cost-externalisation and bring out efficient rules,[154] which may in turn facilitate competition. When the parties in arbitration are given more flexibility to bargain for the law to govern their arbitration case or are less restricted by mandatory rules or unseen boundaries (*i.e.*, unclear practices), exit costs can be lowered simply because the parties do not have to be physically attached to a particular

---

150 See generally, Maxwell L. Stearns and Todd J. Zywicki, *Public Choice Concepts and Applications in Law*, St. Paul: West (2009).

151 In the jurisdictional competition context, a federal system is more often defined as a regime composed of constituent jurisdictions bound by a common constitution under which some regulatory powers are reserved for the central government. Here, a "federal" system may be used in analogy to a global regime even though some key features may not be in existence, for example, a central government or centralised regulatory body. The function of the central government in a "federal" system is not for decorative purposes only. At a more substantial level, a centralised regime is put in place to minimise potentially destructive competition. It must be pointed out that in a true federal system, federal judges and arbitrators have no incentives to uphold state law. This line of analysis can be found in Alan Schwartz, 'Contracting about Bankruptcy', (1997) 13 *Journal of Law, Economics and Organization* 127. In any event, the international setting and other types of federal systems offer fruitful contexts for the study and application of jurisdictional competition theory.

152 Other typical consensual settings include bankruptcy, securities regulations and marriage, to which the principle of free choice of law can be applied. The principles of contractual choice of law can also be extended to some unconventional areas such as torts. However, many torts such as product liability and legal and medical malpractice arise out of consensual relationships.

153 However, "rule-makers" here, in terms of their role of making efficient rules to "move" arbitration cases, should not include arbitrators, who have no personal reason to set precedents but only compete for adjudication business through efficient dispute resolution. See Robert D. Cooter, 'The Objectives of Private and Public Judges', (1983) 41 *Public Choice* 107, 129–30; Gordon Tullock, *Trials on Trial: The Pure Theory of Legal Procedure*, New York: Columbia University Press (1980) p. 129.

154 The efficiency of a jurisdiction's law depends on two parameters: the jurisdiction's ability to externalise costs and the ability of an external to redress the harm by contracting for the applicable law.

place for relevant arbitration activities to take place. Despite local rule-makers' incentives to impose stricter arbitration rules in order to "trap" arbitration activities in their own jurisdictions, the parties in arbitration have more power to choose not only the law applicable to their contract (*i.e.*, arbitration agreement) but also the venue where they would arbitrate their disputes.

A flexible approach requires the local rules to be less harsh as regards recognising the validity or effectiveness of an annulled award, which would entitle rule-makers to some "rents",[155] *i.e.*, money generated from arbitration businesses, and strengthen parties' confidence in that jurisdiction for arbitrating their disputes.[156] Wealth transfers are likely to spur corrective, if not collective, action by losing jurisdictions.[157] Rule-makers in other forums may correspondingly adopt similarly less-harsh rules. Under "harsh" rules, as can be anticipated, arbitrating parties are still able to exit those jurisdictions inexpensively by contracting *ex ante* for the application of a particular law and/or arbitration in a particular forum rather than avoid regulating jurisdiction physically.[158] Enforcing "harsh" rules may also hurt interest groups (including governments and arbitration organisations) that would benefit from the business (such as taxing and regulating arbitration for the government). These considerations may suggest that there are no policy incentives for the rule-makers to maintain "harsh" rules in this respect.

In a global "federal" setting, several factors may change the dynamics of a true federal system. For instance, there is a greater risk of opportunistic action by the citizens of a foreign state, but a lack of the same level of reliability and sophistication in emerging or transnational economies.[159] More relevant is the disparity of political or market power among citizens and non-citizens that is likely to be greater than that in a true federal system. Against these, one way to reduce exit costs as well as contracting costs is for the rule-makers to supply standard (or uniform) form rules unifying general practices in dealing with the

---

155 For a detailed account of rent extraction, see Maxwell L. Stearns and Todd J. Zywicki, above n. 150, 67–68.

156 The opposite possibility may be that rule-makers and judicial counterparts want to protect rents (the concept of which can be extended wider to cover legislative benefits of avoiding regulatory arbitrage) by resisting enforcement of annulled awards.

157 For background information, see generally, Mancur Olson, *The Logic of Collective Action: Public Goods and the Theory of Groups*, Cambridge, MA: Harvard University Press (1971); Robert E. McCormick and Robert D. Tollison, *Politicians, Legislations, and the Economy: An Inquiry into the Interest-Group Theory of Government,* Boston: Martinus Nijhoff (1981); Robert D. Tollison, 'Public Choice and Legislation', (1988) 74 *Va. L. Rev.* 339. In this sense, the ability of arbitrating parties to select the governing law or forum is a counterweight to the tendency of local rule-makers' interests to expropriate wealth from their non-local counterparts.

158 Physically moving away from the jurisdiction and its regulation refers to moving to or travelling in a particular forum before engaging in or being subject to the relevant conduct. See generally, Erin Ann O'Hara and Larry E. Ribstein, 'Interest Groups, Contracts, and Interest Analysis', (1997) 48 *Mercer Law Review* 765.

159 Geoffrey P. Miller, above n. 142.

legality of annulled awards. This is more important internationally because of the greater differences among legal regimes concerning their willingness to make durable commitments. Further, this is more pragmatically difficult than in a true federal system due to the lack of shared constitutional rights[160] and a concrete tradition of comity.[161] The supply of such uniform rules may therefore be a great challenge left to the unfinished task of improving or reforming the New York Convention.[162]

3.5.1. LEGITIMATE EXPECTATIONS OF PRIVATE PARTIES IN ARBITRATION

Unlike litigation in courts, arbitration is a default means of resolving disputes. Assuming that both parties are sophisticated and are well-informed of the costs and benefits of their dispute resolution options, it seems sensible in the context of international commercial arbitration that parties will agree to arbitrate if the marginal benefits of arbitration over litigation exceed the marginal costs. The parties to arbitration show their preference for a specific jurisdiction by submitting their disputes to a specific place for arbitration. The preference represents trust and high expectation of the fairness and neutrality of a legal system as well as its court system.

Although it may be true that one party might take advantage of its stronger bargaining power to persuade or force the other side to accept the arbitration venue, the opposing party may well have compromised on the *situs* of arbitration as well as the governing law, in anticipation of reciprocal concessions or benefits from the other party. In addition, the parties look forward to the simplicity and predictability of the proceedings, which is a criterion or factor in assessing the feasibility of the approach in dealing with the annulled awards.[163] The place of

160 For instance, the US constitution contains a "full faith and credit rule". Article 4 reads: "Full Faith and Credit shall be given in each State to the public Acts, Records, and judicial Proceedings of every other State. And the Congress may by general Laws prescribe the Manner in which such Acts, Records and Proceedings shall be proved, and the Effect thereof."

161 States in the regional arrangement may have a longer tradition of comity for a "community" depending on reciprocal respect for the views of its members. David Jackson, 'Mandatory Rules and Rules of "Ordre Public"', in P.M. North (ed.), *Contract Conflicts*, Amsterdam: North Holland (1982) p. 59 and pp. 61–62.

162 The theory of jurisdictional competition may support the conclusion that local laws may be more efficient than critics of "federalism" have argued. However, this conclusion while well-founded in a true federal system may need to be adjusted a bit in a global "federal" system given the "corrective" function of the "federal" law and the mess of competition among national laws. "Federal" law (*i.e.*, treaty or international-level law) can be used sparingly to correct supposed problems of national laws. This adjustment deserves some cautious thought. At a later stage of state competition, the "federal" law may be worse than the ultimate national rule.

163 Some courts also take into account delay and fairness when deciding whether to adjourn the enforcement proceedings. Other threshold tests include whether the proceedings to set aside

arbitration is in a better position than any other places to determine the regularity of the arbitration proceedings due to its close connection to the dispute. On the other hand, the parties to the dispute do not expect unnecessary complexity of the arbitration proceedings. If a vacated award is regarded as a completely dead one, then no party will even try to seek enforcement of the award in another jurisdiction because parties are aware of the impossibility of having the award recognised by any court anywhere. Therefore, the game is over.[164] This is the rationale of the "traditional approach", that is, a vacated award is a nullity and shall not be enforced in any jurisdiction.[165]

Besides its intervening side-effect, the annulment procedure obviously is an effective means adopted by the home jurisdiction to guarantee the quality and regularity of arbitration. The annulment process, however, is time-consuming and costly. The judicial review of an arbitral award does not leave the parties significantly worse off with respect to time than would litigation. As a matter of fact, parties may even be better off because they can enjoy the benefits of arbitration along with court-provided assurance of basic fairness in the arbitral process. Does enforcement of an annulled award by a court, in a given transnational transaction or activity, defeat the legitimate or justified expectations of the parties who instead choose the seat of arbitration? At first glance, it seems that the parties' autonomy and their choice of arbitration have not been respected if an annulled award is enforced by an overseas court because, without an "invitation" from the parties, courts in another country may not extend their jurisdiction to the dispute. In *Chromalloy*, the place of arbitration was chosen by the parties and the courts in France and the United States were incidentally involved in the arbitration proceeding simply because one party's assets were located in these two countries. In practice, however, it is not a general rule that a choice of the seat of arbitration is freely or mutually decided by the parties to a dispute. This may effectively mean that the courts in the seat of arbitration may not necessarily have any material relationship with the dispute or parties. Put differently, fairness or neutrality to the parties or the dispute is not only dependent on the seat of arbitration. The involvement of another jurisdiction is practically possible and justifiable and would not necessarily severely affect the parties' interests.

It has been argued that a full-scale protection of the parties to arbitration requires that an annulled arbitral award not be enforced in any country. To grant international legal effect to an annulled award would effectively allow the party

---

the award have been commenced in the appropriate court of the originating jurisdiction, and whether there is a potential prejudice to the party seeking the adjournment should the court refuse the adjournment and enforce the award, only to have the original jurisdiction set aside the award. *Powerex Corp. v. Alcan Inc.* [2004] BCSC 876 at [24] to [26].

164 Albert Jan van den Berg, above n. 47, 15.

165 William Laurence Craig, above n. 94, 177 ("in practice it would be extraordinary that an enforcement court abroad would give effect to an award annulled in its home jurisdiction").

in whose favour the award is rendered to seek to have that award enforced all over the world until one flexible jurisdiction accepts the application for enforcement of the award.[166] The international legal effect granted to an annulled award may create a new regime or mechanism by which the winning party in arbitration may take advantage of this situation. The finality of the arbitration proceedings and award, which is a well-established and widely accepted arbitration norm, will be severely undermined. This reasoning makes sense provided that the award is set aside for proper or fair reasons, which are adopted by most, if not all, jurisdictions when setting aside an award in similar situations. In this case, an annulled award shall not be lawfully effective anywhere, not only in its home jurisdiction but also any other foreign countries. Logically, an award which is set aside for any well-recognised reason, *i.e.*, any serious substantive or procedural defects, may not be enforced by a court in any event. If so, the control at the rendering stage of the arbitral award is simply so that one party in arbitration will not bear any risk associated with execution of a defective award. However, in the real world, arbitral awards may be set aside for improper or unfair reasons. For instance, the grounds for annulling an award may not be universally accepted or adopted in most jurisdictions. The annulment of an arbitral award on a "bad" ground is not fair and just to the parties. The protection of parties' interests requires such awards to have a very narrow (or local) legal effect so that their interests would not be damaged worldwide. Therefore, control at the enforcement stage is necessary, and enforcement of an annulled award may become the last resort to protect a winning party's legal interests and eventually save the reputation and legitimacy of arbitration. There exists no internationally accepted category of unfair or improper grounds for annulment of arbitral awards. Some grounds can easily be classified as "bad" in terms of general norms in international commercial arbitration.[167] An award may be set aside in one jurisdiction merely for a typically local reason specific to that jurisdiction where the award is rendered. It is then unreasonable or unjust to subject the parties to an international dispute over a specific local ground outside the national boundaries. To recognise and enforce an award annulled on that basis no doubt exports very local, likely very low, standards to other jurisdictions. Such practice may in turn lower the well-established standards of international arbitration. The interdependence of various jurisdictions as regards the legal effect of a specific arbitral award will result in a "race to the bottom" and the international arbitration regime would be undermined.

---

[166] That jurisdiction must have some means, such as assets owned by the party which loses the case, to enforce the award. In other words, there must be some connection between the enforcing jurisdiction and the parties or parties' assets. This view has won some support in the international arbitration community. For instance, Albert Jan van den Berg said that: "In the case of a questionable award, a party cannot stop around the world in order to find a flexible court somewhere which is willing to enforce such an award". See Albert Jan van den Berg, above n. 47, 15.

[167] See Jan Paulsson, above n. 50, 14.

To misapply local laws to an award and for a local court subsequently to set aside an award is another "bad" reason in this context. The Court of Appeal of Cairo made a mistaken judgment in *Chromalloy*.[168] The Court set aside an award issued in Cairo on the basis of Article 53(1)(d) of Egyptian Law No. 27 of 1994 on arbitration,[169] and held that the arbitral panel, by applying Egyptian civil law (rather than administrative law) indeed failed to apply the law agreed upon by the parties to govern the subject matter in the dispute.[170] The Court also re-characterised, if not mis-characterised, the nature of the disputed contract so that the so-called appropriate laws could be applied.[171] This departed from the usual practice because the Court then had to review the merits of the case and revise the award.[172] In international commercial arbitration, it is well established that the court is only entitled to "open the box" under very limited circumstances and is restricted to reviewing only the substance of the dispute and award. Enforcement of an award annulled by a court which breaks this "golden" rule in effect raises the review level by inviting the court to intervene in the arbitration proceedings and ultimately diminishes the credibility of the arbitration panel.

To grant legal effect to an annulled award on a worldwide basis would truly put an award to an end since the international effect attached to an annulled award would prevent that award from being enforced on a worldwide basis.[173] This is a substantial risk to the parties in the sense that any non-existing or future grounds for setting aside an award in the home jurisdiction may eventually make the winning party lose its rights entirely. The parties' interests cannot justify merely leaving unrestricted discretion to a jurisdiction where an award is rendered. In contrast, the rule which does not grant international legal effect to an annulled award would discourage the court in the arbitral *situs* from

168 See *Ministry of Defence v. Chromalloy Aero Services Company*, in (1998) 4 *Rev. Arb.* 723, a note by Leboulanger.

169 Article 53(1)(d) of Egyptian Law No. 27 for 1994 promulgating the law concerning arbitration in civil and commercial matters provides (English translation appearing in the ICCA International Handbook on Commercial Arbitration): "An arbitral award may be annulled only … if the arbitral award failed to apply the law agreed upon by the parties to govern the subject matter in dispute".

170 The contract provided that: "it is … understood that both parties have irrevocably agreed to apply Egyptian Laws and to choose Cairo as the seat of the court of arbitration". In this case, the arbitral tribunal held that the legal issues in dispute were not affected by the characterisation of the contract, and applied the rules of Egyptian civil law to the contract. See (1998) 11(8) *Mealey's Int'l Arb. Rep.* C-1.

171 The Court was widely criticised. See Philippe Fouchard, 'La portée internationale de l'annulation de la sentence arbitrale dans son pays d'origine', (1997) 3 *Rev. Arb.* 330, 349; Gary H. Sampliner, above n. 16, 18.

172 It was also argued that the re-characterisation of the contract made the Court surpass the powers conferred upon it by Egyptian Law No. 27 of 1994 on arbitration, which clearly prohibited any review on the merits of awards. See Philippe Fouchard, above n. 171, 349; Albert Jan van den Berg, above n. 47, 27.

173 Philippe Fouchard, above n. 171, 348 (noting that: "It is not legitimate to grant to the judges of a State the power to annihilate on a worldwide basis an award which they dislike").

adopting any "bad" grounds for setting aside an award. As far as the enforcement of arbitral awards is concerned, permitting the prevailing party in arbitration to enforce a vacated award in another jurisdiction serves as a potential constraint on the prevailing party's risk of losing rights on a worldwide basis. Non-enforcement of arbitral awards, on the basis of any ground, bad or good, would not finally "kill" an award but would still leave the possibility for the winning party to seek enforcement of an award in other jurisdictions. This will become an effective competitive policy tool to limit the arbitral *situs*'s motivation to adopt "bad" grounds for setting aside arbitral awards.

As a matter of fact, the parties' legal interests and legitimate expectations need a mechanism through which judicial powers can be balanced among various jurisdictions. Apart from judicial or arbitral systems, the parties should be allowed to resolve the dispute through contracts or contractual arrangements. As economic analysis has suggested, the parties are more likely to maximise their joint utility if they must choose prior to the action triggering the problem. *Ex ante* choice can create mutual benefits while *ex post* choice is a zero-sum game. In economic models of choosing the dispute resolution forum, the parties will be driven by economic incentives to choose an arbitral forum when the benefits of that forum net of its costs exceed those from a judicial forum.[174] The "contract" approach allows the parties to reduce potential risks of arbitration by contracting for certain judicial supervision in the arbitral *situs*. The selection of the arbitral *situs* subjects the parties to the national arbitration law of the *situs*, including its standards for vacating awards, which sets out the degree of court supervision in the *situs*. The "contract" approach also allows the parties to agree to a greater or lesser degree of court supervision[175] such as *de novo* review of legal issues by courts.[176] At least some parties to arbitration prefer more court supervision on arbitral awards than otherwise provided by law.[177] The "contract" approach can further allow the parties to agree that a vacated award would be enforceable. Under the French approach, vacated awards are enforceable without regard to the agreement of the parties. Under the "traditional" approach, vacated awards are unenforceable no matter what the parties have agreed in the contract.

---

174 See Keith N. Hylton and Christopher R. Drahozal, 'The Economics of Litigation and Arbitration: An Application to Franchise Contracts', (2001) (Boston U. Working Paper No. 01–03); Keith N. Hylton, 'Agreements to Waive or to Arbitrate Legal Claims: An Economic Analysis', (2000) 8 *Sup. Ct. Econ. Rev.* 209; Steven Shavell, 'Alternative Dispute Resolution: An Economic Analysis', (1995) 24 *J. Legal Stud.* 1.

175 For example, English arbitration law allows parties to conduct out-of-court review of legal issues in arbitration. The Swiss and Belgian arbitration laws authorise foreign parties to contract out of court supervision in the situs. Several American courts have upheld agreements specifying a greater degree of court supervision than otherwise provided in the Federal Arbitration Act.

176 Christopher R. Drahozal, '"Unfair" Arbitration Clauses', (2001) *University of Illinois Law Review* 695, 731.

177 See *Lapine Tech. Corp. v. Kyocera Corp.*, 130 F.3d 884 (9th Cir. 1997); *Gateway Techs. Inc. v. MCI Telecommunications Corp.*, 64 F. 3d 993 (5th Cir. 1995).

Only under the *Chromalloy* approach do courts look to what the parties agreed in deciding whether to enforce a vacated award. Such an agreement would not be the same as an agreement to limit judicial review in the country of arbitral *situs* as the courts would continue to review the award and any decision in the arbitral *situs* would continue to determine the domestic enforceability of the award. However, a decision by the court in the arbitral *situs* to vacate the award would not preclude the victorious party from enforcing the award elsewhere, therefore providing the parties with greater flexibility in choosing the *situs* of their arbitration. In the interests of legitimacy and future development of international commercial arbitration, the international legal effect granted to an annulled award shall be upheld but limited, if not eliminated, to a certain extent. The appropriate legal framework should facilitate and respect the parties' choice of the level or degree of judicial supervision by the courts in the arbitral *situs* while respecting the mandatory nature of the grounds for vacating awards under most national arbitration laws.

3.5.2. PUBLIC INTERESTS OF NATIONS IN ENFORCING ANNULLED AWARDS

As far as public interests of states involved in the enforcement of annulled awards are concerned, attention must be given to the competitive strategic setting involving the forum of arbitration and forum of enforcement.[178] Two

[178] The struggle between the country of origin and the country of enforcement also exists in other scenarios. One party to arbitration may raise a challenge in the court in the country of origin. The challenge may fail. It is unlikely that a court in the country of enforcement would allow a similar objection to be raised. The outcome of enforcement proceedings may well be affected by the sequence of the proceedings in the country of origin. The *Dallah* saga is a riveting example to illustrate this struggle. The UK Supreme Court decided not to enforce the French award on the grounds that the arbitration agreement was not valid against the Government of Pakistan under French law (the law was chosen as such because the parties had not subjected the arbitration agreement to any law so Aikens J decided the issue under the municipal law of the seat of arbitration). Subsequently, the Paris Court of Appeal dismissed the application filed by the Government of Pakistan to annul the award as the court found that the Government of Pakistan was a party to the arbitration agreement. The French court did not feel itself bound by the finding of the UK court. This type of struggle is termed as "double attempt" cases. *Dallah Real Estate and Tourism Holding Company v. The Ministry of Religious Affairs, Government of Pakistan* [2010] UKSC 46; *Gouvernement du Pakistan – Ministère des Affaires Religieuses v. Dallah Real Estate and Tourism Holding Company* (Case No 09/28533, 17 February 2011, Court of Appeal, Paris). Also White & Case, 'In Dallah, the Paris Court of Appeal and UK Supreme Court Reach Contrary Decisions Applying Same Law to Same Facts', *Insight: International Arbitration* (February 2011) p. 3. It is worth clarifying that if the setting aside attempt before the court of the seat of arbitration has been successful, that would constitute grounds to refuse enforcement according to Article V(1)(e) of the New York Convention. So the question here is really about whether an unsuccessful setting aside attempt before the court at the seat of arbitration creates issue estoppel against reliance on the same grounds to challenge enforcement in the forum of

perspectives can be explored: the specificity of the arbitral process and the nature of an arbitral award.

A court in the state hosting arbitration, either in the forum of arbitration or enforcement, has a desire to create and maintain a reputation of hosting fair arbitration. The court has great incentives to ensure that the arbitration process meets the parties' expectations and conforms to procedural regularities so as to guard against manifest miscarriages of justice. This judicial objective can be achieved through the annulment mechanism, whereby an award may be annulled by the court under certain circumstances. To that end, the court, as is often claimed, possesses the ultimate competence to invalidate an award by setting aside the award where any of the grounds enumerated in Article V of the New York Convention or similar grounds listed in national arbitration laws appears. This will stop a defective award from coming into force in its own legal order. Similarly, the state can adopt legislation to the effect that an annulled award would not be enforced somewhere else when its own legal order has treated the award as a defective or invalid one.

Furthermore, the home jurisdiction[179] has a legitimate claim to protect its image in the international community as an arbitration-friendly country where

enforcement. In a "double attempt" case, public interests of the state of origin and state of enforcement are different from those in the context of *Chromalloy*-type cases. The struggle between the state of origin and state of enforcement is more related to the possibility for the parties to have "two bites at the cherry". In legal terminology, the struggle concerns an issue estoppel. A simple way to describe it can be borrowed from Rix LJ's view in the Court of Appeal judgment in *Dallah Real Estate* (CA): "As for the case of a successful or unsuccessful (or waived) challenge in the courts of the country of origin, that is a more controversial area. My own view is that a successful challenge is not only in itself a potential defence under the Convention or our statute but likely also to raise an issue estoppel. As for an unsuccessful challenge, that may also set up an issue estoppel. As for a waived challenge, that cannot in itself set up an issue estoppel and is unlikely to be of significance, save possibly in the rare case where the residual discretion is in play". *Dallah Estate and Tourism Holding Company v. The Ministry of Religious Affairs, Government of Pakistan* [2009] EWCA Civ 755 at [90]. The common law courts opined that the option of applying to set aside the award at the seat of the arbitration and the option to resist enforcement at the forum of enforcement are alternative or exclusive rather than cumulative. *Newspeed International Ltd. v. Citus Trading Pte. Ltd.* [2003] 3 SLR(R) 1 at [26] to [28]. This judicial approach to tackle this struggle between the seat of arbitration and enforcement forum is closer to the concept of avoidance of "double recovery" in contract law or injustice in public law. The lack of the concept of issue estoppel in civil law countries may make it difficult to develop jurisprudence in this line of cases in the context of the New York Convention. Even in common law jurisdictions, the judicial approaches on this struggle are not uniform. For instance, the Hong Kong Court of Final Appeal was of the opinion that the defendant was not bound to choose between the two options. *Hebei Import & Export Corp. v. Polytek Engineering Co. Ltd.* [1999] 2 HKC 205.

179 It is generally agreed that "the law under which the award was made" refers to the law of the place where the award was made. Alan Redfern and Martin Hunter, *Law and Practice of International Commercial Arbitration*, London: Sweet & Maxwell (4th edn. 2004) pp. 10–49. However, this is not the only possibility. The "home jurisdiction" here in theory is not a fixed term but can be (i) where the arbitration proceeding is conducted; (ii) where the parties' arbitration agreement refers to; or (iii) where the substantive law governs the underlying dispute. These possibilities are caused by the New York Convention's failure to define the

the principle of party autonomy is fully respected as a founding doctrine in international commercial arbitration and any arbitral award would not be easily set aside even though the award may be defective or may result from arbitration in violation of some well-established norms. There are two limbs to this policy concern. The first limb is that the home jurisdiction needs to maintain a certain level of judicial control over arbitral awards. The second limb puts the onus on the necessity for the court to balance its secondary role in resolving legal issues in arbitration. Accordingly, an appropriate level of involvement in the award review in the arbitral *situs* needs to be tailored. Overly extensive judicial review and local control of arbitral awards is not ideal: it will encourage parties to arbitrate elsewhere and possibly discourage investment by those parties who will be deterred by the thought of likely national court resolution of future disputes despite an agreement to arbitrate.[180] A limited level of judicial control in the arbitral *situs* is appropriate.

It is one of the prerogatives of the state (in which, or under the arbitration law of which, an award was made other than other less relevant states) where a judgment is issued to set aside an arbitral award if it is found that the award is rendered in an objectionable manner. The interest of the home jurisdiction (or seat of arbitration) is to ensure that, according to its own legal standards, a defective award in its territory would not come into force and become enforceable elsewhere. In this case, the home jurisdiction is allowed to enjoy the "primary" jurisdiction or discretion as to the substantive and procedural standards to be followed for the annulment within its own boundaries. This is in line with the New York Convention which leaves the signatory countries some discretion to set aside awards for reasons the courts see appropriate.[181] The Model Law also contains a separate list of grounds in Article 34 by which an arbitral award can be set aside by the court in the country of rendition. Obviously, this interest of the arbitral *situs* requires international recognition as to the legal effect of an annulled award. Nevertheless, worldwide legal effect cannot be granted where an award is set aside by a court for any unfair or

term "under the law of which the award was made" in Article V(1)(e). The scenario (iii) is practically possible. The parties may agree to arbitrate a dispute in Country A according to the procedural law of Country B. Likely, the award may be set aside by the courts of Country B. Based on English law, enforcement of this award in England may be refused. C.M.V. Clarkson and Jonathan Hill, *The Conflicts of Laws*, Oxford: Oxford University Press (3rd edn. 2006) p. 263. Although the case of (iii) is less likely to be seen, it took place at least once in *Venture Global Engineering v. Satyam Computer Services* [2008] INSC 40, 233 Fed Appx 517 (CA 6 (Mich)). The Indian Supreme Court held that an award rendered in London that was the object of enforcement proceedings in the United States could be set aside in India on the exclusive basis that the parties had chosen Indian law to govern the substance of the dispute.

180 See William W. Park, 'Duty and Discretion in International Arbitration', (1999) 93 *American Journal of International Law* 805, 823 (claiming that "should commercial actors find a country's review standards burdensome or inadequate, the market will direct their next arbitration to a place more compatible with the desired level of judicial control").

181 Philippe Fouchard, above n. 171, 349.

improper grounds. This will cause potential negative impact on an incorporated company or an individual resident in the home jurisdiction. For example, let us assume an award is rendered in Country A against a company incorporated in Country A for payment of a significant amount to a foreign entity which is another party in arbitration. In the international arbitration regime, the final say cannot belong solely to the court in the seat of arbitration or home jurisdiction as this would strike an imbalance between the rendering and enforcing jurisdictions. The serious consequence caused by this imbalance would be that the home jurisdiction would take advantage of its earlier position in the chain of arbitration proceedings to set aside an arbitral award first according to its local standards so that its local interests can be protected if the court in the country of enforcement must accept this annulment decision as the status quo. It is likely that the enforcing jurisdiction may be reluctant to support cross-border arbitration because of the obvious unfairness and partiality arising out of its disadvantageous "secondary" position in arbitration.[182] The side-effect would be that a dispute may ultimately end up in a jurisdiction where impartiality and fairness are not guaranteed. Of more concern is the fact that the international arbitration regime would collapse because of the lack of trust and confidence between rendering and enforcing states.

The court in the arbitral *situs* is legitimately entitled to possess judicial power and discretion to set aside arbitral awards issued in its jurisdiction. However, such judicial power does not justify full-scale international effect or worldwide recognition, offered by courts in other jurisdictions, to the annulled award. In addition, the court in the arbitral *situs* has no effective means to compel courts in other jurisdictions not to enforce the annulled award. The home jurisdiction is a separate regime independent from other jurisdictions, which enjoy their own judicial independence and powers, though secondary to the foremost powers enjoyed by the courts in the country of rendition. Therefore, the next question is whether enforcement of an award outside the territory of the country of rendition constitutes a threat to the legal order of the home jurisdiction. The enforcement of an annulled award in other jurisdictions may not necessarily bring substantial damages to the home jurisdiction of the award. This is because the award has been neutralised after it was annulled by the court in the home jurisdiction. Further actions taken by courts in other jurisdictions would not revive this award in the home jurisdiction or bring any accountability or discredit to the home jurisdiction. Therefore, enforcement of an annulled award abroad should not become a concern to the home jurisdiction or damage the legitimacy and reputation of the legal order in the home jurisdiction. This line of argument is consistent with the territorial conception of arbitration.

---

182 By way of clarification, "secondary" jurisdiction of the court at the enforcement forum is ranked after the primary jurisdiction enjoyed by the court at the seat of arbitration. Courts in other less relevant jurisdictions may enjoy "secondary" jurisdiction compared to the court at the seat of arbitration in terms of the jurisdictional power to set aside an arbitral award.

The role or function of the courts is to protect the legal order in one jurisdiction as a representative of the interests or sovereign of the country. Through its initial review, the court in the arbitral *situs* ensures that arbitral awards leaving its borders for recognition or enforcement have a certain level of national approval and international acceptability, *i.e.*, due process or substantive fairness. However, the court in the arbitral *situs* cannot replace the role of the courts in the enforcement regime by playing a judicial role in its own legal order. The judicial scrutiny by courts at the arbitral *situs* cannot avoid repetition of review by the court in the enforcement forum even though the *situs* court's judicial review may have provided the parties and the enforcement forum courts with a level of confidence in the fairness and justice of the arbitral award. When an annulled award floats to an enforcement forum, international (judicial) comity also encourages the court in the enforcement forum to conduct a constrained level of judicial review over the award in order to ensure that there is no reason to refuse enforcement under the New York Convention standards enumerated in Article V.[183] It is hard to centralise the court review merely in the arbitral *situs* because the *situs* courts are not capable of interpreting and applying the national laws in the enforcement forum. In addition, Article V of the New York Convention itself is clear in granting a discretion whether or not to recognise the award to courts in the country of enforcement.[184] Therefore, the courts in the enforcement forum play a role as a gatekeeper in approving the arbitral awards regardless of the local or global legal effect of those awards. The enforcement forum is usually connected to the dispute only because one or two parties' assets are located there.[185] This connection also supports a policy of reviewing an award rendered abroad, so that investments and assets in the enforcement forum will be protected against unripe claims raised abroad. The legal effect of a decision by a foreign court to enforce an annulled award is theoretically limited to its own territory.[186] Given such limitations, it was

---

183 Some courts have given heed to judicial comity and the possibility of inconsistent judgments. *Powerex Corp. v. Alcan Inc.* [2004] BCSC 876 at [24] to [26].

184 If the text is read literally, that "recognition and enforcement will not be refused … unless" the award has been annulled or suspended, it appears that the reviewing court is not required to refuse enforcement of the award in all cases. Put differently, there would still be no positive obligation to enforce the annulment decision. See Jan Paulsson, above n. 77, 22 (noting that Article V "does not command a refusal to enforce when there has been an annulment"); Gary B. Born, *International Commercial Arbitration in the United States: Commentary and Materials*, Deventer/Boston: Kluwer Law and Taxation Publishers (1994) p. 649 (noting that the French version of Article V is equally authoritative as English in providing that "Article V's exceptions permit, but do not require, non-recognition").

185 See W. Michael Reisman, William Laurence Craig, William W. Park and Jan Paulsson, *International Commercial Arbitration, Cases, Materials and Notes on the Resolution of International Business Disputes*, New York: The Foundation Press Inc. (1997) p. 1099.

186 In practice, it is possible that a court may recognise a judgment rendered in a foreign country which had granted enforcement of an award in its jurisdiction. Nevertheless, this is entirely that court's decision to recognise such a judgment.

proposed to reduce the "secondary" court's control in the enforcement forum,[187] which can be achieved with respect to the individual grounds for refusal set out in Article V of the New York Convention, such as Article V(1)(e).

It is generally accepted in Europe that the 1961 European Convention limited the effect of the setting aside of an award in a contracting state to the Convention when seeking the recognition and enforcement of the award in other contracting states. The approach is "conventional" rather than "revolutionary" in terms of its underlying territorial conception of arbitration. According to Article IX of the European Convention, the setting aside of an award in a contracting state only constitutes grounds for refusal for recognition and enforcement in another contracting state where the setting aside took place in a state in which or under the law of which the award has been made for one of the reasons listed in Article IX of the Convention.[188] These reasons are close to the grounds listed in Article V(1)(a) to (d) of the New York Convention.[189] Nevertheless, the annulment of an award for violation of public policy of the state in which or under the law of which the award has been rendered does not constitute grounds for refusing recognition and enforcement of such an award in other contracting states.

The Austrian Supreme Court applied Article IX of the European Convention in *Radenska*.[190] An arbitral tribunal rendered an arbitral award in Belgrade, Yugoslavia in 1988. The panel applied Yugoslavian law and ordered DO Zdravilisce Radenska, a Yugoslavian company, to pay Kajo-Erzeugnisse, Essenzen GmbH, an Austrian company, around 30 million Austrian schillings and interest for Radenska's breach of a manufacturing and distribution contract of a non-alcoholic beverage in Yugoslavia. The award was set aside by the Slovenian Supreme Court in July 1992 on the grounds that the contract was in a monopolistic form which was against public policy. Radenska requested the Austrian Supreme Court not to enforce the award for the annulment in the country of rendition. Nevertheless, the Austrian Supreme Court rejected this request according to Article IX(2) of the European Convention, which limited the effect of Article V(1)(e) of the New York Convention. The Austrian Supreme Court held that, according to Article IX of the European Convention, the setting aside of an award in Slovenia on the grounds of public policy cannot justify the refusal of the enforcement of an award in Austria. Thereafter, Radenska started fresh proceedings to oppose the enforcement decision made by the court in Austria. Nevertheless, the Austrian Supreme Court turned down Radenska's request and confirmed the lower court's decision and reasoning.

---

187 Gerold Herrmann, above n. 56, 235.

188 As Albert Jan van den Berg pointed out, this provision has been only tested once. See Albert Jan van den Berg, above n. 47, 20.

189 Article IX(1) of the European Convention.

190 See *Radenska v. Kajo*, Austrian Supreme Court, 20 October 1993, XX *Yearbook* (1995) 1051; (1998) 2 *Rev. Arb.* 419, with note by Senkovic and Lastenouse; Austrian Supreme Court, 23 February 1998, (1999) 2 *Rev. Arb.*, with note by Senkovic and Lastenouse.

The European Convention is not an exception to the principle of limiting the legal effect of annulment. Rather, it provides a platform for the home jurisdiction to claim the region-wide legal effect of an annulment under enumerated circumstances. The European Convention also excludes the potential incorporation of particularities for setting aside an award contained in the arbitration law of the country of origin into the grounds for refusal of enforcement under the Convention.[191] This effectively avoids a confusing circumstance where an enforcement regime may be subject to the Convention as well as the local law of another contracting state. It seems that the lawmakers of the European Convention intend to restrict the regional legal effect of an annulled award to a limited degree. This may explain why the New York Convention does not seem to function effectively in this respect. The New York Convention still maintains the territorial concept by leaving more discretion in annulling an award to courts in the arbitral *situs*. Meanwhile, it gives some leeway to the enforcing courts by allowing them to have more favourable legislation for enforcing an annulled award. In substance, the New York Convention does not grant any judicial power to a jurisdiction so as to represent the entire international community. This approach makes sense in the bigger picture since Member States may not reach any agreement as to the unified or common meaning and understanding of the grounds for setting aside an award.

3.5.3. DUAL CONTROL MECHANISM, DELOCALISATION AND JUDICIAL COMPETITION

In a gaming setting, players are likely to end up in a confession-confession setting if they have conflicting interests and if there is no uniform and clear guidance governing the actions of players. In the context discussed here, a natural question is whether recognition and enforcement of annulled awards necessarily creates or increases the "disorder" at the international level. The question that follows is whether it would breach the harmony of legal orders among various signatory countries to the New York Convention.[192]

The modern development and popularity of international commercial arbitration has been made possible by the willingness of an increasing number of countries to permit matters traditionally reserved for the courts to be settled by private processes of dispute resolution. If international arbitration exists at all, this is only because states are willing for it to be that way by sacrificing some judicial powers. Furthermore, it can continue to thrive and develop only if it retains the confidence of lawmakers and courts in jurisdictions where arbitration is conducted or the award is rendered or enforced. Such confidence has been

191 See Albert Jan van den Berg, above n. 47, 20.
192 Ibid.

secured in most countries because of the retention by the state of a minimum level of oversight and control over the arbitral process. The modern international arbitration "compact" that has emerged, as reflected in both the New York Convention and the UNCITRAL Model Law, is founded on a system of dual control by the states, firstly by the original state of arbitration and secondly by the state where an award is enforced.[193] The first type of judicial control occurs in the proceedings of setting aside arbitral awards while the second type of judicial control occurs in the proceedings of enforcing foreign awards. The distinction between these two types of judicial control therefore, in essence, is a distinction between control by the primary jurisdiction and control by the secondary jurisdiction.[194]

The first type of judicial control mainly arises from, but is also restricted by, various grounds on which arbitral awards can be vacated as prescribed in national arbitration laws. A large number of national laws follow the UNCITRAL Model Law on International Commercial Arbitration, which actually has the same list of grounds for non-enforcement of awards as contained in the New York Convention. Some national arbitration laws contain grounds for vacating awards in addition to those in the UNCITRAL Model Law. For instance, in the United States, following dicta in two Supreme Court opinions, a number of courts of appeals have recognised a non-statutory ground for vacating arbitration awards if the awards are in "manifest disregard" of the law.[195] There are also several national laws which contain fewer grounds for vacating arbitral awards than the UNCITRAL Model Law.[196] The degree of judicial control in the setting aside proceedings is reflected in the nature and number of statutory grounds for vacating arbitral awards. In most countries, including several major international arbitration centres, the grounds for vacating arbitral awards are mandatory and the parties are not entitled to contract around them.[197] In the United States, however, some courts have opined that the grounds for vacating an award are a mandatory minimum basis rather than a mandatory maximum

---

193 Article V(1)(e) of the New York Convention also contemplates possible control by an authority of the country "under the law of which the award was made", a provision that has given rise to special difficulties and case-law beyond the scope of this discussion.

194 W. Michael Reisman, *Systems of Control in International Adjudication and Arbitration*, Durham, NC: Duke University Press (1992) pp. 109–20.

195 *e.g.*, *Yusuf Ahmed Alghanim & Sons, W.L.L. v. Toys "R" Us Inc.*, 126 F.3d 15 (2nd Cir. 1997); *Halligan v. Piper Jaffray Inc.*, 148 F.3d 197 (2nd Cir. 1998); *George Watt & Son, Inc. v. Tiffany & Co.*, 248 F.3d 577 (7th Cir. 2001); see *Wilko v. Swan*, 346 U.S. 427, 436 (1953) (dicta), overruled on other grounds, *Rodriguez de Quijas v. Shearson/Am. Exp. Inc.*, 490 U.S. 477 (1989); *First Options of Chicago Inc. v. Kaplan*, 514 U.S. 938, 942 (1995) (dicta). See Gary B. Born, *International Commercial Arbitration: Commentary and Materials*, The Hague: Kluwer Law International (2nd edn. 2001) pp. 727–28 (outlining in detail the split among American courts over the grounds for vacating international arbitration awards made in the United States).

196 Swiss Private International Law Act, Art. 192(1) (18 December 1987).

197 W. Michael Reisman, William Laurence Craig, William W. Park and Jan Paulsson, above n. 185, §28.04(c).

cap. Similarly, in England, "a party to arbitration proceedings may ... appeal to the court on a question of law arising out of an award made in the proceedings" unless the parties agree otherwise.[198] This means that the grounds for setting aside arbitral awards are a mandatory minimum basis and the partùies to arbitration cannot contract for less judicial supervision than stipulated in the statutes, but can contract for more judicial supervision.[199] In other countries, the grounds for vacating international arbitration awards are default rules, especially for arbitrations involving foreign parties.[200]

The annulment stage of an award is very domestic compared to the regime governing recognition and enforcement of foreign arbitral awards. Under the New York Convention, there is no restriction imposed on a state court to adopt any grounds to set aside an award issued. The local law in the seat of arbitration may change from time to time, subject to local conditions. In contrast, the second type of judicial control is less domestic, if not more international. A state court in which enforcement is sought decides on those defences that have been outlined in the New York Convention and may have been decided upon in an action for setting aside the award by the judge of the country of rendition. Nevertheless, it is not the case that the New York Convention tried to take away from the enforcement forum its judicial and legislative powers to regulate and decide non-recognition of a foreign judgment.[201]

The co-existence of judicial control by the state of rendition and the state of enforcement in international commercial arbitration is recognised as a dual control mechanism, which is, to a significant degree, rooted in the "territorial" conception of arbitration.[202] It follows that arbitration is conducted subject to

---

198 UK Arbitration Act 1996, §69.

199 For cases holding that parties cannot contract out of judicial review of arbitral awards, see *Iran Aircraft Indus. v. Avco Corp.*, 980 F.2d 141 (2nd Cir. 1992); *M&C Corp. v. Erwin Behr GmbH & Co.*, 87 F.3d 844 (6th Cir. 1996).

200 Swiss Private International Law Act, Art. 192(1) (18 December 1987) states that "where none of the parties has its domicile, its habitual residence, or a business establishment in Switzerland, they may, by an express statement in the arbitration agreement or by a subsequent agreement in writing, exclude all setting aside proceedings, or they may limit such proceedings to one or several of the grounds listed in Art. 190, para. 2".

201 For a comparative overview of grounds for refusal of recognition, see Permanent Bureau of the Hague Conference on Private International Law, Note on the Recognition and Enforcement of Decisions in the Perspective of a Double Convention with Special Regard to Foreign Judgments Awarding Punitive or Excessive Damages (Enforcement of Judgments: Prel. Doc. No. 4 (1996) pp. 8–17).

202 In a complicated case with the involvement of multiple jurisdictions, a dual control mechanism may turn out to be a multiple one. In addition to the country in which or under the law of which an award is made, there may be involvement of the country where the award is enforced as well as of the country where the award debtor's assets are located. The US Fifth Circuit Court examined various courts' functions in the case of *Karaha Bodas Co. LLC v. Perusahaan Pertambangan Minyak Dan Gas Bumi Negara* and confirmed that a court in a country where the award is made has primary jurisdiction while all other countries are secondary jurisdictions. *Karaha Bodas Co. LLC v. Perusahaan Pertambangan Minyak Dan Gas Bumi Negara* 364 F.3d 287 (5th Cir. 2004).

the law of the place of arbitration, and the resulting award forms part of the legal order of that place, and is therefore legitimately subject to such recourse there as the legal order may provide.[203] The theoretical foundation of the territorial theory is the doctrine of sovereign immunity. The territorialism theory clings to the notion of sovereignty that nothing of legal significance can appear anywhere if it is neither approved nor tolerated by the local sovereign.[204] The UNCITRAL Model Law and other modern arbitration legislation recognise a traditional "territorial" view. "The UNCITRAL Model Law makes the place of arbitration the legal touchstone for international arbitration procedure and judicial recourse. ... One of the surprising effects of the legislative reform movement has been to reinforce the concept of the territorial application of arbitration law and the importance of the law of the seat of the arbitration".[205]

An extreme theory at odds with territorialism is the "delocalisation" of international arbitration, which claims that there is no link whatsoever between the arbitral proceeding in the territory and the state's legal regime, and, as a result, arbitral awards rendered in the country of rendition should be considered a-national awards.[206] Both *Chromalloy* and *Hilmarton* challenge the conventional "territorial" conception, and somehow adopt an anti-territorial or delocalised view, though the reasoning may technically differ. The French court in *Hilmarton* stresses the international legal effect of an award from the very early beginning and states that: "... the award rendered in Switzerland was an international award that was not integrated into the legal order of that State, so that its existence remained established despite its annulment..."[207] This was the basis for the Paris Court of Appeal's decision to allow the enforcement of the *Chromalloy* award in France. The decision of the US District Court in *Chromalloy* did not make similar comments.[208] Instead, the Court assumed from the outset that, despite its annulment, there still remained in existence an award capable of being enforced. It seems that both French and US courts upheld the view that an annulled award still has legal effect, either because of its continuous existence or its integration into the international regime from the outset. These two cases, inconsistent with the traditional "territorial" concept, may be justified by the delocalisation theory or the dual control regime, either of which triggers a parallel relaxation of the level of judicial review exerted by local courts in both countries of rendition and enforcement for "international" arbitral awards. The antithesis of the territorial view is that enforcement of

---

203 Ibid.

204 See Jan Paulsson, above n. 77, 20.

205 See William Laurence Craig, 'Some Trends and Developments in the Laws and Practice of International Commercial Arbitration', (1995) 30(1) *Texas Int'l L.J.* 36, 57.

206 Ibid. 23.

207 *Hilmarton c/OTV, Cass. Civ. 1re (Hilmarton)*, (1994) *Rev. Arb.* 328.

208 There is nothing in its decision to suggest that the Court consciously sought to embrace the theory of the "stateless" award.

awards annulled abroad is not impeded when the award in question has been annulled in the country of origin, as a court in the enforcement regime can attribute that award to its existence or effect that is independent from the legal order of the home jurisdiction (arbitral *situs*). The theory of delocalisation effectively suggests that, due to the detachment from the sovereignty, an arbitral award may become stateless and float in the international firmament, capable of being enforced wherever it may touch down.

The primary feature of the delocalisation theory is the notion of party autonomy in determining two key aspects of arbitration. One is the movement toward the delocalisation of the arbitral proceedings, and the other is the trend toward delocalising the applicable law in arbitration. Both developments aim at freeing arbitration from the peculiarities of national laws. As to the delocalisation of arbitral procedure, the objective is to remove arbitration proceedings from the place of arbitration. The ultimate goal is to prevent the law of the place of arbitration from placing undue burden on the arbitration proceedings. However, the present move toward the harmonisation of national laws on arbitration would make delocalisation of arbitration proceedings relatively unnecessary. Therefore, the other development, delocalising applicable law, largely the substantive law, is of more significance. In international commercial arbitration, the governing law of arbitration is often the law of the state where the arbitration is conducted, the *lex loci arbitri*. In practice, the place of arbitration is often chosen because of practical considerations such as a matter of convenience or a matter of connection.[209] The delocalisation theory aims to disconnect arbitration from the place of arbitration,[210] and subject the arbitrating parties to non-national law, such as the *lex mercatoria* and global law.[211] As an obvious example, if the parties to a state contract were to select international law as the governing law and the contract were not supplemented by a particular national law, the dispute has nothing to do with any state law but rather international law, apart from its proclamations of *pacta sunt servanda* and similar generalities.

The motive behind the delocalisation theory is to make international arbitration independent from the rigorous national legal systems, which may impose excessive judicial interference on party autonomy and deprive parties to arbitration of the predictability, finality and confidentiality to which they attach so much importance in arbitration. The notion of delocalised arbitration allows the parties to arbitration to enjoy neutrality and the convenience of the place of arbitration, without resorting to the intricacies of local rules. This concept also suggests that the arbitral procedure and any resulting award shall be autonomous, being disconnected from any national legal system and deriving

---

209 A.F.M. Maniruzzaman, 'Conflict of Law Issues in International Arbitration: Practice and Trends', (1993) 9(4) *Arb. Int'l* 385.

210 Hans Smit, above n. 92, 632.

211 See Chapter 4 of this book.

their legal force solely from the agreement of the parties. On the topic we are discussing here, the concept of delocalised arbitration certainly supports the relaxation of judicial control exerted by the courts in both annulment and enforcement regimes. However, the concept of delocalised arbitration, a theory in favour of the complete detachment of the substance of the dispute from the ambit of national laws, will encounter practical difficulties.[212] For instance, the Court of Appeal in England has supported the view that the procedural law governing arbitration is that of the forum of the arbitration, as this was the system of law with which the agreement to arbitration in the particular forum will have the closest connection.[213] It has also been argued that a large number of provisions in the New York Convention such as Articles II(1), II(3), V(1)(a), V(1)(d), V(1)(e) and VI explicitly recognise the principle of *lex loci arbitri*. The counter argument, however, is that Article VII in the New York Convention allows *lex loci arbitri* to be bypassed, since it establishes the right of the enforcement states to take a more pro-enforcement stance by enforcing a foreign award under its more arbitration-friendly rules despite the award's annulment by the court of rendition where the annulment is not a ground under the domestic law for refusal of recognition of the award.

The dual control mechanism has some benefits. From an economic perspective, the key difference between arbitration and litigation is that governments ordinarily subsidise court systems, with the plaintiff paying only a small filing fee, whereas arbitration institutions charge administration fees to manage the arbitration proceedings. In any event, arbitration may be more or less costly than litigation, but arbitrators and arbitration institutions, as discussed previously in a market setting, are competing under market pressures. The damage awards from the process may be different and are distributional in nature.[214] The differing expected damage awards have "deterrence benefits"[215] and affect the parties' contractual performance and behaviours. If the expected damage award in arbitration is closer to the optimal level than the expected damage judgment in litigation, all else being equal, arbitration will better deter wrongful conduct in arbitration than litigation.[216] Along with its greater deterrence benefits than litigation, arbitration has inherent risks, one of which is the arbitration panel's aberrational award. Unlike in court systems, an appeals process is uncommon in arbitration. The economic reason for this phenomenon

[212] Albert Jan van den Berg, above n. 47, 33.

[213] *Bank Mellat v. Helleniki Technicki SA* [1983] 3 WLR 783–89; *Naviera Amazonica Peruana S.A. v. Compania Internacional de Seguros del Peru* [1988] 1 Lloyds Rep. 116.

[214] One party may require the other party to transfer payment before the disadvantaged party will agree to arbitrate.

[215] Deterrence benefits can result either from the increasing level of deterrence if the expected damages in court are too low (avoiding under-deterrence), or from the decreasing level of deterrence if the expected damages in court are too high (avoiding over-deterrence).

[216] See Keith N. Hylton, 'Agreements to Waive or to Arbitrate Legal Claims: An Economic Analysis', above n. 174, 220.

is that arbitrators face market sanctions for poor decisions. Thus, the risk of an aberrational arbitration award should be theoretically less than the risk of an aberrational trial court decision.[217] However, the market sanctions do not guarantee a zero aberrational award. The parties in arbitration, on the other hand, have little incentive to support or request the law-making function of appellate judges, the benefits of which are purely external to the parties. The lack of an internal appeals process requires an external regime to supervise the regularity and quality of arbitral awards. The court supervision of arbitral awards is a natural substitute in terms of risk management. The availability of judicial review and control by an enforcement court can reduce the risk of aberrational decisions by a court in the arbitral *situs* in two respects. First, enforcing courts can serve a constraint on or protection against an erroneous failure to vacate an award at the arbitral *situs* so that the prevailing party can still collect on the arbitral award. Second, if the award should have been vacated, enforcing courts can always refuse to enforce that award. As Park rightly pointed out, "judicial review of arbitral awards constitutes a form of risk management designed to safeguard against perverse arbitrators and shameless intermeddlers".[218]

The dual control mechanism, nonetheless, gives rise to tremendous uncertainties in practice. Depending upon which approach the court of the enforcement forum will take, either the territoriality or delocalised approach or a combination of both, various models can be used in dealing with the enforcement of an arbitral award that is set aside by the court in the country of rendition. The first model is a strict territoriality model in which the law of the enforcing state requires its courts to refuse enforcement of an arbitral award that has been set aside by a court of competent jurisdiction. This model is adopted by Italy and the Netherlands.[219] The second model is largely the same as the first model except that under the laws of the enforcing state, the grounds for refusal of enforcement of a foreign arbitral award are more limited than those of Article V and preclude the grounds of the setting aside of the award under the *lex loci*

---

217 Gordon Tullock, above n. 153, 123; Robert D. Cooter, above n. 152, 107; Robert D. Cooter and Daniel L. Rubinfeld, 'Trial Courts: An Economic Perspective', (1990) 24 *L. & Soc'y Rev.* 533, 545.

218 William W. Park, above n. 180, 808.

219 Article 840(5) of the Italian Code of Civil Procedure provides as follows:

> The Court of Appeal shall refuse recognition and enforcement of the foreign award if in the opposition proceedings the party against whom the award is invoked proves any of the following circumstances: ... (5) the award has not yet become binding on the parties or has been set aside or suspended by a competent authority of the State in which, or under the law of which, it was made.

Article 1076(1)(A)(e) of the Netherlands Private International Law Act provides as follows:

> If no treaty concerning recognition and enforcement is applicable, or if applicable treaty allows a party to rely on the law of the country in which recognition and enforcement is sought, an arbitral award made in a foreign State may be recognised in the Netherlands and its enforcement may be sought in the Netherlands ... unless: ... (e) the arbitral award has been set aside by a competent authority of the country in which the award is made.

arbitri. However, under this model, the award that has been set aside in the country of rendition may still be entitled to enforcement by the court in the enforcing jurisdiction according to the "most favoured right" provision (Article VII) of the New York Convention if the requirements of the law of the enforcement forum are satisfied. The third model recognises the territoriality rule by respecting the decision of a foreign court of competent jurisdiction to set aside the award subject to rights of impeachment in cases such as procedural unfairness or obtaining a judgment by fraud. This model grants a certain level of discretion to the courts in the enforcement forum. England,[220] Mexico,[221] Germany[222] and Switzerland[223] adopt this model. The fourth model is likely not to recognise an annulment order in the court of origin either as grounds in itself for refusing enforcement of the award or as any kind of presumption that such an order establishes facts which would bring the case within a possible ground under the law of the enforcing state. The fifth model is based upon the delocalisation theory and has been adopted by French courts. In a series of cases, the Court of Cassation held that the setting aside or suspension of an award by a court in the country of origin did not deprive the party obtaining the award of his right to have the award enforced in France in the conditions permitted by French law.[224] Under the French model, Article V of the New York Convention would rarely be applied and can be almost regarded as a dead letter. The sixth model is an extreme and unique model adopted by Belgium. According to the Belgian legislation, no court in Belgium could set aside an award unless at least one party to arbitration is Belgian. The model effectively endorses the delocalisation theory and reflects such a theory in the annulment rather than enforcement stage. In brief, the possibility of various legislative or judicial models is likely to cast uncertainties over the enforcement practice and policies and spread scepticism and reluctance towards arbitration among international law- and policy-makers. Lack of certainty may also result in inconsistent judgments by foreign courts and multiple jeopardy, as has been demonstrated by *Hilmarton* and *Chromalloy*.

The dual control mechanism also causes conflicts of interest and inherent inefficiencies. Conflicts of interest arise between the annulment of an award in the home jurisdiction and enforcement of an annulled award in a foreign jurisdiction because enforcement of an annulled award may be regarded by its home jurisdiction as showing a lack of respect for the court's decision in setting

220 Article 103(2) of the UK Arbitration Act 1996.

221 Article 1462 of the Mexican Commercial Code.

222 Article 1061 of the German Code of Civil Procedure.

223 Article 194 of the Swiss Private International Law Act 1987.

224 *Pabalt Tikeret Sirketi v. Norsolor*, Cass. 1ere civ., 9 October 1984 (1985) *Rev. Arb.* 431; *Polish Ocean Line v. Jolasry*, Cass. 1ere civ. 10 March 1993 (1993) *Rev. Arb.* 255; *Hilmarton Ltd. v. Omnium de Traitement et de Valorisation (OTV)* Cass. 1ere civ., 23 March 1994 (1994) *Rev. Arb.* 327; *Arab Republic of Egypt v. Chromalloy Air Services*, CA Paris, 14 January 1997 (1997) *Rev. Arb.* 395.

aside the award. The French courts were criticised for their approach in dealing with *Hilmarton* where the Swiss Supreme Court's decision to set aside the award was not duly respected. In *Hilmarton*, the French Court of Cassation did not recognise the regularity and legitimacy of the decision made by the Swiss Supreme Court but applied French law to the case. According to French law, the annulment of a foreign award in the jurisdiction where the award is issued is not a ground for rejecting an application to recognise and enforce the award in France. In this sense, the French courts' approach was criticised as a unilateralist or imperialist one.[225] Nevertheless, from a legal perspective, for a court to apply its own law in its own territory would not be considered imperialist regardless of public international law. In *Chromalloy*, the interest of Egypt was undermined by the decision made by the US Court since the integrity of its legal system, in particular the arbitration system, was destroyed to a certain extent. In reality, conflicts of interest may cause more practical difficulty and inefficiency. It is likely that the dual control mechanism may be transformed into a multi-party control practice. It is possible under Article V(1)(e) that the courts in two or more countries, namely the country where the award is rendered and the country under the law of which the award is rendered, may find that they both have jurisdiction to set aside an award and that the two decisions may be inconsistent.[226] Furthermore, the country where the award is enforced may also find that it actually has jurisdiction to decide whether an annulled award shall be enforced or not. The judgment rejecting an appeal to set aside the award in the country where it is rendered leaves complete freedom to the court in the country where enforcement is sought to refuse enforcement of such awards.[227] A bizarre consequence would be that after an action to set aside the award has been rejected in Country A where the award was issued, enforcement of the award may be refused in Country B but granted in Country C.[228] Inefficiency is also reflected by an increasingly significant cost in the possibility of multiple enforcement actions faced by the parties. Enforcement of arbitral awards may take place in any jurisdiction that recognises an annulled award and where the losing party has assets. A party that fails in an attempt in one jurisdiction can bring successive actions to other jurisdictions until it ultimately realises its credit of the award. The exposure to a multiplicity of proceedings in a number of different countries undermines the economic efficiency in arbitration, and induces profligacy and the wasteful use of resources.

---

[225] See Sebastien Besson and Luc Pittet, 'La reconnaissance à l'étranger d'une sentence annulée dans son Etat d'origine – Reflexions à la suite de l'affaire Hilmarton', (1998) 3 *Bulletin ASA* 515.

[226] See Philippe Fouchard, above n. 171, 332.

[227] Philippe Fouchard, above n. 171; Philippe Fouchard, 'Suggestions pour accroître l'efficacité internationale des sentences arbitrales', (1998) 4 *Rev. Arb.* 666; J.F. Poudret, 'Quelle solution pour en finir avec l'affaire Hilmarton? Réponse à Philippe Fouchard', (1998) 1 *Rev. Arb.* 17.

[228] See the case discussed in XXIII *Yearbook* (1998) 754.

A related question arising out of *Chromalloy* is how arbitration and litigation can co-exist in the trend of globalisation. Put differently, the question is how to balance the need for judicial review and for private autonomy based on the principle of party autonomy. Notwithstanding the theory of "internationalism", as opposed to "territorialism", the *Chromalloy* decision, along with its Belgian and French predecessors, brings sovereign rules into doubt. The court's tendentious pragmatism is not apt to preserve sovereignty, and the enforcement of an annulled award constitutes a violation of the implicit allocation of sovereignty among national courts under international law,[229] even though such sovereignty is recognised by the New York Convention.

The New York Convention does not provide a solution to the chaos caused by *Chromalloy* and *Hilmarton*. Article VI of the New York Convention endeavours to reduce the discrepancy that arises between annulment in the country of origin and enforcement in another jurisdiction by providing that the enforcement court may adjourn the enforcement proceedings pending a decision of the annulment court. The proceedings in the country of rendition and in the country of enforcement are coordinative due to their closeness. In theory, the coordination can be achieved by giving priority to the court first seised. However, Article VI is not able to bring international harmony to the chaos caused by the dual control mechanism between the country of origin and the country of enforcement since it, together with Article V(1)(e), provides the most important procedural weapon to respondents seeking to resist enforcement. The combined effect of Articles V(1)(e) and VI of the New York Convention is to enable the courts in the country of enforcement to refuse or postpone enforcement if the award "has not yet become binding on the parties" or if it has been "set aside or suspended by a competent authority of the country in which it was made". As previously discussed, both limbs give rise to practical and theoretical problems.

3.5.4. TENSIONS BETWEEN RENDITION AND ENFORCEMENT FORUMS AND GAMING SETTINGS

The New York Convention may be characterised by fundamental tensions between the courts of the enforcing forum versus those of the arbitral *situs*.[230] Traditionally, arbitration is regarded as an important branch of customary international law,

[229] See Albert Jan van den Berg, above n. 47, 15 (stating that an arbitral award would not be vested with a practically irrefutable regularity at the moment of its issue).

[230] As discussed before, the forum of arbitration can be several jurisdictions and the forum of enforcement generally only refers to the jurisdiction in which enforcement of the award is sought. Although it is possible for the parties to apply for the enforcement of the award even after it is set aside first in the same jurisdiction, in practice this rarely takes place. To simplify the discussion, the tension here is limited to the one between the forum of arbitration (the country of origin) and enforcement.

which is often understood as a general practice of states developed out of a sense of legal obligation. However, game theory principles suggest that customary norms are in fact the result of self-interested states acting in various strategic situations. States do not respect and comply with customary arbitration rules out of a sense of legal obligation. Rather, they act out of their rational self-interest in their interactions with other states. The felicific calculus is difficult because it is not certain how other states will react to alternative measures. Economic analysis makes an assumption that the state, like an individual person, is a "rational economic person" or a rational maximiser of its satisfaction.[231] The discussion and analysis here are premised upon this conception of rationality.

In principle, regularities exist in behavioural models among states. In terms of influencing state behaviours, the implications for a game theory critique extend to both custom and treaties, and appear to imply that neither source of law can be relied on to influence state behaviour when interests change. Even if this theoretic presumption is true, international law can continue to be used instrumentally to enhance international cooperation when desired. The feasibility of using customary norms or treaties to influence behaviours or not depends on the assessment of the level of functioning of and compliance with legal norms. In this sense, customary norms do not reflect a single unitary logic. Instead of a set of rules established by a general and consistent practice followed out of a sense of legal obligation, customary arbitration rules actually refer to behavioural regularities that emerge out of self-interested state interactions in various strategic settings. It appears that a new insight can be gained by identifying those situations in which behavioural regularities among states arise. There are four basic models that give rise to such regularities: coincidence of interest, coercion, cooperation, and coordination.

Coincidence of interest occurs "where states engage in behavioural regularities simply because each obtains private advantages from a particular action (which happens to be the same action taken by the other state) irrespective of the action of the other".[232] Assuming that an arbitral award is issued by an

[231] For the concept of "rational economic person", see Robin Paul Malloy, *Law in a Market Context: An Introduction to Market Concepts in Legal Reasoning*, Cambridge: Cambridge University Press (2004) pp. 144–46. For instance, if a state will achieve more of what it wants to achieve by taking step A rather than step B, *homo economicus* will, by definition, take step A; to do otherwise would, by definition, be acting irrationally. The felicific calculus is also problematic because of empirical difficulties in finding out what states do in fact want. What a state wants is, by definition, what a state is willing to pay for – either in money, or by the development of some other resource that a state has, such as time and effort. For all that happens to a state can be reduced to things a state will pay to have or pay to be without, the solvent of a hypothetical market. For more accounts of applying the rationality concept in the study of law and economics, see Avery Wiener Katz, *Foundations of The Economic Approach to Law*, New York: Foundation Press (1998) pp. 296–340.

[232] Jack L. Goldsmith and Eric A. Posner, 'A Theory of Customary International Law', (1999) 66 *U. Chi. L. Rev.* 1113, 1122.

arbitration panel which accepted bribes from both sides, the courts in the place of arbitration and the enforcement forum share the same interest in mitigating the negative effects generated by this award.[233] Under certain conditions, it is simply more beneficial for the courts in both states to act without regard for the other state's action. The payoff for ignoring the other's judicial action is higher than extending its jurisdiction towards a judgment made by the other state, the side effect of which is to damage the relationship between two states. Moreover, the fact that two states refrain from "attack" is coincidental. The third model dealing with enforcement of an annulled award, discussed in Section 5.3.1 *supra*, adopted by England, Mexico, Germany and Switzerland, can be seen as a coincidence model.

Coercion takes place when "one state, or a coalition of states with convergent interests, forces other states to engage in actions that serve the interest of the first state or group of states".[234] For example, the European Union and the United States use coercion to codify their preferences in international law and "forum-shopping" among different governmental organisations to advance their interests by pushing international law to their desired ends.[235] The strategy employed first involves an agreement among a coalition of the willing, followed by enticing the resisting sovereign states to agree. The true basis of the legal prohibition is economic efficiency, rather than some other normative concept.[236] In our context, the powerful state could threaten to destroy a weaker state's judgment if it attacks or damages the stronger state's commercial interests. The stronger state could do so if the costs of carrying out the threat are relatively low. The weaker state, realising that its payoff for attacking the stronger state's commercial interests is very low, will not do so or will stop doing so. If the stronger state can make better use of its advantageous position, it will not necessarily attack the weaker state's legal system.[237] A different but possible scenario is retaliation. An arbitral *situs* might retaliate against an enforcement court that enforces an award vacated in the *situs* either by enforcing vacated awards originating from the enforcement jurisdiction or by refusing to enforce

233 See the *Paquete Habana* decision 175 U.S. 677 (1900), in which each of two belligerent states that patrol the same body of water can choose between attacking or ignoring commercial fishing vessels of the other state. Under certain conditions, it is simply more beneficial for each state to ignore the other state's fishing boats than it is to attack them. The payoff for ignoring the other's boats is higher than it is for attacking, and the fact that the two states refrain from attack is coincidental. "The outcome is no more surprising than the fact that states do not sink their own ships".

234 Jack L. Goldsmith and Eric A. Posner, above n. 232.

235 Daniel W. Drezner, 'On the Balance between International Law and Democratic Sovereignty', (2001) 2 *Chicago Journal of International Law* 321, 323, 329, 332.

236 So-called *mala in se,* such as murder, assault, rape and theft, are examples of coerced transactions. See Richard A. Posner, *Economic Analysis of Law,* New York: Aspen Publishers (4th edn. 1993) pp. 251–252.

237 Jack L. Goldsmith and Eric A. Posner, above n. 232, 1124.

all awards from that jurisdiction.[238] In a coercive model, some value is transferred from the weaker state to the stronger one without proper bargaining.[239] Again, the regularity in the behavioural models cannot be simply explained by a general rule. Rather, the explanation may be given by reference to states' rational response to a given strategic situation. In this context, the obvious imbalance between two states may stop both sides from taking any direct actions towards the other state. A stronger state, in terms of its commercial advantages and privileges in the international community, at a relatively lower price, may pressure a weaker state not to take any actions against it or otherwise discredit the weaker state's judicial decision. There are however practical difficulties in assessing damages in these circumstances.

Cooperation takes place when states find themselves in a bilateral repeated prisoner's dilemma.[240] The logic of the prisoner's dilemma, as previously illustrated in this chapter, is such that it would be mutually beneficial if two states in such a dilemma were to cooperate. If the game is played only once, the only "rational" thing to do is to defect. Over repeated interactions, though, states realise that it is more beneficial to cooperate so long as the other side does not defect. However, several conditions must be met for the purpose of cooperation. First, states must be aware of the benefits of cooperation in a repeated prisoner's dilemma. Second, states must believe that they will continue to encounter each other in the foreseeable future. Third, both parties must care about the future, which means that they must both be willing to defer a present payoff for future gains.[241] In other words, states must believe that cooperation is better than other means to protect or realise their own interests. Finally, the payoffs for defection must not be too high relative to the payoffs for cooperation.[242] Due to these conditions, the behavioural regularity among states through cooperation is less likely to arise than through coincidence of interest or coercion. Nevertheless, when such conditions exist, true cooperation among states does occur.[243] The

---

238 See Eric A. Schwartz, above n. 91, 135 ("I fear the more likely consequence of decisions such as *Chromalloy* may be to undercut the efforts of those who have been laboring for years to restore confidence in the international arbitration process in Egypt and elsewhere in the Middle East, where international arbitration has long been viewed with suspicion"). Also see Emmanuel Gaillard, above n. 42, 521–23.

239 For instance, in a criminal law context, some value is transferred from the victim to the delinquent without proper bargaining. The law then penalises the thief, not because theft is in some non-economic sense "wrong", but in order to persuade the thief to use the market. The reason for punishment is that the cost to the delinquent needs to be greater than mere compensation in order to provide him with the necessary incentive to refrain.

240 Jack L. Goldsmith and Eric A. Posner, above n. 232, 1125–26.

241 This means that the future discount must be low.

242 Jack L. Goldsmith and Eric A. Posner, above n. 232, 1126.

243 Ibid. at 1127. For purposes of this section, the concept of "true" cooperation is used to refer to instances of behavioural regularities that are not merely the product of coincidence of interest or of coercion. More positively, it is a decision that it is preferable to cooperate with or coordinate one's strategy with another's.

cooperative setting can also evolve from the coincidental setting where the common advantages become a common scenario. For instance, where the annulment court has not been impartial in handling the case,[244] *i.e.*, the relevant judgment was obtained by fraud, or there has been a serious procedural irregularity,[245] or there exists a previously made contrary judgment of the forum which is *res judicata* there,[246] the annulment and enforcement regimes recognise similar defects in an award and it is in the common interests of both the enforcement and rendition forums to see non-enforcement of an annulled award.

The New York Convention can fit into and constitute a cooperative setting, just as it envisages a mechanism which depends on the cooperation of national courts in Member States. The cooperative setting here is based on reciprocal trust and confidence as well as comity. The reciprocity or comity would be impaired if any court in any one Member State is biased against other States' nationals, as other States may show bias in favour of their own nationals. In order for its own nationals to be equally and fairly protected, the national court's only sensible choice is to cooperate by taking a pro-arbitration (or pro-enforcement) stance. The cooperative setting needs the courts in various jurisdictions to act in a "federal" type of legal regime framed by the New York Convention. Seen from this angle, the court in the enforcement forum may not deserve judicial discretions if harmony or unity were conceived of as the primary goal of the New York Convention.

Finally, coordination between states can arise when each state's best move depends on the move of the other state. In this situation, State 1 prefers to take action X if State 2 takes action X, and State 1 prefers to take action Y if State 2 takes action Y. The problem, however, is that there must be some way to know or communicate in advance what the other state will do so as to make coordination possible; otherwise, the states must choose by guessing as to what the other will do. In a legal context, access to an international treaty which adopts a reciprocal treatment may effectively inform the international community of a state's own position. Similarly, the state can predict judicial actions or standings of other Member States to the treaty on the same issue. The international treaty functions as a communicative tool. This again proves the need for a convention or a higher

---

244 Park discussed the possibility of biased or corrupt judiciaries in William W. Park, 'National Law and Commercial Justice: Safeguarding Procedural Integrity in International Commercial Arbitration', (1989) 63 *Tul. L. Rev.* 647 (referring to "dishonestly annulled" awards).

245 *e.g.* the defendant has not been duly summoned or was otherwise not given an adequate opportunity to present his case.

246 The Brussels Convention Article 27(3); the Hague Convention Article 5(3)(b). That case is sometimes considered to fall under the general ground of contrariety to public policy. See the Convention on the Reciprocal Recognition of Judicial Decisions (Athens, 4 November 1961), Act 4305/1963, [1963] Official Gazette of the Hellenic Republic, No. A78, Article 3(1)(a) (Federal Republic of Germany-Greece).

level of supervision mechanism in the field of international commercial arbitration.

Most behavioural regularities among states that purport to serve as a basis for customary norms can be explained by coincidence of interest or coercion. It is often claimed that the legal validity of a rule is a matter of that rule's derivability from some basic conventional criterion of legal validity accepted in the particular legal system. Although most behavioural regularities among states can be understood as self-interested responses in one or more of the foregoing four types of gaming settings, it is still necessary to posit a universal customary norm that explains such behaviour in terms of predictability and stability. Apparently, the collision of domestic and international standards in an unguided context threatens to create strife in judicial relations between nations. Cooperative universal behavioural regularities, however, are not illusory. Indeed, states have now moved beyond the stage of self-restraint and towards active international cooperation through various means, such as legislation and international activism in promoting cross-border collaboration in specific fields. In the present context, cooperation can be formed as a result of all state players' recognition of a repeated prisoner's dilemma or coordinative game. It has been proposed that the court, without being bound to deny recognition of an award that has been set aside, may consider the award and the foreign judgment, together with the pertinent interests and policies, before deciding which decision should be given effect.[247] This approach indeed acknowledges the superior position of the foreign court to review the arbitration. At the international level, cooperation in these circumstances is probably not common and, therefore, requires wider recognition of some basic norms or a systematic legal reform so as to build up an effective legal framework. This is partly due to the fact that universality implies a large number of actors. In the case of the n-person repeated prisoner's dilemma, however, the game eventually raises the public good or tragedy of the common problems. In spite of cooperation among a large number of players, one will always find it advantageous to defect or free-ride. In the case of coordination, the sheer number of players makes such coordination very difficult. Given these problems, it appears that a form of cooperation among states can be more realistically accomplished through enacting treaties.[248] After all, law is a matter of a rule having been established in some recognised sources, such as a statute or a binding precedent. If rationalistic motivation is not to be hoped for, public measures should seek to balance conflicting aspirations by

---

247 Stephen T. Ostrowski and Yuval Shany, '*Chromalloy*: United States Law and International Arbitration at the Crossroads', (1998) 73 *NYU L. Rev.* 1692.

248 For instance, the New York Convention itself achieved uniformity which in turn creates a safer and more stable legal environment for arbitration to prosper and minimises forum shopping. See Hamid G. Gharavi, '*Chromalloy*: Another View', (1997) 12 *Mealey's Int'l Arb. Rep.* 21–22.

giving as much satisfaction to each actor in the game as possible. From an economical perspective, in settings in which the cost of allocating resources by voluntary transactions is prohibitively high, making the market an infeasible method of allocating resources, the common law prices behaviour in such a way as to mimic the market.

Alternatively, cooperation can be achieved if most states truly recognise party autonomy by treating the rule of enforceability or non-enforceability of vacated arbitral awards as a default rule rather than a mandatory rule. After all, party autonomy itself is a widely recognised arbitration norm and a "majoritarian" default rule, which most parties would likely acknowledge with full information and low bargaining costs. Besides, the decision by the enforcement court to enforce or not enforce a vacated award will be based on the parties' agreement, rather than a mandatory rule of the enforcement jurisdiction. Therefore, there is less reason for the arbitral *situs* to take retaliatory actions. This would reduce the likelihood of conflicts of interests among states or of the wrong choice of the default rule. A cooperative model will guarantee that the courts in different jurisdictions are more likely to grant the same courtesy in future situations by deferring to the court decisions in respect of the validity of awards in another jurisdiction, when the reviewing and enforcing roles are reversed. Therefore, international comity, or a community-based reciprocal respect for the laws of other states, would potentially benefit a party seeking to enforce abroad an award affirmed or vacated in one jurisdiction, for example, by saving the extra trouble and expense of convincing another set of courts in the enforcement forum that the award should be recognised and enforced. In this way, observance of court review guards against the possibility of enforcing an unfair arbitral award and increases the universality of award recognition and enforcement, which are necessary for the smooth functioning of an international system of dispute resolution by arbitration.

Annulment of an arbitral award is still relatively local, rather than international, in the sense that annulment of an award rendered in State A by State B does not influence any other jurisdictions' decision to recognise and enforce this award. At a practical level, it is rare to see the arbitral *situs* exporting its conception of arbitration outside its border. Largely, this is because the grounds for setting aside an award, unlike those for refusing recognition and enforcement of a foreign award, have not been standardised yet. That is to say, those grounds are specific to the legal order of the country of rendition. The New York Convention does not regulate the grounds on which an arbitral award can be vacated and does not seek to harmonise the grounds of annulment of awards. However, the competition among jurisdictions for international arbitration business may influence the standards for vacating awards set out in national arbitration laws since serving as a *situs* for international arbitration proceedings can be lucrative.[249] Consequently, jurisdictions compete to provide favourable arbitration settings including providing favorable legal standards, norms and environment.[250] International arbitration proceedings are so mobile that parties can choose a different arbitral *situs* in future agreements to arbitrate if a national arbitration law is seen as unfavourable.[251] It is also in the interest of private parties and arbitration institutions to avoid locating arbitration in a jurisdiction with legal standards they find harsh and objectionable.[252] Although some have decried inter-jurisdictional competition among arbitral sites as a "race to the bottom",[253] in other areas such competition has been beneficial in improving the quality of regulation.[254] Technically speaking, the grounds listed in Article V(1)(a) to (d) of the New York Convention for refusing enforcement of an award are essentially the same as those grounds on which the judges may set aside an award in the arbitral *situs*. This is the case since more and more jurisdictions have adopted UNCITRAL Model Law, which is in turn modelled on the New York Convention. In terms of promoting arbitration and ameliorating the regulatory environment, the UNCITRAL Model Law provides for fairly uniform standards. Its continuous spread should eventually result in a diminishing number of local standards in annulment practice. This would be the case even

---

249 See, *e.g.*, UK Department of Trade and Industry, Departmental Advisory Report 69 (1996) ("The fact is that this country has been very slow to modernize its arbitration law and this has done us no good in our endeavour to retain our pre-eminence in the field of international arbitration, a service which brings this country very substantial amounts indeed"), quoted in W. Michael Reisman, William Laurence Craig, William W. Park and Jan Paulsson, above n. 185, §28.06.

250 Thomas E. Carbonneau, *Cases and Materials on the Law and Practice of Arbitration*, New York: Juris Publishing (2nd edn. 2000) p. 1143 ("Many jurisdictions have flung their regulatory authority to the winds in order to climb upon the 'hospitable-jurisdiction-to-arbitration' bandwagon and advertise their availability as venues to arbitration"); See Klaus Peter Berger, *International Economic Arbitration*, Deventer/Boston: Kluwer Law and Taxation Publishers (1993) pp. 8–9.

251 W. Michael Reisman, William Laurence Craig, William W. Park and Jan Paulsson, above n. 185, §28.06 ("Particularly at the margins of venue selection, a reputation for a good or bad arbitration law will often cause a migration among otherwise plausible locations"); Filip De Ly, 'The Place of Arbitration in the Conflict of Laws of International Commercial Arbitration: An Exercise in Arbitration Planning', (1991) 12 *NW J. Int'l L. & Bus.* 48–49; Jacques Werner, 'International Commercial Arbitrators: From Merchant to Academic to Skilled Professional', (1998) *Dispute Resolution Magazine* 22.

252 Stephen R. Bond and Christopher R. Seppala, 'The New (1998) Rules of Arbitration of the International Chamber of Commerce', (1997) 12(5) *Mealey's Int'l Arb. Rep.* 33–38.

253 In the case of Belgian arbitration law, competition has resulted in more oversight of arbitration at the arbitral *situs*. This will be discussed below. However, it should be pointed out that some parties may prefer a higher level of court supervision in arbitration even though not every party does. In this sense, a higher level of judicial supervision may be regarded as a more favourable feature of that jurisdiction by some parties.

254 Roberta Romano, 'State Competition for Corporate Charters', in John Ferejohn and Barry R. Weingast (eds.), *The New Federalism: Can the States be Trusted?* Stanford, CA: Hoover Institutions Press (1997) p. 129 ("the best available evidence indicates that, for the most part, the race is towards the top but not the bottom in the production of corporate laws"); and Richard L. Revesz, 'Rehabilitating Interstate Competition', above n. 109, 1210.

though various grounds for setting aside awards and different understandings of the scope and requirements of these grounds are in existence and can be chaotic. This task of harmonising the standards for setting aside an award should be at the core of the new regulatory or legislative regime which has yet to be established by the New York Convention.

Enforcing an annulled award may cause the forum shopping which the international legal community has made great efforts to eliminate in the field of international litigation. Forum shopping will also attack the purpose of arbitration which tries to avoid most serious defects of the court system and international commercial litigation, and to become a reliable substitute. The grant of international legal effect to an annulled award would indeed provide the home jurisdiction with a controlling discretion over disputes arbitrated within its territory. This excessive discretion amounts to giving the state courts the discretionary power to choose a possibly favourable result for the dispute, and, along with the tensions and conflicting interests between the rendition and enforcement forums, further encouraging the local standard for annulment, which is described by Paulsson as "annulments on the basis of ... other criteria than those which are internationally accepted".[255] It is therefore very likely that local courts may be inclined to protect the local party in a dispute by applying more biased local standards. This sort of local tendency is often described as local protectionism, which, as a matter of fact, is more popular in developing countries. Local protectionism is shown in the annulment standards, procedurally or substantively. A clear distinction has been made between local and international annulment standards, which consist of four grounds contained in Article V(1)(a) to (d) of the New York Convention, the exclusive grounds for annulment in modern domestic laws, as well as Article 36(2)(a) of the UNCITRAL Model Law.[256] As a result, any international commercial dispute with parties from developing countries may largely rely on the court or judicial systems in those countries because relevant parties from these jurisdictions have confidence in their home jurisdictions for local protection. The potentially defeated party may search for a jurisdiction which adopts local annulment standards.

Forum shopping in international litigation may occur again in international arbitration. To eliminate the forum shopping in international commercial arbitration also requires cooperation within the international community. Ideally, annulling decisions based on such grounds would be accorded deference by the courts in the enforcement forum, which conforms to the principle of

---

255 Jan Paulsson, above n. 77, 20.

256 Under this presumption, an arbitral award can be set aside if it violates fundamental legal principles, for example, the principle of *pacta sunt servanda*, the protection against the misuse of a right, the principle of good faith, or the protection against expropriation without remuneration. See Nathalie Voser, 'Mandatory Rules of Law as a Limitation on the Law Applicable in International Commercial Arbitration', (1996) 7 *Am. Rev. Int'l Arb.* 334.

international comity embodying such notions as mutual courtesy and respect.[257] Annulment based on any other local grounds needs to be denied extraterritorial effect.[258] This scenario is close to the coincidental model because, in order to realise its self-interest to win international recognition of the locally vacated awards, the state will "allow the arbitral process to become truly international", which "will create incentives for national courts to conform to internationally accepted standards".[259] In effect, this scenario becomes a competitive model, reputation costs of which certainly ensure optimal deference of the state mistakes or misconducts. The competitive behavioural model will possibly eliminate a "race to the bottom" if other jurisdictions are attracted to protect their own nation's commercial and legal interests and not to lower their annulment standards. In the judicial competition, the host country's economic motivation to provide a desirable setting for future international commercial arbitrations, thereby promoting potential investors' confidence in the country, makes its courts consider the appropriateness of adopting local annulment standards in the first phase of an arbitral award review. Since attracting international commercial arbitration requires a high level of fairness and impartiality, decent legal infrastructure, and sufficient attention to foreign parties' legitimate concerns, the host state has to consider such factors when it reviews awards made within its territory. Expectation of fairness and impartiality by the international arbitration community requires courts in the home jurisdiction not to lower their annulment standards. Therefore, a "race to the top" is more likely to take place, and the interstate interactions, in a model of perfect competition, would be welfare-enhancing. For instance, US courts are willing to recognise an award rendered in New York governing two foreign parties as a "foreign award"[260] which then falls in the regime of New York Convention and is entitled to a more liberal and international enforcement standard. This effectively is a beneficial consequence of the "race to the top" whereby the US courts adopt a more lenient approach to arbitral awards even if those awards are rendered locally and therefore attract more arbitration.

In our context, there is also a "race to the bottom," a result of external competition for the supply of law. In order to make Belgium an attractive forum

---

257 A general comity jurisprudence may be in place allowing the application of foreign law. It is said that the consideration of comity of nations is the only basis for a national interest in upholding a foreign law. J.J. Fawcett, 'Evasion of Law and Mandatory Rules in Private International Law', (1990) 49(1) *Cambridge Law Journal* 44, 55. Following this line of thinking, where the foreign mandatory law is pro-arbitration or both local and foreign laws are pro-arbitration, the application of such laws is no longer an issue.

258 Certainly, there may be some practical wisdom behind that construction, but it is entirely outside the language of the spirit of the New York Convention.

259 Jan Paulsson, above n. 77, 31.

260 *Bergesen v. Joseph Muller Corp.*, 710 F.2d 928 (2nd Cir. 1983). In this case, the award concerned a Swiss and Norwegian party and was made in New York. The court held that the award was a "foreign award", which could then be enforced in the US under the New York Convention.

for international arbitration, Belgium introduced a provision excluding the power of Belgian courts to entertain an application for annulment of an award unless at least one party to the arbitration is a Belgian as defined.[261] This provision effectively removes the possibility of annulment by the Belgian courts, leaves the parties who wanted judicial assistance or had good grounds for annulment with nowhere to go, and gives the control over the arbitral awards *de facto* to the forum where the enforcement is sought. In effect, this provision makes Belgium a forum to be avoided by the international arbitration community.[262] The International Court of Arbitration at the ICC did avoid Belgium as a place for arbitration when it was able to determine the place of arbitration itself.[263] The business community generally does not want to risk a forum for dispute resolution which removes any possibility of appeal from the outset. In response to the criticisms from the international arbitration community,[264] Belgium, along with Sweden[265] and Tunisia,[266] followed the lead of the Swiss Private International Law Act[267] and changed its law by enabling the parties to exclude the request for annulment rather than a complete exclusion of it by operation of law.[268] This is a real example to show the existence of judicial competition in reality and the need for a rational design in the competitive setting. This is also a strong example effectively indicating that the parties to arbitration do need judicial scrutiny in order to protect their interests.

A critique against the separatist proposition is that local law may subvert international uniformity.[269] For instance, the French position is that an award may be invalid in the rendition forum but still valid in France, which is close to a relativity theory in legal regime. By giving no weight to the judicial review on the

---

261 Judicial Code Article 1717(4).

262 Herman Verbist, 'Reform of the Belgian Arbitration Law (the Law of 19 May 1998)', (1998) 7 *Int'l Bus. L.J.* 843; Luc Demeyere, '1998 Amendments to Belgian Arbitration Law: An Overview', (1999) 15 *Arb. Int'l* 295, 308 (translation of Judicial Code, Art. 1717.4) ("[Former Article 1717.4] was highly criticized and for some, including arbitration institutions, Belgium became a forum to be avoided").

263 Luc Demeyere, above n. 262.

264 William W. Park, above n. 244, 647; Marcel Storme and Bernadette Demeulenaere, *International Commercial Arbitration in Belgium: A Handbook,* Antwerp: Kluwer Law and Taxation International (1989) p. 22; Bernadette Demeulenaere, 'The Place of Arbitration and the Applicable Procedure Law: The Case of Belgium', in Marcel Storme and Filip De Ly (eds.), *The Place of Arbitration,* Ghent: Mys and Breesch (1992) p. 67.

265 Swedish Arbitration Act 1999 s 51.

266 Tunisian Arbitration Act Article 78–6.

267 Private International Law Act Article 192(2).

268 It reads: "through an explicit declaration in their arbitration agreement or by a later agreement, parties may exclude all requests to nullify an arbitral award if none of the parties is a natural person of Belgian nationality or a natural person whose habitual residence is in Belgium or a legal person with its principal place of business or a branch in Belgium".

269 See Bruno Leurent and Nathalie Meyer-Fabre, 'La reconnaissance en France des sentences rendues à l'étranger, l'exemple Franco Suisse', (1995) 13 *Bulletin ASA* 118; Hamid G. Gharavi, above. 248, 21.

award by the court in the arbitral *situs* and viewing the arbitral award as separate from the national judicial regime, France upholds party autonomy to resolve disputes. This in turn supports the proposition that the benefits of arbitration, *i.e.*, faster determination of issues and the ability to select a neutral forum, far outweigh any positive aspects of observing *situs* court review. Under this approach, enforcement of arbitral awards would dispel the parties' unease because the thought and action of litigating in the courts of the opposing party's home country would not be upheld in France. However, this relativity theory may hinder uniformity in the process of international commercial arbitration and award recognition[270] and then further subvert any notion of international judicial cooperation and comity. Apparently, the French approach undermines international interaction necessary for the smooth functioning of the international market. The relativity theory of the French practice may lead to a "multi-localisation" as opposed to a complete detachment from national laws, or "delocalisation", of international arbitral awards.[271] The assumption of such criticism is that the courts of the state of origin have a legitimate claim to support annulment proceedings, and that the courts will apply the same grounds for setting aside awards as under Article V(1)(a) to (d) of the New York Convention.[272] However, it has been argued that the enforcement forum has a better claim to determine the validity of an international award than the rendition forum.[273] The French theory is explicitly stated in the *Chromalloy* opinion by the Paris Court of Appeal: "[T]he award made in Egypt is an international award which, by definition, is not integrated in the legal order of that state so that its existence remains established despite it being annulled and its recognition in France is not in violation of international public policy".[274] The theory is consistent with common practice in France that the French legal order would not consider it an offence to its sovereignty for an enforcement forum to

270 See Erica Smith, above n. 38, 367.

271 See Pierre Meyer, 'L'insertion de la sentence dans l'ordre juridique francaise', in Yves Derains et al (ed.), *Droit et Pratique de l'Arbitrage International en France*, Paris: Fondation pour l'étude du droit et des usages du commerce international (1984) p. 81 and pp. 82–84.

272 This proposition is believed to reflect principles of international jurisdiction and sound policy that each State must provide for annulment jurisdiction for awards rendered in its territory, subject to proof that the parties have expressly provided that another State's arbitration law will be the *lex arbitri* and that State will assume annulment jurisdiction. This is the crux of the problem with French law. Exorbitant grounds for awards are still current, though the propagation of the UNCITRAL Model Law and the modernisation of arbitration laws around the world will gradually bring about a greater degree of uniformity. If the grounds for annulment in the State of origin tally with the grounds for refusal of enforcement, the same result would be achieved by both forums. See Gary B. Born, above n. 184, pp. 167–168.

273 See Emmanuel Gaillard, 'Enforcement of a Nullified Foreign Award', (1997) 3 *New York Law Journal* 218.

274 *Arab Republic of Egypt v. Chromalloy Aeroservices, Inc.* (*Cour d'Appel* Paris, 14 January 1997), in XXII *Yearbook* (1997) 693.

disregard an annulling French decision.[275] The French theory and practice appear to reflect some features of a cooperative behavioural model. At least, the French courts have been aware of a repeated prisoner's dilemma and deferred a present payoff for future gains. If other states move forward by following a coordinative behavioural model, that is, by adopting the French approach, according to game theory, a higher level of cooperation may be formed without international written guidance or legislation.

It is the general principle of law that a party who is in pursuit of a particular course of conduct upon which the other party reasonably relies cannot subsequently follow another course inconsistent with the position he previously took. This principle of estoppel is widely adopted in litigation. For instance, an English court will preclude a party from re-litigating the issue in England if a foreign judgment has already been rendered against that party by a court of competent jurisdiction unless there are strong grounds to impeach the judgment. Practically speaking, it makes sense that the defendant in enforcement proceedings shall be estopped from raising annulment as a defence if the party should have had an opportunity to raise a ground for such annulment in the arbitration proceedings.[276] The justification for this proposition is that such party should have exhausted all means to protect its rights and interests in the arbitral *situs*, where the arbitral tribunal shall be given a full opportunity to review all aspects of the dispute and correct any defects, substantive or procedural, in the arbitration proceedings.[277] This proposition is endorsed by arbitration rules and domestic arbitration laws,[278] and suggests that the litigant's failure to raise the matter in the arbitral proceedings is either due to its intention for its arbitration or litigation tactics to have a second chance, or due to negligence, both of which may lead to estoppel. However, the estoppel doctrine may not be applicable to such defences that are raised for the first time in annulment proceedings. The underlying rationale of the estoppel doctrine is the preclusive effect of Article V(1)(a) to (d) defences admitted in enforcement proceedings.[279]

---

275 See Sebastien Besson and Luc Pitter, above n. 225, 498, 510.

276 See Gary H. Sampliner, above n. 16, 162–63.

277 cf. the purpose of the requirement of exhaustion of local remedies applicable in diplomatic protection proceedings; see the *Ambatielos* arbitration (1956) 23 ILR 306, 12 RIAA 83 (*Greece v. UK ad hoc* 1956); Article 35(1) of the European Convention on Human Rights (as amended by Protocol No. 11 of 1994).

278 See LCIA Rules (1998), Article 32(1); Rules of the Arbitration Institute of the Stockholm Chamber of Commerce (1988), Section 24. Code of Civil Procedure, Article 1076(2) (the Netherlands); *Code Judiciaire,* Article 1704(4) (Belgium). Also see *Hebei Import and Export Corp. v. Polytec Engineering Co. Ltd*, judgment of 9 February 1999 at http://www.info.gov.hk/jud (*per* Justice Litton PJ, discussing whether the concept of estoppel may properly apply to the Convention provisions).

279 See Hong Kong High Court, *Qinhuangdao v. Million Basic Trading*, XIX *Yearbook* (1994) 675, 676.

3.6. "SECOND LOOK" AT THE NEW YORK CONVENTION[280]

3.6.1. GOALS OF THE NEW YORK CONVENTION

The proper application of the New York Convention requires a careful consideration of its goals. The extreme view is that "a core objective of the New York Convention is to free the international arbitral process from the domination of the law of the place of arbitration". However, the mainstream view is that two primary objectives of the New York Convention are for greater enforceability of arbitral awards[281] and greater uniformity and certainty of enforcement practice.[282] The New York Convention enhances enforceability of arbitral awards by and large through the simplification of enforcement proceedings.[283] The goal of increasing uniformity of enforcement proceedings is realised though the enumeration of limited and exclusive grounds in Article V of the Convention, by which signatory states could refuse to enforce an award.[284] It is explicitly stated in Article III that: "each contracting state shall recognise arbitral awards as binding and enforce them in accordance with the rules of procedure of the territory where the award is relied upon, under the conditions laid down in [these] articles". Article VII further establishes a "more favourable right" regime, leaving a loophole or opening the floodgates to the application of a diversity of national arbitration rules and solutions. The combined effect of Articles III, V(1) and VII effectively confirms that the New York Convention did not seek to establish a uniform regime and harmonise solutions to all problems in international commercial arbitration at the international level, but leaves most of the problems such as procedural flexibility to a specific territory. For this reason, the Convention did not impose or propose any common rules such as procedural rules in relation to the recognition and enforcement of arbitral awards. In addition, the New York Convention mainly focuses on the recognition and enforcement of foreign arbitral awards other than all related or ancillary issues

280 "Second look" is a doctrine used by US courts to examine the public policy issue in enforcing arbitral awards. See Chapter 5 of this book. This term is borrowed here to stress the need to review the spirit and legislative background of the New York Convention when scrutinising relevant issues under it.

281 See Fali S. Nariman, 'The Convention's Contribution to the Globalisation of International Commercial Arbitration', in *Enforcing Arbitration Awards under the New York Convention: Experience and Prospects – New York Convention Day 9*, New York: United Nations (1998).

282 See Stephen T. Ostrowski and Yuhal Shany, above n. 247, 1656; Robert Briner, 'New York Convention – Philosophy and Objectives of the Convention', in *Enforcing Arbitration Awards under the New York Convention: Experience and Prospects – New York Convention Day 9*, New York: United Nations (1998).

283 In particular by abolishing the cumbersome double exequatur procedure required by its predecessor, the 1927 Geneva Convention on the Execution of Foreign Arbitral Awards.

284 See Hamid G. Gharavi, above n. 248, 21–22, and Stephen T. Ostrowski and Yuval Shany, above n. 247, 1657.

such as enforcement of an award set aside in its home jurisdiction. Obviously, the objective and approach adopted by the New York Convention are realistic.

For the time being, there have been no harmonised procedural rules for the recognition and enforcement of foreign awards in the Member States of the New York Convention. Given the non-harmonious approach, inconsistent decisions are inherent and permissible under the New York Convention and will continue to exist even if the rule that annulled awards may never be enforced is established. This is because Article V(2) of the New York Convention leaves a lot of room for the courts in the jurisdictions where the enforcement of a foreign award is sought to decide whether an enforcement application can be rejected or not on the grounds of arbitrability and public policy according to the law of the enforcing state. The practice and legislation concerning the arbitrability of disputes and other issues have not been and will not be unified. Moreover, the public policy ground gives more flexibility and leeway to courts in various jurisdictions involved in international commercial arbitration. The New York Convention did not provide any guidance or place any restriction as to the exact content of and practical application to the notion of public policy. Therefore, signatory states indeed enjoy greater freedom to enforce or refuse to enforce a foreign award for any reason which may be only slightly connected with the ground of public policy. This is a source of disparity of treatment of awards at the international level. In the absence of a uniform scope of arbitrable matters and a common definition of, or approach to, dealing with public policy in all signatory states, it is very likely that an award granted in one jurisdiction may be found unacceptable in another due to different standards of arbitrability or public policy. It can also be anticipated that an award is not able to be enforced in one jurisdiction but enforced in the other. The New York Convention's pragmatic ambition, goal and approach did not purport to establish a single and uniform regime for the enforcement of foreign awards in all respects in all signatory states.[285]

3.6.2. LIMITS FOR DISCOUNTING ANNULMENT UNDER THE NEW YORK CONVENTION

The New York Convention is also an open-ended text. Articles V(1) and VII are two limbs of this text. Article V(1) provides for discretion without detailed guidance as to when and how such discretion should be exercised. Article VII makes domestic law prevail over the Convention if that law contains a more favourable regime for enforcement of foreign arbitral awards. Accordingly, there would be two routes open to an award creditor seeking to have an annulled award enforced elsewhere. The award creditor must convince the enforcing court

[285] See Jan Paulsson, above n. 50, 17.

to either discount a particular annulling decision or discard annulment altogether without going into its merits. The former case falls under "may" in Article V(1) whilst the latter falls under the "more favourable right" regime of Article VII. In other words, Articles V(1) and VII outline two separate legal routes for the enforcement of annulled awards.[286] The enforcing court can exercise its discretion under the more flexible "may" regime of Article V(1) by granting enforcement. The "may" regime allows the court in the enforcement forum not to exercise such discretion under its law on whether to grant or refuse enforcement. A more straightforward approach is to apply Article VII as long as a more favourable domestic law does not make annulment grounds for refusal of enforcement. Under Article VII, the award creditor would be entitled to enforcement of an annulled arbitral award under the domestic law of the enforcement forum. In substance, this is a right to have the annulling decision discounted or the award's validity re-examined or even restored despite the separate existence of the judicial decision. The award creditor usually initiates the enforcement proceedings, rather than claiming for a declaration of non-existence of the annulling decision, not to have the annulling decision recognised.[287] In this sense, Articles VII and V(1) are applied altogether.

As to Article VII of the New York Convention, the conditions have several layers. First, there must be domestic laws applicable to foreign awards defined in Article I of the Convention. Second, these domestic laws must be more favourable than laws in other jurisdictions. The French jurisprudence, as illustrated in *Hilmarton*, does not take account of an annulling decision of the court in the country of rendition under Article VII because annulment under the domestic law is not a ground to refuse enforcement. In a recent case, the *Cour de Cassation* suggested that a proper analysis is to compare relevant French rules with the provisions under the New York Convention.[288] This comparison leads to an understanding of Article VII as allowing "cherry-picking". However, this selective approach to using domestic rules was criticised by some commentators, who upheld the view that domestic rules should apply either *en bloc* or not at all.[289] This proposition is not easy to fit into reality. An award creditor cannot benefit from a more favourable provision in a foreign legal system but can still be caught by a less favourable law, even though a specific plea is necessary for the application of domestic law. Moreover, this proposition is

286 See Fali S. Nariman, 'Some Thoughts on the Fortieth Anniversary of the New York Convention 1958', [1998] *Int. ALR* 163, 165.

287 It is more appropriate to use the term of "denial of *res judicata*" instead. However, most national laws may treat the grant of recognition and *res judicata* as substantially same.

288 See Cass. Civ. 1ere, 24 March 1998, *Société Excelsior Film TV, SRL v. Société UGC-PH* (1999) 126 *J.D.I* 155, note Kahn (the case concerned the *exception d'ordre public* of Articles 1502(5) NCPC and V(2)(b) of the Convention); Paris, 2 April 1998, *Technip v. Asmidal*, summarised and commented on by Gaillard [1998] *Int. ALR* N-80 (cumulatively applying French law and the Convention).

289 See Albert Jan van den Berg, above n. 50, 85–86.

also inconsistent with the nature of an international treaty which purports to step aside, as it were, in favour of domestic law only where and to the extent that the latter contains more favourable provisions.

It is beyond doubt that arbitration is an indispensable means of dispute resolution in today's global economy. It is the nature of a multilateral framework like the New York Convention to require the order and stability of the governing norms. Reliability and predictability are among the key features that make international commercial arbitration even more attractive. In order to preserve the effect and functioning of such institutions, lawmakers, courts, but first and foremost its main proponents, the arbitration community, should make great efforts to stabilise arbitration within the setting of international jurisdictional interdependencies. To continue the enforcement practice initiated by the *Chromalloy* court would make arbitration increasingly unpredictable and undesirable. Enforcement of vacated awards may lead to the coexistence of inconsistent judgments as regards the same award concerning the same dispute between the same parties, and therefore may violate the well-established uniformity of the international arbitral process.[290] The outcome of *Hilmarton* is evidence of this chaotic consequence.[291] Furthermore, under the present unsatisfactory situation, there may be two or more awards in respect of the same dispute. For instance, apart from the spectacle of the French courts paying no heed to the decisions of their Swiss neighbours, two distinct and inconsistent awards were in circulation and, indeed, even if the French Court of Cassation decided that the second award should not be recognised in France, it will presumably still be capable of enforcement in other jurisdictions.[292] The situation created by *Chromalloy* and *Hilmarton* may be even worse than the "race to the bottom" or confess-confess scenario in a prisoner's dilemma. This is because the effect of annulment of an award in some legal systems may restore the ordinary competence of the courts so that a fresh proceeding may lead to a judgment which is required to be enforced elsewhere under bilateral or regional conventions such as the Brussels Convention 1968.[293] This situation hardly contributes to the harmonious and uniform international treatment of arbitration awards and the lofty goals of those who crafted both the New York Convention and the Model Law. Ultimately, the parties can no longer rely upon the judicial control of the state where arbitration takes place, but have to fear

---

290 Hamid G. Gharavi, above n. 248, 23.

291 Paulsson discounts the relevance of *Hilmarton* and then goes on to argue that "anyone who maintains that inconsistent results are intolerable anathema ... would, in order to be intellectually honest, have to accept that enforcement should never be granted until any possibility of challenge to the award in its country of origin has been disposed of". See Jan Paulsson, above n. 77, 28–9.

292 Albert Jan van den Berg made the statement that "[i]f an award is set aside in the country of origin, a party still can try its luck in France". See XIX *Yearbook* (1994) 592.

293 See a brief discussion of the Brussels Convention 1968 in Chapter 2.

that, despite an annulment, the vacated award will be caught and enforced somewhere in the world and the enforcement proceedings become an endless game.

3.7. UPGRADING THE NEW YORK CONVENTION: PRELIMINARY THOUGHTS

The provisions of the New York Convention and interpretations of them can be examined from various perspectives, e.g., the enforcement forum, the state of rendition or a truly international law point of view. As to the validity of an award, the law of the state of rendition shall have a primary control over the proceedings and the effectiveness of the award. There are two exceptions to this general rule. First, the annulling judgment fails to pass the test for *res judicata* in and under the law of the enforcement forum. Second, the enforcement forum has a law which does not treat annulment of an award as a circumstance precluding enforcement. These two exceptions can exist at the same time under the framework of Articles V(1) and VII of the New York Convention. Article V(1)(e) reflects a difficult cohabitation between provisions which have different underlying philosophies. Article V(1)(e) does not create or spell out the rule of allocating international competencies among multiple regimes.[294] Instead, Article V(1)(e) indeed allocates international competencies between the home jurisdiction and enforcement forum. In an ideal judicial economy, the enforcement forum would either have complete freedom in evaluating an award within the boundaries set by the New York Convention, namely, the grounds contained in Article V(1)(a) to (d) and (2), or be absolutely bound by a decision of the forum of origin, subject to the grounds set out in Article V(2). This may indicate that the enforcement forum is a strong point of anchorage for foreign awards, and the rendition forum does not have the sole legitimate connection. Article VII of the New York Convention is a doctrinal development. The purpose of this article is to ensure that the New York Convention will not inhibit the diversity of national practice and enforcement of a foreign arbitral award in a contracting state in the event that there is a distinct and more liberal regime for the enforcement of foreign awards in that country. In order to avail itself of Article VII, a party must therefore establish that the grounds for enforcement of a foreign award under domestic laws or an applicable treaty are more favourable than those set out in the New York Convention.

As a matter of fact, the New York Convention abolished the requirement to have an award confirmed in the place of rendition, which was once the old rule

[294] See W. Michael Reisman, above n. 194, 111–114.

adopted in the Geneva Convention.[295] The New York Convention then established the notion that an award is valid and effective once it is rendered in the state of origin. It is widely agreed that it is neither desirable to restore the old rule under the Geneva Convention nor ideal to eliminate the mechanism of setting aside arbitral awards for any "good" grounds.[296] The New York Convention does not seem to support the proposition that an annulled award shall be effective in the enforcement forum. On the other hand, the New York Convention does not exclude such a possibility entirely. The *travaux préparatoires* show that the issue was yet to be elaborated by the drafters of the New York Convention. However, this does not necessarily prove that the issue was outside the contemplation of the law as well. A neutral understanding of this issue would be that the New York Convention left the issue open to the enforcement forum,[297] which is subject to a higher-level but relatively abstract rule that a uniform regime should be created. The spirit of the New York Convention seems to require that international arbitral awards be truly capable of enforcement notwithstanding the annulment by local courts in the jurisdiction where these awards are issued in the first place. To allow enforcement of an annulled award would protect the legitimate expectation and interests of the parties to arbitration and eventually enhance the creditability of arbitration as an effective means of international commercial arbitration. However, from a technical point of view, without a centralised ICSID-type body responsible for supervising all local systems of setting aside awards issued in contracting countries, a certain level of international legal effect over annulled awards is evidently not desirable.

Although we have been living in a truly "globalised world" in the 21st century,[298] it appears that there is a force that from time to time pushes the resolution of international commercial disputes to national courts. In the US, the "emphatic federal policy in favour of arbitral dispute resolution" which currently prevails as a "policy [which] applies with special force in the field of international commerce"[299] may be overturned. In the face of the trend of globalisation, it appears that the original obstacles faced by international merchants seem to diminish. Future lawmakers of the world shall envisage the New York Convention's "full potential".[300]

A brief analysis of game theory in the context of the New York Convention seems to provide various options for the path of convergence. However, in

---

295 See *Union Nationale des Cooperatives Agricoles de Céréales v. Robert Catterall & Co. Ltd.* [1959] 2 QB 44, 53–54 (CA).

296 It is good for the parties to have a setting aside procedure in place so that they may obtain relief from the local judicial system and start a new arbitration when the award is defective.

297 See Richard A. Posner, 'The Jurisprudence of Skepticism', (1988) 86 *Michigan L. Rev.* 827, 881.

298 See Thomas L. Friedman, *The World Is Flat: The Globalized World in the 21st Century*, Harmondsworth: Penguin Books (2006).

299 *Mitsubishi Motors Corp. v. Soler Chrysler-Plymouth Inc.*, 473 US 614, 631 (1985).

300 See Jan Paulsson, above n. 50, 14.

reality, Nash equilibrium is rarely achieved instantaneously. This is so because the key conditions that state players are rational and know the payoff functions of all players, and that they know their opponents are rational and know the payoff functions, are almost impossible to satisfy. Therefore, we may have to rely upon a higher level of regulatory coordination, which may not necessarily require identical standards.[301] The uniform standards may often be too strict to respond to the wide diversity of political and economic conditions that exist in various jurisdictions.[302] By reference to the jurisprudence of natural law, law is treated as a body of commands laid down by a supreme legislative body in a legal system.[303] Accordingly, we may have a superior framework to deal with annulled awards. To this end, it has been proposed that a supranational court or a *renvoi* to an existing supranational court such as the International Court of Justice can be established and that such a supranational court will deprive jurisdiction from national courts so as to have exclusive jurisdiction over the control of arbitral awards.[304] Once this superior framework has commenced its task, any individual enforcement actions must cease, and any individual attachments must be repaid to the collective pool,[305] which would be shared by relevant states. This pool would be dealt with in a manner determined by a uniform decision-making process or an independent higher-level regime.[306] The supranational regime is able to guide and justify the conduct or even to order the use of coercive measures such as punishment. The normative nature of the supranational regime

301 The regulatory diversity has played a role in the ratcheting upwards of regulatory standards: in the long run it is welfare-enhancing for some political jurisdictions to have stricter regulations than others.

302 Even within a particular country – a point which has been repeatedly made by critics of regulatory harmonisation. See Richard Revesz, 'Rehabilitating Interstate Competition' above n. 109, 1210.

303 Bentham and Austin endeavoured to provide a firm foundation for the separation of expository and censorial jurisprudence by their general theories of law. In their view, law is a body of commands laid down by the sovereign, a supreme law-making body in every single legal system. See Jeremy Bentham, *An Introduction to the Principles of Morals and Legislation*, Oxford: Clarendon Press (1789).

304 Hamid G. Gharavi, *The International Effectiveness of the Annulment of an Arbitral Award*, The Hague: Kluwer International Arbitration Law (2002) pp. 157–162.

305 More characteristic of the economic analysis school is the importance it attaches to notional markets. Its adherents seek to draw implications for legal "wrongs" of all kinds from notional re-allocations within a total wealth-pie taken to be fixed at a particular moment of time. Granted zero transaction costs, every right would end up vested in the person who values it most – value being determined by each party's willingness to pay. Where transaction costs frustrate such re-allocations, the law should impose the "efficient" solution. See Ronald H. Coase, above n. 122, 1. Coase's analysis purports to demonstrate that where real transactions are impracticable, stand in the way of rights being accorded to those who would (if they could) pay most for them.

306 The normative implications of economic analysis of law are, probably, most challenging when it is claimed that a real (not just notional) market should be introduced in respect of some sensitive area of social interactions.

might be treated as predictions of what other states are likely to do, for example in the application of sanctions.

In the state strategic setting, it is now no longer irrational to cooperate.[307] Indeed, "cooperate" now dominates "enforce", with the result that the bottom-right cell, in which both players choose "cooperate", has become the dominant strategy equilibrium. In our context, inspired by the UNCITRAL Model Law, the establishment of criteria for enforcement that do not take account of annulment in the country of origin is not and should not be the current legislative trend.[308] It is not necessary to subscribe to the view that the enhancement of efficiency should be the sole, or even the most important or ultimate, goal of the solution to the enforcement of annulled awards under the New York Convention. An appreciation of the costs of "rights" distress and the incentive effects of various legal responses is surely an important precondition in designing legal rules which will succeed in implementing any given policy. In fact, it has been proposed that the New York Convention needs to be rewritten. At most, this reform suggestion remains at the level of legislative proposal. In any event, the New York Convention should be updated or upgraded to acknowledge the judicial review in the country that hosts arbitration.[309] The New York Convention, or its supplement in the form of a model law or guidelines, as an enabling framework, should outline international standards and standards for adopting the result of that review to ease the task of the recognition and enforcement forum[310] but leave the detail of ever-changing practices to national arbitration laws and arbitration rules. As long as an annulment follows from one of those standards, recognition or enforcement should be allowed. The upgrading of the New York Convention would ultimately lead to a more harmonised mechanism or system of award review and enforcement.

---

307 The game theory explains why states cooperate or do not, but it does not explain anything new about the scope of the problem of international cooperation.

308 Jan Paulsson, above n. 50, 14.

309 Hamid G. Gharavi, above n. 304 (discussing the possibility of "adoption of a new convention or an amendment or protocol to the New York Convention" to cover "jurisdiction over annulment and the extent of oversight of arbitral awards during annulment proceedings"). However, there is no point in harmonising annulment grounds through a new convention if the interpretation of these grounds rests entirely in the hands of State courts.

310 Ibid. 169–193 (asserting that the interaction of international arbitration and national judicial systems can take one of two directions: "harmonisation, *i.e.*, the synchronisation of national laws, [or] unification, *i.e.* [sic] the formation of an exclusively international legal regime through the establishment of a *supra*-national court vested with exclusive jurisdiction over the control of arbitral awards").

CHAPTER 4

LEX MERCATORIA AND THE NEW YORK CONVENTION

The significance of *lex mercatoria* lies in the issue of the applicable law or choice of law in international commercial arbitration, which is dealt with under the New York Convention. The exact meaning, scope and nature of *lex mercatoria* are contested both in scholarship and in practice. What is generally accepted, however, is that *lex mercatoria* involves an array of principles not necessarily defined by any nation's statutory law.[1] Where international commercial arbitration involves *lex mercatoria,* arbitration panels or arbitrators have to look outside the national law ordinarily applicable to the dispute.

4.1. CONCEPTUALISATION OF *LEX MERCATORIA*

Lex mercatoria lacks a universally accepted definition. It has been defined as "a set of principles and customary rules ... in a framework of international trade ... without reference to a particular national system of law",[2] "a single autonomous body of law created by the international business community",[3] or "a uniform law developed by parallelism of action in various national systems in an area of optional law in which the state is disinterested".[4] These definitions are wide enough to include the Hague and Vienna Conventions Establishing Uniform Laws for the International Sale of Goods, the United Nations Convention on Contracts for the International Sale of Goods (CISG) and "national legislation whose specific and exclusive object is international trade".[5]

1 A. Claire Cutler, *Private Power and Global Authority*, Cambridge: Cambridge University Press (2003) p. 104.

2 See Berthold Goldman, *Lex Mercatoria*, Antwerp: Kluwer Law and Taxation Publishers (1983).

3 Bernardo Cremades and Steven Plehn, 'The New *Lex Mercatoria* and the Harmonisation of the Laws of International Commercial Transactions', (1984) 2 *B.U. Int'l L.J.* 324.

4 Clive Schmitthoff, 'Nature and Evolution of the Transnational Law of Commercial Transactions', in Norbert Horn and Clive Schmitthoff, *The Transnational Law of International Commercial Transactions*, Antwerp: Kluwer Law and Taxation Publishers (1982) p. 22.

5 Berthold Goldman, 'The Applicable Law: General Principles of Law – The *Lex Mercatoria*', in Julian D.M. Lew (ed.), *Contemporary Problems in International Arbitration,* Dordrecht: Martinus Nijhoff Publishers (1987) p. 113. Michael Bridge, 'Foreword', in Fan Yang, *Contracts*

Generally speaking, the term is defined as the "rules of law which are common to all or most of the States engaged in international trade or to those States that are connected with a dispute, and if not ascertainable, then the rules which would appear to be the most appropriate and equitable".[6] Nevertheless, a group of less enthusiastic commentators may support the view that *lex mercatoria* is "a non-national or transnational commercial law"[7] which has sources both in national and international laws and in the vaguely defined region of general principles of law or "transnational law".[8] It may be suggested that *lex mercatoria* is "a sort of shadowy, optional, aleatory, international commercial congeries of rules and principles".[9]

These definitions point out several key qualities of *lex mercatoria*, which are its detachment from any particular national system[10] as well as its flexibility and adaptability to various international commercial activities.[11] Accordingly, *lex mercatoria* can, at one time or another, include trade usages, a set of customary rules or general principles relating to international commercial transactions,[12] uniform rules accepted in all countries,[13] an autonomous system of law, an international body of law founded on commercial understandings and practices,[14] certain equitable principles, as well as the entirety of transnational legal norms affecting international commercial operations.[15] Therefore, *lex mercatoria* may be seen as an evolving body of customary rules or principles, of a private law nature, arising out of or in connection with commercial activities

for the Sale of International Sale of Goods in China, Hong Kong: Wolters Kluwer Law & Business (2012) p. xii.

6 Ole Lando, 'The *Lex Mercatoria* in International Commercial Arbitration', (1985) 34 *ICLQ* 747–68.

7 Julian D.M. Lew, 'The Case for the Publication of Arbitration Awards', in Jan C. Schultse and Albert Jan van den Berg (eds.), *The Art of Arbitration, Essays on International Arbitration, Liber Amicorum for Pieter Sunders*, Antwerp: Kluwer Law and Taxation Publishers (1982) pp. 223–232.

8 Horacio A. Grigera Naón, *The Transnational Law of International Commercial Transactions* (1984) p. 89, cited in Nikitas E. Hatzimihail, 'The Many Lives – and Faces – of *Lex Mercatoria:* History as Genealogy in International Business Law', (2008) 71 (Summer) *Law and Contemporary Problems* 169, 170 n. 10; also in Horacio A. Grigera Naón, *Choice-of-law Problems in International Commercial Arbitration*, Tübingen: J.C.B. Mohr (Paul Siebeck) (1992).

9 Keith Highet, 'The Enigma of the *Lex Mercatoria*', (1989) 63 *Tul. L. Rev.* 613, 618.

10 Berthold Goldman, above n. 5, 116.

11 See Paul Freeman, '*Lex Mercatoria*: A Legal Basis for the Resolution of International Disputes', in Martin Odams De Zylva and Reziya Harrison (eds.), *International Commercial Arbitration – Developing Rules for the New Millennium*, Bristol: Jordans (2000) p. 123.

12 Clive Schmitthoff, above n. 4, 19.

13 Clive Schmitthoff, *Commercial Law in a Changing Economic Climate*, London: Sweet & Maxwell (2nd edn. 1981) p. 20.

14 Harold Berman and Colin Kaufman, 'The Law of International Commercial Transactions (*Lex Mercatoria*)', (1978) 19(1) *Harvard International Law Journal* 273.

15 William W. Park, 'Arbitration of International Contract Disputes', (1984) 39 *Business Lawyer* 1783.

or relationships of the transnational community, which is free from the assumptions inherent in any particular national regulatory regime.

It is worth mentioning that *lex mercatoria* is distinguishable from the concept of *amiable composition* or *ex aequo et bono*, which is frequently confused or used as a synonym. *Amiable composition* is a term used in continental legal systems to refer to the power to decide a dispute without reference to any fixed system of law. An arbitrator exercising such power is sometimes said to be deciding *ex aequo et bono*, which is said to be "a kind of international law ... that may provide the necessary flexibility within legal limits".[16] Parties who authorise the arbitrator to act as an *amiable compositeur* may be deemed to have waived the right to challenge the award. Even the most impassioned proponents of *lex mercatoria* would agree that if a contract expressly stipulates a choice of governing law and if the arbitrator is not an *amiable compositeur*, then the arbitrator cannot properly apply *lex mercatoria* in preference to the chosen law. The point to be made is that, at least in the eyes of the classical mercatorist,[17] *lex mercatoria* is more akin to law, albeit imperfect and evolving, rather than some intangible and subjective notion. When *lex mercatoria* is expressly incorporated into an arbitration agreement, there is some room for arbitration panels or arbitrators to impose their own rules while contractual norms should *prima facie* be binding and enforceable according to the principle of *pacta sunt servanda*.[18]

4.2. EVOLUTION OF *LEX MERCATORIA*: A HISTORICAL PERSPECTIVE

"The criterion for determining the ambit of *lex mercatoria* ... does not solely reside in the object of its constituent elements, but also in its origin and its customary, and thus spontaneous nature".[19] A review of the evolution of *lex mercatoria* reveals a dialectical movement in the balance between merchant autonomy and state power in transnational capitalism.[20]

---

16 Francisco Orrego Vicuna, *International Dispute Settlement in an Evolving Global Society: Constitutionalization, Accessibility, Privatization*, Cambridge: Cambridge University Press (2004) p. 111.

17 Berthold Goldman, above n. 5, 124; Ole Lando, above n. 6, 754. The difference between quality and rules of law was clearly stated in *Sapphire International Petroleum v. NIOC* (1984) 12 *ICLQ* 987.

18 In the Middle Ages, it was not the custom of the court of the lord king to protect private agreements. This illustrates the limited extent to which local legal systems regarded the regulation of commerce as their legitimate domain. See A. W. B. Simpson, *A History of the Common Law of Contract*, Oxford: Clarendon Press (1975).

19 Berthold Goldman, '*Lex Mercatoria*', (1983) 3 *Forum Internationale* 1, 6.

20 Harold Berman and Colin Kaufman, above n. 14, 221–78.

4.2.1. MEDIEVAL LAW MERCHANT AND SELF-REGULATION OF COMMERCE

The origin of *lex mercatoria* can be traced back to Italian cities and market towns in medieval times.[21] As commerce expanded and trading communities grew, a system of law drawing upon ancient Greek and Italian maritime customs, the Roman law of sales, debt and general civil obligations, as well as the Roman *jus gentium* (law of nations), emerged.[22] Prior to the emergence of modern regulatory states, this system of law governing domestic commercial activities, international trade and commerce evolved within a self-regulating framework, free from government interference. Medieval merchants constituted a relatively independent class, separate from the feudal political economy and municipal system of law, in special places such as fairs, markets and seaports. The members of domestic and transnational commercial community voluntarily and cooperatively created, adjudicated and enforced this system of law,[23] the essence of which departed considerably from forms of property and ownership associated with the feudal system, and was aimed at avoiding feudal transaction restrictions.[24] The social, legal and economic order, as well as the processes and institutions of law-creation and dispute resolution, was then an autonomous, informal, privatised and customary one, which is very different from a state-centred order in the modern world.

Throughout the sixteenth and seventeenth centuries mercantile law evolved in England and continental Europe.[25] Although the development of mercantile law reflected the contrasting requirements of local traders and merchants, the foundations of the law merchant, the early generation of *lex mercatoria,* focused primarily upon commercial matters and the ability to meet the demands of the business community, and remained unchallenged in both civil and common law systems. Generally, the law merchant regulated merchant conduct without the coercive assistance of state governments.[26] The law merchant was largely self-enforcing, in that a party failing to comply with a mercantile law or a merchant court's decision risked damage to his reputation and could be excluded from trading at the fairs.[27]

---

21 Paul Freeman, above n. 11, 122.

22 A. Claire Cutler, above n. 1, 113.

23 Bruce L. Benson, 'The Spontaneous Evolution of Commercial Law', (1989) 55 *Southern Economic Journal* 644, 647.

24 A. Claire Cutler, 'Historical Materialism, Globalisation, and Law: Competing Conceptions of Property', in Mark Rupert and Hazel Smith (eds.): *Historical Materialism and Globalisation*, New York and London: Routledge (2002) pp. 230–56.

25 The evolution of *lex mercatoria*, in England at least, can be closely linked to the development of principles of equity in the Chancery Division where, to some extent, *lex mercatoria* and law of equity have tended to clash. See, for example, the decision in *Gibson v. Carruthers* (1841) 8 *M&W* 321, at 338.

26 Bruce L. Benson, above n. 23, 649.

27 Bernardo Cremades and Steven Plehn, above n. 3, 319.

Some imagination is necessary to understand how a merchant jurist functions and how its role differs from the role envisioned for judges under the present positivist conception of the judiciary. In medieval times, merchants were guided by "merchant" rules.[28] The law merchant, together with church law, feudal law, manorial law and urban law, constituted normative and institutional pluralism in the medieval authority structure, which made local political and religious authorities unable to enforce merchant law; hence mercantile disputes had to be channelled to merchant courts.[29] Unlike royal, ecclesiastical or common law courts, merchant courts, which were not composed of professional judges but merchants themselves, achieved a high degree of independence. Like modern arbitrators, the merchant judges relied on their knowledge of and expertise in commercial custom and trade usages, and on their familiarity with the evolving needs of commerce to resolve commercial disputes among merchants.[30] Merchant courts were able to apply commercial norms that merchants observe in practice, to uphold and enforce transactions otherwise unenforceable in other courts,[31] and to support equity, in the medieval sense of fairness, as an overriding principle.[32] At the procedural level, the merchant courts provided the most utilised institutional framework for settling commercial disputes. Like contemporary arbitration tribunals, merchant courts operated privately, speedily and informally.[33] Jurists examined the truth themselves, without regard to the formal legal rules of evidence and proof,[34] and then tailored justice to specific facts by employing merchant custom. The fair courts and merchant jurists, with the assistance of guilds which provided facilities and discipline for members,[35] also played an influential role in articulating merchant law and custom, building up an efficacious and private dispute settlement system, and established the foundations for the modern Continental courts of commerce.

---

28 Friedrich A. Hayek, *Law, Legislation and Liberty Vol. 1 Rules and Order*, Chicago: Chicago University Press (1973) p. 19.

29 This is also consistent with the pluralism in the political authority structure: "in early modern Europe, at least at first, a government could be an Italian city, a feudal principality, the Hanseatic League, or a more familiar empire or kingdom". See Michael N. Pearson, 'Merchants and States', in James D. Tracy (ed.), *The Political Economy of Merchant Empires*, New York: Cambridge University Press (1991) pp. 41–116.

30 Bernardo M. Cremades and Steven L. Plehn, above n. 3, 317, 319.

31 Frederick Pollock, 'The Early History of the Law Merchant in England', (1901) 67(3) *Law Quarterly Review* 232–51.

32 Harold Berman and Colin Kaufman, above n. 14, 221–78.

33 Leon E. Trakman, *The Law Merchant: The Evolution of Commercial Law*, Littleton, CO: Fred B. Rothman and Co. (1983).

34 Clive M. Schmitthoff (ed.), *The Sources of the Law of International Trade*, New York: Praeger (1964).

35 Avner Greif, Paul Milgrom and Barry Weingast, 'Coordination, Commitment and Enforcement: The Case of the Merchant Guild', (1994) 102(4) *Journal of Political Economy* 745–76.

Sovereign rulers did not object to an a-national regime governing the legal relationship among merchants as long as merchant activities could generate tax revenues and bring in foreign goods. This laissez-faire attitude facilitated the development of independent rules of conduct.[36] No local ruler, legislator or jurist ever "made" the law merchant, which indeed was customary and self-regulatory in both law creation and dispute resolution. The customary character of the law merchant reflects the more general autonomy of the merchant class from the feudal class system. The order of the law merchant occupied a space external to the local political economy and feudal mode of production. Therefore, the law merchant is a form of "unconscious" and self-enforcing law departing from "rational and systematic legislation" which is a product of "conscious human law-making".[37] The words "custom" and "statute" were used interchangeably, and most commercial statutes were merely compilations of existing custom[38] rather than the "creation of legislature".[39] Merchants were free to develop their own legal institutions in light of their own commercial needs. The customs and laws governing maritime trade and commerce formed the foundation of the law merchant.[40] The Amalfian Table, a collection of maritime laws produced by the Italian Republic of Amalfi, was adopted by all Italian cities,[41] and a collection of maritime judgements of the Court of Oleron on the French coast was widely adopted by the seaport towns of the Atlantic, the North Sea and England.[42] Various sea laws governing maritime transportation, insurance and instruments had their origin in, and gained their currency and efficacy through, commercial custom.[43] These laws and customs spread to other commercial centres in Europe.[44] A body of law regulating overland trade in the markets and fairs of England, Germany and northern France and in the city-states in Italy and southern France[45] was also developed in inland towns. The fairs and city-states

36 William Laurence Craig, William W. Park and Jan Paulsson, *International Chamber of Commerce Arbitration*, New York: Oceana Publications and ICC Publishing (1995) para. 35.01.

37 Max Weber, 'Economy of Law' or 'Society of Law', Vols. I and II, in Guenther Roth and Claus Wittich (eds.), *Max Weber, Economy and Society: An Outline of Interpretive Sociology, Vol. 2*, Berkeley: University of California Press (1978) pp. 753–8.

38 Frederic R. Sanborn, *Origins of the Early English Maritime and Commercial Law*, London: Century Co. (1930) p. 183.

39 William Mitchell, *An Essay on the Early History of the Law Merchant*, Cambridge: Cambridge University Press (1904) pp. 141–155.

40 Merchants in ports drew upon the Sea Law of Rhodes transmitted to Western Europe by the Greeks and Romans. See A. Claire Cutler, 'Private Authority in International Trade Relations: The Case of Maritime Transport', in A. Claire Cutler, Virginia Haufler and Tony Porter (eds.), *Private Authority and International Affairs*, Albany, NY: SUNY Press (1999).

41 Frederic R. Sanborn, above n. 38.

42 William Mitchell, above n. 39.

43 See Alan Cafruny, *Ruling the Waves: The Political Economy of International Shipping*, Berkeley: University of California Press (1987).

44 Shepard B. Clough and Charles W. Cole, *Economic History of Europe*, Boston, MA: D.C. Heath & Co. (revised edn. 1946).

45 Frederic R. Sanborn, above n. 38, 31.

allowed the evolution of a complete and ingenious system of the law merchant, separate from the authority of a sovereign. These platforms were important in facilitating the growth of commerce, providing security and safe conduct for merchants, and universalising the merchant custom. In many European city-states of the early Middle Ages, for example, the merchant guilds, which had traditionally arbitrated disputes among their members, gradually evolved into commercial courts with general jurisdiction over all commercial matters.[46]

Although *lex mercatoria* developed throughout medieval Europe in numerous small states at varying rates, virtually all commentators have been struck by its near universal uniformity. Most have found that "despite some local variations, ... the law was common and uniform",[47] and that the usages of commercial cities tended to conform to the general usage of merchants throughout Europe. It is also observed that "each country ... had its own variety of Law Merchant, yet all were but varieties of the same species. Everywhere the leading principles and the most important rules were the same, or tended to become the same".[48] There are both economic and political reasons for this unplanned uniformity, which was not achieved through international treaties or conventions that did not yet exist.[49] Rather, the law merchant gradually progressed towards and achieved considerable uniformity and universality through the expansion of commerce and trade as well as the mobility of capital and the transmissibility of property in the European trading world.[50] The medieval law merchant contained principles facilitating exchange through informal and flexible standards, and was easy to adopt and implement in commercial circles. In substance, the medieval law merchant system "does not derive its normative claims from treaties amongst sovereign states"[51] but is a de-territorialised and predominantly private legal order. The law merchant granted more autonomy and discretion to merchants who in turn strengthened the independence of their social status as a separate class. Although a great deal of conscious borrowing of law occurred, it was never done with the intent to

46 See William C. Jones, 'An Inquiry into the History of the Adjudication of Mercantile Disputes in Great Britain and the United States', (1958) 25 *U. Chi. L. Rev.* 445, 450; Louise Hertwig Hayes, 'Note, A Modern *Lex Mercatoria*: Political Rhetoric or Substantive Progress?', (1977) 3 *Brook J. Int'l L.* 210, 212 n. 13.

47 Frederic R. Sanborn, above n. 38, 126.

48 William Mitchell, above n. 39, 9.

49 Foreign merchants were granted immunities from municipal laws, for example, in England. See William S. Holdsworth, 'The Development of the Law Merchant and Its Courts', in John Henry Wigmore, Ernst Freund, and William Ephraim Mikell (eds.), *Selected Essays in Anglo-American Legal History*, Vol. I, Boston: Little, Brown & Company (1909) pp. 289–331.

50 See generally Henri Pirenne, *Economic and Social History of Medieval Europe*, London: Kegan Paul (1937); Robert Lopez, *The Commercial Revolution of the Middle Age, 950–1350*, Cambridge: Cambridge University Press (1971) pp. 950–1350; and Stephard B. Clough, *The Economic Development of Western Civilisation*, New York: McGraw-Hill Book Co. Inc. (1959).

51 See Boaventura de Sousa Santos, *Toward a New Common Sense: Law, Science, and Politics in the Paradigmatic Transition*, London and New York: Routledge (1995) p. 289.

create a uniform law, but arose from the merchants' desire to emulate the successful commercial practices of their more prosperous neighbours.

Although local or municipal authorities regulated trade and production with the aim of ensuring adequate production and a fair and reasonable price level, municipal governments were relatively accommodating to the merchants due to their reliance on commerce for tax revenue, and were therefore anxious to promote business and trade in markets and fairs within their borders. Thus, despite the rather primitive state of economic knowledge, governors were prudent enough to discern that merchants were best left to regulate their own affairs.[52] Governments best contributed to the growth of commerce and trade at this time by merely keeping the peace at fairs and market towns and by protecting the trade routes. Merchant courts seldom required the assistance of state governments to enforce their judgments because a variety of private remedies were available that were usually sufficient.[53] In summary, during the medieval phase, merchants were able to privately generate and enforce legal norms in response to commercial developments and the needs and expectations of merchants. Such merchant-made norms constitute the main body of *lex mercatoria*, which is an autonomous legal order separate from the nation-state system.

4.2.2. NATIONALISATION OF LAW MERCHANT AND DECLINE OF *LEX MERCATORIA*

Starting in the sixteenth century, the rise of the sovereign state substantially changed the medieval landscape. The state-building process changed the balance between public and private spheres, and shifted in favour of the former. The states became the major players in commercial development and mercantilism, and economic state-building involved the use of national policies and practices in order to secure economic unity through a national economy. As states grew more powerful and merchants disappeared as a separate class, the state authority replaced the overlapping authority structure of the medieval period and sought dominant control over commercial activities, economic process and actors over which the church, town and guild authorities had hitherto weakened controls.[54] Thus, merchants gradually lost their autonomous status and the law merchant became a tempting target for nationalisation.[55]

52 The principal threat to trade from government at this time was not over-regulation per se, but rather over-taxation. Greedy rulers often inadvertently taxed lucrative fairs out of existence.

53 Bernardo M. Cremades and Steven L. Plehn, above n. 3, 319.

54 Eli Heckscher, *Mercantilism*, New York: Macmillan (1955).

55 Thomas E. Carbonneau and Marc S. Firestone, 'Transnational Law-Making. Assessing the Impact of the Vienna Convention and the Viability of Arbitral Adjudication', (1986) 1 *Emory Journal of International Dispute Resolution* 61.

Along with the rise of capitalism, the process of legal nationalisation was carried out in every country, but in different manners and degrees due to local conditions and traditions.[56] In England, nationalisation occurred on two fronts: the consolidation of substantive merchant law into the common law applicable to all persons[57] and the absorption of the specialised courts into the common law courts.[58] As a result, the commercial law was based fundamentally on the customs of merchants but retained a cosmopolitan flavour.[59] In the United States, nationalisation occurred in the nineteenth and twentieth centuries through the adoption of English commercial law and the unification of state commercial law and practices. Unification of state laws in the form of the Uniform Commercial Code in the twentieth century had an impact on international transactions by rendering American commercial norms more consistent with international usage.[60] France took a different course and the French Revolutionary values separated special personal status from the special status of commercial transactions.[61] The Napoleonic commercial code established the pattern of separate and distinct treatment of commercial matters, a practice subsequently adopted by many other civil law countries.[62] In Germany, codification and unification of law aimed at securing political unification constituted the main feature of legal nationalisation.[63] The German Commercial Code was borrowed by Austria and Japan, and the latter codes appeared to bear a greater likeness to the medieval law merchant.

Regardless of these differences, legal nationalisation has been reflected in two respects: commercial relations were subject to increasingly state-based rules and the law merchant was gradually juridified, formalised and incorporated into the territorial-based national regulatory and court systems, rendering it subject to the vagaries of each nation's particular legal order.[64] As the political counterpart

---

56 Clive M. Schmitthoff, 'International Business Law: A New Law Merchant', in Clive M. Schmitthoff, *Current Law and Social Problems 2,* Canada: University of W. Ontario Press (1961) pp. 129–53.

57 William S. Holdsworth, above n. 49, pp. 289–331. In *Pillans v. van Mierop* 3 Burr. 1663, 97 Eng. Rep. 1035 (KB 1765) Lord Mansfield held that the rules of the law merchant were questions of law to be decided by the courts and not matters of customs to be proved by the parties.

58 Denis Tallon, 'Civil Law and Commercial Law', in *International Encyclopedia of Comparative Law: Specific Contracts,* Vol. III, Ch. 2, The Hague: Martinus Nijihoff (1983) pp. 103–4.

59 Philip W. Thayer, 'Comparative Law and the Law Merchant', (1936) 6(2) *Brooklyn Law Review* 139–54.

60 John Honnold, 'The Influence of the Law of International Trade on the Development and Character of English and American Commercial Law', in Clive M. Schmitthoff (ed.) *The Sources of the Law of International Trade,* New York: Praeger (1964) pp. 70–87.

61 Denis Tallon, above n. 58, 103–14.

62 Ernst von Caemmerer, 'The Influence of the Law of International Trade on the Development and Character of Commercial Law in the Civil Law Countries', in Clive M. Schmitthoff (ed.), *The Sources of the Law of International Trade,* New York: Praeger (1964) pp. 88–100.

63 Clive M. Schmitthoff, above n. 56, 136.

64 Bernardo M. Cremades and Steven L. Plehn, above n. 3, 320.

of mercantilism and as part of the political process, the codification or nationalisation of the law merchant or *lex mercatoria* in Europe resulted in a nationalised, rationalised, systematic and positivist[65] form of legal regulation adapted to the needs of major trading nations according to principles of territorial sovereignty and legal positivism.[66] The state regulations contained and formed part of the measures adopted and implemented by state authorities to gain control over economic activities in the era of state building, mercantilism and capitalism.

The localising tendency of national regulation and the incorporation of *lex mercatoria* into the municipal law continued throughout the eighteenth and nineteenth centuries.[67] By the twentieth century jurists had begun to assert that municipal law was the only law that could govern transnational transactions.[68] The autonomous and self-supporting law merchant order was so much less compatible with economic expansion and state dominance that merchant autonomy in law creation and dispute resolution declined. As merchant courts became incapable of dealing with transnational disputes due to the geographic expansion of commercial relations and the inadequacy of self-enforcement systems, merchants were forced to yield disputes to non-merchant judges of state courts, which became dominant in the legal sphere and had far-reaching jurisdiction in commercial disputes.[69] The self-imposed sanctions attached to the notion of *lex mercatoria* became difficult to enforce as markets proliferated. During this period, the expansion of trade through colonisation and the functioning of private and autonomous law merchant was contingent on national intervention.[70]

Perhaps even worse, from the merchant's perspective, the previously uniform law of international commerce disintegrated as *lex mercatoria* became embedded in the "myopic prism of national adjudicatory sovereignty".[71] The role of commercial customs declined as it gave way to national legislation and case law

65 The codification engendered an attitude of legal positivism being aggravated by nationalist sentiments. René David and J.E.C. Brierley, *Major Legal Systems in the World Today: An Introduction to the Comparative Study of Law*, London: Stevens & Sons (1978) p. 62.

66 Leon Trakman, 'The Evolution of the Law Merchant: Out Commercial Heritage', (1980) 12 *Journal of Maritime Law and Commerce* 153.

67 By the beginning of the 19th century, municipal jurists had convinced themselves that they were not to take the law from merchant custom, but that merchants were to take their law from the courts and legislatures – thus completely halting the dynamic evolution of the law merchant. See Clive Schmitthoff, above n. 56, 136.

68 Christopher W.O. Stoecker, 'The *Lex Mercatoria*: To What Extent Does it Exist?', (1990) 7 *J. Int'l Arb.* 101, 103.

69 Thomas E. Carbonneau and Marc. S. Firestone, above n. 55, 62.

70 See generally Robert Cox, *Production, Power and World Order: Social Forces in the Making of History*, New York: Columbia University Press (1987).

71 Thomas E. Carbonneau and Marc. S. Firestone, above n. 55, 62.

which were regarded by both states and merchants as definitive sources of law.[72] The movement from a delocalised system of customary mercantile law to a localised and positive state regulatory regime, though elements of commercial custom persisted, was a crucial development in the growth of capitalism,[73] and in the erosion of *lex mercatoria* as an independent legal order governing legal relationships among merchants. At the international level, state laws incorporated international mercantile custom retaining significant universality, while states replaced individuals, private associations and corporations as the main subjects in international law. These phenomena reflect the acceptance of national sovereignty and political autonomy, the expansion of public regulatory authority in enforcing commercial agreements, and reinforcement of national particularism, during this period.

Nationalisation brought about not only the fragmentation but also the sterilisation of *lex mercatoria*. The argument was that municipal courts were easily confused by commercial innovation, whereas new business practices develop and spread quickly among merchants.[74] Therefore, judges were reluctant to admit evidence of innovation once custom had been codified by legislators or officially recognised by the courts,[75] and merchants required certainty in business.[76] However, the conclusion seems to be that nationalisation did not eradicate the law merchant. Although the law merchant persisted and influenced the development of rules governing financial transactions, insurance and shipping beyond the medieval period, it is important to recognise disjunctures and discontinuities. In substance, during this period, the law merchant became more localised and less universal due to the increasing state power.[77] Merchant autonomy in commercial law was transformed into modern contract law, which replaces the medieval notion of equity in contracting and stresses the freedom of contract. This contractual freedom, together with the new political economy, facilitated commercial exchange and substantially increased efficiency,[78] because the courts could play a more facilitative role by enforcing contracts with minimum judicial intervention into business activities and substantive contractual terms. Contrary to the medieval phase, merchant autonomy

---

72 René David, 'Sources of Law', in *International Encyclopaedia of Comparative Law*, Vol. II (1972) Ch. 3, para. 3-404.

73 Piers Beirne, 'Ideology and Rationality in Max Weber's Sociology of Law', in Piers Beirne and Richard Quinney (eds.) *Marxism and Law*, New York: John Wiley & Sons (1982) pp. 44–62.

74 See generally John H. Baker, *An Introduction to English Legal History*, Oxford: Oxford University Press (3rd edn. 1990) p. 418.

75 *Goodwin v. Robarts*, 10 L.R.-Ex. 337, 357 (1875); see also Robert W. Aske, *The Law Relating to Custom and the Usages of Trade*, London: Stevens and Sons (1909) p. 23; and Harold J. Berman and Colin Kaufman, 'The Law of International Transactions (Lex Mercatoria)', (1978) 19 *Harvard International Law Journal* 221, 227.

76 Harold J. Berman and Colin Kaufman, above n. 14, 226.

77 Bruce Benson, above n. 23, 644–61.

78 Patrick Atiyah, *The Rise and Fall of Freedom of Contract*, Oxford: Oxford University Press (1979).

operated with the sanction and support of state authorities as territorially individuated states became stronger in economic, political and ideological senses.

Positivism is the ideology that legitimised the nationalisation of *lex mercatoria*. It is a jurisprudence that regards law "as a deliberate construction based on empirical knowledge of the effects it would have on the achievement of desirable human purposes".[79] This line of thinking reflects the impact of capitalism on moral theology, which became more consistent with the capitalist business techniques and mercantilist doctrine, "a new degree of freedom from religious constraints on individual enterprise and individual aspirations for economic betterment".[80] The juridification of commerce is shaped by a juridical ideology that departed from the medieval tradition of substantive justice, which was based upon the belief that the justification of contractual obligation is derived from the inherent justice or fairness of exchange.[81] Thus, the juridical ideology helps to distinguish the judicial function of the judiciary from economics, politics and morality. The ideology of market economy, as well as modern contract law, proclaims that all men are equal. Such ideology fundamentally transformed the philosophical foundations of rules and legal systems.

Today "international business occurs within a myriad of independent national legal systems".[82] Each nation filters the once uniform law merchant through its own unique historical, cultural and political experiences.[83] Needless to say, the regulatory variation arising from the national legal order both distorts and disrupts international commerce.[84] As it has been rightly pointed out, "... the way in which international commerce is regulated today ... relates to the nationalisation of law that took place in the 19th century, it is as unsatisfactory as it could be".[85] Similarly, the jurisprudence of positivism today is so embedded in many judicial systems that many judges are reluctant to recognise other sources of law, because the application of *lex mercatoria* by a national court would be likely to render part of a State's sovereignty into the invisible hands of a constantly changing community of merchants. The jurisprudence of positivism may not support a theory postulating the development of a legal regime outside

---

79 Friedrich A. Hayek, above n. 28, p. 19.

80 Max Weber, *The Protestant Ethic and the Spirit of Capitalism*, London: Allen and Unwin (1978); and Jacob Viner, *Religious Thought and Economic Society*, Durham, NC: Duke University Press (1978).

81 Morton Horwitz, 'The Historical Foundations of Modern Contract Law', (1974) 87(5) *Harv. L. Rev.* 917–56.

82 Bernardo M. Cremades and Steven L. Plehn, above n. 3, 317.

83 Ibid.

84 Gerald Malynes, *Consuetudo, Vel, Lex Mercatoria: Or, the Ancient Law-Merchant: In Three Parts, According to the Essentials of Traffick*, The Lawbook Exchange, Ltd. (reprint edn. 2009) p. 3.

85 A note of the transactions of the 2nd UNIDROIT Congress of Private Law, Rome, September 1976 published in *New Directions in International Trade,* New York: Oceana Publications (1977) p. 5.

of the national legal order.[86] A law merchant developed in such a fashion could at times go against the interests of a State or its government.[87]

4.3. THE NATURE OF *LEX MERCATORIA* IN THE LEGAL REALM

Lex mercatoria is often regarded as the private customary law of international commerce,[88] an autonomous legal order "independent of any one national legal system".[89] Arguably, *lex mercatoria* functions as conduits by which the law is enriched to allow more space for concepts not encompassed by one particular legal order. In this sense, *lex mercatoria* can be regarded as "a quasi-legal recognition of rules of common sense, equity and reasonableness",[90] which may provide the increased flexibility necessary in developing legal relationships.[91] Alternatively, *lex mercatoria* can be seen as a tool "to clarify, to fill gaps, and to reduce the impact of peculiarities of individual countries' laws, often not designed for international transactions at all".[92]

4.3.1. RELATIONSHIP BETWEEN *LEX MERCATORIA* AND NATIONAL LAWS

There are two aspects to the relationship between *lex mercatoria* and national law. The first aspect is the "disconnection" between national laws and *lex mercatoria*. The reality, as the second aspect, is that both are closely related. The difference between the state laws and *lex mercatoria* is not one of degree but of kind. The practice of *lex mercatoria* proceeds on different lines from any other kind of law.[93] For instance, *lex mercatoria* can include or refer to those principles of

---

86 Bernardo M. Cremades and Steven L. Plehn, above n. 3, 317.

87 Christopher W.O. Stoecker, above n. 68, 108.

88 Thomas E. Carbonneau and Marc. S. Firestone, above n. 55, 51, 57.

89 Andreas F. Lowenfeld, 'Lex Mercatoria: An Arbitrator's View', in Thomas E. Carbonneau (ed.), *Lex Mercatoria and Arbitration: A Discussion of the New Law Merchant*, New York: Kluwer Law International; Yonkers/Cambridge, MA: Juris (revised edn. 1998) p. 49.

90 Keith Highet, above n. 9, 628.

91 Ibid.

92 Andreas F. Lowenfeld, above n. 89, 56.

93 International law may be closer to *lex mercatoria* than state laws. The majority of the rules of international law are generally observed by all nations without actual compulsion, for it is generally in the interest of all nations concerned to honour their obligations under international law. *Lex mercatoria* may not impose such obligations upon states. Nevertheless, states may have great economic interests in respecting *lex mercatoria*. A nation will likewise be reluctant to disregard *lex mercatoria* since the benefits that it expects from the recognition given to *lex mercatoria* by other states would be complementary to those anticipated by the latter. The state may stand to lose more than it would gain by not respecting *lex*

municipal systems common to each other and common to international law.[94] Likely, *lex mercatoria* can bring into its own sphere some of the particular aspects of commercial activities which at present lie between the "domestic" and non-domestic jurisdictions. A related question is how much weight the arbitrator should place on national laws and *lex mercatoria* in deciding substantive issues of the dispute. The question in itself can be complicated in the absence of a choice of law made by the parties or where the parties have chosen a variety of "general principles of law" instead of a specific national law. The second aspect concerns the reaction of national courts to an a-national award. The real concern is whether the court of the place where arbitration takes place or where the enforcement is sought will agree to enforce an award that is based upon *lex mercatoria.*[95]

There are two further perspectives relevant to these two aspects of the fundamental issue of which is more the important, national laws or *lex mercatoria,* in a commercial context. A traditional view may hold that national laws are the authority in determining and evaluating *lex mercatoria.* In contrast, it has been asserted that *lex mercatoria* takes precedence over national laws,[96] and avoids the effect of relatively unsophisticated national laws unsuited to international transactions.[97] In both theory and practice, *lex mercatoria* performs a useful and indeed a necessary function in international society, especially in the international business community, in enabling business entities to carry on their day-to-day intercourse along orderly and predictable lines. Most norms of *lex mercatoria* serve such complementary interests. Following this classical mercatorist view, the arbitrator should avoid all references to national laws and thus a conflict between the two would not arise. This view appears in a few arbitral awards. For example, in the *Pyramids* case, the tribunal proceeded by interpreting Egyptian law as conforming to the general principle exemplified in Article 42(1) of the ICSID Convention, and then applying it in that sense.[98]

Two lines of argument in favour of each side can be found in the *Rakoil* case.[99] In the dispute between Deutsche Schachtbau- und Tiefbohrgesellschaft

---

mercatoria. This is particularly so in the long run, since a nation that has the reputation of disregarding its commercial obligations will find it hard to conclude commercial treaties beneficial to itself.

94 David W. Rivkin, 'Enforceability of Arbitral Awards based on *Lex Mercatoria*', (1993) 9(1) *Arb. Int'l* 68.

95 See Chapter 3 of this book.

96 See Ole Lando, above n. 6, 759 ("It is now established by ... the Convention [of 18 March 1965 on the Settlement of Investment Disputes between States and Nationals of Other States, which instituted the International Centre for the Settlement of Investment Disputes (ICSID)] that, in the case of a conflict between the law of a Contracting State and 'the rules of international law, the latter rules may be given preference to the former.'")

97 David W. Rivkin, above n. 94, 67.

98 *SPP (Middle East) v. The Arab Republic of Egypt*, IX *Yearbook* 111.

99 See *DST v. R'As al-Khaimah National Oil Co.* [1987] 3 WLR 1023; the Court of Appeal in the *Rakoil* case was called upon to interpret the scope of Art 13(3) of the ICC Rules; and XIV *Yearbook* (1989) 111 (unpublished award).

mbH (DST), a consortium of oil companies, and the Government of R'As al-Khaimah, via a government-owned oil company (Rakoil), an agreement included an ICC arbitration clause providing for arbitration in Geneva. The dispute related to a 1973 concession agreement and two oil exploration agreements, and the alleged inducement by misrepresentation. The contract contained no choice of law clause but the arbitration tribunal held instead that the proper law was "internationally accepted principles of law governing contractual relations". The arbitrators derived such power from Article 13(3) of the ICC Rules which empowers them to apply the law designated by appropriate conflicts of law rules if the parties have not chosen the proper law. The arbitration tribunal focused on the "common" practice of arbitrators adjudicating oil exploration disputes to select general principles, and concluded that the practice "must have been known to the parties" and thus represents their "implicit will".[100] Eventually, the alleged misrepresentation was not established and there were no other grounds for holding that the agreement was invalid. Both the High Court in London and the arbitral tribunal appeared to support the idea that the national law does not necessarily rank ahead of *lex mercatoria* as long as the parties, through the ICC Rules or arbitration clause, allow the tribunal to apply *lex mercatoria* to the dispute.[101] The Court of Appeal dismissed Rakoil's appeal, which sought to resist enforcement of the award in England on the basis that a reference in the award to international principles was contrary to English public policy. Rakoil argued that public policy prevented enforcement where the party's rights and obligations were based on "unspecified, possibly ill-defined, internationally accepted law".[102] In sharp contrast to the traditional English hostility to anything akin to *lex mercatoria* or an a-national standard, the court rejected this argument and pointed out that "parties can validly provide for some other system of law to be applied to an arbitration tribunal. ... The parties could validly agree that their legal relationships should be decided by the arbitral tribunal ... perhaps on the basis of principles of international law".[103] This judicial view is consistent with Lord Denning's opinion expressed in the case of *Eagle Star v. Yuval* that both the contract and the arbitration clause requiring an "equitable rather than a strictly legal interpretation" are valid.[104]

In *Rakoil*, Donaldson MR proposed a three-pronged test to determine the validity and enforceability of an award based upon a-national law: (a) the state shall not interfere with the dispute if the parties intend to create legally

---

100 XIV *Yearbook* (1989) 117 (unpublished award).

101 See XIII *Yearbook* 532, and Hunter (1987) *Lloyd's Maritime and Commercial Law Quarterly* 277 at 279.

102 *DST (FR Germany) v. (1) R'as Al Khaimah National Oil Co. (UAE); (2) Shell International Co., Ltd. (UK)* [1987] 2 Lloyd's Rep. 246–258, [1987] 2 All ER 769–784; extract reprinted in XIII *Yearbook* (1988) 522, 530.

103 XIII *Yearbook* (1988) 532.

104 [1978] 1 Lloyd's Rep. 357.

enforceable rights and obligations; (b) whether the resulting agreement is sufficiently certain to constitute a legally enforceable contract; (c) whether it would be contrary to public policy to enforce the award using the coercive powers of the state.[105] This test actually gives the court a broad nod and a wink to the proponents of *lex mercatoria*. Without an express choice of law by the parties, the arbitrator has a mandate to decide that he will apply "internationally accepted principles of law" in appropriate circumstances.[106] The three-pronged test then demonstrates the court's willingness and flexibility to recognise *lex mercatoria*, at least in co-existence with national law. Lord Mustill down-played the importance of the *Rakoil* case as regards *lex mercatoria* and stressed that the judgment did not address the question of whether, under English law, a contract is effective if it does not contain any explicit choice of the "general principles". The established proposition may be that a contract cannot exist *in vacuo* and nor can it be stateless if the parties wish to seek enforcement by a court.[107] Although this line of argument is probably against the tide of academic opinion, it raises a critical question: how can *lex mercatoria*, as a law, operate without the support of a legal system? In a positivist sense, the functioning of *lex mercatoria* may rely upon the recognition of nation-states. Nevertheless, the servicing function of *lex mercatoria* strongly explains why the rules in *lex mercatoria* are generally self-enforced, as discussed below.

4.3.2. *LEX MERCATORIA*: EFFECTIVE TOOL TO FILL GAPS IN COMMERCIAL CONTRACTS?

The power of arbitrators to review and fill gaps in commercial contracts is the most controversial arbitral doctrine.[108] The discussion started in the last century[109] but did not arrive at a satisfactory solution due to a seemingly clear cut dogma: the procedural character of arbitration may be incompatible with the substantive nature of contractual gap-filling.

The drawback of complex long-term "relational" contracts lies in the fact that contracts are vulnerable to the change of technological, political or economic circumstances or the omission of detailed contractual terms. Arbitrators are theoretically entitled to deal with any issue arising from such a contract. Nevertheless, this power is subject to two opposing principles of contract law: the principle of *pacta sunt servanda*, which stands for the sacrosanct character of

105 XIII *Yearbook* (1988) 534.
106 Martin J. Hunter, 'Lex Mercatoria – Deutsche Schachtbau- und Tiefbohrgesellschaft mbH v. R'As Al Khaimah National Oil Co.' (1987) *Lloyd's Maritime and Commercial LQ* 277, 279.
107 Michael Mustill, 'The New Lex Mercatoria: The First 25 Years', (1988) 4 *Arb. Int'l* 86; and Keith Highet, above n. 9, 614–5.
108 See William Laurence Craig, William W. Park and Jan Paulsson, above n. 36, 143.
109 Clive Schmitthoff, 'Hardship and Intervener Clauses', (1980) *Journal of Business Law* 82.

the parties' initial agreements, and the notion of *clausula rebus sic stantibus*, which reflects a necessary flexibility in interpreting the contract so that the initial economic equilibrium can be maintained. It appears that the degree of the arbitrator's discretion to modify or fill gaps in contracts is dependent on how the dilemma between the need for commercial flexibility and the ideal of sanctity of contracts is resolved.

The role of arbitrators in practice is in some ways quite narrow and is confined to making a simple judgement on the non-performance or violation of contractual duties.[110] Such a traditional role of the arbitrator is reflected in the UNCITRAL Model Law and other domestic arbitration laws[111] but is incompatible with the reality that arbitrators may be compelled to play a more constructive role in evaluating economic issues and modifying the contract. In practice, the line between gap-filling and contractual interpretation is not easy to draw and is a matter of degree. Under German civil law, if a contractual stipulation for a specific issue has been omitted from the contract, arbitrators may apply the principle of the "supplementary construction" (*erganzende Vertragsauslegung*) of contractual terms derived from Section 157 of the German Civil Code so that gaps in the contract can be closed, if and to the extent that this is in line with the hypothetical will of the parties.[112] This part of the arbitrator's decision-making still falls under the arbitrator's general task of applying the *lex causae*. A tribunal acting under English law may avoid the unenforceability of "to be agreed" clauses by applying the principle of construction and assuming an implied term in the contract where the parties have commenced performing the contract.[113] Similarly, under US law, an arbitral tribunal may supply an omitted contract term by "implication" based upon the expectations of the parties or the principles of justice and fairness.[114] The Uniform Commercial Code (UCC) defers to the authority of *lex mercatoria* for gap-filling purposes and "the principles of law and equity, including the law merchant ... shall supplement its provisions".[115] Thus, private parties' commercial or legal objectives can be satisfied without resorting to the legal

110 See the statement made by the German delegation in drafting Model Law in UN Doc. A/CN.9/263, para. 15: the activity of the arbitral tribunal is concentrated on the interpretation and application of contractual agreements and legal provisions.

111 See Article 7(1) of the UNCITRAL Model Law.

112 See Fritz Nicklisch, 'Agreement to Arbitrate to Fill Contractual Gaps', (1988) 3(5) *J. Int'l Arb.* 38.

113 *Hillas & Co. v. Arcos Ltd* [1932] All ER 494; *Foley v. Classique Coaches* [1934] 2 KB 1.

114 E. Allan Farnsworth, 'Pre-contractual Liability and Preliminary Agreements: Fair Dealing and Failed Negotiations', (1987) 87 *Colum. L. Rev.* 259–60. E. Allan Farnsworth, *Contracts*, New York: Aspen Law & Business (3rd edn. 1999) §7.16.

115 UCC 1–103 (1992). In fact, the authors of the UCC proclaimed it to be a modern *lex mercatoria*. Friedrich K. Juenger, 'The *Lex Mercatoria* and the Conflict of Laws', in Thomas E. Carbonneau (ed.), *Lex Mercatoria and Arbitration: A Discussion of the New Law Merchant*, Yonkers, New York: Kluwer Law International (revised edn. 1998).

system. In essence, *lex mercatoria* is regarded as an addition, rather than an alternative, to state law.[116]

The admissibility of contract adaptation or supplementation by arbitrators ultimately boils down to a clash of two basic ideas: the adjudication of pre-existing rights is a matter of procedural law; and the contractual intervention to create rights is a matter of substantive contract law. The distinction relates to the filling of "initial" and "supervening" gaps.[117] Initial gaps are those deliberately left open by the parties in negotiating the contract. Therefore, the arbitrator has not been granted any discretion to fill such gaps. In contrast, supervening gaps occur after the conclusion of the contract. Since such gaps are not foreseen by the parties in the drafting stage, arbitrators may be entitled to fill such gaps if conditions of substantive and procedural laws are satisfied. Such a distinction triggers various concerns in procedural and substantive aspects of law. From a procedural perspective, initial gaps are left by the parties at the outset with an intention to settle any future ambiguities by themselves when the contract is being performed. No dispute is actually left for arbitration. For instance, in the case of "indefinite agreements" in English and American contract law, courts may refuse to enforce a mere "agreement to agree" or a "contract to negotiate" since terms are too vague to shape any legal remedies according to the parties' intent.[118] Certainly, if the parties fail to reach an agreement in filling the gap, it

---

116 E. Allan Farnsworth, above n. 114, §7.16.

117 See Pieter Sanders, *Quo Vadis Arbitration? Sixty Years of Arbitration Practice, A Comparative Study*, The Hague: Kluwer Law International (1999) p. 141; Wolfgang Peter et al., *Arbitration and Renegotiation of International Investment Agreements,* The Hague: Kluwer Law International (2nd edn. 1995) p. 254.

118 *May and Butcher v. R.* [1934] 2 KB 17; *Walford v. Miles* [1992] 2 AC 128; Ewan McKendrick, *Force Majeure and Frustration of Contract,* Lloyd's of London Press (2nd edn. 1995) p. 110. *Lahaina-Maui Corp. v. Tau Tet Hew,* 362 F.2d. 419; *Transamericana Equipment Leasing Corporation v. Union Bank*, 426 F.2d 273, 275; *Joseph Martin Ju., Delicatessen v. Schumacher,* 52 NY 2d. 105; *Magna Development Co. v. Reed,* 228 Cal. App. 2d. 230, 236; *White Point Company v. Paul B Herrington et al.*, 268 Cal. App. 2d. 458, 468. The general approach to an agreement to agree under English law is that a failure to agree on all essential terms of a bargain is generally fatal to a finding that there is a contract. Michael Furmston, *The Law of Contract,* UK: LexisNexis (4th edn. 2010), para. 2.156. There have been some new developments on this issue. Some courts in England have seen an express agreement to negotiate in good faith as an unenforceable agreement to agree. *Barbudev v. Eurocom Cable Management Bulgaria EOOD* [2012] EWCA Civ 548, esp. at [44] to [46]; *Shaker v. Vistajet Group Holding SA* [2012] EWHC 1329 (Comm), at [7]. In the US, overwhelming weight of authority holds that courts will not enforce an agreement to negotiate *(Honolulu Waterfront Ltd. v. Aloha Tower Dev.* 692 F. Supp. 1230 (D. Haw. 1988)), this being the starting point, albeit some courts have shown their willingness to enforce agreements to negotiate (*Itek Corp. v. Chicago Aerial Industries* 248 A.2d 625, 629 (Del. 1968) and *Hill v. Waxberg* (237 F.2d 936, 938–939 (9th Cir. 1956)). It was once pointed out that "[it] would be difficult to find a less predictable area of contract law". E. Allan Farnsworth, 'Pre-contractual Liability and Preliminary Agreements: Fair Dealing and Failed Negotiations', (1987) 87 *Colum. L. Rev.* 259–60.

may suffice to establish the competence of a tribunal for arbitration.[119] This risk remains in some common law jurisdictions such as England and America where such agreements to agree are not enforceable by international arbitral tribunals. In order to avoid such problems, the parties may clearly convey to arbitrators the power to fill in gaps under the principle of *lex mercatoria*.

In the drafting of the UNCITRAL Model Law, besides the distinction between contract modification and gap filling, the distinction between authorisation and non-authorisation was put forward,[120] and was adopted in some well-known arbitration cases such as *AMINOIL*.[121] With authorisation,[122] the principle of *pacta sunt servanda* is in favour of the arbitrator's competence to reshape the contract.[123] The party autonomy in international commercial arbitration builds up a strong theoretical ground for arbitrators to exercise the discretion to adapt or fill gaps in contracts.[124] Without express or implied authorisation, arbitrators and arbitral tribunals must look for legal authority to interfere with the contract. Such authority may be found in the applicable law but the principle of sanctity of contacts makes this difficult.[125] Some recent cases have indicated a tendency of arbitrators' greater willingness to apply the doctrine of *lex mercatoria* to determine various issues such as the validity of the arbitration agreement even though the parties had not chosen *lex mercatoria* (or transnational general principles, usages of international trade, or law of merchants) as the law applicable to the arbitration agreement.[126]

---

119 See s 82(1) of the UK Arbitration Act (1996) which reads: "in this part ... dispute includes any difference ..."

120 See Alan Redfern and Martin Hunter, *Law and Practice of International Commercial Arbitration* London: Sweet & Maxwell (3rd edn. 1999) No. 8–17 *in fine*; also see the proposals to include in the Model Law a provision dealing with the arbitrator's authority to adapt contacts and fill gaps and requiring an "express authorisation" by the parties, UN Doc. A/CN.9/WG.II/WP.41, para. 11; A/CN.9/WG.II/WP.44, para 32.

121 See *Kuwait v. The American Independent Oil Company*, ILM (1982) 976, 1015: "there can be no doubt that ... a tribunal cannot substitute itself for the parties in order to make good a missing segment of their contractual relations – or to modify a contract – unless that right is conferred upon it by law, or by the express consent of the parties".

122 For instance, the parties may authorise the tribunal to decide on "all disputes arising out of the contract including a change of the contract itself". See ICC (Partial) Award No. 7544 in (1999) Clunet 1062, 1063 with note Hascher, *ibid*, at 1064, 1065.

123 Ugo Draetta, Ralph B. Lake and Ved P. Nanda, *Breach and Adaptation of International Contracts: An Introduction to Lex Mercatoria*, New York: Matthew Bender & Co. (1992) p. 202.

124 It should be inherent in the principle of party autonomy that the parties may entrust a third party to decide on how a contract should be adapted or supplemented. See the UNCITRAL Working Group in UN Doc. A/CN.9/233, para. 16.

125 The German delegation emphasised that a stricter approach should be taken where the parties have not authorised the arbitrators because "if the parties do not want an arbitration of this kind, it should not be imposed on them". See UN Doc. A/CN.9/263, para. 15.

126 *Dallah Real Estate and Tourism Holding Company v. The Ministry of Religious Affairs, Government of Pakistan* [2010] UKSC 46.

4.3.3. *LEX MERCATORIA* AND PRINCIPLES OF GOOD FAITH AND FAIRNESS

Law includes enforceable rules of conduct or transaction that the community recognises as binding and that convey signals to business decision-makers about the community goals, norms and values. The principles of good faith and fair dealing are important components of *lex mercatoria*[127] and have become the benchmarks for the "social control" of business behaviours and agreements.[128] As a supplement (but not substitute) to legal rules, such principles, together with other norms or values in *lex mercatoria*, reach toward general notions of "rights" that may be in tension with the dictates of the state, and appeal to commands of morality or ethics beyond those expressed in statutes and court decisions. The emphasis on such principles signals the transition to a new form of contractual morality in international business and the emergence of a more flexible and pragmatic approach than the sanctity of contractual rules. This approach is in consonance with commercial common sense and reflects the fact that various extra-contractual devices such as cooperation and flexibility involving the "entangling strings of friendship, reputation, interdependence, morality and altruistic desires",[129] and the intrinsic willingness of the parties to adjust terms, can operate to help to reduce the rigid use and inefficiency of contract law. Arbitration certainly matches and facilitates such an approach as well as the application of principles of good faith and fair dealing.

The *Norsolor* case seems to suggest that arbitrators' sense of fairness is not simply a rule but indeed the primary rule of decision.[130] Legal rules do not necessarily provide the predictability that business people need in planning business strategies, evaluating commercial risks and making commercial choices. Although dispute resolution according to non-legal criteria is unlikely to be far more successful than state-centred legal rules in bringing community standards to bear on the allocation of values and resources that affect third parties, in meeting the needs of cross-border business and protecting public interests, *lex mercatoria* and *ad hoc* justice are needed in the long run in the international business community.

---

127 David W. Rivkin, above n. 94, 68.

128 See Allan Farnsworth, 'Duties of Good Faith and Fair Dealing under the UNIDROIT Principles, Relevant International Conventions, and National Laws', (1994) 3(1/2) *Tulane J. Int'l and Comp. L.* 45; Michael Joachim Bonell, 'Policing the International Commercial Contract Against Unfairness under the UNIDROIT Principles', (1994) 3(1/2) *Tulane J. Int'l and Comp. L.* 73; Arthur Hartkamp, 'The Concept of Good Faith in the UNIDROIT Principles for International Commercial Contracts', (1994) 3(1/2) *Tulane J. Int'l and Comp. L.* 65.

129 K.M. Sharma, 'From "Sanctity" to "Fairness": An Uneasy Transition in the Law of Contracts', (1999) 18 *NY Law School Journal of International and Comparative Law* 95.

130 IX *Yearbook* (1984) 109. See also *Mechema v. Troisem* [1980] *Rev. Arb.* 560.

To the extent that commercial law lags behind norms, principles and standards shared by the business community, arbitration according to principles of good faith and fair dealing rather than legal rules may occasionally promote and satisfy the parties' commercial needs and expectations. *Lex mercatoria* adds a new dimension to the arbitrator's dilemma in navigating among the legal mandates. Many arbitrators are inclined to include the application of this a-national customary business law on the basis of "general principles of law" or "equitable considerations", in rendering arbitral awards without relying on a particular national legal system. For instance, in continental European countries arbitration in equity or *ex aequo et bono*, where arbitrators act as *amiables compositeurs*, is an institution in itself.[131] Arbitrators may find their way to a contractual interpretation under Article 13(5) of the ICC Arbitration Rules, which commands arbitration in all cases to "take account of … relevant usages", or a "commercial custom" which is of binding force under the CISG.[132]

4.3.4. *LEX MERCATORIA* AND LEGAL PROCESS

In terms of the predictability, authoritativeness and accessibility that a "proto-typical system of legal rules" carries,[133] *lex mercatoria* arguably does not have the same "force" of law even though both the Hague Convention and the CISG are said to be the products of *lex mercatoria*.[134]

4.3.4.1. *Uniformity and Predictability of the Proceedings*

Lex mercatoria can be argued to be particularly suitable for arbitration proceedings in three ways. First, arbitrators often follow a common understanding of what is "fair" in the business world.[135] "Most arbitrators have common ethics and common notions of how business should be conducted".[136] Second, *lex mercatoria* is regarded as a necessary supplement to the strict rules

---

131 Jacques Covo, 'Commodities, Arbitrations and Equitable Considerations', (1993) 9(1) *Arb. Int'l* 61. According to Article 26 of the 1957 European Convention for the Peaceful Settlement of Disputes of 29 April 1957, an arbitral decision may be adopted *ex aequo et bono* in absence of a *compromis*.

132 Allan E. Farnsworth, 'Unification and Harmonisation of Private Law', (1996) 27 *Canadian Business Law Journal* 48.

133 Keith Highet, above n. 9, 624.

134 See the Hague Convention Providing a Uniform Law on the International Sale of Goods, 1 July 1964, 834 UNTS 107 (1972) and the CISG, concluded at Vienna, 1 April 1980, UN Doc. A/Conf.97/18 (1990), reprinted in 19 ILM (1980) 671.

135 Ole Lando, above n. 6, 747.

136 Ibid. 753.

of law,[137] and a "useful tool for arbitrators ... when faced with dissatisfying answers from their initial inquiries", supplying an addition rather than an alternative to the applicable law.[138] Third, the changing and unforeseeable circumstances that arise in the international business community need a more permissive and flexible legal or quasi-legal regime,[139] and *lex mercatoria* can play this role well.

However, the paradox is that while the application of *lex mercatoria* is meant to be a method of getting closer to the participating parties' expectations of fairness, a choice of *lex mercatoria* may result in arbitrary and capricious decisions, in particular as perceived by the losing party. In the absence of choice by the parties, arbitrators may exercise their unrestricted freedom. In most cases, they may choose the fundamental principles of equal treatment of the parties and due process (or natural justice). The possible inability of *lex mercatoria* to achieve fairness may be largely due to the unlimited discretion that the arbitrators may actually exercise and the uncertainty surrounding the content of *lex mercatoria* itself, and that prevents practitioners from being able to predict the outcome of arbitration. Practically speaking, arbitrators are likely to apply *lex mercatoria* "either in accordance with their own comparative law interpretation of general principles and trade customs or refer to their favourite school of thought and ... published arbitral awards".[140] If parties, courts or legislatures give arbitration panels or arbitrators the freedom "to pursue more perfect justice by ignoring otherwise applicable law that the arbitrator finds inconvenient in the case at hand",[141] arbitrators act as *de facto* "legislators", defining and applying their own concept of fairness and thus implicating a personal creative process into arbitration, and the result may be abstract or *ad hoc* justice.

The *ad hoc* justice of *lex mercatoria* to some extent affects the degree of predictability and may result in a loss of confidence in "the system". Indeed, the deficiency of the consensus on the scope or nature of *lex mercatoria* will add uncertainty to transactions.[142] One function of adjudication is the delineation of acceptable goals, values and norms for commercial activities. However, *lex*

---

137 Andreas F. Lowenfeld, above n. 89, 51, 57.

138 Ibid. 51.

139 William Laurence Craig, William W. Park and Jan Paulsson, above n. 36, 138, 310 n. 1, 312–13; and René David, *Arbitration in International Trade,* Deventer: Kluwer Law and Taxation (1985) p. 336.

140 Wolfgang Peter, above n. 117, 172–176.

141 William W. Park, 'Control Mechanisms in the Development of a Modern Lex Mercatoria', in Thomas E. Carbonneau (ed.), *Lex Mercatoria and Arbitration: A Discussion of the New Law Merchant,* Yonkers, NY: Kluwer Law International / Cambridge, MA: Juris (1990) pp. 110–113.

142 Wolfgang Peter, above n. 117, 178. Professor Pierre Lalive disagrees by stating that "the difficulties of determination or application of the general principles [of *lex mercatoria*] are greatly exaggerated", but he is in the minority in holding this position.

mercatoria may not provide sufficient guidance to the community as regards commercial behaviour and may discourage consistent application over time.

As previously discussed, *lex mercatoria* may function as a conduit by which law is enriched and expanded to allow greater room for concepts and standards not encompassed by domestic laws. The next question is then whether arbitration is the proper forum for the development and elaboration of *lex mercatoria* due to the lack of precedential value created by arbitral awards. As precedent is the foundation upon which the growth of law depends, particularly in common law countries,[143] the relative imprecision of *lex mercatoria* is necessarily unable to provide sufficient support for such growth. Arbitral tribunals and arbitrators are more concerned with finding a solution appropriate for the dispute *per se* than with the evolution of the law.[144]

4.3.4.2. *Judicial Review by the Court*

The business community's desire to free international arbitration from *de novo* review by the court is understandable and must be satisfied to some extent. The parties to international arbitration and the states involved generally exclude the jurisdiction of national courts to review the merits of arbitral awards. As a result, an arbitrator has the ability to invoke the power of *lex mercatoria* without risking judicial review. Under *lex mercatoria*, arbitration is vastly uncontrolled and the parties to arbitration cannot expect community but individual justice. However, a total freedom from judicial control may not be realistic and may lead to unfairness.[145] Without judicial review in place, the losing party in arbitration where the arbitrator has exceeded the authority granted to him, either by incorrectly applying *lex mercatoria* or applying *lex mercatoria* without the permission of the parties, may have no recourse in the country where the award is rendered or where the enforcement is sought. Moreover, the losing party will have no access to any enforcement forum since there will be no award to enforce and the party will be forced to resort to litigation or a second arbitration. The viability of transnational arbitration requires that the national legal system ensure the integrity of arbitration. The trend of "justice without law" may injure

[143] René David, above n. 139, 106 (arguing that "arbitration [in general] will in all probability gradually assume the same features as the justice administered by the courts".).

[144] Thomas E. Carbonneau, *Resolving Transnational Disputes Through International Arbitration*, Charlottesville, VA: University of Virginia Press (1984) p. 88 (arguing that because arbitrators do not risk being overruled for errors in their legal reasoning, they "can be expected to give reasoned awards more frequently", thereby contributing to the development of a modern "law merchant, or *lex mercatoria*").

[145] Total freedom may also cause the interests national courts have in "ensuring the integrity of proceedings conducted within their national borders" to be ignored, and may result in the devaluation of these awards abroad in terms of enforceability. William W. Park, above n. 15, 1795.

the arbitrating parties as well as the legitimate public interest that law is designed to protect.

4.4. *LEX MERCATORIA* AND INTERNATIONAL COMMERCIAL ARBITRATION

The reluctance of the business community to use national courts raises a key question of whether national courts can be expected to recognise *lex mercatoria*. Merchants in many countries are convinced that municipal judges do not understand the complexities of international business. Both national courts and laws are designed by national governments for domestic purposes and, therefore, are rarely suited to international commerce. This has been the merchants' perennial complaint since nationalisation of *lex mercatoria* began in the seventeenth century.[146]

4.4.1. INHERENT FEATURES OF ARBITRATION AND *LEX MERCATORIA*

Arbitration itself is a business-friendly customary tool developed by merchants over the last several centuries. Compared to litigation in a national court, arbitration meets the needs of business better than national courts. Arbitration is preferable to litigation because arbitration is informal, faster, less costly, equitable, a way to avoid unfavourable publicity, relatively conciliatory, and requires less time. Most importantly, arbitration is seen as providing the best chance to preserve the parties' goodwill and therefore save their underlying business relationship.[147] In arbitration, businessmen can choose arbitrators who possess specific expertise in trade or industry and who are better able to deal with technical questions than municipal judges whose expertise is limited to municipal law.[148] Because arbitrators are more familiar with practices and technical aspects of international commerce, they are better equipped than municipal judges to determine and apply customary usages that meet the parties' expectations. Further, the business community is eager to assess the risks they face if a contract is breached, or if collection of debts proves difficult, or if the dispute arises. Arbitration under *lex mercatoria* likely makes the risk assessment

---

146 Daniel R. Coquillette, 'Ideology and Incorporation II: Sir Thomas Ridley, Charles Molloy, and the Literary Battle for the Law Merchant, 1607–1676', (1981) 61 *Boston University Law Review* 315, 361.

147 James E. Meason and Alison G. Smith, 'Non-Lawyers in International Commercial Arbitration: Gathering Splinters on the Bench', (1991) 12 *NW J. Int'l L. & Bus.* 27–28.

148 Bernardo M. Cremades and Steven L. Plehn, above n. 3, 331.

much easier.[149] Resort to *lex mercatoria* through arbitration "eliminates the risks inherent in political resolutions of controversies" whether through the mandatory application of some national "public policy" or in the local bias often found in national courts.[150] The degree of uncertainty is then reduced through carefully drafted arbitration provisions.[151]

Arbitration is a reflection of the inherent jurisdictional power of the international merchant community. The business community possibly provides nothing substantial in contracts, leaving arbitrators free to select a governing law according to their views of justice and appropriateness. Arbitrators are then given power to act as *amiables compositeurs* and to dispense with the law or to apply *lex mercatoria*. Merchants also need to re-establish their own adjudicatory institutions to articulate and apply private law based on transnational commercial customs.[152] Such desire to "keep transnational commercial disputes out of the national courts, and thereby beyond the reach of local laws ... has become nearly universal".[153] International commercial arbitration is the preferred method for realising this desire, and its customary nature not only matches but also supports *lex mercatoria* in arbitration. Merchants are reluctant to have their contracts governed by a particular national law and sometimes authorise arbitrators to resolve disputes *ex aequo et bono* or as *amiable compositeurs*. In the former case, arbitrators may depart from a law and decide the case according to equity and good sense. In the later case, arbitrators will use their goodwill to engineer an amicable settlement. Since arbitration does not derive its authority from the coercive power of national governments,[154] but from an agreement between two private parties, merchants may contract outside of municipal law or a-national private law embodied in *lex mercatoria* and applied in arbitration.[155] Through constant use by the business community and a large number of international arbitral institutes such as the ICC Court of Arbitration,[156] *lex mercatoria* may grow rapidly due to its strong link with

---

149 Nicholas de B. Katzenbach, 'Business Executives and Lawyers in International Trade', in ICC International Court of Arbitration (ed.), *60 Years of ICC Arbitration: A Look at the Future* (1984) pp. 67–69.

150 Ibid.

151 Ibid.

152 Berthold Goldman, above n. 19, 8.

153 Friedrich K. Juenger, above n. 115, 213.

154 Carlo Croff, 'The Applicable Law in an International Commercial Arbitration: Is It Still a Conflict of Laws Problem?', (1982) 16 *International Law* 613.

155 Russell B. Stevenson, Jr., 'An Introduction to ICC Arbitration', (1980) 14 *Journal of International Law and Economics* 382.

156 The ICC is a private institution, founded and financed exclusively by the enterprises that are its members and by the users of the services it offers. Its organisation and rules have been designed specifically to meet the needs of international arbitration. Arthur Tompkins, 'A Practical Guide to International Commercial Arbitration', (1991) 47 *New Zealand Law Journal* 274, 276.

international arbitration.[157] Both the ICC Rules[158] and the UNCITRAL Model Law[159] require the arbitrator to consider the provisions of the contract, as well as relevant trade usages, when rendering an arbitral award and permit at least a reference to *lex mercatoria*.[160]

Arbitration is recognised as one of a few functionally acceptable dispute resolution processes available to parties from different jurisdictions who want to depart from a national legal system, which may be unfairly biased or conciliatory. The concern with the distortion of the arbitral process by national laws may justify the modern trend toward "a-national" arbitration. However, the a-national and autonomous legal order of *lex mercatoria* attracts its most resonant criticism.[161] It has been argued that "the fostering of a *lex mercatoria* has nothing to do with the harmonisation of trade law. The aim of the latter is to minimise the differences between the law of individual nations, so as to provide a stable and uniform basis for commerce. To the mercatorist, the laws of individual States are irrelevant, save as a quarry from which to draw the raw materials for generalised rules".[162] In essence, "a-national" arbitration may be realised by not applying any municipal law and by instead applying general principles of international business and equity. The exercise of self restraint by governments is inspired less by any solicitude for merchant self-regulation than by the practical difficulties encountered by governments in attempting to reach agreement on a uniform transnational law of trade.[163]

4.4.2. NECESSITY OF ARBITRATORS' DISCRETION

Arbitrators often regard themselves as morally and legally bound to apply the law chosen by the parties, expressly or tacitly. Arbitrators also regard themselves as

157 See Carlo Croff, above n. 154, 634–35.

158 Article 13(5) of the ICC Rules. Note that under the current ICC Rules, the ability to provide for amiable composition no longer depends on whether the procedural law of the seat of arbitration would permit such use. The 1975 version of the Rules, unchanged in the 1988 version, made this change from the 1955 version, which placed an additional condition on the power to act as *amiable compositeur* besides requiring that the parties agree to the use of such power: such use "[must] not in any way interfere with the legal enforcement of the award".

159 Article 33(3) of the UNCITRAL Model Law. Isaak I. Dore, *Arbitration and Conciliation Under the UNCITRAL Rules: A Textual Analysis*, Boston: Martinus Nijhoff Publishers (1986) p. 65 and p. 209.

160 See ICC Rules Art 13(3); Model Law Art 28(2) and the same wording used in Art. 23 of the UNCITRAL Rules; see also *DST v. R'As al-Khaimah National Oil Co.* [1987] 3 WLR 1023, CA; see also later elaboration in this chapter.

161 Frederick A. Mann, 'England Rejects 'Delocalised' Contracts and Arbitration', (1984) 33 *ICLQ* 193; and Michael Mustill, above n. 107, 86; Frederick A. Mann, 'Private Arbitration and Public Policy', (1985) 4 *Civil Justice Quarterly* 257, 264.

162 Michael Mustill, above n. 107, 88.

163 Mark A. Buchanan, 'Public Policy and International Commercial Arbitration', (1988) 26 *American Business Law Journal* 511–12.

bound by the applicable law contained in arbitration rules such as the ICC Rules or the UNCITRAL Rules, to which the parties have subjected their arbitration. Where there is no choice of law by the parties, the arbitrators' task is exceptionally difficult and they may simply make awards as they think fair and just. This can be justified by the fact that both parties choose justice according to their own standards, and the parties choose arbitrators to make a decision for fairness and justice. It is not surprising to see that a different approach, which enjoys the strong support of some commentators, is to eschew national laws altogether, and to apply what is often described as *lex mercatoria*. This "transnational" or "a-national" school of thought views arbitrators as autonomous "judges" independent from any national legal system. Proponents of the "transnational" or "a-national" approach would prefer to apply *lex mercatoria* in determining the law applicable to the merits.

It follows that an arbitrator would be more like a creative jurist – "an inventor" – by "taking advantage of [his] freedom to select the better rule of law which courts sometimes miss".[164] This flexible dimension is reflected in the arbitration rules of various arbitration institutions. For instance, Articles 15 and 17 of the ICC Rules on International Commercial Arbitration allow arbitrators to apply the law they deem appropriate.[165] According to the American Arbitration Association Commercial Arbitration Rules, arbitrators can exercise their discretion to conduct the proceedings with a view to expediting the resolution of the dispute.[166] Whether this is a viable approach, and whether it should be adopted if the parties in their contract or arbitration agreement have not sanctioned it, is a matter of practice and controversy.[167] At least, this approach to applying *lex mercatoria* fits an "a-nationalist" arbitrator's role well.

4.4.3. RECOGNITION OF *LEX MERCATORIA* IN MAJOR JURISDICTIONS

No national courts have directly applied *lex mercatoria* in cases, as *lex mercatoria* is not a national law. The enforceability of arbitral awards rendered on the basis of *lex mercatoria* depends entirely upon the national system where enforcement is sought, and is now almost uniformly accepted.[168] Historically, the most revealing difference between England, France and the United States in terms of

---

164 Ole Lando, above n. 6, 752–53.
165 http://www.iccwbo.org/court/english/arbitration/.
166 American Arbitration Association Commercial Arbitration Rules (as amended and effective as of 1 July 2003), Rule 30.
167 Frederick A. Mann, '*Lex Facit Arbitrum*', (1986) 2 *Arb. Int'l* 244.
168 David W. Rivkin, above n. 94, 74.

arbitration policy is the attitude towards the purpose of the arbitral process: is arbitration viewed as a strict substitute for adjudication or as a method of reaching settlement between the parties? The judicial attitude towards the role of arbitration partly reflects the level of recognition of *lex mercatoria* in the legal system.

4.4.3.1. England and Other Common Law Jurisdictions

English courts have traditionally been unreceptive to the application of *lex mercatoria* in arbitration. Commercial disputes were once resolved only according to common law, and law merchant was simply regarded as commercial customs and practices that were questions of law to be decided by courts[169] in each case "to the satisfaction of twelve reasonable and ignorant jurors".[170] It was the position of English law prior to 1979 that arbitrators must apply English law,[171] and the courts consistently rejected the validity of clauses calling for a non-state legal standard, on the grounds that "arbitrators in general are bound to apply a fixed and recognisable system of law".[172] The clear proposition was that *lex mercatoria* is not a law at all.[173] It was argued that an arbitrator who intentionally applies rules other than English law exceeds his jurisdiction and that his award should be set aside or remitted for misconduct by arbitrators as manifest disregard of choice of law by the parties,[174] under the court's powers to supervise arbitration. This proposition rests on two grounds: (i) the long-standing belief in extensive judicial supervision of and interference in arbitral matters; and (ii) the suspicion of the legitimacy, credibility and predictability of awards based on non-legal criteria. The judicial attitude since the passage of 1979 Arbitration Act has inclined towards non-intervention,[175] and pointed the way towards favouring, if not encouraging, enforceability of an

---

169 *Pillans v. Mierop*, 3 Burr. 1663, 97 Eng. Rep. 1035 (KB 1765); *Orion Compania Espanola de Seguros v. Belfort Maatschappij von Algemene Verzekgringeen* [1962] 2 Lloyd's Rep. 251 (Q.B. Com. Ct.).

170 Theodore Frank Thomas Plucknett, *Concise History of the Common Law,* Boston: Little, Brown & Company (5th edn. 1956) p. 660; and C.H.S. Fifoot, *English Law and Its Background,* London: G. Bell and Sons (1932) p. 105.

171 Lawrence Collins (ed.), *Dicey & Morris on The Conflict of Laws*, London: Sweet & Maxwell (12th edn. 1993) p. 543 (stating that an English arbitrator cannot apply any substantive law other than that of a fixed and recognisable system. In the 19th century the most important parts of the commercial law contained in common law cases were embodied in various statutes such as Bills of Exchange Act 1882 and Sales of Goods Act 1893).

172 *Maritime Insurance Co., Ltd. v. Assecuranz-Union Von 1865* [1935] 52 Ll.L.R. 16; *Orion v. Belfort*, [1962] 2 Lloyd's Rep. 251 (Q.B. Com. Ct.); and *Czarnikow v. Roth, Schmidt & Co.* [1922] 2 KB 478 and (1922) Ll.L.R. 195.

173 See Michael J. Mustill and Steward C. Boyd, *Law and Practice of Commercial Arbitration in England,* London: Butterworths (2nd edn. 1989) pp. 80–82.

174 Ibid. 497–9.

175 *Pioneer Shipping v. BTP Tioxide Ltd.: The Nema* [1982] AC 724 (HL).

award on the basis of a chosen extra-legal criterion.[176] In the case of non-domestic arbitration without a substantial connection with England, the courts generally would not interfere with the arbitrator's failure to apply English law[177] or foreign law.[178] Nevertheless, the English court may take an incongruous approach in cases with the English connection whereby the resort to *lex mercatoria* may not be well recognised. Public policy may preclude the validity of an arbitration agreement that allows the arbitral tribunal to determine the merits of the dispute by recourse to considerations that are purely equitable, or standards that are recognised and followed within the industry itself.[179] The policy distinction may be made between the cases precluding English and foreign laws respectively.

The judiciary in England used to view *lex mercatoria* and *amiable composition* with great scepticism. An equity clause may be a good substitute. However, it has been said that such a clause would imply that there was no contract at all "because the parties did not intend the contract to have legal effect".[180] Indeed, in England, equity is a "system of rules and remedies which form part of the law and do not in any way lie outside it".[181] The judicial attitude towards *lex mercatoria* has changed over time. In the Court of Appeal's *Eagle Star Insurance Co. Ltd. v. Yuval Insurance Co. Ltd.*, an arbitration clause provided that the arbitrators "should not be bound by the strict rules of law but ... settle any difference referred to them according to an equitable rather than a strictly legal interpretation of the provisions of this contract".[182] The Court of Appeal however rejected the established view that an equity clause makes the contract no contract.[183] Rather, the Court held that the clause was valid, having the effect of "not ousting the jurisdiction of the courts"[184] but ousting "technicalities and strict constructions",[185] and enabling arbitrators "to view the matter more

---

176 Julian D.M. Lew, *Applicable Law in International Commercial Arbitration: A Study in Arbitration Awards*, Dobbs Ferry, NY: Oceana Publications (1978) p. 123.

177 Michael J. Mustill and Steward C. Boyd, above n. 173, 603–4.

178 *e.g.*, in the case of *Deutsche Schachtbau- und Tielfbohrgesellschaft mbH v. R'As al-Khaimah National Oil Co.*, the English Court of Appeal saw that there was no policy reason for refusing to enforce in England an award determined in Switzerland in accordance with Article 13(3) of the ICC Rules, *i.e.*, whereby the tribunal applied "internationally accepted principles of law governing contractual relations". [1987] 2 All ER 769.

179 *Home and Overseas Insurance Co Ltd. v. Mentor Insurance Co (UK) Ltd* (in liq) [1989] 3 All ER 74.

180 *Orion Compania Espanola de Seguros v. Belfort Maatschappij Voor Algemene Verzekgringeen* [1962] 2 Lloyd's Rep. 257.

181 Michael Kerr, '"Equity" Arbitration in England', (1991) 2 *Am. Rev. Int'l Arb.* 295.

182 [1978] 1 Lloyd's Rep. 357.

183 *Orion Compania Espanola de Seguros v. Belfort Maatschappij Voor Algemene Verzekeringen* [1962] 2 Lloyd's Rep 257.

184 [1978] 1 Lloyd's Rep. 357.

185 Lord Denning MR [1978] 1 Lloyd's Rep 362.

leniently and having regard more generally to commercial considerations than would be done if the matter were heard in Court".[186]

In the *Rakoil* case,[187] the Court of Appeal in England was concerned with the enforcement of an arbitral award made in Switzerland regarding a contract with an ICC arbitration clause, which provides that in the absence of the choice of law by the parties, the arbitrator shall apply the law designated by the rule of conflict. The arbitrators held the proper law of the contract to be the "internationally accepted principles of law governing the contractual relations". The respondents contended that it would be contrary to English public policy to enforce an award in which rights and obligations are determined otherwise than on the basis of the particular national law. The effect of the judgment of John Donaldson MR was however to recognise "a clause which purports to provide that the rights of the parties shall be governed by some system of 'law' which is not that of England or any other state or is a serious modification of such a law", so long as the parties intended to create legally enforceable rights and duties and the agreement is not too uncertain. The court held that there was no national public policy objection to the enforcement in England of an arbitral award according to *lex mercatoria*. English arbitration law apparently is finally moving in the direction of countries such as France and the United States in accepting equity-type clauses.[188] The greater freedom, and the emphasis placed upon the broadest possible understanding of the scope of "party autonomy", can be found in the English Arbitration Act 1996, which now clearly permits arbitrating parties to choose *lex mercatoria* as their governing law or to invest their tribunal with the power to act as *amiable compositeurs*.[189]

The riveting case in which the UK Supreme Court directly applied *lex mercatoria* was *Dallah Real Estate and Tourism Holding Company v. The Ministry of Religious Affairs, Government of Pakistan*. The court seemed to show some sympathy to the application of transnational general principles and usages of international trade (comparable to the concept of *lex mercatoria*) by the tribunal (even without the parties' choice of *lex mercatoria* as the law applicable to the arbitration agreement) when it came to determine the validity of the arbitration agreement even though common law jurists commonly argue against the concept of *lex mercatoria*.[190]

English law is widely used as the governing law in international arbitration. Its common law tradition is found in a large number of jurisdictions including Canada, Australia, New Zealand, Singapore and Hong Kong. However, common

186 Carlo Croff, above n. 154, 636.
187 [1987] 2 All ER 769 (CA); [1987] 2 Lloyd's Rep. 246 (Eng. CA).
188 Michael Kerr, above n. 181.
189 Section 46 of the English Arbitration Act 1996.
190 *Dallah Real Estate and Tourism Holding Company v. The Ministry of Religious Affairs, Government of Pakistan* [2010] UKSC 46.

law systems do not guarantee a common approach because common law systems have increasingly begun to diverge from one another. For instance, the law on equitable compensation is tending in different directions in Canada, Australia and England.[191] Australia may be more liberal in the application of *lex mercatoria*. The New South Wales Commercial Arbitration Act explicitly allows "determination to be made according to law or as *amiable compositeur* or *ex aequo at bono*;" and "if the parties to an arbitration agreement so agree in writing, the arbitrator or umpire may determine any question that arises for determination in the course of proceedings under the agreement by reference to considerations of general justice and fairness".[192] More importantly, English law is a national legal system and is unlikely to be distilled by different national cultures. The purpose of English judges' developing, for example, contract law principles, was to make the principles of law similar to those of the other nations that England traded with.[193] Much of English law remains precedent-based but, as the number of precedents has increased enormously with the natural progression of the years, the principles have become obscured.[194] Then the question of whether English law in its current state is really apt for international arbitration, and whether it provides sufficient easily graspable international commercial principles, becomes a real one.

4.4.3.2. France and Other Continental European Countries

In continental Europe, the appearance of national legislation in the age of mercantilism led to the decline of custom-based merchant law and its universality.[195] France had a reputation of being a jurisdiction in which international arbitration was relatively free from judicial interference.[196] With the enactment of the Decree of 12 May 1981,[197] the French acknowledgment of, and even deference to, the ability to decide arbitration by reference to *lex mercatoria* or as *amiable composition* became clear.[198] The Decree permits "almost unlimited freedom" in the choice of law to be applied in international

---

191 Martin Odams De Zylva and Reziya Harrison, above n. 11, xxxii.

192 Section 22 of the New South Wales Commercial Arbitration Act.

193 Best J in *Cox v. Troy* (1822) 5 B & Ald. 474; 106 ER 1264: "This is a question of the law merchant, and it is desirable, that that law should be the same in this as in every other commercial country".

194 Steyn LJ in the Court of Appeal in England complained of the inadequacy of the practice on the part of counsel of simply reading large numbers of cases to the court rather than elucidating for the court the 'argument' that lay behind the cases. *White v. Jones* [1995] 2 AC 207, CA at 235.

195 Ernst von Caemmerer, above n. 62, 90.

196 Gerald Pointon and David Brown, *France: Resolving Disputes*, Euromoney Supp. (1991) p. 13.

197 Decree of 12 May 1981, 1 J.O. 1492, translated in (1981) 20 ILM 878, 917.

198 Under Articles 12 and 58 of the *Nouveau code de procedure civile*, even a judge can be given the power to decide as an *amiable compositeur*.

commercial arbitration by providing that "the arbitrator shall decide the dispute in conformity with the rules of law chosen by the parties; in the absence of a party choice, he shall decide according to the rules that he deems appropriate".[199] In this respect, the French Code "appears to go farther than any other document on international commercial arbitration" by allowing the use of *lex mercatoria* when expressly chosen by the parties.[200] The Decree of 1981 also set out very limited grounds for judicial intervention by setting aside arbitral awards. In domestic arbitrations expressly established under the powers of *amiable composition*, Article 42 of the Decree provides that, except in certain specific instances, the arbitral award is not subject to appeal unless the parties agree otherwise.[201]

Several cases such as the *Norsolor* case demonstrate the judicial acceptance of *lex mercatoria*. In 1982, an arbitral tribunal established under ICC Rules rendered an award based upon *lex mercatoria*, where the parties, a French company, Norsolor, and its Turkish agent, Pabalk, had not chosen any specific national law and nor had they granted the power to arbitrate under *amiable composition*.[202] Without a clearly specified national law, the arbitrators considered that, given the international character of the contract, it was appropriate to avoid any national law, but to apply *lex mercatoria*.[203] The arbitrators also stated that the principles on which *lex mercatoria* is based are good faith and fair dealing, which exist in the formation and performance of contracts and imply trade usage and a moral rule of behaviour. The proceedings for enforcement were commenced in France brought by Pabalk, whilst Norsolor, the loser, simultaneously brought proceedings in Vienna (where arbitration took place) for annulment of the award. One complaint made was that the arbitral award had been decided on equitable grounds in excess of the arbitrators' jurisdictional mandate. However, the Paris *Tribunale de Grande Instance* in the enforcement proceedings held that the award did not offend any "mandatory

---

199 Ibid.

200 Other provisions in the French Code allow for *amiable composition* as long as the parties choose it. See French Code Art. 1474 ("The arbitrator decides the dispute according to the rules of law, unless in the Terms of Reference, the parties give the arbitrator permission to act as *amiable compositeur*"); Art. 1483 ("The judge may act as *amiable compositeur* if the arbitrator was given such permission"); Art. 1497 ("The arbitrator may act as *amiable compositeur* if the Terms of Reference give the arbitrator such permission").

201 Those instances are: absence or invalidity of an arbitration agreement; excess of jurisdictional authority; lack of due process; improperly appointed tribunal; non-compliance with form requirements; or violation of domestic public policy. Steven J. Stein and Daniel R. Wotman, 'International Commercial Arbitration in the 1980s: A Comparison of the Major Arbitral Systems and Rules', (1983) 38 *Bus. Law* 1685.

202 *Pabalk Ticaret Limited Sirketi (Turkey) v. Norsolor S.A. (France)*, award 26 October 1979, reprinted in IX *Yearbook* (1984) 109.

203 Judgment of 9 October 1984 (*Pabalk Ticaret v. Norsolor*), Cass., Pourvoi N# 83–11.355 (Fr.), reprinted in (1985) 24 ILM 360 (English translation).

norms" of the forum in applying *lex mercatoria*. The court also found that the arbitrators, in selecting *lex mercatoria*, had acted within the scope of their mandate under Article 13 of the ICC Rules and therefore did not wrongly act as *amiable compositeurs* without party authority. The French *Cour de Cassation* also upheld enforcement upon failing to find a violation of public policy.[204] The enforcement proceedings succeeded.

Norsolor challenged the award in Austria where the award had been rendered, arguing that the arbitral tribunal had based its decision on *lex mercatoria* whereas "there exists no *lex mercatoria* equivalent to a legal system, and one may refer to general principles of commerce and of good faith only if the specific rules of the law ... take precedence over general rules ..."[205] The Commercial Court of Vienna dismissed this claim and declared that "... the principles of good faith and loyalty, applied by the arbitral tribunal in conformity with *lex mercatoria*, ... constitutes a general principle of law".[206] On appeal, the Viennese Court of Appeal criticised the tribunal's reference to *lex mercatoria* as violating ICC Rule 13(3). *Lex mercatoria*, the Court asserted, is of global uncertainty and has no connection to any national legal order.[207] The Austrian Supreme Court found that the tribunal's application of *lex mercatoria* justified and reversed the Court of Appeal. The Court confirmed that the application of equity by the arbitral tribunal without special authorisation from the parties does not involve a transgression of its competence.[208] In the Court's view, the arbitrators had applied private law principles which did not violate mandatory provisions of either French or Turkish law and the award was thus enforceable.[209] The claim for setting aside the award failed.

At the very least, the courts in both France and Austria recognised the status of *lex mercatoria* as a valid and enforceable body of law and were satisfied that arbitrators had validly rendered the award in accordance with general principles of law in international trade. While the French court accepted *lex mercatoria* as a genuine system of law, the Austrian Supreme Court did not share the same view even though it did uphold the validity of the award. In

---

204 (1995) 24 ILM 360.

205 *Société Norsolor v. Société Pabalk Ticaret Ltd. Sirketi*, 108 J.D.I. 836, 839 (*Trib. Gr. Inst.* 1981) (Fr.).

206 (1983) *Rev. Arb.* 513, 515–16 (*Handelsgericht* Wien 1981) (Aus.).

207 (1984) *Rev. Arb.* 513, discussed in Berthold Goldman, above n. 5, 124.

208 *Norsolor v. Pabalk Ticaret Ltd. Sirketi* (1983) *Yearbook* 362 (*Cour d'Appel* Paris 1981); *Norsolor v. Pabalk Ticaret Ltd.* (1984) *Yearbook* 154 (*Oberster Gerichtshof* 1982) (Aus.) 160. "It should be stressed that the basic issues before the Court were whether a decision based on *bona fides* considerations (Grundsatz von Treu und Glauben) and equity (Billigkeit)" exceeded the arbitrators' powers under Austrian law. Ibid. at 163. Note W. Melis: "Although it would have been desirable for the Supreme Court to have taken a stand on the legal qualification of the lex mercatoria, this was not necessary under the circumstances".

209 1983 *Recht der Internationalen Wirtschaft* 29, 868 (Supreme Court of Austria, decision of 18 November 1982); excerpts printed in IX *Yearbook* (1984) 159; Ole Lando, above n. 6, 757.

effect, the Austrian litigation was not an endorsement of *lex mercatoria* so much as the recognition of a court's limited power where a tribunal's reasoning was under attack.[210] By contrast, the French *Cour de Cassation* did lend support to the mercatorists but only to the extent that the court did not repudiate the notion of *lex mercatoria*.[211]

The French courts again upheld the validity of the arbitrator's choice of a-national law in the *Fougerolle* case. The dispute related to an agency agreement between Fougerolle, as an intermediary assigned to negotiate a contract, and the Banque, which however terminated the agency.[212] The arbitrators in the ICC arbitration, in the absence of a clear mandate to act as *amiables compositeurs*, rendered an award on the basis of "general principles of obligations generally applicable in international trade". The respondent first contested the award before the Court of First Instance claiming that the tribunal had wrongly decided as *amiables compositeurs*, and that the award had exceeded the scope of submission and was thus invalid. This claim was rejected. Rather, the court found the arbitrators had implicitly referred to usages of international trade "evidently in force" and had thus based the award on a rule of law, acting within the scope of submission.[213] Eventually, both the Court of Appeal and the *Cour de Cassation* upheld the award. The *Cour de Cassation* even expressly stated that the general principles of international commerce form a part of law, and that the arbitrators had duly fulfilled their duties under the Terms of Reference to define the applicable law,[214] and that *lex mercatoria* was a valid source of law in international trade.

A case decided in 1989 by the Paris *Cour d'Appel* also upheld the application of *lex mercatoria*, where the parties could not agree which national law was applicable but did not expressly authorise the use of *lex mercatoria*. The parties had, however, agreed to arbitration under ICC Rules, which do permit the use of *lex mercatoria*. The *Cour d'Appel* held that the arbitrator, who had applied "general principles of the conflicts of laws" and *lex mercatoria*, had properly fulfilled the terms of reference.[215]

French law encompasses a doctrine that every contract is subject to national law, although an international contract can be subject to commercial usages. Some French scholars define *lex mercatoria* as a term containing a collection of practices and usages which are a spontaneous non-law system relevant to the

---

210 Michael J. Mustill, above n. 107, 106.

211 Ibid. 107.

212 *Fougerolle (France) v. Banque de Proche Orient (Lebanon)* [1982] *Rev. Arb.* 183; 1982 *J. Droit Int'l* (Clunet) 931 (*Cour de Cassation*, 9 December 1981).

213 109 *J. Droit Int'l* (Clunet) 231 (1982) (decision of 12 June 1980).

214 [1982] *Rev. Arb.* 1983; 109 *J. Droit Int'l* (Clunet) 931 (1982) (decision of 9 December 1981).

215 Gerald Pointon and David Brown, above n. 196, 70.

object of the law.[216] The judicial definition refers to *lex mercatoria* as "the body of international commercial rules consecrated by practice and approved by national courts".[217] In practice, the arbitrator must comply with fundamental notions of procedural fairness, must not violate public policy in the terms of the award, and must give reasons for the award. The court will use its power to lay down modifications "in a very sparing fashion".[218] In theory, the French courts can accord great deference to the arbitral tribunal.

The judicial practice in France seems to have spread to other European jurisdictions. For instance, as far as the Austrian courts are concerned, a more specific endorsement of *lex mercatoria* was given by the Commercial Court, which, although referred to in a derogatory way by the Vienna Court of Appeal, was not specifically condemned by the Austrian Supreme Court. There has also been a significant decision approving the concept of *lex mercatoria* in Italy.[219] The Supreme Court of Italy has expressly recognised law merchant: "the law in which such arbitration operates is transnational being independent of the laws of the individual states. Since 'mercantile' law comes into existence through adhesion of merchants to the values of their milieu, merchants comply with those values, because of necessity, [and because of] that merchants [do not] belong to a state ... *lex mercatoria* exists". Accordingly "mercantile" law comes into existence when binding values are recognised and complied with, and merchants coordinate their conduct on the grounds of common rules.[220] It appears that the European courts have been moving cautiously towards approving certain rules beyond the purely national commercial laws. To a certain extent, *lex mercatoria* is distinct from any national system of law but is emerging as a system of law in its own right.

4.4.3.3. The United States

Lex mercatoria is not explicitly recognised in American statutes or case law, nor in the arbitration rules of the American Arbitration Association (AAA). Nevertheless, it is used in practice perhaps even more frequently by US arbitrators than French arbitrators.[221] This is partly because US arbitrators "do not think of themselves as doing anything special in so acting".[222] In the US, equity is an integral part of "the law". Thus, every arbitrator ought to make

---

216 Philippe Kahn, 'La *Lex Mercatoria*: Point de Vue Français Apres Quarante Ans de Controverses', (1992) 37 *McGill L.J.* 413.

217 Jean-Pierre Ancel, 'French Judicial Attitudes Toward International Arbitration', (1993) 9(2) *Arb. Int'l* 128.

218 William Laurence Craig, William W. Park and Jan Paulsson, above n. 36, 314.

219 *Soc. Pabalk Ticaret Ltd., Sirketi v. Soc. Anon. Norsolor.*

220 Thomas E. Carbonneau and Marc. S. Firestone, above n. 55, 56.

221 William Laurence Craig, William W. Park and Jan Paulsson, above n. 36, 137.

222 Ibid.

equitable considerations part of the body of law on which decisions are based, even without express authorisation by the parties in arbitration.

Although *lex mercatoria* is essentially foreign to American law, it appears that an American court would not likely challenge an agreement to which such a system is applied.[223] As a matter of fact, in the United States, a powerful and consistent pro-enforcement bias in both public policy and case law has made state and federal courts reluctant to overturn arbitral awards on legal grounds.[224] In *Scherck v. Alberto-Culver Co.*, the US Supreme Court stated that the purpose of adhering to the New York Convention was to encourage recognition and enforcement of arbitral agreements in international contracts and to unify standards of enforcement.[225] In this vein, arbitration clauses are liberally construed in favour of enforcement. The leading case in this regard is *Mitsubishi Motors Corp. v. Soler Chrysler-Plymouth, Inc.*, in which the Supreme Court concluded that "the international arbitral tribunal owes no prior allegiance to the legal norms of particular states".[226] This effectively gives a green light to *lex mercatoria.*[227]

In addition, the defences to enforcement permitted under Article V of the New York Convention are narrowly interpreted to be exclusive. According to US law, the only grounds to challenge an international arbitral award are the fundamental fairness of the proceedings, the arbitrability of the subject matter, and the scope and validity of the arbitration agreement.[228] Typically, a party may not be allowed to challenge an arbitrator's findings of law or fact; "the interpretation of the law by the arbitrators … [is] not subject, in the federal courts, to judicial review for error in interpretation".[229] Thus, the US law apparently shelters from judicial review arbitral awards rendered under *lex mercatoria*, a non-national standard. Indeed, the court in *International Standard Electric Corp. v. Bridas Sociedad Anonima Petrolera, Industrial y Commercial* stated that the 1958 New York Convention would not allow a court to refuse enforcement of the arbitral award due to "manifest disregard of the law"[230] even if an arbitrator were to act as *amiable compositeur* without authority. The Court held the view that the objective of the New York Convention would be frustrated if judges were permitted to make a *de novo* inquiry into whether the law supposedly applied by the arbitrators was properly applied.[231] In the case of

223 Ole Lando, above n. 6, 759.
224 See, *e.g., Wilko v. Swan*, 346 US 427, 436–37 (1953).
225 417 US 506, 520 (1974).
226 473 US 614 (1985).
227 Restatement (Third) of the Foreign Relations Law of the United States, §488 (1987).
228 Gerald Pointon and David Brown, above n. 196.
229 *San Martine Compania de Navegacion, S.A., v. Saguenay Terminals Ltd.*, 293 F.2d 796 (1961), cited in Ole Lando, above n. 6, 759.
230 See 745 F. Supp. 172 (SDNY 1990) and 3 UST 2517, reprinted in (1968) 7 ILM 1042.
231 International Standard, 745 F. Supp. at 182.

Ministry of Defence of the Islamic Republic v. Gould, Inc., the US Court of Appeals for the Ninth Circuit upheld the District Court's jurisdiction to enforce, pursuant to the New York Convention, an award for Iran against an American corporation, rendered by the Iran-US Claims Tribunal.[232] Gould sought an interlocutory review by asserting that Article V(1)(e) of the New York Convention implies that the Convention applies only to awards rendered under a "national arbitration law". The Ninth Circuit rejected this argument on the grounds, among others, that the discrepancy between Article V(1)(d), which seemed to give primacy to the parties' choice of arbitral law, and Article V(1)(e), which seemed to require the award be made under a national arbitration law, led to the conclusion that the only possible intended interpretation was for the Convention to apply to national and non-national awards.[233] The US case law and pro-enforcement bias appear to secure the likelihood that the freedom to apply *lex mercatoria*, even if not expressly acknowledged as such, is *de facto* recognisable in the US.

4.5. REVIVAL OF *LEX MERCATORIA* AND INTERNATIONAL COMMERCIAL ARBITRATION

4.5.1. *LEX MERCATORIA* AND GLOBALISATION: AN EVOLUTIONARY PERSPECTIVE

Lex mercatoria must be placed in the historical context of evolving global capitalism. Globalisation implies the self-deconstruction of the hierarchy of legal norms.[234] The evolution of *lex mercatoria* in the twentieth century is a revival of "medieval internationalism"[235] and the emergence of "global capital's own law"[236] liberalising the state and world order and economy. Alongside the separation of the state and economy and the distinctions between politics and economics and the public and private spheres, commercial relations re-appear to be privatised, juridified and pluralised through an intensification process

232 See *Gould Marketing, Inc. v. Ministry of Defence of the Islamic Republic of Iran*, 6 Iran-USCTR 272 (award No. 136-49/50-2, 22 June 1984).

233 887 F.2d at 1365, referring in support to the Dutch Supreme Court's decision in *SEEE v. Yugoslavia, HR* (*Hoge Raad der Nederlanden*) NJ 74, 361 (1974) (holding that no examination of the relationship between the award and a national law is warranted until a party pleads and undertakes to prove the existence of an Article V impediment to enforcement). Robert P. Lewis, 'What Goes Around Comes Around: Can Iran Enforce Awards of the Iran-US Claims Tribunal in the United States?', (1988) 26 *Columbia Journal of Transnational Law* 515.

234 Gunther Teubner, 'Breaking Frames – Economic Globalisation and the Emergence of *Lex Mercatoria*', (2002) 5(2) *European Journal of Social Theory* 199–217.

235 Clive M. Schmitthoff, above n. 56, 139–40.

236 Boaventura de Sousa Santos, above n. 51, 288.

associated with transnationalised social forces,[237] which in turn results in a "transnationalisation of the legal field".[238]

As discussed in Chapter 2, according to Darwinian theory, speciation occurs spontaneously through natural selection in the natural world, which consists of, first, mutations and rearrangements of the germ-line that are responsive to external forces of change; and second, sorting by the environment of the most adaptive organisms. In the legal sense, the environment, or more precisely, social force, is a decisive element in determining the survival of individual organisms which are transformed through the meme over the time. More specifically, in our context, the most sensible explanation for the rise or decline of *lex mercatoria* in various historical periods is the socioeconomic development and change as the primary driving environmental force.

In terms of the environment, there are crucial distinctions between the contemporary and the medieval orders. Conditions are profoundly different in the sense that the sheer volume of overseas transactions is different. Of great importance is the difference in the political economies of the two periods. In the medieval trading world, merchants engaged in foreign trade and business were autonomous in the absence of political authorities that did not desire to or were incapable of disciplining their activities. Local political authorities exercised limited control by mainly granting trade charters, maintaining safe conduct of merchants and securing the peace of the markets and fairs. The commercial law governing business exchange emerged from the customs generated by the merchant community and dispute settlement was a private engagement amongst merchants.

In the modern age, the capitalist model of production, market and economic exchange has transformed substantially, and capital is no longer constrained by national borders,[239] both of which contribute to the re-patterning and re-transformation of state-society relations like the restructuring process of nation-states right after the medieval period. As a result, the current commercial environment is comprised of both private and public spheres, which is a unique feature of the modern mercantilism.[240] There are two limbs. First, the contemporary process of reconfiguration is historically unprecedented in the sense that it has gradually involved a massive "shake-out" of societies, economics and institutions of governance and obscures any clear distinction between international and domestic, external and internal affairs. Political authorities make great efforts to reconfigure the relationships between politics and economics and between the public and private spheres so that the state regulatory authority and sovereign power may be partly delegated to or assumed by private groups or

---

237 Robert Cox, above n. 70, 357–359.

238 Boaventura de Sousa Santos, above n. 51, 276.

239 Stephen Gill and David Law, *The Global Political Economy: Perspectives, Problems and Policy*, Baltimore: John Hopkins University Press (1988).

240 Philip Cerny, *The Changing Architecture of Politics: Structure, Agency and the Future of the State*, London: Sage Publications (1990) p. 23.

institutions or intergovernmental institutions. Meanwhile, merchant autonomy operates with the strong support of state authorities, and they now have both administrative and legal infrastructures to exercise concrete but limited control over business activities, and have often adopted, enacted and enforced private commercial regulations. Second, the reconstituting and delegation of state power, functions and authority enhances the diversity and pluralism of market actors and mercatocracy. National regulatory authorities are weakening as decisions or actions over capital resources and commercial activities are made increasingly by private commercial actors over the time.[241] Furthermore, the state is emerging as a "commodifying agent" in the private sphere and is functioning as a market player in an alliance with corporate actors in the broader mercatocracy. The alliance of public and private actors favours merchant custom as a source of legal norms and private arbitration over adjudication in national courts. The diagram below shows how the private-public dimension changes during various periods.

Diagram: Public-Private Spheres in Various Periods

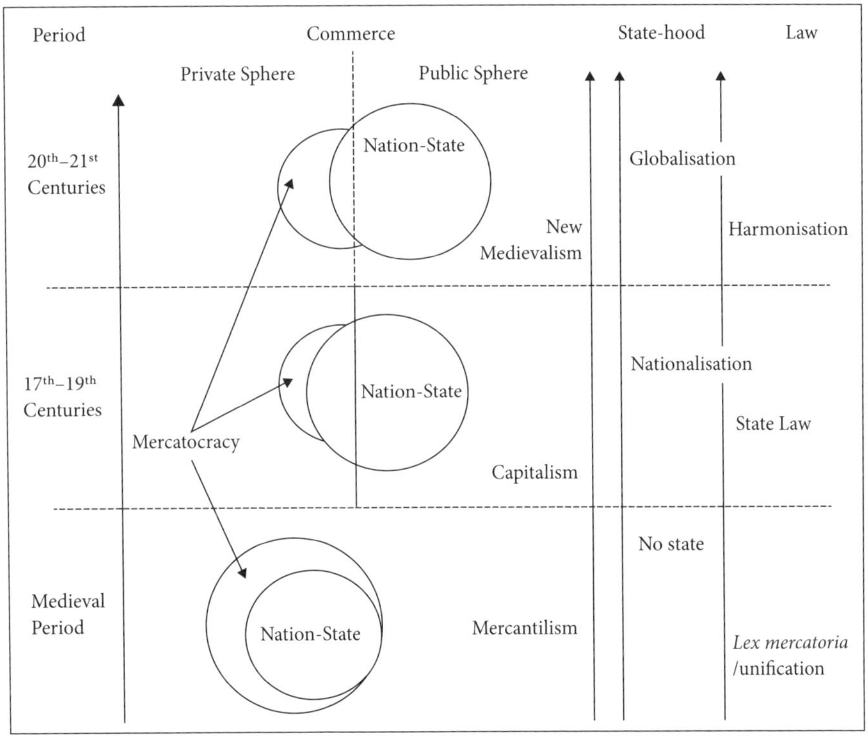

Second, the global mercatocracy, as a transnationalised social force, appears with an elite association of public and private organisations engaged in the unification and globalisation of transnational merchant law. This elite association is the

241 Susan Strange, 'The Defective State', (1995) 124(2) *Daedalus* 55–74.

"organic intellectuals" of the transnational capitalist or managerial class,[242] which shares the same concern to maintain the system that enables the class to remain dominant.[243] The global capitalist system and global economy transcend nation-states to the extent that private rather than national interests prevail across borders. The mercatocracy plays a critical role in furthering such major focal goals in globalisation as the formation of a borderless global economy, the denationalisation of substantive and procedural aspects of business activities and the eradication of economic nationalism.[244] In this sense, the modern mercatocracy is part of the global effort and neoliberal commitment to consolidate capitalism and to the further expansion of capital.[245] The transnational capitalist class, the contemporary counterpart to the nascent merchant class, is the main driver of a series of globalising practices in the global economy and is the leading force in the emergence of a global capitalist system.[246] Through its material links to transnational capital, its monopoly of expert knowledge and its controlling influence in the institutional framework of the new *lex mercatoria*, the transnational capitalist class is in a process of exercising near hegemonial influence in a material, ideological and institutional way. The influence is an instance of "disciplinary neoliberalism" or "new constitutionalism", which advances a blurring of the distinction between public and private spheres. The neoliberalism confers privileged rights of citizenship and representation on corporate capital and imposes disciplines on public institutions for interference with property rights,[247] which constitutes the juridical and ideological underpinnings of the contemporary world social, economic and legal order. The business class therefore becomes relatively autonomous, operating locally and transnationally in a separate regime parallel to the state system.

The third trend in modern capitalism is the emergence of the global civil society as the civil society matures and exceeds the territorial confines of the state worldwide.[248] The civil society is a "civilising process"[249] through which independent groups of citizens are concerned with substantive empowerment of

242 Robert Cox, above n. 70, 359.

243 Ibid. 359–60.

244 David Held, Anthony McGrew, David Goldblatt and Jonathan Perraton, *Global Transformations: Politics, Economics, and Culture*, Cambridge: Polity Press (1999).

245 Stephen Gill, 'Theorising the Interregnum: The Double Movement and Global Politics in the 1990s', in Bjorn Hettne (ed.) *International Political Economy: Understanding Global Disorder*, Halifax: Fernwood Publishing (1995); David Held, *Democracy and the Global Order: From the Modern State to Cosmopolitan Governance*, Palo Alto, CA: Stanford University Press (1995).

246 Antonio Gramsci, *Selections from Prison Notebooks*, London: Lawrence and Wishart (1971) pp. 103–104.

247 Stephen Gill, 'Globalisation, Market Civilisation, and Disciplinary Neoliberalism', (1995) 24(3) *Millennium: Journal of International Studies* 399–423.

248 Andrew Arato and Jean L. Cohen, *Civil Society and Political Theory*, Cambridge, MA: MIT Press (1995); John Keane, *Civil Society: Old Images, New Visions*, Cambridge: Polity Press (1998).

249 Norbert Elias, *The Civilising Process: State Formation and Civilisation*, Oxford: Blackwell (1982).

citizens, disseminate values of rule of law and counter-control abuses of power by the state.[250] When this civilising process or social movement operates across national boundaries, the civil society has a global dimension. The global civil society is a natural consequence of the spread of neoliberal ideas and democratisation, the collapse of previously closed societies, the dramatic developments in information technologies and the intensifying process of global interconnectedness, which is a political, economic and social transnational process. The rising of the global civil society, in substance, reflects the demand for a radical extension of personal autonomy and a more advanced level of self-organisation in increasingly complex and uncertain post-modern societies as well as the growth of a variety of actors such as state government authorities, international governmental organisations, non-governmental institutions, corporations and individuals. As a result, the global civil society becomes a self-ordering regime,[251] which constrains the autonomy and narrows the freedom of the state. Although nation-states remain the focus of politics, some of the key political and economic decisions are now no longer made at the level of the nation-states but taken in international fora, an autonomous space with citizens' groups and market players. The key feature of global civil society, the new mercantalism or neoliberalism is that the mercatocracy unites private and public authorities, both of which are committed to expanding capitalism, disembedding international commerce from national and social controls and then re-embedding it into the private sphere. The contemporary concept of a global civil society has ideological, societal and geographical significance. Ideologically, the modern capitalist era has restored the belief in the self-sufficiency and autonomy of *lex mercatoria*, which are the philosophical and juridical underpinnings of the modern merchant order. In a societal sense, the civil society has replaced the state-centred thinking with more individual-based empowerment and autonomy. Geographically, the intensifying interconnectedness has made the nation-state less important in restructuring social relations. Put differently, it is no longer possible to sustain a civil society within the territorial confines of the state.[252] The institutional foundation of the global civil society is global civic networks including new transnational social movements and non-governmental organisations.

Fourth, although sovereignty is of great ideological and legal significance, it is substantially transformed even though the nation-state retains its power in the modern era and its role as a primary actor in the world order.[253] In the

---

250 Ernest Gellner, *The Conditions of Liberty: Civil Society and its Rivals*, London: Hamish Hamilton (1994).

251 Philip Allott, *Eunomia, New Order for a New World*, Oxford: Oxford University Press (2004) Ch. 16.

252 David Held, Anthony McGrew, David Goldblatt and Jonathan Perraton, above n. 244.

253 Paul Hirst and Grahame Thompson, *Globalisation in Question: The International Economy and the Possibilities of Governance*, Cambridge: Polity Press (1996).

nationalisation period, the concept of sovereignty has two distinct dimensions. Internally, sovereignty is "a final and absolute authority in the political community",[254] which allows a state government to exercise supreme command over a given society. In an international dimension, sovereignty is "the supreme legal authority of the nation to … enforce the law within a certain territory",[255] which is a key quality reflected in the fact that a state is independent in all matters of internal politics from the authority of any other nation under international law.[256] The scale of economic exchange generates a demand for an international regime, a set of formal and informal rules that facilitate cooperation among states[257] and guarantee the *ex ante* creditability of commitments. Interactions among states are changing the identity and interests of a state, in that states are now "internalising sovereignty norms" to "rely more upon the institutional fabric of international society".[258] Accordingly, sovereignty today neither remains intact under existing forms of complex interdependence nor is it wholly eroded. Instead, sovereignty becomes "less a territorially defined barrier" but "a bargaining resource for a politics characterised by complex transnational networks",[259] or "an order of liberal international sovereignty, which seeks to limit the nature and scope of state power".[260] Consequently, given a broader framework of governance in which states are increasingly but one site for the exercise of authority,[261] a vacuum is created in the international order.[262] This vacuum is likely to be filled by "a multi-centric system of diverse types of other collectives"[263] and the merchant class is a critical component of collectives or cosmopolitanism.[264]

In modern capitalism, it is conceivable that a new mercatocracy has emerged in that the functions of sovereign states might have been eroded and been replaced by a modern and secular equivalent of the kind of universal political

254 F.H. Hinsley, *Sovereignty*, Cambridge: Cambridge University Press (2nd edn. 1986) p. 1.

255 Hans J. Morgenthau, *Politics among Nations*, New York: Knopf (4th edn. 1967) p. 305.

256 F.H. Hinsley, above n. 254.

257 Stephen D. Krasner (ed.) *International Regimes*, Ithaca, NY: Cornell University Press (1982); Robert O. Keohane, *After Hegemony: Cooperation and Discord in the World Political Economy*, New Jersey: Princeton University Press (1984).

258 Alexander Wendt, 'Anarchy is What State Makes of It?', (1992) 46(2) *International Organisation* 414–5.

259 Robert O. Keohane, 'Hobbes's Dilemma and Institutional Change in World Politics: Sovereignty in International Society', in Hans-Henrik Holm and Georg Sorensen (eds.), *Whose World Order? Uneven Globalisation and the End of the Cold War*, Jackson, TN: Westview Press (1995).

260 David Held, *Law of States, Law of Peoples, Legal Theory*, Cambridge: Cambridge University Press (2002) pp. 1–44.

261 Ibid.

262 Susan Strange, *The Retreat of the State: The Diffusion of Power in the World Economy*, Cambridge: Cambridge University Press (1996).

263 James N. Rosenau, 'Governance in a New Global Order', in David Held and Anthony McGrew, *Governing Globalisation*, Cambridge: Polity Press (2002).

264 Pippa Norris, 'Global Governance and Cosmopolitan Citizens', in Joseph S. Nye and John D. Donahue, *Governance in a Globalising World*, Washington DC: Brookings Institution Press (2000).

regime that existed in Western Christendom in the Middle Ages.[265] The idea of returning to the medieval period, more precisely, refers to the development of a modern and secular counterpart of the medieval model which embodies a central characteristic: a system of overlapping authority and multiple loyalty.[266] It may be envisaged that states would come to share the authority with citizens and other authorities to the extent that state sovereignty and supremacy over its territory and people becomes less important and a non-state-centred status would prevail over the globe. In substance, the return to the medieval period is not a repetition of earlier times but an appearance of a neo-medieval form of universal political order in the new century. The return to a neo-medieval mercatocracy also represents a superior path to the world order since it theoretically avoids a structural overlapping of authorities and loyalties in a sovereign state-based universal society, and the overt concentration of power in a world government. The neo-mercatorist world structure is likely to provide a firm basis for the realisation of elementary goals of social and economic life in the trend of globalisation. In any event, even a return to medieval times does not guarantee a pure repetition of previous historical experiences because any future form of society will have certain features that are unique to the future society and do not resemble an old systemic form. The table below outlines major social, economic and legal features during different periods, and demonstrates some features in the current world which resemble those in the medieval period and support a revival of *lex mercatoria* or appearance of new mercatorism.

Table: Major Social, Economic and Legal Features in Various Periods

Periods / Indicator	Medieval Period	16th–19th Centuries	20th–21st Centuries
Commerce/ Economy	- Expansion of commerce - Growth of trading community	- Rise of capitalism - Expansion of national economy - National capital accumulation	- Expansion of cross-border transactions - Market-dominated - Modern capitalism - Privatisation
Merchant Class	- Merchant class - Separate from the feudal political economy - Self-regulatory autonomy	- Lost independence - Subject to state intervention - Target for nationalisation	- Appearance of global mercatocracy - Rise of global capitalist class - Dominance of multinational corporations

265 Hedley Bull, *The Anarchical Society: A Study of Order in World Politics*, London: Macmillan (1977).

266 Ibid.

Periods / Indicator	Medieval Period	16th–19th Centuries	20th–21st Centuries
State-hood	– City-states	– Nation-states – State-building – Political unification – Colonisation	– Modern states
Public/Private Dimension	– Merchantalism – Dominance of private sphere	– Nationalisation – State intervention – Dominance of public sphere	– Globalisation – Re-patterning of state-society relations – Mix of public/private spheres
Key "Actor"	– Merchant class	– Nation-states	– Pluralism of "actors" – Proliferation of public/private agencies
Authority	– Merchant autonomy	– Territorial sovereignty	– Pluralisation of authority including sovereignty – Sharing of sovereignty by other "actors" – Increase of business autonomy – State is experiencing a loss of control
Social Order	– Autonomous – Informal – Privatised – Customary	– State-centred – Formal – Publicalised – Mandatory	– Rational and systematic – Mixture of autonomous and nationalised natures
Legalisation of Business	– Juridification – Unification	– Nationalisation – Rationalisation – Codification – Fragmentation of *lex mercatoria*	– Pluralisation – Harmonisation
Law Merchant	– Uniformity achieved through the universality of merchant customs – Unifying influence of norms and procedures – Merchant courts	– Nationalisation of regulation of business – Dominance of national courts and domestic/municipal laws – Incorporation of customs into domestic laws	– Proliferation of legal sources – Modern *lex mercatoria* – Private regulation – "Soft" law

Indicator \ Periods	Medieval Period	16th–19th Centuries	20th–21st Centuries
Sources of International Law	– Trade usages and merchant customs	– Classic international law – "Hard" law	– International conventions – Regional conventions – "Soft" law such as model law
Legal System	– Law as autopoietic system[267]	– Law as discipline[268]	– "Law as game"[269]
Trend	– Law merchant is a central and spontaneous mechanism – Self-enforcing/ voluntary – Autonomous	– Being localised and territorialised – Statutory and binding	– Being delocalised and deterritorialised – Increasing soft, voluntary, informal and discretionary regulations of legal relations – A-political
Ideological Foundation	– Mercatorism	– Positivism	– Disciplinary neoliberalism – Global capitalism

Along with the foregoing social forces, there is also a unification or harmonisation movement seeking to recreate the medieval tradition of *jus commune* which disappeared in the nationalisation period. The modern unification movement is an integral aspect of the juridification of commerce although contemporary juridification, as a variation to the meme, differs from an earlier version which occurred through the processes of state-building and national capital accumulation, and is intensified through delocalising and transnationalising legal disciplines that both reflect and facilitate the expansion of capitalism and related commercial practices. The modern unification movement is engaged more in harmonising, unifying and, more fundamentally, globalising merchant law as a result of the proliferation of national differences in the period of nationalisation, the decline of state sovereignty and competition derived from universal imperatives of deregulation, privatisation and the restrictions of public intervention in economic processes.[270]

---

267 Niklas Luhmann, *Das Recht der Gesellschaft*, Frankfurt: Suhrkamp (1993), cited in Gunther Teubner, above n. 234, 203.

268 Michel Foucault, *Surveiller et punir: la naissance de la prison*, Paris: Gallimard (1975).

269 This is a term created by Gunther Teubner to summarise the key feature of various legal philosophies. Gunther Teubner, *Law as An Autopoietic System*, Oxford: Blackwell (1993). This term is used here to describe the complexity of the current status of law.

270 Robert Cox, 'Critical Political Economy', in Bjorn Hettne (ed.), *International Political Economy: Understanding Global Disorder*, Halifax: Fernwood Publishing (1995) pp. 31–45.

4.5.2. UNIFICATION OF COMMERCIAL LAW AND RISE OF "SOFT LAW"

The modern unification process is to facilitate exchange and transnational mobility of capital[271] by reducing national and territorial legal barriers to exchange through delocalised laws, procedures and dispute settlement mechanisms. In essence, legal unification, again, is a global restructuring or re-patterning process.[272] Transnationalised business blurs the boundary between the public and private domains by narrowing the jurisdiction and powers of the public sphere and broadening those of the private sphere, which has important implications for understanding the relationship between *lex mercatoria* and world order. As a result, the modern unification movement becomes a cooperative strategy for managing conflicting nationally-based commercial laws and is a changing process that shifts the structural power from nationally to transnationally-based interests.[273] This structural shift is evident in increased pluralism in the subjects of law, with private business associations and transnational corporations as *de facto* legal "subjects" and with a host of other identities aspiring to status as "subjects" of law. This structural shift is also manifested in the growing pluralism of sources of law, evident in the growing preference for non-binding "soft law" over binding "hard law", and a renewed emphasis on merchant custom as a source of law. Given the devolution of the public authority in creating and enforcing commercial norms, merchant autonomy in the private sphere promotes merchant norms to be operative substantive rules. Parallel to the revival of substantive but "soft" law, which only provides normative guidance, private arbitration offers a private infrastructure for enforcement of commercial norms so as to avoid excessive interference from national courts. The practical aspects of such structural shift form the essential components of neoliberal restructuring of the state and society, which are consistent with globalised trends.

As a critical part of the unification movement, many of the values embodied in the medieval law merchant regain their significance in transnational businesses. These values include substantive norms upholding party autonomy in creating contractual relationships, the self-disciplining and self-regulating abilities and capacities of merchants,[274] and procedural norms in support of private dispute settlement, speed and informality. The renewed values include

271 William Robinson, 'Beyond the Nation-State Paradigms: Globalisation, Sociology, and the Challenge of Transnational Studies', (1998) 13(4) *Sociological Forum* 561–94.

272 Roland Robertson, *Globalisation: Social Theory and Global Culture*, London and Thousand Oaks, CA: Sage (1992) p. 53.

273 Philip Cerny, 'Paradoxes of the Competition State: The Dynamics of Political Globalisation', (1997) 32(2) *Government and Operation* 251–74; Stephen Gill, 'New Constitutionalism, Democratisation and the Global Political Economy', (1998) 10(1) *Pacifica Review* 23–38.

274 Bruce Benson, above n. 23, 644–61.

variations of medieval values and have adopted the primacy of liberal capitalist values. Regardless of the current environmental differences with the medieval age, the code of the meme remains unchanged and the fundamental value and operative principle of the new *lex mercatoria* is merchant autonomy. According to the "new political economy" and utilitarianism, freedom to transact is an indispensable component in the evolution of international business.[275] On the basis of merchant autonomy, commercial conventions or merchant customs delineate and codify permissive and facultative commercial practices of merchants' business habits. The functioning of the merchant autonomy still relies upon the self-regulating ability of merchants to manage their own affairs, and, more importantly, a delegation by the state to private parties to maximise the freedom of contracting.[276]

The merchant community has redeveloped its own laws and adjudicatory institutions. Recognising that the expansion of international commerce and trade and growing economic interdependence demand the privatisation of commercial regulations and rules, merchants and lawyers are working together to re-establish an autonomous transnational regime of private customary law.[277] Their efforts have enabled the *lex mercatoria* to undergo a tremendous revival in the past several decades. For instance, the nineteenth century codification of sales law in England did not spell out the principles of fair dealing for sales contracts, but translated the effect of the fair dealing principle into standard implied terms for the sale of goods. Fair dealing terms of a more global nature are now experiencing a revival.[278] Another example is the principle of "good faith", signifying the ancient origin of the fair dealing principle, which however is still regarded as "foreign" by the majority of English lawyers.[279] Continental lawyers are already looking into various ways in which the English and European systems may be harmonised.[280] This old principle has never been abolished and even today remains underpinned by the force of a number of primary legislatures.[281] The US UCC provides for good faith in commercial contracts, but stipulates that: "good faith in the case of a merchant means honesty in fact and the observance of reasonable commercial standards of fair dealing in the trade".[282]

---

275 Leon E. Trakman, above n. 23, 97.

276 Bernado M. Cremades and Steven L. Plehn, above n. 3, 328.

277 Thomas E. Carbonneau and Marc. S. Firestone, above n. 55, 62.

278 European Council Directive on Unfair Terms in Consumer Contracts [1993] OJ L 95/25.

279 It is still be fair to say that many English lawyers remain sceptical about the existence of an English law of good faith. Reziya Harrison, *Good Faith in Sales*, London: Sweet & Maxwell (1997); and Roger Brownsword, Norma J. Hird and J. Rubery (eds.), *Good Faith in Contract: Concept and Context*, Dartmouth: Ashgate (1999).

280 C.E.C. Jansen, *Towards a European Building Contract Law*, Deventer: Kluwer (1998).

281 Trade Practices Act 1974 (Cth) and the US UCC.

282 UCC Article 2-103(1)(b).

Lex mercatoria does not only refer to a general practice but also to local or regional customs, which can be found in the practice of global, regional or even local business communities or groupings. Most rules of *lex mercatoria* are only conventional or contractual in their origins but may have passed into the general corpus of international commercial law or customary law. These rules are now accepted as such by the *opinio juris* so as to have become binding even for those which may have never accepted them.[283] Local customs may supplement or derogate from general customary rules, which can be described as constant and uniform usage accepted as rules. A customary system of law, regardless of the rarity of new universal customary law, can never be adequate to satisfy the needs of a modern society, only a primitive one. However, in order to deal with frequent clashes, *lex mercatoria*, an advanced level of customary system of law, should be recognised as reflecting the modern needs of globalisation. *Lex mercatoria* will never play a really effective part in a "global" world until it has become a source of "law". A very critical trend in the modern world is the increasing reliance upon "soft law" which is not directly enforceable in domestic courts or international tribunals.[284] In contrast with "hard law" such as conventions and customary international law which are usually enacted by international organisations and have binding legal effect, "soft law" is composed of non-binding, informal and discretionary standards. "Soft law" is not "weak law"[285] as it binds market players on a voluntary basis. Recent examples include the Equator Principles, which were put together by leading banks to determine and manage environmental and social risks in project financing. In the first year of its launch, 27 banks had signed up representing, over 75 percent of global project financing funds.[286] In addition, soft law usually helps establish a legal foundation for treaties.[287]

As previously discussed, the contemporary world has seen a multiplicity of "actors" in global socioeconomic development, which is also reflected in the

283 Hersch Lauterpacht defined *opinio necessitates juris* as all uniform conduct of state governments. See Hersch Lauterpacht, *The Development of International Law by the International Court*, New York: Praeger (1958) p. 380.

284 Hugh M. Kindred, J. G. Castel, W. Graham, A. De Mestral, L. Reif, I. Vlasic and S. Williams, *International Law: Chiefly as Interpreted and Applied in Canada*, Toronto: Emond Montgomery Publishers Ltd. (5th edn, 1993), p. 78.

285 Roy Goode, 'Rule, Practice, and Pragmatism in Transnational Commercial Law', (2005) 54 *ICLQ* 547, 549.

286 Jane Monahan, 'Principles in Question', (2005) *The Banker* 60.

287 Thomas Walde, 'International Standards in Transnational Investment & Commercial Disputes: The Role of International Standards, Soft Law, Guidelines, Voluntary and Self-regulation in International Arbitration, Negotiation and Other Forms of Dispute Management – Preliminary Study, Transnational Dispute Management', October 2004, available at: http://www.transnational-dispute-management.com; and Stephane Brabant, 'Designing Petroleum Contracts and Emerging Principles of International Law, Transnational Dispute Management', December 2004, available at: http://www.transnational-dispute-management.com.

resurgence of *lex mercatoria*, that is, the diversity of agencies, intergovernmental or non-governmental, private or public, global or regional, involved in the harmonisation of commercial laws and principles. The main intergovernmental organisations are the United Nations Commission on International Trade Law (UNCITRAL), the International Institute for the Unification of Private Law (UNIDROIT), the Hague Conference on Private International Law, the International Maritime Organisation (IMO)[288] and the United Nations Conference on International Trade and Development (UNCTAD).[289] The main non-governmental agencies are the International Chamber of Commerce (ICC),[290] the International Law Association (ILA) and the Comité Maritime International (CMI).[291] According to the classic international legal personality doctrine, individuals, corporations or private institutions lack formal legal personality as subjects of the law. However, in reality, they do actively and constructively participate in formulating commercial rules by undertaking a harmonisation initiative as *de facto* subjects of the law.[292] Their participation now becomes ever more influential, along with the deepening of juridified, pluralised and privatised commercial relations. Numerous efforts by international, regional and transnational organisations to produce guidelines, codes, recommendations and other "soft law" norms would be a major contribution to the development of modern *lex mercatoria*.

Without the requisite international legal personality to create "hard law", international private organisations such as the ICC, the ILA, the CMI may have to develop "soft law", an autonomous system from the international law regime which, though legally non-binding, acquires binding force and influential effect through its voluntary adoption by the private parties in cross-border transactions and the supportive enforcement by the state. The ICC, for instance, has formulated a number of codes that are universally recognised by the merchant community, by arbitral institutions, and even by many national courts. Among these are Incoterms, Uniform Customs and Practice for Documentary Credits,[293] Uniform Rules for a Combined Transport Document, and the International Code of Standards of Advertising Practice.[294] The ICC has also

---

288 IMO, a specialised agency set up in 1948 and entering into effect in 1958, has engaged in a number of projects unifying private maritime law.

289 UNCTAD was created as an organ of the General Assembly in 1964 and has engaged in unifying regulations of bills of lading, marine insurance, charter-parties, shipowners' liabilities and flags of convenience.

290 ICC was founded as a private French association of national chambers of commerce and engaged in a number of projects aimed at unifying international commercial law.

291 CMI was created in 1897 for the purpose of unifying private maritime law.

292 A. Claire Cutler, 'Critical Reflections on the Westphalian Assumptions of International Law and Organisation: A Crisis of Legitimacy', (2001) 27(2) *Review of International Studies* 133–50.

293 Michael Rowe, 'The Contribution of the ICC to the Development of International Trade Law', in Norbert Horn and Clive Schmitthoff (eds.), *The Transnational Law of International Commercial Transactions*, Deventer: Kluwer Law and Taxation Publishers (1982) pp. 51–60.

294 Carol Croff, above n. 154, 636.

issued ground rules for an electronic version of its uniform customs and practices for documentary credits (UCP) entitled Uniform Rules of Conduct for Interchange of Trade Data by Teletransmission (UNCID),[295] which aims to "lay down minimum standards of professional care and behaviour for commercial parties engaged in trade transactions involving electronic data interchange".[296] The efforts undertaken by the ICC to unify trade and business terms resulted in influential rules such as the Incoterms governing transportation costs and liabilities in carriage of goods by sea. Although Incoterms is not mandatory in nature, reliance upon Incoterms has become so common that it has acquired the status of customary international law.[297] In contrast to the work of the ICC and Incoterms, unification efforts for bills of lading, bills of exchange, promissory notes and letters of credit, being first initiated by private associations, are subsequently taken over by intergovernmental associations and codified in the form of binding international conventions.

UNIDROIT's Principles of International Commercial Contracts (the "Principles")[298] is a good example to show why "soft law" is becoming more "popular" in practice. The Principles were formulated on the basis of idea that private law can be unified by other than legislative means, with the aim to "establish a balanced set of rules designed for use throughout the world irrespective of the legal traditions and the economic and political conditions of the countries in which they are to be applied".[299] Accordingly, in view of the manifold national legal orders, the Principles referred to the UCC, the Restatement (Second) of the Law of Contracts, the 1980 Vienna Sales Convention, Incoterms, and the Uniform Customs and Practice for Documentary Credits, and included those principles that were common to the existing national legal systems and seemed best adapted to the particular needs of international commercial contracts. However, the key question was whether the Principles would be functional in meeting the needs of international community. One point of view is that rules which spring out of no country's background lack an essential foundation.[300] Moreover, it has been argued that the work of UNIDROIT is aimed at, or at least more suited to, developing legal systems;[301] thereby seeking to provide a platform of legal principles for such

---

295 Paul Murphy, 'Automation up to a Point', (1988) *The Banker* 89.

296 Ibid.

297 Jan Ramberg, 'Incoterms 1980', in Norbert Horn and Clive Schmitthoff (eds.), *The Transnational Law of International Commercial Transactions*, Deventer: Kluwer (1982) p. 146.

298 At its 83rd session (2004) the Governing Council of UNIDROIT adopted the new edition of the UNIDROIT Principles of International Commercial Contracts, available at http://www.unidroit.org/english/principles/contracts/main.htm.

299 UNIDROIT, *UNIDROIT Principles of International Commercial Contracts*, "Introduction", Rome, (1994) p. viii.

300 This problem has been addressed by the draftsmen of the proposed European Civil Code. See A.S. Hartkamp et al, *Towards a European Civil Code*, Nijmegen: Ars Aequi Libri (1994).

301 See the 1989 Report of the Mustill Committee as to the incorporation of the Model Law in the English legislative panorama.

jurisdictions.[302] Nevertheless, it is worth noting the legislative methodology adopted in the drafting of Principles, which is deliberately not packaged as a treaty or model law. Instead, the Principles are elaborated to include basic contract rules such as freedom of contract,[303] openness to usage,[304] *favor contractus*,[305] and good faith and fair dealing,[306] that are flexible enough to accommodate the changing circumstances brought about by the technological and economic developments but without a binding force so that the acceptance of the Principles would be exclusively dependent on the persuasive power and the authority of UNIDROIT.[307] In addition, the legislative techniques adopted in drafting the Principles are consistent with the overall methodology. For instance, the Principles deliberately avoid using terminology that is peculiar to any given national legal system.[308] The search for legal ideas and principles common to various national and international legal systems has been thoroughly undertaken by means of comparative analysis.[309] The openness to usages and customs, as a tool responsive to new commercial practices developed by the merchant community, is considered in determining the rights and duties of the parties in each contract.[310] These static features make the Principles a distinct modern and systematic legal order closely linked to *lex mercatoria*.[311]

As part of this burgeoning "soft law" trend, even UNCITRAL has been pushing for the progress of harmonising international sale of goods, payments and commercial arbitration,[312] by focusing more of its efforts on "soft law" and promoting the adoption of uniform rules, standard contract terms, general standards, trade terms and other measures. UNCITRAL has become the leading international body for harmonising private commercial law[313] and has an

302 United Nations Convention on Contracts for the International Sales of Goods 1980. This may be because the Convention is designed to obviate the need to refer to national law, which is anathema to national pride.

303 Article 1.1 of UNIDROIT Principles.

304 Article 1.8 of UNIDROIT Principles.

305 Articles 2.11, 2.14, 2.22 and 6.2.1–6.2.3 of UNIDROIT Principles.

306 Article 1.7 of UNIDROIT Principles.

307 UNIDROIT, above n. 299, ix.

308 Comment 2 to Article 1.6 of UNIDROIT Principles.

309 Klaus Peter Berger, 'Die UNIDROIT-Prinzipien fur Internationale Handelsvertrage-Indiz für ein autonomes Weltwirtschaftsrecht?' (1995) 94 *Zeitschrift fur vergleichende Rechtswissenschaft* 226.

310 Article 1.8 of UNIDROIT Principles.

311 *Lex mercatoria* is clearly identified in the Preamble of the Principles.

312 The policy of UNCITRAL is centred on the belief "that international trade cooperation among States is an important factor in the promotion of friendly relations and, consequently in the maintenance of peace and security".

313 Harmonisation of international trade law was previously the stated objective of the UNIDROIT, which was set up in 1926 as an auxiliary organ of the League of Nations, which, following the League's demise, was re-established in 1940 by way of a multilateral agreement entitled 'the UNIDROIT Statute'. Apart from producing the highly respected UNIDROIT terms of international sales, this organisation seems largely to have been overtaken by the more efficient and radical UNCITRAL.

impressive record of achievements, including such model laws and advisory documents dealing with various international commercial sectors as the Model Law on Procurement of Goods, Construction, and Services (1993), the Model Law on International Commercial Arbitration (1985), and the Model Law on Electronic Commerce (1996). Thus, it is important not to overlook the great success of international agencies such as UNCITRAL in establishing internationally acceptable rules to regulate various aspects of commercial relations.

Gradually, "soft law", through customary usage or transformation into the public domain, can be evolved into customary international law.[314] The growing trend in the use of soft law and voluntary or non-binding arrangements signals the increasing salience of the private ordering of commercial relations that grants maximum scope to merchant autonomy and flexibility. The private regulation of commerce is natural, neutral and consensual and can produce greater efficiencies by reducing transaction costs and achieving greater economies and thus represent a new ordering of international commerce. Regardless of various national legislative variations and judicial interpretations of these international uniform and model laws, the development of customary business rules and the harmonising and compromising efforts in the "soft law" process are part of the formation of new *lex mercatoria*.

4.5.3. INFRASTRUCTURE OF *LEX MERCATORIA* AND ARBITRATION

Lex mercatoria that is preferred by the business community now has a well-shaped legal infrastructure in place. For instance, the intergovernmental trade associations respond to the requirements of international commerce and are able to harmonise the cross-border trading environment by distilling the operative common principles and, with the benefit of having a huge bureaucracy, they can enforce such self-disciplinary commercial rules and norms. These bodies are concerned, and well placed to deal, with the requirements of corporate and other commercial actors in the market place.

Probably of equal importance is the need for a "safety-net" regime under which users could enjoy certain basic protections. It is claimed that *lex mercatoria* has a weakness in enforcement because there is no police force that makes a system of traditional rules strong and respected. Many informal mechanisms also contribute to the unchallenged enforcement of business agreements, including business norms such as good faith, commercial honesty and the paramount anxiety to protect business reputation.[315] The

314 Michael C. Rowe, above n. 293, 51–60.

315 Ibid. 348–49.

imperative character of *lex mercatoria* may be felt, and obedience to it has become a matter of habit within a highly civilised community and has been spread to most developing countries along with the development of globalisation. There are a variety of private sanctions and disciplinary rules established by many professional organisations, arbitral institutions, chambers of commerce, stock exchanges and commodity exchanges.[316] As in medieval times, one potent sanction is the exclusion from the industry's professional association or exchanges, which often is tantamount to a complete commercial boycott.[317] The power of trade associations, exchanges and arbitral institutions to deny recalcitrant parties benefits, membership, or access, and to blacklist them, gives them the ability to inflict substantial economic harm. The institution of international reputational sanctions would make *lex mercatoria* effective. In addition, national law has developed a machinery of borrowing and adoption.

Arbitration also plays a constructive role in shaping such an infrastructure for the development of *lex mercatoria*. For instance, international commercial arbitration succeeds in abolishing the distinctions between the traditional practices and philosophies of the common law and civil law systems by providing a fusion of their best aspects.[318] Arbitration in different locations may well follow a similar course, that is, a pro-arbitration bias or a *favor arbitrandum* stand. In essence, arbitration derives its binding authority from a contractual arrangement between the parties, not from national law. Due to its nature as an autonomous, independent and a-national institution,[319] arbitration is an important component and supportive infrastructure in both the revival of *lex mercatoria* and the modern unification movement, although it has lost its early simplicity and become more complex, legalistic and institutionalised. A simple international commercial arbitration case may require reference to as many as three different national systems or rules of law. First, there is the law which regulates the arbitration proceedings. Second, there is the law or a set of rules which the tribunal has to apply to substantive matters in the dispute. Finally, there is the law that governs enforcement of the award made by the arbitral

316 Pierre Lalive, 'Enforcing Awards', in International Chamber of Commerce (ed.), *International Arbitration, 60 Years of ICC Arbitration: A Look at the Future*, Paris: ICC Publishing (1984) p. 348.

317 Ibid.

318 The traditional distinction exists between the so-called adversarial and inquisitorial systems in common and civil law systems respectively. In terms of *lex mercatoria*, there is sharp difference between common law and civil law. While common law jurists commonly argue against *lex mercatoria*, civil law jurists uphold it as a perfectly feasible and ascertainable set of international commercial principles. For a summary of debate, see Michael Pryles, 'Application of the *Lex Mercatoria* in International Commercial Arbitration', (2004) 78 *ALJ* 396.

319 Roy Goode, 'The Role of the *Lex Loci Arbitri*', (2001) 17(1) *Arb. Int'l* 19; Jan Paulsson, 'Delocalisation of International Commercial Arbitration: When and Why it Matters', (1983) 32 *ICLQ* 53.

tribunal. Each arbitration is a "national" one in the sense that it must be bound by the national law of one country in order to manifestly possess its legal effect.[320] Meanwhile, each arbitration is an "a-national" one in that the trend in modern arbitration is moving towards the delocalisation or denationalisation of conflict of laws rules because the mechanical relation between arbitration and a national law does not necessarily arise.

It may be of little use to enforce an obligation to arbitrate by reference to law or the rule of law in one specific country if arbitration is conducted in an autonomous regime. Theoretically, an international arbitration agreement is better given an effect world-wide, rather than merely in the place where the agreement is made. In Darwinian terms, the meme of the international effect of arbitration was first recognised in the Geneva Protocol of 1923, one of the first multilateral conventions on arbitration.[321] The Protocol provides that the courts of the contracting state, on being seised of a dispute to which an arbitration agreement covered by the Protocol applies, "shall refer the parties on the application of either of them to the decision of the arbitrators".[322] The New York Convention is silent as to *lex mercatoria*. Neither Article I, outlining the scope of its application, nor Article V, enumerating defences to the enforcement of an arbitral award, refers to reliance upon a non-national law *per se*. Although the New York Convention does not clearly deal with the concept of a stateless award or arbitration, or, as claimed by some scholars, its legislative history may not have intended it to cover an "a-national" award,[323] it appears happy to bypass some territoriality-based arbitration procedural rules such as *lex loci arbitri*, which indirectly support substantive a-national arbitration.[324] For instance, in the *Rakoil* case, as discussed above, the Court of Appeal in England regarded the award based on a non-national law or extra-legal criteria as valid under the New York Convention.[325] In addition, Article 42(1) of the ICSID Convention binding the UK, the US and other signatory countries allows a tribunal to incorporate non-national law in its awards.

Arbitrators may decline to apply the strict letter of a national law to the merits of the dispute. Instead, arbitrators may be tempted to resolve the dispute in a semi-regime which consists of three components. First, arbitrators may have

320 Frederick Mann, above n. 167, 244.

321 League of Nations Treaty Series (1924) Vol. XXVII p. 158 No. 678.

322 Geneva Protocol of 1923, Art. 4. The New York Convention extends similar recognition to the international force and effect of arbitration agreements in Art. II(3).

323 Albert Jan van den Berg, *The New York Arbitration Convention 1958: Towards a Uniform Judicial Interpretation,* Netherlands: Kluwer Law and Taxation Publishers (1981) pp. 29–43.

324 Ibid. 33 (stating that "the detachment of the substance from the ambit of national laws will generally not encounter difficulties" and "the 'de-nationalisation' of the substance in international arbitration is, in fact, increasingly gaining acceptance"). Also Albert Jan van den Berg, 'When is an Arbitral Award Nondomestic Under the New York Convention of 1958?', (1985) 6 *Pace Law Review* 25.

325 XIII *Yearbook* 534.

their own notion of justice and fairness, which appears in the international law of contract or general principles of law. Second, there are well-established arbitration norms such as *forum non conveniens*, *lex fori*[326] and *lex loci arbitri*[327] in arbitration practice. Third, arbitrators may interject into the awards elements of commercial or trade usages to supplement a national legal system that the parties choose to govern the dispute. Seduced away from the rules of the otherwise applicable law, the arbitrator may take on unauthorised powers of *lex mercatoria* or *amiable composition*. It has been sometimes argued that international commercial arbitration should be freed from the constraints of national law and regarded as denationalised or delocalised.[328] Liberating international arbitration from the constraints of national legal systems has several implications, one of which relates to the choice of law. The controversy surrounding a-national arbitration and *lex mercatoria* seems unnecessary and could be resolved by more astute use of conflicts of law principles which may help supplement the ambiguity of *lex mercatoria* by designating an appropriate governing national law. However, the variety of choice of law clauses found in international contracts makes it difficult to generalise the limits of arbitral autonomy. The viability of transnational arbitration and the adoption of *lex mercatoria* require the national legal systems that make arbitration binding to also ensure its integrity. Otherwise, the trend toward transnational norms and "justice without law" may injure the parties, as well as the legitimate public interest that law is designed to protect. This argument justifies a certain level of judicial control or review of the arbitrators' use of *lex mercatoria*.

A number of enforcement devices for arbitral awards are expressly premised on reputation considerations. A possible sanction involves the publication of the arbitral award or the fact of a party's non-compliance with it.[329] A particularly effective device is the prohibition from recourse to institutional arbitration in the future.[330] A more refined version of the prohibition sanction involves the ability of a defendant to refuse arbitration initiated by a party who has previously refused to comply with an award.[331] For example, the world's largest insurance companies resort almost exclusively to arbitration in settling disputes arising under reinsurance contracts. Arbitration clauses usually provide that insurance experts act as the arbitrators. Enforcement of these awards by national courts is rarely necessary because failure to comply with the terms of an award will result

---

326 A.F.M. Maniruzzaman, 'Conflict of Law Issues in International Arbitration: Practice and Trends,' (1993) 9(4) *Arb. Int'l* 375.

327 Roy Goode, above n. 319, 19.

328 An early mention of this revolutionary theory appears in Philippe Fouchard, *L'Arbitrage Commercial International*, Paris: Dalloz (1965) pp. 30–31.

329 Pierre Lalive, above n. 316, 348 (stating that "Such a threat ... is provided by a number of rules or by-laws of professional associations").

330 Ibid.

331 Ibid.

in an economically damaging loss of reputation.[332] The modern doctrine of *lex mercatoria* attaches international currency to the award and represents a delocalised trend in arbitral practice which matches the social environment in the 21st century compared to the medieval and nationalisation periods.

4.5.4. COMMERCIAL JUSTIFICATION OF *LEX MERCATORIA* IN THE COMMERCIAL WORLD

It must be recognised that "the law tends to respond to social realities".[333] The twentieth century has seen increasing internationalisation of commerce, trade and investment. However, the complexity of modern cross-border business and finance "has led to an awareness that general rules in an international instrument are no longer sufficient and need to be supplemented by rules which in varying degrees are problem-oriented and fact-specific".[334] A growing body of international business principles and techniques, together with their similarity and wide acceptance, led to the rediscovery of *lex mercatoria*.[335]

The speed, complexity, diversity and sophistication of modern business activities and non-traditional markets also challenge the legitimacy, efficiency, suitability and adequacy of existing national commercial law and push commercial law to keep up with the needs of the commercial community.[336] National laws have been adapting to the needs and demands of international business community but always lag behind and are divorced from reality,[337] and yet demonstrate hostility towards mercantile customs. However, the application of diverse but inadequate and less-updated national laws including over-complicated conflicts of law rules[338] inherently impedes the mobility and growth of global commerce, which calls for a regime of rules founded on a mutual understanding among merchants, and perhaps a revival of *lex mercatoria*.[339] On the other hand, the international character of commercial law has started to move away from the restrictions of national law to a universal and international concept of international business law. A strong argument for the application of *lex mercatoria* in international transactions and arbitrations is the need of the international business community for a system which allows a departure from national rules. This need arises because (i) national laws are generally meant for

---

332 Bernardo M. Cremades and Steven L. Plehn, above n. 3, 325–26.
333 Friedrich K. Juenger, above n. 115, 219.
334 Roy Goode, above n. 285, 539, 541.
335 Clive Schmitthoff, above n. 13, 19.
336 Andre Tunc, 'English and Continental Commercial Law', (1961) *Journal of Business Law* 237; Ole Lando, above n. 6, 754.
337 Harold J. Berman and Colin Kaufman, above n. 14, 224.
338 Aleksandar Goldstajn, 'The New Law Merchant Reconsidered', in F. Fabricius (ed.), *Law and International Trade*, Frankfurt: Athenaum Verlag (1973) p. 171.
339 Aleksandar Goldstajn, above n. 338, 182; Christoph W.O. Stoecker, above n. 68, 106.

domestic "consumption" rather than for the application in international context; (ii) national legal systems are largely, if not necessarily, one-sided, which may result in inequitable judicial intervention or even outright injustice; (iii) a national system of law may be inadequate to respond to the changing circumstances of modern international business and to accommodate the multilateral aspects of contemporary commerce. The regime of *lex mercatoria* will be essential to viable commercial practice across national boundaries,[340] better accommodate the multilateral aspects of contemporary commerce,[341] and have a wider application and recognition in both nation-states and the commercial community. This notion has been reflected in the Incoterms, EU treaties and UN conventions, and, more importantly, has led to the public recognition and support of an autonomous commercial law regime, independent from national legal systems.[342]

Business decision-makers contemplating a cross-border sale, loan or acquisition want to predict how potential commercial disputes will be adjudicated. By opting for binding arbitration, international businesspeople are indicating their desire for a more simplified and straightforward procedure than that in a national court. However, the business community is not opting for abandonment of legal rules. The lack of reasonable certainty, familiarity and predictability regarding the applicable norms of legal regimes will not enhance cross-border commerce, finance or investment. Without a set of rules for arbitration, the business community may lose confidence in the arbitration process. No party to the arbitration agreement would like to see the dispute resolved according to an adjudicator's intuitive sense of fairness. Rather, the business community will likely prefer the greater level of stability and predictability, from both substantive and procedural perspectives, offered by a choice of national legal rules or a fixed legal regime governing the merits of any dispute.[343] On the other hand, the business community is inclined to abandon the diverse and rigorous rules of law in favour of the more fluid principles of fairness and equity. The involvement of various legal systems suggests that these systems may have different, if not contradictory, legal rules, values and principles that hamper the flow of international commerce and investment. To have disputes involving the parties from multiple jurisdictions resolved by reference to a national system of law allows for the possibility of inequitable intervention or impasse due to claims of sovereign immunity or even outright injustice should

340 Leon Trakmann, above n. 66, 173–4.

341 Michael Medwig, 'The New Law-Merchant: Legal Rhetoric and Commercial Reality', (1993) 24 *Law and Policy in International Business* 615.

342 EU legalisation and the growth of harmonised private law with enforcement by the ECJ may undermine the argument here, as will be discussed below.

343 English law is frequently chosen to govern international insurance and maritime agreements. See Lawrence Collins et al (eds.), *Dicey & Morris on the Conflicts of Laws*, London: Sweet & Maxwell (13th edn. 2000) pp. 549–51.

the national law deliberately be changed or interpreted so as to favour one party.[344] In order to maintain a certain level of uniformity and flexibility in the governing law, arbitrators who are not empowered to decide as *amiables compositeurs* sometimes may hold the view that the more fluid but uniform principles of fairness and good faith, based on a common origin and a faithful reflection of mercantile customs, may be in the best interests of the business community. The selected law may incorporate nebulous terms such as "fair play" or "good faith". *Lex mercatoria* contains commonly accepted legal and commercial norms which are supposed to get around the conflicts of law question as there is only one possible law to apply.[345] As such, *lex mercatoria* reflects the commercial need to promote business based upon party autonomy and freedom of contract and recognises the capacity of merchants to regulate their own affairs through their customs, usages and practices,[346] even though businessmen used to certain national practices actually prefer protection under national rules. Another justification for permitting resort to *lex mercatoria* is party autonomy and expectations; that is, the parties to international contracts are generally relational rather than adversarial, and thus expect autonomy and fairness rather than a strict legal interpretation of their rights and duties. Why shouldn't courts give effect to the parties' choice to empower the arbitral tribunal to disregard the law and resolve the dispute according to its own sense of fairness and good conscience? Party autonomy is certainly not an evil to be avoided.

There has been sufficient jurisprudence to establish that *lex mercatoria* obviously exists, despite the fact that some writers vehemently reject it or claim that *lex mercatoria* is not a law at all.[347] Therefore, we perhaps should not be overly concerned with theoretical questions of how *lex mercatoria* exists and whether it is a law seeking to oust national jurisdictions, so long as a system of norms or principles exists[348] which is recognised and valued by the business community. Such factors as accessibility or general applicability, authoritativeness and consistency, and predictability and fairness[349] can be used to determine if a convincing system of legal rules may be regarded to be in place. Does *lex mercatoria* provide the business community with a set of rules which is sufficiently accessible and certain to permit the efficient conduct of transactions? Has *lex mercatoria* been developed to the stage that it can be inserted into an agreement in a manner which would do the client a positive service? An

---

344 See Keith Highet, above n. 9, 613; David W. Rivkin, above n. 94, 67.

345 Ole Lando, above n. 6, 754.

346 Leon Trakman, above n. 33, 8.

347 Frederick A. Mann, 'Private Arbitration and Public Policy', above n. 161, 264; Michael Mustill, 'Contemporary Problems in International Commercial Arbitration: A Response', (1989) 17 *International Business Law* 163.

348 Highet offers a *principia mercatoria* in lieu of *lex mercatoria* in Keith Highet, above n. 9, 616 and 627.

349 Keith Highet, above n. 9, 614–5.

unwritten law, understood amongst merchants, does exist and does something to fill the contractual vacuum that arbitrators stumble on from time to time.[350] In this sense, the general principles of the law merchant offer at least as much predictability as the occasionally unexpected law of a given country, particularly if it is a law not selected by the parties.[351] Andreas Lowenfeld takes a much more pragmatic approach to the subject of the application of *lex mercatoria*. In terms of an evolving body of principles, in the *principia mercatoria* rather than in the *lex mercatoria*, there is something of benefit available to arbitrators and businessmen alike. Lowenfeld offers a number of illustrations of cases where *lex mercatoria* provides a just solution to a problem where national systems of law fall short of the task. It is argued that arbitrators offer resort to principles of the usages of a particular trade (*lex mercatoria)* without drawing attention to the fact that they are doing so.[352] *Lex mercatoria* also matches a flourishing global commercial culture. There are signs that jurists are becoming increasingly sensitive as to how local legal norms and principles continue to thrive in the transnational commercial setting. Assuming that global private law is possible and global law and business are situated as cultural artefacts, they likely evince some of the same connectedness to the society in which they evolve.[353] Some attention has been given to the transnational law in the European Union,[354] and, more occasionally, to Europe's evolving shared *jus commune*.[355]

4.5.5. POSITIVIST RHETORIC AND JURISPRUDENTIAL JUSTIFICATION OF *LEX MERCATORIA* IN A GLOBALISED PERIOD

Many scholars have responded to *lex mercatoria* with fear and loathing. Some have expressed their doubt as to the existence of *lex mercatoria*[356] due to the fact that *lex mercatoria* has not been enacted and lacks authority as a substantial legal order or system.[357] Others have argued that "such rules are not at present part of the international legal system"[358] and that "a source of *lex mercatoria* is of

350 Andreas F. Lowenfeld, above n. 89, 150.

351 Ibid. 133.

352 Ibid. 142–3.

353 Hugh Collins, 'European Private Law and the Cultural Identity of States', (1995) 3 *European Review of Private Law* (1995) 354.

354 See Cianco, *Elargissement et problèmes de traduction*, in Report of the Semaine de Bruges, *Une communauté a douze? L'impact du nouvel élargissement sur les communautés européennes* (1978) p. 113.

355 Walter Van Gerven et al (eds.), *Cases, Materials, Text on National, Supranational and International Tort Law; Scope of Protection*, Oxford: Hart (1999) p. xviii.

356 Michael J. Mustill and Stewart C. Boyd, above n. 173, 611.

357 Frederick Mann, 'England Rejects "Delocalised" Contracts and Arbitration', above n. 161, 196; Frederick A. Mann, 'Private Arbitration and Public Policy', above n. 161, 264.

358 See Hans Smit, 'A-National Arbitration', (1989) 63 *Tul. L. Rev.* 633.

doubtful validity".[359] *Lex mercatoria* was once described as an "elusive and often frightening subject"[360] and "a myth … an enigma".[361] These writings indicate that positivist jurisprudence does not recognise the "validity" of *lex mercatoria* as a legal order. However, there may arguably be objections to viewing *lex mercatoria* through the lens of legal positivism. For instance, many positivists maintain that a contract governed by law merchant and arbitrated by a private tribunal is a stateless contract and therefore a nullity.[362] Positivists hold that the force of the obligation in a contract comes from "the force of the legal system that creates the obligation".[363] Accordingly, the state is the only legal system sufficiently potent to "create" a contractual obligation.[364] The positivist criticism of *lex mercatoria* flows from the belief that *lex mercatoria* has "no connexion with any definable society" and does not "amount in positivist terms to a legal system at all".[365] In substance, the positivists adopt a formalistic approach that ignores the fact that international business is often conducted in such a manner as to be beyond national laws. Under positivist theory, the international merchant community and arbitral institutions do not constitute a "legal system", nor do agreements created with reference to this system constitute "contracts". However, the arbitrating parties, who are part of the business community, deserve a certain level of flexibility to have their dispute arbitrated according to the merchant rules they choose to comply with. Therefore, the national and largely positivist character of legal ideology is ill-suited to international commerce. The positivist theory cannot account for what was, and is, against the trend of the strict legalistic view that only state rules that have a binding effect should be rejected. Contemporary lawyers should be aware that state rules are not indispensable components of efficient commerce. For centuries during the Middle Ages lawyers were excluded from many commercial courts because their slavish adherence to tedious formalities made dispute resolution costly, slow, uncertain and unfair.[366]

There are also jurisprudential grounds for recognising *lex mercatoria*. The criticisms of *lex mercatoria* and of de-nationalised arbitration are similar to those made of public international law. It was argued that, in light of the recognition afforded to customary international public law, "there is no

---

359 Christopher W.O. Stoecker, above n. 68, 27.

360 Keith Highet, above n. 9, 613.

361 Ibid.

362 This argument is based on the positivist premise that "freedom of contract is a delegation by the state to individuals of the power to enter into binding contracts". Bernardo M. Cremades and Steven L. Plehn, above n. 3, 328.

363 Keith Highet, above n. 9, 614.

364 Georges R. Delaume, 'Comparative Analysis as a Basis of Law in State Contracts: The Myth of the *Lex Mercatoria*', (1989) 63 *Tul. L. Rev.* 582.

365 David Suratgar, 'Considerations Affecting Choice of Law Clauses in Contracts Between Government and Foreign Nationals', (1962) 2 *Indian Journal of International Law* 311.

366 Frederic R. Sanborn, above n. 38, 196.

fundamental theoretical opposition to the existence of *lex mercatoria*", except the lack of a "formal" system for the enforcement of arbitral awards provided in the merchant society. In this respect, however, *lex mercatoria* is even more effective than the public international law regime.[367] First, the New York Convention provides for compulsory enforcement of awards through the network of national courts. There is nothing in Article V of the New York Convention requiring the denial of recognition of an award based on *lex mercatoria*. Second, *lex mercatoria* is also enforced through private action within the merchant community. Third, institutional arbitration rules, the major source of arbitration laws, provide arbitrators with freedom to apply *lex mercatoria*. For example, Article 13(3) of the ICC Rules allows the arbitrator to apply the proper law by the rule of conflict which he deems appropriate in the absence of the parties' choice of applicable law. Article 28 paragraph 4 of the Model Law also allows the arbitral tribunal to decide "in accordance with the terms of the contract and take into account the usages of the trade applicable to the transaction". Both the "proper law" under ICC Rules and "usages" under the Model Law may refer to *lex mercatoria*.

Some positivists argue that, because it allegedly contains no delineated set of general principles, arbitration "results become unpredictable, and parties to agreements have little ground on which to base their expectations".[368] It is even argued that: "the relative clarity of the legal process … is simply far less for *lex mercatoria* than for the established national legal systems …"[369] Other arguments include that the application of *lex mercatoria* "provides a court with a diminished level of guidance" that creates uncertainty.[370] These assertions, indeed, are only a variation of the dubious argument that *lex mercatoria* consists of "rules of uncertain existence and content".[371] A similar objection arises from the purported "lack of binding precedent", the lack of an obligation to follow what precedents there are for guidance,[372] and the "lack of consistent, specific sources".[373] The underlying logic of these arguments seems to suggest that the inherent defects of *lex mercatoria* will yield a system that is "unlikely to produce

---

367 Ibid.

368 B. Wortmann, 'General Principles of Law in International Commercial Arbitration', (1988) 101 *Harv. L. Rev.* 1819.

369 William W. Park, above n. 141, 111. Park described the law merchant as "a catch all phrase of uncertain content", and also suggested that "the *lex mercatoria* is too uncertain a set of rules to be regarded as a law that binding for everyone". Christopher W.O. Stoecker, above n. 68, 125; or that "the lack of clear definition renders these rules inadequate for the choice of law", Craig M. Gertz, 'Comment, The Selection of Choice of Law Provisions in International Commercial Arbitration: A Case for Contractual Depecage', (1991) 12 *NW J. Int'l L. & Bus.* 176.

370 B. Wortmann, above n. 368, 1819.

371 Hans Smit, above n. 358, 633.

372 Bernardo Cremades and Steven L. Plehn, above n. 3, 336.

373 Craig M. Gertz, above n. 369, 176.

a uniform interpretation of custom and practice".[374] Nevertheless, it appears from the published awards that the content of *lex mercatoria* is neither vague nor uncertain. Practically speaking, merchants are more familiar with the uniform practices of their own trade than with the vagaries of various municipal regulations or the niceties of conflicts doctrine. Likewise, the development of a common law of international business should enhance predictability rather than diminish it.[375] It is clearly not true that the state is the exclusive source of law, as classic positivism has concluded. The most compelling argument in favour of *lex mercatoria* may lie in its practical evolution: the continued growth of international business simply demands a reconstituted, if not new, *lex mercatoria* capable of accommodating the multinational aspects of contemporary international commerce. New economists claim that commerce is an evolving process of interaction and reciprocity which is simultaneously facilitated by, and leads to, an evolving system of commercial law.[376] Carl Menger claimed that the origin, formulation and the ultimate process of all social institutions, including law, is essentially the same as the "spontaneous order".[377] For instance, markets guided by Adam Smith's invisible hand coordinate interactions, and so is customary law. Accordingly, these institutions develop because, through a process of trial and error, the actions they are intended to coordinate are performed more effectively and efficiently under one institutional arrangement or process than under another. Thus, in a Darwinian sense, the more effective institutions and practices replace the less effective ones. Merchants have a long history of legal autonomy, and any argument against the viability of a transnational and self-regulating system of commercial law is belied by the history of *lex mercatoria*.[378] In the case of the customary commercial law, traditions and practices evolve to produce the observed spontaneous order. *Lex mercatoria*, in the form of customary commercial law, continues to be made by the international merchant community despite government efforts to monopolise such law.[379]

Lex mercatoria is far more conducive to economic growth than national law. International merchants want to do business, hope to make a profit and expect their contracting partners to perform the contract with the willingness to do so on their own part. Considering that new technologies and political realities are continuously altering the dynamics of international business, the merchant community cannot wait for state governments or courts to initiate legal changes

374 Bernardo Cremades and Steven L. Plehn, above n. 3, 336.

375 Nicholas de B. Katzenbach, above n. 149, 77.

376 Bruce L. Benson, above n. 23, 648.

377 Carl Menger, tr. Francis J. Nock, *Investigations into the Method of the Social Sciences with Special Reference to Economics*, New York: New York University Press (1986) (laying out the essential blue print for "bottom up" spontaneous order or unintended consequences type explanations).

378 Thomas E. Carbonneau and Marc. S. Firestone, above n. 55, 79.

379 Bruce L. Benson, above n. 23, 644.

in favour of international merchants. Only *lex mercatoria* can immediately adapt to the changing circumstances and practices of transnational commerce. National legislation takes much longer; and by the time the agreement is reached on international treaties, the law embodied within them is already obsolete due to the divergence of interests of contracting states. Furthermore, merchants have better incentives to develop practices that facilitate rather than obstruct transnational business, and are better equipped than state governments to articulate and to enforce these customary rules.[380] The ultimate justification for *lex mercatoria* is its conforming to and effectuating what merchants understand or expect to be the consequences of contractual undertakings or business arrangements. From the economic point of view, the avoidance of conflict is far more important than the resolution of it. While both international arbitration and *lex mercatoria* aim to facilitate private transactions by reducing conflicts, the advocates of positive national law institutionalise conflicts within the nation-state through the attempts to localise international commerce in national legal systems. As such, national law runs counter to the object and purpose of the international commercial relationship. The opponents of *lex mercatoria* are concerned less with the promotion of international business than with the protection of their own prominent position in the regime of regulatory states. This form of legal protectionism has become increasingly obstructive to economic growth.[381] It has been rightly observed that "the way in which international trade rules nowadays, in relation with the nationalisation of law in the 19th century, is unsatisfactory".[382] The proponents of national systems of commercial laws are afraid of their shrinking jurisdictions and are reluctant to lose any more business to a-national systems. While the rationalities of negotiated orders such as *lex mercatoria* are recognised,[383] their existence and real function "are actually effaced."[384] Neither the future development of private international law nor the continued growth of international business should be held hostage to the narrow pecuniary and ideological interests of domestic theorists and bureaucrats: "the strongly legalistic view that rules can only have a binding force if enacted by state authorities has to be rejected".[385]

---

380 It should not be ignored that *lex mercatoria* may also be imposed in hindsight and therefore may not give businesses the *ex ante* clarity they desire. Nevertheless, compared to coded law, *lex mercatoria* is theoretically more responsive to the needs of the business community.

381 Michel Gaudet, 'The International Chamber of Commerce Court of Arbitration', (1986) 4 *International Tax & Business Law* 216.

382 René David in Rapport Général at UNIDROIT in 1977.

383 "They involve a different orientation to the normative repertoire from those of state law; decision-making is through agreement, reached through cyclical processes of information exchange and learning, rather than the imposed order of a third party; different forms of trust are necessarily involved." Simon Roberts, 'After Government? On Representing Law without the State', (2005) 68(1) *Mod. L. Rev.* 1.

384 Ibid. 23.

385 Christopher W.O. Stoecker, above n. 68, 119.

4.6. NEW *LEX MERCATORIA* AND NEO-NEW YORK CONVENTION

The role of arbitration in cementing international commerce is undisputed. What is more open to question is whether arbitration, in addition to its procedural contribution, can and should yield a uniform law of international commerce. If so, the existence and continued development of *lex mercatoria* are real and undeniable, and should be encouraged and supported.

International transactions, by their very nature, usually involve parties from one or more countries and who will have differing perceptions of the principles of law. They will probably also have differing interpretations of their rights and duties as understood by the legal system of the party with whom they are doing business, or of the place where a contract is to be performed, or even of the place where they have chosen to resolve their disputes. Parties who decide to enter a cross-border transaction are faced with a significantly increased level of complexity compared with entities that trade exclusively within their familiar domestic jurisdiction. It is for this reason that the interaction of different legal rules can tend towards a disruption of international transactions. Globalisation requires commonly accepted practice to cut across differing juridical and commercial traditions, drawing from each of those elements that are considered to be most universally practical. In business, certainty is highly valued, the support of which needs rules. Rules are derived from principles, and practice, as well as legal reasoning, has a hand in shaping principles. Commercial practice in a global economy will increasingly tend to reflect conditions, concerns and expectations that are common, that is, transnational, rather than purely local. This process of harmonisation is, to a large degree, a product of sustained effort by proponents of a principled system of international commercial arbitration.

Over the years, the business community, driven by the desire to make honest profits in marketplaces, has developed a relatively sophisticated system comprised of laws, trade practices, custom and usages, to manage and balance the risks of the marketplace with the opportunities of business. Freedom of international business calls for transnational principles and customary rules, spontaneously and progressively produced by the *societas mercatorum*. Many customary practices and mercantile principles have been well-understood, adopted and codified, almost in an organic fashion, in much national legislation.[386] While most international arbitrators are conscientious in respecting the bounds of their missions, some have been bold and known to try their skills in finding ways to bypass the established rules of the party-chosen law. To circumvent the prescribed limits of their authority, they have discerned

---

386 For an interesting politico-legal account as to developments, see Alan Rodger, 'The Codification of Commercial Law in Victorian Britain', (1992) 108 *LQR* 570.

"emerging trends" that lead in a contrary direction, or have implemented new commercial principles and *lex mercatoria*. Legislators and policymakers alike can appreciate the international arbitrators' desire for freedom from substantive and procedural national legal constraints. Today, commercial practices and rules are expanding and have obtained international currency. This may not support the view that *lex mercatoria* can claim to constitute a complete but separate legal order. However, it at least can claim a right to exist.[387]

Lex mercatoria is spoken of under a number of names, including international, transnational, or supranational commercial law; international customs or usages; general principles of international commercial law; and merchant law.[388] Regardless of the label, the same phenomenon – a set of rules encompassing commercial practices of the international merchant community – is being described.[389] *Lex mercatoria* is a manifestation of the commercial community's growing disenchantment with national legal systems. Over the last century, merchants have slowly begun to extricate their commercial disputes from the tangled regulatory web of the national legal order. In order to escape the labyrinth of conflicting national laws, international merchants submit their disputes to a-national arbitral bodies, and increasingly, arbitrators are resolving disputes by applying an a-national body of private customary law – *lex mercatoria*.

A new *lex mercatoria* is rapidly developing in the world of international commerce. There exists an autonomous commercial legal regime that has grown independently of the national systems of law. It is the desire of the business community to have an efficient and self-enforcing system of law that has led to the emergence of a new *lex mercatoria*, the universality of which can promote cross-border transactions. The evaluation of *lex mercatoria* is central to the elaboration of a trans-border rule of law and to efforts to harmonise world adjudicatory practices.[390] The New York Convention's popularity in different legal, political and economic systems reflects its flexibility and compatibility with *lex mercatoria*. The provisions in the New York Convention continue to be widely accepted although the Convention has been in existence for around sixty years. Furthermore, its popularity is also demonstrated by the fact that the chapter on recognition and enforcement of arbitral awards in the UNCITRAL Model Law was closely modelled on the main provisions of the New York Convention, and that the solutions of the New York Convention have been

387 *Soc. Pabalk Ticaret Ltd., Sirketi v. Soc. Anon. Norsolor.*

388 Carlo Croff, above n. 154, 623.

389 Mark A. Buchanan, 'Public Policy and International Commercial Arbitration', (1988) 26 *Am. Bus. L.J.* (1988) 511.

390 There are projects aimed at making *lex mercatoria* principles more readily identifiable, notably the Transnational Law Database set up by the University of Cologne's Centre for Transnational Law, through what has been termed as "creeping codification". See http://www.tldb.uni-koeln.de.

incorporated into multilateral and many bilateral international treaties. The development of *lex mercatoria*, however, requires the members of the New York Convention to demonstrate their further willingness, through the judiciaries, to recognise and embrace more self-governing rules of the international commercial community. This kind of willingness needs a new level of flexibility in implementing the New York Convention, eventually a neo-New York Convention.

CHAPTER 5

PUBLIC POLICY AND THE NEW YORK CONVENTION

Public policy, along with the closely related issue of the role and function of the state courts in commercial arbitration, is the most open-ended, ambiguous and controversial issue in the New York Convention and is the key topic of this chapter.

A discussion of public policy can be far-reaching but the focus of this chapter is from a more macro perspective. This chapter starts with the basic concept of public policy and focuses on two constitutive aspects of public policy within the framework of the New York Convention. The issue of arbitrability appears in the early stage of arbitration proceedings where courts can exert judicial discretion to conduct substantive or procedural review over the question of whether the dispute is arbitrable or not by reference to public policy. At the end of an arbitration proceeding, courts have the last resort not to recognise and enforce arbitral awards on the grounds that arbitral awards are in violation of public policy.

A review of judicial approaches to public policy law follows in Part 2. Currently, the major judicial approaches to dealing with public policy in international commercial arbitration are, respectively, to draw a distinction between substantive and procedural laws and/or to distinguish national and international disputes. Attention needs to be given to the fact that most courts may only mention public policy or describe what public policy is but rarely explain the underlying rationale, which is classified as the distinction between prescriptive and normative public policy. Normative public policy is analysed in Part 3 in detail. In addition to the core concept of normative public policy, the discussion will focus on the options available for achieving normative public policy according to game theory. Public policy is a major concern to most states in international commercial arbitration. However, the development of international commercial arbitration needs more recognition of party autonomy and less judicial intervention from the states. Therefore, the role and function of states in the era of globalisation will be studied so that the significance of public policy and party autonomy can be understood in a wider context.

Part 4 tries to explore the possibility of framing the normative public policy theory in the "real world". The basic idea is to assess the possibility of forming normative public policy based on game theory. For instance, the critical issue can be whether the normative public policy regime can be built up through a "federalism" model and global legislation. In Part 5, jurisprudential analysis will be applied in discussing the possibility of building up a world legal framework so that public policy will not be manipulated by states to constrain, but rather to facilitate, international commercial arbitration. Market economic theory and democratic process have become defining elements of contemporary international law. Is normative public policy compatible with these fundamental theories? This part of the discussion is more focused on the problems of globalisation such as the transplant of the notion of normative public policy to developing countries. Part 6 would discuss how to make use of the current international legal system to solve the divergence of local practice and to strengthen the convergence of harmonised practice. The chapter will conclude in Part 7 with a brief summary.

5.1. CONCEPT AND PRACTICE OF PUBLIC POLICY

Public policy is not a determinate but rather a malleable legal concept which has been judicially compared to "a very unruly horse and when once you get astride it you never know where it will carry you".[1]

5.1.1. ARBITRABILITY AND PUBLIC POLICY

According to Article V(2)(a) of the New York Convention, enforcement of an arbitral award may be refused "if the competent authority in the country where recognition and enforcement is sought finds that the subject matter of the difference is not capable of settlement by arbitration under the laws of that country". The concept of arbitrability reflects the level of judicial control the court exerts over arbitration. When one party submits the dispute to arbitration, the other party is entitled to stay the proceedings. The courts will consider whether national public policy denies the parties' right to arbitration or should reserve the matter for the exclusive jurisdiction of its national courts.[2] In light of their interconnections, the matter of arbitrability can form part of or even be subsumed under the public policy ground.[3] The current position in the

---

1 *Richardson v. Mellish* (1824) 2 Bing 228 at 252.

2 Stephen M. Schwebel and Susan G. Lahne, 'Public Policy and Arbitral Procedure', in Pieter Sanders (ed.), *Comparative Arbitration Practice and Public Policy in Arbitration*, The Hague: Kluwer (1978) p. 205–208.

3 It is claimed that "the issue of 'arbitrability' under the New York Convention is an issue for the law of the enforcement State and, being governed largely by questions of public policy,

international regime is that no uniform standard is set nor exists among all states on the scope of arbitrable matters.[4]

Apart from those explicitly excluded from arbitrable matters by statutes, courts will judicially determine a number of matters as non-arbitrable according to public policy. Some obvious examples are disputes relating to family law,[5] criminal law or disputes in which a compromise cannot be reached through arbitration. As a result, matrimonial disputes and cases involving parent–child relationships are non-arbitrable.[6] Also, these non-arbitrable disputes include public law concerns such as those arising under the Constitution or mandatory laws. For example, Article 2060 of the French Code does not permit arbitration of personal injury, tort, employer–employee, or insurance contract claims.[7] Along the same lines, in England, an award concerning the illegality or criminality of a transaction cannot be enforced. Therefore, these matters are exclusively reserved for state courts due to the nature of public law and the protection of public interests.[8] Similarly, a dispute concerning a contract tainted by bribery, fraud or corruption is not suitable for arbitration because the dispute is no longer a contractual one in nature and because of "the general principles denying arbitrators the power to entertain disputes of this nature".[9] In *Argentinian Bribery*, Judge Lagergren held that contracts tainted by bribery, fraud or corruption could not be enforced by arbitral tribunals or judges (*ex turpi causa action non oritur).*[10] Lagergren declined jurisdiction after it was established that "the agreement between the parties contemplated the bribing of Argentine officials". In his view, "parties who ally themselves in an enterprise of [such] nature must realise that they have forfeited any right to ask for assistance of the machinery of justice (national Courts or arbitral tribunals) in settling

---

varies from State to State". Nigel Blackaby and Constantine Partasides (eds.), *Redfern and Hunter on International Arbitration*, Oxford: Oxford University Press (5th edn. 2009) p. 655.

4 G. Gaja, *International Commercial Arbitration: New York Convention*, 3 Vols, Dobbs Ferry, NY: Oceana Publications (1990) I B 2.

5 In the US, marital status and capacity are within the exclusive jurisdiction of the courts of law. Thomas E. Carbonneau, 'A Consideration of Alternatives to Divorce Litigation', (1986) *U. Ill. L. Rev.* 1119, 1159. However, arbitration in most areas of family law has been gradually accepted by US courts. Stephen W. Schlissel, 'A Proposal for Final and Binding Arbitration of Initial Custody Determination', (1992) 26 *Family Law Quarterly* 76–77.

6 Florian F. Haase, 'Arbitration Awards in German International Business Relations', [2005] *ICCLR* 143.

7 Ark. Stat. Ann. §34–511 (Supp. 1985),.

8 Jason C.T. Chuah, *Law of International Trade*, London: Sweet & Maxwell (1998) p. 416.

9 See *Argentinian Bribery* case, ICC Award No. 1110; Gillis J. Wetter, 'Issues of Corruption before International Arbitral Tribunals: The Authentic Text and True Meaning of Judge Gunnar Lagergren's 1963 Award in ICC Case No. 1110', (1994) 10 *Arb. Int'l* 277.

10 ICC Award No. 1110; see also Gillis J. Wetter, above n. 9, 277. The case concerned a contract between a British company and an Argentine intermediary who was engaged to obtain a public works contract in Argentina. In return, the intermediary was to receive a commission of 10% of the contract value. The British company then refused to pay the promised commission, and the dispute was referred to Judge Lagergren as a sole arbitrator.

their disputes". It was found later that this may not be the best approach to dealing with such cases.[11] Assuming that any initial illegality did not directly impeach the arbitration clause, the arbitrator should assume jurisdiction according to the principles of severability and *kompetenz-kompetenz* even if the contract itself is null and void. The arbitrator should rule that the contract is null and void because it is tainted by fraud, corruption or bribery. Such approach has been expressed very eloquently by the US Supreme Court[12] and the Court of Appeal in England.[13]

Most commercial and civil matters do not pose the problem of arbitrability. Nevertheless, there are some subject matters in which it is not entirely clear whether they can be resolved by arbitration, or which aspects of the dispute are arbitrable. National laws may exclude them from the arbitrable category of disputes due to the expansion of public policy concern. In Australia, for example, disputes concerning insurance contracts[14] and carriage of goods by sea[15] are of limited arbitrability according to express legislative provisions. Trade practices disputes have also been a murky area. The Australian courts were previously more cautious in dealing with such disputes even though the courts of the US and New Zealand have held that trade practice disputes are fully arbitrable.[16] More recently, however, Australian courts held that an arbitration clause was broad enough to encompass trade practices disputes.[17] Likewise, bankruptcy and labour disputes are not arbitrable in some jurisdictions. These matters are of overwhelming public interest and are often heavily influenced by political policy

---

11 ICC Award No. 5622; *Hilmarton v. OTV*, XIX *Yearbook* (1994) 214.

12 "… [I]f the claim is fraud in the inducement of the arbitration clause itself – an issue which goes to the 'making' of the agreement to arbitrate – the federal Court may proceed to adjudicate it. But the statutory language does not permit the federal Court to consider claims of fraud in the inducement of the contract generally". *Prima Paint Co. v. Flood & Conklin Manufacturing Corp.*, 388 US 395 (1967).

13 "In English law the principle of separability of an arbitration clause contained in a written contract could give jurisdiction to an arbitrator under that clause to determine a dispute over the initial validity or invalidity of the written contract provided that the arbitration clause itself was not directly impeached. Furthermore, an issue as to the initial illegality of the contract was also capable of being referred to arbitration, provided that any initial illegality did not directly impeach the arbitration clause. In every case the logical question was not whether the issue of illegality went to the validity of the contract, but whether it went to the validity of the arbitration clause". *Harbour Assurance Co (UK) Ltd. v. Kansa General International Assurance Co. Ltd. and ors* [1993] 3 All ER 897 (English Court of Appeal).

14 Section 43 of the Insurance Contracts Act 1984 (Cth), although parties are free to agree after a dispute has arisen to refer that dispute to arbitration (s 43(2)).

15 Section 2C of the International Arbitration Act, saving the continued operation of s 9 of the Sea Carriage of Goods Act 1924 (Cth) and the operation of ss 11 and 16 of the Carriage of Goods by Sea Act 1991 (Cth).

16 For the US, see *Mitsubishi Motors v. Soler Chrysler-Plymouth*, 473 US 614 (1984); and for New Zealand, see *AG v. Mobil Oil New Zealand* [1989] 2 NZLR 649.

17 The New South Wales Court of Appeal, *IBM Australia Ltd. v. National Distribution Services Ltd.*, (1991) NSWLR 466. A similar finding was made in *QH Tours Ltd v. Ship Design and Management (Aust) Pty Ltd.* (1991) 33 FCR 227.

considerations. Accordingly, labour arbitration is separate from commercial arbitration and often falls into the category of administrative law.

Non-arbitrable matters, at one time or another, have included disputes concerning patent and trademark filings,[18] competition law,[19] securities claims,[20] foreign illegality and punitive damages. These are categorised as "public law claims" which were, for much of the 20th century, deemed non-arbitrable by national courts and legislatures,[21] and are still rarely arbitrated internationally.[22] These matters are of great importance to the public interest and even to "the democratic capitalism of the regime".[23] For example, in respect of competition-related matters, as Adam Smith pointed out, the proper functioning of the market is an important matter of public interest.[24]

---

18 The granting of a trademark or patent is a monopolistic right and a prerogative of the State. Disputes regarding the granting of such rights between the State and the applicant, which is a vertical relationship and administrative law in nature, are not capable of settlement by arbitration. The ICC's Final Report on IP Disputes and Arbitration states that: "the existence, extent, meaning and application of such rights could legally only be definitively investigated, reviewed, ... revoked or confirmed by the authority which issued or granted the right ... This had the effect that rights and entitlements to intellectual property, and the legal issues which flowed from those rights, could not usefully be referred to or considered by an arbitration tribunal", (1998) 9(1) *The ICC International Court of Arbitration Bulletin* 38. The disputes concerning patent infringement, validity of a copyright, and trademark claims are arbitrable. Joseph T. McLaughlin, 'Arbitrability: Current Trends in the United States', (1996) 12(2) *Arb. Int'l* 135. These disputes involve a horizontal relationship between the parties to the commercial transaction.

19 In the US, the Sherman Antitrust Act prohibits contracts, combinations and conspiracies in restraint of trade in interstate commerce, and creates both civil rights for damages against antitrust violators and criminal sanctions for violations. Any person who monopolises or attempts to monopolise, or combines with others to monopolise trade or commerce, shall be guilty of a felony and punishable by fine (including treble damages) or imprisonment. Civil actions may be filed by the Federal government or a private party.

20 The arbitrability of securities disputes was extended in 1987 to the domestic case of *Shearson v. McMahon*, 482 US 220; 107 S.Ct. 2332 (1987). A survey in 1995 showed that over 10 million of the contracts contained arbitration clauses. See Constantine N. Katsoris, 'Foreword to the New York Stock Exchange, Inc. Symposium on Arbitration in the Securities Industry', (1996) 6(3) *Fordham Law Review* 1495, 1525. Customers seem to insist that the brokerage firms honour arbitration clauses. The reason for this can be seen in the investor-friendly *Mastrobuono v. Shearson Lehman Hutton* decision, 115 S.Ct. 1212; 89 AJIL (1995) at 601.

21 Gary Born, *International Commercial Arbitration: Commentary and Materials*, The Hague: Kluwer Law International (2nd edn. 2001) pp. 245–247.

22 Dora Marta Gruner, 'Accounting for the Public Interest in International Arbitration: The Need for Procedural and Structural Reform', (2003) 41 *Colum. J. Transnat'l L.* 923, 945.

23 See Sigvard Jarvin, 'Arbitrability of Anti-trust Disputes: The Mitsubishi v. Soler Case', (1985) 2(3) *J. Int'l Arb.* 69; *American Safety Equipment Corp. v. Maguire (J.P.) & Co.*; 391 F.2d 821 (2nd Cir. 1968). One of the four reasons the Court of Appeal listed in support of non-arbitrability of antitrust cases was "the fundamental importance to American democratic capitalism of the regime of the antitrust laws and the pivotal role played by private parties – by means of the private action for treble damages – in aiding enforcement of the antitrust laws".

24 Adam Smith, *An Inquiry into the Nature and Causes of the Wealth of Nations*, Chicago: University of Chicago Press (1977).

Competition and antitrust laws protect the market from distorting practices such as cartels[25] and, as a result, protect the essential fabric of a market economy. Currently, cases involving antitrust disputes are still not arbitrable in domestic US disputes on the grounds of public policy. Restrictions on the right to waive recourse to courts in favour of private arbitration are naturally imposed if courts perceive the private dispute as implicating a public policy issue so sensitive that it should be reserved for decision by public authorities, *i.e.*, state courts. The underlying rationale of this proposition rests in part on the "mistrust of arbitration".[26] Historically, it was claimed that "public law issues are too complicated for arbitrators"[27] to apply the proper law, legal skills and theories to such issues. For example, in the opinion of the court in the case of *Wilko v. Swan*, arbitration of a claim under the Securities Act "requires subjective findings on the purpose and knowledge of an alleged violator of the Act" and the arbitrator will make this determination under the strain of no "judicial instruction of law".[28] Besides, the court held that arbitration lacked the judicial system's ability to provide investors with the level of protection necessitated by the Securities Act.[29] There is a risk that the entire community loses out as a result of the arbitrator's failure to interpret and apply the law appropriately when arbitrators must interpret a statute that implicates the public policy.

There are other policy considerations for non-arbitrability such as non-recognition of a foreign law which is penal only,[30] which may result in a punitive award, involvement of arbitrators chosen from a foreign business community,[31] and the public law nature of competition law to promote trade other than private rights and to impose criminal penalties other than merely monetary damages.[32] Disputes arising out of or in connection with illegal contracts are not arbitrable because foreign revenue and penal laws are generally not enforceable in one

25 Article 81 of EC Treaty.

26 482 US at 233.

27 William W. Park, 'National Law and Commercial Justice – Safeguarding Procedural Integrity in International Arbitration', (1989) 63 *Tul. L. Rev.* 648, 700.

28 346 US 435–436 (1953).

29 Ibid. The Court of Appeal in the case of *American Safety Equipment Corp. v. Maguire (J.P.) & Co.;* 391 F.2d 821 (2nd Cir. 1968) was of the opinion that "antitrust issues, prone to complication, require sophisticated legal and economic analysis, and are thus ill-adapted to the strengths of the arbitral process, *i.e.*, expedition, minimal requirements of written rationale, simplicity, resort to basic concepts of common sense and simple equity".

30 *Laminoirs, etc. v. Southwire Co.*, 484 F. Supp. 1063 (N.D. Ga. 1980).

31 *American Safety Equipment Corp. v. Maguire (J.P.) & Co.*, 391 F.2d 821 (2nd Cir. 1968). The Court of Appeal claimed that "decisions as to antitrust regulation of business are too important to be dealt with by arbitrators chosen from the business community – particularly those from a foreign community that has had no experience with or exposure to US law and values".

32 As far as the UK and EU are concerned, the determination of anti-competitive practices is primarily a matter for the jurisdiction of the administrating body such as the EU Commission.

country at the suit of a foreign government.[33] As Lord Denning said, "these Courts do not sit to collect taxes for another country or to inflict punishments for it".[34] Therefore, these disputes are legitimately in the sole jurisdiction of national courts and arbitration on these disputes may not be judicially allowed.

The current judicial trend, however, is towards a pro-arbitration bias, or a smaller category of disputes being reserved solely to the jurisdiction of courts.[35] Courts have more confidence in arbitration procedures[36] and recognise the capacity of arbitral tribunals to deal with factual and legal complexities of statutory claims[37] and to provide sufficient protection to investors.[38] The other trends towards containing costs, and the support of international arbitration by national legislation, are also said to be the contributing factors to this trend.[39] Accordingly, courts have been more inclined to bring new subject matters such as antitrust and competition issues into the arbitrable domain.[40] This liberalisation approach in turn becomes a strong national public policy and the importance of some policy concerns decreases. In Germany, for example, the liberalising reform allows arbitration of revocation or declaring patents void.[41] In some jurisdictions such as Belgium, legislation has been changed to allow arbitral tribunals to order payment of a penal sum.[42] As a practical matter, the jurisprudence of arbitrability of securities claims has "established that most disputes in the securities industry will be resolved not in the courts but through arbitration".[43] In principle, non-arbitrable disputes are outside the purview of the New York Convention. This paradigm rule is catered for by national laws such as section 103(3) of the UK Arbitration Act which provides that enforcement of an award may be refused if the award is in respect of a matter which is not capable of settlement by arbitration.

---

33 However, a party to a civil action may plead the foreign illegality of a contract even if the illegality is in respect of a law of a penal or revenue nature. D.M. Day and Bernardette Griffin, *The Law of International Trade*, London: Butterworths (1993) p. 178.

34 In *Regazzoni v. K C Sethia (1944) Ltd.* [1956] 2 QB 490 at 515.

35 *ICCA's Guide to the Interpretation of the 1958 New York Convention: A Handbook for Judges*, International Council for Commercial Arbitration (2011) p. 104.

36 482 US at 233–34.

37 *Mitsubishi v. Soler Chrysler*, 473 US 614 (1985).

38 *Shearson/American Express v. McMahon*.

39 *ICCA's Guide*, above n. 35, 104.

40 Antoine Kirry, 'Arbitrability: Current Trends in Europe', (1996) 12(4) *Arb. Int'l* 373; John Beechey, 'Arbitrability of Anti-trust/Competition Law Issues – Common Law', (1996) 12(2) *Arb. Int'l* 188.

41 Daniel Paul Simms, 'Arbitrability of Intellectual Property Disputes in Germany', (1999) 15(2) *Arb. Int'l* 195.

42 Traditionally the Belgian doctrine has held that an arbitral tribunal could not order payment of a penal sum which was changed by the new Article 1709*bis* JC. See Marcel Storme and Bernadette Demeulenaere, *International Commercial Arbitration in Belgium: A Handbook*, Antwerp: Kluwer Law and Taxation International (1989) p. 73.

43 Lewis D. Lowenfels and Alan R. Bromberg, 'Securities Industry Arbitration: An Examination and Analysis', (1989) 53 *Albany Law Review* 755, 757.

5.1.2. PUBLIC POLICY IN ARTICLE V(2)(B) OF THE NEW YORK CONVENTION

The public policy ground is codified in Article V(2)(b) of the New York Convention as follows:

> "The recognition or enforcement of the award would be contrary to the public policy of that country".

It is unclear from the wording what the exact meaning of public policy is. This can potentially open the floodgates to the second-guessing of arbitral tribunals' findings on points of fact or law for bias in favour of the enforcement court's own nationals.

The fundamental importance of public policy in the arbitration regime relates to the enforcement of arbitral awards. Judges may review an arbitral award at the enforcement stage. Blackmun J made this clear in *Mitsubishi*:

> "Having permitted the arbitration to go forward, the national Courts of the United States will have the opportunity at the award enforcement stage to ensure that the legitimate interest in the enforcement of the ... laws has been addressed. The [New York] Convention reserves each signatory country the right to refuse enforcement of an award where the 'recognition and enforcement of the award would be contrary to the public policy of that country'. Article V(2)(b). While the efficacy of the arbitral process requires that substantive review at the award-enforcement stage remains minimal ... "[44]

Article V(2)(b) of the New York Convention allows the court in which enforcement of a foreign arbitral award is sought to refuse enforcement on the defendant's motion or *sua sponte,* if "enforcement of the award would be contrary to the public policy of [the forum] country". While the term "public policy" is used in the English text of Article V, the term "*ordre public*" appears in the French text and is adopted in such civil law countries as Germany and France.[45] It is well recognised that "no single English expression is equivalent to '*ordre public*' as it is much broader than 'public policy'.[46] Although Article V(2)(b) is the only provision in the New York Convention explicitly mentioning the term "public policy", other provisions may be of relevance in interpreting or applying that term. Article V(1)(b), for example, allows a court to refuse

---

44 *Mitsubishi Motors Corp. v. Soler Chrysler-Plymouth Inc.*, 473 US 614; 105 S.Ct. 3346; 87 L.Ed.2d 444 (1985).

45 Article 16 of the Rome Convention was entitled "*Ordre Public*": "The application of a rule of the law of any country specified by this Convention may be refused only if such application is manifestly incompatible with the public policy 'ordre public' of the forum".

46 Kurt H. Nadelmann and Arthur T. von Mehren, 'Equivalences in Treaties in the Conflicts Field', (1966/1967) 15 *American Journal of Comparative Law* 195, 200.

enforcement of an award if the award violates basic standards of due process.[47] The legislative history of this provision provides no definite guidance as to its construction. Its precursors in the Geneva Convention and the New York Convention's *ad hoc* committee draft extended the public policy exception to awards contrary to "principles of the law" and awards in violation of "fundamental principles of law", respectively. The uncertainty still exists in most jurisdictions and is likely to be interpreted by the judiciary widely enough to cover many other ways in which an award can offend public policy.

Many of the judicial decisions refusing enforcement of arbitral awards are made on the grounds of such public policy concerns as due process, fraud or the breach of natural justice. The US court in *Parsons v. Whittemore* held that Article V(2)(b) of the New York Convention "essentially sanctions the application of the forum state's standards of due process".[48] The English court must also be satisfied that the rules of natural justice have been complied with in the arbitration proceedings and the making of the award.[49] This requirement has several aspects. Where the party against whom the enforcement of award is sought is not given sufficient notice to present his case, the enforcement of award must be refused. Where a party is under some legal incapacity and is not properly represented, this too would constitute a breach of procedural justice and there can be no enforcement of that award.[50] Errors of law do not *per se* conflict with public policy. However, awards in deliberate and manifest disregard of the law may not be enforced.[51] The courts of England, France and the United States have all attempted in recent years to facilitate the conduct of international arbitration by loosening the public policy restraint on arbitration. England has incorporated a public policy favouring the autonomy of contracting parties to choose arbitration as a means of dispute resolution which "prevails over the public policy favouring judicial review of arbitration awards".[52] This "facilitative" way of interpreting and applying public policy, like a new memetic code, has been spread to other common law jurisdictions. In Singapore, for example, it was held by the Court of Appeal that "the legislative policy [is to] give primacy to the autonomy of arbitral proceedings and uphold the finality of arbitral awards".[53]

---

47 Article V(1)(b) is intended to be raised by the party defending against enforcement ("at the request of the party against whom it is invoked") while Article V(2)(b) is to be raised by the court itself ("may be refused if the competent authority in the country where recognition and enforcement is sought").

48 *Parsons & Whittemore Overseas Co., Inc. v. Société Générale de l'Industrie du Papier (RAKTA)*, 508 F. 2d 969, 975 (2nd Cir. 1974).

49 Jason C.T. Chuah, above n. 8, 413.

50 Section 37(2)(b) of the UK Arbitration Act 1950.

51 *Sidarma Societa Italiana etc. v. Holt Marine*, 515 F. Supp. 1362 (1981).

52 Steven J. Stein and Daniel R. Wotman, 'International Commercial Arbitration in the 1980s: A Comparison of the Major Arbitral Systems and Rules', (1983) 38 *Bus. Law.* 1685.

53 *AJT v. AJU* [2011] SGCA 41 at [410] to [460].

Public policy is also implemented in the setting-aside stage of an arbitral award.[54] At a technical level, there is no difference in the concept of public policy for the purpose of setting aside an award under the Model Law or for the purpose of enforcement under the New York Convention. One exception is this: grounds for setting aside an award are normally based on public policy principles of the country of rendition rather than the country of enforcement. As the purpose of the setting-aside proceedings is to ensure that a minimum standard of fairness is provided to parties in arbitration, the power of the court may be seen as a means to check the overall compliance of the award with the fundamental principles of the state. In contrast, Article V(2)(b) is a permissive mandate which means that the court has a certain discretion to overrule the defence and to grant the enforcement of the award if the court considers that the violation of the public policy of the award is not of such a nature and extent as to prevent enforcement of the award.

5.2. JUDICIAL APPROACHES TO PUBLIC POLICY

The issue of judicial approaches to public policy is, to some extent, the same as the issue of the relationship between national courts and arbitrators as well as between national laws and applicable law in arbitration. There are basically two aspects. From the perspective of the court, national courts used to view any agreement between the parties to arbitrate as an effort to oust the courts' supervisory powers, which is contrary to public policy and therefore is null and void.[55] A measure of control needs to be exercised by the court over arbitrations such as the conduct of arbitration, the making of awards, and the application of laws. From the perspective of arbitration, the similarity in the arbitral territory and the consensual nature of the process bred by national legal traditions makes for a process that functions within defined parameters under the umbrella of the national judicial system. Arbitrators are bound to consider the provisions in the agreement between the parties as well as the applicable law and to observe the prevailing legal norms of fairness and justice in the proceedings within the confines of the state. It is certain that minimum standards of natural justice or due process shall be observed and adhered to in the arbitration proceedings. Unlike domestic arbitration, the entire situation becomes more complicated once a dispute transcends sovereignty boundaries. Although the imperatives guiding international arbitration vary from those directing arbitrators and judges operating within the framework of national legislation and judicial systems, national laws play a role in sustaining and supporting the international system of dispute resolution through arbitration. Apart from the struggles

---

54 See Chapter 3 of this book.

55 *Czarnikow v. Roth, Schmidt & Co.* [1922] 2 KB 478, CA.

between courts and arbitration tribunals, the other source of problems is the inconsistent ways that different national courts would apply the grounds of public policy to refuse enforcement. Inconsistency lies in the diversity of cultural, social and economic values, regardless of law and legal values, in divergent societies, which inevitably results in different concepts of public policy. It is not realistic to expect conceptual harmony in the near future.

5.2.1. SUBSTANTIVE PUBLIC POLICY VERSUS PROCEDURAL PUBLIC POLICY[56]

The distinction between substance and procedure is a principal element of international commercial arbitration. The International Law Association Commercial Arbitration Committee's final report on public policy made a distinction between substantive international public policy and procedural international public policy.[57] This segregation of the law applicable to the substantive side of the dispute from the law applicable to the arbitration procedure indicates that the arbitral process may be independent from the system of law that regulates the rights and obligations of the parties. The segregation also implicitly acknowledges that the choice and application of two sets of applicable laws may be subject to different considerations. Therefore, the public policy relating to the substantive and procedural sides of the dispute will not be the same. The explanatory memorandum that accompanied the Australian International Arbitration Act Bill in 1988 adopted this distinction by requiring compliance with the "procedural justice as well as substantive principles of law and justice".

As far as the law governing arbitration proceedings is concerned, there is much to be said for setting an international standard by which international

---

56 A dichotomy between common law and civil law is not listed here as a separate pair or division in handling the public policy issue. Even in common or civil law, judicial pronouncements of public policy can vary greatly. For example, as discussed below, in common law jurisdictions, public policy can be a violation of the most basic notions of morality and justice; so fundamentally offensive to (the jurisdiction's) notions of justice; a great departure from basic concepts of justice. The list of these notions is not meant to be exhaustive. There have been some efforts to mould a so-called objective-criteria approach to re-frame public policy rules. Teresa Cheng, 'Celebrating the Fiftieth Anniversary of the New York Convention', in Albert Jan van den Berg, *50 Years of the New York Convention*, The Hague: Permanent Court of Arbitration (2009) p. 687. This approach suggests another dichotomy between objective criteria and subjective criteria. With respect, the most objective criteria can turn out to be subjective depending on how judiciary interprets and applies these criteria. Hence, the harmonising efforts should not be focussed on the objectiveness of criteria but on the scope of criteria.

57 International Law Association Final Report (presented at the ILA's 17th Conference in New Delhi), 2002, available at http://www.ila-hq.org/download.cfm/docid/032880D5-46CE-4C, Recommendation 1(c).

arbitration should be superintended, as opposed to leaving each State to enact and enforce its own local standards, which may run contrary to the aspirations of foreign arbitrating parties. The current trend is moving towards the harmonisation of international arbitral practices through the uniform adoption of internationally accepted standards for the conduct of the arbitration proceedings, one of which is enforcement of arbitral awards. Significantly, both the New York Convention and the Model Law, which are the two major pieces of global legislation on international commercial arbitration, demand that the arbitration process conform to international minimum standards such as the restriction imposed on the substantive review of arbitral awards by the court, while it respects the doctrine of party autonomy. The prevailing view is that disregard for or ignorance of imperative procedural requirements in the domestic law of the arbitral *situs* constitutes a breach of public policy.[58] These requirements are usually in the form of "international due process" or "procedural irregularities" which often includes equal treatment of the parties, proper notices as regards the conduct of the proceedings and appointment of arbitrators, fair and equal opportunity to present the case and evidence, or *ex parte* of relevant evidence, etc.[59] In the same vein, a statute of limitations defence may not be an arbitrable matter as well due to its mandatory nature.[60] Legislative efforts have been made in some jurisdictions, such as England, to draw up an exhaustive list of what constitutes serious irregularity affecting the proceedings.[61] Nonetheless, no agreement has been reached as to the scope or coverage of "procedural irregularities" among all jurisdictions.[62]

As to the substance or merits of the dispute, the doctrine of party autonomy prevails in "virtually all international conventions dealing with arbitration and contract law".[63] However, the true situation is more complicated than this stand-

---

58 Julian D.M. Lew, *Applicable Law in International Commercial Arbitration: A Study in Arbitration Awards*, Dobbs Ferry, NY: Oceana Publications (1978) p. 536.

59 *Totem Marine Tug & Barge Inc. v. North American Towing Inc.* 607 F.2d 649 (5th Cir. 1979).

60 *Smith Barney et al. v. Luckie*, 85 NY 2d 198 (1995).

61 These are: (a) failure of the tribunal to comply with its general duty contained in s. 33; (b) the tribunal exceeding its powers; (c) failure by the tribunal to conduct the proceedings in accordance with the procedure agreed by the parties; (d) failure by the tribunal to deal with all the issues that were put to it; (e) any arbitral or other institution or person vested by the parties with powers exceeding its powers; (f) uncertainty or ambiguity as to the effect of the award; (g) the award being obtained by fraud or the award or the manner in which it was procured being contrary to public policy; (h) failure to comply with the requirements as to the form of the award; (i) admitted irregularity in the conduct of proceedings. Section 68(2) of the English Arbitration Act 1996.

62 It seems that, at least in the EU, the finality of arbitration proceedings may prevail over the consideration of arbitrability. For example, the ECJ concluded in the case of *Eco Swiss* that the competition provisions under Article 81 (ex 85) were not so fundamental as to override otherwise valid procedural rules relating to limitation periods and the finality of arbitration proceedings. *Eco Swiss China Time Ltd. v. Benetton International NV*, Case C-126/97, [1999] ECR 3055 (ECJ).

63 Okezie Chukwumerije, *Choice of Law in International Commercial Arbitration*, Westport, CT and London: Quorum Books (1994) pp. 130–31.

alone principle. The controversy surrounding party autonomy in choosing the substantive law, for example, can be that the parties will resort to *lex mercatoria*.[64] Equally controversial is the parties' decision to allow the arbitrator to act as an *amiable compositeur*, freeing him from the designated responsibility to apply systemised principles of law.[65] These controversial areas may necessitate the states to exert judicial or legislative discretion and impose public policy restraints on arbitrators who are then bound to observe some mandatory rules. In most jurisdictions, judicial review over the merits of arbitral awards is usually allowed, in the context of both domestic and international arbitrations.

Mandatory rules of national law are frequently applied by international arbitration tribunals regardless of the choice made by the parties. This seems inevitable because the parties' choice of law in no way precludes a tribunal from determining the applicable law which may have connections with a jurisdiction. Every arbitrator has to consider the importance of preserving commercial arbitration as an independent instrument for the settlement of international disputes. On the other hand, like the courts that arbitrators or tribunals replace, arbitral tribunals or arbitrators must consider the public policy of a country that is closely connected with and relevant to the dispute.[66] The reputation of arbitration may suffer and the judicial support of the state courts may deteriorate if arbitration itself is used as means to evade public policies of those countries which have a stake in the subject-matter of the dispute. Therefore, a natural question is how and to what extent arbitral tribunals or arbitrators should apply mandatory rules of a state. In determining the particular national public policy system to be implemented in the arbitral process, as proposed, "the requisite test should be the connection of the jurisdiction (whose policy is at issue) to the dispute and the nature of the policy involved"[67] regardless of the fact that the national law of that jurisdiction is not the governing law chosen by the parties to the dispute.

This "close connection" test may not be workable in a more liberal arbitration regime. The restrictive and intervening effect of a country's public policy and mandatory rules is neither consistent nor compatible with the spirit of party autonomy and may further nullify the parties' agreement or an arbitral award, in whole or in part. Such a test usually invalidates self-contained arbitration rules on the basis of party autonomy and underpins the legitimacy of the arbitration regime. It seems implausible that arbitral tribunals or arbitrators should depart from the decision which they would otherwise make in order to further the interests and public policy of all countries which are connected with a cross-border and multi-party dispute. In other words, due to the lack of a functional

64 See Chapter 4 of this book.

65 Okezie Chukwumerije, above n. 63, 117.

66 Ole Lando, 'The Lex Mercatoria in International Commercial Arbitration', (1985) 34 *ICLQ* 764–8.

67 Okezie Chukwumerije, above n. 63, 203.

definition, the "close connection" test does not appear to be workable in particular when a dispute has close connections with various jurisdictions. Technically, multi-nationals sometimes seek escape from an onerous public policy restraint by choosing to have their contracts governed by the law of a country with more liberal norms. If there is a risk that such a choice of law clause might be declared invalid for being again

the public policy, one way of avoiding the potential invalidity would be to submit future disputes to arbitral tribunals or arbitrators who do not share the judicial respect for the mandatory public norms in question. These strategic devices may prove to be of great utility in practice.

The next question is whether mandatory rules should take priority over the doctrine of party autonomy as well as the arbitral tribunal or arbitrator's prerogative to promote fairness and justice in arbitration. The application of public policy may be dependent upon the express agreement by the parties in the arbitration clause,[68] the mandatory requirement in national laws and regulations, or arbitrators' own consciences or personal standards of morality and propriety. An individual party's preference to apply mandatory rules to arbitration may be rare. Nevertheless, these moral and justice considerations do exist in reality. The standard of morality would oblige arbitral tribunals or arbitrators to take into account public policy in arbitrating such disputes as contracts obtained by, or involving, corruption or other wrongdoings.[69] Internationally recognised defences also include duress, mistake, fraud,[70] waiver or a breach of fundamental policies of the forum state.[71] The notion of justice may also oblige arbitral tribunals or arbitrators to consider the public policy in cases, for example, where, after the making of the contract, specific performance was prohibited by the law of the country where that performance would result in criminal penalty.[72] A better view is that arbitral tribunals or arbitrators should only apply public policy and mandatory rules which are designed to protect public interests rather than the interest of a particular party to the dispute. The application of public policy and mandatory rules by arbitrators or arbitration tribunals is indeed supplementary to the mandatory rules and public policy to be applied by courts at the set-aside and enforcement stages. Courts can still set

---

68 It is argued that an express choice of a governing law should not in itself lead to the application of that law's invalidating rules: A.J.E. Jaffey, 'Essential Validity of Contracts in the English Conflicts of Law', (1974) 23 *ICLQ* 3–8.

69 Ole Lando, above n. 66, 765; Julian D.M. Lew, 'Determination of Arbitrators' Jurisdiction and Public Policy Limitations', in Julian D.M. Lew (ed.), *Contemporary Problems in International Arbitration*, The Hague: Martinus Nijhoff Publishers (1987) pp. 82–85.

70 *Renshaw v. Queen Anne Mansions Co.* [1897] 1 QB 662.

71 *Tennessee Imports, Inc. v. Pier Paulo Filippi and Prix Italia SRL*, 5 *Mealey's Int'l Arb. Rep.* (1990) E7; *Rhone Mediterranee Compagnia v. Lauro*, 712 F.2d 50 (3rd Cir. 1983).

72 In English law this is the rule in *Ralli Brothers v. Compania Naviera Soyay Aznar* [1920] 2 KB 287 that arbitrators might not apply it in respect of an illegality existing at the time of the contract, on the grounds that the party concerned should have anticipated this predicament.

aside or refuse to enforce an arbitral award that operates in tandem with a choice-of-law clause as a "prospective waiver" of sensitive public policy.[73]

5.2.2. DOMESTIC PUBLIC POLICY VERSUS INTERNATIONAL PUBLIC POLICY

The applicability of public policy in many jurisdictions such as France, the US and Argentina traditionally requires an international but not a domestic dimension. National public policy focuses on interests and values cherished by the national community at large. Accordingly, the application of national public policy contemplates the absolute exclusion of foreign law and legal principles contradictory to national public policy, as is the case in Argentina.[74] In contrast, courts in England, for example, used to be given considerably more leeway to intervene in and exercise various supervisory powers over international arbitrations and awards.[75] As part of the judicial effort, the current trend has been moving in the direction of limiting judicial involvement in the cross-border arbitration process. Hence, international arbitration is generally treated more liberally, with greater respect for the doctrine of party autonomy and far less judicial intrusion in the arbitration process than in domestic arbitration.

As some leading cases have indicated, there is growing judicial predilection to expand the ambit of arbitrability in transnational disputes. This trend originated in the US which used to hold a hostile attitude towards arbitration but now, more often than not, permits businesspeople to arbitrate some matters that were previously considered non-arbitrable. In the well-known case of *Mitsubishi Motors Corporation v. Soler-Chrysler-Plymouth Inc.*,[76] the US Supreme Court stated in a 5:3 decision that antitrust claims are arbitrable in an international context since: "[t]he *Bremen* and *Scherk* [cases] establish a strong presumption in favour of enforcement of freely negotiated contractual choice of forum provisions. ... Thus we must weigh the concerns ... against a strong belief in the efficacy of arbitral procedures for the resolution of international commercial disputes and an equal commitment to the enforcement of freely negotiated choice of forum clauses. ... Accordingly, we 'require this representative of the American business community to honour its bargain' ... by holding this agreement to arbitrate 'enforce[able]'..."[77] In response to the argument that anti-

---

73 W. Michael Reisman, William Laurence Craig, William W. Park and Jan Paulsson, *International Commercial Arbitration, Cases, Materials and Notes on The Resolution of International Business Disputes*, New York: The Foundation Press Inc. (1997) pp. 381–382.

74 Article 14(2) of the Argentine Civil Code.

75 J. Kodwo Bentil, 'Making England a More Attractive Venue for International Commercial Arbitration by Less Judicial Oversight', (1988) 5(1) *J. Int'l Arb.* 50.

76 See Sigvard Jarvin, above n. 23, 69.

77 *Mitsubishi Motors Corp. v. Soler Chrysler-Plymouth Inc.*, 473 US 614; 105 S.Ct. 3346; 87 L.Ed. 2d 444 (1985).

trust claims were inappropriate for arbitration owing to the "pervasive public interest" in enforcing anti-trust law, the US Supreme Court stated that "concerns of international comity, respect for the capacities of foreign transnational tribunals, and sensitivity to the need of the international system for predictability in the resolution of disputes require that we enforce the parties' agreement, even assuming that a contrary result would be forthcoming in a domestic context".[78] The US Supreme Court "powerfully advocates the need for international comity in an increasingly interdependent world. Such respect is especially important, in this Court's view, when parties mutually agree to be bound by freely negotiated contracts".[79]

Wilko v. Swan clearly established that securities transactions are not arbitrable.[80] In the decade following *Wilko*, US courts, relying on *Wilko*, applied the non-arbitrability doctrine to a wide range of statutory claims, such as antitrust, employment discrimination, patent rights, and other statutory claims. However, the 1974 decision of *Fritz Scherk v. Alberto-Culver* foreshadowed this case-based principle. The US Supreme Court recognised the validity of an ICC arbitration clause in a contract by which an American company acquired shares of a German citizen's business. The Court held that federal securities claims in the international context are arbitrable. It reached this decision even though the claim concerned fraudulent representation of the status of the trademark rights, which is a violation of section 10(b) and Rule 10b-5 of the Securities Exchange Act of 1934.[81] As a practical matter, *Wilko*'s holding with respect to the arbitrability of federal securities claims is a dead letter after the judgments of *McMahon*[82] and *Rodriguez de Quijas*,[83] and arbitration since then has been "no longer an alternative to litigation … but widespread practice" in securities disputes.[84]

The trend of expanding the domain of arbitrable matters also spreads to other jurisdictions such as Belgium.[85] The judicial trend, on the other hand, is reflected in limiting the use of public policy in commercial arbitration. For instance, in England, the practice has been changed to minimise the judicial interference in international commercial arbitration. The English High Court was precluded from allowing a party to an international arbitration to appeal to

78 473 US 614 at 629.

79 *Sonatrach (Algeria) v. Distrigas Corp.* (District Court of Massachusetts, US), XX *Yearbook* (1995) 795; also *Wong v. Tenneco, Inc.*, 702 P.2d 570 (Cal. 1985).

80 *Wilko v. Swan*, 346 US 427 (1953).

81 *Scherk v. Alberto-Culver Co.*, 417 US 506 (1974).

82 *Shearson/American Express v. McMahon*, 482 US 220 (1987).

83 *Rodriguez de Quijas v. Shearson/American Express*, 490 US 477 (1989). The court made it clear that *Wilko* was wrongly decided.

84 Robert S. Clemente, 'Trends in Securities Industry Arbitration', (1996) *New York State Bar Journal* 20.

85 Luc Demeyere, '1998 Amendments to Belgian Arbitration Law: An Overview', (1999) 15(3) *Arb. Int'l* 303.

it on a question of law arising from an award if the parties to the dispute in question have entered into a written agreement which excludes the right of appeal.[86] This is consistent with the English courts' effort to let the public policy principle give way to the need for greater finality in arbitral awards.[87]

What drives this change then? The rationale in *Mitsubishi* allowing a case that essentially involved antitrust matters to be settled by arbitration rested mainly on the international nature and dimension of the dispute. In the US, the courts make a distinction between international and domestic agreements or transactions and are of the opinion that "the [New York] Convention does not contemplate the expression of local public policy as a barrier to the arbitrability of claims".[88] For example, in *Scherk*, the court recognised the nature of the agreement as "the significant and crucial difference between *Wilko* and *Scherk*" because the agreement in *Scherk* "was a truly international agreement" which implicated "considerations and policies significantly different from those found controlling in *Wilko*".[89] Similarly, the international nature of the transaction in *Mitsubishi* was also a determinative factor.

This distinction between international and domestic transactions and the recognition of the international nature of the transaction indicates the courts' increasing concern over the cry of non-arbitrability which impairs the effectiveness and efficiency of arbitration in providing a neutral forum for adjudication of international business disputes. In a legitimate sense, for instance, if American courts fail to uphold an arbitration agreement on the basis that the dispute touches on non-arbitrable subject matters under US law, courts in other countries may be tempted to do the same when their nationals are conducting business with Americans. In such case, all parties concerned will suffer as they may have no alternative but go before non-neutral courts to argue or defend their cases in foreign languages under unfamiliar procedures according to foreign laws.

The judges, in particular Justice Stewart, in *Scherk* appreciated that US businesses are not able to do business in the world market exclusively on US terms, governed by US laws, and resolved in US courts.[90] This line of reasoning has also appeared in other cases. The US Supreme Court held in *The Bremen v. Zapata* that: "[T]he expansion of American business and industry will hardly be encouraged if, notwithstanding solemn contracts, we insist on a parochial concept that all disputes must be resolved under our laws and in our Courts" and re-emphasised the judicial position that "[US businesses] cannot have trade

86 Section 3(1) of the English Arbitration Act 1979.

87 [1983] 2 Lloyd's Rep. 423; *Antaios Compania Naviera S.A. v. Salen Rederierna A.B.* [1985] 1 AC 191, [1984] 3 WLR 592, [1984] 3 All ER 229.

88 *Develop. Bank of Philippines v. Chemtex Fibres Inc.*, 617 F. Supp. 55, 57 n. 12 (SDNY 1985).

89 *Scherk v. Alberto-Culver Co.*, 417 US 506 (1974) 515.

90 Ibid.

and commerce in world markets … exclusively on our [US] terms, governed by our laws and resolved in [US] Courts".[91] American courts have gradually showed their preference for "the international marketplace as a whole" over the "economic or social organisation of the United States".[92]

The judges in *Mitsubishi Motors* explicitly listed such distinctive considerations in cross-border transactions as the principle of international comity, a basic level of respect for international arbitrators, and sensitivity to the needs of international trade as decisive factors. Likewise, American courts have been abundantly sensitive to "concerns about international comity and foreign enforcement".[93] This distinction is also drawn by courts in New Zealand because "international trade and commercial relationships are of critical importance" even to a small country.[94] A French court also enforced a Belgian award "in the absence of any demonstration … of a flagrant, real and concrete violation of international public policy".[95] The English courts have tended to discourage the exercise of judicial control in international commercial arbitration so as to impress upon the international business community the attractiveness of England as a venue for settling disputes by international arbitration in contemporary times.[96] On occasion, a distinction has been made between English domestic public policy and foreign domestic public policy. In *Westacre Investments Inc. v. Jugoimport-SDPR Holding Co. Ltd.*, it was held that "there is nothing which offends English public policy if an Arbitral Tribunal enforces a contract which does not offend the domestic public policy under either the proper law of the contract or its crucial law, even if English domestic public policy might have taken a different view".[97] It appears to suggest that, at least in some English (and Commonwealth) cases,[98] domestic public policy should not be cited as grounds to refuse enforcement of an international arbitral award.

These concerns or policy considerations drive the courts to distinguish between domestic and cross-border disputes and to adopt different approaches in dealing with the arbitrability and public policy issues in two scenarios. The chief purpose of these considerations is to facilitate and favour international

---

91 *The Bremen v. Zapata Off-shore Co.*, 407 US 1 (1972); 92 S.Ct. 1907; 32 L.Ed. 2d 513 (1972).

92 ICC Case No. 6320, XX *Yearbook* (1992) 62, 156. In that case, a federal district court stayed the RICO suit in favour of arbitration. RICO refers to the Racketeer Influenced and Corrupt Organizations Act, a United States federal law, that provides for extended criminal penalties and a civil cause of action for acts performed as part of an ongoing criminal organisation.

93 *North South Finance Corp. v. Al-Turki*, 100 F.3d 1046 (2nd Cir. 1996).

94 *Attorney-General of New Zealand v. Mobil Oil New Zealand Ltd.* [1989] 2 NZLR 668.

95 *SNF SAS v. Cytec Industries BV* (*Cour d'Appel* Paris, 23 March 2006) in (2007) 2 *Stockholm Int'l Arb. Rev.* 99.

96 Lord Hacking, 'Where We Are Now: Trends and Developments Since the Arbitration Act 1979', (1985) 2 *J. Int'l Arb.* 7, 14.

97 *Westacre Investments Inc v. Jugoimport-SDPR Holding Co Ltd* [2000] QB 288.

98 An Indian case is also illustrative on this point: *Renusagar Power Co. Ltd. (India) v. General Electric Co. (US)*, XX *Yearbook* (1995) 681.

trade over an expansive application of domestic laws such as the securities law.[99] As a result, some matters that are not arbitrable in a domestic context may be arbitrated when the controverted event covered by the arbitration clause has an international aspect. Gradually, the distinction of international public policy and national public policy has been adopted in national legislation and court decisions.[100] The distinction between international and domestic disputes is also adopted in judicial review under the Model Law.[101] Such a double standard might be justified by the objectives of fostering international commercial and economic intercourse, reciprocity, harmony, and unification of international economic transactions, as well as the particular need for neutrality in trans-border commercial dispute resolution and overly better results in game theory.

It has been claimed that there is a category of "transnational public policy" including globally accepted norms of conduct with respect to international transactions.[102] The concept is said to constitute private international law that represents the "international consensus as to universal standards or accepted norms of conduct that must always apply and provide limitations to public as well as private international relationships and transactions".[103] A similar concept was adopted by the International Law Association.[104] French law clearly adopts such a concept. French private international law draws a distinction within the realm of public policy between *ordre public interne* that is mandatory only when the legal transaction or relationship is governed by French law, and *ordre public international* that is mandatory when the legal transaction or relationship is

99 *Scherk v. Alberto-Culver*, 417 US 506 (1974).

100 Decision of 11 May 1983 No. 3 Ob 30/83, 38 Osterr. Juristen-Zeitung, pp. 519–21, Evidenzblatt No. 142 (1983) 113 Clunet, p. 395 (1986), 56 Entscheidungen des osterr. Obersten Gerichtshofes in Zivil- und Justizverwaltungssachen (SZ) No. 77 (1983). To the same effect, Austrian Supreme Court, 23 February 1983, No. 3 Ob 185/82 38 Osterr. Juristen-Zeitung 327, Evidenzblatt No. 84 (1983); 24 Zeitschrift für Rechtsvergleichung 206 (1983).

101 Article 34(1) of the Model Law provides: "recourse to a court against an arbitral award may be made only by an application for setting aside in accordance with paragraphs (2) and (3) of this article". Paragraph (2) sets out the grounds for setting aside an award, which are, in material respects, exactly the same as the grounds upon which an application for enforcement of the award may be refused under Article 36. The only difference is that Article 36 is intended to apply to any international arbitral award irrespective of the country in which it was made, whereas Article 34 applies only to awards made within the country in which the application for setting aside is made. Consequently, the Model Law does not permit an arbitral award to be set aside on the grounds of error committed within a jurisdiction, whether such error relates to a question of fact or of law.

102 See Mark A. Buchanan, 'Public Policy and International Commercial Arbitration', (1985) 26 *American Business Law Journal* 511, 514–15. In international investment arbitration, "transnational public policy" is understood to mean "an international consensus as to universal standards and accepted norms of conduct that must be applied in all for a". *World Duty Free Co. Ltd. v. Republic of Kenya*, ICSID Award, Case No. ARB/00/7, 4 October 2006, 46 ILM 339 (2007).

103 Ibid. 514.

104 ILA Final Report, above n. 57, para. 11.

subject to a law other than the law of France. In the latter case, the law consists of some of the most essential, fundamental and universal norms.

There has been some judicial support for a proposition distinguishing between *ordre public international* and *ordre public interne*. The Supreme Court of France has interpreted certain restrictive domestic policies as inapplicable to international commercial arbitration.[105] In the US case of *Parsons and Whittemore Overseas Co. v. Société Générale de L'Industrie du Papier*, public policy was interpreted as "those mandatory norms that comprise a State's most basic notions of morality and justice".[106] The Court of Appeals, the Second Circuit, held that the concept of public policy employed in Article V(2)(b) of the New York Convention is narrower than the notion of national policy. Accordingly, the court rejected an objection to the enforcement of an arbitral award in favour of an Egyptian defendant on the ground that it violated the current US foreign policy towards Egypt. The narrower scope of public policy in international commercial arbitration was elaborated in a number of cases. The District Court of Massachusetts summarised the position in the case of *Sonatrach* that "the line of decisions which conclusively tip the judicial scale in favour of arbitration [is] rather a line of United States Supreme Court opinions which enthusiastically endorse an international approach towards commercial disputes involving foreign entities". These decisions – *Bremen*, enforcing the forum selection clause in an international commercial contract, *Scherk*, enforcing the international arbitration clause in conflict with federal securities law, and *Mitsubishi*, holding the international arbitration clause enforceable when in conflict with federal antitrust laws – eschew the parochial tendencies of domestic tribunals in retaining jurisdiction over international commercial disputes. The Austrian Supreme Court also invented the equivalent concepts of "supranational public policy" and "a common European *ordre public*" in the case of *VAG*.[107] English law too has gradually developed so as to invoke public policy in cases involving an international element.[108] However, common law rules in this regard are still rare because of the difficulty of identifying these rules.[109]

A technical question naturally arises from this approach: what can be considered to be national or international public policy? The scope of national

---

105 Steven J. Stein and Daniel R. Wotman, above n. 52, 1685; Thomas E. Carbonneau, 'The Elaboration of a French Court Doctrine on International Commercial Arbitration: A Study In Liberal Civilian Judicial Creativity', (1980) 55 *Tul. L. Rev.* 1.

106 *Parsons Whittemore Overseas Co. Inc. v. Société Générale de l'Industrie du Papier (RAKTA)* 508 F.2d 969, 974 (2nd Cir. 1974). Also see *MGM Productions Group Inc. v. Aeroflot Russian Airlines* 2004 WL 234871 (2nd Cir. (NY)).

107 The Austrian Supreme Court held that the New York Convention simply refers to the public policy of the country where enforcement of the award is sought.

108 Lawrence Collins et al (eds.), *Dicey, Morris & Collins on The Conflict of Laws*, London: Sweet & Maxwell (14th edn. 2006) pp. 1626–1627.

109 Peter North and J.J. Fawcett, *Cheshire & North's Private International Law*, Oxford: Oxford University Press (13th edn. 1999) p. 582.

public policy theoretically includes all mandatory rules of domestic law[110] or economic policy of sufficient importance.[111] However, it is unlikely that every mandatory rule forms part of public policy.[112] The term of "national public policy" or "mandatory rules of domestic law" is at risk of being interpreted widely.[113] For example, "mandatory rules" is defined as "... an imperative rule of law that cannot be excluded by agreement of the parties".[114] Therefore, the concept of "mandatory rules" may embody the public regulatory and economic policies of the enacting state which can further stretch out to cover a variety of policy areas.[115] In the Anglo-American legal context, "public policy" probably comprises all the elements of due process of law.[116] This is same as the requirement of complying with certain procedural formalities in civil law jurisdictions such as Germany.[117] The wide coverage of such concepts may endanger the party autonomy principle in arbitration as courts in the forums of enforcement would occasionally take an expansive approach in applying these concepts. It has been held by an Indian court that a dispute arising from an international agreement for the transfer of technology is not arbitrable under Indian law "because such agreement implicates national economic policies".[118]

---

110 *J. H. v. Brunn, Zur Nachprufbarkeit von Schiedsspruchen*, 22 Neue Jur. Wochenschift (1969) 826. The category of mandatory rules is said to include two groups of norms: one group dealing with protection of certain contract parties, and the other group touching upon fundamental policies of the enacting states. Hannah L. Buxbaum, "Mandatory Rules in Civil Litigation: Status of the Doctrine Post-Globalisation", in George A. Bermann and Loukas A. Mistelis (eds.), *Mandatory Rules in International Arbitration*, New York: Juris Net LLC (2011) p. 38.

111 Christopher B. Kuner, 'The Public Policy Exception to the Enforcement of Foreign Arbitral Awards in the United States and West Germany Under the New York Convention', (1990) 7(4) *J. Int'l Arb.* 88.

112 Karl-Heinz Bockstiegel, 'Public Policy and Arbitrability', in Pieter Sanders (ed.), *Comparative Arbitration Practice and Public Policy in Arbitration*, The Hague: Kluwer Law International ICCA Congress Series No. 3 (1987) p. 183.

113 There appear some subtle differences between the concepts of "public policy" and "mandatory rules" despite their similarity and overlap. For example, mandatory rules are positive ones requiring an application, while public policy is more negative in its exclusory nature and the courts may exclude the application of rules based on public policy. Peter North and J.J. Fawcett, above n. 109, 132.

114 International Law Association Final Report (presented at the ILA's 17th Conference in New Delhi 2002, available at http://www.ila-hq.org), para. 48.

115 Marc Blessing used "mandatory rules" as an umbrella to cover the following categories of rules: (i) those protecting monetary interests of the enacting state (*i.e.*, exchange control regulations); (ii) those of a fiscal nature (*e.g.*, customs regulations); (iii) those safeguarding economic interests of the enacting state (*e.g.*, import and export restrictions); (iv) those protecting the welfare of certain individuals (*e.g.*, rules protecting the weaker contract party); (v) those serving political or military interests (*e.g.* embargoes); (vi) those aimed at protecting environmental welfare; and (vii) those protecting open markets (competition law). Marc Blessing, *The Impact of the Extraterritorial Application of Mandatory Rules on International Contracts*, Frankfurt am Main: Helbing und Lichtenhahn (1999) pp. 14–15.

116 Kurt H. Nadelmann and Arthur von Mehren, above n. 46, 195, 200.

117 Christopher B. Kuner, above n. 111.

118 M. Sornarajah, 'The UNCITRAL Model Law: A Third World Viewpoint', (1989) 6(4) *J. Int'l Arb.* 7.

The scope of international public policy is difficult to define partly because "international" itself is a vague concept in international arbitration. A rather vague definition is supplied in Article 1492 of the French Code of Civil Procedure, which provides that "arbitration is international if it implicates international commercial interests". French case law has broadly construed this statutory definition by holding that the international character of arbitration is determined by the international feature of the economic transaction in question, such as a cross-border flow of goods, persons and services, rather than the nationality of the parties or the governing law.[119] A more precise definition appears in Article 176(1) of the Swiss Federal Code of Civil Procedure Law, which provides that: "the provisions of this chapter shall apply to all arbitrations if the seat of the arbitral tribunal is in Switzerland and if, at the time of the conclusion of the arbitration agreement, at least one of the parties had neither its domicile nor its habitual residence in Switzerland".

Article 1(3) of the Model Law provides a more detailed definition of "international arbitration" in which the parties to an arbitration agreement can be from different states, or the parties have expressly agreed that the subject-matter of the arbitration agreement relates to more than one country. All these definitions are of great practical value but have an inherent problem in certain situations. The New York Convention itself simply applies to any award made in another contracting state and does not require that an award relate to an international arbitration.

"The goal of the New York Convention … was to encourage the recognition and enforcement of commercial arbitration agreements in international contracts and to unify the standards by which agreements to arbitrate are observed and arbitral awards are enforced in the signatory countries".[120] However, the New York Convention fails to provide for the content of public policy. Courts in some countries such as Germany regarded "public policy" in Article V(2) of the New York Convention merely as having a declaratory effect.[121] It is noted that the New York Convention's failure to include similar language in its earlier draft signals a narrowing of the non-enforcement defence.[122] The counter-argument is that this omission may be regarded as an indication of the intention to widen the non-enforcement defence.[123] More constructive

[119] Jean-Pierre Ancel, 'French Judicial Attitudes Toward International Arbitration', (1993) 9(2) *Arb. Int'l* 121.

[120] 417 US 506 (1974) at n. 15.

[121] Ignaz Seidl-Hohenveldern, 'Austrian Public Policy and the Enforcement of Foreign Arbitral Awards', (1988) 4(4) *Arb. Int'l* 328.

[122] See Paolo Contini, 'International Commercial Arbitration The United Nations Convention on the Recognition and Enforcement of Foreign Arbitral Awards', (1959) 8 *Am. J. Comp. L.* 283, 304.

[123] See Leonard V. Quigley, 'Accession by the United States to the United Nations Convention on the Recognition and Enforcement of Foreign Arbitral Awards', (1961) 70 *Yale L.J.* 1049, 1070–71.

inferences can be drawn from the history of the New York Convention as a whole. The general pro-enforcement bias which is the New York Convention's supersession of the Geneva Convention points toward a narrow reading of the public policy defence. An expansive construction of this defence would vitiate the New York Convention's basic effort to remove pre-existing obstacles to enforcement of arbitral awards.[124]

A circumscribed public policy doctrine contemplated by the New York Convention's framers indicated that a country, in acceding to the Convention, meant to subscribe to this super-national effort.[125] Therefore, enforcement of foreign arbitral awards may be denied on the basis of public policy only where enforcement would violate the forum state's most basic notions of morality and justice.[126] The public policy provision in the New York Convention surely "was not meant to enshrine the vagaries of international politics under the rubric of public policy".[127] Equating "national" policy with state "public" policy or national political interests may seriously undermine the New York Convention's objectives, namely utility and efficacy. Similarly, a state's foreign policy shall not be regarded as part of the public policy recognised under the New York Convention. To this end, the distinction between domestic and international disputes suggests that an international arbitrator has to ensure that domestic public policies have a legitimate claim for application in the international arena, whereas national courts are more ready and willing to look only to the domestic public policy.[128] International or transnational public policy in theory is a product of many legal sources including natural law, *jus cogens*, and the norm of justice and equality universally applied in most nations today.[129] Therefore, the material content of "international public policy" seems to include general principles of law to be found in the domestic law of all countries such as rules on good faith, and against corruption and bribery.[130]

Efforts have been made to clarify the scope or meaning of "international public policy". It has been suggested that "international public policy" requires the application of particular rules designed to be used in cases involving

---

124 See Donald B. Straus, 'Arbitration of Disputes between Multinational Corporations', in American Arbitration Association, *New Strategies for Peaceful Resolution of International Business Disputes*, Dobbs Ferry, NY: Oceana Publications (1971) pp. 114–115.

125 cf. *Scherk v. Alberto-Culver Co.*, 417 US 506, 94 S.Ct. 2449, 41 L.Ed.2d 270(1974).

126 cf. 1 Restatement (Second) of the Conflict of Laws §117, comment (c) at 340 (1971); *Loucks v. Standard Oil Co.*, 224 N.Y. 99, 111, 120 N.E. 198 (1918).

127 *Parsons & Whittemore Overseas Co., Inc. v. Société Générale de l'Industrie du Papier (RAKTA)*, 508 F.2d 969, 974 (2nd Cir. 1974).

128 Okezie Chukwumerije, above n. 63, 44.

129 Julian D.M. Lew, *Applicable Law in International Commercial Arbitration: A Study in Commercial Arbitration Awards*, Dobbs Ferry, NY: Oceana Publications (1978) p. 535.

130 Berthold Goldman, 'Les conflits des lois dans l'arbitrage international de droit privé', (1963 II) 109 *Recueil des Cours* 432.

international commerce[131] as the term "international" at least rules out any resort to either domestic or foreign municipal law. In this case, "national policy" in the diplomatic or foreign policy sense would not be taken into account.[132] The recommendations of the International Law Association in 2002 defined "international public policy" to include (i) fundamental principles, pertaining to justice or morality, that the state wishes to protect even when it is not directly concerned; (ii) rules designed to serve the essential political, social or economic interests of the state, these being known as "*lois de police*" or "public policy rules"; and (iii) the duty of the state to respect its obligations towards other States or international organisations.[133] In spite of some efforts to clarify the definition, a line between domestic and international public policy is still not clear-cut in theory and practice.[134]

In theory, "international public policy" is taken to be narrower than "national public policy".[135] It can also be argued that the concept of "national public policy" is, from the application perspective, more parochial but less lenient than "international public policy".[136] Reference can be made to *Mitsubishi* setting out

---

131 Pierre Lalive, 'Transnational (or Truly International) Public Policy and International Arbitration', in Pieter Sanders (ed.), *Comparative Arbitration Practice and Public Policy in Arbitration*, The Hague: Kluwer Law International (1987) p. 275.

132 *Waterside Ocean Navigation Co., Inc. v. International Navigation Ltd.* 737 F.2d. 150 (2nd Cir. 1984) at 152.

133 Emmanuel Gaillard and Domenico di Pietro, *Enforcement of Arbitration Agreements and International Arbitral Awards: the New York Convention in Practice*, London: Cameron May (2008) p. 797.

134 The recommendations of the International Law Association issued in 2002, available at http://www.ila-hq.org/download.cfm/docid/032880D5-46CE-4C, Clause 1(d).

135 Udo Kornblum, '"Ordre public transnational", "ordre public international" und "ordre public interne" im Recht der privaten Schiedsgerichtsbarkeit', in Walther J. Habscheid and Karl Heinz Schwab, *Beitrage zum internationalen Verfahrensrecht und zur Schiedsgerichtsbarkeit: Festschrift fur Heinrich Nagel zum 75. Geburtstag*, Munster: FS Nagel (1987) pp. 140, 155.

136 In terms of practicability, the ILA fails to offer further details as to how to apply the concept of "international public policy" expect for some guidance. Relevant guidance is in Recommendations 3(b) to 3(d). Recommendation 3(b): "A court should only refuse recognition or enforcement of an award giving effect to a solution prohibited by a rule of public policy forming part of its own legal system when: (i) the scope of said rule is intended to encompass the situation under consideration; and (ii) recognition or enforcement of the award would manifestly disrupt the essential political, social or economic interests protected by the rule". Recommendation 3(c): "When the violation of a public policy rule of the forum alleged by a party cannot be established from a mere review of the award and could only become apparent upon a scrutiny of the facts of the case, the courts should be allowed to undertake such reassessment of the facts." Recommendation 3(d): "When a public policy rule of the forum enacted after the rendering of the award prohibits the solution implemented by said award, a court should only refuse the award's recognition or enforcement if it is plain that the legislator intended said rule to have effect as regards awards rendered prior to its enactment." Some commentators meanwhile have outlined some elements for the purpose of evaluating whether a public policy rule is violated. Marc Blessing included the following elements into the consideration: (i) the rule in question must be a norm of a mandatory character; (ii) the rule must be such as to impose itself irrespective of the applicable law; (iii) the preconditions regarding the application (as per the mandatory rule) must be given, the

the high requirement that illegality for attracting judicial notice must be so blatant as to "knock your eyes out".[137] As a result, the application of "international public policy" by a court in the enforcement forum may be less far-reaching than the national one.[138] The bottom line appears to be that, in the current context, the term "international public policy" should not be used as "a parochial device protective of national political interests",[139] but only to refer to "super-mandatory" rules (as opposed to just mandatory rules) in modern transnational commercial law texts.[140] Courts in more jurisdictions showed a readiness to limit the public policy defence to enforcement by reference to "international public policy".

---

scope of the mandatory rule must be construed narrowly; (iv) there must be a close connection between the subject matter of the parties' contract and the jurisdictional area or State that had promulgated the mandatory rule or norm; (v) the rule or norm must appear to be "application-worthy"; (vi) the result must, in view of all circumstances, qualify as an "appropriate result"; and (vii) the result must, therefore, satisfy scrutiny under the perspectives, the demands and the supplementing or sometimes corrective notions of a truly international public policy. Marc Blessing, *Introduction to Arbitration – Swiss and International Perspectives*, Swiss Commercial Law Series, Vol. 10, Frankfurt am Main: Helbing und Lichtenhahn (1999) pp. 266–267. Although this checklist approach seems inherently logical, it still fails to provide clear guidance. For instance, the starting point of ensuring a mandatory character in the norm is of little use in determining the scope of "mandatory norms". Points (v) to (vii) look into the result of applying mandatory rules, which turns the application of mandatory rules to the outcome rather than focusing on the application or rule itself. This appears cyclical because some of these elements focus on the results of applying the rule and this contributes little to the problem of how to apply the rule.

137 The French decision in *SA Thales Air Defense v. GIE Euromissile* 2005 *Rev. Arb.* 751 (*Cour d'Appel* Paris, 2004) goes even further than *Mitsubishi*. The court held that any violation of public policy must – so as not to call into question the finality of the award – be "manifest" or "flagrant". Because it was a "complex dispute" requiring factual inquiry into the agreement's "specific circumstances" and "possible negative effects", it could not be said that the illegality was so clear as to "knock one's eyes out".

138 The arbitral tribunal's application of public policy rules would be different in two scenarios given the differences between domestic and international public policy. While the tribunal sits in one country but expects to see the award enforced in the other country, it may need to apply international public policy in the forum of enforcement in order to ensure enforcement. However, the tribunal may need to apply domestic public policy if its award would be enforced in a domestic court. Whether the tribunal should consider mandatory rules or public policy in a foreign legal system is a difficult question to answer. A recurring question is to what extent can the mandatory rules of a country whose law is neither the *lex fori* nor the *lex contractus* affect the rights of the parties. Most likely, the rules or public policy of the place of performance would kick in. In English law, it is not likely that an award that is contrary to a mandatory rule of a foreign legal system could be appealed on a point of law or challenged as being contrary to English public policy unless English law and the foreign legal system shared the same public policy or because of compelling reasons of international comity. Sections 68(2)(g) and 69 of the Arbitration Act. Also see *Tamil Nadu, Electricity Board v. ST – CMS Electric Co. Private Ltd.*, [2007] EWHC 1713.

139 *Parsons & Whittemore Overseas Co., Inc. v. Société Générale de l'Industrie du Papier (RAKTA)*, 508 F.2d 969, 974 (2nd Cir. 1974).

140 Roy Goode, Herbert Kronke and Ewan McKendrick, *Transnational Commercial Law: Text, Cases, and Materials*, Oxford: Oxford University Press (2007) paras. 2.48–2.57.

5.2.3. PRESCRIPTIVE PUBLIC POLICY VERSUS NORMATIVE PUBLIC POLICY

The traditional judicial approach in dealing with public policy purports to reflect what the courts actually are doing rather than presenting a normative theory of how they should deal with it. To that end, the legislation may simply describe the key components or main factors in public policy rules. For instance, section 19 of the Australian International Arbitration Act defines two scenarios as the violation of "public policy", that is, the making of the award being induced or affected by fraud or corruption, and a breach of the rules of natural justice having occurred in connection with the making of the award. Similarly, the arbitration law in Zimbabwe also adopted this two-pronged definition of public policy,[141] which is the standard proposed by the Model Law.

Prescriptive public policy is potentially helpful in predicting future results from past cases based upon prescriptive rules. The resulting clarity has advantages over seemingly disparate court rulings, including facilitating *ex ante* public policy and satisfying the public expectation of judicial efficiency. However, the defects of a prescriptive approach are also obvious. First, the prescriptive approach says nothing about the merits of any rule and only has value in comparison to a regime in which courts say one thing and do another. The judges are likely to be over mechanical by using "escape devices" to reach more intuitively satisfying results[142] or advocate their own proposals on prescriptive grounds.[143] Second, the prescriptive approach forces the courts to take the issue into account regardless of the formal method the judges are supposed to use. The criticism of formalistic theorists on this issue is that courts actually are using criteria to make public policy decisions without considering the underlying rationale of legal criteria. The two aspects of "public policy" listed in the Australian arbitration law, for example, fail to provide the court with guidance in interpreting "natural justice", which ultimately makes the application of this two-prong standard very hard and unpredictable. Third, the prescriptive rules may not guarantee efficient judicial results because judges may serve their own, interest groups' or legislators' interests rather than those of the society as a whole. Judges are likely to favour particular interest groups such as local lawyers who prefer to attract litigation[144] and may have influence on judicial selection, or

---

141 An award is in conflict with the public policy of Zimbabwe if (a) the making of the award was induced or effected by fraud or corruption; or (b) a breach of the rules of natural justice occurred in connection with the making of the award. Articles 34(5) and 36(3).

142 See Brainerd Currie, 'Married Women's Contracts: A Study in Conflict-of-Laws Method', (1958) 25 *U. Chi. L. Rev.* 227 99–107 (criticising the opportunistic use of escape devices).

143 See Robert A. Leflar, 'Choice-Influencing Considerations in Conflicts Law', (1960) 41 *NYU L. Rev.* 267, 324–252.

144 See Michael E. Solimine, 'An Economic and Empirical Analysis of Choice of Law', (1989) *24 Georgia L. Rev.* 49, 73 (noting that judges may favour the bar through decisions that will generate litigation as the bar may fund judicial election campaigns).

a particular group of companies such as energy companies in a highly energy dependent economy. "Such countries may not lightly accept the notion in the Model Law that [exploitation agreements and concessions] could be removed from the public law sphere by a mere commercial contract"[145] since these agreements and concessions "are subject to the doctrine of permanent sovereignty over natural resources, a doctrine which, whatever its validity in international law may be, is constitutionally enshrined in many countries".[146] Judges may also favour forum law, partly to serve the legislators that determine judges' pay and perquisites, and partly because this simplifies the judges' judicial task. Following this line of analysis, the dominant prescriptive approach is naturally pro-resident and pro-forum biased.[147]

There has, indeed, been a kind of "race to the bottom" in formulating and implementing public policy rules. Although judges usually start with a rule-based approach that might deter them from indulging their own preferences or interests by making departures over-obvious and dramatic, the courts have often tended to develop a more open-ended approach that facilitates a more discretion-orientated judicial decision-making process. This approach may be attributable to a prisoner's dilemma type of game among the states, that is, individual states and their courts gain judicial advantages by abandoning a socially or globally optimal approach or standard. Courts in larger states could adopt a wider range of constraints in the public policy framework in order to protect or serve their self-interests. The more attractive markets of larger states, in terms of the availability of rich resources, market transactions and commercial opportunities in these states, make it harder for business entities to avoid contracts that create a basis for exerting jurisdiction. Smaller states could not easily compete for arbitration or litigation business by giving potential arbitrating parties a "safe harbour" from a tough public policy regime. Therefore, courts in the smaller states would have little incentive to sacrifice their own self-interests by forgoing more flexible public policy rules. In short, it would not pay for most national state courts to retain a more self-restrictive approach to public policy. Certainly a dynamic might appear through the jurisdictional competition that overcomes these barriers to efficiency. That is particularly true now that innovations in business, communications and transportation, such as the Internet (or cyberspace), give business firms more flexibility about where to do business and chances to move to a more business-friendly regime. For the time being, there is a legitimate reason to cast doubt on the efficiency of at least some rules developed by state courts.

---

145 M. Sornarajah, above n. 118, 7.

146 Ibid.

147 Stuart Thiel, 'Choice of Law and the Home Court Advantage: Evidence', (2000) 2 *American Law and Economics Review* 291; and George L. Priest and Benjamin Klein, 'The Selection of Disputes for Litigation', (1984) 13 *J. Legal Stud.* 17 (claiming that litigated disputes are biased toward those that are on the margin).

Compared to the prescriptive approach, the normative approach takes a different course by recognising the normative role that public policy plays in legislation, adjudication and compliance.[148] The emphasis on the normative value of public policy reflects the normative jurisprudence which is concerned with the moral underpinnings of law and morality of commercial lawmaking.[149] This jurisprudence has traditionally concentrated on legislative legitimacy and justice in the field of public law such as criminal law and human rights law. Nevertheless, it should be also compatible with commercial law for several reasons. First, like public law, the prospective and facilitative role of commercial law demarcates commercial rights of business participants and provides guidance for the conduct of commercial actors. Second, virtues such as clarity and certainty are also moral imperatives for commercial law so that it can carry out its prospective (*i.e.*, regulatory) and retrospective (*i.e.*, adjudicative) functions adequately, and so that the commercial players are able to ascertain without doubt when, where, how and with whom they will be doing business. Third, the "rule of law" requires a commitment made by the legislature and judiciary, in both public and commercial laws, to certain procedural and substantive accounts which have the same moral notions. These moral notions include the generality of rules, ascertainability to the public, non-retroactivity, consistency and coherency.[150] As early as the beginning of the twentieth century, close to the position advocated here, Judge Cardozo put forward the judicial formula of public policy according to which the courts will not refuse to enforce or recognise a foreign right unless it would "violate some fundamental principle of justice, some prevalent conception of good morals, some deep-rooted tradition of the common weal".[151] As regulation is viewed as a "free good",[152] there is a

148 Ronald Dworkin defined the normative theory of law in detail. In his opinion, the normative part of the law is about a theory of legislation, of adjudication, and of compliance from the standpoints of a lawmaker, a judge, and an ordinary citizen respectively. Ronald Dworkin, *Taking Rights Seriously*, London: Duckworth (2005) Introduction, pp. vii-viii.

149 In the opinion of Dworkin, "the normative theory will be embedded in a more general political and moral philosophy which may in turn depend upon philosophical and theories about human nature or the objectivity of morality". Ibid.

150 Lon Fuller, *The Morality of Law*, New Haven: Yale University Press (1969) (listing such 8 principles as (i) rules must apply standards on a general, not an *ad hoc* or *ad hominem*, basis; (ii) rules must be publicly ascertainable; (iii) legislation must not be retroactive; (iv) rules must be expressed in terms comprehensible to citizens or their advisers; (v) the legal system must be internally consistent and coherent; (vi) rules must not be impossibly onerous nor standards unachievable; (vii) laws laid down must not be changed too frequently; and (viii) congruence between the rules as they are declared and the rules as they are administered is a matter of administrative, not legislative, fairness.

151 *Loucks v. Standard Oil Co.*, 224 NY 99, 111 (1918). Cardozo's formulation of public policy was approved by some well-known scholars such as Dicey. See Lawrence Collins et al, above n. 108, 1627.

152 See generally Charles Goodhart, Philipp Hartmann, David T. Llewellyn, Liliana Rojas-Suarez and Steven Weisbrod, *Financial Regulation: Why, How and Where Now?* London: Routledge (1998).

strong social bias against any laws intervening in the ordinary conduct of business and narrowing or diminishing existing rights of business actors. Therefore, the overall moral objective requires legislation to have some key features. First, the law should be drafted in ascertainable and specific terms, the application of which can be reliably predicated. Second, the law should adopt concepts and principles which are consistent. Third, the law should not impose intolerable or unreasonable costs or burdens. For example, the law should contain fixed rules rather than flexible standards so that people can focus on the literal or plain meaning of the text other than purposive or contextual methods. According to the "internal morality of law", Article V(2)(b) of the New York Convention is not ideal. The term "public policy" is an ambiguous and abstract definition that lacks specificity, certainty and clarity such that its application cannot accurately be predicted as most marginal cases have indicated.[153] As a result, there is a large room for the improvement of public policy rules so as to avoid "cumulative infringement of legal morality".[154]

At the technical level, the normative approach does not try to define the term or identify boundaries or parameters of public policy. Instead, the normative approach is principles-based. The concept of principles-based regulation is not new and, in the context of commercial laws, was first originated by Sir David Walker, the then Chairman of the UK Securities and Investments Board in the late 1980s. The importance and popularity of such a concept was waning in the mid-1990s when more prescription and greater certainty became the fashion in legislation. The concept has experienced a revival in the European Union when Charlie McCreevy, the European Commissioner for Internal Market and Services, re-adopted the approach to "well-regulate" rather than "over-regulating" the market.[155] In the same vein, the UK Financial Services Authority in December 2005 published a "Better Regulation Action Plan" which moved to a more principles-based approach for regulation.[156] Principles-centred arbitration legislation is not rare either. For instance, the English Arbitration Act 1996 started with an express statement of several key principles in commercial arbitration,[157] which is viewed as a commendable innovation. The principles-

153 There are no paradigmatic cases that are crystal clear on the term "public policy".

154 Charles Goodhart et al., above n. 152, 92.

155 Charlie McCreevy, German-Irish Chamber of Industry and Commerce, Ireland: Making the Most of the Internal Market, 9 December 2005; and Europe's Capital Markets in a Global Marketplace, 4th Annual Financial Services Conference, Brussels, 31 January 2006.

156 The Financial Services Authority is already a principles-based regulator. It set out 11 high-level Principles for Businesses which are supposed to be complied with by financial services firms. FSA Handbook PRIN 2.

157 These principles are found in Section 1 of the Arbitration Act 1996 which provides:
The provisions of this Part are founded on the following principles, and shall be construed accordingly:
(a) the object of arbitration is to obtain the fair solution of disputes by an impartial tribunal without unnecessary delay or expense;

based normative approach does not mean that the approach would not consider some key legislative norms. Rather, principles-based regulation needs to take account of legal rationality. As far as the public policy is concerned, the underlying judicial rationality was clearly pointed out in *Egerton v. Brownlow* where the court described public policy as "that principle of law which holds that no subject can lawfully do that which has a tendency to be injurious to the public or against the public good".[158]

Principles-based regulation also needs to utilise some major economic factors such as efficiency and wealth-maximisation to guarantee the functioning of public policy rules. For example, it is argued that one of the failings of the rules-based approach is that prescriptive rules are often introduced too late to rectify market misconduct that has occurred. The high level principles, instead, will reduce market misconducts because they establish the nature and limits of the market players' duty to obey the law in different forms of state and are easier for compliance than the minutiae of prescriptive rules. In the same vein, the morality of commercial law-making regards proportionality as a critical measuring tool or safeguard test.

The philosophical idea of maximising the "good" such as utility, happiness, pleasure or other human positives, requires individual rights or interests be subsumed and aggregated in a general calculation about what is best for the general population or overall majority. In light of "proportionality", the decision-makers shall assess whether the rule or decision limiting the right was necessary, for example, meeting a pressing social need. As far as public policy is concerned, the assessment should be made on whether the judicial interference is really proportionate to the legitimate aim being pursued, judicially or administratively. The assessment would then rule out such judicial interference with commercial rights that is disproportionate to the policy objectives in question.

Under the normative approach, prescriptive standards or rules would be replaced by high level principles focusing on how best to act in a general situation, rather than simply following a mechanistic process such as a tick-box approach to prescriptive rules. The key principles incorporated in the normative public policy may include (i) a narrow construction of public policy in light of the overriding purpose of the New York Convention; (ii) an avoidance of applying vague, abstract or all-encompassing terms such as "principles of the law", and (iii) an increased application of a *favor arbitrandum* stance. As a general rule, the normative approach is moving towards "attenuated" rather than "strict" public policy norms and is fundamentally centred on the notion of public choice. Like a choice-of-law system that allocates political power among

---

(b) the parties should be free to agree how their disputes are resolved, subject only to such safeguards as are necessary in the public interest;
(c) in matters governed by this Part, the court should not intervene except as provided by this Part.

158 (1853) 4 HLCI.

the states, the normative approach to public policy also tends to achieve the similar objective among the state courts, arbitration institutions and arbitrating parties.

The prescriptive public policy in substance is a form of "interest analysis", which focuses on the states' political objectives and values as reflected in the legislation. In contrast, the emphasis on the state interests and powers is misguided in the normative public policy because political leaders including legislators cannot be expected to maximise social welfare. As Commissioner McCreevy observed, "politicians are not there to dictate to market participants what they should do or not do".[159] The political decision-making is infected by agency costs that inevitably follow the delegation of power. Normative public policy can help to alleviate political agency costs by letting the parties involved in arbitration avoid inefficient mandatory rules by individual action[160] because they, as economic players, can make their own choice of locating the enforcement forum based upon sound economic reasoning (*e.g.*, comparing different results in various jurisdictions).[161]

Is normative public policy likely to produce an efficient result? Traditionally, it had been up to the courts to articulate the philosophy underlying arbitration laws. A clear theory can serve as a focal point that augments the effect of jurisdictional competition in moving the law towards efficiency and efficacy, without sacrificing clarity and predictability. This is illustrated by contrast with a system that lacks a clear theory, *i.e.*, a kind of grand description accommodating all of the various judicial approaches to public policy,[162] or a baseline presumption that courts can ignore if a multi-faceted analysis indicates that another state's law most appropriately applies.[163] This system ends up sanctioning whatever the courts want to do, thereby contributing to the judicial agency costs, and further frustrates parties who seek to determine the law applicable to the proceedings before they engage in it.

The principle-based normative approach, in its robust form, supports and articulates a legislative or judicial standard by which judicial decisions on arbitrable matters and public policy can be more critically evaluated. Although

---

159 Charlie McCreevy, Speech at EP Hearing on Cross-border Consolidation, 31 January 2006.

160 This argument has been made in the securities law context. See Roberta Romano, 'Empowering Investors: A Market Approach to Securities Regulation', (1998) 107 *Yale L.J.* (1998) 2359, 2395–99, 2415–18 (arguing that more favorable securities laws can result under the choice-of-law clause approach if state regulatory competition replaces federal securities regulation).

161 Charlie McCreevy, Speech at EP Hearing on Cross-border Consolidation, 31 January 2006.

162 See William A. Reppy, Jr., 'Eclecticism in Choice of Law: Hybrid Method or Mishmash?', (1983) 34 *Mercer L. Rev.* 645, 655–66.

163 Compare Jason E. Pepe, 'Comment, Kansas's Conflict of Laws Rules for Insurance Contract Cases: It's Time to Change Policies', (1998) 46 *University of Kansas Law Review* 819, 828–29 (noting that some jurisdictions essentially ignore the presumptive rule in favour of the most significant relationship test).

the normative approach applies public policy on a case-by-case, issue-by-issue and *ad hoc* basis, taking into account the specific subject-matter and dispute at stake, it may exclude some technical or mechanical defects of arbitration, *i.e.*, the arbitrator's mistake in his findings of law or evidence,[164] and a breach of a domestic statute[165] or regulation.[166] Taken at face value, the normative rule is likely to result in a reduction in detailed and complex rules and standards. The outcome of this normative device therefore is a narrowing range of public policy, which may only target "palpable and indisputable illegality",[167] and must involve a violation of the most basic notions of morality and justice,[168] drawing universal or near universal condemnation from the world's legal systems.

Seen in this light, normative public policy is in essence a pro-arbitration policy, a value shared in common with almost all jurisdictions,[169] applicable not only to reciprocal enforcement of foreign arbitral awards but also to restrain judicial intervention in international commercial arbitration. Accordingly, any easy or quick reliance on, or reference to, the public policy defence may constitute a breach of public policy in the international arbitration arena. Corresponding to this outcome-determinative rule, the steady case law jurisprudence has also shown that, for instance, in the United States, all non-penal statutes are eligible for arbitral enforcement. The normative public policy, in a plain but powerful phrase, is, as *Mitsubishi* posited, an "emphatic … policy in favour of arbitral dispute resolution".[170] Both statutes and case law in many

164 Case law is not uniform on this. For instance, the Indian Supreme Court held in *Oil & Natural Gas Corporation Ltd. v. SAW Pipes Ltd.*, AIR 2003 SC 2629 that an arbitral award which was wrong in law was "patently illegal" and liable to be set aside on the ground that it was in conflict with the public policy of India. Neither the Malaysian High Court nor the Singapore courts agreed with this approach. *Colliers International property Consultants (USA) v. Colliers Jordan Lee and Jaafar (Malaysia)*, Suit Nos R3(1)-24-06-2008 and R3(1)-24-07-2008 (High Court, Malaysia) at pp. 32–33.

165 *Omnium de Traitment et de Valorisation SA v. Hilmarton Ltd.* [1999] 2 Lloyd's Rep 222, 224. In the instant case, a Switzerland-seat ICC tribunal found that an underlying agreement had violated an Algerian statute (the law of the place of performance) but was lawful under Swiss law (the governing law of agreement). The tribunal dismissed an allegation of bribery. Walker J enforced the award in England on the grounds that what needed to be adjudicated on was enforcement of an arbitral award based on Swiss law.

166 *Colliers International Property Consultants (USA) v. Colliers Jordan Lee and Jaafar (Malaysia)*, Suit Nos R3(1)-24-06-2008 and R3(1)-24-07-2008 (High Court, Malaysia).

167 *Soleimany v. Soleimany* [1999] QB 785.

168 *AJT v. AJU* [2011] SGCA 41 at [38]; *Parsons & Whittemore Overseas Co., Inc. v. Société Générale de l'Industrie du Papier (RAKTA)*, 508 F.2d 969 (2nd Cir. 1974). However, the International Law Association Commercial Arbitration Committee made a distinction between mandatory rules and fundamental principles of justice and morality. International Law Association Final Report (presented at the ILA's 17th Conference in New Delhi 2002, available at http://www.ila.hq.org), Recommendations.

169 The term is borrowed from Bernhard Grossfeld and C. Paul Rogers, 'A Shared Values Approach to Jurisdictional Conflicts in International Economic Law', (1983) 32 *ICLQ* 931, 939.

170 *Mitsubishi Motors Corp. v. Soler Chrysler-Plymouth Inc.*, 473 US at 631.

other countries are becoming equally pro-arbitration.[171] The solution devised here is a doctrinal approach that articulates a new vision of arbitration, an idiosyncratic standard of a choice-of-law system,[172] that not only entirely relies upon party autonomy but also balances party autonomy with other fundamental judicial or policy considerations. The main technical thrust of this normative approach is a narrower interpretation of "public policy", which will in great measure give rise to greater success of the New York Convention.[173] Reliance on a normative approach, in metaphors, may well help rein the "unruly horse" from leaping into the dark.

5.3. NORMATIVE PUBLIC POLICY IN THE GAMING CONTEXT

The notion of public policy is a changing concept in line with a state's level of development, economic, legal, religious or political persuasions. Therefore, no matter what approach a state court takes, "the content of the [public policy] rules should vary from country to country and from era to era".[174] The prescriptive public policy theory may be less able to reflect this changing character of public policy and has revealed the defects and drawbacks in current legislation and case law that merely explain the inferiority of modern public law and call for a higher level of regulation of public policy. Besides, the diversity and divergence of national public policy may make the determination of an independent internationally acceptable minimum both imperative and difficult.[175] This Part explores what normative public policy is, whether the normative public policy method is feasible in practice and which institution, if any, should take the lead in assisting the production of normative public policy. Section 3.1 defines normative public policy on the basis of efficiency and explains problems of inefficient laws and causes of such problems. Sections 3.2 to 3.4 introduce various theories as to viable approaches to deal with inefficient public policy. Section 3.2 discusses the route by which the private parties can avoid a hostile jurisdiction by escaping to another jurisdiction. Competition and cooperation are analysed in sections 3.3 and 3.4 respectively as alternative long-term methods of overcoming impediments to insufficient public policy.

---

171 George A. Bermann, 'The Origin and Operation of Mandatory Rules', in George A. Bermann and Loukas A. Mistelis (eds.), *Mandatory Rules in International Arbitration*, New York: Juris Net LLC (2011) p. 19.

172 See generally, Horatia Muir Watt, 'Choice of Law in Integrated and Interconnected Markets: A Matter of Political Economy', (2003) 9 *Colum. J. Eur. L.* 383, 407.

173 Joseph Lookofsky and Ketilbjorn Hertz, *Transnational Litigation and Commercial Arbitration – An Analysis of American, European, and International Law*, Copenhagen: Juris Net LLC (3rd edn. 2011) p. 921.

174 *CBI NZ Ltd. v. Badger Chiyoda* [1989] 2 NZLR 669 at 674.

175 Karl-Heinz Bockstiegel, above n. 112, 176, 178–181.

5.3.1. NORMATIVE PUBLIC POLICY – EFFICIENCY-CENTRED APPROACH TO PUBLIC POLICY

Compared to prescriptive public policy, normative public policy is not made up of an exhaustive list of items that are deemed to be critical to public interests nor a complete description of basic components or features of public policy which have been scattered throughout a large number of cases and legislation.[176] Instead, the major standard underlying normative public policy should be efficiency or efficacy, which is a key economic factor in determining the value, justifying a norm or system and measuring aggregate welfare from minimum to maximum. The public policy rule is closely linked to the choice-of-law or contractual choice principle. To apply this comparison at the judicial level, the public policy grounds should be construed or applied extremely narrowly. The narrow construction of public policy is also reflected in a broader range of arbitrable matters, which in turn indicates the judicial recognition of arbitration as an important and growing tool in procuring the speedy, efficient and fair resolution of disputes. The perverse effects of inefficient public policy rules can be mitigated to the extent that parties may avoid the application of these laws[177] by escaping from the hostile jurisdiction or altering the contract. On the other hand, the parties' ability to choose and evade laws reduces the benefits generated by efficient public policy.

The problem of inefficient public policy is best described by using simple algebra. It can be assumed that, if parties cannot avoid the dispute or settle their dispute on their own, *i.e.*, through mediation or friendly consultation, and then have to apply a law, the law generates aggregate benefits B while imposing social costs C. If those burdened by the law have some ability to opt out of its application, the costs are reduced by the amount $C[e]$. Also, the law's benefits might be reduced by an amount $B[e]$ through parties' ability to avoid application of the law. The rule of thumb is that a *law* is efficient if $B - B[e] > C - C[e]$. As the law may be subject to the parties' free choice, exit is an important element in calculating the efficiency of law. Exit may not only mitigate the effect of an enacted law but also deter the enactment of a law. Increasing the availability of

176 These basic features or components include global justice and equality, uniform moral values, international institutional and economic order, international democracy, civil and political human rights, right to a standard of living adequate for the health and well-being, etc. See Thomas W. Pogge, 'Priorities of Global Justice', in Thomas W. Pogge (ed.), *Global Justice*, Boston: Blackwell (2001). Since these elements are largely morality-based, they are not a better target for the legal study compared to the efficiency, which can be "economically" measured. However, these moral values can become a universal minimum of the efficiency-centred public policy.

177 See Bruce H. Kobayashi and Larry E. Ribstein, 'Contract and Jurisdictional Competition', in F.H. Buckley (ed.), *The Fall and Rise of Freedom of Contract*, Durham, NC: Duke University Press (1999) p. 325 (arguing that validating choice-of-law clauses will lead parties to opt out of inefficient laws, promoting jurisdictional competition between states to pass efficient laws).

exit increases both *B[e]* and *C[e]*. A law allowing an exit is efficient if *C[e]* > *B[e]*, which suggests that exit reduces the law's overall costs by more than it reduces the law's benefits.[178] Exit is also important in the discussion of public policy. The efficiency of public policy depends upon the extent to which the rules increase social wealth by enabling exit from inefficient laws or, conversely, reduce social wealth by blocking access to efficient laws. As the effect of law on those benefiting from the law and those suffering costs from the law will vary from one person or transaction to another, there is no reason to believe that law, *i.e.*, a public policy rule, will affect *B[e]* and *C[e]* equally.[179] The normative public policy rules, nevertheless, are in support of an exit since the non-prescriptive rules allow more flexibility in choice-of-law by the parties. The normative public policy may be used to enhance *C[e]* while simultaneously preserving *B* as the reduction of exit costs may increase both *B[e]* and *C[e]* and higher exit costs can increase social welfare for the law with high *B* and low *C*. Therefore, in theory, normative public policy is able to strengthen efficient laws while mitigating inefficient ones. Such rules should help ensure the application of laws that produce efficiencies but not those that produce inefficiencies. In other words, a *law* that is supported by or compatible with normative public policy is efficient if *B* – *B[e]* > *C* – *C[e]*. A full scale discussion will touch upon the basic problem of inefficient laws, the exit as a potential solution, the potential for choice of law to facilitate an exit from inefficient laws.

Certainly, it is still necessary to define "efficiency" first. There are many theoretical and practical ways to define efficiency or to determine *a priori* the relevant costs and benefits of a particular law. In the context of arbitration, the notion of efficiency may also contain the element of efficacy, which is often considered by legislature, courts, arbitrators and commentators.[180] In a jurisprudential sense, the term "efficiency" is an ethical criterion in social decision-making, *i.e.*, the extent to which courts enhance the democratically enacted law. If so, the parties should not be able to escape even the law, the primary effect of which is to transfer social wealth. Economically, the term efficiency denotes that allocation of resources in which value is maximised.[181] Accordingly, an inefficient law may be characterised as one that primarily redistributes wealth while imposing deadweight transfer costs. However, the

---

178 The overall efficiency of law can be analysed in light of the public choice implications of the law. By reducing the effect of laws, exit can decrease both the support of interest group proponents and the opposition of those who would be burdened by laws. See Erin A. O'Hara, 'Opting Out of Regulation: A Public Choice Analysis of Contractual Choice of Law', (2000) 53 *Vanderbilt Law Review* 1551.

179 This tension between *B[e]* and *C[e]* cannot be easy to resolve without empirical data on the efficiency of law.

180 *e.g.*, "Arbitration needs the support of national law if it works effectively". Alan Redfern, 'International Commercial Arbitration: Jurisdiction Denied: The Pyramid Collapses', [1986] *JBL* 15.

181 Richard A. Posner, *Economic Analysis of Law*, New York: Aspen Publishers, Inc. (5th edn. 1998) p. 13.

society as well as the judicial and legislative bodies may regard the redistribution itself as an aspect of *B* rather than of *C*. In practice, the efficiency of a law can also depend upon the extent to which it suits individual parties or transactions that are subject to the law.[182] In other words, if a law is ill-suited for some parties or transactions, *C* rises with the number of these parties and transactions and with the magnitude of the costs imposed upon these parties or transactions.

The concept of normative public policy, the legitimacy of which is based on party autonomy, is arguably an optimal legislative or judicial method of allocating resources. This is the case because party choice is made on the basis of contracts, which produces few externalities and in turn reduces transaction costs. In addition, the normative approach greatly streamlines the process of collaboration between arbitration institutions and domestic courts on the dispute settlement. The allocation of judicial resources would be optimised as courts also have incentives to uphold private bargaining[183] and put heavy hands off the public policy cases. Consistency, a product of this approach, would further enhance the court's expertise and reputation in performing its functions.

In most cross-border arbitration cases, multinational companies are key players (either as claimants or respondents). The national courts may choose to apply a restrictive judicial approach towards the international arbitral awards, which means the court may narrowly interpret the term "public interest" or "public policy" and restrictively intervene into the arbitrators' ruling power. The underlying rationale of this judicial approach, is to promote international trade and investment. By doing so, the courts may ignore or show less respect for the counter parties' rights or interests.[184] Thus, the normative approach, through recognising and promoting party autonomy, itself serves a regulatory function, largely correcting overly intrusive public policy and thereby improving global welfare.[185] To borrow law and economics terminology, in a semi-strong form, this approach may eliminate many uncertainties or vagueness surrounding the concept of public policy. In its strongest form, it can help reduce the likelihood of applying public policy rules.[186]

---

182 This refers to default rules as well as to mandatory rules because of the potential costs of drafting around default rules. See Ronald H. Coase, 'The Problem of Social Cost', (1960) 3 *J. L. & Econ.* 1, 15–19 (discussing the significance of transaction costs for legal rules). Public policy rules arguably make an entire body of state law a "default" rule and may be a less costly alternative to drafting around each rule individually because of lower transaction costs.

183 Michael Whincop and Mary Keyes, 'Putting the "Private" Back into Private International Law: Default Rules and the Proper Law of the Contract', (1997) 21 *Melbourne University Law Review* 515, 542.

184 Joel R. Paul, 'Comity in International Law', (1991) 32 *Harv. Int'l L.J.* 1, 65.

185 Increasing legislative or judicial efficiency increases welfare. In a global setting, the availability of more sophisticated rules for the regulation of particular transactions to "outsiders" (private parties, arbitrators, arbitration institutions, courts and legislatures) also increases global welfare. For the latter argument, see Erin Ann O'Hara, 'Economics, Public Choice, and the Perennial Conflict of Laws', (2002) 90 *Geo. L.J.* 941, 943.

186 The theory has been developed in other branches of law such as securities regulation and bankruptcy law. See generally, Stephen J. Choi and Andrew T. Guzman, 'Portable Reciprocity:

The efficiency of public policy rests on the extent to which it suits the society or community as a whole. The analysis here focuses on two limbs of efficiency. First, it is important to spot potential inefficiencies in statutory law, including judicial and administrative interpretation and application of statutes. The costs and benefits of a statute depend on the baseline of case law,[187] customary rules, judicial interpretation or other legal rules. Efficiency of legal rules is likely to occur in an evolutionary mechanism in which inefficient rules are more likely to be challenged and ruled out through litigation and arbitration[188] due to temporary balances in rent-seeking pressures.[189] Second, it is also important to assess exit costs which critically impact the formation of efficiency-centred public policy. Given the focus of this book, the approach adopted here is to analyse which institution is able to formulate efficient public policy. In commercial arbitration, the main institutions involved are two state bodies, that is, legislatures and courts, and one non-public body, *i.e.*, arbitration institutions and arbitrators, all of which have a natural duty to promote and protect the efficiency of the legal system. The discussion will also indicate why inefficient public policy exists and how to deal with such inefficiency.

5.3.1.1. Legislatures

As the political agent, legislatures and legislators are responsible for enacting laws, either efficient or inefficient. Agency costs always exist whenever the power, whether administrative or judicial, is delegated to agents such as political representatives and government agencies. However, it is difficult to closely monitor the exertion of the delegated power by the legislators or legislature. It is claimed that statutes, made by the legislative or administrative agencies,[190] are not efficient, as legislators are rent creators or seekers for interest groups[191] and extract rents from interest groups in return for forbearing from regulating.[192] For the purpose of rent-seeking, legislators may increase their campaign contributions, lobbying efforts and other perks by brokering wealth transfers

Rethinking the International Reach of Securities Regulation', (1998) 71 *S. Cal. L. Rev.* 2003; Robert K. Rasmussen, 'A New Approach to Transnational Insolvencies', (1997) 19 *Michigan Journal of International Law* 1.

187 For arguments that common law is efficient, see George L. Priest, 'The Common Law Process and the Selection of Efficient Rules', (1977) 6 *J. Legal Stud.* 65–66 (arguing that efficient outcomes of common law are largely immune to individual biases of judges). For arguments to the contrary, William M. Landes and Richard A. Posner, 'Adjudication as a Private Good', (1979) 8 *J. Legal Stud.* 280–84.

188 Paul H. Rubin, 'Why is the Common Law Efficient?', (1977) 6(1) *J. Legal Stud.* 51–52.

189 Martin J. Bailey and Paul H. Rubin, 'A Positive Theory of Legal Change', (1994) 14 *International Review of Law and Economics* 467, 468–69.

190 J.W. Harris, *Legal Philosophies*, London: Butterworths (2nd edn. 1997) p. 49.

191 See Robert D. Tollison, 'Public Choice and Legislation', (1988) 74 *Va. L. Rev.* 339, 361–62.

192 See Fred S. McChesney, 'Rent Extraction and Rent Creation in the Economic Theory of Regulation', (1987) 16 *J. Legal Stud.* 101, 102–05.

that end up favouring some interest groups at the expense of others.[193] Logically, most statutes are the products of the pressures brought by the competing interest groups.[194] The winning interest groups are those who can organise most effectively and least expensively to raise and spend funds, or to mobilise political resources, *i.e.*, votes.[195] The resulting legislation may fail to serve the interests of a majority of voters but only of a particular group of people. In our context, for example, it is common to see large corporations requiring their employees to sign labour contracts which have a standard arbitration clause arbitrating all disputes involving discrimination, harassment or termination. A lobby of trial lawyers in the US has also led many states to enact legislation to "protect" consumers or employees from arbitration.[196] More importantly, from the perspective of social welfare, the proponent interest group's gains from the law may not outweigh the losses for the rest of society. In an extreme case, the State of Alabama, for example, regards enforcement of arbitration clauses agreed prior to the origin of the dispute, *i.e.*, an arbitration clause in standard form contract, as being against public policy.[197]

Even legislatures and legislators motivated to enhance social welfare are not necessarily perfect agents in reality. First, legislatures or legislators lack perfect knowledge and foresight about the effects of laws. Second, legislatures or legislators with perfect knowledge and foresight may still be unable to craft efficient regulation because of a lack of legislative skills. Third, given the incentives and self-interests of legislators and interest groups, a piece of well-crafted legislation may not be efficient because the law may impose net costs on some people even if it has net benefits as applied to others. For example, it may be understandable for the legislature, perhaps after the lobbying efforts of interest groups such as state-owned giants, to pass the law or adopt the public policy to protect the state-owned sector and state-owned assets from being the subject of enforcement of foreign arbitral awards. Nevertheless, such protection offered by the legislation may harm other economic sectors and eventually harm the neutrality of the arbitration regime, the entire legal system and the interests of the whole society. Fourth, the efficiency of law is also closely linked with the market. The incidence of burdens and benefits depends upon elasticities of

---

193 See Robert E. McCormick and Robert D. Tollison, *Politicians, Legislation, and the Economy: An Inquiry into the Interest Group Theory of Government,* Boston, The Hague and London: Martinus Nijhoff Publishing (1981) (applying interest group theory to legislatures).

194 J.W. Harris, above n. 190, 49.

195 See Mancur Olson, *The Logic of Collective Action: Public Goods and the Theory of Groups,* Cambridge, MA: Harvard University Press (1971) pp. 53–57 (arguing that these features have made small groups historically effective).

196 David J. Branson, 'Arbitrability and Pre-emption: More Litigation in the United States', (1996) 12(2) *Arb. Int'l* 163.

197 Ibid.

supply and demand in particular markets.[198] As it has been rightly pointed out, "virtually any individual piece of legislation will generate both a plausible private-interest and a plausible public-interest explanation".[199] For example, the forum-biased public law can expand litigation opportunities. Should public policy grant discretionary power to the courts to supervise arbitrators and tribunals' malpractice or misconduct for the purpose of protecting society and interest parties in the case? Is it a justifiable public policy to ensure that only foreign arbitral awards will have the privilege of being the subject of procedural review only, thus limiting party autonomy of domestic parties which are subject to substantive review in local arbitration or vice versa? The difficulty of determining whether any particular law or public policy is efficient suggests the necessity of preserving a role for individuals and firms to decide for themselves the laws that apply to them.

5.3.1.2. Courts

Courts play a critical role in effecting and implementing black letter rules and making rules functional. Courts also play a critical role in making law efficient[200] because judges "legislate new legal rights and apply them retrospectively to the case at hand",[201] and the significance of judges' residual function is increasingly more important while the court is being re-conceptualised explicitly as a supervised negotiated order.[202] As a result of judicial intervention, courts have placed themselves in a pivotal position to influence the pace, pattern and direction of legal evolution and integration on matters of economic and social regulation. In theory, courts are at least able to use judicial interpretations or precedents to mitigate inefficiencies created by legislation. However, courts may not be expected to play a constructive role in checking legislative efficiency or inefficiency and bargains because courts are also rent-seeking and the judicial lawmaking process involves agency costs.[203] It would be highly unlikely that every doctrine and decision adjudicated by the court is efficient given the nature of judges' incentives. State court judges have some incentives to respond to legislators' interests and concerns to the extent

198 See Erin O'Hara and Larry E. Ribstein, 'Interest Groups, Contracts and Interest Analysis', (1997) 48 *Mercer L. Rev.* (1997) 765, 766–67.

199 See Jerry L. Mashaw, *Greed, Chaos and Governance: Using Public Choice to Improve Public Law*, New Haven: Yale University Press (1997) p. 37.

200 See Robert Cooter and Lewis Kornhauser, 'Can Litigation Improve the Law Without the Help of Judges?', (1980) 9 *J. Legal Stud.* 139, 140–41 (arguing that unguided evolution of law does not by itself maximise economic efficiency).

201 Ronald Dworkin, above n. 148, 81.

202 See Simon Roberts, 'What is a Court?' (unpublished paper in 2007, on file with the author).

203 See Bruce Hay, 'Conflicts of Law and State Competition in the Product Liability System', (1992) 80 *Geo. L.J.* (arguing that the courts have competing incentives to entice plaintiffs or favour local litigants).

that the latter control judges' salary[204] and tenure.[205] In this case, judges might actually increase the durability and value of the legislature and guarantee the stability of interest group deals by enforcing the legislation within the state.[206] In addition, judges may also have incentives to serve the interest group,[207] which substantially affects their ability to maximise the wealth of society.

Judges may experience difficulties in acting in the public interest as an independent body due to the difficulties in isolating themselves from the pressures of legislature or interest groups. Judges may be particularly responsive to the interests of domestic lawyers, who are motivated to compete for and protect their own interests as well as the economic and social interests of local interest groups.[208] For example, lawyers are claimed to have competing interests to push for limited liability company statutory provisions in a jurisdiction.[209] The interdependence and correlation between judges and lawyers would also require judges to respond to or act in respect of the domestic lawyers' agenda. In some countries, judges may be nominated and recommended by bar associations. Most judges may seek to return to practice or work in the legal profession after they leave the bench. Judges are naturally attuned to the lawyers' interests or thinking because of their legal training and professional association. Lawyers' concerns such as the increased litigation costs are often reflected in judgments[210] and would influence the court's attitudes towards legal changes.[211] Lawyers are often politically motivated to protect local interests. For instance, lawyers

204 See Gary M. Anderson, William F. Shughart II and Robert D. Tollison, 'On the Incentives of Judges to Enforce Legislative Wealth Transfers', (1989) 32 *J. L. & Econ.* 215, 217, 220–26 (arguing with empirical evidence that legislative control of judicial salaries is used as a reward for upholding legislative output).

205 See Edward Hartnett, 'Why Is the Supreme Court of the United States Protecting State Judges from Popular Democracy?', (1997) 75 *Tex. L. Rev.* 907, 975 (only three states in the US grant *de facto* life tenure).

206 William M. Landes and Richard A. Posner, 'The Independent Judiciary in an Interest-Group Perspective', (1975) 18 *J. L. & Econ.* 875, 877–88.

207 Richard S. Murphy and Erin A. O'Hara, 'Mistake of Federal Criminal Law: A Study of Coalitions and Costly Information', (1997) 5 *Sup. Ct Econ. Rev.* (1997) 217, 274–76 (giving an example of how court rulings on mistake of law can strengthen an interest group bargain made with the legislature).

208 See Erin A. O'Hara and William R. Dougan, 'Redistribution Through Discriminatory Taxes: A Contractarian Explanation of the Role of the Courts', (1998) 6 *Geo. Mason U. L. Rev.* 869, 914–16 (arguing that the Delaware bar has an incentive to lobby for seemingly innocuous statutory changes for the purpose of extracting rents from the initial wave of clarifying litigation).

209 Larry E. Ribstein, 'Statutory Forms for Closely Held Firms: Theories and Evidence from LLCs', (1995) 73 *Wash. U. L. Q.* 369, 412–30.

210 Larry E. Ribstein, 'The Mandatory Nature of the ALI Code', (1993) 61 *Geo. Wash. L. Rev.* 984, 1023 (claiming that lawyers' support for changes to the corporate governance code is due to the differential impact of increased litigation costs).

211 Jonathan R. Macey, 'Judicial Preferences, Public Choice, and the Rules of Procedure', (1994) 23 *J. Legal Stud.* (1994) 627, 628 (stating that the bar is unlikely to support procedural changes that serve to minimise the cost of litigation).

actively attract litigation to the state as business, whether or not the litigation produces efficient incentives. To this end, lawyers may participate in drafting uniform laws and creating complex and vague provisions in order to serve their institutional interests.[212] Given their close relationship with the local bar, judges may have personal biases such as self-interests or social status privileges (or prejudices) that skew their decisions.[213] It was argued that "Delaware lawyers, in essence, are the Delaware legislature, at least insofar as corporate law is concerned".[214] Although appellate courts and reputational considerations may discipline judges at the lower level,[215] such constraints are imperfect and of limited practical value simply because court decisions are effectively insulated from reversal on appeal in arbitration cases, as "a judge's managerial decisions are interlocutory in nature".[216] In any event, arbitral awards are subject to a lenient "abuse of discretion" in the judicial review process. Since very few precedents have been created in the area of public policy, lower-level judges may be tempted to do justice in individual cases without taking into account the effect on future cases.[217]

Given both information asymmetry and agency costs, there is little reason to assume that judges' decisions on the scope and content of public policy would be significantly more efficient than those made by legislators or, in particular, by the parties themselves. Practically speaking, even well-motivated judges lack the investigative and policymaking apparatus necessary to reliably or accurately evaluate the relative efficiency of public policy in the case of arbitration. Judges may be faithful agents of the legislature and government in effectuating legislators' interest group deals and may have self-interested reasons for implementing forum-based and restrictive public policy. The legislature is certainly in a position to monitor the enforcement of public policy and to amend legislation when judicial decisions go awry.[218] Nevertheless, it has been

---

212 See Jonathan R. Macey and Geoffrey P. Miller, 'Toward an Interest-Group Theory of Delaware Corporate Law', (1987) 65 *Tex. L. Rev.* 469, 505 (discussing that the Delaware bar "has some interest in reducing the clarity of Delaware law to enhance the amount of litigation").

213 See Richard A. Epstein, 'The Independence of Judges: The Uses and Limitations of Public Choice Theory', (1990) *BYU L. Rev.* 827, 831–38.

214 Larry E. Ribstein, 'Delaware, Lawyers, and Contractual Choice of Law', (1994) 19 *Del. J. Corp. L.* 999, 1007–12.

215 See Erin Ann O'Hara, 'Social Constraint or Implicit Collusion?: Toward a Game Theoretic Analysis of Stare Decisis', (1993) 24 *Seton Hall L. Rev.* 746, 767–68.

216 See Jonathan T. Molot, 'How Changes in the Legal Profession Reflect Changes in Civil Procedure', (1998) 84 *Va. L. Rev.* 955, 1004.

217 See Stewart E. Sterk, 'The Marginal Relevance of Choice of Law Theory', (1994) 142 *U. Pa. L. Rev.* 949, 993–96 (citing the comments of Charles D. Breitel, former Chief Judge of the New York Court of Appeals that judges first approach cases by asking themselves which party deserved to win and then move on the question: what harm to the jurisprudence will result if I do justice in the individual case?).

218 See Martin H. Malin and Robert F. Ladenson, 'Privatising Justice: A Jurisprudential Perspective on Labor and Employment Arbitration from the Steelworker's Trilogy to Gilmer', (1993) 44 *Hastings Law Journal* 1187, 1237–38.

recognised that courts normally view the forum's law as "better".[219] It is likely that courts would lean on local public policy, efficient or inefficient. In reducing the effect of inefficient public policy while preserving its ability to monitor arbitration efficiently, courts could either try to determine which public policy is more efficient and apply it, or apply rules that allow affected parties make the decision themselves. This latter alternative seems consistent with the doctrine of party autonomy in commercial arbitration. Therefore, in order to make public policy more efficient, it is important to decrease the chances and occasions where courts may intervene in the business community by resorting to public policy, and increase arbitrating parties' opportunity to choose among competing legal regimes.[220] This so-called "self-restraint" approach has been adopted by courts in some cases,[221] and is more favoured over the more traditional but expansive approach, that is, a judicial re-examination of allegations of illegality, propounded in other cases.[222]

Amid the globalisation evidenced by the demands of transnational commerce and the growing interdependence of states, there emerged a need for greater international cooperation in the judicial field. The role of courts in the trend towards globalisation can be important on some disparate issues such as the globalisation of the judiciary, that is, "judicial globalisation," through judicial networks, the proliferation of tribunals at the international level, and the use of foreign law in local judicial decision-making processes. Judicial cooperation may take a variety of forms including heightened communication across courts and greater willingness to review or accept foreign decisions when interpreting domestic standards.[223] Within this climate, there are more chances to see a resurgence of interest in the application of uniform public policy standards as one specific form of judicial cooperation in cross-border arbitration cases.[224]

---

219 See Robert A. Leflar, 'Choice-Influencing Considerations in Conflicts Law', (1966) 41 *NYU L. Rev.* 267, 298–99.

220 Richard A. Posner, above n. 181, 570 (claiming that a judge will naturally ask which of the competing activities is more valuable in an economic sense).

221 *Westacre Investments, Inc. v. Jugoimport-SDPR Holding Co. Ltd.* [2000] QB 740 at 767–8 and 784 (*per* Colman J); *Westacre Investments, Inc. v. Jugoimport-SDPR Holding Co. Ltd.* [2000] QB 288 at 316–17 (*per* Mantell LJ) and at 317 (*per* Sir David Hirst); *AJT v. AJU*, SGCA 41 at 41–60.

222 *Westacre Investments, Inc. v. Jugoimport-SDPR Holding Co. Ltd.* [2000] QB 288, at 314–5; *Soleimany v. Soleimany* [1999] QB 785, at 800 and 803.

223 38, 39 and 40 *Tex. Int'l L.J.* (2003, 2004 and 2005) (symposia on judicial globalisation providing an overview of these issues).

224 In international litigation, the line of cases, as suggested by some commentators, suggests a trend towards narrowing the scope of application of forum mandatory rules. Meanwhile there has been no trend towards increased application of foreign mandatory rule, which is less relevant to the topic here. Hannah L. Buxbaum, 'Mandatory Rules in Civil Litigation: Status of the Doctrine Post-Globalisation', above n. 110, 47.

5.3.1.3. *Arbitration Institutions, Arbitral Tribunals and Arbitrators*

The role of arbitrators, arbitration institutions, or arbitration tribunals is closely related to the question whether they have a duty or obligation to pay more attention to, apply or enforce public policy. There are basically two lines of thinking: either considering them as nothing more than "the servant of the parties" with allegiances to the parties that appoint them or to the state that supports them,[225] or identifying them as "jurists whose first dedication is to law".[226] These are two opposite schools of thought: while one is a contract-based private role, the other leans towards a social or jurisdictional model. Correspondingly, arbitrators or arbitration institutions are under no obligations to apply or enforce public policy from the lenses of contract. Nonetheless, they would be bound by such duties if arbitration were viewed as adjudication.[227] These two schools of thought somehow match the other pair of competing "philosophies", which have been reflected in law and practice in various jurisdictions. England and Germany have taken a "territorial" approach taking the view that the position of arbitrators is akin to that of judges at the seat of arbitration.[228] By contrast, France has conceived of arbitrators as truly international judges anchored in a multitude of legal orders and subject to an autonomous legal order.[229]

Arbitrators can be regarded as the agents of the parties. In *George Watts & Son v. Tiffany & Co*,[230] Judge Easterbrook used an agency perspective to argue for greater deference to arbitrator's interpretation of law. The agency theory developed by Judge Easterbrook is that arbitrators, being agents of the parties, ought to be able to exercise powers delegated to them by their principals. The classic problem surrounding the agency problem is that the agent may ignore the wishes of the principal and act in his own interest. To reduce agency slack, a certain level of screening is necessary. Review of awards becomes a device for agency control.[231] However, under this theory, judicial review is no longer suitable because the private parties have not granted any power to judges in

225 Marc Blessing, 'Mandatory Rules of Law versus Party Autonomy in International Arbitration', (1997) 14(4) *J. Int'l Arb.* 23, 40; Andrew Barraclough and Jeff Waincymer, 'Mandatory Rules of Law in International Commercial Arbitration', (2005) 6 *Melbourne J. Int'l L.* 205, 206.

226 Andreas F. Lowenfeld, 'The Mitsubishi Case: Another View', (1986) 2 *Arb. Int'l* 178, 188.

227 A third, more positivist, approach is that the arbitrator's duty is imposed by the arbitration rules. For example, Article 35 of the Rules of Arbitration of the International Chamber of Commerce requires arbitrators "to make every effort to make sure that the Award is enforceable at law". This approach has not pierced the veil of an arbitrator's function or role at the theoretical level.

228 Emmanuel Gaillard, *Aspects philosophiques du droit de l'arbitrage international*, Leiden: Martinus Nijhoff Publishers (2008) pp. 34–46.

229 Ibid. 46–100.

230 248 F.3d 577 (7th Cir. 2001).

231 Screening in the labour market or hiring a second agent to monitor the first one is not feasible in the context of arbitration. Arbitration is confidential so there is not an open market for

order to monitor arbitration. Instead, the courts (or judges) are more appropriately categorised as agents of the legislature or the public as a whole, who may suffer if the arbitrating parties can call on judges' limited time or resources for their own private purposes. Enhancing judicial economy (*i.e.*, not subsidising private dispute resolution by courts) requires less involvement of mandatory rules in the first place in solving disputes and less policing over arbitration later on. In other words, an agency perspective would allow the parties, and ultimately arbitrators, more freedom in agreeing on the scope (or standard) of review.[232] The contract-based agency framework essentially limits a regime of *de novo* review.

Alternatively, arbitration institutions (or arbitrators) can be theoretically regarded as sub-agents of courts given the court's view of delegating judicial power to arbitrators in adjudicating "disputes". Consequently, as a practical matter, the ability of arbitrators is better recognised by the courts to make a reasonable choice among all the bodies of law that purport to apply to a given dispute.[233] In *Mitsubishi*, for example, the US courts constructed the domain of the evanescent "second look" suggesting, albeit in a more attenuated or theoretical way, that the arbitrator in shaping his award needs to consider mandatory rules of other jurisdictions where the award might ultimately be brought for enforcement.[234] Refusal to consider mandatory rules may open the door to review on a "second look" by the court.[235] The "second look" doctrine is "a problematic safety valve"[236] effectively trapping the arbitrator between two completely different concerns,[237] and leading to multiple adjudication (including one arbitration and two or more litigations).

Characterising an arbitrator, tribunal or institution as a delegated "judicial" or "quasi-judicial" organ requires consideration of the agency problem that results from any delegation. As a sub-agent, arbitration institutions certainly involve more agency costs than courts. Confidential, private and self-managed arbitration is thought to present significant dangers to the public interests. Arbitral awards and the publicity surrounding these awards do not generate

picking better arbitrators. Having a second arbitrator review the first arbitrator's work is a *de facto* appeal system, which is not recognised by arbitration law.

232 Alan Scott Rau, 'Fear of Freedom', (2006) 17 *American Review of International Arbitration* 469.

233 Luca G. Radicati di Brozolo, 'Antitrust: A Paradigm of the Relations Between Mandatory Rules and Arbitration – A Fresh Look at the "Second Look"', [2004] *Int'l Arb. L. Rev.* 23, 27.

234 Other relevant cases are *SNF SAS v. Cytec Industries BV* (*Cour d'Appel* Paris, 23 March 2006), 2 *Stockholm Int'l Arb. Rev.* (2007) 99; *Tensacciai v. Terra Armata* (Trib. Fed. Switz. 2006), *Rev. Arb.* (2006) 763, 768–69.

235 William W. Park, *Arbitration of International Business Disputes: Studies in Law and Practice*, US: Oxford University Press (2006) 130.

236 William W. Park, 'Private Adjudicators and the Public Interest: The Expanding Scope of International Arbitration', (1986) 12 *Brooklyn J. Int'l L.* 642.

237 Serge Lazareff, 'Mandatory Extraterritorial Application of National Law', (1995) 11 *Arb. Int'l* 137, 140.

uniform standards to shape public policy.[238] Confidential decisions may hinder the creation of precedent and the development of the law because "arbitration is based on an avoidance of the outcome of litigation" which is different from litigation based on a prediction of the outcome of litigation.[239] Without sufficient and easy access to arbitral awards, the arbitrating parties may find it difficult or impossible to evaluate a pattern of practice and predict the application of public policy. As a result, the parties to arbitration are not certain to what extent arbitration institutions, arbitral tribunals and arbitrators should apply mandatory rules, such as public policy rules, of countries with which the parties or the contracts may be connected.

Courts will be reluctant to delegate powers unless they believe agents serve their interest. Courts must have mechanisms for limiting the agency problem or have other benefits out of arbitration.[240] It has therefore been suggested[241] that arbitrators in international commercial arbitration are under a certain duty to apply the public policy and mandatory rules of countries closely connected with the contract or dispute even though they may not have to regard themselves as bound to apply any country's mandatory rules. As Lando has pointed out:

> "[A]lthough the arbitrator derives his authority from the will of the parties, he cannot have regard to their interests only. Like the courts of law which he replaces, he must consider any strong principle of public policy of a country closely connected with the contract ... Furthermore, every arbitrator has to consider the importance of preserving commercial arbitration as an instrument for the settling of international disputes ... If ... arbitration is used as means to evade the relevant policies of those countries which have an interest in the subject-matter of the dispute, the reputation of arbitration will suffer".[242]

In reality, arbitration institutions, arbitration tribunals and arbitrators are not state authorities. They have neither a forum nor *lex fori*. In international commercial arbitration, from the perspective of arbitration institutions, tribunals and arbitrators, all state laws are on an equal footing and none of them has a privileged status. Therefore, they do not have the duty, even a moral one, to apply

238 Katherine van Wezel Stone, 'Mandatory Arbitration of Individual Employment Rights: The Yellow Dog Contracts of the 1990s', (1996) 73 *Denv. U. L. Rev.* 1043.

239 See Christine Godsil Cooper, 'Where Are We Going with Gilmer? – Some Ruminations on the Arbitration of Discrimination Claims', (1992) 11 *St. Louis U. Pub. L. Rev.* 203, 214–15.

240 One benefit an arbitrator, arbitral tribunal or arbitration institution may bring to courts is its "gatekeeper" role in the discovery proceedings of finding evidence. Arbitrators can assess the reasonable proportionality between the burden of producing a document and the potential that the document will enlighten the tribunal. William W. Park, above n. 235, 465; Giacomo Rojas Elgueta, 'Understanding Discovery in International Commercial Arbitration Through Behavioral Law and Economics: A Journey Inside the Minds of Parties and Arbitrators', (2011) 16 *Harvard Negotiation L. Rev.* 165, 180.

241 Ole Lando, above n. 66, 764–768.

242 Ibid.

foreign policy laws and will not act as the guardian of state public policy, since neither domestic nor foreign public policy, but only policy laws foreign to the *lex contractus*, are binding on them. They are merely constrained by the possibility of judicial review by the courts to reflect or comply with public policy according to the standards imposed by the courts. The role of courts is to satisfy themselves with the arbitrators' choice of law from their a-national perspective. As a matter of fact, numerous arbitrators remain strongly opposed to the application of foreign policy rules.[243] In this sense, arbitration institutions, tribunals and arbitrators are not in a dominant position in making efficient positivist public policy at least in the current arbitration regime. However, they may be the best candidates to make efficient public policy in favour of international commercial arbitration given their basic instinct to promote arbitration.

The International Law Association Arbitration Committee is reformulating its view on the issue of *jura novit curia*. According to ILA Arbitration Committee's Report, a tribunal may have to be proactive. At a minimum, a tribunal should not ignore the likely existence of rules that may be mandatory and should seek comment from the parties.[244] The underlying rationale of this approach rests on an arbitrator's instinct to insulate his award from possible judicial attack and achieving this requires the arbitrator to align his decision with the most rigorous and intrusive public policy of the contending regulatory regimes. This matches the evidence that international arbitrators are deeply concerned about their reputation for respecting mandatory rules.[245]

5.3.2. VOICE OR EXIT AS A POTENTIAL SOLUTION TO INEFFICIENT PUBLIC POLICY[246]

If interest groups and other agency costs are likely to prevent legislative or judicial bodies from generating efficient public policy, then the question is how to deal with inefficient public policy so as to improve efficiency of public policy.

243 ICC award no. 1512 of 1970, Jarvin and Derains, [1974–1985] ICC Arbitral Awards 554.

244 Report on Ascertaining the Contents of the Applicable Law in International Commercial Arbitration (presented at the ILA's 73rd Conference in Rio de Janeiro, August 2008), available at http://www.ila-hq.org. Recommendation 13: "In disputes implicating rules of public policy or other rules from which the parties may not derogate, arbitrators may be justified in taking measures appropriate to determine the applicability and contents of such rules, including by making independent research raising with the parties new issues (whether legal or factual), and giving appropriate instructions or ordering appropriate measures insofar as they consider this necessary to abide by those rules or protect against challenges to the award".

245 Eric A. Posner, 'Arbitration and the Harmonisation of International Commercial Arbitration: A Defense of *Mitsubishi*', (1999) 39 *Va. J. Int'l L.* 647, 668.

246 Albert O. Hirschmann's framework of Exit, Voice and Loyalty provides a tool for understanding these options here. Albert O. Hirschmann, *Exit Voice and Loyalty: Responses to Decline in Firms, Organisations, and States*, Cambridge, MA: Harvard University Press (1970); Joseph H.H. Weiler, 'The Transformation of Europe', (1990) 100 *Yale L.J.* 2403, 2411.

There are two ways to eliminate inefficient public policy. First, in theory, the local political, judicial or legislative process can involve, if not facilitate, public participation and monitoring of their representatives in producing efficient public policy or improving efficiency of public policy. This voice option, however, has limited practical effect. Individuals or firms must use scarce resources, including time, energy, money and human resources, to obtain and analyse information and then to form and express their views, which are not necessarily to be heard or adopted by the legislative body. Individual voters may have few or inadequate incentives to use private resources or to suffer personal burdens in order to generate laws that have public benefits. In the global era, foreign individuals and companies may have even less incentive to change inefficient public policy in a specific foreign locality because no locality is indispensable.

At the international level, states can exercise voice in two types of mechanisms. At the level of individual decisions, a state does not have to communicate to other states about its displeasure. Its court can simply ignore or overrule a particular decision by refusing recognition and enforcement of a foreign award. Private parties in a given case can also communicate with the court by ignoring the decision, resulting in an ineffective court ruling. In a more general manner, a state has options to form its own judicial or legislative stance. In extreme cases, a state may tighten up its own regime (by broadening the scope of public policy). This may constitute an attack to the court.

The mobility of individuals and firms allows exit to function as a second means. Exit is not an option that substitutes for the voice option in the political, judicial or legislative process. Rather, it effectively complements the voice option[247] by sorting people by preferences. As no political organisation or sovereign state has infinite jurisdiction, the governed can escape from a "harsh" legal regime they do not like by gravitating towards more appealing legal systems. It has been vividly argued that the governed can effectively vote with their feet.[248] For example, consumer-voters can choose their preferred level of public goods such as taxes and expenditures by moving to another place.[249] Similarly, individuals and companies may be inclined to take the exit route when the costs of exit are less than the costs they would incur or the burden they would bear by remaining in the jurisdiction. Forum-shopping is a typical and strong example of the exit route. In this sense, exit is a disciplinary mechanism which would discipline, directly or indirectly, lawmakers or judicial bodies, to opt out of inefficient laws and promote "better" laws and public policy. Costs of exit are not uniform across states within a given regime. However, in the current

[247] See Albert O. Hirschman, above n. 246.

[248] See Chapter 3 of this book.

[249] Charles M. Tiebout, 'A Pure Theory of Local Expenditures', (1956) 64 *J. Pol. Econ.* 416, 418–21, 423–24.

context, exit can be used as a relatively inexpensive strategy by relying upon the choice of law or choice of venue clause in the arbitration agreement.

In the long run, both voice and exit oblige politicians, lawmakers and judges to consider the public interests and the efficiency of public policy so as to avoid losing clientele in the community. While politicians, lawmakers and judges are motivated to compete[250] for clientele if business players are mobile,[251] they are also subject to other economic factors, especially in a cross-border context. Legislators may not be able to gain benefits from the competition because other jurisdictions can easily free ride on their efforts by copying successful legislation. Public policy rules are domicile-centred and may impose potentially higher exit costs on individuals and firms who will move to avoid dealing with over-restrictive jurisdictions.[252] The costs of exit would be lowered if the exit can be realised through the choice of governing law of another jurisdiction. The problem of inefficient public policy may disappear once the cost of exit falls to zero. In international commercial arbitration, enforcement must take place in a specific jurisdiction and the choice-of-applicable-law by the arbitrating parties does not guarantee the zero cost of exit. Although the exit route can eliminate inefficient laws, it has side effects and can reduce the benefits of efficient regulation. The businesses' leaving the regulating states may make unilateral state regulatory efforts less effective and meaningful.

Efficiency (or efficacy) of public policy is a critical dimension to the debate over the nature of regulation and private ordering.[253] The key is whether contracting parties should be allowed to waive statutory protections, regardless of efficiency, through the choice-of-law mechanism or forum shopping. Among other things, legislators, courts and interested private parties internalise at least some of the influences of the laws in the home jurisdiction since the laws politically affect the parties located in that state, thereby giving legislators or courts an incentive not to regulate or deregulate inefficiently merely for the purpose of attracting out-of-state transactions or parties. Contractual choice may be a reasonable compromise between oppressive laws and complete circumvention of regulations. The arbitrating parties, however, may not make the right choice on some occasions because of information asymmetries, bargaining imbalance, third-party pressures, or judgment biases, which may not justify judicially or legislatively imposed restrictions on the contractual choice or other exit routes. The public policy inquiries thwart certainty, objectiveness

---

250 Some commentators are sceptical about such motivation to compete. Douglas J. Cumming and Jeffrey G. MacIntosh, 'The Role of Interjurisdictional Competition in Shaping Canadian Corporate Law: A Second Look', (2000) 20 *Int'l Rev. L. & Econ.* 141.

251 For articles discussing the importance of mobility to jurisdictional competition, see Frank H. Easterbrook, 'Antitrust and the Economics of Federalism', (1983) 26 *J. L. & Econ.* 23, 34–35.

252 A restrictive law may be efficient to the extent that it protects against erroneous choices such as those attributable to cognitive biases and asymmetric information.

253 Bruce H. Kobayashi and Larry E. Ribstein, above n. 177.

and predictability, which will not be achieved by legislation that is influenced by interest group pressure and not focused on public choice or *ad hoc*, case-by-case public policy cases and public interest inquiries made by the state courts. In this sense, public policy must be designed with a view to improving and strengthening efficiency and efficacy of arbitration. To maximise efficiency and efficacy, public policy should, in general, facilitate individual choice and recognise and respect the doctrine of party autonomy. This involves greater enforcement of the contractual choice clauses.

5.3.3. JURISDICTIONAL COMPETITION AS AN ALTERNATIVE TO FORMULATE EFFICIENT PUBLIC POLICY

Public policy has side effects, such as nurturing local protectionism and excessive judicial interference. This will ultimately damage a state's long term benefits of having a neutral and internationally recognisable arbitration regime. There may be another way out of this conundrum. Similar to market competition, jurisdictional competition may create effective pressures on states to adopt necessary reforms[254] for better or more efficient public policy and more restrictive state intervention.[255] This would give the state a competitive advantage that attracts capital and labour and then enhances social welfare.[256] The judicial competition can be traced to the historical developments of markets and business,[257] which were rooted in the liberal concept of individuals as being self-interested, and the assumption that the behaviour is best mediated by the market. Ultimately, law has both "demand" and "supply" sides. Parties to disputes are likely to find it worthwhile to pay the legal expenses and filing fees

---

254 See Wolfgang Kerber and Viktor Vanberg, 'Competition among Institutions: Evolution within Constraints', in Luder Gerken (ed.), *Competition among Institutions*, London: MacMillan (1995) p. 35 and pp. 42–48 (stating that jurisdictions that "introduce new superior institutions or abolish old ones" would outlive their usefulness).

255 See Luder Gerken, 'Institutional Competition: An Orientative Framework', in Luder Gerken (ed.), *Competition among Institutions*, London: MacMillan (1995) (claiming that legislatures of different states compete with one another, leading to a more limited government intervention).

256 Bruno S. Frey and Reiner Eichenberger, 'Competition among Jurisdictions: The Idea of FOCJ', in Luder Gerken (ed.), *Competition among Institutions*, London: MacMillan (1995) (advocating a framework that would encourage competition among all levels of government in the EU, thus enhancing social welfare). Arthur Laffer and Stephen Moore, 'The (Tax) War between the States', *The Wall Street Journal*, 11 December 2007, at 19 (claiming that noncompetitive states may be plagued by falling housing values, a shrinking tax base, business outmigration, capital flight and high unemployment rates, and less money for schools, roads and aging infrastructure).

257 See B. Buchell, S. Deakins, J. Michie and J. Rubery (eds.), *Systems of Production: Markets, Organisations and Performance*, London: Routledge (2002).

associated with switching jurisdictions,[258] if they find that there is a jurisdiction in which compliance costs are lower. Incentives to customise the arbitration law regime to the needs of businesses do exist. On the supply side, states are motivated to amend or even reform their laws to make them more user-friendly.[259] Developing jurisdictions reserve a higher level of judicial review by imposing more public policy constraints on arbitral proceedings and awards. Even though there is a lack of reciprocity, developed jurisdictions do not seem to move downwards by imposing more restrictions or exerting more control over arbitral awards. Instead, more and more jurisdictions are moving upwards by building a more flexible and arbitration-friendly regime, showing more respect to the party's autonomy and implementing public policy in fewer circumstances.

Judicial competition can achieve efficiency in several ways. First, states may be pressured to adopt facilitative rather than intervening public policy rules in arbitration. Individuals and firms can avoid one state's law by breaking off all contact with that state. Modern communication technology substantially lowers exit costs. In particular, the Internet increases the viability of exit.[260] For example, firms using blocking software to target sales can swiftly avoid states that impose onerous taxes or regulation. In this sense, firms now are less vulnerable to changes in the law in their home states. The state has to retain those who would otherwise physically flee by allowing them to contract out of the application of rigid public policy[261] or adopt better public policy. Interested parties may accede to a more favourable jurisdiction with choice-favouring or user-friendly public policy.[262] Parties usually prefer to choose the national law of an economically sophisticated state, often the location of a significant financial, business or arbitration centre. Although the firms' costs to avoid jurisdictional connections with a large state are higher, the increasing international business and jurisdictional competition is able to influence and constrain larger states as well.

Second, the interest parties' pressure to leave stringent and intervening jurisdictions may create a competitive atmosphere. Private parties will gravitate toward better commercial law, therefore motivating interest groups to urge their states to join the competition in order to preserve business.[263] Some jurisdictions have ambitions to make arbitration in the local jurisdiction an appealing

258 Brian Cheffins, *Company Law: Theory, Structure and Operations*, Oxford: Oxford University Press (1997) p. 431.

259 In the US, Delaware company law is dominant in company codes and the judiciary and legislature in Delaware give strong confidence to the managers and owners of the companies. See generally Roberta Romano, *The Genius of American Corporate Law*, Washington DC: AEI Press (1993).

260 The Internet may ultimately uncouple applicable law from its territorial roots and lead to a system that is based on individual interests rather than political power.

261 See Larry E. Ribstein, 'Choosing Law by Contract', (1993) 18 *J. Corporation Law* 247; Bruce H. Kobayashi and Larry E. Ribstein, above n. 177, pp. 331–32.

262 Erin A. O'Hara, above n. 178.

263 Larry E. Ribstein, above n. 214, 1016–18.

proposition. Pro-arbitration rules will bring economic benefits to the jurisdiction together with an expansion of employing other professionals in related areas of services. The overall result is important to determine the direction of improvement in response to the local economic needs. The US experience suggests that, over time, regulatory competition in commercial law leads to a fairly high level of convergence among states, the empirical value of which is to confirm the possibility of regulatory convergence surrounding a single and efficient system or model in a competitive setting.

Third, rather than simply avoiding contacts within the regulating jurisdiction, disadvantaged parties may choose to stay and fight against the rigid public policy in a jurisdiction. The larger the public policy levy imposed on the disadvantaged party, the more likely it will be willing to incur the costs of opposing such policy. The interested parties will determine their support or opposition based on the costs and benefits of the statutes net of the effect of exit respectively. Interested parties such as foreign investors and lawyers can coordinate in the arbitration proceedings as well as in legislative action, thereby fostering the gradual evolution of more narrowly defined public policy rules compatible with those in other jurisdictions. Both litigators and commercial lawyers specialising in dispute resolution may want their states to respect the doctrine of party autonomy by enforcing contractual choice of law. Corporations may contractually designate the forum in order to arbitrate in a jurisdiction where courts are most likely to enforce their contracts. Courts, in turn, may be more willing to enforce choice-of-forum rather than choice-of-law clauses because the former does not force courts to deal with potentially contentious issues such as the application of foreign law that conflicts with the public policy and local values. Legislature may also gain by making local adjudication, legislation and legal values attractive to contracting parties. Through opposing rigid public policy, disadvantaged parties may gain more from substantially softening public policy rules than from exit.

The fundamental question here is whether jurisdictional competition, a theory contemplating the process towards efficiency, is able to improve public policy, which is "interventionist" rather than "facilitative" in nature. Competitive forces do not operate spontaneously, instantaneously and perfectly, and are not likely to result in a convergence, as the state response to the preference over the content of public policy and the level of legal intervention and protection may vary significantly. In addition, the transboundary externalities may alter the effect of competition. Despite the competitive dynamics, the efficiency-enhancing forces discussed in this section co-exist with the evolutionary theory discussed in Chapter 2, according to which evolution should occur without any assumptions of altruism by state legislatures or courts. This evolutionary theory also does not depend upon the states' conscious willingness to forgo short-term gain for long-term efficiency. Rather, jurisdictional competition can be seen as an application of Darwinian theory that competitive pressures can produce efficient results over time with the public actors' view of consciously generating such results by diminishing their intervening role and causing efficient ones to thrive.[264] In summary, even if legislators or courts lack the knowledge, motivation and foresight to formulate or supply efficient public policy, legal evolutionary theory suggests that efficient public policy may ultimately emerge through competition.[265] Market players who have an incentive to minimise their transaction and information costs and possess the capability to choose a more user-friendly legal regime or a more efficient and restricted public policy may cause that public policy to evolve towards efficiency, if only because inefficient regimes end up governing fewer and fewer market players and transactions.

5.3.4. COOPERATION AMONG STATES TO FORMULATE EFFICIENT PUBLIC POLICY

States are players in a repeat-play game and have long-term incentives to cooperate over choice of applicable law.[266] The same applies to public policy, which is a residual product of the choice of law. In the context of cross-border arbitration, the formulation and implementation of public policy may be viewed as a prisoner's dilemma game in which each state has a strong incentive to cooperate because (i) defection is likely to happen because state courts cannot easily monitor, let alone discipline, the uncooperative courts of other states;[267] and (ii) the joint losses from defection substantially exceed the benefits unilaterally enjoyed by a defecting state. In theory, in order to make cooperation feasible, (i) the long-term and joint gains from cooperation must exceed the short-term benefits from defecting via the application of forum law; and (ii) the present discounted value of each state's long-term gains from cooperation must exceed that of its short-term gains from defecting or "unjustified distributive effects".[268] The state law may end up evolving towards an efficient equilibrium through cooperation rather than competition if these conditions can be satisfied.

Judicial cooperation may create an atmosphere of reciprocity that motivates states to apply uniform laws or local laws containing widely accepted normative standards, and to defer to other states' interests, which in turn protects its own

264 Martin J. Bailey and Paul H. Rubin, above n. 189 (positing model of legal change in which legal rules reflect temporary balances in rent-seeking pressures).

265 See Armen A. Alchian, 'Uncertainty, Evolution, and Economic Theory', (1950) 58 *J. Pol. Econ.* 211, 213 (claiming that an "economic natural selection" of the market may be more fruitful than that of individual motivation).

266 See Larry Kramer, 'Rethinking Choice of Law', (1990) 90 *Colum. L. Rev.* 342–44 (applying prisoner's dilemma to model choice-of-law situation between states).

267 See Stewart E. Sterk, above n. 217, 949, 1008–10 (claiming enforcement and information problems undercut the emergence of stable reciprocity).

268 See John Rawls, *The Law of Peoples*, Cambridge, MA: Harvard University Press (1999) p. 43.

interests.[269] Judicial cooperation ultimately fosters comity,[270] which further provides a legal regime where enforcement is uniform and predictable and facilitates multiple jurisdiction activities. Likewise, judicial cooperation also facilitates diminishing forum shopping and promotes efficient behaviours and public policy in arbitration. In the context of arbitration, there is a strong chance that judicial cooperation among states and arbitration institutions on public policy would enhance efficiency or party autonomy. This is so because states are partially, if not entirely, isolated from the arbitration regime and a uniform position on public policy taken by the states would help avoid the prisoner's dilemma. Therefore, cooperation may dominate over defection in the prisoner's dilemma. This line of thinking, however, may overlook the practical difficulty in achieving reciprocity. Governance at the international level is a constantly evolving discourse involving multiple actors whose influence and roles vary across time and policy realms. A legitimate and effective model of global governance such as judicial cooperation needs a delicate balance between international cooperation and national sovereignty.[271]

Judicial cooperation differs significantly from judicial competition in that it requires either coordination or interstate monitoring. Cooperation among state courts requires them to monitor and discipline defections, which is difficult to implement via the classic tit-for-tat enforcement strategies.[272] Monitoring other state courts' public policy decisions is costly, ineffective and inefficient.[273] Retaliation is also not an effective monitoring tool for three reasons. First, an interstate dispute will not arise so often as to enable a disadvantaged state to retaliate against the defector.[274] Second, states possess different levels of retaliatory power. Larger plaintiff-favouring states would have more opportunities to defect than smaller states. Third, the reputation cost may restrict retaliation. Therefore, the remaining feasible cooperative mechanics are multilateral or bilateral treaties which can facilitate states' monitoring or disciplining each other. The treaty-model is a more transparent, inclusive, participatory and legitimacy-enhancing decision-making process among state and non-state actors, and can decrease accountability and uncertainty

---

269 Larry Kramer, above n. 266, 314 ("From a selfish and parochial point of view, it may still be in State A's interests to apply other states' laws in some true conflicts in State A courts, thereby inviting reciprocal action that advances State A policies in cases brought elsewhere").

270 Ibid, 313 (arguing that states share "multistate policies" that may point toward the application of another state's law or policies like comity toward other states).

271 Daniel W. Drezner, 'On the Balance between International Law and Democratic Sovereignty', (2001) 2 *Chi. J. Int'l L.* 321, 323.

272 See Robert Axelrod, *The Evolution of Cooperation*, New York: Basic Books (1984).

273 See Larry Kramer, above n. 266, 343 (noting that monitoring and punishing defections will be among the most likely impediments to cooperation).

274 Stewart E. Sterk, above n. 217, 1008–11 (claiming that the discounting of potential gains from cooperation is likely to be very high, and that defection will not always be obvious to each court).

concerns.[275] The often-used technique is the introduction of a uniform approach or uniform standards to narrow the scope of public policy, which would not only reduce the uncertainty but also increase aggregate certainty and welfare. A certain degree of equivalence in state arbitration laws is necessary to disincentivise the "movement" of disputes from one state to another. There is evidence that states generally adopt uniform rules and practices where uniformity is functional and efficient.[276] Prominent examples include the adoption of uniform grounds on which enforcement of an award can be rejected under the New York Convention and the Model Law. However, efficient uniformity failed in formulating public policy in arbitration.[277] Even if uniformity emerges in certain areas, the result may not be optimal. This is a potential problem not only with uniform laws but also with other mechanics for achieving uniformity. It has been argued that state cooperation can be fostered by soft law such as the Model Law.[278] However, soft law may not be a panacea in that it reflects the agenda of various interest groups and hence the very purpose of having the soft law may be compromised.[279]

5.4. CONSTRUCTION OF NORMATIVE PUBLIC POLICY IN INTERNATIONAL ARBITRATION

Evolutionary game theory indicates that judicial cooperation can be structured to achieve diverse distributional effects[280] and that states ultimately will evolve to adopt efficiency-maximising public policy. As a gaming theoretic approach, evolutionary game theory may lead to another equilibrium depending on the operative assumptions concerning, among others, risks as well as payoffs from cooperation and defection.[281] Constraints on policy-makers' time, resources and information limit their ability to develop new public policy theories, methodologies or norms. The "federalism" court model is likely to provide

---

275 Robert Howse, 'Transatlantic Regulatory Cooperation and the Problem of Democracy', in George A. Bermann et al (eds.), *Transatlantic Regulatory Cooperation*, Oxford: Oxford University Press (2000) p. 469 and p. 471.

276 See Larry E. Ribstein and Bruce H. Kobayashi, 'An Economic Analysis of Uniform State Laws', (1996) 25 *J. Legal Stud.* 131.

277 Other failing efforts to adopt uniformity rules include the service of judicial documents and taking evidence abroad. The Convention on Service Abroad of Judicial and Extrajudicial Documents in Civil and Commercial Matter, 15 November 1965, 20 UST 361 and the Convention on the Taking of Evidence Abroad in Civil or Commercial Matters, 27 July 1970, 23 UST 2555.

278 See Chapter 4 of this book.

279 See Alan Schwartz and Robert E. Scott, 'The Political Economy of Private Legislatures', (1994) 143 *U. Pa. L. Rev.* 595, 596–97.

280 John Rawls, *Political Liberalism*, New York: Columbia University Press (1996) pp. 265–267.

281 See Randal C. Picker, 'Simple Games in a Complex World: A Generative Approach to the Adoption of Norms', (1997) 64 *U. Chi. L. Rev.* 1225.

national courts with a mechanism to look to foreign courts' judgments, which is one way to achieve convergence and efficiency of public policy. Lawmakers may rely on external guidance when formulating public policy. International treaties and model laws are major guiding tools for legislators.

5.4.1. IMPEDIMENTS TO ADOPTION OF A "FEDERALISM" COURT

State courts are unlikely to turn from politics to efficiency in formulating public policy. First, judges are likely to adhere closely to the local case law, statutes, and jury instructions they are familiar with rather than foreign law or international law. Second, in response to local protectionism such as pressures from local bars and domestic business giants including state-owned enterprises and special interest groups, judges may apply forum law, which increases the demand for forum lawyers' expertise and systematic support from the domestic community. States often act through their governmental bodies. The question arises as to how the division can be drawn between state agencies, which can be private entities and shall not enjoy state immunity, and which, at least in the given situation, act as agents for the state. It is difficult to suggest a clear-cut test in determining whether or not a legal entity is a state agency.[282] The state courts may implement different legal principles in cases involving a state agency or state-owned commercial enterprise.[283] In light of these considerations, it is not surprising that judges have favoured prescriptive public policy, with its bias in favour of forum law. Third, even if some judges do focus on the normative virtues or principles of public policy, the efficiency-centred public policy requires consistent application of efficiency principles across many states. Spontaneous coordination world-wide seems unlikely, and differentiation and experimentation at the state level may exist for the time being.

A balance between sovereignty and globalisation cannot be achieved by solely relying upon a traditionally state-centred governance regime without reflecting on the multiplicity of actors now engaged in international policymaking. Unregulated judicial competition or cooperation among states may not guarantee that the system which eventually prevails would be the most efficient. A governance regime at the global level serves a substantive policy goal to perfect international commercial arbitration. What if we have a global court modelled on a federal court in a federal country? Since a federal court is more detached from local interests and is less likely than state courts to be biased in

---

282 *Muellenger v. New Brunswick Development Corporation* [1971] All ER 593.

283 See *Bank Markazi Iran v. The Federal Reserve Bank of New York*, Award No. 595-823-3, para. 75–76 (holding that, even if the Federal Reserve Bank of New York were considered an entity controlled by the government of the US, it could, under some circumstances, invoke *force majeure* since it has its own legal personality distinct from the state).

favour of forum state law, theoretically it would help decrease local particularities and influences in international arbitral processes[284] and promote efficiency-centred public policy in "federal diversity" cases. This proposition seems convincing in the context of cross-border arbitration.[285] Suggestions have been made for the formation of an international court for the enforcement of international arbitral awards applying truly international public policy.[286]

A "federalism court" governance model raises several legitimacy concerns. First, there is a growing concern over the "policy space" available to sovereign countries.[287] The empirical evidence and long-range historical records have shown that the policy space of sovereign countries is shrinking. Virtually all policy areas such as democracy, judicial reform, trade, industrial development, corporate governance, education and health care are now subject to the influence of the outside world economically, and are systematically dominated by institutions such as the World Bank, IMF and WTO.[288]

The dominance of Western capitalist countries in the WTO, the IMF and probably any future "federalism" court causes the suspicion of "neo-colonialism". From a historical perspective, there has been a constant attempt to reduce the

---

284 Albert Jan van den Berg, 'Some Practical Questions Concerning the 1958 New York Convention on the Recognition and Enforcement of Foreign Arbitral Awards', in United Nations (ed.), *Uniform Commercial Law in the 21st Century, Proceedings of the Congress of the United Nations Commissions on International Trade Law, New York, 18–22 May 1992*, New York: United Nations (1995) p. 219.

285 See Larry E. Ribstein, above n. 261, 284–85 (finding that in the United States federal courts are more likely to enforce choice-of-law clauses than state courts). The latest global financial crisis calls for greater coordinated efforts to tackle some pressing regulatory and governance challenges worldwide. Some proposals have been made to rely on more global institutions to supplement or even replace the existing piecemeal and *ad hoc* intergovernmental responses to sovereign debt crisis so that global systemic risks can be handled or mitigated in a more effective and efficient manner. For instance, it has been proposed that an international debt restructuring court can be put in place. This will be a more structured framework for international cooperation in this area. Joseph E. Stiglitz, *The Stiglitz Report. Reforming the International Monetary and Financial Systems in the Wake of the Global Crisis*, New York and London: The New Press (2010) pp. 178–80. However, the mainstream scholarship seems to support the view that international law is self-enforcing due to the lack of an external enforcement agent such as world government or court. Eric A. Posner and Alan O. Sykes, *Economic Foundations of International Law*, Cambridge, MA and London: Harvard University Press (2013) p. 3.

286 Stephen M. Schwebel, 'A Celebration of the United Nations New York Convention on the Recognition and Enforcement of Foreign Arbitral Awards', (1996) 12(1) *Arb. Int'l* 84; Howard Holtzmann, 'A Task for the 21st Century: Creating a New International Court for Resolving Disputes on the Enforceability of Arbitral Awards', in Martin Hunter, Arthur Marriott and V.V. Veeder (eds.), *The Internationalisation of International Arbitration: The LCIA Centenary Conference*, London and Boston: Graham & Trotman and Martinus Nijhoff Publishers (2nd edn. 1995) p. 109.

287 K. Gallagher, *Putting Development First – The Importance of Policy Space in the WTO and IFIs*, London: Zed Press (2005).

288 Ha-Joon Chang, *Why Developing Countries Need Tariffs – How WTO NAMA Negotiations Could Deny Developing Countries' Right to a Future*, Oxford: Oxfam Publishing (2005).

currently available policy space,[289] and a "federalism court" regime may be logically characterised as part of such efforts. The experience of the World Bank and the IMF may persuasively indicate the likelihood of a "federalism court" expanding its initially fairly restricted mandate (*i.e.*, with the focus on the enforcement of cross-border arbitral awards), which will threaten the sovereignty of national states. Like the result of shrinking policy space in the economic realm, a "federalism court" may also have an enormous influence on a country's ability to achieve judicial development, to the point of making the use of any meaningful policy for judicial construction impossible. Second, there is little prospect of comity among various jurisdictions in a "federalism" regime. Although it is in the interest of all nations to create an effective regulatory regime globally, the apprehensions of sovereign countries cannot be disregarded in imposing a "federalism" model. States are less bound to recognise the laws of other states than states in a federal country. This may suggest that enforcement of efficiency-centred public policy by a global court may be less effective than by the US Supreme Court. The federal court is as unlikely as the state courts to coordinate around general principles of public policy. The "federal court" may oblige an enforcing state to recognise another state's law without preventing the affected state from applying more stringent or local public policy rules.[290] Therefore, a state in a "federalism" regime may still resort to self-help to maintain a basic level of comity as the legal pressure on the defecting state is not that strong.

A "federalism" governance model may not be compatible with modern international law, under which supranational institutions are not self-legitimating but derive their legitimacy from the constitutional structures of Member States. The dilemma of the "federalism" governance has two limbs. First, it is critical to balance the sovereign prerogatives of Member States and the overall legitimate interest of the institution, failure of which would undermine the functioning of the institution. Second, it is important to achieve the benefits of international cooperation without sacrificing legitimate concerns over the democracy in the decision-making process. It suffices to say that a federal-type of judicial resolution provides a new way of thinking – a coordinative forum can marginally discipline local public policy at the state level. The state court can somehow be mandated to implement some basic norms or principles and non-discriminatory public policy, thereby adopting an even-handed system like the choice-maximising rules. Given the effect of a federal court in a real federal country,[291] the proposal for greater involvement of a federal-type of institution at the global level may have little chance of success.

---

289 Ha-Joon Chang, *Kicking Away the Ladder – Development Strategy in Historical Perspective*, London: Anthem Press (2002).

290 See Michael Whincop and Mary Keyes, 'The Recognition Scene: Game Theoretic Issues in the Recognition of Foreign Judgments', (1999) 23 *Melb. U. L. Rev.* 416, 422.

291 There have been some doubts about the functioning of a "federalism court". In the US context, a federal court sitting in diversity cases holds diversity jurisdiction in low regard and

5.4.2. GLOBAL LEGISLATION

The formulation of normative public policy in a single jurisdiction may vary from one jurisdiction to another. The French way of developing a doctrine of "international public policy", for example, is dependent upon a series of decisions by the courts. The judicial decisions bring together those rules and principles that are considered to have normative status under all circumstances in the area of international legal relations.[292] For obvious reasons, the ultimate decision on whether to adopt efficiency-centred public policy at the international level may be based on legislatures rather than courts. First, the legislature is best situated to make factual and policy findings that are necessary to determine the value, propriety and model of the public policy regime. Second, legislatures can make efficiency-centred public policy operate as default rules that give notice to the parties who can fashion or plan their behaviours accordingly. Third, legislatures can overrule explicit statutes by as many externalities as possible and minimise public choice difficulties inherent in the legislation-making process, so as to effectively formulate efficiency-centred public policy. Fourth, embodying public policy in statutes promotes efficiency-enhancing jurisdictional competition. When the burdens of the domestic legislation become too high, the burdened parties may overcome compliance and coordination costs and organise in opposition to the law,[293] which in turn limits wealth transfers.

Legislation of public policy at the global level is a harmonising process of national laws, by which states may not only develop local practices but also conform to model practices. This is more akin to "co-evolution", which assumes that a variety of diverse systems, each with their own viability, may co-exist within an environment.[294] Given the impediments to state coordination and competition, "interventionist" rules such as public policy are arguably better governed by global legislation in order to promote a level of predictability in local practice. Global legislation could take several possible forms, *e.g.*, mandatory unification measures or voluntary codes.[295] International

even federal judges are likely to apply the public policy followed in the state in which it is located. See 'Federalisation of Crimes: Chief Justice Rehnquist on Federalisation of Crimes', 33 *Prosecutor* 9, 15 (Mar-Apr 1999) (quoting Justice Rehnquist's remark that federal diversity jurisdiction should be repealed). *Klaxon Co. v. Stentor Electric Manufacturing Co.*, 313 US (1941) 487, 496 (holding that in diversity cases the federal court must decide conflict of laws issues according to the prevailing law in the state in which it sits). State courts always could trump federal diversity precedents. See generally Henry J. Friendly, 'The Historic Basis of Diversity Jurisdiction', (1928) 41 *Harv. L. Rev.* 483 (summarising the history of diversity jurisdiction in order to set up a re-examination of the doctrine).

292 Jean-Pierre Ancel, above n. 119, 127.

293 See Gary Becker, 'A Theory of Competition Among Pressure Groups for Political Influence', (1983) 98 *Quarterly Journal of Economics* 371, 372–73, 381–88.

294 Gunther Teubner, *Law as an Autopoietic System*, Oxford: Blackwell (1993) p. 53.

295 See Larry E. Ribstein and Bruce H. Kobayashi, above n. 276, 168–169 (providing evidence of evolutionary efficiency concerning the demand for uniform statutory provisions and

organisations can promulgate international conventions ensuring enforcement of contractual choice-of-forum or choice-of-applicable-law provisions as "the most important international commercial usage [... holding] the parties to their agreements".[296] An international convention may simply adopt the principle of *favor arbitrandum* which forces the contracting states to take a pro-arbitration bias on the public policy issue in enforcing foreign arbitral awards. It seems acceptable to the judiciary that "an agreement to arbitrate ... should not be permitted to decline enforcement ... on the basis of parochial views of their desirability or in a manner that would diminish the mutually binding nature of the agreements".[297] In other words, the arbitration agreement should become the foundation for interpreting or applying public policy. Uniform and narrowly defined treaties could minimise the level of judicial intervention and solve the forum-shopping problem. For instance, if the law governing the agreement declares a dispute capable of being settled by arbitration, the court should declare its incompetence.

Global legislation may encounter the risk of losing state support according to the support-maximising theory of federalism.[298] Accordingly, international legislatures should refrain from internationalising an area of law if they would lose more support than they would gain from legislating. This may occur if the global regulation would dissipate a substantial state capital investment in regulation,[299] if economic, social, or political environments vary across states, or if controversial issues threaten to damage the political agenda, process and image of a state. When one state specialises in formulating valuable regulation, such as English commercial law and German civil law, the party choice may enhance the value of that asset but international legislation may weaken the national characteristics. When the environments vary, the choice-maximising approach enables each state to exercise its comparative regulatory advantage rather than substituting its own substantive policy. However, global legislation may not recognise the differences between the states. Global legislation adopting a less intervening approach towards public policy may increase the likelihood of opposition from developing states as these states are not likely to see private

claiming that uniform laws that have the greatest net social benefit are also those adopted by the greatest number of states).

296 William Laurence Craig, William W. Park and Jan Paulsson, *International Chamber of Commerce Arbitration,* Dobbs Ferry, NY: Oceana Publications, Inc. (3rd edn. 2000) p. 81.

297 760 F. Supp. 1030 (1991); *Yearbook* (1992) 686.

298 Jonathan R. Macey, 'Federal Deference to Local Regulators and the Economic Theory of Regulation: Toward a Public-Choice Explanation of Federalism', (1990) 76 *Va. L. Rev.* 265, 267.

299 Ibid. "Delaware's dominant position in the market for corporate charters represents a valuable capital asset that generates revenues for Delaware corporations, corporate lawyers, investment bankers, and for the state itself. ... These capital assets would be destroyed if the federal government enacted a pervasive system of federal corporate law that pre-empted the field", at 279.

parties completely escape from public policy. By contrast, global legislation adopting more restrictive public policy may ruin the developed states' past attempts to adopt an advanced level of public policy and eventually block the evolving path of developing more efficiency-centred public policy globally. These factors remind us that global legislation may have side-effects or defects. A uniform approach has to take account of the varying economic, social or political status of the states. In reality, there is a chance that the global statute might gain support from various economic players, possibly including state governments. Global public policy-related statutes would serve the global interest of enhancing international trade, investment and other economic activities by removing local barriers. Foreign actors are more concerned about the risk of exposure to unfavourable state law or biased judicial treatment in a jurisdiction, *i.e.*, insufficient recognition of party autonomy, restrictive public policy or local protectionism.[300] State governments or economic lobbying groups favouring increased foreign trade and investment and fair legal and business environments are likely to endorse public policy adopted in and implemented by the global legislation which will minimise local protectionism and excessive judicial or administrative intervention.

The empirical reason to be sceptical about the prospect of efficiency-centred global public policy is the lack of any real examples, except the existence of some regional public policy focusing on the harmonisation of the regional legal order or the internal market. In the EU, competition law is a matter of regional public policy,[301] *order public communautaire*,[302] where the EU Commission serves as the guardian. The EU Commission's own administrative authority and manpower will conduct due investigation into a case to the extent that an arbitral tribunal is not capable of doing so. The public policy nature of EU competition law is reflected in the limited involvement of arbitration tribunals, which have jurisdiction to rule on EU competition matters only if the EU Commission does not have exclusive power. In other words, the tribunal can only settle private disputes *inter partes*.[303] For instance, the tribunals and national courts cannot grant individual exemptions under Article 81(3) of the EC Treaty since this is an exclusive power possessed by the EU Commission and the tribunals cannot even

300 This consideration has influenced the Court in civil procedure cases. See, for example, *Helicopteros Nacionales de Columbia, SA v. Hall*, 466 US 408, 418–19 (1983) (holding that the minimal activities of a foreign corporation within a state were insufficient for that state to assert general jurisdiction over the corporation); *The Bremen v. Zapata Off-Shore Co.*, 407 US 1, 8–9 (1972) (holding that a forum-selection clause should be upheld because of the interest of preserving and expanding trade).

301 Article 81 (ex Article 85) of the Treaty of Rome.

302 *Eco Swiss China Time Ltd v. Benetton International NV* (European Court of Justice, 1 June 1999). Also Christoph Liebscher, 'European Public Policy After Eco Swiss', (1999) 10(1) *Am. Rev. Int'l Arb.* 81.

303 See Philippe Fouchard, Emmanuel Gaillard and Berthold Goldman, *International Commercial Arbitration*, The Hague: Kluwer Law International (1999) p. 350.

refer cases to the European Court of Justice.[304] It was once held in *Eco Swiss v. Benetton* that a national court must deny enforcement if the award violates Article 81,[305] provided that its domestic procedures provide for annulment on grounds of public policy violation, which is the case in all Member States to the New York Convention.[306] Failure by the arbitral tribunal to make its decision in compliance with EU competition laws may constitute public policy grounds for a court to refuse enforcement of the award.[307] EU Member States have, to a significant extent, ceded their sovereignty to a supranational body, which has resulted in a common policy regime, an essential component of economic integration and the creation of the single market.[308] By contrast, nothing substantial has been achieved in unifying public policy in civil and commercial laws after World War II because of the dilemma between the harmonisation of law and sovereignty in global governance. The threat of a loss of sovereignty generates the fear that international integration of public policy would prevent state governments from delivering preferred benefits to their citizens.[309] This indicates the difficulty of full reliance on the global bodies to frame the public policy world-wide.

---

304 The arbitral tribunal is not a "Court or Tribunal of a Member State" in the sense of Article 234 of EC Treaty. *Nordsee Deutsche Hochseefischerei Nordstern GmbH v. Reederei Mond Hochseefischerei Nordstern AG & Co*, Case 102/81 (ECJ, 23 March 1982); *Bulk Oil (Zug) v. Sun International Ltd.* [1983] 1 Lloyd's Rep. 655.

305 The ECJ ruled that Article 81 (ex 85) EC "constitutes a fundamental provision which is essential for accomplishment of the tasks entrusted to the Community and, in particular, for the functioning of the internal market" and that where "its domestic rules of procedure require a national court to grant an application for annulment of arbitration award where such an application is founded on a failure to observe national rules of public policy, it must also grant such an application where it is founded on failure to comply with the prohibition laid down in Article 85(1) of the [EC] Treaty". *Eco Swiss China Time Ltd v Benetton International NV*, Case C-126/97, [1999] ECR 3055 (ECJ), paras. 36 and 37.

306 *Eco Swiss China Time Ltd. v. Benetton International NV*, Case C-126/97 (European Court of Justice, 1 June 1999). See Christoph Liebscher, above n. 302, 81; Vincent Smith, 'Arbitration in International Telecommunications: The Way Ahead?', in Martin Odams De Zylva and Reziya Harrison (eds.), *International Commercial Arbitration – Developing Rules for the New Millennium*, Bristol: Jordans (2000) p. 193.

307 Here, the violation of EU competition law probably, but unnecessarily, lead to the setting aside or non-enforcement of an arbital award. In the case of *Thales v. GIE Euromisslile*, the French Court of Appeal held that the possible violation of EU competition law did not provide a basis for annulling an award on public policy grounds. See *Thales Air Defence BV v. GIE Euromissile* (Paris Court of Appeals, 18 November 2004); Denis Bensaude, 'Defining the Limits of Scrutiny of Awards Based on Alleged Violations of European Competition Law', (2005) 22(3) *J. Int'l Arb.* 239.

308 See Treaty Establishing the European Community, 2002 O.J. (C 325).

309 Eleanor M. Fox, 'Antitrust and Regulatory Federalism: Races Up, Down, and Sideways', (2000) 75 *NYU L. Rev.* 1781, 1801.

5.5. PUBLIC POLICY, RULE OF LAW AND GLOBALISATION

Despite fruitful law and economics literature over the last three decades, economic analysis has made little inroad into one of the most perplexing legal areas – the rationales and rules of determining what kind of public policy applies to an interstate dispute. The critical issue is whether sovereign states shall accept uniform public policy rules while the compatibility of uniform public policy rules in different legal systems seems questionable. This section mainly discusses several macro theories even though their economic underpinnings have not been made explicit or are of little relevance at first glance. Legal rationality is discussed in Section 5.1 by reference to the theory of rights hypothesis which focuses on the concepts of rights and predictability. Political economic theory is important in that developed countries have different legal systems although they may share the same moral value in political institutions. The focus of Section 5.2 is on the market and globality according to the political economy theory. The situation is different in developing countries as the legal system in these countries is largely developed through transplant, which is no longer popular in the 21st century. Therefore, the systematic question must be encountered as to whether uniform public policy can be introduced through transplant again, which is the topic in section 5.3.

5.5.1. LEGAL RATIONALITY, RIGHTS HYPOTHESIS AND PREDICTABILITY

An important school of thought in institutional economics is the Rights Hypothesis which claims that business development and economic growth require a legal order securing stable and predictable rights of contract and property and offering the security of enforcement. Without such a legal order, the risks of a large number of otherwise beneficial transactions will far outweigh their expected return. As a result, trade, investment and business will neither occur nor succeed. The role of legal institutions in the economy, as Weber pointed out, is that: "the universal predominance of the market consociation requires … a legal system the functioning of which is calculable in accordance with rational rules".[310] The law and development movement in the 1960s advanced the view that "modern law promotes the development of markets and hence economic growth" "through legal institutions such as

---

310 Max Rheinstein (ed.), *Max Weber on Law in Economy and Society*, Cambridge, MA: Harvard University Press (1954); Max Weber, *The Protestant Ethic and the Spirit of Capitalism*, London: Allen & Unwin (Talcott Parsons trans., 1958) p. 25 ("Modern rational capitalism has need … a calculable legal system and of administration in terms of formal rules").

contract and private property rights".[311] More recently, it has been asserted that "the inability of societies to develop effective, low-cost enforcement of contracts is the most important source of … historical stagnation and contemporary underdevelopment …"[312]

5.5.1.1. *The Idea of Rights*

According to the Rights Hypothesis, inviolable property rights, enforceable contracts and adjudication are necessary for productive capitalism.[313] The real concern in our context is whether the security of expectations and promises only comes from a well-functioning legal system protecting contract and properties rights or a wise government that prudently declines to exercise the power it has to interfere with adjudication in order to maximise its ultimate revenue from taxing the income stream. For all types of transactions except one-shot deals, it is possible in principle for other mechanisms to provide the necessary security and protection. In reality, arbitration, together with other alternative dispute resolution mechanisms, is an effective replacement for, or supplement to, a formal legal system or adjudication even though such a legal institution is autonomous and then is expensive to maintain.[314] As the substantial literature on informal and social sanctions, repeated games, and self-enforcement mechanisms[315] has suggested, this effectively means that governmental intervention is not necessarily the only means to achieve economic development. Other quasi-government and non-governmental agencies also play a role in adjusting the relations between parties and promoting security of expectations and enforcement. The New York Convention is "the most important … attainment in promoting a more effective and universal rule of law".[316] As a legal institution, the New York Convention should also promote rights. The approach widely prevalent in major jurisdictions is the law of *situs*. The "rights" rationale

311 David M. Trubek, 'Toward a Social Theory of Law: An Essay on the Study of Law and Development', (1982) 82 *Yale L.J.* 1 (criticising this conception); and David M. Trubek and Marc Galanter, 'Scholars in Self-Estrangement: Some Reflections on the Crisis in Law and Development Studies in the United States', (1974) *Wisconsin Law Review* 1062.

312 Douglass C. North, *Institutions, Institutional Change and Economic Performance,* Cambridge: Cambridge University Press (1990) p. 54.

313 Ibid. 35, and Douglass C. North and Robert P. Thomas, *The Rise of the Western World: A New Economic History,* Cambridge: Cambridge University Press (1973). This proposition may not be empirically convincing because enforcement through government coercion is not in fact the only effective mechanism available, one-shot deals exist between people who intend to remain strangers, and businesspeople sometimes resort to self-help.

314 See Simon Johnson, John McMillan and Christopher Woodruff, 'Courts and Relational Contracts', (2002) 18 *J. L., Econ. & Org.* 221, 227.

315 See Bernard Black and Reinier Kraakman, 'A Self-Enforcing Model of Corporate Law', (1996) 109 *Harv. L. Rev.* 1911; Clive Bull, 'The Existence of Self-Enforcing Implicit Contracts', (1987) 102 *Q. J. Econ.* 147; Lester G. Telser, 'A Theory of Self-Enforcing Agreements', (1980) 53 *J. Bus.* 27.

316 Stephen M. Schwebel, above n. 286.

underlying this approach has led to a set of rules delineating the territorial boundaries of lawmaking and enforcement authority. Under this approach, once an individual's rights are vested in one time and place, that jurisdiction determines the extent of the rights. Therefore, courts in that jurisdiction are entitled to impose local public policy on the individuals and their disputes. This theory emphasises the territorial origin of the states' political power to control the parties and the outcome of a dispute.

The cornerstone of modern arbitration law is the notion of party autonomy which is "rights"-based with the aim of liberalising arbitration law from judicial restraints. The concept of party autonomy has substantially changed the relationship between courts and arbitration tribunals and the extent of judicial supervision of national courts and governments. As a result, more freedom has been granted to participants in the arbitral process. This freedom is extended, among other things, to the choice of arbitrators, the jurisdiction of the arbitral tribunal, the choice of law governing the substance of dispute and arbitration proceedings, etc. The concept is embedded in the Geneva Protocol of 1923, the Geneva Convention of 1927, the New York Convention and the UNCITRAL Model Law. Article 2 of the Geneva Protocol of 1923 provided that "the arbitral procedure, including the constitution of the arbitral tribunal, shall be governed by the will of the parties, and by the law of the country in whose territory the arbitration takes place".

One of the prerequisites for recognition and enforcement of awards stipulated in Article 1 of the Geneva Convention of 1927 was that the arbitral tribunal was "constituted in the manner agreed upon by the parties and in conformity with the law governing arbitral procedure". The New York Convention also embodied the concept of party autonomy. For example, Article V(1)(d) provides that recognition and enforcement of an award may be refused if "the arbitral procedure was not in accordance with the agreement of the parties or, failing such agreement, was not in accordance with the law of the country where the arbitration took place". One fundamental principle of the Model Law is to recognise the freedom of the parties within minimal restriction.[317] The autonomy of the parties is subject to public policy and applicable mandatory rules of national laws. Section 1 of the English Arbitration Act 1996 embodied the concept of party autonomy by providing that "the parties are free to agree how their disputes are resolved, subject only to such safeguards as are necessary in the public interest". In furtherance of this concept, the Act grants the parties the freedom to design their arbitral framework by, *inter alia*, choosing the seat of arbitration, selecting their arbitrators and deciding the arbitral procedure.[318]

[317] Gerold Hermann, 'The Role of the Courts under the UNCITRAL Model Law Script', in Julian D.M. Lew (ed.), *Contemporary Problems in International Arbitration*, London: Centre for Commercial Law Studies (1986) p. 173.

[318] Sections 25 and 34 of the English Arbitration Act 1996.

The support of party autonomy is to support arbitration, but not interfere with it.[319] Therefore, the judicial intervention is limited to a certain extent. For instance, in resorting to the irregularity, the English courts must be satisfied that such irregularity is of a kind which "has caused or will cause substantial injustice to the applicant".[320] The requirement of "substantial injustice" is aimed at reinforcing the autonomy of the arbitral process. The concept of party autonomy has been highly respected by French courts in numerous cases involving international arbitration clauses whereby the existence and validity of a given arbitration clause is determined without referring to any municipal law.[321]

5.5.1.2. *The Notion of Predictability*

The "rights" theory actually owes nothing to the economic analysis of predictability, which may be a more constructive focus than the presence or absence of enforceable legal rights.[322] Assuming that all other things are equal, it is more conducive to economic development to have predictability than not to have it since predictability has economic value and can further economic development, *inter alia*, the enforcement of contract rights and the security of property rights even though predictability many not come from an autonomous legal system and a regime of rights. As a matter of fact, predictability is a critical factor in applying public policy in arbitration by courts. For instance, the court in *Mitsubishi v. Soler* considered, among other factors, "sensitivity to the need of the international commercial system for predictability in the resolution of dispute" when deciding to take a pro-arbitration stance.[323] Similarly, the US Supreme Court placed weight on predictability, which is "essential to any international business transaction" when it had to decide whether to recognise an arbitration agreement in an anti-trust case.[324] In practice, it is important to distinguish between predictability and rights. Activities in arbitration depend on predictability of matters in respect of which the disputing parties may have no legal rights. For example, the arbitration institution or panel will proceed with the arbitration proceedings step by step, which is a legal order that contains no rights in some aspects but operates in a predictable manner.

---

319 Toby T. Landau, 'Introductory Note – United Kingdom: Arbitration Act of 1996', (1997) 36(1) ILM (1996) 155, 159; Departmental Advisory Committee, Report on the Arbitration Bill (February 1996) 196.

320 Section 68(2) of the English Arbitration Act 1996.

321 Jean-Pierre Ancel, above n. 119, 123.

322 Modern critical social and legal theory does deny that law in Western societies is autonomous, rational, and determinate, and therefore challenges the central causal claim of the Rights Hypothesis. See Albert Chen, 'Rational Law, Economic Development and the Case of China', (1999) 8 *Social and Legal Studies* 97. Critical theory does not deny that there is predictability in societies.

323 473 US 614 (1985).

324 *Scherk v. Alberto-Culver*, 417 US 506 (1974).

The inquiry into predictability touches upon the issue of predictability for whom? In theory, there must be predictability for private economic actors because economic development requires a market and a market requires private actors. This is so even though non-private actors such as government agencies are capable of fulfilling the role of private actors leading to flourishing markets and economic growth. What the market does require in order to have meaningful bargaining over prices are actors that are trying to buy low and sell high. Therefore, the rationale of the legal system shall not be merely interpreted from the government's point of view. In our context, it appears convincing that the legal rationale shall be agreeable to the private actors in the marketplace. Obviously it is important in the 21st century that the government shows sufficient respect to the private actors' choice of law and choice of dispute resolution to protect and enforce their own rights simply because that choice itself is rational from the perspective of private actors.

The analysis in this section has policy implications in addition to academic ones. Public policy is supposed to preserve a role for government regulation by prohibiting party choice of law or by making it contingent upon the satisfaction of procedural protections and protection of fairness. The legal rationality requires substantial improvement of "governance" and "the rule of law". An effective and functioning legal system shall contain some basic components: (a) there is a set of rules which is known to the public in advance; (b) such rules are in force; (c) mechanisms exist to ensure the proper application of the rules and to allow for departure from them as needed; (d) conflicts in the application of the rules can be resolved through an independent judicial or arbitral body; and (e) there are clearly-made procedures for amending the rules when they no longer serve their purpose.[325] The state shall devote its resources to creating a legal system that could fairly adjudicate contract disputes and enforce their decisions. However, without a better public policy by which the state can intervene in adjudication and rule of law, the *sine qua non* of economic development cannot be secured.[326] This supports a better set of public policy rules that enhance *ex ante* predictability.

An efficiency-centred public policy attempts to minimise the sum of the costs that public policy decisions may entail. These include the extra litigation costs associated with legal uncertainty,[327] the parties' costs of predicting the applicable

---

325 Ibrahim Shihata, 'The World Bank and "Governance" Issues in Its Borrowing Members', in Ibrahim Shihata (ed.), *The World Bank in a Changing World,* The Hague: Martinus Nijhoff Publishers (1991) p. 85, cited in Frank K. Upham, 'Speculations on Legal Informality: On Winn's "Relational Practices and the Marginalisation of Law"', (1994) 28 *Law & Soc'y Rev.* 233.

326 For a review of "rule of law" rhetoric in policymaking circles concerned with economic development, see John K.M. Ohnesorge, 'The Rule of Law, Economic Development, and the Developmental States of Northeast Asia', in Christoph Antons (ed.), *Law and Development in East and Southeast Asia,* London: Routledge Curzon (2003) p. 91.

327 These costs are not a focus of this Chapter but have been discussed in the legal and economic literature on litigation. See Louis Kaplow, 'A Model of the Optimal Complexity of Legal

law at the time of relevant conduct, the social costs of inefficient laws and violation of basic public interests, and the lost benefits of evasion of or non-compliance with public policy rules through exit routes such as the choice of law and un-regulated behaviours. A principle-based public policy rule plus the contractual choice approach might effectively decrease some of these unnecessary costs because (a) a mechanism that facilitates individual choice has the potential to dilute the effect of inefficient law and to diminish the level of judicial intervention due to less application of local public policy rules; and (b) if courts always apply public policy principles on a necessity basis, their decisions would be simple and predictable *ex post*, and extra litigation costs would be reduced. In this regard, the courts in England are supposed to provide the parties with sufficient freedom in arbitration "subject only to such safeguards as are necessary in the public interest".[328] However, in terms of predictability, public policy still causes uncertainty about the applicable law *ex ante* and would reduce beneficial interstate competition. A principle-based public policy rule should have a legitimate foundation and clear direction. A prevailing desire to promote the primacy of international arbitration can be a strong foundation for policy consideration to design public policy rules, which should adopt a pro-arbitration bias in honouring, or at least acquiescing to, the interests of a coordinate sovereign, and the principle of party autonomy while enforcing arbitral awards.[329] This direction will result in a narrow or restricted construction of public policy by courts.

5.5.2. LEGAL ORDER AND TRANSPLANT

Montesquieu wrote in *L'Esprit des Lois* in 1748 that the political and civil laws should be tailored for each nation and that it would be a great coincidence should they fit other people equally well.[330] Montesquieu argued that the spirit of each

Rules', (1995) 11 *J. L. Econ. & Org.* 150; Richard A. Posner, *Economic Analysis of Law*, Boston: Little, Brown & Company (4th edn. 1992) 554–60 (discussing how uncertainty affects the decision to settle or to go to trial); Isaac Ehrlich and Richard A. Posner, 'An Economic Analysis of Legal Rulemaking', (1974) 3 *J. Legal Stud.* 257, 265 (positing that a clear legal rule will facilitate more settlements and diminish the need for litigation, which is generally a more costly method of settling disputes).

328 Section 1(b) of the UK Arbitration Act 1996.

329 Comity here is tied inextricably to political imperatives, and relies upon a base level of similarity in the policies expressed by competing rules. If there is no "normative" public policy upholding the similar or same value, *i.e.*, pro-arbitration or party autonomy, it is easy to envisage that the court of the forum would be inclined to give priority to effect to its own domestic public policy in the event that any aspect of foreign public policy were found to be in irreconcilable conflict therewith. However, with shared values in common, the court of the forum would be more inclined to recognise domestic public policy, which is basically the same as the foreign public policy.

330 Montesquieu, *The Spirit of Laws* (1977) p. 30 (in Book 1 Chapter 3) (stating that "law in general is human reason, inasmuch as it governs all the inhabitants of the earth; the political

nation's law closely reflects its type of government, geography and climate as well as religion, history and culture. Today, this Darwinian type of proposition may seem like an anachronism as people around the globe have by and large converged on the Western type of formal law or global law both for political (*i.e.*, constitutional) and civil laws. Historically, the existing formal legal order in a large number of countries was shaped by transplanting law that had evolved in several European countries in the eighteenth and nineteenth centuries.[331] In the context of commercial arbitration, transplant is a common phenomenon. In defining the scope of public policy, a number of jurisdictions, such as Australia, Zimbabwe, Bermuda, Singapore, Malta and India, adopted a two-pronged definition of public policy, that is, the making of the award being induced or effected by fraud or corruption; and a breach of the rules of natural justice, both of which originated in the Model Law.[332] Even Western countries are transplanting norms and rules in regional or international conventions or model laws. For instance, the Model Law led to a revolution in the practice of arbitration in England,[333] and has been entirely transplanted into arbitration laws in Australia, Canada and recently Japan.[334] EU law influences directly the content of public policy in the laws of Member States at the stage of enforcement of arbitral awards. For instance, Article 81 (ex Article 85) is regarded as a mandatory rule within all EC Member States, including England.[335] The EU law's influence has also extended to the procedural side of arbitration law, leaving its trace on the interpretation and application of "lack of impartiality and independence" under the English law[336] when the courts have to decide whether the requirements that an arbitrator be impartial[337] and conduct arbitration fairly and with due process[338] are satisfied. Yet, convergence has often been confined to the law on the

and civil laws of each nation ought to be only the particular cases in which this human reason is applied. They should be adapted in such a manner to the people for whom they are made, as to render it very unlikely for those of one nation to be proper for another").

331 For example, the Japanese Civil Code (1898) was modelled on the German Civil Code of 1896, which came into force only in 1900.

332 Also see section 2.3 of this Chapter.

333 Bruce Harris, Rowan Planterose and Jonathan Tecks, *The Arbitration Act 1996 – A Commentary*, Oxford: Blackwell (1996) p. 1.

334 Masatsugu Suzuki, 'Japan's New Arbitration Law', [2005] *Asian DR* 18–19.

335 See generally, Christoph Liebscher, *The Healthy Award, Challenge in International Commercial Arbitration*, The Netherlands: Kluwer Law International (2003); Phillip Louis Landolt, *Modernised EC Competition Law in International Arbitration*, The Netherlands: Kluwer Law International (2006) Ch. 6.

336 The English courts have held that the test for lack of impartiality under s. 24 should be the same as the test applied by the European Court of Human Rights under Article 6(1) for lack of impartiality and independence, whether a fair-minded and informed observer having considered the facts would conclude that there was a real possibility that the arbitrator was biased. *Magill v. Porter* [2001] UKHL 67. In other words, the English courts acknowledged that the procedural rights enshrined in Article 6(1) of the European Court of Human Rights are sufficiently protected by the mandatory provisions of the Arbitration Act.

337 UK Arbitration Act 1996, s. 24(1).

338 UK Arbitration Act 1996, s. 33.

books and the functioning and effectiveness of legal institutions continue to diverge substantially.

Under the transplant theory, countries that receive their legal order from other countries have to come to grips with a substantial mismatch between the pre-existing conditions and the imported legal order.[339] The social, economic, cultural, political and institutional context often differs so remarkably between the originating and transplant countries that the imported legal order may not be effectuated in the transplant country. Transplant countries are likely to suffer from the transplant effect, *i.e.*, a mismatch between local conditions and institutions, as well as the side-effect of transplanted law on society. Transplant error often occurs in transplanting arbitration laws. In the arbitration laws of India and Pakistan, there is a "section 9(b)" problem relating to the provision dealing with the enforcement of foreign arbitral awards in both countries. The effect of section 9(b) is that in cases in which the governing law of the arbitration agreement is the law of India or Pakistan, awards made outside these territories are treated as domestic and thereby subject to the judicial review on the merits by the courts. As a result, an award rendered in such locations as Paris, London or New York will be subject to judicial control in India or Pakistan on arbitration as long as the substantive law of the dispute is the law of India or Pakistan. The problem originated from section 6(b) of Part I of the English Arbitration (Foreign Awards) Act 1930,[340] which was subsequently re-enacted in section 40(b) of Part II of the Arbitration Act 1950.[341] Section 40(b) was only concerned with the enforcement of awards pursuant to the Geneva Convention of 1927 and soon became a dead letter in England. However, when the 1930 Act was transplanted into over 30 Commonwealth countries, India and Pakistan adopted this provision into section 9(b) of their then respective statutes. The effect of applying section 9(b) has been something of a disaster, that is, to treat foreign awards in the same way as domestic awards and to subject arbitration conducted outside India and Pakistan to the control of the national courts. From a jurisprudential perspective, the history of section 9(b) is unfortunate because nothing in the Geneva Convention 1927 justified the original section 6(b) of the

339 For inconsistencies between informal indigenous norms and Western formal law in Asia, see Carol A.G. Jones, 'Capitalism, Globalisation and Rule of Law: An Alternative Trajectory of Legal Change in China', (1994) 3 *Soc. & L. Stud.* 195; and Jane Kaufman Winn, 'Relational Practices and the Marginalisation of Law: Informal Financial Practices of Small Businesses in Taiwan', (1994) 28 *Law & Soc'y Rev.* 193.

340 The draftsman of section 6(b) was inspired by the case of *Spurrier v. La Cloche* in 1902 ([1902] AC 446) in which the Privy Council gave effect to an English *Scott v. Avery* arbitration clause (1856 HL Cas. 811, making arbitration and an award a condition precedent to any resort to the courts) by setting aside a Jersey judgment on the merits and decided that the matter had to be referred to arbitration under the English Arbitration Act 1889. This case resulted in section 6(b) which states that "nothing in Part of this Act shall apply to any award made on an arbitration agreement governed by the law of England".

341 This section now continues in force due to section 99 of the Arbitration Act 1996 in relation to "foreign" awards excluding New York Convention awards.

1930 Act and there is no persuasive justification for construing section 6(b), and later section 40(b), in the English Arbitration Acts and section 9(b) in arbitration laws of India and Pakistan. More surprisingly, the mis-transplanted section 9(b) was still in force in India and Pakistan governing New York Convention awards until 1996, even though there was no trace of it in the English Arbitration Act 1975 due to the recommendation made by the Fifth Report by the Private International Law Committee to the Lord Chancellor in 1961 concerning the accession of the United Kingdom to the New York Convention to remove section 40(b) of the 1950 Act.[342] The side effect or error of legal transplant suggests that the absolute or complete transplant of a legal order or norm into another country may not guarantee that the inherent features of the legal order will function effectively locally. Similarly, the arbitration principles or norms that work well in some jurisdictions may not necessarily function in others. The risk exists to less intervening or restrictive pubic policy which may not be as functional in a developing country as in a developed country.

States that have developed their legal orders internally have a comparative advantage in creating effective legal institutions over countries on which a formal legal order was imposed externally. This proposition is empirically supported by the rejection of the earlier transplant practice under colonialism, and the recent attempts to use Western law as a tool to promote socioeconomic developments. This claim is also consistent with the notion that law is a cognitive institution in which laws that are compatible with the pre-existing social norms are more likely to be well-received and therefore effectuated.[343] Legal evolution theory ably explains why this comparative advantage exists in some countries. Where law evolves internally through a process of trial, error and correction, with the involvement of users of the law such as legal professionals and other interest groups, legal institutions tend to be more responsive to local conditions and adopt locally-tailored solutions. Legislature and judiciary can build on domestic knowledge and take full advantage of complementarities between new and old conditions as well as between new and old institutional arrangements. This is most explicit for case law, where new legal rules are generated from litigated cases.[344] By contrast, where foreign law is transplanted, legal institutions become less responsive and legal evolution becomes external rather than internal. The functioning and legality of transplant is largely dependent upon the demand for law, which, in turn, results in more voluntary compliance with law and more willingness of a society to invest in the legal institutions necessary for upholding the legal order. Therefore, a good fit of foreign law with local conditions may not be just a lucky coincidence, but can be achieved by

342 See the Fifth Report to the Lord Chancellor of the Private International Law Committee, Parliamentary Papers Vol. 18, Cmnd. 1961 No. 1515, App 3, p. 23.

343 Cass R. Sunstein, 'Social Norms and Social Roles', (1996) 96 *Colum. L. Rev.* 903, 925.

344 See Friedrich A. Hayek, *Law, Legislation and Liberty, Vol. 1: Rules and Order*, Chicago: Chicago University Press (1973).

constructive adaptation. Attempts must be made to induce a self-sustaining demand for legal change, or in Darwinian terms, evolution. Internal legal evolution can improve the legality of the transplanted law by adopting more adaptive measures to localise the law and to match local conditions. This requires a more constructive borrowing and undoubtedly takes as much time as for the enactment of optimally designed laws. After two hundred years of "colonial" or external legal transplant, more patience with the internal legal evolution seems necessary. In this sense, an effective legal reform shall be a voluntary transplant which can improve the legal receptivity of transplanted law. A voluntary transplant requires a substantial adaptation of the foreign legal order to the local context. Therefore, local conditions must be considered and workable modifications need to be made to transplanted rules or institutions. It is logical to conclude that an involuntary transplant of foreign or international public policy may not be compatible with local conditions of countries which have their own level of public intervention. The making of hard law at the international level may not constitute and result in a voluntary transplant.

5.6. HARMONISATION OF PUBLIC POLICY RULES AND INTERNATIONAL LAW-MAKING PROCESS

Despite the fact that the regulation of international business has a framework of norms, principles and rules, the sheer force of the world economy has resulted in more and more commercial disputes among states and international commercial players. International arbitration and other alternative dispute settlement methods have proved effective in the global marketplace and have a considerable impact on the transaction costs and security of international business. International commercial arbitration, therefore, should be seen as a key device for structuring and maintaining the international markets and for guiding the transactional behaviours of international economic players.[345] Although there have been international and regional conventions facilitating the "arbitralisation" of commercial disputes, there are still problems facing arbitrators, arbitration institutions, arbitration panels and private parties involved in transnational commercial arbitration. It is imperative that the parties agree on the system of law applicable to their particular agreement to proceed with arbitration, as well as the law applicable to the actual process and to the merits of their dispute. This perspective is eclectic, in particular because of the "dynamic interaction between the will of the arbitrating parties and the interest of various national legal

345 See Yves Dezlay and Bryant G. Garth, *Dealing in Virtue: International Commercial Arbitration and the Construction of a Transnational Legal Order*, Chicago and London: University of Chicago Press (1996) p. 7.

systems in ensuring justice and fairness of the arbitral process and its respect for vital and appropriate national interests".[346]

Legal culture and history are legitimate and reasonable sources of differentiation in transnational commercial law. The hypothesis of a "culturally neutral, universal language of law" is theoretically possible but realistically difficult still.[347] It has been argued that, paradoxically, legal integration has a disintegrating effect on law in that it distances human beings from formal law[348] and local conditions. Along with globalisation, the concept of floating or de-localised arbitration has become popular but has received a less enthusiastic response as even the previously enthusiastic transnationalist campaigners start to appreciate that international commercial arbitration is not wholly distinct from national arbitration laws.[349] In other words, local characteristics are still in existence in the globalisation of law. There is no legislative or judicial authority empowered at the international level so far to provide "official" meaning for or to define the scope of public policy in the global body of law. The process for the emergence of a uniform public policy is different from the usual way in which the legal standard takes on the "official" or uniform legal meaning given the absence of a transnational legislative body. Whatever the degree of ascendency of global law or transnational commercial law is, the emergence of a uniform public policy in transnational arbitration is not a spontaneous process as law's "naming of persons and types of transactions links private law systems closely to the culture of communities in which they evolve".[350]

There have always been hues and cries as to the necessity of harmonising national laws, *inter alia*, on public policy at the international level so that international commercial arbitration can be conducted in a more foreseeable and uniform manner worldwide. The persuasive response to this claim is same as the answer to the question whether a country shall be a member of the New York Convention. The substance and form of the New York Convention appears to have passed two important tests. First, the New York Convention has been accepted by and adapted to different legal, political and economic systems. Second, the Convention continues to be effective even though it has been in

346 Okezie Chukwumerije, above n. 63.

347 Peter Sack, 'Law, Language and Culture: Verbal Acrobatics and Social Technology', (1998) 41 *Journal Legal Pluralism* 15.

348 Thomas Wilhelmsson, 'Legal Integration as Disintegration of National Law', in Hanne Petersen and Henrik Zahle, *Legal Polycentricity: Consequences of Pluralism in Law,* Aldershot: Dartmouth Publishing Co. (1995) p. 139 ("the further away from the individual citizen the legal instruments are created, the greater is the possibility that disintegration as alienation from law will occur").

349 Jan Paulsson, 'Delocalisation of International Commercial Arbitration: When and Why it Matters', (1983) 32 *ICLQ* 53; Frederick A. Mann, 'England Rejects "Delocalised" Contracts and Arbitration', (1984) 33 *ICLQ* 193.

350 Hugh Collins, 'Good Faith in European Contract Law', (1994) 14 *Oxford Journal Legal Studies* 229.

existence for around five decades. This is proven by the fact that the chapter on recognition and enforcement of arbitral awards in the UNCITRAL Model Law was closely modelled on the provisions of the New York Convention, and that the solutions of the New York Convention have been incorporated into many national legislation and multilateral international treaties. Expanding the membership of the New York Convention enables commercial entities in one country to rely on the growing network of the regime for recognition and enforcement of arbitral awards. It is, therefore, in the interests of a country to be a member of the New York Convention and to adhere to the standards, principles and norms therein so that its interaction with the international business community can be promoted.

The only reason that a country could conceivably be against adopting the New York Convention is to preserve for the legislative body and courts a degree of autonomy in dealing with foreign arbitral awards. However, this argument is superficial and should not be a decisive factor. There are more convincing counter-arguments in favour of being a member of the New York Convention. The privately-contracted adjudicators in international arbitration should be left to manage the legal construction of the public sphere without rigorous supervision by the courts. The judicial power of national courts should not be a great concern. In addition, participants in international business need reasonable confidence in the enforceability of an arbitral award regardless of the jurisdiction in which the assets are located and will be enforced against. Without such confidence, it will be more difficult to expand the trade, investment and business to non-traditional markets and to establish business ties with new partners in untested jurisdictions.[351] Parties that have refused to comply with an award are often black-listed; on the other hand, a jurisdiction which adopts more non-enforcement grounds justified by the New York Convention will not be internationally respected. The adoption of the New York Convention does not mean that a country has signed a *carte blanche* compelling recognition and enforcement of foreign awards. Rather, the New York Convention offers reasonable leeway for non-enforcement of a foreign arbitral award. Foreign business partners are more willing to accept the place of arbitration in a country that is a party to the New York Convention. Therefore, the Member States will enjoy an advantageous edge in the marketplace. By contrast, it is short-sighted for a country not to be part of the uniform regime and that country is likely to be marginalised in international commercial circles.

Inherent in the international law-making process is the recognition of diversity as well as different levels of inception of uniform legal norms and standards. The genesis of the harmonisation of commercial law is the theory of

351 In addition to the legal system, foreign partners also tend to require a higher degree of security, which may complicate contract negotiations and increase the costs of the transaction.

sources of law.[352] There are several layers of source of law in transnational commercial law. First, the United Nations reformed or at least recast the international laws with the weight of supranational sovereign rules. The United Nations has spawned a number of international, quasi-political and inter-governmental economic organisations, which seek to achieve harmonisation in the legal field.[353] The Vienna-based UNCITRAL has swiftly developed into the core agency of the UN legal services and has contributed decisively to legal harmonisation worldwide.[354] The New York Convention is among the most successful unification instruments not only in the area of arbitration but in the entire field of international commercial law. Nevertheless, the Convention does not eliminate all obstacles including inappropriate levels of judicial intervention, which calls for a new generation of international rules. Second, the Hague Conference on Private International Law,[355] UNIDROIT,[356] and organisations of merchants such as the ICC[357] formulate important rules and principles and have become a strong force in the unification and harmonisation of international commercial law. The UNIDROIT Principles, UNCITRAL Model Law and other soft laws are being so aggressively transposed into national black letters as part

---

352 Bruno Oppetit, 'L'emergence de la lex mercatoria', in Bruno Oppetit, *Droit et modernité* (1998) p. 53.

353 Ernst-Ulrich Petersmann, *E-U in International Trade Law and the GATT/WTO Dispute Settlement System*, Boston: Kluwer Law International (1977) p. 5.

354 UNCITRAL's most prominent contributions include the United Nations Convention on Contracts for the International Sale of Goods, which has achieved worldwide success and recognition. UN Doc. A/CONF.97/18, Annex I, English version reprinted in 52 Fed. Reg. 6264 (1987) and in 19 ILM 668 (1980), and the UNCITRAL Arbitration Rules, UN Doc. A/31/17, para. 57 (1976), reprinted in 15 ILM 701 (1976). Other products the UNCITRAL produced include the United Nations Convention on the Carriage of Goods by Sea (1978), the Convention on the Limitation Period in the International Sale of Goods (New York, 1974); Legal Guide on International Transactions (1992); UN Convention on the Liability of Operators of Transport Terminals in International Trade, Model Law on Procurement of Goods, Construction and Services (1994); Legal Guide on Drawing Up International Contracts for the Construction of Industrial Works (1988); UN Convention on International Bills of Exchange and International Promissory Notes (New York, 1988); Legal Guide on Electronic Funds Transfers (1987); Model Law on International Credit Transfers (1992); UN Convention on Independent Guarantees and Stand-by Letters of Credit (New York, 1995); Recommendation on the Legal Value of Computer Records (1985); Model Law on Electronic Commerce (1996); Model Law on Cross-Border Insolvency (1997).

355 The work of the Hague Conference includes the Convention on Service Abroad of Judicial and Extrajudicial Documents in Civil and Commercial Matter, 15 November 1965, 20 UST 361 and the Convention on the Taking of Evidence Abroad in Civil or Commercial Matters, 27 July 1970, 23 UST 2555.

356 UNIDROIT's conventions include the Convention on International Financial Leasing, 28 May 1988, 27 ILM 931 and the Convention on International Factoring, 28 May 1988, 27 ILM 943, as well as the Restatement-like Principles of International Commercial Contracts (1994).

357 Few sets of international commercial rules are as widely used as the ICC Incoterms, ICC Pub. No. 460 (1990) and the Uniform Customs and Practice for Documentary Credits, ICC Pub. No. 500 (1993).

of the scheme of rendering the uniform rules and standards globally. Participants in international arbitration are increasingly conscious of local obstacles. The most effective way for a country to reassure all participants in arbitration about the quality of its law on international arbitration is perhaps to enact the UNCITRAL Model Law. The Model Law usefully extends the enforcement regime of the New York Convention to all international arbitral awards irrespective of the country where the award was made.

Along with globalisation and the international law-making process, the neo-liberal dogma of free trade, investment and business would also have resulted in a predominantly market-oriented political economy at the international level. Even arbitration has now become more market-oriented and has been in the process of marketisation. Nevertheless, there has been widespread discomfort with marketisation of everything including the legal order and public policy, for various reasons. First, most countries are considerably less market-oriented than a truly *laissez-faire* economy, so the level of administrative, legislative and judicial intervention varies to different degrees. Second, markets do not deal well with all public externalities, a combination of inadequate information, public process bias, and traditional economic externalities. The increasing integration of the world economy is more likely to intensify conflicts in international business, which impose pressures on each nation to conform to some kind of world standard for political economy[358] such as a more tolerant and flexible judiciary, a more limited level of judicial review and more recognition of party autonomy of business players. In the long run, such pressures may produce a much greater degree of convergence of legal orders or legal systems. Some types of "international standards" are necessary if the world arbitration community is going to be perceived as having a minimal level of fairness and justice. However, the convergence will not develop smoothly or quickly as the differences in political economy are rooted in history and are not amenable to change through rational discourse. If the reality of the difficulties of legal convergence in political economies is rightly observed, the challenge is to build a legal order that sufficiently satisfies justice and legitimacy based on radically different approaches to public policy and party autonomy in the commercial community. There are few options left so far. First, it is advisable to build up a supranational framework. With the fast growth of international business, some regulation of international arbitration in a systematic fashion in a centralised manner is definitely preferred. Unlike the European Union, however, there are no political, regulatory or judicial bodies at the centre of international political and legal systems that have any real resemblance to the sovereign organs of a true state. This may suggest that there is not a centralised legal order to maintain desirable

358 "Political economy", in a political sense, essentially reflects the dominant philosophy in each country about the proper role of government in assuring general welfare and the way the dominant philosophy is institutionalised in the country's economic and political structures.

markets. The question then is how and how much power can and must be transferred from national governing bodies to a regional or international body in order to make markets workable. Second, in addition to a uniform legal order, voluntary regulation is also a possibility. It is possible that greater convergence will be achieved through a spontaneous and internal process of constructing the legal order, although this will not be an easy, smooth or quick process.

5.7. SUMMARY

The vulnerable process of international arbitration is under pressure to change. The pressures arise from diverse sources: the contemporary cross-border commercial environment, the acceleration of cross-cultural influences, globalisation, the growing experimentation with less formal and rigid dispute resolution mechanisms, more supportive judicial attitudes towards commercial arbitration, more respect demanded by the business community from the courts to party autonomy, less judicial and government intervention, and finally, the consumer demand for a faster, more efficient and less expensive arbitration process. Innovations like judicialisation of certain procedures, expansion of mechanisms for obtaining evidence and information, imposition of case-management techniques, commitment to less formal processes, adoption of less intervening public policy and a narrower scope of judicial review clearly respond to these pressures. It seems that continued pressures from arbitrating parties, arbitral institutions and courts will effect an alteration to many aspects of international commercial arbitration.

There is a pressing need for a clear consideration of modernity, locality, nationality, internationality and globality. The twentieth century experienced an important change, that is, the dilution, the dissipation, and, in some extreme cases, the disappearance of state power. The "delocalised" arbitration is free from the procedural safeguards traditionally imposed by those national legal systems. This shift in the locus of authority reflects a widespread popular realisation, but also a critical controversy, that the collective public responsibility of the state does not fully substitute on a broad basis for individual responsibility privately exercised. So far a three-tiered global system, consisting of private adjudication under agreed rules, supported by national regulations necessary to ensure its integrity, and an international exercise or non-exercise of state power to the extent required to guarantee enforcement of arbitral awards, has been set up. The dilution of state power strengthens the mechanism whereby parties of different nationalities agree to mandatory arbitration of disputes between them, pursuant to a particular set of arbitration rules. Statutes in major industrial jurisdictions have been modernised so as to minimise state or judicial intervention in the arbitral process, while offering judicial review under a "small" umbrella of public policy to the extent merely necessary to ensure the integrity of the process by which the arbitral tribunal arrived at its award. These evolving trends, however, have not been fully reflected in the global legislation of international commercial arbitration. The New York Convention only deals with arbitration proceedings indirectly (by providing principles which must not be violated) or partially (by dealing with some aspects of the validity of the arbitration agreement). The Model Law and UNCITRAL Arbitration Rules are of a contractual nature and, as a result, their good functioning depends on the mandatory procedural legislation in individual states governing the case. In any event, neither the New York Convention, the Model Law nor the UNCITRAL Arbitration Rules deal with judicial intervention, such as public policy and due process, at a mandatory level or in a more functional manner.

Under the label of globality, there are undeniably strong pressures towards harmonisation and homogenisation of legal orders, systems or norms such as public policy, as significant differences in local law stand as impediments to international business and dispute resolution. The attempt to harmonise the substantive law in cross-border litigation has been going on for a while. In the context of international commercial arbitration, such an attempt has not been substantially made on several critically important issues such as the law on public policy. The needs of modern day arbitration mandate that states moderate and harmonise their traditionally parochial views of public policy relating to the enforcement of foreign arbitral awards. In this respect, the French approach to distinguishing domestic and international public policy has been regarded as an innovative approach and has been gradually recognised by more states. However, this approach is over-pragmatic yet lacks practical guidance. The principle-based and efficiency-centred normative public policy, which supports the presumption in favour of enforcement of contractual choice among the parties, shall be able to compensate for such defects. Where the parties cannot contract explicitly, public policy shall allow the parties to determine, at a low cost and *ex ante*, that the given conduct will trigger the application of the law of a specific state. The parties may be able to plan and structure their behaviour so as to avoid laws ill-suited to their affairs. Moreover, party autonomy and the contractual choice mechanism shall minimise the costs of contracting for efficient laws or avoiding inefficient ones. In the absence of an explicit contract, courts should apply the state law that the parties most likely would have selected had they contracted explicitly before their legal dispute arose.[359] Assuming that the parties would typically prefer to be governed by the law that maximises their joint welfare,[360] they would be expected to choose the law of the state with the comparative regulatory advantage. In order to preserve the parties' rights and *ex ante* predictability, comparative regulatory advantage should be employed not as a general standard but rather as a criterion for developing specific and predictable rules.

---

359 See Richard A. Posner, above n. 181, 646.

360 Ibid.

The attractiveness of normative public policy rests with its ability to provide for reasonable and predictable standards of commercial practice and an acceptable benchmark for judicial intervention. Ideally, normative public policy law and practice can be legalised in statutes at an international level. Given the weakness of international hard law, such normative public policy may be coded in soft law but with a more mandatory flavour. It has been suggested that a detailed list of non-arbitrable matters be elaborated in a model law type of legal document. Given the considerable difficulties in reaching a worldwide consensus on an exhaustive list in a new multilateral treaty, a non-exhaustive list may be proposed to states for domestic adoption or implementation by a model law or a supplementary protocol to the model law. States are then "compelled" to list thereafter any other issues deemed necessary according to local laws.[361] The advantage of this approach is that it is able to channel "local information" to outsiders and to channel "outside information" to the local context, thereby "compelling" states not to over-extend the scope of non-arbitrable matters. The legal norms or standards in soft law will be adeptly transplanted into other countries, especially into a large number of developing countries, which are not willing to transplant foreign legal norms into their local legal order in a dramatic and mechanical manner. Once legal norms contained in soft law are locally accepted, they may become the foundational elements of harmonised public policy in international commercial arbitration.

[361] Gerold Herrmann, 'Does the World Need Additional Uniform Legislation on Arbitration?', (1999) 15(3) *Arb. Int'l* 219.

CHAPTER 6

NEO-NEW YORK CONVENTION: A PRELIMINARY CONCLUSION

This chapter summarises the whole book, which essentially consists of the study of four dilemmas in the New York Convention, two research methodologies adopted, and one core question relating to the globalised world in the 21st century. The focus of this book has two limbs. First, although the book touches upon four dilemmas in the New York Convention, the scope of this book is indeed beyond the traditional topics in commercial arbitration and extends to some theoretical topics in globalisation such as judicial competition and international governance, which are not traditionally linked to the New York Convention. Second, consistent with the topics covered in this book, the analytical methods adopted are also beyond traditional methodologies such as case studies and positivist approaches.

6.1. FOUR DILEMMAS OF THE NEW YORK CONVENTION

6.1.1. DILEMMA OF THE PAST, PRESENT AND FUTURE OF THE NEW YORK CONVENTION

The New York Convention is a product of evolution with two primary objectives, *i.e.*, greater enforceability of arbitral awards and greater uniformity of enforcement practice. These objectives are actually the two primary objectives of the Geneva Protocol of 1923 on Arbitration Clauses in Commercial Matters and the 1927 Geneva Convention on the Execution of Foreign Arbitral Awards.[1] The New York Convention achieved these two objectives largely through the simplification of enforcement proceedings, in particular by abolishing the cumbersome double exequatur procedure required under the provisions of its predecessor, namely the 1927 Geneva Convention, and by setting out certain

1 See Chapter 2 of this book.

exclusive grounds in Article V by which signatory states could refuse to enforce an award.[2]

In Darwinian terminology, the New York Convention inherited, through a "natural selection process", core memetic codes from the two previous generations' "organism", and evolved into a higher level of "organism" by transmitting codes and information from the environment into the "gene" and adapting itself into a new environment. Ultimately, the New York Convention provides a more stable legal regime under which arbitration can prosper for the next several decades. However, according to Darwinian legal theory, change is a universal characteristic of the world and law is a cognitive institution. Therefore, the New York Convention should not be a close-ended regime. Rather, it should be part of the evolving universal change which needs to respond to external forces and possess features that co-evolve with the surroundings. As fifty-five years have passed since its birth, some adjustments to account for new developments, legal, technological, political and economic, must be made to the New York Convention.

6.1.2. DILEMMA OF TENSIONS BETWEEN RENDITION AND ENFORCING FORUMS

The purposes of the New York Convention are to preserve expectations of both contracting states of rendition and enforcement as well as private parties, thereby minimising forum shopping.[3] Unfortunately, however, the pursuit of these goals often encounters difficulties in practice since the enforcement of awards ultimately relies upon the implementation of uniform standards by contracting states of the New York Convention. A compelling issue is how the court in the enforcement forum should deal with an arbitral award which has been set aside by the court in the country of rendition. The plain language of Article V, in its use of the term "may", seems to show the discretionary character of the defences to enforcement of awards available under that Article. This discretion stands in stark contrast to Article III, which in setting out the Convention's central obligation, provides that courts of "each contracting state shall recognise … and enforce" foreign arbitral awards.

---

2 Article V enumerates an exclusive list of grounds on which recognition or enforcement of a foreign arbitral award may be withheld: (1) incapacity of the parties to agree to arbitrate or other invalidity of the arbitration agreement; (2) inability to present a party's case during the arbitration proceedings; (3) award exceeding the scope of the submission to arbitration; (4) irregularities in the composition and procedure of the arbitral tribunal; (5) award not binding, set aside or suspended at the *situs* of the arbitration; (6) non-arbitrability of the subject matter of the dispute; and (7) award contravening public policy. See Article V of the New York Convention.

3 See Hamid G. Gharavi, 'Chromalloy: Another View', (1997) 12 *Mealey's Int'l Arb. Rep.* 21, 21–22 (noting parties may purposely try to arbitrate in forum where arbitral awards can be more easily overturned under local law).

Taken together, the interplay between the two Articles illustrates that a decision to enforce an award despite an Article V(1)(e) defence, such as annulment of the award in the country of rendition, would be not only permissible under the Convention, but would accord with its pro-enforcement goals.[4] Nonetheless, it has been argued that no matter what the technical wording of Article V(1)(e), an enforcing court should always defer to the judgment of a court at the *situs*, and that Article V(1)(e) could never really be construed to permit enforcement of an award under such circumstances.[5] The New York Convention is therefore characterised by fundamental underlying tensions between the roles of the courts of the enforcing forum versus those of the *situs*.

The cases of *Hilmarton* and *Chromalloy* are two vivid examples illustrating such a chaotic dilemma. Yet there are strong arguments for vesting in the courts of the *situs* or of the enforcement the primary competence to review arbitral awards. Obviously, the flexibility and vagueness provided by the New York Convention on a myriad of potential defences to enforcement possibly leads to a loss of a significant measure of uniformity[6] and potential chaos in practice. Without uniform guidance and being bound by the treaty or a "federal" type of institutional structure, individual contracting states could slow the development of international standards by adopting and implementing domestic laws that mainly protect local interests and which vary considerably from international norms.[7]

6.1.3. DILEMMA OF HARD LAW, SOFT LAW AND *LEX MERCATORIA*

The New York Convention can be understood as a nod towards greater enforcement of foreign arbitral awards at the expense of a degree of uniformity, given the manner in which it effectively imports domestic norms into the

---

4 See Gary H. Sampliner, 'Enforcement of Foreign Arbitral Awards After Annulment in Their Country of Origin', (1996) 11 *Mealey's Int'l Arb. Rep.* 22, 23 ("As one indication of the 'pro-enforcement bias' … [the Convention's] authors knew to use the mandatory 'shall' language in the articles contemplating enforcement of awards, while not using such language in the article that sets forth defenses to enforcement").

5 See Albert Jan van den Berg, 'Consolidated Commentary', XIX *Yearbook* (1994) 475, 590–93 (arguing that Article V(1)(e) automatically vests setting aside of award with extraterritorial effect, precluding enforcement elsewhere).

6 See Chapter 3 of this book.

7 For example, the Egyptian law of arbitration at the heart of the *Chromalloy* case included "two uniquely Egyptian" grounds for annulment of awards, namely "if the arbitral award fails to apply the law agreed by the parties to the subject matter of the dispute" and "if nullity occurs in the arbitral award, or if the arbitral proceedings are tainted by nullity affecting the award". Jan Paulsson, 'Rediscovering the New York Convention: Further Reflections on Chromalloy', (1997) *Mealey's Int'l Arb. Rep.* 21.

operation of an international legal instrument. Although most countries have made great efforts to adhere to the uniform standards laid out in Article V,[8] the tension between diversity in enforcement practice on the one hand and uniformity on the other, however, still exists.

It is not the ambition of the New York Convention to resolve the discrepancies in substantive and procedural arbitration law and practice in state signatories, in particular, between common law and civil law jurisdictions as well as between developed and developing states. Accordingly, even with the growth of international commercial arbitration, local practices, such as those in existence in common and civil law systems as well as in developed and developing jurisdictions are unlikely to converge because, in either Darwinian terminology or a jurisdictional competition norm, the "change can be better characterised as incremental adaptation rather than the wholesale adoption or replacement of the ... system".[9]

As far as the applicable law in commercial arbitration is concerned, *lex mercatoria* has become more popular and is used to denote a new approach or standard in favour of the application of non-national legal standards rather than the use of standards stemming from a particular national legal system. The concept of *lex mercatoria* is compatible with the trend of delocalisation of commercial arbitration and the self-regulation character of international commercial arbitration.[10] Although arbitral awards based on *lex mercatoria* are statistically rare, they are invariably recognised and enforced by national courts.[11] The study of *lex mercatoria* inevitably needs to touch upon the jurisprudential tension between hard law and soft law. Hard rules and associated sanctions often cause hesitancy and decrease of the likelihood of an agreement among states. By contrast, soft law, such as voluntary codes of conduct, non-binding recommendations, and informal agreements on cooperation, promotes a common approach to arbitration. The reliance on soft law as a tool to harmonise international arbitration law and practice allows for policy

8 For example, Article 36(1) of the UNCITRAL Model Law, see Report of the UN Comm. on Int'l Trade L., UN GAOR 40th Sess., Supp. No. 17, at 92, UN Doc. A/40/17 (1985), from which a number of national arbitration laws have been derived, is almost an exact replica of Article V of the New York Convention. See Kenneth T. Ungar, 'The Enforcement of Arbitral Awards Under UNCITRAL's Model Law on International Commercial Arbitration', (1987) 25 *Colum. J. Transnat'l L.* 717, 732–34, 743–53 (noting similarity between rules laid down in Article 36 and the New York Convention).

9 Sigurt Vitols, Steven Casper, David Soskice and Stephen Woolcock, *Corporate Governance in Large British and German Companies: Comparative Institutional Advantage or Competing for Best Practice*, London: Anglo-German Foundation for the Study of Industrial Society (1997) p. 36.

10 See AAA International Rules Article 28; ICC Article 17; LCIA Article 22.3; Arbitration Rules of the Institute of the Stockholm Chamber of Commerce Article 24. Also see the UNCITRAL Rules Article 33.

11 See Chapter 4 of this book.

experimentation and more deference to party autonomy in arbitration, and further permits flexibility and adaptability of law to local circumstances.[12]

6.1.4. DILEMMA OF PUBLIC POLICY AND PARTY AUTONOMY

The New York Convention has its roots in Article III which provides that courts of "each contracting state shall recognise ... and enforce" foreign arbitral awards, thereby protecting party autonomy. The introduction of harmonising measures in the field of arbitration law is essentially ancillary to the principle of party autonomy. On the other hand, Article V, in particular the non-arbitrability and public policy provisions, has created some tensions with the principle of party autonomy because non-arbitrability and public policy exceptions provide courts in the country of enforcement with some leeway in enforcing arbitral awards and have created the possibility for the enforcing courts to effectively import domestic norms into the operation of the New York Convention.

A more controversial aspect of the New York Convention is Article VII, which has been often regarded as a "more favourable right" rule calling for the application of a state's domestic law if such law provides more liberal grounds for enforcement than under the New York Convention.[13] This allows the party seeking enforcement to choose a body of law more favourable to its dispute.[14] The New York Convention therefore represents a minimum standard from which signatory states cannot derogate but are allowed to retain existing liberal norms or take further unilateral steps to facilitate enforcement.

The deeper tension is then a potential conflict between Articles VII and V(2) because the former is where judicial competence to evaluate awards lies and the latter should exercise control in the event of conflict. The state-centred and non-

---

12 See Brian Portnoy, 'Constructing Competition: Antitrust and the Political Foundations of Global Capitalism', (2000) 75, 204 (unpublished Ph.D. dissertation, University of Chicago; on file with the University of Chicago), cited in Anu Piilola, 'Assessing Theories of Global Governance: A Case Study of International Antitrust Regulation', (2003) 39 *Stan. J. Int'l L.* 207.

13 See Albert Jan van den Berg, *The New York Arbitration Convention of 1958: Towards a Uniform Judicial Interpretation*, the Netherlands: Kluwer Law and Taxation Publishers (1981) p. 88 and n. 225; see also Jan Paulsson, 'Rediscovering the New York Convention: Further Reflections on Chromalloy', (1997) 12(4) *Mealey's Int'l Arb. Rep.* 20 (noting that Article VII provides that "national rules or indeed other treaties shall be given preference if they are more favourable to enforcement"); 'Problems in Enforcement of Foreign Arbitral Awards', (1995) 6 *World Arbitration & Mediation Report* 77 (noting that Article VII allows domestic forum to apply its own arbitration law if that law is more pro-enforcement than under the Convention).

14 See Albert Jan van den Berg, above n. 13, 84 (arguing that language must pertain only to the party seeking enforcement in order to avoid results "wholly inconsistent with the pro-enforcement bias of the Convention and the aim of the [more favourable right] provision itself").

harmonising public policy exception of the New York Convention does not seem to be compatible with the general "pro-enforcement bias" of the New York Convention.[15] Given the lack of clear guidance, the public policy rule of the New York Convention represents a withdrawal from the core objective of upholding party autonomy in commercial arbitration and achieving uniformity of practice among state signatories.[16]

6.2. TWO "NEW" THEORIES

Two main research methodologies have been adopted and their technical aspects and application to the New York Convention have been thoroughly discussed in this book. They are "innovative" in the sense that they have been rarely used in the study of the New York Convention and international commercial arbitration, most questions of which are practical and procedural in nature. These two methodologies also have significant jurisprudential value to the core question of the entire book at the macro-level study.

6.2.1. GAME THEORY AND JUDICIAL COMPETITION

The dynamics among states can be explained by reference to game theory, the focus of which is the self-interest, reputation and competition of various players in repeated transactions.[17] The theory supports the view that judicial competition and cooperation are in co-existence and can lead to credible commitments. Competing or cooperating states are subject to peer pressure and are conscious of the reputation and self-interest which would be endangered by the breaking of commitments. The players in the gaming setting have a stronger incentive in the upkeep of their reputations in the community. As a result, a federal or centralised convention and governance regime (or a "pool" in an economics sense) facilitates the emergence of shared expectations and concerns, development of behavioural standards and eventually a "race to the top".

Although the existence of many international organisations across a large number of fields have demonstrated their valuable role in international policymaking, an effective international governance regime does not necessarily

---

15 *Parsons & Whittemore Overseas Co. v. Société Générale de l'Industrie du Papier*, 508 F.2d 969 (2nd Cir. 1974).

16 See Chapter 5 of this book.

17 Giandomenico Majone, 'International Regulatory Cooperation: A Neo-Institutionalist Approach', in George A. Bermann, Matthias Herdegen and Peter L. Lindseth (eds.), *Transatlantic Regulatory Cooperation: Legal Problems and Political Prospects*, Oxford: Oxford University Press (2000) p. 136 and p. 138.

require a full scale of institutionalisation, which does not guarantee the efficiency of global governance.[18] Game theory provides a reliable theoretical model of the global economic order and provides the necessary level of flexibility and benefits to the existing institution-based governing regime. The potential and strength of a new governance regime accordingly depends on its ability to define common goals as well as the state actors' good faith, internal cohesion, mutual trust and ability to reach consensus.

6.2.2. DARWINIAN THEORY AND EVOLUTION OF LAW

According to Darwinian theory, history and environment matter, because both determine the way in which institutions can change or evolve; efficiency is not necessarily a decisive factor. In international commercial arbitration, the New York Convention itself is a product of Darwinian development and indicates the interdependence between the meme, legal norm and social environment that are key factors in social evolution.

The significance of Darwinian theory is reflected in its supplementary role to game theory. In real life it is rare that the competitive or cooperative setting is achieved instantaneously, as the players are not necessarily rational and aware of the payoff functions of other players. The question is whether the equilibrium can persist in an increasingly competitive global market. Arguably, as markets globalise and market players (including individuals, corporations and states which are subject to very different governance systems) are compelled to compete head to head (in product, labour and capital markets), a Darwinian struggle becomes possible, out of which, in theory, the most efficient norm should emerge dominant. Indeed, it has been predicted that such a competition implies an "end to history" for some laws.[19]

A relevant but newer proposition is the "path dependency" theory that explains the path of the convergence and further postulates that institutions evolve along path-dependent trajectories, which are heavily shaped by initial starting points and pre-existing conditions.[20] In employing such a methodology to measure the degree of legal change, "there is a strong tendency towards convergence of formal legal rules as the result of extensive legal reforms", and

---

18 Ibid. 136.

19 Frank H. Easterbrook and Daniel R. Fischel, *The Economic Structure of Corporate Law*, Cambridge, MA: Harvard University Press (1996) pp. 4–15; and Henry Hansmann and Reinier Kraakman, 'The End of History for Corporate Law', (2001) 89 *Georgetown Law Journal* 439.

20 Lucian Arye Bebchuk and Mark J. Roe, 'A Theory of Path Dependence in Corporate Ownership and Governance', (1999) 52 *Stan. L. Rev.* 127; Amir N. Licht, 'The Mother of All Path Dependencies: Toward a Cross-Cultural Theory of Corporate Governance Systems', (2001) 26 *Del. J. Corp. L.* 147.

"law reform has been primarily responsive to economic change rather than initiating or leading it".[21]

Darwinian theory is a strong jurisprudential tool to confirm the necessity and way of reforming the New York Convention. For instance, for the sake of consistency, a revision of the New York Convention to resolve the discrepancy between national laws in precautionary remedies in enforcement of foreign arbitral awards[22] is not feasible since this would substantially change the memetic code of the New York Convention.

6.3. ONE CORE QUESTION: IMPROVING THE NEW YORK CONVENTION IN THE GLOBALISED WORLD IN THE 21ST CENTURY

We are currently witnessing an increase in all forms of international commercial transactions and a resurgence in pro-free trade and investment attitudes at different levels in the world. Global commerce has expanded with flourishing multinational corporations, sophisticated electronics and data processing systems, and the dramatically increasing volume of transnational transactions. In this respect, it is now common practice for businesses to cross their national borders to enter foreign markets. Although the pressure from different types of protectionist interests at the international level is still considerable, progress has been made towards globalisation. Trade relations and capital investments are now being "rationalised" in a new international economic order.

The worldwide liberalisation is being influenced by a number of virtually universal trends: deregulation or re-regulation aimed at promoting enhanced competition; increased competitive pressures among different market players; and efforts of state authorities to coordinate, harmonise and strengthen the rule of law and legal systems. Along with liberalisation, the absolute authority of the sovereign is constrained by law; however, the legal system furthers the decentralisation of power in society, which makes possible private law-making and the growth of self-regulatory bodies such as arbitration institutions.

Due to globalisation and economic liberalisation and integration, it is harder for any contracting state to manage and regulate a more dynamic, market-driven and international economic order alone. Global governance can exist in different modes but state governments must face the dilemma of balancing national

---

21 Katharina Pistor, 'Patterns of Legal Change: Shareholder and Creditor Rights in Transition Economies' (Eur. Bank for Reconstruction & Development Working Paper No. 49/2000, 2000), available at http://www.ebrd.com/english/region/workingp/wp49.pdf.

22 Bernardo M. Cremades, 'Is Exclusion of Concurrent Courts' Jurisdiction over Conservatory Measures to be Introduced through a Revision of the Convention?', (1989) 6(1) *J. Int'l Arb.* 171.

interests with international obligations, and of complying with international obligations without compromising national sovereignty. Game theory assumes that the behaviour and self-interest of the state are best mediated by the market, which ensures both individual interests and general economic welfare. Judicial competition, as well as market competition, liberates the self-interest of individual states while at the same time constraining its misuse. The neo-liberal global governance now makes better use of "soft law" in pursuit of cooperation and voluntary convergence rather than coercion. In modern times, the global governance regime created through norms of reciprocity, trust and consensus is superior to a regime advancing the rule of law through regulatory imperialism and mandatory sanctions.

Most laws remain predominantly national. The conventional way to deal with international legal issues such as enforcement of foreign arbitral awards set aside by the court in the country of rendition is to rely on a unilateral application of national laws, which often causes trouble and tension. There is an ongoing debate over whether there is a need for an international regime that could better respond to the new economic environment, increased cross-border business activities, and the integration of markets. An effective transnational regime is viewed as a useful tool to reduce transaction costs, increase efficiency and cultivate legal predictability and certainty. Achieving convergence by compelling nations to harmonise their policies and rules with a common vision can lead to successful public policies and effective global governance.[23] Nevertheless, the establishment of an international regime may hinder any positive attempts to internalise the regulatory convergence. Expanding bilateral and regional cooperative arrangements is a possibility. The establishment of unified supranational rules is a more controversial approach, which lacks sufficient support in the real world.[24] The other alternative solution would be the harmonisation of national laws. It is however hard to find a satisfactory equilibrium.

Harmonisation of law in the early days gave way to more flexible approaches which placed greater stress on Member States' autonomy. For instance, in the process of harmonising corporate law in Europe, harmonising measures appeared in different ways and were reflected in the first, second, third and

[23] cf. Giandomenico Majone, above n. 17 (arguing that "where such mutual trust is not forthcoming, regulatory cooperation may have to be supported by formal institutions and centralised procedures", although it is noted that agreements often lack credibility when the level of implementation is uncertain and the importance of trust-building is not well recognised by all the players).

[24] See Joel I. Klein, 'Time For A Global Competition Initiative?', Address at the EC Merger Control 10th Anniversary Conference in Brussels (14 September 2000), http://www.usdoj.gov/atr/public/speeches/6486.htm. The United States has opposed this approach most notably, yet US leaders have more recently recognised that some measures at an international level are inevitable. Eleanor M. Fox, 'Antitrust and Regulatory Federalism: Races Up, Down, and Sideways', (2000) 75 *NYU L. Rev.* 1781, 1803.

fourth generation directives. The early generation directives are more prescriptive, whereas the approach of more recent directives is to lay down basic standards in the form of a set of options which essentially represent the predominant approaches in operation in various Member States.[25] The third generation directives reflected the "new approach" to harmonisation with the initiation of the single market program. The "new approach" establishes the principle that community intervention should be limited to the harmonisation of essential requirements. At that point, the decentralising approach is applied and a range of regulatory issues are explicitly left with the Member States.[26] The fourth generation measures are even less detailed and closer to a "framework" model, which favours general principles or standards rather than rigid prescriptive rules.[27]

The harmonisation approach in the new generation is indeed a reflexive one. The essence of the approach is to base the effect of the regulatory harmonisation (or intervention in some sense) on the "second order effects" on the part of Member States, rather than on direct prescriptive or intervening rules. The rationale of this reflexive harmonising approach is to recognise the need to underpin autonomous processes of adjustment in the context of economic regulation, and the infeasibility of imposing any specific distributive outcomes. The theory effectively encourages the coupling of external regulation with self-regulatory processes. If this approach is implemented in practice, the legislation shall devolve or confer rule-making powers on self-regulatory processes or bodies. As is relevant to our discussion, the objective of reflexive harmonisation is therefore not to be a substitute for state-level regulation. The transnational standards would not operate as monopolistic regulators to occupy the field but would instead be used to promote diverse and local-level approaches to regulating problems. The technique adopted to achieve this mode is to set basic standards as a "floor of rights", which would help rule out certain factors associated with the "race to the bottom" and allow Member States to develop their own standards. Thus, the "floor of rights" prevents "downwards" derogations. Eventually, the reflexive harmonisation operates to push individual states to enter into a "race to the top" by competing to withdraw protective standards.

---

25 Charlotte Villiers, *European Company Law: Towards Democracy?* Aldershot: Dartmouth Publishing Co. (1998).

26 Kenneth Armstrong and Simon Bulmer, *The Governance of the European Single Market*, Manchester: Manchester University Press (1998) p. 152.

27 A good example is the draft Thirteenth Directive on Takeover Bids, the general principles of which are implemented through local-level action by self-regulatory bodies such as the City Panel on Takeovers and Mergers, a professional association in the finance sector in the UK.

6.4. HOW TO REFORM THE NEW YORK CONVENTION?

The New York Convention is "the most important international treaty relating to international commercial arbitration",[28] and "the most effective instance of international legislation in the entire history of commercial law".[29] However, the New York Convention is "now beginning to show its age".[30] Besides, the New York Convention causes some striking conflicts in international arbitration resulting from the inherent vagueness and simplicity of some provisions, inadequacies in legislative enactment in contracting states, and deficiencies in the application of the provisions by national courts.[31]

The New York Convention only covers the enforcement of arbitration agreements and arbitral awards and leaves many theoretical and practical issues in arbitration untouched. Unharmonised national practices may make the functioning of international commercial arbitration overly burdensome or even impossible. In this sense, harmonisation should aim for the virtual unification of national arbitration laws. For instance, as discussed in Chapter 2, some scholars suggest a wholesale change to the "writing requirement" in the New York Convention in national arbitration laws.[32] The harmonisation of national arbitration laws may represent a good chance to capture beneficial aspects of regulatory competition, in terms of evolutionary adaptation, within the framework of globalisation. In fact, many aspects of international commercial arbitration still lie within the sphere of competence of national laws. The method of wholesale change to national arbitration reflects such a reality.

The aim of harmonisation is not to eliminate the autonomy and diversity of national legal systems. The diversity is a bonus to the development and evolution of law. Co-evolution based on diversity at the level of national legal systems, coupled with the transplanting of transnational norms, is more likely to be a path of future development than the type of convergence around a single, dominant regime which appears in other harmonising processes of substantive norms. By and large, the proposal to amend the New York Convention, *i.e.*, Article VII, a so-called stumbling block to encouraging states to bypass Article V and to invoke their own laws,[33] to the effect of restricting the scope and

---

28 Alan Redfern and Martin Hunter, *Law and Practice of International Commercial Arbitration*, London: Sweet & Maxwell (3rd edn. 1999) p. 67.

29 Stephen Schwebel, 'A Celebration of the United Nations – New York Convention', (1996) 12(1) *Arb. Int'l* 83, 85.

30 Alan Redfern and Martin Hunter, above n. 28.

31 Michael Kerr, 'Concord and Conflict in International Arbitration', (1997) 13(2) *Arb. Int'l* 141.

32 Michael Marks Cohen, 'Arbitration "Agreement in Writing": Notes in the Margin of the Sixth Goff Lecture', (1997) 13(3) *Arb. Int'l* 273.

33 Roy Goode, 'The Role of the *Lex Loci Arbitri* in International Commercial Arbitration', (2001) 17(1) *Arb. Int'l* 39.

removing the part of the "more favourable right" provision, is not a sensible one. Instead of "damaging the process of international arbitration which the New York Convention itself has done so much to foster",[34] Article VII actually provides contracting states with a certain level of flexibility to diversify the practice and "race to the top" so that other states may follow a better lead. Article VII, while recognising the importance of diversity, helps steer the process of evolutionary adaptation of rules at the state level.

The model for legal harmonisation can be based on a reflective harmonising approach. Arbitration-related legislation is essentially comprised of two layers: basic political choices which can be articulated as broad, but sufficiently precise, framework rules; and detailed technical measures, which conform to and implement the objectives of the framework rules. A multi-layer approach to harmonisation on the basis of this duality can be explored. For instance, principles, or basic political choices, can be adopted in a framework (in the form of treaties or conventions) in accordance with normal treaty legislative procedures. The New York Convention has achieved the purpose of this layer of harmonisation. Next to the conventions and treaties is the model law recommended by international organisations which would play a supplementary role. The UNCITRAL Model Law on International Commercial Arbitration has been put in place to supplement the New York Convention. A significant number of bilateral treaties and regional conventions with provisions on the enforcement of awards is also a very important source of law in this regard. By contrast, detailed technical measures would be adopted by arbitration institutions, national legislation or court precedents in a semi "law-making" manner. The substance of these detailed measures would conform to the principles set out in the convention or the rules recommended in the model law.

The "hard law" approach to revising the New York Convention could not be seriously entertained due to the practical difficulties.[35] In multilateral settings, it is usually difficult to build amendment into the treaty design. In practice, the more parties involved, the more difficult any amendments will be to conclude. The New York Convention involves more than 145 countries. The transaction costs of making any amendment to such a multilateral treaty will be very high. It is necessary to make "escape" (or exit) difficult so that commitments made by the contracting states can be effective.

In response to the proposal to revise the New York Convention addressing the court intervention in arbitral proceedings, the United Nations Commission on International Trade Law, which took over the legislative role of the New York Convention from the United Nations Economic and Social Council and initiated the UNCITRAL Arbitration Rules and Model Law on International Commercial

---

34 Ibid.

35 Michael Kerr, above n. 31, 143.

Arbitration, was against the idea to negotiate an additional protocol.[36] Instead, the UNCITRAL adopted a model law approach. Special considerations were given to the difficulty of obtaining ratification by a sufficient number of countries, the failure of which would be counterproductive and harm the cause of aiding harmonisation of arbitration law and practice.[37] The impact of the Model Law has been significant in certain areas, such as the harmonisation of arbitration proceedings, simplification of the enforcement procedures and unification of enforcement standards. The Model Law presents to national legislators around the world a sample of a statute which accommodates the need for modern arbitration. The model law technique, as compared to the treaty-making approach, has proven to be effective not only in terms of the speed of implementation but also in terms of the level of harmonisation.[38] The significant influence of the Model Law is reflected in its wholesale adoption by some major trading states such as Canada and Australia and, more often, partial revisions to existing national arbitration statutes. Deviations from the Model Law text have, as a general rule, rarely been made. Nevertheless, the continuing divergence between the "insider systems", which stress the judicial attitudes towards party autonomy in arbitration and judicial systems in the home jurisdiction, and "outsider systems", which place a strong emphasis on the uniform enforcement standards and judicial systems in other enforcement jurisdictions, is reflected in the failure of the Member States to reach agreement on a number of key proposals, in the very early beginning, and then on some tricky practical issues such as the enforcement of annulled arbitral awards and application of *lex mercatoria* and public policy in practice. It has to be recognised that the Model Law, together with the New York Convention, falls a long way short of establishing a systematic code relating to the uniformity in international commercial arbitration.

In its recent assessment of various options to modernise the New York Convention, UNCITRAL's Working Group again concluded that a minimalist approach not to revise the Convention was preferable.[39] A minimalist approach, however, does not suggest a no-action solution. Rather, it must be applied together with a "soft law" approach that matches the jurisprudential foundation or desired balance of the New York Convention, that is, setting a minimum

---

36 Jacques Werner, 'Should the New York Convention be Revised to Provide for Court Intervention in Arbitral Proceedings?', (1989) 6(3) *J. Int'l Arb.* 114, 118 (stating that the United Nations Commission on International Trade weighed the pros and cons of extending the New York Convention to the conduct of the arbitral proceedings proposed by the Asian-African Legal Consultative Committee in 1977 and rejected the proposal).

37 Ibid.

38 Gerold Herrmann, 'The UNCITRAL Arbitration Law: A Good Model of A Model Law', (1998) 3 *Uniform Law Review* 483.

39 Herbert Kronke, Patricia Nacimiento, et al (eds.), *Recognition and Enforcement of Foreign Arbitral Award: A Global Commentary on the New York Convention*, the Netherlands: Kluwer Law International (2010) p. 4.

standard to safeguard more liberal national treatments of arbitration agreements and enforcement of arbitral awards. For instance, UNCITRAL's Thirty-ninth Session in 2006 revised Article 7 of the UNCITRAL Model Law to relax the writing requirement.[40] The UNCITRAL made a Recommendation Regarding the Interpretation of Article II, Paragraph 2, and Article VII, Paragraph 1, of the Convention on the Recognition and Enforcement of Foreign Arbitral Awards to harmonise judicial interpretations of these provisions.[41] Non-binding recommendations were also issued to promote a liberal interpretation of the written form required by Article II(2) of the New York Convention.[42] These "soft law" type of guidelines are more useful than "hard law" amendments to the New York Convention. The operation of the New York Convention, though dynamic, diverse or even messy as it may look, actually moves towards clarity and efficiency, especially when more jurisdictions have tried or are trying to take a pro-arbitration stance and follow these guidelines.

According to the analysis in the gaming strategy, it is advisable to put in place a centralised or federal-type governing system. A strong proposal has been made to create an International Court for Resolving Disputes on Enforceability of Arbitral Awards or an International Court of Arbitral Awards.[43] Although the functions of these "supranational" bodies have not been clearly outlined by their proponents,[44] in the game theory, they are supposed to play a governing, supervisory and co-ordinating role in harmonising enforcement practices by

---

40 Two alternative options are offered to the states. One is to liberalise the "in writing" requirement. The other allows for oral arbitration agreements. The adopted text is in document A/CN.9/606 of 13 April 2006, para. 4. Also see the Official Records of the General Assembly, Sixty-first Session, Supp. No. 17 (A/54/17), paras. 163–67.

41 Recommendation Regarding the Interpretation of Article II, Paragraph 2, and Article VII, Paragraph 1, of the Convention on the Recognition and Enforcement of Foreign Arbitral Awards, in Herbert Kronke, Patricia Nacimiento, et al, above n. 39, 564–65.

42 The adopted text is contained in Official Records of the General Assembly, Sixty-first Session, Supp. No. 17 (A/61/17), Annex II.

43 Stephen Schwebel, 'The Creation and Operation of an International Court of Arbitral Awards', and Howard Holtzmann, 'A Task for the 21st Century: Creating a New International Court for Resolving Disputes on the Enforceability of Arbitral Awards', in Martin Hunter, Arthur Marriott and V.V. Veeder (eds.), *The Internationalisation of International Arbitration*, Kluwer Law International (1995) p. 115 and p. 109 respectively.

44 There are at least two possibilities. One is an independent and permanent court or tribunal exclusively dealing with all enforcement-related disputes among states as well as states and private parties. The other possibility is dependent courts or tribunals appointed by the parties. This binary distinction has a law and economics implication. Most public international lawyers may prefer independent to dependent tribunals, as the former can generate compliance and will be more utilised. An independent tribunal can expect a steady stream of cases presenting similar issues so as to choose effective rules and generate compliance in future cases. Laurence R. Helfer and Anne-Marie Slaughter, 'Why States Create International Tribunals: A Response to Professors Posner and Yoo', (2005) 93 *California Law Review* 2–58; Tom Ginsburg and Richard McAdams, 'Adjudicating in Anarchy: An Expressive Theory of International Dispute Resolution', (2004) 45 *William & Mary Law Review* 1229.

contracting states to the New York Convention. This is so because the procedural scheme for enforcement of awards is not regulated by the New York Convention and needs special attention and oversight. At the regional level, such functions may be first tested by some existing regional judicial bodies, for example, the European Court of Justice, according to existing regional conventions such as the Brussels Convention on Jurisdiction and the Enforcement of Judgments in Civil and Commercial Matters.[45]

Aside from some limited regional progress, the idea of having a world court of international arbitral awards with exclusive jurisdiction[46] to determine whether recognition and enforcement of an international arbitral award may be refused for any of the reasons set out in Article V of the New York Convention is still an "impossible dream".[47] This scepticism is evidenced by international courts' limited instrumental value for states, despite the proliferation of international courts world-wide.[48] There are other drawbacks which may hinder the realisation of this institutional design. For instance, there will be the potential ineffectiveness of an independent international tribunal (which can, among other criteria, be permanent, staffed by judges with fixed terms, and enjoy compulsory jurisdiction over certain enforcement-related disputes) as regards its possible imposition of rules on states, leading to constraints over sovereignty.[49] While review by a second decision-maker provides substantial benefits, such as minimising error costs and heightening uniformity across arbitration or arbitral award enforcement cases, placing a superior decision-maker on the top of all arbitration institutions, arbitral tribunals as well as national courts would introduce other costs such as procedural delay and, more detrimentally, the shifting costs (and the remedial costs that may follow) that move power away from decision-makers who are closer to the primary inquiry. Also worth mentioning is some difficulty, even among advocates of judicial discourse and the "new world order", over holding international tribunals or judges accountable.[50] These considerations have not touched upon some practical

45 Dominique T. Hascher, 'Recognition and Enforcement of Arbitration Awards and the Brussels Convention', (1996) 12(3) *Arb. Int'l* 265.

46 Charles N. Brower, 'The Coming Crisis in the Global Adjudication System', (2003) 19 *Arb. Int'l* 34.

47 Nigel Blackaby and Constantine Partasides, *Redfern and Hunter on International Arbitration*, Oxford: Oxford University Press (5th edn. 2009) p. 640 n. 73.

48 Eric A. Posner, *The Perils of Global Legalism*, Chicago: Chicago University Press (2009) p. xv.

49 Eric A. Posner and John Yoo, 'A Theory of International Adjudication', (2005) 93(1) *Cal. L. Rev.* 3–74; Jack L. Goldsmith and Eric A. Posner, *The Limits of International Law*, Oxford: Oxford University Press (2005); Symposium, 'The Proliferation of International Tribunals: Piecing Together the Puzzle', (1999) 31 *NYU J. Int'l L. & Pol.* 679; Cesare P. Romano, 'The Proliferation of International Judicial Bodies: The Pieces of the Puzzle', (1999) 31 *NYU J. Int'l L. & Pol.* 709.

50 Anne-Marie Slaughter, 'Sovereignty and Power in a Networked World Order', (2004) 40 *Stan. J. Int'l L.* 283.

difficulties in passing a treaty to establish the tribunal and grant judicial capacity to judges regardless of effective and efficient enforcement mechanisms.

In addition, in order to enhance the correct implementation, progressive interpretation and gradual liberalisation of convention provisions by national courts, it has been advocated that a new interpretative text of the New York Convention should be produced in the form of UNCITRAL Guidelines[51] or a Model Law Supplement,[52] which can improve the implementation, interpretation and application of the New York Convention. This proposal takes into account both "soft law" and new harmonisation theories, and fully makes use of both the "instrumentalist" and "deregulatory" sides of the judicial harmonising trend of the 21st century. The emphasis of instrumentalism lies in the self-regulation of social and legal systems and resistance to external regulatory interference, whilst the deregulatory theory tries to diminish, if not remove, the external regulatory controls.[53]

Beyond the New York Convention, it is anticipated that a new generation of "soft" law or, less likely, "supranational" harmonising bodies in international commercial arbitration will appear in due course.

---

51 Michael Kerr, above n. 31, 142–43.

52 Gerold Herrmann, 'Does the World Need Additional Uniform Legislation on Arbitration?', (1999) 15(3) *Arb. Int'l* 213.

53 Simon Deakin and Alan Hughes, 'Economic Efficiency and the Proceduralisation of Company Law', (1999) 3 *Company, Financial and Insolvency Law Review* 169–189. Also see Gunther Teubner, *Law as an Autopoietic System*, Oxford: Blackwell (1993).

BIBLIOGRAPHY

Abrams, David S. and Yoon, Albert H., 'The Luck of the Draw: Using Random Case Assignment to Investigate Attorney Ability' (2007) 74 *U Chi L Rev* 1145

Adler, Ruth (tr), Teubner, Gunther and Bankowska, Anne, *Law as an Autopoietic System* (Blackwell, Oxford 1993)

Albrow, Martin (tr), Luhmann, Niklas, *A Sociological Theory of Law* (Routledge & Kegan Paul, London 1985)

Alchian, Armen A., 'Uncertainty, Evolution, and Economic Theory' (1950) 58 *J Pol Econ* 211

Allen, Thomas I.A., 'Institutional Rules: Straitjacket or Scaffold?', in De Zylva, Martin Odams and Harrison, Reziya (eds), *International Commercial Arbitration – Developing Rules for the New Millennium* (Jordans, Bristol 2000)

Allott, Philip, *Eunomia – New Order for a New World* (Oxford University Press, Oxford 2004)

Alschuler, Albert W., *Law Without Values: The Life, Work, and Legacy of Justice Holmes* (University of Chicago Press, Chicago 2000)

Alstott, Anne L., 'Federalism and U.S. Social Welfare Policy: Fundamental Change and New Uncertainties' (1996) 2 *Colum J Eur L* 441

Ancel, Jean-Pierre, 'French Judicial Attitudes Toward International Arbitration' (1993) 9(2) *Arb Int'l* 121

Anderson, Gary M., Shughart, William F. II and Tollison, Robert D., 'On the Incentives of Judges to Enforce Legislative Wealth Transfers' (1989) 32 *J L & Econ* 215

Appelbaum, Richard P., Felstiner, William L.F. and Gessner, Volkmar (eds), *Rules and Networks, The Legal Culture of Global Business Transactions* (Hart Publishing, Oxford 2001)

Arato, Andrew and Cohen, Jean L., *Civil Society and Political Theory* (MIT Press, Cambridge, MA 1995)

Armstrong, Kenneth and Bulmer, Simon, *The Governance of the European Single Market* (Manchester University Press, Manchester 1998)

Arsic, Jasna, 'International Commercial Arbitration on the Internet' (1997) 14(4) *J Int'l Arb* 219

Arthur, Brian, 'Competing Technologies, Increasing Returns, and Lock-in by Historical Events' (1989) 99 *Econ J* 116

Aske, Robert W., *The Law Relating to Custom and the Usages of Trade* (Stevens and Sons, London 1909)

Atiyah, Patrick, *The Rise and Fall of Freedom of Contract* (Oxford University Press, Oxford 1979)

Aunger, Robert (ed), *Darwinising Culture: The Status of Memetics as Science* (Oxford University Press, Oxford 2001)

—, 'Introduction', in Aunger, Robert (ed) *Darwinising Culture: The Status of Memetics as a Science* (Oxford University Press, Oxford 2001)
Axelrod, Robert, *The Evolution of Cooperation* (Basic Books, New York 1984)
Bailey, Martin J. and Rubin, Paul H., 'A Positive Theory of Legal Change' (1994) 14 *Int'l Rev L & Econ* 467
Baker, John H., *An Introduction to English Legal History* (3rd edn, Oxford University Press, Oxford 1990)
Balkin, Jack M., *Cultural Software: A Theory of Ideology* (Yale University Press, New Haven 1998)
Barkow, Jerome H., Cosmides, Leda and Tooby, John, *The Adapted Mind: Evolutionary Psychology and the Generation of Culture* (Oxford University Press, Oxford 1992)
Barraclough, Andrew and Waincymer, Jeff, 'Mandatory Rules of Law in International Commercial Arbitration' (2005) 6 *Melb J Int'l L* 205
Bebchuk, Lucian Arye and Roe, Mark J., 'A Theory of Path Dependence in Corporate Ownership and Governance' (1997) 52 *Stan L Rev* 127
Becker, Gary, 'A Theory of Competition Among Pressure Groups for Political Influence' (1983) 98 *Q J Econ* 371
Beechey, John, 'Arbitrability of Anti-trust/Competition Law Issues – Common Law' (1996) 12(2) *Arb Int'l* 188
Beirne, Piers, 'Ideology and Rationality in Max Weber's Sociology of Law', in Beirne, Piers and Quinney, Richard (eds), *Marxism and Law* (John Wiley & Sons, New York 1982)
Bensaude, Denis, 'Defining the Limits of Scrutiny of Awards based on Alleged Violations of European Competition Law' (2005) 22(3) *J. Int'l Arb.* 239
Benson, Bruce L., 'The Spontaneous Evolution of Commercial Law' (1989) 55 *Southern Economic Journal* 647
Bentham, Jeremy, *An Introduction to the Principles of Morals and Legislation* (Clarendon Press, Oxford 1789)
Bentil, Kodwo J., 'Judicial Intervention and International Commercial Arbitration' (1986) 130 *Solicitors' J* 191
—, 'Making England a More Attractive Venue for International Commercial Arbitration by Less Judicial Oversight' (1988) 5(1) *J Int'l Arb* 50
Berger, Klaus Peter, *International Economic Arbitration* (Kluwer Law and Taxation Publishers, Deventer/Boston 1993)
—, 'Die UNIDROIT-Prinzipien für Internationale Handelsverträge-Indiz, fur ein autonomes Weltwirtschaftsrecht?' (1995) 94 *Zeitschrift für vergleichende Rechtswissenschaft*
—, *The Creeping Codification of Lex Mercatoria* (Kluwer Law and Taxation Publishers, The Hague/Boston 1999)
—, 'The New Law Merchant and the Global Market Place: A 21st Century View of Transnational Commercial Law' (2000) *Int'l Arb L Rev* 91
Berman, Harold and Kaufman, Colin, 'The Law of International Commercial Transactions (*Lex Mercatoria*)' (1978) 19(1) *Harv Int'l L J* 273
Bermann, George A., 'The Origin and Operation of Mandatory Rules', in Bermann, George A., and Mistelis, Loukas A., (eds), *Mandatory Rules in International Arbitration* (Juris Net LLC, New York 2011)

Besson, Sebastien and Pittet, Luc, 'La reconnaissance à l'étranger d'une sentence annulée dans son état d'origine – Reflexions à la suite de l'affaire Hilmarton' (1998) 3 *Bulletin ASA* 515

Binder, Peter, *International Commercial Arbitration and Conciliation in UNCITRAL Model Law Jurisdictions* (3rd edn, Sweet & Maxwell, London 2009)

Bingham, Thomas, 'The Price of Justice' (1994) 60 *JCIArb* 247

Black, Bernard and Kraakman, Reinier, 'A Self-Enforcing Model of Corporate Law' (1996) 109(8) *Harv L Rev* 1911

Black, Julia, *Rules and Regulators* (Oxford University Press, Oxford 1998)

Blackaby, Nigel, Lindsey, David and Spinillo, Alessandro, *International Arbitration in Latin America* (Kluwer Law International, The Hague 2003)

Blackaby, Nigel and Partasides, Constantine, *Redfern and Hunter on International Arbitration* (5th edn, Oxford University Press, Oxford 2009)

Blackmore, Susan, *The Meme Machine* (Oxford University Press, Oxford 1999)

Blackstone, William, *Commentaries on the Laws of England Vol. I* (Clarendon Press, Oxford 1765–1769)

Blessing, Marc, 'Mandatory Rules of Law versus Party Autonomy in International Arbitration' (1997) 14(4) *J Int'l Arb* 23

—, *The Impact of the Extraterritorial Application of Mandatory Rules on International Contracts* (Helbing und Lichtenhahn, Frankfurt am Main 1999)

—, *Introduction to Arbitration – Swiss and International Perspectives* (Swiss Commercial Law Series Vol. 10, Helbing und Lichtenhahn, Frankfurt am Main 1999)

Bockstiegel, Karl-Heinz, 'Public Policy and Arbitrability', in Sanders, Pieter (ed), *Comparative Arbitration Practice and Public Policy in Arbitration* (ICCA Congress Series No. 3, Kluwer Law International, The Hague 1987)

Bond, Stephen R. and Seppala, Christopher R., 'The New (1998) Rules of Arbitration of the International Chamber of Commerce' (1997) 12(5) *Mealey's Int'l Arb Rep* 33

Bonell, Michael Joachim, 'Policing the International Commercial Contract Against Unfairness under the UNIDROIT Principles' (1994) 3(1/2) *Tulane J Int'l and Comp L* 73

Born, Gary B., *International Commercial Arbitration in the United States: Commentary and Materials* (Kluwer Law and Taxation Publishers, Deventer/Boston 1994)

—, *International Commercial Arbitration: Commentary and Materials* (2nd edn, Kluwer Law International, The Hague 2001)

Boyd, Robert and Richerson, Peter J., *Culture and the Evolutionary Process* (University of Chicago Press, Chicago 1985)

—, 'Memes: Universal Acid or A Better Mousetrap?', in Aunger, Robert (ed) *Darwinising Culture: The Status of Memetics as a Science* (Oxford University Press, Oxford 2000)

Boyd White, James, *The Legal Imagination. Studies in the Nature of Legal Thought and Expression* Little, Brown and Company, Boston 1973)

—, "Law as Language: Reading Law and Reading Literature" (1982) 60 *Tex L Rev* 415

Brabant, Stephane, 'Designing Petroleum Contracts and Emerging Principles of International Law, Transnational Dispute Management' (December 2004), available at http://www.transnational-dispute-management.com

Braithwaite, John and Drahos, Peter, *Global Business Regulation* (Cambridge University Press, Cambridge 2000)
Branson, David J., 'Arbitrability and Pre-emption: More Litigation in the United States' (1996) 12(2) *Arb Int'l* 163
Bridge, Michael, 'Foreword', in Fan Yang, *Contracts for the International Sale of Goods in China* (Wolters Kluwer Law & Business, Hong Kong, 2012)
Briner, Robert, 'New York Convention – Philosophy and Objectives of the Convention', in *Enforcing Arbitration Awards under the New York Convention: Experience and Prospects – New York Convention Day* 9 (United Nations, New York 1998)
Brownsword, Roger, Hird, Norma J. and Howells, Geraint G. (eds), *Good Faith in Contract: Concept and Context* (Ashgate, Dartmouth 1999)
Buchanan, Mark A., 'Public Policy and International Commercial Arbitration' (1988) 26 *Am Bus L J* 511
Buchell, B., Deakin, S., Michie, J. and Rubery, J. (eds), *Systems of Production: Markets, Organisations and Performance* (Routledge, London 2002)
Bull, Clive, 'The Existence of Self-Enforcing Implicit Contracts' (1987) 102 *Q J Econ* 147
Bull, Hedley, *The Anarchical Society: A Study of Order in World Politics* (Macmillan, London 1977)
Burstein, Matthew, 'Conflicts on the Net: Choice of Law in Transnational Cyberspace' (1996) 29(1) *Vanderbilt J Trans L* 75
Butler, Henry N. and Macey, Jonathan R., 'The Myth of Competition in the Dual Banking System' (1988) 73 *Cornell L Rev* 680
— —, 'Externalities and the Matching Principle: The Case for Reallocating Environmental Regulatory Authority' (1996) 14 *Yale L & Pol'y Rev* 29
Buxbaum, Hannah L., 'Mandatory Rules in Civil Litigation: Status of the Doctrine Post-Globalisation', in Bermann, George A., and Mistelis, Loukas A. (eds), *Mandatory Rules in International Arbitration* (Juris Net LLC, New York 2011)
Caemmerer, Ernst von, 'The Influence of the Law of International Trade on the Development and Character of the Commercial Law in the Civil Law Countries', in Schmitthoff, Clive M. (ed), *The Sources of the Law of International Trade* (F.A. Praeger, London 1964)
Cafruny, Alan, *Ruling the Waves: The Political Economy of International Shipping* (University of California Press, Berkeley 1987)
Calabresi, Guido and Melamed, A. Douglas, 'Property Rules, Liability Rules, and Inalienability: One View of the Cathedral' (1972) 85 *Harv L Rev* 1089
Calabresi, Steven G., 'The Era of Big Government Is Over' (1998) 50 *Stan L Rev* 1015
Caldwell, Casey J., 'The Black Diamond of Harmonisation: The Alpine Convention as A Model for Balance Competing Objectives in the European Union' (2003) 21 *Boston U Int'l L J* 137
Cappelletti, Mauro and Garth, Bryant (eds), *Access to Justice: A World Survey* (4 Vols. Siftoff & Noordoft, London/Boston/Milan 1978–9)
— and Tallon, Denis (eds), *Fundamental Guarantees of the Parties in Civil Litigation* (Giuffre, Milan/Oceana Publications, Dobbs Ferry, NY 1973)
Carbonneau, Thomas E., 'The Elaboration of a French Court Doctrine on International Commercial Arbitration: A Study In Liberal Civilian Judicial Creativity' (1980) 55 *Tulane L Rev* 1

— (ed), *Resolving Transnational Disputes Through International Arbitration* (University of Virginia Press, Charlottesville, VA 1984)

—, 'A Consideration of Alternatives to Divorce Litigation' (1986) *U Ill L Rev* 1119

— (ed), *Lex Mercatoria and Arbitration: A Discussion of the New Law Merchant* (revised edn, Kluwer Law International, Yonkers, New York/Juris, Cambridge, MA 1998)

—, *Cases and Materials on the Law and Practice of Arbitration* (2nd edn, Juris Publishing, New York 2000)

—, and Firestone, Marc S., 'Transnational Law-Making: Assessing the Impact of the Vienna Convention and the Viability of Arbitral Adjudication' (1986) 1 *Emory J Int'l Disp Resol* 51

Casella, Alessandra, 'On Market Integration and the Development of Institutions: The Case of International Commercial Arbitration' (1996) 40 *Eur Econ Rev* 155

Cashin, Sheryll D., 'Federalism, Welfare Reform, and the Minority Poor: Accounting for the Tyranny of State Majorities' (1999) 99(3) *Colum. L. Rev.* 552

Cavalli-Sforza, Luigi Luca and Feldman, Marcus W., *Cultural Evolution and Transmission: A Quantitative Approach* (Princeton University Press, Princeton 1981)

Cerny, Philip, *The Changing Architecture of Politics: Structure, Agency and the Future of the State* (Sage Publications, London 1990)

—, 'Paradoxes of the Competition State: The Dynamics of Political Globalisation' (1997) 32(2) *Government and Operation* 251

Chan, Leng Sun, *Singapore Law on Arbitral Awards* (Academy Publishing, Singapore 2011)

Chang, Ha-Joon, *Kicking Away the Ladder – Development Strategy in Historical Perspective* (Anthem Press, London 2002)

—, *Why Developing Countries Need Tariffs – How WTO NAMA Negotiations Could Deny Developing Countries' Right to a Future* (Oxfam Publishing, Oxford 2005), also available at http://www.marketradefair.com/en/assets/English/sctadp.pdf

Cheffins, Brian, *Company Law: Theory, Structure and Operations* (Oxford University Press, Oxford 1997)

Chen, Albert, 'Rational Law, Economic Development and the Case of China' (1999) 8 *Soc & L Stud* 97

Cheng, Teresa, 'Celebrating the Fiftieth Anniversary of the New York Convention', in van den Berg, Albert Jan, *50 Years of the New York Convention* (Permanent Court of Arbitration, The Hague 2009)

Choi, Stephen J. and Guzman, Andrew T., 'Portable Reciprocity: Rethinking the International Reach of Securities Regulation' (1998) 71 *S Cal L Rev* 2003

Chuah, Jason C.T., *Law of International Trade* (Sweet & Maxwell, London 1998)

Chukwumerije, Okezie, *Choice of Law in International Commercial Arbitration* (Quorum Books, Westport, Connecticut and London 1994)

Clarkson, C.M.V. and Hill, Jonathan, *The Conflicts of Laws* (3rd edn, Oxford University Press, Oxford 2006)

Clemente, Robert S., 'Trends in Securities Industry Arbitration' (Sep/Oct 1996) *New York State Bar J* 20

Clough, Shepard B., *The Economic Development of Western Civilisation* (McGraw-Hill Book Co. Inc., New York 1959)

Clough, Shepard B. and Cole, Charles W., *Economic History of Europe* (revised edn, Heath & Co., Boston, MA and Washington DC 1946)
Coase, Ronald H., 'The Problem of Social Cost' (1960) 3 *J L & Econ* 1
Coffee, John C., Jr., 'Racing Towards The Top? The Impact of Cross-Listings and Stock Market Competition on International Corporate Governance' (2002) 102 *Colum. L. Rev.* 1757
Cohen, Michael Marks, 'Arbitration "Agreement in Writing": Notes in the Margin of the Sixth Goff Lecture' (1997) 13(3) *Arb Int'l* 273
Cohn, E.J., 'The Rules of Arbitration of the International Chamber of Commerce' (1965) 14(1) *Int'l & Comp L Q* 132
Collins, Hugh, 'Good Faith in European Contract Law' (1994) 14 *Oxford J. Legal Stud.* 229
—, 'European Private Law and the Cultural Identity of States' (1995) 3 *Eur Rev Pr L* 354
Collins, Laurence, et al. (eds) *Dicey, Morris & Collins on The Conflict of Laws* (12th edn, Sweet & Maxwell, London 1993)
—, *Dicey, Morris & Collins on The Conflict of Laws* (13th edn, Sweet & Maxwell, London 2000)
—, *Dicey, Morris & Collins on The Conflict of Laws* (14th edn, Sweet & Maxwell, London 2006)
Cona, Frank A., 'Internet Arbitration of International Commercial Disputes' (1996), available at http://www.ipwarehouse.com/IP_Library/general_articles/arb_art.htm
—, 'Application of Online Systems in Alternative Dispute Resolution' (1997) 45 *Buffalo L Rev* 975
Contini, Paolo, 'International Commercial Arbitration The United Nations Convention on the Recognition and Enforcement of Foreign Arbitral Awards' (1959) 8 *Am J Comp L* 283
Cooper, Christine Godsil, 'Where Are We Going with Gilmer? – Some Ruminations on the Arbitration of Discrimination Claims' (1992) 11 *St. Louis U Pub L Rev* 203
Cooter, Robert D., 'The Objectives of Private and Public Judges' (1983) 41 *Public Choice* 107
— and Kornhauser, Lewis, 'Can Litigation Improve the Law Without the Help of Judges?' (1980) 9 *J. Legal Stud.* 139
— and Rubinfeld, Daniel L., 'Trial Courts: An Economic Perspective' (1990) 24 *L & Society Rev* 533
Coquillette, Daniel R., 'Ideology and Incorporation II: Sir Thomas Ridley, Charles Molloy, and the Literary Battle for the Law Merchant, 1607–1676' (1981) 61 *Boston U L Rev* 351
Corbin, Arthur, 'The Law and the Judges' (1914) 3 *Yale L J* 234
Cotterrell, Roger, *Law, Culture and Society – Legal Ideas in the Mirror of Social Theory* (Ashgate, Aldershot 2006)
—, *The Sociology of Law – An Introduction* (2nd edn, Butterworths, London 1992)
Covo, Jacques, 'Commodities, Arbitrations and Equitable Considerations' (1993) 9(1) *Arb Int'l* 61
Cox, Robert, *Production, Power and World Order: Social Forces in the Making of History* (Columbia University Press, New York 1987)

—, 'Critical Political Economy', in Hettne, Bjorn (ed), *International Political Economy: Understanding Global Disorder* (Fernwood Publishing, Halifax 1995)

Craig, William Laurence, 'Uses and Abuses of Appeal from Awards' (1988) 4(3) *Arb Int'l* 174

—, 'Some Trends and Developments in the Laws and Practice of International Commercial Arbitration' (1995) 30(1) *Tex Int'l L J* 36

—, Park, William W. and Paulsson, Jan, *International Chamber of Commerce Arbitration* (Oceana Publications and ICC Publishing, New York 1995)

—, *International Chamber of Commerce Arbitration* (3rd edn, Oceana Publications, Dobbs Ferry, NY 2000)

Cremades, Bernardo M., 'Is Exclusion of Concurrent Courts' Jurisdiction over Conservative Measures to be Introduced through a Revision of the Convention?' (1989) 6(3) *J Int'l Arb* 105

— and Plehn, Steven, 'The New *Lex Mercatoria* and the Harmonisation of the Laws of International Commercial Transactions' (1984) 2 *Boston U Int'l L J* 324

Crick, Francis, 'The Origin of the Genetic Code' (1968) 38 *J Molecular Biology* 367

Croff, Carlo, 'The Applicable Law in an International Commercial Arbitration: Is It Still a Conflict of Laws Problem?' (1982) 16 *Int'l Lawyer* 613

Cumming, Douglas J. and MacIntosh, Jeffrey G., 'The Role of Interjurisdictional Competition in Shaping Canadian Corporate Law: A Second Look' (2000) 20 *Int'l Rev L & Econ* 141

Currie, Brainerd, 'Married Women's Contracts: A Study in Conflict-of-Laws Method' (1958) 25 *U Chi L Rev* 227

Cutler, A. Claire, 'Private Authority in International Trade Relations: The Case of Maritime Transport', in Cutler, A. Claire, Haufler, Virginia and Porter, Tony (eds), *Private Authority and International Affairs* (SUNY Press, Albany, New York 1999)

—, 'Critical Reflections on the Westphalian Assumptions of International Law and Organisation: A Crisis of Legitimacy' (2001) 27(2) *Rev Int'l Stud* 133

—, 'Historical Materialism, Globalisation, and Law: Competing Conceptions of Property', in Rupert, Mark and Smith, Hazel (eds), *Historical Materialism and Globalisation* (Routledge, New York and London 2002)

—, *Private Power and Global Authority* (Cambridge University Press, Cambridge 2003)

Darby, W. Evans, *International Tribunals: A Collection of Various Schemes, Which Have Been Propounded and Instances Since 1815* (Peace Society, London 1899)

Darian-Smith, Eve, 'Structural Inequalities in the Global Legal System' (2000) 34(3) *L & Society Rev* 826

Darwin, Charles, *On the Origin of Species by Means of Natural Selection or the Preservation of Favoured Races in the Struggle for Life* (John Murray, London 1859)

—, 'The Origin of Species', in Porter, Duncan M. and Graham, Peter W. (eds), *The Portable Darwin* (Penguin Books, Harmondsworth 1993)

David, Paul, 'Clio and Economics of QWERTY' (1985) 75 *Am Econ Rev* 332

David, René, *Arbitration in International Trade* (Kluwer Law and Taxation, Deventer 1985)

— and Brierley, J.E.C., *Major Legal Systems in the World Today: An Introduction to the Comparative Study of Law* (Stevens & Sons, London 1978)

— and Tunc, André, 'The International Unification of Private Law', in Zweigert, K. and Drobnig, K. (eds), *International Encyclopedia of Comparative Law. Volume II, The Legal System of the World; Their Comparison and Unification* (Paul Siebeck and Martinus Nijhoff Publishers, The Hague/Boston/London 1972)

—, 'Sources of Law', in *International Encyclopaedia of Comparative Law*, Vol. II, (1972) Ch. 3

Dawkins, Richard, *The Blind Watchmaker* (Norton & Company, Inc., London 1986)

—, *The Selfish Gene* (2nd edn, Oxford University Press, Oxford 1989)

Day, D.M. and Griffin, Bernardette, *The Law of International Trade* (Butterworths, London 1993)

De Ly, Filip, 'The Place of Arbitration in the Conflict of Laws of International Commercial Arbitration: An Exercise in Arbitration Planning' (1991) 12 *Northwestern J Int'l L & Bus* 48

—, *International Business Law and Lex Mercatoria* (Elsevier Science, North Holland, Amsterdam/London 1992)

Deakin, Simon and Hughes, Alan, 'Economic Efficiency and the Proceduralisation of Company Law' (1999) 3 *Company, Financial and Insolvency L Rev* 169

Delaume, Georges R., 'Introductory Note: France: Court of Appeal of Rouen Decision in Société Europééne d'Etudes et d'Enterprises v. Yugoslavia, et al. (Recognition of Arbitral Award) (November 13, 1984)' (1985) 24(1–3) *International Legal Materials* 345

—, 'Comparative Analysis as a Basis of Law in State Contracts: The Myth of the *Lex Mercatoria*' (1989) 63 *Tulane L Rev* 582

Demeulenaere, Bernadette, 'The Place of Arbitration and the Applicable Procedure Law: The Case of Belgium', in Storme, Marcel and De Ly, Filip (eds), *The Place of Arbitration* (Mys and Breesch, Ghent 1992)

Demeyere, Luc, '1998 Amendments to Belgian Arbitration Law: An Overview' (1999) 15 *Arb Int'l* 295

Dennett, Daniel C., *Darwin's Dangerous Idea* (Simon & Schuster, New York 1995)

Deshpande, V.S., '"Foreign Award" in the 1958 New York Convention' (1992) 9(4) *J Int'l Arb* 51

Dezalay, Yves and Garth, Bryant, *Dealing in Virtue – International Commercial Arbitration and the Construction of a Transnational Legal Order* (University of Chicago Press, Chicago 1996)

Di Pietro, Domenico and Platte, Martin (eds), *Enforcement of International Arbitration Awards – The New York Convention of 1958* (Cameron May, London 2001)

Distin, Kate, *The Selfish Meme – A Critical Reassessment* (Cambridge University Press, Cambridge 2005)

Dore, Isaak Ismail, *Arbitration and Conciliation Under the UNCITRAL Rules: A Textual Analysis* (Martinus Nijhoff Publishers, The Hague 1986)

Draetta, Ugo, Lake, Ralph B. and Nanda, Ved P., *Breach and Adaptation of International Contracts: An Introduction to Lex Mercatoria* (Matthew Bender & Co., New York 1992)

Drahozal, Christopher R., '"Unfair" Arbitration Clauses' (2001) *U Ill L Rev* 695

Drezner, Daniel W., 'On the Balance between International Law and Democratic Sovereignty' (2001) 2 *Chi J Int'l L* 321

Durham, William H., 'Advances in Evolutionary Culture Theory' (1990) 19 *Annual Rev of Anthropology* 197
Dworkin, Ronald, *Taking Rights Seriously* (Duckworth, London 2005)
Easterbrook, Frank H., 'Antitrust and the Economics of Federalism' (1983) 26 *J L & Econ* 23
— and Fischel, Daniel R., *The Economic Structure of Corporate Law* (Harvard University Press, Cambridge, MA 1996)
Ehrlich, Isaac and Posner, Richard A., 'An Economic Analysis of Legal Rulemaking' (1974) 3 *J Legal Stud* 257
El-Ahdab, Abdul Hamid, 'Enforcement of Arbitral Awards in the Arab Countries' (1995) 11(2) *Arb Int'l* 230
Eldredge, Niles, *Reinventing Darwin: The Great Evolutionary Debate* (Phoenix Giant, London 1995)
— and Gould, Stephen Jay, 'Punctuated Equilibria: An Alternative to Phyletic Gradualism', in Eldredge, Niles, *Time Frames: The Rethinking of Darwinian Evolution and the Theory of Punctuated Equilibria* (Heinemann, New York 1986)
Elias, Norbert, *The Civilising Process: State Formation and Civilisation* (Blackwell, Oxford 1982)
Elliott, E. Donald, 'The Evolutionary Tradition in Jurisprudence' (1985) 85 *Colum L Rev* 38
—, 'Law and Biology: The New Synthesis?' (1997) 41 *St Louis U L J* 595
—, 'The Tragi-Comedy of the Commons: Evolutionary Biology, Economics and Environmental Law' (2001) 20 *Vermont Environmental L J* 17
Epstein, Richard A., 'The Independence of Judges: The Uses and Limitations of Public Choice Theory' (1990) 5 *Brigham Young U L Rev* 827
Esty, Daniel C., 'Environmental Protection in the Information Age' (2004) 79 *NYU L Rev* 115
Farnsworth, Edward Allan, 'Unification of Sales Law at the Regional and International Level: Why They Behave Like Americans', in Ziegel, Jacob and Foster, William (eds), *Aspects of Comparative Commercial Law: Sales, Consumer Credit, and Secured Transactions* (Oceana Publications, Dobbs Ferry, NY 1969)
—, 'Duties of Good Faith and Fair Dealing under the UNIDROIT Principles, Relevant International Conventions, and National Laws' (1994) 3(1/2) *Tulane J Int'l and Comp L* 45
—, 'Unification and Harmonisation of Private Law' (1996) 27 *Can Bus L J* 48
—, *Contracts* (3rd edn, Aspen Law & Business, New York 1999)
—, 'Pre-contractual Liability and Preliminary Agreements: Fair Dealing and Failed Negotiations' (1987) 87 *Colum L Rev* 259–60.
Fawcett, J.J., 'Evasion of Law and Mandatory Rules in Private International Law' (1990) 49(1) *Cambridge L J* 44
Ferguson, Robert B., 'The Adjudication of Commercial Disputes and the Legal System in Modern England' (1980) 7 *British J L and Society* 141
Fields, Karen E. (tr), Durkheim, Emile, *The Elementary Forms of the Religious Life* (Simon & Schuster Ltd, New York 1997)
Fifoot, C.H.S., *English Law and Its Background* (G. Bell and Sons, London 1932)

'Final Award in the Arbitration of Chromalloy Aero-Services and Arab Republic of Egypt' (1996) 11(8) *Mealey's Int'l Arb Rep* C-1
Fletcher, George, 'The Universal and the Particular in Legal Discourse' (1987) 2 *Brigham Young U L Rev* 335
Flinn, Mark R., 'Culture and the Evolution of Social Learning' (1997) 18 *Evolution and Human Behaviour* 23
Florescu, Grigore, 'The Evolution of Commercial Arbitration in Romania' (1993) 10(1) *J Int'l Arb* 95
Foucault, Michel, *Surveiller et punir: la naissance de la prison* (Gallimard, Paris 1975)
Fouchard, Philippe, *L'Arbitrage Commercial International* (Dalloz, Paris 1965)
—, 'La portée internationale de l'annulation de la sentence arbitrale dans son pays d'origine' (1997) 3 *Revue de l'arbitrage* 330
—, 'Suggestions pour accroître l'efficacité internationale des sentences arbitrales' (1998) 4 *Revue de l'arbitrage* 666
—, Gaillard, Emmanuel and Goldman, Berthold, *Traite de l'Arbitrage Commercial International* (Litec, Paris 1996)
—, — and —, *International Commercial Arbitration* (Kluwer Law International, The Hague 1999)
Fox, Eleanor M., 'Antitrust and Regulatory Federalism: Races Up, Down, and Sideways' (2000) 75 *NYU L. Rev.* 1781
Francis, Mark, *Herbert Spencer and the Invention of Modern Life* (Acumen, Stocksfield, UK 2007)
Frank, Joshua, 'Applying Memetics to Financial Markets: Do Markets Evolve Towards Efficiency?' (1999) 3(2) *Journal of Memetics - Evolutionary Models of Information* 87
Freeman, Paul, '*Lex Mercatoria*: A Legal Basis for the Resolution of International Disputes', in De Zylva, Martin Odams and Harrison, Reziya (eds), *International Commercial Arbitration - Developing Rules for the New Millennium* (Jordans, Bristol 2000)
Frey, Bruno S. and Eichenberger, Reiner, 'Competition among Jurisdictions: The Idea of FOCJ', in Gerken, Luder (ed), *Competition among Institutions* (MacMillan, London 1995)
Fried, Michael S., 'The Evolution of Legal Concepts: the Memetic Perspective' (1999) 39 *Jurimetrics* 291
Friedman, Lawrence M., 'The Law and Society Movement' (1986) 38 *Stanford L Rev* 763–780
Friedman, Thomas L., *The World is Flat - The Globalised World in the Twenty-First Century* (Penguin Books, Harmondsworth 2006)
Friendly, Henry J., 'The Historic Basis of Diversity Jurisdiction' (1928) 41 *Harv L Rev* 483
Fuller, Lon, *The Morality of Law* (Yale University Press, New Haven 1969)
Furmston, Michael, *The Law of Contract* (4th edn, LexisNexis, London 2010)
Gaillard, Emmanuel, 'Introductory Note: France: Court of Cassation Decision in Pabalk Ticaret v. Norsolor (Enforcement of Arbitral Awards; Lex Mercatoria) (October 9, 1984)' (1985) 24(1–3) *International Legal Materials* 360
—, 'Enforcement of a Nullified Foreign Award' (1997) 3 *New York L J* 218

—, 'Compagnie Française d'Etudes et de Construction Technip v. Entreprise Nationale des Engrais et des Produits Phytasanitaires' (1998) 5 *Int'l Arb L Rev* N-80
—, 'Enforcement of Awards Set Aside in the Country of Origin: The French Experience', in van den Berg, Albert Jan (ed) *Improving The Efficiency of Arbitration Agreement and Awards: 40 Years of Application of the New York Convention* (Kluwer Law International, The Hague 1999)
—, *Aspects philosophiques du droit de l'arbitrage international* (Martinus Nijhoff Publishers, Leiden 2008)
—, 'The Urgency of Not Revising the New York Convention', in van den Berg, Albert Jan (ed), *50 Years of The New York Convention* (The Permanent Court of Arbitration, Peace Palace, The Hague 2009)
— and di Pietro, Domenico, (eds), *The Enforcement of Arbitration Agreements and International Arbitral Awards, The New York Convention in Practice* (Cameron May, London 2008)
— and Savage, J. (eds), *Fouchard, Gaillard and Goldman on International Commercial Arbitration* (Kluwer Law International, The Hague 1999)
Gaja, G., *International Commercial Arbitration: New York Convention* (3 Vols, Oceana Publications, Dobbs Ferry, NY 1990)
Gallagher, Kevin P., *Putting Development First – The Importance of Policy Space in the WTO and IFIs* (Zed Press, New York/London 2005)
Gatherer, Dan, 'Why The Thought Contagion Metaphor Is Retarding The Process Of Memetics' (1998) 3 *Journal of Memetics – Evolutionary Mechanisms of Information Transmission*, available at http://www.cpm.mmu.ac.uk/jom-emit.1998/vol12/gatherer_d.html
Gaudet, Michel, 'The International Chamber of Commerce Court of Arbitration' (1986) 4 *Int'l Tax & Bus Law* 216
Gelb, Betsy D., 'Creating "Memes" Whilst Creating Advertising' (1997) 37(6) *J Advertising Research* 57
Gellner, Ernest, *The Conditions of Liberty: Civil Society and its Rivals* (Hamish Hamilton, London 1994)
Gerken, Luder, 'Institutional Competition: An Orientative Framework', in Gerken, Luder (ed), *Competition among Institutions* (MacMillan, London 1995)
Gertz, Craig M., 'Comment, The Selection of Choice of Law Provisions in International Commercial Arbitration: A Case for Contractual Depecage' (1991) 12 *Northwestern J Int'l L & Bus* 176
Geu, Thomas E., 'Chaos, Complexity, and Coevolution: The Web of Law, Management Theory, and Law Related Services at the Millennium' (1998) 65 *Tenn L Rev* 925
Gharavi, Hamid G., 'Enforcing Set Aside Awards: France's Controversial Steps Beyond the New York Convention' (1996) 6 *J Trans L & Pol* 93
—, '*Chromalloy*: Another View' (1997) 12(1) *Mealey's Int'l Arb Rep* 21
—, 'A Nightmare Called Hilmarton' (1997) 12(9) *Mealey's Int'l Arb Rep* 20
—, *The International Effectiveness of the Annulment of an Arbitral Award* (Kluwer International Arbitration Law, The Hague 2002)
Giddens, Anthony, *The Constitution of Society* (University of California Press, Berkeley, CA 1986)

Gill, Stephen, 'Theorising the Interregnum: The Double Movement and Global Politics in the 1990s', in Hettne, Bjorn (ed), *International Political Economy: Understanding Global Disorder* (Fernwood Publishing, Halifax 1995)

—, 'Globalisation, Market Civilisation, and Disciplinary Neoliberalism' (1995) 24(3) *Millennium: J Int'l Stud* 399

—, 'New Constitutionalism, Democratisation and the Global Political Economy' (1998) 10(1) *Pacifica Rev* 23

— and Law, David, *The Global Political Economy: Perspectives, Problems and Policy* (John Hopkins University Press, Baltimore 1988)

Gillies, Peter and Moens, Gabriel, *International Trade and Business: Law, Policy and Ethics* (Cavendish Publishing, Australia 1998)

Ginsburg, Tom and McAdams, Richard, 'Adjudicating in Anarchy: An Expressive Theory of International Dispute Resolution' (2004) 45 *William & Mary Law Review* 1229

Goldman, Berthold, 'Les conflits des lois dans l'arbitrage international de droit privé' (1963 II) 109 *Recueil des Cours* 432

—, *Lex Mercatoria* (Kluwer Law and Taxation Publishers, The Hague 1983)

—, *Lex Mercatoria'* (1983) 3 *Forum Internationale* 6

—, *Forum Internationale: Lex Mercatoria* (Kluwer Law International, The Hague 1984)

—, 'The Applicable Law: General Principles of Law – The *Lex Mercatoria*', in Lew, Julian D.M. (ed), *Contemporary Problems in International Arbitration* (Martinus Nijhoff Publishers, The Hague 1987)

Goldsmith, Jack L. and Posner, Eric A., 'A Theory of Customary International Law' (1999) 66 *U Chi L Rev* 1113

—, *The Limits of International Law* (Oxford University Press, Oxford 2005)

Goldštajn, Aleksandar, 'The New Law Merchant Reconsidered', in Fabricius, F. (ed), *Law and International Trade* (Athenaum Verlag, Frankfurt 1973)

Goode, Roy, 'Usage and Its Reception in Transnational Commercial Law' (1997) 46 *Int'l & Comp L Q* 1

—, 'The Role of the Lex Loci Arbitri in International Commercial Arbitration' (2001) 17(1) *Arb Int'l* 19

—, 'Rule, Practice, and Pragmatism in Transnational Commercial Law' (2005) 54 *Int'l & Comp L Q* 539

—, Kronke, Herbert and McKendrick, Ewan, *Transnational Commercial Law: Text, Cases, and Materials* (Oxford University Press, Oxford 2007)

Goodenough, Oliver R., 'Biology, Behaviour and the Criminal Law: Seeking a Responsible Approach to an Inevitable Interchange' (1997) 22 *Vermont L Rev* 263

Goodenough, Ward H., 'Outline of a Framework for a Theory of Cultural Evolution' (1999) 33 *Cross-Cultural Research* 84

Goodnow, Frank Johnson, 'The Geography of China: The Influence of Physical Environment on the History and Character of the Chinese People' (1927) 51 *National Geographic Magazine* 661

Goodhart, Charles, Hartmann, Philipp, Llewellyn, David T., Rojas-Suarez, Liliana and Weisbrod, Steven, *Financial Regulation: Why, How and Where Now?* (Routledge, London 1998)

Gould, Stephen Jay, *The Individual in Darwin's World* (Edinburgh University Press, Edinburgh 1991)

—, *The Structure of Evolutionary Theory* (Harvard University Press, Cambridge, MA 2002)

— and Lewontin, Richard, 'The Spandrels of San Marco and the Panglossian Paradigm: A Critique of the Adaptationist Programme' (1979) B205 *Proceedings of the Royal Society* 581

— and Verba, Elizabeth, 'Exaptation: A Missing Term in the Science of Form' (1981) 8 *Paleobiology* 4

Gramsci, Antonio, *Selections from Prison Notebooks* (Lawrence and Wishart, London 1971)

Greenberg, Simon, Kee, Christopher and Weeramantry, J. Romesh, *International Commercial Arbitration: An Asia-Pacific Perspective* (Cambridge University Press, Cambridge 2011)

Greif, Avner, Milgrom, Paul and Weingast, Barry, 'Coordination, Commitment and Enforcement: The Case of the Merchant Guild' (1994) 102(4) *J Pol Econ* 745

Griffiths, John, 'What is Legal Pluralism?' (1986) 24 *J Legal Pluralism and Unofficial L* 1

Grimaldi, J.V., 'Microsoft, Justice Remain Far Apart; Sources Say Pact Unlikely by Tuesday' *Washington Post*, 25 March 2000, E1

Grossfeld, Bernhard and Rogers, C. Paul, 'A Shared Values Approach to Jurisdictional Conflicts in International Economic Law' (1983) 32 *Int'l & Comp L Q* 931

Gruner, Dora Marta, 'Accounting for Public Interest in International Arbitration: The Need for Procedural and Structural Reform' (2003) 41 *Colum J Transnat'l L* 923

Guerra, Marc D., 'The Delusion of Darwinian Natural Law' (2001) 11(4) *Religion & Liberty* 6

Guzman, Andrew T., Choice of Law: New Foundations' (2002) 90 *Geo L J* 883

Haase, Florian F., 'Arbitration Awards in German International Business Relations' (2005) *ICCLR* 143

Hancock, John, 'Finding A Solution: How To Have Free Trade While Upholding International Labour Standards' (2002) 11 *MSU-DCL J Int'l L* 23

Hansmann, Henry and Kraakman, Reinier, 'The End of History for Corporate Law' (2001) 89 *Geo L J* 439

Harris, Bruce, Planterose, Rowan and Tecks, Jonathan, *The Arbitration Act 1996 - A Commentary* (Blackwell, Oxford 1996)

Harris, J.W., *Legal Philosophies* (2nd edn, Butterworths, London 1997)

Harrison, Reziya, *Good Faith in Sales* (Sweet & Maxwell, London 1997)

Hartkamp, Arthur S., 'The Concept of Good Faith in the UNIDROIT Principles for International Commercial Contracts' (1994) 3(1/2) *Tulane J Int'l and Comp L* 65

—, von Bar, Christian, Hesselink, Martijn W., Hondius, Ewoud, Joustra, Carla and Du Perron, Edgar (eds), *Towards a European Civil Code* (Ars Aequi Libri, Nijmegen 1994)

Hartnett, Edward, 'Why Is the Supreme Court of the United States Protecting State Judges from Popular Democracy?' (1997) 75 *Tex L Rev* 907

Hascher, Dominique T., 'Recognition and Enforcement of Arbitration Awards and the Brussels Convention' (1996) 12(3) *Arb Int'l* 233

Hass, Ulrich, 'Convention on Recognition and Enforcement of Foreign Arbitral Awards, New York 1958', in Weigand, Frank-Bernd, (ed), *Practitioner's Handbook on International Arbitration* (C.H. Beck, Munich 2002)

Hawkins, Mike, *Social Darwinism in European and American Thought 1860–1945: Nature as Model and Nature as Threat* (Cambridge University Press, Cambridge 1997)

Hay, Bruce L., 'Conflicts of Law and State Competition in the Product Liability System' (1992) 80 *Geo L J* 617

Hayek, Friedrich A., *Law, Legislation and Liberty, Vol. 1: Rules and Order* (University of Chicago, Chicago 1973)

—, *The Road to Serfdom* (Routledge Press, UK 1944)

Hayes, Louise Hertwig, 'Note, A Modern *Lex Mercatoria*: Political Rhetoric or Substantive Progress?' (1977) 3 *Brooklyn J Int'l L* 210

Heckscher, Eli, *Mercantilism* (Macmillan, New York 1955)

Held, David, *Democracy and the Global Order: From the Modern State to Cosmopolitan Governance* (Stanford University Press, Palo Alto, CA 1995)

—, *Law of States, Law of Peoples, Legal Theory* (Cambridge University Press, Cambridge 2002)

Held, David, McGrew, Anthony, Goldblatt, David and Perraton, Jonathan, *Global Transformations: Politics, Economics, and Culture* (Polity Press, Cambridge 1999)

Helfer, Laurence R. and Slaughter, Anne-Marie, 'Why States Create International Tribunals: A Response to Professors Posner and Yoo' (2005) 93 *California L Rev* 2

Henkin, Louis, *How Nations Behave: Law and Foreign Policy* (2nd edn, Columbia University Press, New York 1979)

Hermann, Gerold, 'The Role of the Coruts under the UNCITRAL Model Law Script', in Lew, Julian D.M. (ed), *Contemporary Problems in International Arbitration* (Centre for Commercial Law Studies, London 1986)

—, 'The UNCITRAL Arbitration Law: A Good Model of A Model Law' (1998) *Uniform L Rev* 483

—, 'Does the World Need Additional Uniform Legislation on Arbitration? The 1998 Freshfields Lecture' (1999) 15(3) *Arb Int'l* 211

Highet, Keith, 'The Enigma of the *Lex Mercatoria*' (1989) 63 *Tulane L Rev* 613

Hill, Richard, 'The Internet, Electronic Commerce, and Dispute Resolution: Comments' (1997) 14 (4) *J Int'l Arb* 103

—, 'On-line Arbitration: Issues and Solutions' (1999) 15(2) *Arb Int*'l 199

— and Walden, Ian, 'The Draft UNCITRAL Model Law for Electronic Commerce: Issues and Solutions' (1996) 13(3) *The Computer Lawyers* 18

Hinsley, F. H., *Sovereignty* (2nd edn, Cambridge University Press, Cambridge 1986)

Hirschman, Albert O., *Exit, Voice and Loyalty: Responses to Decline in Firms, Organisations, and States* (Harvard University Press, Cambridge, MA 1970)

Hirst, Paul and Thompson, Grahame, *Globalisation in Question: The International Economy and the Possibilities of Governance* (Polity Press, Cambridge 1996)

Ho, Daniel E. and Imai, Kosuke, 'Randomization Inference with Natural Experiments: An Analysis of Ballot Effects in the 2003 California Recall Election' (2006) 101 *J Am Stat Ass'n* 888

Hobhouse, Leonard T., *Morals in Evolution: A Study in Comparative Ethics* (6th edn, Chapman & Hall, London 1906)

Hodgson, Geoffrey, 'Is Social Evolution Lamarckian or Darwinian?', in Laurent, John and Nightingale, John (eds), *Darwinism and Evolutionary Economics* (Edward Elgar, Cheltenham, UK 2001)

Hoftstadter, Richard, *Social Darwinism in American Thought* (Beacon Press, Boston 1955)

Holdsworth, William Searle, 'The Development of the Law Merchant and Its Courts', in Wigmore, John Henry, Freund, Ernst and Mikell, William Ephraim (a panel of Association of American Law Schools) (eds), *Select Essays in Anglo-American Legal History Vol. I* (Little, Brown & Company, Boston 1909)

— et al., *A History of English Law Vol. XIV* (Methuen, London 1964)

Holmes, Oliver Wendell, Jr., *The Common Law*, (first published in 1881, Courier Dover Publications, New York 1991)

—, 'Law in Science and Science in Law' (1899) 12 *Harv L Rev* 433

Holtzmann, Howard, 'A Task for the 21st Century: Creating a New International Court for Resolving Disputes on the Enforceability of Arbitral Awards', in Hunter, Martin, Marriott, Arthur and Veeder, V.V. (eds), *The Internationalisation of International Arbitration: The LCIA Centenary Conference* (2nd edn, Graham & Trotman/Martinus Nijhoff, London/Boston 1995)

Honnold, John, 'The Influence of the Law of International Trade on the Development and Character of English and American Commercial Law', in Schmitthoff, Clive M. (ed), *The Sources of the Law of International Trade* (F.A. Praeger, New York 1964)

Horning, Richard Allan, 'Deferral of Enforcement of New York Convention Awards for Prudential Reasons' (1997) 1 *Int'l Arb L Rev* 3

Horwitz, Morton, 'The Historical Foundations of Modern Contract Law' (1974) 87(5) *Harv L Rev* 917

Howse, Robert, 'Transatlantic Regulatory Cooperation and the Problem of Democracy', in Bermann, George A. et al. (eds), *Transatlantic Regulatory Cooperation* (Oxford University Press, Oxford 2000)

Hunter, Martin J., 'Lex Mercatoria – Deutsche Schachtbau- und Tiefbohrgesellschaft mbH v. R'As Al Khaimah National Oil Co.' (1987 Part 3) *Lloyd's Maritime and Commercial L Q* 277

—, 'Publication of Arbitration Awards and Lex Mercatoria' (1988) 54 *JCIArb* 55

—, Marriott, Arthur and Veeder V.V. (eds), *The Internationalisation of International Arbitration: The LCIA Centenary Conference* (2nd edn, Graham & Trotman/ Martinus Nijhoff, London/Boston 1995)

Hunter, Robert, 'Anticipating Trends in Dispute Resolution', in De Zylva, Martin Odams and Harrison, Reziya (eds), *International Commercial Arbitration: Developing Rules for the New Millennium* (Jordans, Bristol 2000)

Huth, William E., 'Mastrobuono v. Shearson Lehman Hutton, Inc. 115 S Ct 1212, U.S. Supreme Court, March 6, 1995' (1995) 89(3) *Am J Int'l L* 601

Hylton, Keith N., 'Agreements to Waive or to Arbitrate Legal Claims: An Economic Analysis' (2000) 8 *Sup Ct Econ Rev* 209

— and Drahozal, Christopher R., 'The Economics of Litigation and Arbitration: An Application to Franchise Contracts' (Boston University Working Paper No. 01–03) (2001)

ICCA's *Guide to the Interpretation of the 1958 New York Convention: A Handbook for Judges* (International Council for Commercial Arbitration 2011)

Jackson, David, 'Mandatory Rules and Rules of "Ordre Public"', in North, P.M. (ed), *Contract Conflicts* (North Holland, Amsterdam 1982)

Jaffey, A.J.E., 'Essential Validity of Contracts in the English Conflict of Laws' (1974) 23 *Int'l & Comp L Q* 1

Jansen, C.E.C., *Towards a European Building Contract Law* (Kluwer, Deventer 1998)

Jarvin, Sigvard, 'Arbitrability of Anti-trust Disputes: The Mitsubishi v. Soler Case' (1985) 2(3) *J Int'l Arb* 69

Jennings, R. and Watts, A., *Oppenheim's International Law* (Longman, London 1992)

Jessup, Philip C., *Transnational Law* (Yale University Press, New Haven 1956)

Johnson, Simon, McMillan, John and Woodruff, Christopher, 'Courts and Relational Contracts' (2002) 18 *J. L. Econ. & Org.* 221

Jones, Carol A. G., 'Capitalism, Globalisation and Rule of Law: An Alternative Trajectory of Legal Change in China' (1994) 3 *Social & Legal Studies* 195

Jones, William C., 'An Inquiry into the History of the Adjudication of Mercantile Disputes in Great Britain and the United States' (1958) 25 *U Chi L Rev* 445

Juenger, Friedrich K., 'The *Lex Mercatoria* and the Conflict of Laws', in Carbonneau, Thomas E. (ed), *Lex Mercatoria and Arbitration: A Discussion of the New Law Merchant* (revised edn, Kluwer Law International, Yonkers, New York/Juris, Cambridge, MA 1998)

Kahn, Philippe, 'La Lex Mercatoria: point de vue français après quarante ans de controverses' (1992) 37 *McGill L J* 413

Kaplan, J., 'Hong Kong: Supreme Court of Hong Kong, High Court 2 February 1994, Oonc Lines Ltd v. Sino-American Trade Advancement Co. Ltd.' (1994) 3 *Arb and Disp Resol L J* 291

—, 'Hong Kong: Supreme Court of Hong Kong, High Court 18 August 1994 Aster-Reiniger Joint Venture v. Argos Engineering Co. Ltd.' (1995) 4 *Arb and Disp Resol L J* 41

Kaplan, Neil, 'Is the Need for Writing as Expressed in the New York Convention and the Model Law out of Step with Commercial Practice?' (1996) 12(1) *Arb Int'l* 27

Kaplow, Louis, 'A Model of the Optimal Complexity of Legal Rules' (1995) 11 *J. L. Econ. & Org.* 150

Katsh, Ethan and Rifkin, Janet, *Online Dispute Resolution: Resolving Conflicts in Cyberspace* (Jossey-Bass: A Wiley Co., San Francisco 2001)

Katsoris, Constantine N., 'Foreword to New York Stock Exchange, Inc. Symposium on Arbitration in the Securities Industry' (1995) 63(5) *Fordham L Rev* 1495

Katz, Avery Wiener, *Foundations of The Economic Approach to Law* (Foundation Press, New York 1998)

Katzenbach, Nicholas de B., 'Business Executives and Lawyers in International Trade', in International Chamber of Commerce (ed), *International Arbitration, 60 Years of ICC Arbitration: A Look at the Future* (ICC Publishing, Paris 1984)

Keane, John, *Civil Society: Old Images, New Visions* (Polity Press, Cambridge 1998)

Kelsen, Hans, *Principles of International Law* (Rinehart, New York 1952)

Keohane, Robert O., *After Hegemony: Cooperation and Discord in the World Political Economy* (Princeton University Press, New Jersey 1984)

—, 'Hobbes's Dilemma and Institutional Change in World Politics: Sovereignty in International Society', in Holm, Hans-Henrik and Sorensen, Georg (eds), *Whose World Order? Uneven Globalisation and the End of the Cold War* (Westview Press Inc., Jackson, TN 1995)

Kerber, Wolfgang and Vanberg, Viktor, 'Competition among Institutions: Evolution within Constraints', in Gerken, Luder (ed), *Competition among Institutions* (MacMillan, London 1995)

Kerr, John J., Jr., 'Arbitrability of Securities Law Claims in Common Law Nations' (1996) 12(2) *Arb Int'l* 176

Kerr, Michael, 'The Arbitration Act 1979' (1980) *Modern L Rev* 45

—, 'International Arbitration v. Litigation' (1980) *J Bus L* 164

—, '"Equity" Arbitration in England' (1991) 2 *Am Rev Int'l Arb* n 295

—, 'Concord and Conflict in International Arbitration' (1997) 13(2) *Arb Int'l* 121

Kessler, Friedrich, 'Arthur Linton Corbin' (1969) 78 *Yale L J* 571

Kindred, Hugh M., Castel, J.G., Graham, W., De Mestral, A., Reif, L., Vlasic, I., and Williams, S., *International Law: Chiefly as Interpreted and Applied in Canada* (5th edn, Emond Montgomery Publishers Ltd., Toronto 1993)

King, Michael and Thornhill, Chris (eds), *Luhmann on Law and Politics – Critical Appraisals and Applications* (Hart Publishing, Oxford 2006)

Kirry, Antoine, 'Arbitrability: Current Trends in Europe' (1996) 12(4) *Arb Int'l* 373

Klein, Joel I., 'Time For A Global Competition Initiative?' a paper presented at the EC Merger Control 10th Anniversary Conference in Brussels (14 September 2000), available at http://www.usdoj.gov/atr/public/speeches/6486.htm

Kobayashi, Bruce H. and Ribstein, Larry E., 'Contract and Jurisdictional Competition', in Buckley, F.H. (ed), *The Fall and Rise of Freedom of Contract* (Duke University Press, Durham, NC 1999)

Kornblum, Udo, '"Ordre public transnational", "ordre public international" und "ordre public interne" im Recht der privaten Schiedsgerichtsbarkeit', in Habscheid, Walther J. and Schwab, Karl Heinz, *Beiträge zum internationalen Verfahrensrecht und zur Schiedsgerichtsbarkeit: Festschrift fur Heinrich Nagel zum 75. Geburtstag* (FS Nagel, Munster 1987)

Kramer, Larry, 'Rethinking Choice of Law' (1990) 90 *Colum. L. Rev.* 342

Kramer, Ludwig, *EC Treaty and Environmental Law* (2nd edn, Sweet and Maxwell, London 1995)

Kuner, Christopher B., 'The Public Policy Exception to the Enforcement of Foreign Arbitral Awards in the United States and West Germany Under the New York Convention' (1990) 7(4) *J Int'l Arb* 71

Krasner, Stephen D. (ed), *International Regimes* (Cornell University Press, Ithaca, New York 1982)

Kronke, Herbert, and Nacimiento, Patricia, et al (eds), *Recognition and Enforcement of Foreign Arbitral Award: A Global Commentary on the New York Convention* (Kluwer Law International, The Hague 2010)

Laffer, Arthur and Moore, Stephen, 'The (Tax) War between the States', *The Wall Street Journal*, 11 December 2007, 19

Laland, Kevin N. and Brown, Gillian R., *Sense and Nonsense: Evolutionary Perspectives on Human Behaviour* (Oxford University Press, Oxford 2002)

Laland, Kevin N., Odling-Smee, John and Feldman, Marcus, 'Authors' Response: Niche Construction Earns Its Keep' (2000) 23 *Behavioral and Brain Sciences* 164

Lalive, Pierre, 'Enforcing Awards', in International Chamber of Commerce (ed), *International Arbitration, 60 Years of ICC Arbitration: A Look at the Future* (ICC Publishing, Paris 1984)

—, 'Transnational (or Truly International) Public Policy and International Arbitration', in Sanders, Pieter (ed), *Comparative Arbitration Practice and Public Policy in Arbitration* (Kluwer Law International, The Hague 1987)

Landau, Toby T., 'Introductory Note – United Kingdom: Arbitration Act of 1996' (1997) 36(1) *International Legal Materials* 155

Landes, William M. and Posner, Richard A., 'Adjudication as a Private Good' (1979) 8 *J. Legal Stud.* 280

— —, 'The Independent Judiciary in an Interest-Group Perspective' (1975) 18 *J L & Econ* 875

Lando, Ole, 'The *Lex Mercatoria* in International Commercial Arbitration' (1985) 34 *Int'l & Comp L Q* 747

Landolt, Phillip Louis, *Modernised EC Competition Law in International Arbitration* (Kluwer Law International, The Netherlands 2006).

Lasswell, Harold D. and McDougal, Myres S., *Jurisprudence for a Free Society: Studies in Law, Science, and Policy* (Martinus Nijhoff Publishers/New Haven Press, New Haven 1992)

Lastenouse, Pierre, 'Why Setting Aside an Arbitral Award is Not Enough to Remove it from the International Scene' (1999) 16(2) *J Int'l Arb* 25

Lauterpacht, Hersch, *The Development of International Law by the International Court* (F.A. Praeger, New York 1958)

Lawson, Tony, *Economics and Reality* (Routledge, London 1997)

Layton, Robert, 'Changing Attitudes Toward Dispute Resolution in Latin America' (1993) 10(2) *J Int'l Arb* 123

Lazareff, Serge, 'Mandatory Extraterritorial Application of National Law' (1995) 11 *Arb Int'l* 137

LeBeouf, Jacques, 'The Economics of Federalism and the Proper Scope of the Federal Commerce Power' (1994) 31 *San Diego L Rev* 555

Leflar, Robert A., 'Choice-Influencing Considerations in Conflicts Law' (1966) 41 *NYU L. Rev.* 267

Leurent, Bruno, 'Reflections on the International Effectiveness of Arbitration Awards' (1996) 12 *Arb Int'l* 269

— and Meyer-Fabre, Nathalie, 'La reconnaissance en France des sentences rendues à l'étranger, l'exemple Franco-Suisse', (1995) 13 *Bulletin ASA* 118

Lew, Julian D.M., *Applicable Law in International Commercial Arbitration: A Study in Arbitration Awards* (Oceana Publications, Dobbs Ferry, NY 1978)

—, 'The Case for the Publication of Arbitration Awards', in Schultse, Jan C. and van den Berg, Albert Jan (ed), *The Art of Arbitration, Essays on International Arbitration, Liber Amicorum for Pieter Sunders* (Kluwer Law and Taxation Publishers, The Hague 1982)

—, 'Determination of Arbitrators' Jurisdiction and Public Policy Limitations', in Lew, Julian D.M. (ed), *Contemporary Problems in International Arbitration* (Martinus Nijhoff Publishers, The Hague 1982)

Lewis, Robert P., 'What Goes Around Comes Around: Can Iran Enforce Awards of the Iran-US Claims Tribunal in the United States?' (1988) 26 *Colum J Trans L* 515

Lewontin, Richard, 'Gene, Organism and Environment', in Bendall, D.S. (ed), *Evolution from Molecules to Men* (Cambridge University Press, Cambridge 1983)

Licht, Amir N., 'The Mother of All Path Dependencies: Toward a Cross-Cultural Theory of Corporate Governance Systems' (2001) 26 *Del J Corp L* 147

Liebscher, Christoph, 'European Public Policy After Eco Swiss' (1999) 10(1) *Am Rev Int'l Arb* 81

—, *The Healthy Award, Challenge in International Commercial Arbitration* (Kluwer Law International, The Netherlands 2003)

Lieders, Adriana, 'A New Chapter in Brazil's Oil Industry: Opening the Market While Protecting the Environment' (2001) 13 *Geo Int'l Environmental L Rev* 781

Likosky, Michael (ed), *Transnational Legal Process: Globalisation and Power of Disparities* (Butterworths/LexisNexis, London 2002)

Littman, Mark, 'England Reconsiders "The Stated Case"' (1979) 13 *Int'l Lawyer* 253

Lookofsky, Joseph and Hertz, Ketilbjorn, *Transnational Litigation and Commercial Arbitration - An Analysis of American, European, and International Law* (3rd edn, JurisNet LLC, Copenhagen 2011)

Lopez, Robert, *The Commercial Revolution of the Middle Age, 950–1350* (Cambridge University Press, Cambridge 1971)

Lord Goff, 'The Future of the Common Law' (1997) 46 *Int'l Comp L Q* 745

Lord Hacking, 'The "Stated Case" Abolished: The United Kingdom Arbitration Act of 1979' (1980) 14 *Int'l Lawyer* 95

Lord Hacking, 'Where We Are Now: Trends and Developments since the Arbitration Act (1979)' (1985) 2(4) *J Int'l Arb* 7

Lord Justice Saville, '1996 Report on the Arbitration Bill' (1997) 13(3) *Arb Int'l* 275

Lowenfeld, Andreas F., 'The *Mitsubishi* Case: Another View' (1986) 2 *Arb Int'l* 178

—, '*Lex Mercatoria*: an Arbitrator's View' (1990) 6 *Arb Int'l* 133

—, '*Lex Mercatoria*: An Arbitrator's View', in Carbonneau, Thomas E. (ed), *Lex Mercatoria and Arbitration: A Discussion of the New Law Merchant* (revised edn, Kluwer Law International, Yonkers, New York/Juris, Cambridge, MA 1998)

Lowenfels, Lewis D. and Bromberg, Alan R., 'Securities Industry Arbitration: An Examination and Analysis' (1989) 53 *Albany L Rev* 755

Lowry, Houston Putnam, 'The United States Joins the Inter-American Arbitration Convention' (1990) 7(3) *J Int'l Arb* 83

Luhmann, Niklas, 'Evolution des Rechts' (1970) 1 *Rechtstheorie* 3

Lynch, Katherine, *The Forces of Economic Globalization: Challenges to the Regime of International Commercial Arbitration* (Kluwer Law International, The Netherlands 2003)

Macey, Jonathan R., 'Federal Deference to Local Regulators and the Economic Theory of Regulation: Toward a Public-Choice Explanation of Federalism' (1990) 76 *Va L Rev* 265

—, 'Judicial Preferences, Public Choice, and the Rules of Procedure' (1994) 23 *J Legal Stud* 627

— and Miller, Geoffrey P., 'Toward an Interest-Group Theory of Delaware Corporate Law' (1987) 65 *Tex L Rev* 469

MacNeil, Ian, 'Restatement (Second) of Contracts and Presentation' (1974) 60 *Va L Rev* 589
Maine, Henry James Sumner, *Village Communities in the East and West* (Henry Holt and Company, New York 1876)
—, *On Early Law and Custom* (John Murray, London 1890)
—, *Early History of Institutions* (John Murray, London 1890)
—, *Ancient Law* (John Murray, London 1894)
Majone, Giandomenico, 'International Regulatory Cooperation: A Neo-Institutionalist Approach', in Bermann, George A. et al. (eds), *Transatlantic Regulatory Cooperation: Legal Problems and Political Prospects* (Oxford University Press, Oxford 2001)
Malin, Martin H. and Ladenson, Robert F., 'Privatising Justice: A Jurisprudential Perspective on Labor and Employment Arbitration from the Steelworker's Trilogy to Gilmer' (1993) 44 *Hastings L J* 1187
Malloy, Robin Paul, *Law in a Market Context – An Introduction to Market Concepts in Legal Reasoning* (Cambridge University Press, Cambridge 2004)
Malynes, Gerald, *Consuetudo, Vel, Lex Mercatoria: Or, the Ancient Law-Merchant: In Three Parts, According to the Essentials of Traffick* (reprint edn, The Lawbook Exchange Ltd)
Maniruzzaman, A.F.M., 'Conflict of Law Issues in International Arbitration: Practice and Trends' (1993) 9(4) *Arb Int'l* 371
Mann, Frederick A., 'England Rejects "Delocalised" Contracts and Arbitration' (1984) 33 *Int'l & Comp L Q* 193
—, 'Private Arbitration and Public Policy' (1985) 4 *Civil Justice Quarterly* 257
—, 'The UNCITRAL Model Law – *Lex Facit Arbitrum*' (1986) 2 *Arb Int'l* 241
Mashaw, Jerry L., *Greed, Chaos and Governance: Using Public Choice to Improve Public Law* (Yale University Press, New Haven 1997)
— and Calsyn, Dylan S., 'Block Grants, Entitlements, and Federalism: A Conceptual Map of Contested Terrain' (1996) 14 *Yale L and Policy Rev* 297
McChesney, Fred S., 'Rent Extraction and Rent Creation in the Economic Theory of Regulation' (1987) 16 *J. Legal Stud.* 101
McCormick, Robert E. and Tollison, Robert D., *Politicians, Legislation, and the Economy: An Inquiry into the Interest-Group Theory of Government* (Martinus Nijhoff Publishing, Boston, The Hague and London 1981)
McKendrick, Ewan, *Force Majeure and Frustration of Contract* (2nd edn, Lloyd's of London Press 1995)
McLaughlin, Joseph M., *Supplementary Practice Commentaries, N.Y. Civ. Prac. Law & Rules §7502: 4* (Cum. Ann. Pocket Part, McKinney, New York 1990)
McLaughlin, Joseph T., 'Arbitrability: Current Trends in the United States' (1996) 12(2) *Arb Int'l* 135
Meason, James E. and Smith, Alison G., 'Non-Lawyers in International Commercial Arbitration: Gathering Splinters on the Bench' (1991) 12 *Nw J Int'l L & Bus* 27
Medwig, Michael, 'The New Law-Merchant: Legal Rhetoric and Commercial Reality' (1993) 24 *Law and Policy in International Business* 615
Meessen, Karl M., 'An International Antitrust Challenge: Competition of Competition Laws' (1989) 10 *Northwestern J Int'l L & Bus* 17

Mehren, Arthur T. von, Varady, Tibor and Barcelo, John J., *International Commercial Arbitration: A Transnational Perspective* (West Group, St. Paul 1999)
Menger, Carl, tr. Nock, Francis J., *Investigations into the Method of the Social Sciences with Special Reference to Economics* (New York University Press, New York 1986)
Meyer, Pierre, 'L'insertion de la sentence dans l'ordre juridique française', in Derains, Yves, et al. (eds) *Droit et Pratique de l'Arbitrage International en France,* (Fondation pour l'étude du droit et des usages du commerce international, Paris 1984)
Miller, Geoffrey P., 'Choice of Law as a Precommitment Device', in Buckley F.H. (ed), *The Fall and Rise of Freedom of Contract* (Duke University Press, Durham, NC/London 1999)
Milgrom, John and Roberts, Paul, *Economics, Organisation and Management* (Prentice-Hall, Englewood Cliffs 1992)
Mistelis, Loukas A., 'Regulatory Aspects: Globalisation, Harmonisation, Legal Transplants and Law Reform' (2000) 34(3) *Int'l Lawyer* 1055
Mitchell, William, *An Essay on the Early History of the Law Merchant* (Cambridge University Press, Cambridge 1904)
Modelski, George, 'An Evolutionary Theory of Culture?' (1999) 3 *Journal of Memetics – Evolutionary Models of Information Transmission*, available at http://jom-emit.cfpm.org/1999/vol3/modelski_g.html
Mokyr, Joel, *The Lever of Riches: Technological Creativity and Economic Progress* (Oxford University Press, US 1990)
Molot, Jonathan T., 'How Changes in the Legal Profession Reflect Changes in Civil Procedure' (1998) 84 *Va L Rev* 955
Monahan, Jane, 'Principles in Question' (2005) *The Banker* 60
Montesquieu, *The Spirit of Laws* (1977)
Morgan, Lewis H., *Ancient Society* (MacMillan & Company, London 1877)
Morgenthau, Hans J., *Politics among Nations* (4th edn, Knopf, New York 1967)
Murphy, Paul, 'Automation up to a Point' (1988) *The Banker* 89
Murphy, Richard S. and O'Hara, Erin Ann, 'Mistake of Federal Criminal Law: A Study of Coalitions and Costly Information' (1997) 5 *Sup Ct Econ Rev* 217
Mustill, Michael J., 'The New *Lex Mercatoria* – the First Twenty-Five Years' (1988) 4 *Arb Int'l* 86
—, 'Contemporary Problems in International Commercial Arbitration: A Response' (1989) 17 *Int'l Bus Lawyer* 161
—, 'Arbitration: History and Background' (1989) 6 *J Int'l Arb* 43
—, 'Is It a Bird…', in *Liber Amicorum Claude Reymond* (Editions du Juris-Classeur, Paris 2004)
— and Boyd, Steward C., *Law and Practice of Commercial Arbitration in England* (2nd edn, Butterworths, London 1989)
Nadelmann, Kurt H. and Mehren, Arthur T. von, 'Equivalences in Treaties in the Conflicts Field' (1966/1967) 15 *Am J Comp L* 195
Nader, Laura, 'From Legal Processing to Mind Processing' (1992) 30(4) *Family and Conciliation Courts Rev* 468
Naón, Horacio A. Grigera, 'The UN Convention on Contracts for the International Sale of Goods', in Horn, Norbert and Schmitthoff, Clive. M. (eds), *The Transnational*

Law of International Commercial Transactions: Studies in Transnational Economic Law (Kluwer, Deventer 1982)

Nariman, Fali S., 'The Convention's Contribution to the Globalisation of International Commercial Arbitration', in *Enforcing Arbitration Awards under the New York Convention: Experience and Prospects – New York Convention Day 9* (United Nations, New York 1998), available at http://www/uncitral.org/pdf/enough/texts/arbitration/MY-conv/NYCDay-e.pdf

—, 'Some Thoughts on the Fortieth Anniversary of the New York Convention 1958' (1998) 5 *Int'l Arb L Rev* 163

Nice, Richard (tr), Bourdieu, Pierre, *Outline of a Theory of Practice* (Cambridge University Press, Cambridge 1977)

Nicklisch, Fritz, 'Agreement to Arbitrate to Fill Contractual Gaps' (1988) 3(5) *J Int'l Arb* 35

Norris, Pippa, 'Global Governance and Cosmopolitan Citizens', in Nye, Joseph S. and Donahue, John D., *Governance in a Globalising World* (Brookings Institutions Press, Washington DC 2000)

North, Douglass C., *Institutions, Institutional Change and Economic Performance* (Cambridge University Press, Cambridge 1990)

— and Thomas, Robert P., *The Rise of the Western World: A New Economic History* (Cambridge University Press, Cambridge 1973)

North, Peter and Fawcett, J.J., *Cheshire & North's Private International Law* (13th edn, Oxford University Press, Oxford 1999)

'Notes: General Principles of Law in International Commercial Arbitration' (1988) 101(8) *Harv L Rev* 1816

O'Hara, Erin Ann, 'Social Constraint or Implicit Collusion?: Toward a Game Theoretic Analysis of Stare Decisis' (1993) 24 *Seton Hall L Rev* 746

—, 'Opting Out of Regulation: A Public Choice Analysis of Contractual Choice of Law' (2000) 53 *Vanderbilt L Rev* 1551

—, 'Economics, Public Choice, and the Perennial Conflict of Laws' (2002) 90 *Geo L J* 941

— and Dougan, William R., 'Redistribution Through Discriminatory Taxes: A Contractarian Explanation of the Role of the Courts' (1998) 6 *Geo Mason U L Rev* 869

— and Ribstein, Larry E., 'Interest Groups, Contracts and Interest Analysis' (1997) 48 *Mercer L Rev* 765

Ohnesorge, John K.M., 'The Rule of Law, Economic Development, and the Developmental States of Northeast Asia', in Antons, Christoph (ed), *Law and Development in East and Southeast Asia* (Routledge Curzon, London 2003)

Olson, Mancur, *The Logic of Collective Action: Public Goods and the Theory of Groups* (Harvard University Press, Cambridge, MA 1971)

Oppetit, Bruno, 'L'emergence de la lex mercatoria', in Oppetit, Bruno, *Droit et modernité* (1998) 53

Ostrowski, Stephen T. and Shany, Yuval, 'Chromalloy: United States Law and International Arbitration at the Crossroads' (1998) 73 *NYU L Rev* 1692

Pallieri, Giorgio Balladore, 'L'arbitrage privé dans les rapports internationaux', in *Collected Courses of the Hague Academy of International Law*, Vol. 51 (1935- I) 291

Park, William W., 'Arbitration of International Contract Disputes' (1984) 39 *Business Lawyer* 1783

—, 'Private Adjudicators and the Public Interest: The Expanding Scope of International Arbitration' (1986) 12 *Brooklyn J Int'l L* 642
—, 'National Law and Commercial Justice: Safeguarding Procedural Integrity in International Commercial Arbitration' (1989) 63(3) *Tulane L Rev* 647
—, 'Illusion and Reality in International Forum Selection' (1995) 30 *Tex Int'l L J* 135
—, 'Control Mechanisms in the Development of a Modern *Lex Mercatoria*', in Carbonneau, Thomas E. (ed), *Lex Mercatoria and Arbitration: A Discussion of the New Law Merchant* (revised edn, Kluwer Law International, Yonkers, New York/ Juris, Cambridge, MA 1998)
—, 'Duty and Discretion in International Arbitration' (1999) 93 *Am J Int'l L* 805
—, *Arbitration of International Business Disputes: Studies in Law and Practice* (Oxford University Press, US 2006)
— and Paulsson, Jan, 'The Binding Force of International Arbitration Awards' (1983) 23 *Va J Int'l L* 253
Parkinson, C. Northcote, *Parkinson's Law or The Pursuit of Process* (John Murray, London 1958)
Parsons, Talcott (tr), Weber, Max, *The Protestant Ethic and the Spirit of Capitalism* (Allen and Unwin, London 1978)
Paul, Joel R., 'Comity in International Law' (1991) 32 *Harv Int'l L J* 1
Paulsson, Jan, 'Delocalisation of International Commercial Arbitration: When and Why it Matters' (1983) 32 *Int'l & Comp L Q* 53
—, 'Introduction (to the first issue of Arbitration International, a quarterly journal published by The Chartered Institute of Arbitrators, London)' (1985) 1(1) *Arb Int'l* 2
—, 'Problems in Enforcement of Foreign Arbitral Awards' (1995) 6 *World Arb & Mediation Rep* 77
—, 'Rediscovering the New York Convention: Further Reflections on Chromalloy' (1997) 12(4) *Mealey's Int'l Arb Rep* 20
—, 'May or Must under the New York Convention: An Exercise in Syntax and Linguistics' (1998) 14 *Arb Int'l* 227
—, 'Enforcing Arbitral Awards Notwithstanding A Local Standard Annulment (LSA)' (1998) 9(1) *The ICC International Court of Arbitration Bulletin* 14
—, *Denial of Justice in International Law* (Cambridge University Press, Cambridge 2005)
Pearson, Michael N., 'Merchants and States', in Tracy, James D. (ed), *The Political Economy of Merchant Empires* (Cambridge University Press, New York 1991)
Pepe, Jason E., 'Comment, Kansas's Conflict of Laws Rules for Insurance Contract Cases: It's Time to Change Policies' (1998) 46 *U Kan L Rev* 819
Peter, Wolfgang, *Arbitration and Renegotiation of International Investment Agreements: A Study with Particular Reference to Means of Conflict Avoidance under Natural Resources Investment Agreements* (2nd edn, Kluwer Academic Publishers Group, The Hague 1995)
Petersmann, Ernst-Ulrich, *International Trade Law and the GATT/WTO Dispute Settlement System* (Kluwer Law International, Boston 1997)
—, 'Constitutionalism and International Organisations' (1997) 17 *Northwestern U J Int'l L & Bus* 398
Peterson, Paul E., *The Price of Federalism* (Brookings Institution, Washington DC 1995)

Picker, Randal C., 'Simple Games in a Complex World: A Generative Approach to the Adoption of Norms' (1997) 64 *U Chi L Rev* 1225

Piilola, Anu, 'Assessing Theories of Global Governance: A Case Study of International Antitrust Regulation' (2003) 30 *Stan J Int'l L* 207

Pirenne, Henri, *Economic and Social History of Medieval Europe* (Kegan Paul, London 1937)

Pistor, Katharina, 'Patterns of Legal Change: Shareholder and Creditor Rights in Transition Economies' (Eur. Bank for Reconstruction & Dev., Working Paper No. 49/2000, 2000), available at http://www.ebrd.com/english/region/workingp/wp49.pdf

Planel, Philippe (tr), Rouland, Norbert and Planel, Philippe, *Legal Anthropology* (Stanford University Press, Los Altos Hills, CA 1994)

Plotkin, Henry, 'Culture and Psychological Mechanisms', in Aunger, Robert (ed), *Darwinising Culture – The Status of Memetics as a Science* (Oxford University Press, Oxford 2000)

Plucknett, Theodore Frank Thomas, *Concise History of the Common Law* (5th edn, Little, Brown & Company, Boston 1956)

Pogge, Thomas W., 'Priorities of Global Justice', in Pogge, Thomas W. (ed), *Global Justice* (Blackwell, Boston 2001)

Pointon, Gerald and Brown, David, 'France: Resolving Disputes' (Supp. September 1991) *Euromoney* 13

Pollock, Frederick, *First Book of Jurisprudence for Students of the Common Law* (MacMillan and Co. Ltd., London 1896)

—, 'The Early History of the Law Merchant in England' (1901) 67(3) *L Q Rev* 232

Portnoy, Brian, 'Constructing Competition: Antitrust and the Political Foundations of Global Capitalism' (unpublished Ph.D. dissertation, University of Chicago, 2000)

Poser, Norman S., 'The Stock Exchanges of the United States and Europe: Automation, Globalisation, and Consolidation' (2001) 22 *U Pa J Int'l Econ L* 497

Posner, Eric A., 'Arbitration and the Harmonisation of International Commercial Arbitration: A Defense of *Mitsubishi*' (1999) 39 *Va. J. Int'l L.* 647

—, *The Perils of Global Legalism* (Chicago University Press, Chicago 2009).

— and Sykes, Alan O., *Economic Foundations of International Law* (Harvard University Press, Cambridge, MA/London 2013)

Posner, Eric A. and Yoo, John, 'A Theory of International Adjudication' (2005) 93(1) *California L Rev* 3–74

Posner, Richard A., *Economic Analysis of Law* (Little, Brown & Company, Boston 1972)

—, *Economic Analysis of Law* (4th edn, Little, Brown & Company, Boston 1992)

—, *Economic Analysis of Law* (5th edn, Aspen Publishers, New York 1998)

—, *Economic Analysis of Law* (8th edn, Wolters Kluwer 2011)

—, *Law and Literature* (Harvard University Press, Cambridge, MA 2000)

—, 'The Jurisprudence of Skepticism' (1988) 86 *Michigan L Rev* 827

Pospisil, Leopold, *Anthropology of Law: A Comparative Theory* (Harper & Row, New York 1971)

Poudret, J.F., 'Quelle solution pour en finir avec l'affaire Hilmarton? Reponse a Philippe Fouchard' (1998) 1 *Rev Arb* 17

Poundstone, William, *Prisoner's Dilemma* (Doubleday, New York 1992)

Priest, George L., 'The Common Law Process and the Selection of Efficient Rules' (1977) 6 *J. Legal Stud.* 65

— and Klein, Benjamin, 'The Selection of Disputes for Litigation' (1984) 13 *J. Legal Stud.* 17

Pryles, Michael, "Application of the *Lex Mercatoria* in International Commercial Arbitration" (2004) 78 *ALJ* 396

Quigley, Leonard V., 'Accession by the United States to the UN Convention on the Recognition and Enforcement of Foreign Arbitral Awards' (1961) 70(7) *Yale L J* 1049

Radicati di Brozolo, Luca G., 'Antitrust: A Paradigm of the Relations Between Mandatory Rules and Arbitration – A Fresh Look at the "Second Look"' (2004) *Int'l Arb L Rev* 23

Ramberg, Jan, 'Incoterms 1980', in Horn, Norbert and Schmitthoff, Clive M. (eds), *The Transnational Law of International Commercial Transactions* (Kluwer, Deventer 1982)

Rasmussen, Robert K., 'A New Approach to Transnational Insolvencies' (1997) 19 *Mich J Int'l L* 1

Rau, Alan Scott, 'Fear of Freedom', (2006) 17 *American Review of International Arbitration* 469

Rawls, John, *Political Liberalism* (Columbia University Press, New York 1996)

—, *The Law of Peoples* (Harvard University Press, Cambridge, MA 1999)

Raz, Joseph, 'The Rule of Law and its Virtue' 93 (1977) *L Q Rev* 195

Redfern, Alan, 'International Commercial Arbitration – Jurisdiction Denied: The Pyramid Collapses' (1986) *J Bus L* 15

—, *Law and Practice of International Commercial Arbitration* (4th edn, Sweet & Maxwell, London 2004)

— and Hunter, Martin, *Law and Practice of International Commercial Arbitration* (3rd edn, Sweet & Maxwell, London 1999)

Register of Texts of Conventions and other Instruments concerning International Trade Law, Vol. II (United Nations, New York 1973)

Reisman, W. Michael, *Systems of Control in International Adjudication and Arbitration* (Duke University Press, Durham, NC 1992)

—, Craig, William Laurence, Park, William W., and Paulsson, Jan, *International Commercial Arbitration, Cases, Materials and Notes on The Resolution of International Business Disputes* (The Foundation Press Inc., New York 1997)

Reppy, William A., Jr., 'Eclecticism in Choice of Law: Hybrid Method or Mishmash?' (1983) 34 *Mercer L Rev* 645

Revesz, Richard L., 'Rehabilitating Interstate Competition: Rethinking the "Race-to-the-Bottom" Rationale for Federal Environmental Regulation' (1992) 67 *NYU L Rev* 1210

—, 'Federalism and Interstate Environmental Externalities' (1996) 144 *U Pa L Rev* 2341

—, 'Federalism and Environmental Regulation: Lessons for the European Union and the International Community' (1997) 83 *Va L Rev* 1331

—, 'The Race to the Bottom and Federal Environmental Regulation: A Response to Critics' (1997) 82 *Minn L Rev* 535

Rheinstein, Max (ed), *Max Weber on Law in Economy and Society* (Harvard University Press, Cambridge, MA 1954)

Ribstein, Larry E., 'Choosing Law by Contract' (1993) 18 *J Corporation L* 245
—, 'The Mandatory Nature of the ALI Code' (1993) 61 *Geo Wash L Rev* 984
—, 'Delaware, Lawyers, and Contractual Choice of Law' (1994) *19 Del J Corp L* 999
—, 'Statutory Forms for Closely Held Firms: Theories and Evidence from LLCs' (1995) 73 *Wash U L Q* 369
—, 'Contract and Jurisdictional Competition', in Buckley, F.H. (ed), *The Fall and Rise of Freedom of Contract* (Duke University Press, Durham, NC 1999)
Ribstein, Larry E. and Kobayashi, Bruce H., 'An Economic Analysis of Uniform State Laws' (1996) 25 *J. Legal Stud.* 131
Ridley, Matt, *Genome: The Autobiography of a Species in 23 Chapters* (Harper Perennial, London 2000)
Rivkin, David W., 'Enforceability of Arbitral Awards based on *Lex Mercatoria*' (1993) 9(1) *Arb Int'l* 68
—, 'The Enforcement of Awards Nullified in the Country of Origin: The American Experience', in van den Berg, Albert Jan (ed), *Improving the Efficiency of Arbitration Agreement and Awards: 40 Years of Application of The New York Convention* (Kluwer Law International, The Netherlands 1999)
Roberts, Simon, *Order and Dispute: An Introduction to Legal Anthropology* (Penguin Books, London 1979)
—, 'After Government? On Representing Law without the State' (2005) 68(1) *Modern L Rev* 1
—, 'Domesticating the Sociology of Law' (2008) 71(1) *Modern L Rev* 132
—, 'Against a Systemic Legal History' (unpublished paper on file with the author)
—, 'What is a Court?' (unpublished paper on file with the author)
Robertson, Roland, *Globalisation: Social Theory and Global Culture* (Sage Publications, London/Thousand Oaks, CA 1992)
Robinson, William, 'Beyond the Nation-State Paradigms: Globalisation, Sociology, and the Challenge of Transnational Studies' (1998) 13(4) *Sociological Forum* 561
Rodger, Alan, 'The Codification of Commercial Law in Victorian Britain' (1992) 108 *L Q Rev* 570
Rodgers, William H., Jr., 'Where Environmental Law and Biology Meet: Of Pandas, Thumbs, Statutory Sleepers and Effective Law' (1993) 65 *U Colo L Rev* 25
Roe, Mark, 'Chaos and Evolution in Law and Economics' (1996) 109 *Harv L Rev* 641
Roebuck, Derek, 'Sources for the History of Arbitration – A Bibliographical Introduction' (1998) 14(3) *Arb Int'l* 270
Rogers, Andrew, 'Forum Non Conveniens in Arbitration' (1988) 4(3) *Arb Int'l* 240–254
Rogowski, Ralf and Wilthagen, Ton (eds), *Reflexive Labour Law* (Kluwer, Deventer 1994)
Rojas Elgueta, Giacomo, 'Understanding Discovery in International Commercial Arbitration Through Behavioural Law and Economics: A Journey Inside the Minds of Parties and Arbitrators' (2011) 16 *Harv Negotiation L Rev* 165
Romano, Cesare P., 'The Proliferation of International Judicial Bodies: The Pieces of the Puzzle' (1999) 31 *NYU J L Int'l & Pol* 709
Romano, Roberta, *The Genius of American Corporate Law* (AEI Press, Washington DC 1993)

—, 'State Competition for Corporate Charters', in Ferejohn, John and Weingast, Barry R. (eds), *The New Federalism: Can the States be Trusted?* (Hoover Institution Press, Stanford, CA 1997)

—, 'Empowering Investors: A Market Approach to Securities Regulation' (1998) 107 *Yale L J* 2359

Rosenau, James N., 'Governance in a New Global Order', in Held, David and McGrew, Anthony, *Governing Globalisation* (Polity Press, Cambridge 2002)

Roth, Guenther and Wittich, Claus (eds), *Max Weber, Economy and Society* (University of California Press, Berkeley 1978)

Rowe, Michael C., 'The Contribution of the ICC to the Development of International Trade Law', in Horn, Norbert and Schmitthoff, Clive M. (eds), *The Transnational Law of International Commercial Transactions* (Kluwer, Deventer 1982)

Rubin, Paul, 'Why Is the Common Law Efficient?' (1977) 6(1) *J Legal Stud* 51

Ruhl, J.B., 'Complexity Theory as a Paradigm for the Dynamical Law-and-Society System: A Wake-up Call for Legal Reductionism and the Modern Administrative State' (1996) 45 *Duke L J* 849

—, 'The Fitness of Law: Using Complexity Theory to Describe the Evolution of Law and Society and its Practical Meaning for Democracy' (1996) 49 *Vanderbilt L Rev* 1407

Sabalot, Deborah A., 'The World Turned Upside Down: Radical Ideas in Regulation' (2006) 21(4) *Butterworths J Int'l Banking and Financial L* 147

Sacerdote, Bruce, 'Peer Effects with Random Assignment: Results for Dartmouth Roommates' (2001) 116 *Q J Econ* 681

Sack, Peter, 'Law, Language and Culture: Verbal Acrobatics and Social Technology' (1998) 41 *J Legal Pluralism* 15

Saleh, Samir, *Commercial Arbitration in the Arab Middle East* (Hart Publishing, Oxford 2006)

Sampliner, Gary H., 'Enforcement of Foreign Arbitral Awards After Annulment in Their Country of Origin' (1996) 11 *Mealey's Int'l Arb Rep* 22

Samuel, Adam, *The Jurisdictional Problems in International Commercial Arbitration* (Schulthess, Zurich 1989)

Sanborn, Frederic R., *Origins of the Early English Maritime and Commercial Law* (Century Co., London 1930)

Sanders, Pieter, 'The New York Convention', in Sanders, Pieter (ed), *Union International Des Avocats, Arbitrage International Commercial – International Commercial Arbitration*, Vol II. (1960)

—, *Quo Vadis Arbitration? Sixty Years of Arbitration Practice, A Comparative Study* (Kluwer Law International, The Hague 1999)

—, 'Foreword', in the *ICCA's Guide to the Interpretation of the 1958 New York Convention: A Handbook for Judges* (International Council for Commercial Arbitration 2011)

Santos, Boaventura de Sousa, *Toward a New Common Sense: Law, Science, and Politics in the Paradigmatic Transition* (Routledge, London and New York 1995)

Schlissel, Stephen W., 'A Proposal for Final and Binding Arbitration of Initial Custody Determination' (1992) 26 *Fam L Q* 76

Schlosser, Peter, 'The 1968 Brussels Convention and Arbitration' (1991) 7(3) *Arb Int'l* 227

Schmitthoff, Clive M., 'International Business Law: A New Law Merchant', in Schmitthoff, Clive M., *Current Law and Social Problems 2* (University of W. Ontario Press, Canada 1961)

— (ed), *The Sources of the Law of International Trade* (F.A. Praeger, New York 1964)

—, 'Hardship and Intervener Clauses' (1980) *J Bus L* 82

—, *Commercial Law in a Changing Economic Climate* (2nd edn, Sweet & Maxwell, London 1981)

—, 'Nature and Evolution of the Transnational Law of Commercial Transactions', in Horn, Norbert and Schmitthoff, Clive M., *The Transnational Law of International Commercial Transactions* (Kluwer Law and Taxation Publishers, The Hague 1982)

Schwartz, Alan, 'Contracting about Bankruptcy' (1997) 13 *J. L. Econ. & Org.* 127

— and Scott, Robert E., 'The Political Economy of Private Legislatures' (1994) 143 *U Pa L Rev* 595

Schwartz, Eric A., 'A Comment on *Chromalloy*: *Hilmarton* a l'Americaine' (1997) 14(2) *J Int'l Arb* 128

Schwebel, Stephen, 'The Creation and Operation of an International Court of Arbitral Awards', in Hunter, Martin, Marriott, Arthur and Veeder, V.V. (eds), *The Internationalisation of International Arbitration: The LCIA Centenary Conference* (2nd edn, Graham & Trotman/Martinus Nijhoff, London/Boston 1995)

—, 'A Celebration of the UN New York Convention on the Recognition and Enforcement of Foreign Arbitral Awards' (1996) 12(1) *Arb Int'l* 83

— and Lahne, Susan G., 'Public Policy and Arbitral Procedure', in Sanders, Pieter (ed), *Comparative Arbitration Practice and Public Policy in Arbitration* (Kluwer, The Hague 1978)

Seidl-Hohenveldern, Ignaz, 'Austrian Public Policy and the Enforcement of Foreign Arbitral Awards' (1988) 4(4) *Arb Int'l* 328

Seita, Alex Y., 'Globalisation and the Convergence of Values' (1997) 30 *Cornell Int'l L J* 429

Sharma, K.M., 'From "Sanctity" to "Fairness": An Uneasy Transition in the Law of Contracts' (1999) 18 *NY L Sch J Int'l and Comp L* 95

Shavell, Steven, 'Alternative Dispute Resolution: An Economic Analysis' (1995) 24 *J Legal Stud* 1

Shihata, Ibrahim F.I., 'The World Bank and "Governance" Issues in Its Borrowing Members', in Shihata, Ibrahim F.I. (ed), *The World Bank in a Changing World: Selected Essays and Lectures Vol. II* (Martinus Nijhoff Publishers, The Hague 1991)

Shore, Cris and Wright, Susan (eds), *Anthropology of Policy* (Routledge, London and New York 1997)

Simms, Daniel Paul, 'Arbitrability of Intellectual Property Disputes in Germany' (1999) 15(2) *Arb Int'l* 195

Simpson, A.W.B., *A History of the Common Law of Contract* (Clarendon Press, Oxford 1975)

Slaughter, Ann-Marie, 'Governing the Global Economy through Government Networks', in Byers, Michael (ed), *The Role of Law in International Politics: Essays in International Relations and International Law* (Oxford University Press, Oxford 2000)

—, 'Sovereignty and Power in a Networked World Order' (2004) 40 *Stan J Int'l L*283.

Sloss, David, 'Treaty Enforcement in Domestic Courts: A Comparative Analysis', in Sloss, David (ed), *The Role of Domestic Courts in Treaty Enforcement: A Comparative Study* (Cambridge University Press, Cambridge 2009)

Smit, Hans, 'A-National Arbitration' (1989) 63 *Tulane L Rev* 629

Smith, Adam, *An Inquiry into the Nature and Causes of the Wealth of Nations* (University of Chicago Press, Chicago 1977)

Smith, Erica, 'Vacated Arbitral Awards: Recognition and Enforcement Outside the Country of Origin' (2002) 20 *Boston U Int'l L J* 355

Smith, Vincent, 'Arbitration in International Telecommunications: The Way Ahead?', in De Zylva, Martin Odams and Harrison, Reziya (eds), *International Commercial Arbitration – Developing Rules for the New Millennium* (Jordans, Bristol 2000)

Snyder, Francis, 'Governing Economic Globalisation: Global Legal Pluralism and European Union Law' (1999) 5(4) *Eur L J* 334

Solimine, Michael E., 'An Economic and Empirical Analysis of Choice of Law' (1989) 24 *Ga L Rev* 49

Sood, K.T. et al (eds), *Current Legal Issues in International Commercial Litigation* (Faculty of Law, National University of Singapore, Singapore 1997)

Sornarajah, M., 'The UNCITRAL Model Law: A Third World Viewpoint' (1989) 6(4) *J Int'l Arb* 7

Stake, Jeffrey E., 'Are We Buyers or Hosts? A Memetic Approach to the First Amendment' (2001) 52 *Ala L Rev* 1213

Stearns, Maxwell L. and Zywicki, Todd J., *Public Choice Concepts and Applications in Law* (West, St. Paul 2009)

Stein, Peter, *Legal Evolution: The Story of an Idea* (Cambridge University Press, Cambridge 1980)

Stein, Steven J. and Wotman, Daniel R., 'International Commercial Arbitration in the 1980s: A Comparison of the Major Arbitral Systems and Rules' (1983) 38 *Bus Law* 1685

Sterelny, Kim and Griffiths, Paul, *Sex and Death: An Introduction to the Philosophy of Biology* (University of Chicago Press, Chicago 1999)

Sterk, Stewart E., 'The Marginal Relevance of Choice of Law Theory' (1994) 142 *U Pa L Rev* 949

Stevenson, Russell B., Jr., 'An Introduction to ICC Arbitration' (1980) 14 *J Int'l L & Econ* 382

Stiglitz, Joseph E., *The Stiglitz Report. Reforming the International Monetary and Financial Systems in the Wake of the Global Crisis* (The New Press, New York/London 2010)

Stoecker, Christopher W.O., 'The *Lex Mercatoria*: To What Extent Does it Exist?' (1990) 7 *J Int'l Arb* 101

Storme, Marcel and Demeulenaere, Bernadette, *International Commercial Arbitration in Belgium: A Handbook* (Kluwer Law and Taxation International, Antwerp 1989)

Strange, Susan, 'The Defective State' (1995) 124(2) *Daedalus* 55

—, *The Retreat of the State: The Diffusion of Power in the World Economy* (Cambridge University Press, Cambridge 1996)

Straus, Donald B., 'Arbitration of Disputes between Multinational Corporations', in American Arbitration Association, *New Strategies for Peaceful Resolution of International Business Disputes* (Oceana Publications, Dobbs Ferry, NY 1971)

'Study on the Application and Interpretation of the Convention on the Recognition and Enforcement of Foreign Arbitral Awards', UN Doc. A/CN 9/168

Sunstein, Cass R., 'Social Norms and Social Roles' (1996) 96 *Colum. L. Rev.* 903

Suratgar, David, 'Considerations Affecting Choice of Law Clauses in Contracts Between Government and Foreign Nationals' (1962) 2 *Indian J Int'l L* 273

Suzuki, Masatsugu, 'Japan's New Arbitration Law' (2005) *Asian Disp Resol* 18

Symposium, 'The Proliferation of International Tribunals: Piecing Together the Puzzle' (1999) 31 *NYU J Int'l L & Pol* 679

Tallon, Denis, 'Civil Law and Commercial Law', in *International Encyclopedia of Comparative Law: Specific Contracts, Vol. III, Ch. 2* (Martinus Nijihoff Publishers, The Hague 1983), available at http://cisgw3.law.pace.edu/biblio/graffi.html

Tambiah, Stanley J., *Leveling Crowds, Ethnonationalist Conflicts and Collective Violence in South Asia* (University of California Press, Berkeley, CA 1996)

Telser, Lester G., 'A Theory of Self-Enforcing Agreements' (1980) 53 *J Bus* 27

Teubner, Gunther, 'The Two Faces of Janus: Rethinking Legal Pluralism' (1992) 13 *Cardozo L Rev* 1443

—, *Law as an Autopoietic System* (Blackwell, Oxford 1993)

— (ed), *Global Law Without a State* (Dartmouth Pub Co., Aldershot 1997)

—, 'Legal Irritants: Good Faith in British Law, or How Unifying Law Ends Up in New Divergences' (1998) 61 *Modern L Rev* 11

—, 'Breaking Frames – Economic Globalisation and the Emergence of *Lex Mercatoria*' (2002) 5(2) *Eur J Social Theory* 199

Thayer, Philip W., 'Comparative Law and the Law Merchant' (1936) 6(2) *Brooklyn L Rev* 139

Thiel, Stuart, 'Choice of Law and the Home Court Advantage: Evidence' (2000) 2 *Am L & Econ Rev* 291

Thompson, Dennis, 'Court Decision: Soc. Pabalk Ticaret Ltd Sirketi v. Soc. Anon. Norsolor' (1985) 2(2) *J Int'l Arb* 67

Thornton, Anthony, 'Appeals in Construction Arbitrations' (1984) 1 *Construction L J* 103

Tiebout, Charles M., 'A Pure Theory of Local Expenditures' (1956) 64 *J Pol Econ* 416

Tollison, Robert D., 'Public Choice and Legislation' (1988) 74 *Va L Rev* 339

Tompkins, Arthur, 'A Practical Guide to International Commercial Arbitration' (1991) 47 *New Zealand L J* 274

Trakman, Leon E., 'The Evolution of the Law Merchant: Our Commercial Heritage' (1980) 12 *J Marit L & Com* 153

—, *The Law Merchant: The Evolution of Commercial Law* (Fred B. Rothman, Littleton, Colorado 1983)

Trubek, David M. 'Toward a Social Theory of Law: An Essay on the Study of Law and Development' (1982) 82 *Yale L J* 1

— and Galanter, Marc, 'Scholars in Self-Estrangement: Some Reflections on the Crisis in Law and Development Studies in the United States' (1974) 4 *Wisc L Rev* 1062

Tullock, Gordon, *Trials on Trial: The Pure Theory of Legal Procedure* (Columbia University Press, New York 1980)

Tunc, André, 'English and Continental Commercial Law' (1961) *J Bus L* 237

Ulen, Thomas S., 'Economic and Public Choice Forces in Federalism' (1998) 6 *Geo Mason L Rev* 921

Ungar, Kenneth T., 'The Enforcement of Arbitral Awards Under UNCITRAL's Model Law on International Commercial Arbitration' (1987) 25 *Colum J Trans L* 717

Unger, Roberto M., *Law in Modern Society: Towards a Criticism of Social Theory* (Free Press, New York 1976)

UNIDROIT, *New Directions in International Trade Law, Vol. 1* (Oceana Publications, Dobbs Ferry, NY 1977)

—, *Principles of International Commercial Contracts* (Rome 1994)

United Nations Economic and Social Council Docs. E/Conf. 26/2 to E/Conf. 26/7, and E/Conf. 26/SR.1 to E/Conf. 26/SR.24, reprinted in Gaja, G. (ed), *International Commercial Arbitration - New York Convention - Part III - Preparatory Works* (United Nations, Dobbs Ferry, NY 1979)

Upham, Frank K., 'Speculations on Legal Informality: On Winn's "Relational Practices and the Marginalisation of Law"' (1994) 28 *L & Society Rev* 233

Van den Berg, Albert Jan, *The New York Arbitration Convention of 1958: Towards a Uniform Judicial Interpretation* (Kluwer Law and Taxation Publishers, The Netherlands 1981)

—, 'When is an Arbitral Award Nondomestic Under the New York Convention of 1958?' (1985) 6 *Pace L Rev* 25

—, 'The New York Arbitration Convention of 1958: Where is An Award Made? Case Comment House of Lords, 24 July 1991, Hiscox v. Outhwaite', in van den Berg, Albert Jan, *The Place of Arbitration* (Mys and Breesch, Ghent 1992)

—, 'Some Practical Questions concerning the 1958 New York Convention on the Recognition and Enforcement of Foreign Arbitral Awards', in United Nations (ed), *Uniform Commercial Law in the Twenty-First Century, Proceedings of the Congress of the United Nations Commission on International Trade Law, New York, 18–22 May 1992* (United Nations, New York 1995)

—, 'New York Convention of 1958 Consolidated Commentary Cases Reported in Vol. XVII (1992) - XIX (1994)' (1994) 19 *Yearbook Commercial Arbitration* (Kluwer Law and Taxation Publishers, Deventer/Boston 1995)

—, 'Court Decisions on the New York Convention', in Blessing, Marc (ed), *ASA Special Series No. 9*

—, 'The New York Convention: Its Intended Effects, Its Interpretation, Salient Problem Areas', (1996) *ASA Special Series No. 9* (ASA, Zurich 1996)

—, 'Residual Discretion and Validity of the Arbitration Agreement in the Enforcement of Arbitral Awards under the New York Convention of 1958', in Sood, Teo Keang, et al (eds), *Current Legal Issues in International Commercial Litigation* (National University of Singapore Press, Singapore 1997)

—, 'Enforcement of Annulled Awards?' (1998) 9(2) *The ICC International Court of Arbitration Bulletin* 18

—, 'Enforcement of Foreign Arbitral Awards after Annulment in Their Country of Origin' (1998) 9(2) *Mealey's Int'l Arb Rep* 15

—, 'The New York Convention of 1958: An Overview', in Gaillard, Emmanuel and Di Pietro, Domenico, (eds), *The Enforcement of Arbitration Agreements and International Arbitral Awards, The New York Convention in Practice* (Cameron May, London 2008)

—, 'Hypothetical Draft Convention on the International Enforcement of Arbitration Agreements and Awards – Explanatory Note', in van den Berg, Albert Jan (ed), *50 Years of The New York Convention* (The Permanent Court of Arbitration, Peace Palace, The Hague 2009)

Van den Bergh, R., Faure, M. and Lefevere, J., 'The Subsidiarity Principle in European Environmental Law: An Economic Analysis', in Eide, E. and van den Bergh, R. (eds), *Law and Economics of the Environment* (Juridisk Forlag, Oslo 1996)

Van Gerven, Walter, et al. (eds), *Cases, Materials, Text on National, Supranational and International Tort Law; Scope of Protection* (Hart Publishing, Oxford 1999)

Van Wezel Stone, Katherine, 'Mandatory Arbitration of Individual Employment Rights: The Yellow Dog Contracts of the 1990s' (1996) 73 *Denv U L Rev* 1043

Verbist, Herman, 'Reform of the Belgian Arbitration Law (The Law of 19 May 1998)' (1998) 7 *Int'l Bus L J* 843

Vermont, Sam, 'Politics and Literature: New Perspective: Memes and the Evolution of Intellectual Dishonesty in Law' (1998) 22 *Legal Studies Forum* 655

Vicuna, Francisco Orrego, *International Dispute Settlement in an Evolving Global Society: Constitutionalization, Accessibility, Privatization* (Cambridge University Press, Cambridge 2004)

Villiers, Charlotte, *European Company Law: Towards Democracy?* (Dartmouth Pub Co., Aldershot 1998)

Viner, Jacob, *Religious Thought and Economic Society* (Duke University Press, Durham, NC 1978)

Vitols, S., Casper, S., Soskice, D. and Woolcock, S., *Corporate Governance in Large British and German Companies: Comparative Institutional Advantage or Competing for Best Practice?* (Anglo-German Foundation for the Study of Industrial Society, London 1997)

Volokh, Eugene, 'Technology and the Future of Law' (1995) 47 *Stan L Rev* 1400

Vos, Ed and Kelleher, Ben, 'Mergers and Takeovers: A Memetic Approach' (2001) 5(2) *Journal of Memetics – Evolutionary Models of Information and Transmission* 1

Voser, Nathalie, 'Mandatory Rules of Law as a Limitation on the Law Applicable in International Commercial Arbitration' (1996) 7 *Am Rev Int'l Arb* 334

Walde, Thomas, 'International Standards in Transnational Investment and Commercial Disputes: The Role of International Standards, Soft Law, Guidelines, Voluntary and Self-regulation in International Arbitration, Negotiation and Other Forms of Dispute Management – Preliminary Study, Transnational Dispute Management' (October 2004), available at http://www.transnational-dispute-management.com

Waldock, Humphrey, *General Courses on Public of International Law* 106 "Recueil des Cours" 54 (1962-II) (6th edn, Leyde 1963)

Watson, Alan, *The Making of the Civil Law* (Harvard University Press, Cambridge, MA 1981)

Watt, Horatia Muir, 'Choice of Law in Integrated and Interconnected Markets: A Matter of Political Economy' (2003) 9 *Colum J Eur L* 383

Weber, Max, '"Economy of Law" or "Sociology of Law"', in Roth, Guenther and Wittich, Claus (eds), *Max Weber, Economy and Society: An Outline of Interpretive Sociology, Vol. 2* (University of California Press, Berkeley 1978)

—, *The Protestant Ethic and the Spirit of Capitalism* (Allen and Unwin, London 1978)

Weightman, John and Weightman, Doreen (trs), Levi-Strauss, Claude, *The Savage Mind* (University of Chicago Press, Chicago 1966)

Weiler, Joseph H.H., 'The Transformation of Europe' (1990) 100 *Yale L J* 2403

Wendt, Alexander, 'Anarchy is What States Make of It?' (1992) 46(2) *Int'l Organization* 414

Werner, Jacques, 'International Commercial Arbitrators: From Merchant to Academic to Skilled Professional' (1998) *Disp Resol Mag* 22

—, 'Should the New York Convention be Revised to Provide for Court Intervention in Arbitral Proceedings?' (1989) 6(3) *J Int'l Arb* 113

Westfield, Elisa, 'Globalisation, Governance, and Multinational Enterprise Responsibility: Corporate Code of Conduct in the 21st Century' (2002) 42 *Va J Int'l L* 1075

Wetter, J. Gillis, 'The Conduct of the Arbitration' (1985) 2(2) *J Int'l Arb* 7

—, 'The Present Status of the International Court of Arbitration of the ICC: An Appraisal' (1990) 1 *Am Rev Int'l Arb* 91

—, 'Issues of Corruption before International Arbitral Tribunals: The Authentic Text and True Meaning of Judge Gunnar Lagergren's 1963 Award in ICC Case No. 1110' (1994) 10 *Arb Int'l* 277

Whincop, Michael and Keyes, Mary, 'Putting the "Private" Back into Private International Law: Default Rules and the Proper Law of the Contract' (1997) 21 *Melb U L Rev* 515

— —, 'The Recognition Scene: Game Theoretic Issues in the Recognition of Foreign Judgments' (1999) 23 *Melb U L Rev* 416

White and Case LLP, 'In Dallah, the Paris Court of Appeal and UK Supreme Court Reach Contrary Decisions Applying Same Law to Same Facts', *Insight: International Arbitration* (February 2011)

Wiener, Jarrod, *Globalisation and the Harmonisation of Law* (Pinter, London/New York 1999)

Wilhelmsson, Thomas, 'Legal Integration as Disintegration of National Law', in Petersen, Hanne and Zahle, Henrik, *Legal Polycentricity – Consequences of Pluralism in Law* (Dartmouth Pub Co, Aldershot 1995)

Williams, Russell, 'The Business of Memes: Memetic Possibilities for Marketing and Management' (2000) 38(4) *Management Decisions* 272

Wilson, David Sloan, 'The Challenge of Understanding Complexity, Commentary on Laland *et al*: "Niche Construction"' (2000) 23 *Behavioral and Brain Sciences* 165

Wilner, Gabriel M., *Domke on Commercial Arbitration* (revised edn, West Group, St. Paul 1995)

Winn, Jane Kaufman, 'Relational Practices and the Marginalisation of Law: Informal Financial Practices of Small Businesses in Taiwan' (1994) 28 *L & Society Rev* 193

Wortmann, B., 'General Principles of Law in International Commercial Arbitration' (1988) 101 *Harv L Rev* 1819

Wright, Benjamin, *The Law of Electronic Commerce: EDI, Fax and E-mail* (supplement, Little, Brown & Company, Boston 1996)

INDEX

E

F

G

H

I

O

P

R

S

About the Author

Dr Shen Wei

Special Oriental Scholar Professor of Law, Shanghai Jiao Tong University Law School; PhD (LSE), LLM (Cantab), LLM (Michigan), LLM & LLB (ECUPL); Attorney-at-Law, New York, FHKIArb. Professor Shen has been included in Marquis Who's Who (2011 onwards).

Prior to teaching at the law school, Dr Shen practiced in major US and UK firms in Sydney, Shanghai, Chicago and Hong Kong for a decade, primarily assisting multinational clients in their China-related transactions such as foreign direct investment, private equity, mergers and acquisitions, project finance and commercial arbitration. Dr Shen's major research interests include commercial arbitration, international investment law, company law and financial regulations.

Dr Shen has already contributed to 18 books (16 in English and 2 in Chinese) and authored (or co-authored) over 70 articles in English and Chinese law journals.

European Studies in Law and Economics

The European Studies in Law and Economics Series is an initiative of the board of the European Doctorate in Law and Economics programme. It is a peer-reviewed book series for a wide audience, including policy makers, legislators, economists, lawyers and judges. The volumes cover a broad range of topics. Each volume is devoted to promote the understanding of the effects of laws on human behaviour, thus providing the tools for a better assessment of the impact of laws on the economic system.

The European Doctorate in Law and Economics (www.edle-phd.eu) is the academic response to the increasing importance of the economic analysis of law in Europe. It is an excellence programme offered by the Universities of Bologna, Hamburg and Rotterdam and sponsored by the European Commission under the Erasmus Mundus scheme. It offers the unique opportunity to study Law and Economics on a PhD level in three different countries. The programme prepares economists and lawyers of high promise for an academic career in a research field of growing importance or for responsible positions in government, research organizations and international consulting groups.

The editors also invite authors from outside the European Doctorate in Law and Economics to submit publishing proposals. Please contact Ann-Christin Maak (ac.maak@intersentia.co.uk) for further information.